# ABBREVIATIONS FOR CHAPTER TITLES

When your instructor uses one of these abbreviations in marking your paper, you should read or review all the material in the designated chapter.

# WRITING

## A COLLEGE
## HANDBOOK

# James A. W. Heffernan

Dartmouth College

# John E. Lincoln

# WRITING

# A COLLEGE HANDBOOK

W·W·NORTON & COMPANY
NEW YORK    LONDON

Copyright © 1982 by W. W. Norton & Company, Inc.
Published simultaneously in Canada by George J. McLeod Limited, Toronto.
Printed in the United States of America
All Rights Reserved
First Edition

Library of Congress Cataloging in Publication Data

Heffernan, James A    W
    Writing—a college handbook.

    Includes index.
    1. English language—Rhetoric.    2. English
    language—Grammar—1950–    3. Report writing.
    I. Lincoln, John E., joint author.    II. Title.
    PE1408.H438    1982        808'.042        80-17125

W. W. Norton & Company, Inc. 500 Fifth Avenue, New York, N.Y. 10110
W. W. Norton & Company Ltd. 37 Great Russell Street, London WC1B 3NU

2 3 4 5 6 7 8 9 0

# PREFACE

This book is just what its title says—a composition handbook meant for college students. In response to the current and widespread view of what a handbook should be, we wrote this one to be used not only as a reference guide for individual students but also as a classroom text for composition courses. Besides helping students to correct errors on their own, it will provide ample opportunity for classroom discussion of those errors and of what makes writing effective.

Since many teachers like to start by getting students into the rhythm of the writing process as a whole, Part I of this book treats the writing of essays from beginning to end. The first two chapters deal in detail with the vexing problem of getting an essay started. We explain not only how to choose a topic or get a personal grip on an assigned one but also how to use a variety of "prewriting" techniques. Chapter 3 then treats the shaping of an essay as a process of discovering rather than of predetermining its direction. Besides discussing various ways of introducing, developing, and concluding an essay, this chapter explains how to make outlining go hand in hand with thinking. As an alternative to the vertical-list outline, which can be drawn up first only if the student knows in advance what the essay is going to say, we show how to use the tree outline, which can be made to grow and develop as the student thinks about the topic and gradually discovers a thesis.

After thus introducing the writing process as a whole, we closely consider certain aspects of the process. Our discussion includes not only topics that you normally find in a handbook but some that you often don't. As you would expect, we treat description, narration, and various methods of exposition; we explain in a nontechnical way how to write an effective argument; we show how to organize a paragraph by using either one or both of two basic structures; we show how to choose and use individual words effectively; and we give a ten-step guide to revising an essay. But we also offer a section of specific advice on how to invigorate style, and a chapter on how to turn reading into writing: how to use reading matter as a source of stimulation or information, an object of analysis, or a stylistic model to imitate.

Part II, "Writing Sentences," takes a fundamentally positive approach to sentence construction. We give ample space to sentence errors, and our reference system makes it easy to find specific advice on how to correct them. But since this book was written to be read as well as consulted, most of the chapters in Part II begin by explaining and illustrating the rhetorical impact of a particular construction when it is correctly and effectively used. Before we attack the misplaced modifier, we show what a well-placed modifier can do; before we identify the wrong ways of joining independent clauses (for instance, the fused sentence and the comma splice), we show what coordination can do. Using lively examples from student essays as well as from the work of leading writers, we aim to show repeatedly that good writing is not simply the absence of grammatical error, but the presence of rhetorical power.

Our emphasis on rhetorical effect is reinforced by the exercises. Instead of merely calling for the correction of errors, many of them ask students to expand or combine short sentences, to finish sentences that we start for them, or to imitate complete sentences. The exercises will therefore help students to increase the variety of constructions they actually use and the variety of rhetorical effects they can achieve.

This combination of grammatical explanation, error correction, and emphasis on rhetorical effect is something of an innovation in a handbook. In the fall of 1978, therefore, we put an earlier version of "Writing Sentences" into the hands of some six hundred freshman-composition students at sixteen colleges. The results were both instructive and positive. Students' comments and teachers' detailed reports have helped us revise and refine our approach, and have also assured us that it works in classrooms other than our own.

Part III, "The Research Paper and Other Writing Tasks," provides first of all a detailed guide to the preparation and writing of a research paper. We explain not only how to use a library, take notes, cite sources, and avoid plagiarism, but also how to plan and organize the paper, how to keep quotations under control, and how to make them serve an argument or explanation rather than take it over completely. Then, to illustrate the actual process of writing a research paper, we demonstrate how various notes on the subject of dreams grow into the sample paper, "Dreams and Waking Life."

The final chapter of the book moves "beyond Freshman English" into the various kinds of writing that students have to do for other courses and other purposes. With apt illustrations, the chapter shows how to write an examination essay, a résumé and a covering letter for a job application, a business letter, a letter of protest, and a personal statement for an application to a post-graduate program. The chapter tries to demonstrate, in fact, that the ability to write well can have a real and lasting effect upon a student's life.

Many teachers may find that this book by itself serves all the needs of a beginning composition course. But to help you identify the problems of individual students, Bruce Chadwick (Long Island University Brooklyn Center) has prepared diagnostic tests. In addition, we ourselves have prepared a number of supplements. For students who need intensive work on the sentence, we have written *Writing—A College Workbook,* which offers brief instruction and extensive exercises on every aspect of sentence structure treated in Part II of the *Handbook.* For students who wish to check their answers to the exercises in the *Handbook* or the *Workbook,* we have prepared two answer pamphlets, one for each book (you may order one or both of these for your students). Finally, for your own use, we have written an instructor's manual. This provides not only the answers to the exercises in the *Handbook* and the *Workbook* but also a number of suggestions on how to use the *Handbook* in a composition course.

JAMES A. W. HEFFERNAN
JOHN E. LINCOLN

# ACKNOWLEDGMENTS

We have incurred many debts in the preparation of this book, and we are happy to acknowledge them here. It began as *The Dartmouth Guide to Writing*, by John E. Lincoln—a book of lessons and exercises issued by Dartmouth College for its students under a grant from the Lilly Foundation.

We would like to thank those enterprising and gracious teachers, most of them on campuses far removed from ours, who used the preliminary edition of part of this book with their freshman-composition students during the fall of 1978 and told us how it worked. They are Joseph Adams, Northern Virginia Community College; Virginia Bothun, Willamette University; Kenneth Davis and Michael C. Tourjee, University of Kentucky; Elsie Deal, Edinboro State College; Pauline Glover, University of Tennessee; Tom Miles, West Virginia University; Patricia Moody, Syracuse University; S. F. Murray, Old Dominion University; Maureen Potts, University of Texas; Delma E. Presley, Georgia Southern College; Malinda Snow, Georgia State University (who also read the entire manuscript in a later draft); William Walsh, California State University—Northridge; Gregory Waters and Danny Rendleman, University of Michigan; Linda Wells, University of Wisconsin; Karl Zender, University of California—Davis; and Sander Zulauf, County College of Morris.

We are also indebted to many others for various kinds of help and advice: to William Cook, the late James Epperson, Robert Fogelin, G. Christian Jernstedt, John Lanzetta, Chauncey Loomis, Rosalie O'Connell, Karen Pelz, Brenda Silver, William M. Smith, and Henry Terrie, all of Dartmouth College; to Joel Broadkin and

Leslie Freeman, of the New York Institute of Technology; and to Harry Brent, Rutgers University, Camden College of Arts and Sciences; Alma G. Bryant, University of South Florida; Michael Cartwright, California State College—Bakersfield; Lynne Constantine, James Madison University; the late Gregory Cowan, Texas A & M University; Hubert M. English, Jr., University of Michigan; John J. Fenstermaker, Florida State University; Barbara Munson Goff, Cook College of Rutgers University; S. J. Hanna, Mary Washington College; James Hartman, University of Kansas; Joan E. Hartman, College of Staten Island, City University of New York; Francis Hubbard, University of Wisconsin—Milwaukee; Naomi Jacobs, University of Missouri—Columbia; Mildred A. Kalish, Suffolk County Community College; C. H. Knoblauch, Columbia University; James MacKillop, Onondaga Community College; Stephen R. Mandell, Drexel University; John C. Mellon, University of Illinois Chicago Circle Campus; Susan Miller, University of Wisconsin—Milwaukee; James Murphy, California State University—Hayward; Karen Ogden, University of Manitoba; Andrew Parkin, University of British Columbia; Kenneth Roe, Shasta College; Ann Sharp, Furman University; Craig B. Snow, University of Arizona; Ken M. Symes, Western Washington State College; Keith A. Tandy, Moorhead State University; Mary Thysell, University of Waterloo; and Harvey S. Wiener, La Guardia Community College. We especially thank Bruce Chadwick, Long Island University Brooklyn Center, who in addition to reading the manuscript prepared the diagnostic tests that accompany the text; and Ron Fortune, Illinois State University, whose insightful and detailed suggestions guided us through the final revision of the book.

We must record here, too, our indebtedness to the many students who have contributed examples of what they do in their writing—in particular, Mitch Arion, Michelle Carter, Ian Christoph, Barbara Clark, Natica Lyons, and Sarah Watson. We thank Beth Bergeron, Karen James, Annette Kenison, Ken Marcella, Antonia Mulvihill, Nancy Nakano, and Leisa Suhayda, all of whom helped in various ways with the production of the book. Thanks are due as well to Michael Freeman, of Dartmouth College, who helped us considerably with chapter 26, and to several persons who helped us with chapter 28: Frances R. Hall, Dartmouth Medical School; Robert Sokol, Dartmouth College; and Andrew Vouras, New England Telephone Company. In addition, John Lincoln thanks Costas Dourakis, George Savvides, Fred Parker, Charles Rice, and above all Donald Murray.

We also thank our typists, Penelope Walton and Debbie Hodges, and our spouses, Nancy Heffernan and Mary Lincoln, who contributed to the preparation of this book in ways too numerous to mention. We thank our children—Andrew and Virginia Heffernan, and Chris, Brian, and Peter Lincoln—for supplying both vivid samples of student writing and special kinds of information. We thank Ethelbert Nevin II and John E. Neill, who each played a part in persuading us to write the book. And we owe a special debt of gratitude to John W. N. Francis, who is largely responsible for the shape that it gradually assumed.

Finally, we would like to thank members of our publisher's staff for their signal contributions: Esther Jacobson, whose copy editing not only saved us from many errors but ultimately became a substantive contribution to the book; Barry Wade, whose deftness and editorial experience in the field of English composition has helped us solve many problems; and Sydney Wolfe Cohen, Stephen Mautner, Diane O'Connor, Nancy K. Palmquist, Jennifer E. Sutherland, and Jeremy Townsend, whose aid has been invaluable. Lastly and resoundingly, we thank John Benedict, whose editorial zeal and wholehearted cooperation have made it possible for us to bring this book and its supplements to what we hope is a successful completion.

We also wish to acknowledge our debt to the following books and articles: Monroe Beardsley, *Thinking Straight*, 4th ed. (New York: Prentice-Hall, 1975); N. R. Cattell, *The New English Grammar* (Cambridge, Mass.: MIT Press, 1969); Elaine Chaika, "Grammars and Teaching," *College English*, 39 (March 1978), 770–83; Francis Christensen, "A Generative Rhetoric of the Sentence," "Notes toward a New Rhetoric," and "A Generative Rhetoric of the Paragraph," in *The Sentence and the Paragraph* (Urbana, Ill.: NCTE, 1966); Harry H. Crosby and George F. Estey, *College Writing: The Rhetorical Imperative* (New York: Harper & Row, 1968); George O. Curme, *English Grammar* (New York: Barnes and Noble, 1947); Bergen and Cornelia Evans, *A Dictionary of Contemporary American Usage* (New York: Random House, 1957); Charles Fillmore, "The Case for Case," in *Universals in Linguistic Theory*, ed. Emmon Bach and Robert T. Harms (New York: Holt, Rinehart and Winston, 1968); Linda S. Flower and John R. Hayes, "Problem Solving Strategies and the Writing Process," *College English*, 39 (December 1977), 449–61; W. Nelson Francis, *The Structure of American English* (New York: Ronald, 1958); Robert J. Geist, *An Introduction to Transformational Grammar* (New York: Macmillan, 1971); William E. Gruber, " 'Servile Copying' and the Teaching of English Composition," *College English*, 39 (December 1977), 491–97; A. S. Hornby, *A Guide to Patterns and Usage in English* (London, Oxford University Press, 1954); Darrell Huff, *How to Lie with Statistics* (New York: W. W. Norton & Company, 1954); Roderick A. Jacobs and Peter S. Rosenbaum, *English Transformational Grammar* (Waltham, Mass.:

Blaisdell, 1968); Otto Jespersen, *Essentials of English Grammar* (London: George Allen & Unwin, 1959); John C. Mellon, *Transformational Sentence Combining* (Urbana, Ill.: NCTE, 1969); Donald Murray, *A Writer Teaches Writing: A Practical Method of Teaching Composition* (Boston: Houghton Mifflin, 1968), and also various essays and lectures; Frank O'Hare, *Sentence Combining* (Urbana, Ill.: NCTE, 1973), and *Sentencecraft* (Lexington, Mass.: Ginn, 1975); Mina Shaughnessy, *Errors and Expectations: A Guide for the Teacher of Basic Writing* (New York: Oxford University Press, 1977); Harry Shaw, *Errors in English and Ways to Correct Them* (New York: Barnes and Noble, 1970); the *MLA Handbook for Writers of Research Papers, Theses, and Dissertations* (New York: Modern Language Association, 1977); and the *Publication Manual of the American Psychological Association,* 2nd ed. (Washington, D.C.: American Psychological Association, 1974).

J.A.W.H.
J.E.L.

# CONTENTS

# I.

# WRITING ESSAYS

# II.

# WRITING SENTENCES

# III.

# THE RESEARCH PAPER AND OTHER WRITING TASKS

# WRITING

## A COLLEGE
## HANDBOOK

# INTRODUCTION

## Talking and Writing

Talking is something most of us seem to do naturally. We learn to talk almost automatically, first imitating the words we hear and then imitating the ways in which people around us put them together. Well before we learn how to put words on paper, we unconsciously learn how to use them in speech.

But no one learns to write automatically. You cannot write even a single letter of the alphabet without a conscious effort of mind and hand, and to get beyond the single letter, you must be shown how to form words, how to put words together into sentences, and how to punctuate those sentences.

Writing, then, is a means of communication you must consciously learn. And part of what makes it hard to learn is that written words usually have to express your meaning in your absence, have to "speak" all by themselves. When you speak face to face with a listener, you can communicate in many different ways. You can raise or lower the pitch or volume of your voice to emphasize a point; you can grin, frown, wink, or shrug; you can use your hands to shape out a meaning when you don't quite have the words to do it; you can even make your silence mean something. But in writing you have to communicate without facial expressions, gestures, or body English of any kind. You have to speak with words and punctuation alone.

Furthermore, writing is a solitary act. When you talk, you normally talk to someone who talks back, who raises questions, who lets you know whether or not you are making yourself clear. But

3

when you write, you work alone. Even if you are writing a letter to someone you know, that person is not actually standing there to prod or prompt you into speech, to help you fill in the gaps that so often occur when you try to tell a story or give an explanation off the top of your head. To write well, you have to anticipate the reactions of a reader you cannot see or hear.

But writing does have one big advantage over speaking. It gives you time to think, to try out your ideas on paper, to choose your words, to read what you have written, to rethink, revise, and rearrange it, and, most importantly, to consider its effect on a reader. Writing gives you time to find the best possible way of stating what you mean. And the more you study the craft of writing, the better you will use your writing time.

## Standard American English and Other Kinds of English

This book aims to help you write effectively in English. But since there are many kinds of English, you should know which kind this book aims to teach—and why.

The language called "English" is used in many parts of the world. It is spoken not only in England but also in the British West Indies and in countries that were once British colonies—such as Canada, the United States, Australia, India, and Nigeria. These are all "English-speaking" countries, but they have different ways of using English. Sometimes, for instance, they have different words for the same thing:

> truck [U.S.] = lorry [Great Britain]
> pond [U.S.] = billabong [Australia]

Sometimes they have different ways of spelling or pronouncing the same word:

> labor [U.S.] = labour [Great Britain]
> recognize [U.S.] = recognise [Great Britain]
> laugh: pronounced "laff" in the U.S., "lahff" in Great Britain
> paint: pronounced "paynt" in the U.S., "pint" in Australia

Sometimes they use different grammatical forms:

> The jury has reached a verdict. [U.S.]
> The jury have reached a verdict. [all other English-speaking countries]

Probably you have already noticed differences such as these. Even if you have never traveled abroad, you have probably heard

British or Australian speech. When you did, you could undoubtedly tell after just a few words that what you were hearing was different from any kind of English commonly spoken in America. The reason for the difference is that a living language never stands still. Like the people who speak it and the world they speak it in, it changes. And if English-speaking peoples live far enough apart, the English they use will change in divergent ways. That is why English sounds different in different parts of the world.

Just as English varies from one country to another, it also varies from one region of a country to another, and from one cultural or ethnic group to another. Consider these statements:

> She'll say I be talkin.
> She'll say I am talking.

> They ain't got no ponies; they got big horses: I rode one, real big uns.
> They don't have any ponies; they have big horses. I rode one, a really big one.

> I have three brother and two sister.
> I have three brothers and two sisters.

These statements illustrate four dialects—four kinds of English used in America. The first statement in each pair illustrates a regional or ethnic dialect; the second illustrates Standard American English. Each of these dialects has its own distinctive character and rules. But of them all, Standard American English is the only one normally taught in schools and colleges, the only one normally required in business and the professions, and the only one widely used in writing—especially in print. Why does Standard American English enjoy this privilege? Is it always better than any other kind? And if you were raised to speak an ethnic or regional dialect, must you stop speaking that dialect in order to learn the Standard one?

There is no easy answer to the first of those three questions. But the answer to the second one is no. Standard American English is not always better than any other kind. In a spoken exchange, it can sometimes be less expressive—and therefore less effective—than a regional or ethnic dialect. Compare, for instance, the original version of an ethnic proverb with the Standard version:

> You so dumb you can't throw rainwater out of a boot, and the directions say how.
> You are so dumb that you cannot throw rainwater out of a boot, even though the directions explain how.

These two statements strike the ear in different ways. While the first has the expressive vitality of ethnic speech, the second—the

Standard version—sounds comparatively stiff. The original definitely packs more punch.

Part of what makes the original version so effective is the tradition that stands behind it, and because of that tradition, the answer to the third question we raised is also no. A regional or ethnic dialect is not just a way of speaking; it is the living record of a shared heritage and shared concerns. For this reason, no one who speaks such a dialect should be forced to give it up.

But if many people can learn more than one language, most people can learn more than one dialect, and whatever the dialect you were raised to speak, you can and should learn to write Standard American English. Whether or not it is better than any other dialect for purposes of speech, it is what you will normally be expected to use in your writing. During college, it is what teachers will expect you to use in essays, exams, reports, and research papers. After college, it is what others will expect you to use in anything you write for business or professional purposes. For all of these reasons, Standard American English is what this books aims to help you learn.

## Grammar and Rhetoric

The grammar of a language is the set of rules by which its sentences are made. You started learning the rules of English grammar as soon as you started to talk. Well before you learned how to write, you could have said which of these two statements made sense:

> *Eggs breakfast fried I two for had.
> I had two fried eggs for breakfast.

The words in each statement are the same, but you can readily see that only the second arrangement makes sense. You instinctively know that some ways of arranging the seven words are acceptable and others are not. You may not be able to say just why the word order in the first arrangement is wrong, but you know that it is.

Good writing requires a good working knowledge of grammar, a refinement of the basic or instinctive knowledge you already have. But good writing is more than the act of obeying grammatical rules. It is also the art of using rhetoric—of arranging words, phrases, sentences, and paragraphs in such a way as to engage and sustain the reader's attention.

---

* From this point on, nonstandard constructions in this book are marked with a star, except in chapter 17, where sentence fragments are clearly identified in other ways.

The power of rhetoric can sometimes be felt in a single sentence. Patrick Henry said, "Give me liberty, or give me death." Franklin D. Roosevelt said, "The only thing we have to fear is fear itself." General George S. Patton said to his troops after a battle, "You have been baptized in fire and blood and have come out steel." Martin Luther King, Jr., said to a crowd of civil-rights demonstrators, "I have a dream." As these examples help to show, the sentence is at once the basic unit of writing and the basic source of its rhetorical effects. A good sentence not only takes its place with other sentences but also makes a place for itself, striking the reader with its own special clarity and force. One aim of this book, therefore, is to help you maximize the rhetorical impact of every sentence you write.

Yet you do not normally write single sentences in isolation. You write them in sequence, and rhetoric is the art of making that sequence effective—of moving from one sentence to another in a paragraph, and from one paragraph to another in an essay. It is the art of sustaining continuity while continually moving ahead, of developing a description, a narrative, an explanation, or an argument in such a way as to take the reader with you from beginning to end. The ultimate aim of this book, therefore, is to explain the rhetoric of the writing process as a whole.

## Using This Book

You can use this book in one of two ways: as a textbook for a course in composition, or as a reference guide to help you with a large variety of writing tasks in college and afterward.

If you are using this book in a composition course, your teacher will undoubtedly assign certain chapters or sections to the whole class. In addition, after seeing what you individually have written, your teacher will probably assign certain sections and exercises specifically chosen to meet your needs. But since you may want to use this book on your own as well, you should know how it is organized.

The book is divided into three main parts. Part I, "Writing Essays," is a step-by-step guide through the whole writing process, from choosing a topic to proofreading your final draft. Part II, "Writing Sentences," is designed chiefly to explain and illustrate the variety of ways you can use sentence structure. We explain the things you can't or normally shouldn't do, such as writing sentence fragments and misplacing modifiers. But we emphasize the things you can and should do, such as varying your sentence patterns, using modifiers of all kinds, organizing your sentences by means of coordination and subordination, enhancing coordination with parallelism, and controlling emphasis by the way you arrange your words.† Part III, "The Research Paper and Other Writing Tasks," is first of all a guide to the preparation and writing of a research paper, and second a guide to writing in the world "beyond Freshman English," where you will have to compose such things as business letters and covering letters for job applications.

At the end of the book are two alphabetical glossaries. The Glossary of Usage explains many of the words or phrases that writers find troublesome or confusing; the Glossary of Terms defines the terms that are commonly used in discussions of writing. Although the terms we use are printed in **boldface type** in the text and defined where they first appear, you may find this glossary an additional aid.

Since this book is designed for ready reference as well as for steady reading, we have tried to make it as easy as possible for you to locate specific advice on every subject we cover. If you are seeking information on your own, the best places for you to start looking are the summary on the back endpapers—which shows you the layout of the entire *Handbook* in chart form—and the table of contents at the beginning of the book. Both the summary and the contents list every major topic, so all you need to do is turn to the appropriate page. If you can't find the topic you want in either the summary or the table of contents, go to the index, which lists all topics alphabetically and gives the page numbers for each one.

In skimming through the book, you will notice various abbreviations and symbols (such as *mod, mm,* and *//*). These are explained in the two alphabetical lists on the front endpapers: "Abbreviations for Chapter Titles" and "Symbols for Revision." In these lists, each abbreviation and symbol is followed by a chapter title or a brief explanation, along with a reference to the appropriate part of the text.

The abbreviations and symbols are intended for use by your instructor in marking your papers. If, for example, you see *mod, mm,* or *//* on your paper, you can look for it on the front-endpaper lists. There you'll find that *mod* refers you to the "Modifiers" chapter, that *mm* refers you to the section explaining how to correct misplaced modifiers, and that *//* refers you to the section explaining how to correct faulty parallelism.

Alternatively, your instructor may refer you to a specific topic by using one of the section numbers, which are listed, with corresponding titles and page numbers, on the back endpapers and in

---

†To illustrate various constructions we often quote other writers, and we often italicize certain words in their sentences to stress particular points. In all such cases, the italics are ours, not those of the writers.

the table of contents. That is, instead of writing // on your paper, your instructor may write **14.3,** which refers to chapter 14, section 3, where we deal with faulty parallelism. Or your instructor may write **11.10,** which will send you to "Placing Modifiers," or **11.11,** which will send you to "Misplaced Modifiers." Your instructor will tell you whether he or she intends to use numbers or symbols in marking your papers.

One other feature of this book that will help you find specific topics quickly is the reference box in the upper margin of each page. Inside the box is the appropriate section number (e.g.; **11.10, 11.11,** or **14.3**); above the box is the chapter abbreviation (e.g., *mod* or *pc*); and underneath the box, whenever it is needed for reference, is the revision symbol (e.g., *mm* or //). We hope these reference devices will help you find information conveniently both during your composition course and afterward.

# I

# WRITING
# ESSAYS

# 1

# GETTING STARTED

Sometimes the hardest part of writing is getting started. Looking at a sheet of blank white paper is like looking at a snow-covered car on an icy winter morning and wondering if the engine will turn over. When a car doesn't start, of course, there are certain simple things you can do—like calling somebody to come and recharge the battery. But what happens when the mind doesn't start? Where do you get a brain recharged?

Inspiration is a mysterious process, and no one can say just when and how it will strike. What we can say is that it strikes those who work for it much more often than those who simply wait for it. So how do you work for inspiration? How do you create the conditions under which the words will begin to flow? To that question this book has no single, simple answer. Creating an essay is an intensely personal process, and you will finally have to choose the method that works best for you. But it's important to have a method of some kind, to know what to do while waiting for inspiration. Here are our suggestions.

## 1.1   Get in Touch with Your Own Creative Rhythm

For most writers, composing is neither all work nor all inspiration. It's a process of moving back and forth from one to the other, from concentration to relaxation, from pushing ideas to playing with them—and making discoveries in the process. If you push an idea too hard, you may push it into the ground, but if you don't push at all, you may not get anywhere. So it's important to know how and when to push, and when to let up.

Sometimes letting up means simply getting up from your desk and doing something entirely different—walking around the block or going to a movie, or even watching an ant disappear into a crevice. You can't get an essay written by continually interrupting yourself, but you can get the most out of your working periods by alternating them with periods of relaxation. If you've been wrestling with a problem and then set it aside for a while, you will often find when you return to your desk that your subconscious has been working for you in the meantime. That is when inspiration may strike. But you have to earn those magic moments by periods of conscious and concentrated effort.

Before you even start planning the paper, therefore, you should think about your work schedule. Do you really expect to plan and write the paper in one all-night sitting? Maybe you can, but you're taking a risk. Very few writers can work for more than four or five hours without a break, and if you try to do so, you will probably find yourself slowing down or running dry or going around in circles, stuck in a groove because you're too tired to think straight. The smart way to get a paper written is to do it in stages, to set yourself short-term goals to be reached in brief periods of concentrated attention. Every time you sit down to work on your paper, you should set yourself just one specific job—a job you can do in two or three hours.

But creative rhythm is not just a matter of getting up from your desk once in a while and doing something else. It's also a matter of alternating concentration and relaxation while you are at your desk, of allowing space and time for your mind to breathe, and most especially of leaving room for discovery as you write. Work to formulate a searching question; then play with possible answers. Work to think of a good analogy; then let the analogy take shape in your mind. Work to come up with a good idea; then let that idea lead you to another. Allow for the unexpected. Keep yourself open, receptive, free.

Since freedom often leads to discovery, we don't believe that you must always start with a detailed outline, that you must plan every step of your essay in advance. If you like making an outline at the start and working from it, then stay with that method. But don't feel that you must have an outline before you can write anything at all. To make the outline in the first place, you have to know what you are going to write, and that is often what you don't know in advance. Sometimes the mere act of moving a pen across a page can put your mind in motion, making you think of things that would not have occurred to you otherwise. Starting without an outline leaves you open to discovery along the way. After you have made some discoveries, after you have actually written something, you can make an outline to organize what you have discovered.

**EXERCISE 1  Getting Started**

Write a letter to your teacher that begins, "The reason I have trouble getting words down on paper is. . . ." Write for five minutes without stopping. Don't worry about spelling, punctuation, grammar, or even making sense; just write whatever comes to mind. When the five minutes are up, go back and underline anything interesting in the letter that occurred to you for the first time while you were writing.

## 1.2  Choose a Topic You Really Want to Think About

If you're free to choose your own topic, pick one in which you are genuinely interested and about which you want to know more. You have to know something about any topic you write on, but writing is not just an act of transmitting information. It should also be an act of learning.

If you're free to choose any topic at all, you might well try to find something from your own experience, something that will let you explore yourself, perhaps something that you have never fully described or analyzed to anyone, even to yourself. The richest moments of our experience are often born out of conflict. Suppose you recall a time when you were made or asked to do something you did not want to do. When and where did it happen? How did you feel about having to act against your will? How did you feel about the person who asked you to do so? What did you learn from the episode?

Raising questions will help you to think more about any subject. If you know something about ceramics, say, or kayaking, you might ask a specific question about that. What makes kayaking so different from rowing a boat or paddling a canoe? Does centering a clay pot on a wheel have anything to do with finding the center of your own existence? It's always an advantage to write about what you know. But if you start writing on the assumption that you know it all, you drain the life out of the writing process.

**EXERCISE 2  Exploring Yourself**

Recall a time in your life when you felt bullied, cheated, or deceived. When, where, and how did it happen? How did you feel about yourself? How did you feel about the other person? What did you learn from this experience? As you consider these questions, write about them for ten minutes without stopping.

## 1.3 Make an Assigned Topic Your Own

When a topic is assigned, find a way to make it your own. Most of the writing you do in college will be on assigned topics. The way to get started on an assigned topic is to discover how it connects with what you already know, with your own interests and experience. By this means you begin to make the topic your own.

Suppose you are asked to write a term paper for a course in American government—on the presidential election of 1960, for example. If you are eighteen years old or more, you are already entitled to vote in federal elections. Have you ever voted? If so, what led you to vote for one or more particular candidates? This question might lead you to think about the way campaigns are run, about the part that newspapers, magazines, and television play in campaigns, about the building of a candidate's "image." Obviously, consideration of how you voted in 1980, and why, will not supply much information that is directly usable in a paper about the Kennedy–Nixon contest. But it can give you insights into the information you find in other ways, and will help you weigh its meaning and relevance. In other words, this personal way of getting into the topic will give you a firmer grip on it.

Or suppose you are asked to write an essay on the energy crisis for your freshman-composition course. Start by asking yourself how this crisis has affected you. Are you even now shivering because the heat has been turned down to save oil—or sweating because the air conditioner has been turned off to save electricity? Have you ever burned up a gallon or more of gas just looking for an open gas station or inching your way along in a gas line? Have you ever taken part in a demonstration at a nuclear power plant? Once again, any one of these personal experiences could be the wedge that opens up the topic for you.

But don't confuse personal experience with personal opinion. If personal experience can be an opening wedge, personal opinion can be a sledgehammer that pounds a topic flat: "I think the oil companies are ripping all of us off"; "I don't trust politicians." Statements like these say more about you than about your topic. It's better to start not with your opinion but with the *source* of your opinion, with your knowledge and experience of the outside world, with gas lines or icy rooms. If you want to get inside the topic, you will eventually have to get outside yourself.

EXERCISE 3   **Making a Topic Your Own**

Describe a personal experience that you might use to make a point about one of the following topics. Write for ten minutes.

| | |
|---|---|
| computers | crime |
| education | sports |
| farming | music |
| assembly-line manufacturing | housing |
| the selective-service system | |

## 1.4  Cut the Topic Down to Size

Cut the topic down to a size you can manage. One of the biggest obstacles to the success of a short essay is an oversize topic. If you try to write a five-hundred-word essay on the whole energy crisis, you will probably find that you have room only for the most commonplace generalizations about it: we squander energy; we depend too much on foreign oil; we must develop new sources of energy at home. When you fill up a paper with generalizations like these, you leave yourself no room to think and discover, to inject your own experience into the writing process. Also, you bore your readers by telling them what they have already heard many times before.

You probably drive a car on occasion; perhaps you own one. Instead of making generalizations about the whole energy crisis, you could write about your personal troubles in keeping the wheels rolling. How much are you spending—or have you spent—on gas each week? How much has the rising cost of gas affected the way you live? Do you take fewer trips than you once did? Do you ride a bicycle? By cutting the topic down to manageable size, by focusing on a small piece of a big subject, you give yourself the chance to look at it closely and see it with your own eyes.

Exercise 4  Cutting a Topic Down to Size

Take one of the general topics listed in exercise 3, above, and cut it down to a specific topic that you can manage in a short essay. Then ask a question about the specific topic, and write for ten minutes in response to the question.

> Example
> crime
> Specific Topic: shoplifting
> Question: How much should shoplifters be punished, and why?

## 1.5  Read with a Purpose

Whether you've been assigned a topic or have chosen one of your own, a good way of getting started is to read about it. You may not even have to go to the library. In the nearest newspaper or magazine you will find articles on a variety of subjects—articles that generate questions and thus put your mind to work. Why does abortion stir so much controversy? How would gas rationing affect the way we live? What effect does television have on children? How safe is nuclear power? Should homosexuals have a legal right to hold any jobs for which they are qualified—including teaching school? Should the federal government forbid the sale of handguns? Why are taxpayers refusing to support schools in some states? Why is the cost of medical care going through the roof?

You may also find plenty of ideas for essays in a prose reader—a book you may already own. Such a reader customarily includes contemporary as well as "classic" essays on a great variety of subjects, and can serve as your private library. A town or college library, of course, offers many more sources.

Reading is a fine way to fertilize your mind, to help you choose your topic, define it, enrich it, or enlarge it. Reading gives you not only a point of departure but a continuous supply of information. Reading with a purpose, you can often find an important fact or quotation to start a paragraph or even a paper. Suppose you are writing about television. It will help you to know that according to David Sohn (in "A Nation of Videots"), "the average American watches about 1200 hours of TV each year, yet reads books for only five hours per year." It will also help you to know that Robert Lewis Shayon finds TV "a lollipop trap—a pattern of prime-time entertainment programming planned, produced, and directed primarily at the twelve- to seventeen-year-old viewer" ("Consumers, Commercials, and Men about Town"). Facts and quotations like these not only push the paper beyond the limits of your immediate experience; they also generate further questions. Why do people let TV take over so much of their time? How are children and teen-agers presented on TV?

Reading in order to write is a special kind of reading, and we discuss it fully later in the book. (See chapter 9, pp. 171–98.) But the following chapter concerns the next stage in the process of writing: generating the raw material for an essay.

#### EXERCISE 5 Reading with a Purpose

From any printed source available to you—a book, a magazine, or a newspaper—take a single fact or opinion that strikes you as interesting, and write about it for ten minutes.

# 2

# PREWRITING AND FREE WRITING

Once you have chosen your topic, how do you think about it? No one but you can answer that question fully, but we can answer it in part. You need to think purposefully, pointedly, with a pen or pencil in your hand. Well before you start to write your first draft, you need to begin getting your thoughts down on paper. Here are some ways of doing so.

## 2.1 Ask Questions

Hit your topic with every question you can think of. Feel free to ask any questions at all about the topic, and be sure to write every one of them down. You probably won't get around to answering all of the questions you raise; indeed, some of them may not even have answers. But don't worry about the answers for now. Just get the questions down on paper.

What sort of questions? Journalists commonly dig up information by asking certain standard questions about anything that happens: what? who? when? where? how? why? As an essayist, you can use these questions to open up your topic. What happened? Who caused it to happen? When and where did it happen? How was it brought about? Why did it happen—for what purpose? And you might also ask, What was the result?

Not all of these questions will work for every topic. If you ask who caused the most recent nuclear accident, for instance, and what his or her purpose was, you may end up hunting in the dark for a mysterious saboteur or for the equally mysterious hand of

Providence. But every one of these questions can be tried with any topic as a way of opening up its possibilities.

Take television as a sample topic, and use the standard questions to generate further questions:

<u>What</u> is TV? Is it a medium of entertainment? Is it a means of communication? Is it an instrument of mass control? What's the difference between public TV and commerical TV? Is it just the difference between highbrow and lowbrow programming? How do the regular interruptions for advertising on commercial TV affect the viewer? How much of TV programming is aimed at children and teen-agers? What kind of experience are we getting when we watch commercial TV? And what do we get from public TV? What is TV "news"? How much of what really happens on a given day are we shown on the TV screen? How much of the so-called "news" is actually entertainment—stories chosen for "human interest"?

<u>Who</u> produces TV programs? Who writes them? Who sponsors them? Who directs them? Who appears in them? Who decides when to launch a new show or kill an old one? Who writes commercials? Who produces them? Who acts in them? Who directs them? Who controls their content?

<u>When</u> and <u>where</u> are TV programs made? Which programs are made for regional broadcasting and which for national broadcasting? Where are commercials made? How often are they shown? How long are they? How often do we get the news on TV? How often do we get live coverage of news events? When do most people watch TV? How many hours a week? How often do people sit down to watch a specific program? How often do they just turn on the set to watch whatever it offers?

<u>How</u> are TV programs made? On film, the way movies are? As live broadcasts? How are commercials made? And how do TV commercials influence us? Through comedy? Through "scientific proof"? Through appeals to primitive urges (as in images of roaring cars)? Through appeals to anxieties (as in commercials for deodorants, soaps, mouthwashes, travelers' checks)? Through the attraction of pure fun (in children's toys) or of athletic glamor ("the breakfast of champions") or of rejuvenation (as offered in vitamins, face creams, soft drinks)? How do commercials affect the experience of watching TV? How are women presented in commercials, especially commercials for cosmetics and household products like laundry soap? How are women presented in TV shows?

<u>Why</u> are TV programs made? Are they meant to entertain? to inform? to make money for the networks? to make money for

the sponsors? to manipulate the attitudes of the viewer? to get the viewer ready and willing to watch commercials? Why do people watch TV? Is it mainly because they have nothing better to do?

You can also ask about the results. What effect does TV have on the viewer? How much do TV commercials manipulate the consumer? Does violence on TV encourage violence in the real world? Do children grow up faster as a result of watching TV, or do they simply become passive? Does the picture tube weaken their interest in reading and writing? Do commercials turn children into little consumers, perpetually wanting new things? Have Americans grown addicted to TV? What would they do if it were suddenly abolished?

And (as we suggested in sections 1.2–1.3, pp. 15–16) you can ask questions involving yourself: What is my own experience of TV? How much did I watch it as a child? Was I ever deprived of it? How did I feel? What did I do with my time? What programs did I like as a child? What programs do I like now? Is there any particular program that has strongly affected me? Do I watch for entertainment, news, or both? How much of what the commercials tell me do I believe?

The subject of television is of course enormous, and the questions it raises are endless. But once you start asking questions on any topic, you will probably find that one question leads to another, and you should follow those leads wherever they take you—as long as they don't take you off the topic entirely. Use the five or six basic questions to generate others, to liberate your curiosity. And let your curiosity go.

Exercise 1   **Asking Question**

Write down at least ten questions on the topic of "women and careers."

## 2.2   Choose One Question to Give You a Goal

Choose one question to give you a specific writing goal. All of the questions you ask can help to generate material for you to write about, and a good deal of this material may find its way into the paper. But you need one question to focus on, to point you toward a specific writing goal. So after you've put down all the questions you can think of, read the whole list over and look for the question that strikes you as most important, most interesting, or most unusual. It may be one of the questions you have actually written down, or it may be a new question that grows out of those you have before you. In either case, this is the **basic question** you will hope to answer for yourself and your reader as you write the paper. Make it as sharp and specific and pointed as you can.

As soon as you have chosen your basic question, you can put checks beside some of the other questions on your list—questions that may help you pursue the answer to the basic question. You can also look for clusters of questions that might be considered together. For instance, suppose your basic question is, How do commercials affect our experience of television? You will obviously want to check all the questions about TV commercials, and within this category you may decide to group together questions about TV commercials and children, questions about TV commercials and adults, questions about TV commercials and women. This grouping will often look like a rough outline for the paper you will write. But whether or not you decide to make an outline just now, you have already put down and organized a set of questions about the topic, all of which will be available to you as you begin to write.

EXERCISE 2    **Choosing a Writing Goal**

Pick one of the questions you wrote down for exercise 1, p. 21, and make a list of other questions that may help you to pursue this one.

## 2.3    Get Reactions to Your Question

Explain your basic question to a listener, and get his or her reactions. One of the hardest things about writing is that you normally have to do it all by yourself. Before you begin to write, therefore, find someone you can talk to. Try to explain the basic question of your essay and what your own response to the question is likely to be. You may thus prompt your listener to give you a different response. Indeed, you might do well to seek out a listener who is likely to disagree with you. If you think television is nothing but a children's toy, for instance, try to talk with someone who thinks that at least some TV shows are aimed at intelligent adults. Hearing another point of view will make you more sensitive to the complexity of your subject, more skillful in anticipating possible objections to your point of view, and therefore more persuasive in defending it.

EXERCISE 3    **Getting Reactions**

Explain your basic question about "women and careers" to someone you know, and get his or her reaction. Then (1) record that reaction in writing, and (2) comment on it in writing.

## 2.4   Use Analogies

Think of analogies. A single comparison, especially between very different things, can open your eyes to a whole new way of looking at your topic. If you are writing about television, you might compare it with hypnosis, a process designed to make people passive receivers of suggestions or messages. Then you can ask further questions: Does TV control the way we think and act far more than we realize? Does the steady gaze of the newscaster put us into a trance when we watch the news? Do TV commercials subject us to posthypnotic suggestion, so that we feel compelled to buy Dial or Wheaties the next time we go to the store? Does the steady stream of violence on the news and in "entertainment" programs leave us numb, incapable of reacting to real violence?

Thinking up analogies is a purposeful kind of play in which you let your imagination go. Don't worry about being farfetched; if the analogy won't work, you'll find out soon enough. You're not formally writing yet. You're still trying out ideas, and anything goes.

(For more on this topic, see "Using Comparison, Contrast, and Analogy," pp. 59–62.)

EXERCISE 4   Using Analogy

Use an analogy to show how much opportunity you think women have now.

## 2.5   Work with a Nugget

Work with a nugget: a single word, idea, or example that fascinates you. Are you caught up by a particular word, phrase, idea, or example connected with your topic? If so, that may be a nugget for you, a rich source of further ideas. Suppose you are struck by the title of the television show *Happy Days*. Does it express for you a lot of what television programming is all about—nostalgic sweetness calculated to put the viewer in a happy daze of passive contentment? How many TV mini-dramas end in bleak unhappiness? Does TV blind itself to the fact that life is often frustrating, that many human problems cannot be solved in thirty minutes, or at all? And come to think of it, could there be a connection between the thirty-minute solution offered by the crime show or the situation comedy and the thirty-second solution offered by the commercial—the wretched housewife with a pile of "ring-around-the-collar" shirts to clean becoming the happy housewife with a pile of immaculate shirts, thanks to You Know What detergent? A single phrase can sometimes start a whole train of ideas that can be worked into your paper.

EXERCISE 5    **Working with a Nugget**

Write for ten minutes on one of the following:

> ladylike
> blind date
> businesswoman
> mankind
> housewife

## 2.6    Write for One Hour

Write without stopping for one full hour. Now is the time to produce your raw material. Read over everything you have written, get your goal firmly in mind, and write without stopping for an hour. This is called directed free writing. Feel free to plunge in without an introduction. Start with a nugget, with an analogy, with a question, with the one point that interests you more than any other; start anywhere you like, even with your conclusion, but start.

As you write, do not worry about the shape of your paragraphs or the structure of your sentences. You can think about those things later. Your only task now is to put down at least five hundred words—a thousand or more, if you can—in pursuit of the writing goal you have formulated, the answer to your basic question. Keep your mind on your writing goal, and keep writing for the full hour. If your mind stalls, keep your pen or typewriter going by repeating your last word until something new arrives.

Then take a break. If you've just written five hundred to a thousand words in an hour or so, you've certainly earned a breather. Get away from your desk for a while, and think about anything but the paper. You need to relax your brain before you can go on to the next step—which will be to shape the raw material you have just produced.

EXERCISE 6    **Nonstop Writing**

Write for one hour on the topic "women and careers." Use anything you wish to help you develop the topic—including examples drawn from TV programs and commercials. Don't stop until you've written for a full hour.

# 3

# SHAPING YOUR
# MATERIAL

In the previous chapter, we urged you to concentrate on your topic and not worry about anything else. Not even a practiced writer can think of everything at once, and while you are learning to write, you must feel free to concentrate on one thing at a time. So we urged you to be freewheeling, to start anywhere you wanted in pursuit of your topic, and to write without stopping for one full hour.

Now is the time to read your writing critically. If you want to know exactly what you have written, you should first set your writing aside for a time and then read it to yourself out loud. The time away from what you have written will help you consider it objectively, and reading out loud will force you to hear what you actually wrote—not what you think you wrote. Hearing your own words will also make it easier for you to imagine how they would sound to someone else.

As you read, in fact, you should pretend to be someone else. Think of the writer not as "I" but as "he" or "she," someone you don't even know. Though you may have set out to show that television commercials are seductive, "he" or "she" may have wound up saying that they are simply ridiculous. There is nothing wrong with that switch in direction. If you started out to write about TV and wound up discussing firewood, you might have a problem. But a change in your approach to the topic is a healthy sign that you are thinking as you write, that you are willing to discover things you didn't know when you started.

As you read your raw material, therefore, try to recognize the discoveries you have come upon, and then try to make the most of them. If you started with the idea that commercials are seductive and ended with the idea that they are silly, now is the time not to abandon the first idea but to ask yourself about its relation to the second. Is it possible that commercials are seductive *because* they are silly? When a fashion model tells us that she needs only a certain brand of perfume to get her through her day as housewife, career woman, mother, and party hostess, does the sheer absurdity of that claim somehow make it attractive as fantasy? These are the kinds of questions that a critical reading of your own raw material can raise. And as you consider the questions, you should rethink the goal and shape of the essay as a whole.

To help you do so, we recommend the procedures described next.

## 3.1 Outlining Your Raw Material

Once you know what you have written, you can outline it. We recommend that outlining be done now, rather than earlier, because outlining is essentially a way of shaping, and it is often hard to shape something that has not yet been written down. But once you have generated raw material, outlining it helps you to see more clearly which parts need to be expanded, which need to be cut back or cut out, and which need to be rearranged.

Your outline should begin with an indication of your writing goal—the basic question you are trying to answer. Under that question you can outline your raw material in one of two ways: by a vertical list or by a tree diagram.

### The Vertical List

The vertical list is the more common kind of outline, and a simple version of it looks like this:

BASIC QUESTION: How do TV commercials influence us?
    I. Purpose of commercials
        A. Manipulation of viewers' attitudes
        B. Public relations
        C. Selling
            1. Services
            2. Products
    II. Means of influencing viewers
        A. Music
        B. Setting
        C. Characters portrayed
            1. Men

2. Women
3. Children
III. Impact on viewers
   A. On children
   B. On adults

Besides listing all of your points, this outline presents them according to category and importance, showing their relation to the basic question and to each other. It lets you see the structure of the essay you are writing.

## The Tree Diagram

The other way of outlining your material is by the tree diagram. It is so called because it spreads out under the basic question like a family tree or a tree reflected in a lake, as shown on p. 28. The main advantage of the tree diagram is that it lets you see your ideas branching out organically, as you think. For this reason we recommend the tree over the vertical list, and later on, when we show how an outline can grow into an essay, we will be using the tree. A vertical list is a clear-cut way of laying out all your points after you have decided which to include and how to arrange them. But that is exactly what a tree diagram helps you decide. Because the tree is open-ended, you can make it grow by asking questions. What kind of women are portrayed in TV commercials? Some are housewives, and some are career women, so you might add branches for these under *Women*. And what about the quick-solution formula that so many commercials use? You could graft a branch for that onto *Means of influencing viewers*.

The tree lets you see what points are missing from your argument so far—where you need to extend it. The tree may also help you to decide which points are weak, irrelevant, or out of place. In the diagram shown here, for instance, you may decide that *Manipulation of viewers' attitudes* really belongs with *Means of influencing viewers*, or that influence and manipulation of attitude are essentially the same and should be combined under a single heading. Certainly the material to be covered under *Music* and *Setting* will vividly illustrate manipulation; when a TV commercial shows you a brand-new car sitting on the edge of a wave-beaten cliff while a sixty-piece orchestra plays Latin music somewhere offscreen, you know you are being manipulated.

You may notice that the middle branch in the diagram is the only one that is growing. As that happens, you may decide on drastic pruning elsewhere. Perhaps you now see that the center of this topic is *Means of influencing viewers*. If so, you may want to cut the other branches off and let *Means* take over the whole essay. Instead

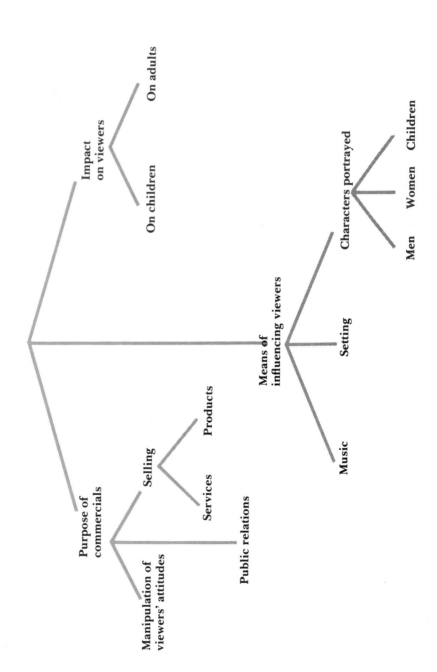

BASIC QUESTION: How do TV commercials influence us?

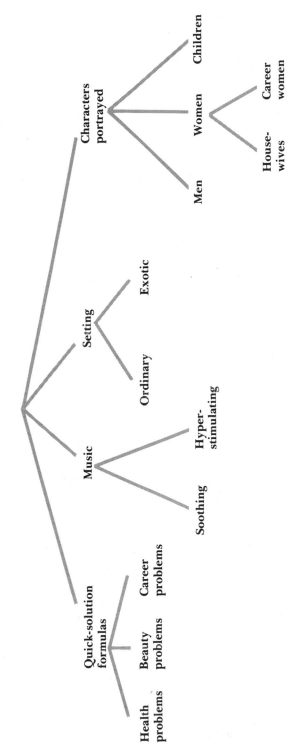

BASIC QUESTION: How do TV commercials influence us?

Quick-solution formulas
- Health problems
- Beauty problems
- Career problems

Music
- Soothing
- Hyper-stimulating

Setting
- Ordinary
- Exotic

Characters portrayed
- Men
- Women
  - House-wives
  - Career women
- Children

of trying to spin out several paragraphs on the obvious point that TV commercials sell products and services, you can mention that point in your introduction, and instead of trying to describe or guess at the actual impact of commercials (something very hard to determine), you can simply concentrate on *how* they sell. In any case, if that branch grows while others wither, it will soon be large enough to fill a whole essay. So now your outline might look like the one on p. 29.

This outline concentrates on the part of the topic that interests you most. Precisely for that reason, you will find that you can make it grow even more as you continue to write. The important thing is to use the outline not just as a record of your thought, but as a means of thinking.

### Formulating Your Thesis

As you think about your outline, you should turn your basic question into a basic answer, a positive statement of your main point. For the basic question about TV commercials, one possible answer is that they influence us by promising instant wish fulfillment: instant solutions to our problems, instant satisfaction of our desires, instant improvement in our lives. When you turn your basic question into an answer of this kind, you define your writing objective in positive terms. You establish the goal of your essay— the thesis you will develop as you shape the essay from beginning to end.

### EXERCISE 1   Outlining

By means of a vertical list or a tree diagram, outline the points made in your raw material on "women and careers"—the material you wrote for exercise 6, p. 24. Then revise the outline to make it as useful as possible, and write (in one sentence) a basic answer to your basic question.

## 3.2   Using Generalizations and Specifics   *spec*

The simplest way to develop any piece of writing is to move back and forth between general ideas and specific details. Whenever you don't know what to write next, ask yourself one of two questions: What specific thing will illustrate the general point I've just made? What's the general effect or general significance of the specific thing I've just mentioned? These two questions will help to energize your writing.

Furthermore, the back-and-forth movement between the general and the specific will help your readers as much as it helps you. A good piece of writing is like a well-marked road. Just as the road has general signs to say where you are headed (NORTH, WEST) and specific signs to say what's just ahead (BUMP, CURVE, CROSS-ROAD), so a good piece of writing has general signs to say where the writer is headed and specific ones to keep the readers' eyes on the road, to hold their attention.

To see how general and specific signs work together, consider this passage:

> My father's reaction to the bank building at 43rd Street and Fifth Avenue in New York City was immediate and definite: "You won't catch me putting my money in *there!*" he declared. "Not in that glass box!"
>
> Of course, my father is a gentleman of the old school, a member of the generation to whom a good deal of modern architecture is unnerving; but I suspect—I more than suspect, I am convinced—that his negative response was not so much to the architecture as to a violation of his concept of the nature of money.
>
> In his generation money was thought of as a tangible commodity—bullion, bank notes, coins—that could be hefted, carried, or stolen. Consequently, to attract the custom of a sensible man, a bank had to have heavy walls, barred windows, and bronze doors, to affirm the fact, however untrue, that money would be safe inside. If a building's design made it appear impregnable, the institution was necessarily sound, and the meaning of the heavy wall as an architectural symbol dwelt in the prevailing attitude toward money, rather than in any aesthetic theory.
>
> But that attitude toward money has of course changed. Excepting pocket money, cash of any kind is now rarely used; money as a tangible commodity has largely been replaced by credit: a bookkeeping-banking matter. A deficit economy, accompanied by huge expansion, has led us to think of money as a product of the creative imagination. The banker no longer offers us a *safe;* he offers us a *service*—a service in which the most valuable elements are dash and a creative flair for the invention of large numbers. It is in no way surprising, in view of this change in attitude, that we are witnessing the disappearance of the heavy-walled bank. The Manufacturers Trust, which my father distrusted so heartily, is a great cubical cage of glass whose brilliantly lighted interior challenges even the brightness of a sunny day, while the door to the vault, far from being secluded and guarded, is set out as a window display.
>
> Just as the older bank asserted its invulnerability, this bank *by its architecture* boasts of its imaginative powers. From this point of view it is hard to say where architecture ends and human assertion begins. In fact, there is no such division; the two are one and the same.                        —Eugene Raskin, "Walls and Barriers"

Raskin starts with a specific situation: one man's reaction to a specific building, at a specific address, with a specific kind of wall (glass). Then he gives us signs of the general direction his essay will take. The father's reaction typifies the attitude of a whole "generation"; the building symbolizes the way the men of that generation thought of their money—as something solid and real. To define this abstract notion, Raskin again resorts to specific objects (*bullion, bank notes, coins*) and specific actions (*hefted, carried, stolen*). He describes the old-fashioned bank in equally specific terms (*heavy walls, barred windows, bronze doors*), and then, after he has helped us to see this old-fashioned bank, he sums up the general impression it gives: *safe, impregnable, sound*. Then he contrasts the general concept of the bank as a safe with another general concept—that of banking as an imaginative service. To illustrate "imagination" and "service," he returns to something specific and visible: the brilliant glass box with which he began. By this back-and-forth movement between the general and the specific, Raskin finally guides us to his highly abstract point that architecture and human assertion "are one and the same." That, in fact, is the general destination of his whole essay.

(For a discussion of general claims and specific evidence in argumentation, see section 5.2, pp. 78–80.)

EXERCISE 2   **Recognizing Generalizations and Specifics**

Identify the ways in which the writer of the following passage moves between general or abstract points and specific details.

> Boys are wild animals, rich in the treasures of sense, but the New England boy had a wider range of emotions than boys of more equable climates. He felt his nature crudely, as it was meant. To the boy Henry Adams, summer was drunken. Among senses, smell
> 5 was the strongest—smell of hot pine-woods and sweet-fern in the scorching summer noon; of new-mown hay; of ploughed earth; of box hedges; of peaches, lilacs, syringas; of stables, barns, cowyards; of salt water and low tide on the marshes; nothing came amiss. Next to smell came taste, and the children knew the taste of
> 10 everything they saw or touched, from pennyroyal and flagroot to the shell of a pignut and the letters of a spelling book—the taste of A-B, AB, suddenly revived on the boy's tongue sixty years afterwards. Light, line, and color as sensual pleasures came later and were as crude as the rest. The New England light is glare, and the
> 15 atmosphere harshens color. The boy was a full man before he ever knew what was meant by atmosphere; his idea of pleasure in light was the blaze of a New England sun. His idea of color was a peony, with the dew of early morning on its petals. The intense blue of the sea, as he saw it a mile or two away, from the Quincy hills; the
> 20 cumuli in a June afternoon sky; the strong reds and greens and

purples of colored prints and children's picture-books, as the American colors then ran; these were ideals. The opposites or antipathies were the cold grays of November evenings, and the thick, muddy thaws of Boston winter. With such standards, the
25  Bostonian could not but develop a double nature. Life was a double thing. After a January blizzard, the boy who could look with pleasure into the violent snow-glare of the cold white sunshine, with its intense light and shade, scarcely knew what was meant by tone. He could reach it only by education.
30      Winter and summer, then, were two hostile lives, and bred two separate natures. Winter was always the effort to live; summer was tropical license. Whether the children rolled in the grass, or waded in the brook, or swam in the salt ocean, or sailed in the bay, or fished for smelts in the creeks, or netted minnows in the salt-
35  marshes, or took to the pine-woods and the granite quarries, or chased muskrats and hunted snapping-turtles in the swamps, or mushrooms or nuts on the autumn hills, summer and country were always sensual living, while winter was always compulsory learning. Summer was the multiplicity of nature; winter was school.

Henry Adams, *The Education of Henry Adams*

EXERCISE 3   **Using Generalizations and Specifics**

Moving back and forth between general ideas and specific details, write a brief essay on one of the following:

| | |
|---|---|
| a circus | a state fair |
| a zoo | an auto race |
| a boxing match | a motorcycle race |
| a football game | a bicycle race |
| a baseball game | a marathon |
| a formal dance | a supermarket |
| a disco party | a hockey game |
| Christmas Day | door-to-door selling |
| a day of surfing | a chess tournament |
| a political campaign | a bar mitzvah |
| a rodeo | |

## 3.3   Discovering Your Strategy

A writing strategy is a way of developing an idea. As we have already shown, the simplest way of developing an idea is to move from the general to the specific and then back again. But to shape your material, you will usually need in addition one or more formal strategies. As you look at your raw material, therefore, ask yourself whether you are mainly describing something, telling a story, explaining something, or seeking to persuade. If you had to identify the main strategy right now, which of these four would it be?

The better you understand your own writing strategy, the better you will write.

Within the framework of your main strategy you may use others. Suppose you want to explain how TV commercials turn children into consumers. You might begin this explanation by telling the story of how you once begged your parents to buy you a triple-decker dollhouse or a remote-control racing car, or by describing how one or the other of these looked when you saw it on TV. On the tree diagram, this story could be an outgrowth of the branch labeled *Children*. Or suppose you want to persuade your readers that TV detergent commercials insult women. Using exposition, you could compare and contrast the life of a woman you know with the lives of the women in the detergent commercials, lives that seem to revolve around a washing machine. Your exposition might then support the main point of your argument.

Whatever strategies you use, however, you should make one of them predominate. If you mainly want to prove a point about what TV does, the story you tell or the comparison you make should concern that point, by leading up to it, supporting it, or illustrating it. A long story of your own experience with TV is fine if what you want is a personal narrative. But if your aim is to present an argument about TV, you need to cut the story down to size and build up an argument around it.

(Because each of the strategies of development is important, we devote two entire chapters to them—chapter 4, pp. 52–74, on description, narration, and exposition, and chapter 5, pp. 75–96, on persuasion.)

## 3.4 Discovering Your Tone

When you hear someone speak, the first thing you are likely to notice is the tone of the speaker's voice. Is it loud or soft? friendly or hostile? sincere or sarcastic? The tone of the speaker's voice usually tells you something about how to interpret what he or she is saying. For instance, read these two questions out loud:

> Would you mind putting out that cigarette?
> Would you *mind* putting out that cigarette?

The words of both questions are exactly the same. Only the tone is different. The first question is polite; the second is insistent.

Obviously, it is harder to "hear" tone in the written word than in the spoken word. Aside from *italics* and **bold print** and exclamation points (!!!), all of which should be sparingly used, there is not much in writing that corresponds to the different ways we can make words sound in speech. Nevertheless, writers do have ways of conveying tone—of expressing an attitude toward their subject, their audience, or both.

Consider the tone in the opening sentences of a student essay about television:

> Why is there so little educational value in TV today? TV has been under fire for its violence in recent years, and it has also been criticized for its de-emphasizing of education. TV is taking away time that could be used to expand one's horizons (like reading, writing, playing an instrument, or practicing a sport) and replacing it with a means of entertainment that requires little or no concentration or imagination.

The student has the beginning of an idea, but the idea is obviously not his own, and the stiff impersonality of the tone shows it. The passive voice (TV "has . . . been criticized") is the voice of someone transmitting what he has heard from others, not of someone speaking for himself. The sentences are roundabout ("de-emphasizing of education") and wordy ("little or no concentration or imagination"). The student is still clearing his throat. But see what happens a few hundred words later:

> Public television has much more to offer than commercial networks do. It challenges you. It makes you think, analyze, and imagine. It compels you to use your mind and concentrate, rather than fall into a hypnotic doze while watching *Alice* or *The Incredible Hulk*. Many people don't watch public television because they think its programs are geared for the elite, sophisticated person. People with this attitude should head for cover because they aren't going to use all of their inner resources. Don't they realize the networks are insulting them by airing no-mind shows?

The writer finds his voice and his subject at the same time. Instead of generalizing about all television, he focuses on the difference between one kind of television and another. Instead of passively echoing the opinions of others, he actively voices his own conviction with verbs like *challenges, makes,* and *compels.* When he refers to the opinions of others this time, it is only to separate his own view from theirs. The tone is no longer leaden and muffled; it is sharp, intense, vigorously assertive. It's the tone of a writer who cares about his subject and wants to wake up his audience.

As you read your own writing, therefore, listen for the point at which you start to hear your own voice—the voice of a human being rather than a word-making machine. Do you hear a voice that breathes contempt for the shallowness of TV commercials? Do you hear a playful tone that mocks their simpleminded vision of life's problems? Or do you hear a poised, judicial tone, the voice of a cool and quietly skeptical observer? If you are pleased with the tone you hear in a certain passage, and especially if you feel that it sounds like you, you may have found the tone that will work best for the finished paper.

Tone is partly controlled by the level of diction you use—the formality or informality of your words. If you aren't sure at this point just what your level of diction is or what you want it to be, see section 7.1, pp. 126–29. And for a discussion of how to catch the tone in what you read, see pp. 176–80.

### EXERCISE 4    Discovering Tone

Here is an essay written by a first-term college freshman. Read it and then do the following: (1) Say what you think is the writer's *prevailing* attitude toward the family tradition. Does she find it admirable or ridiculous? Is she proud of it or ashamed of it? (2) Pick out the phrases or sentences that you think best express this attitude. (3) Rewrite the rest of the essay to make its tone consistent with that of the passages you have selected.

### THE BARTLEY THANKSGIVING

Thanksgiving dinner with my family is rather strange. In fact, if you've never been there before, it can be a bit of a shock treatment.

First of all, people are astonished by the vast amount of
5   humanity present. My mother was one of fourteen children, and a "family dinner" is a long-standing Thanksgiving tradition.

It all started (I think) with Mom's Gramma Bartley. Fifty or so years ago, Gramma Bartley would cook a meal for fifty or so of her brothers and sisters and children and grandchildren—single-
10  handed—for Thanksgiving. She had a very large house, by the way. This went on until she was too insensible to count turkeys. Then the kids took over.

In my younger days, I remember rotating from house to house each year, hitting all the aunts and uncles who still lived in
15  the County (Aroostook County, Me.). Of course, that was when we only had 20–30 people coming to dinner. Now we hire the Mapleton Town Hall every year.

Now you must remember that all these people are my aunts, uncles, and cousins. You must also be aware that my mother's sib-
20  lings have *never* been in one place at one time. In other words, we never have the whole family at Thanksgiving dinner. Those who can come home do, but there are usually about 25–30 people who can't make it home.

All arrangements are made by those already in the County.
25  The women have a meeting about two or three weeks in advance to decide who does what. We have to hire the hall, find beds for all who are coming home, and figure out who does the cooking.

That brings us to "food shock" for most people. We eat five

20 lb. stuffed turkeys, 150 lb. potatoes, 2 extra pans of stuffing,
30 6–10 pies (4–8 different kinds), 5 or 10 lb. peas, squash, lettuce,
milk, butter, gravy, turnip, and salads (green, Jell-o, fruit,
Martian—home recipe for lime and fruit salad, cranberry, cabbage,
coleslaw, and many, many more). There are also many other things
that are too numerous to mention.
35      After this is consumed, all join hands to clean up the hall
and claim silverware and dishes, and then all proceed to the nearest
home for coffee and conversation. Needless to say, we seldom eat
supper on Thanksgiving.

## 3.5   Thinking about Your Readers

While you are thinking about your writing strategy and your tone,
you must also be thinking about your readers. Who will be reading
your essay? How much do they know about TV? How much have
they thought about it? What are they likely to feel about it? If you
want to argue that TV turns us all into consumers, can you expect
that your readers will readily agree, or do most of them tend to
distrust TV commercials? To write effectively, you must try to consider how your readers are likely to think and feel about your subject.

Most of what you write in college will be read by a teacher.
So the question is, What does the teacher want? Some students try
to answer this question by "psyching out" the teacher, learning as
much as possible about his or her attitudes. You may soon find out,
for instance, that Ms. Finch strongly favors gun control and
opposes nuclear energy. If you agree, you will have no trouble
deciding how to write for her on those subjects. But suppose you
disagree? Does writing for particular readers mean that you can
never express your own opinion?

Of course it doesn't. It means only that you should consider
the needs and expectations of your readers, that you should at least
acknowledge the opinions of others before expressing your own.
Most teachers are open-minded enough to consider and even welcome the expression of beliefs they disagree with. But like other
readers, they want their own views to be recognized and respected,
not simply ignored and dismissed. So here are four questions to
keep in mind as you shape your draft.

**1.** How much do your readers know about the topic? Whoever
your readers are, you should try to estimate how much they are
likely to know about your topic. If you underestimate their knowledge, you will bore them by telling them things they already know;
if you overestimate their knowledge, you may confuse them with

unfamiliar terms or incomplete explanations. Try to tell your readers only as much as they need to know in order to understand you.

How much do they need to know? When you write for a teacher, you are writing for someone who probably knows more than you do about a certain subject. But no teacher knows everything about every subject, or even everything about any subject. If you are analyzing a novel or play for a teacher of literature, for instance, you can assume that your teacher knows the plot, but not that he or she has memorized every word of the complete text. If you quote the words of a particular character, you should say who the character is; if you analyze a particular scene or episode, you should explain the circumstances surrounding it and the details that fill it out. The need to explain may be still greater when you are writing about a subject in technical terms. In a lab report written for a chemistry teacher, you can use a word like *fractionation* in full confidence that your reader will understand it. But if you want to use the word in describing a chemistry experiment for your English teacher, you will have to explain what it means.

When writing for general readers, you can assume no more than general information. The wider your audience, the smaller the body of knowledge you can take for granted. If you are writing about boating for a college newspaper or magazine, you can expect your readers to know what a mast and a sail and a rudder are, but you cannot assume that they will know the meaning of *luff* or the specialized meaning of *sheet*. Likewise, if you are writing about high-fidelity components, you can take for granted a general knowledge of what turntables, amplifiers, and speakers do, but you cannot assume that everyone will know the specialized meanings of *wow* and *flutter*.

**2.** How do your readers feel about the topic? Are they likely to favor one side or the other, or will they be undecided or indifferent? It is one thing to defend gun-control legislation when your readers are conservationists, quite another when they are hunters and sportsmen. You can assume that conservationists already favor gun-control legislation and may simply want to arm themselves with arguments for it; but if you want to reach the hunters and sportsmen, you will have to show them that you understand the attractions of hunting and target shooting before you explain the danger of guns in irresponsible hands. To be effective, in other words, you must demonstrate that you understand and respect the feelings of readers who may disagree with you.

**3.** How do your readers expect you to treat the topic? Another way of asking this question is, How does your teacher expect you to treat the topic? But the classroom is not the only place where writ-

ers work under instructions. Professional writers—especially journalists—often work under instructions from editors who tell them
not only what to write about but also how to treat it. When you get
a writing assignment, therefore, you should find out as much as
you can about the approach you are expected to take.

In part that approach will depend on the rules of the game,
the conditions under which you are writing. If your chemistry professor asks for a lab report, you are expected to record what the
experiment showed, not what you felt when you performed it. But
if your English teacher asks for an account of a personal experience
and you decide to describe your first lab experiment, you will
include your feelings, since for this assignment you are expected to
describe what you felt. Students are sometimes confused because
they get conflicting advice about whether or not to start sentences
with *I*, or whether to use *I* at all. The advice is conflicting because
different readers have conflicting expectations. If the reader
expects you to make personal experience a part of your essay,
then you should use *I*; if the reader expects you simply to report
facts and conclusions, you should avoid *I*.

Most of the time, however, readers expect something
between the personal and the impersonal, something between "I
feel" and "it is." If you use *I* in every sentence, you will soon seem
to be floating in a cloud of self-absorption; if you never use *I*, you
may begin to sound like an impersonal machine. Most readers want
objective truth, but they also want to feel that the words they read
have been produced by a human being. In any case, there is no
such thing as a purely impersonal fact. All facts are statements
about what some person has perceived, and now and then, at least,
the person who makes those statements should be willing to
acknowledge his or her own existence.

How you decide to treat a topic will affect not only the number of *I*'s you use but also the strategies of development you select
(see section 3.3, pp. 33–34), the level of your diction (see section
7.1, pp. 126–29), and the extent to which you use and cite sources
for your material (see chapter 27, pp. 449–98, on writing the
research paper). The more you know about all these aspects of
treating a topic, the better you will be able to meet your reader's
expectations.

**4.** <u>How long is the finished essay supposed to be?</u> Often, in college
and afterward, you will be assigned a minimum or a maximum
number of words or pages in which to express your ideas. Aim to
make your first draft half again as long as the minimum—or even
the maximum. When you revise, you will find many words and
even an idea or two that you want to cut out; all authors do, and

many published books and essays include only half of what the author originally wrote, or even less. But if you have written your draft to the prescribed length, pruning that deadwood can seem like cutting away your own flesh. So, in your first draft, write as much as you can about your subject, and do not worry about wasting words. Writing more than you will finally want is liberating. It frees you from the drudgery of counting up words, so you can start making every word count.

With a specific length in mind, with several hundred words of raw material in hand, and with an outline and a general sense of your tone, writing strategy, and audience, you are now ready to begin shaping your essay. Of course, you cannot assume that you are all done thinking about content; as you shape the essay, you will probably have new ideas you want to include in it. But now is the time to put your ideas into a full first draft. The rest of this chapter will show you how to write that draft—how to introduce your essay, determine its general shape, and conclude it.

## 3.6    Introducing Your Essay

In general, the best time to write an introduction is after you have produced at least the raw material for your essay—not before. You will probably confuse your reader and yourself if you try to write your introduction before you know what you are introducing. But by now, if you have followed the steps explained, you should have a fairly clear idea of where your paper is headed.

So how do you get that idea across to your reader? You may have been told that every essay you write should have an introductory paragraph. That advice is good but incomplete. What every essay should have is an **introduction,** and an introduction sometimes takes more than one paragraph. Instead of describing a particular form, therefore, we will focus on the purpose of an introduction.

To write a good introduction, you need to think about the kind of impression you want to make on your reader. Think for a moment about what impresses you when you start reading something. What turns you off after two or three sentences? What turns you on and holds your interest? The better you understand what makes you want to read on, the better you will understand the art of the introduction.

Whatever its length, a good introduction seizes the reader's attention and guides it to the writer's main object. Consider what can be done with just one or two opening sentences:

When I was six or seven years old, growing up in Pittsburgh, I used to take a penny of my own and hide it for someone else to find.　　　　　—Annie Dillard, "Pilgrim at Tinker Creek"

There are more than thirty-three million investors in the United States today. Most of them are losers.
　　　　　—Richard Ney, *Making It in the Market*

The world of religion and philosophy was shocked recently when Henry P. Van Dusen and his wife ended their lives by their own hands.　　　　　—Norman Cousins, "The Right to Die"

According to the Book of Genesis, God first created man. Woman was not only an afterthought, but an amenity.
　　　　　—Elaine Morgan, "The Man-Made Myth"

The recent changes in the technique of war have produced a situation which is wholly unprecedented.
　　　　　—Bertrand Russell, "Co-existence or No Existence: The Choice Is Ours"

Everyone lives on the assumption that a great deal of knowledge is not worth bothering about.
　　　　　—Wayne Booth, "Is There Any Knowledge That a Man *Must* Have?"

The law barring Federal agencies and holders of Federal contracts from discriminating against the physically handicapped has not been actively enforced during its three years of existence.
　　　　　—Nancy Weinberg, "Disability Isn't Beautiful"

Here we have a variety of openings. There are broad generalizations about the creation of man and about knowledge. There are specific statements about discrimination against the handicapped, about a personal experience with pennies, about the suicide of a man and his wife. And there are generalizations with a cutting edge, such as the statement that most of the more than thirty-three million investors in this country are losers.

What do these openings collectively tell us about the art of introducing an essay? Different as they are, all have at least one thing in common: they announce the subject matter of what follows. Together with the titles of the selections, they tell us what the writers plan to discuss: investing, suicide, man and woman, war, knowledge, discrimination against the handicapped. In the first opening, the one that concentrates on personal experience, you cannot yet tell precisely what the subject matter will be, but the author does give a powerful clue; she is introducing an essay on the art of seeing and of finding the beautiful sights hidden around us in nature. In one or two sentences, then, each of these writers indicates what he or she is going to write about.

In addition, these opening sentences catch the reader's attention. The generalizations do it with a wide net that includes us all, or nearly all; the specific and personal openings do it with a sharp hook. When Elaine Morgan cites Scripture on the creation of man, she begins to show how Scripture generates the myth of male dominance. When Wayne Booth cites the universal assumption about knowledge we don't need, he implicitly raises a question about knowledge we do need. Likewise, the specific and personal openings raise provocative questions of their own. Why did Annie Dillard hide pennies, and why does she remember doing so? Why did Henry P. Van Dusen and his wife commit suicide? Why is the law barring discrimination against the handicapped not enforced? The wide and the narrow openings alike raise questions.

Finally, each of these openings is designed to accommodate its audience, the readers for whom it was written. Richard Ney, for instance, is writing for pragmatic readers who would like to make money investing and want to know why they do not. Norman Cousins is writing for the high-minded readers of the *Saturday Review,* and he assumes not only that they are interested in the world of religion and philosophy but also that they must be gently introduced to what will in fact become a defense of suicide. That is probably why he avoids the word *suicide* in his opening sentence, though he does use it later in the paragraph. (For the complete paragraph, see pp. 114–15.)

Now see what one of these writers does with his whole introduction:

> There are more than thirty-three million investors in the United States today. Most of them are losers. Not only do they lose their money; they lose their self-confidence, their security, and the chance they had at one time to use their money to make a killing in the market. Yet the fact is that to get the money needed to invest in the market, most of these people had to be fairly successful in their chosen career. As doctors or lawyers, for example, many of them had demonstrated an ability to think clearly, to make plans for the future, and to carry them out. Why then, employing the same intelligence, do they go wrong when they try to make money in the market? —Richard Ney, *Making It in the Market*

Ney opens with a startling observation and guides us to a provocative question. Asking a sharply worded question is always a powerful way to end an introductory paragraph. It tells us that the writer is seeking answers, and it invites us to share in the search. Note too how Ney prepares us for the question. He opens by speaking of investors as *losers,* and he emphasizes this point by using *lose* twice in the next sentence. Then he gives us a twist, a shift in thought, marked by the transitional *Yet.* The *losers* he has been talking about are *fairly successful* in their own fields. Having thus set up a conflict, Ney poses the question that leads directly into his whole book, How can these winners in medicine and law be losers in the market?

Now here is a two-paragraph introduction:

> When I was six or seven years old, growing up in Pittsburgh, I used to take a penny of my own and hide it for someone else to find. It was a curious compulsion; sadly, I've never been seized by it since. For some reason I always "hid" the penny along the same stretch of sidewalk up the street. I'd cradle it at the roots of a maple, say, or in a hole left by a chipped-off piece of sidewalk. Then I'd take a piece of chalk and, starting at either end of the block, draw huge arrows leading up to the penny from both directions. After I learned to write I labeled the arrows "SURPRISE AHEAD" or "MONEY THIS WAY." I was greatly excited, during all this arrow-drawing, at the thought of the first lucky passerby who would receive in this way, regardless of merit, a free gift from the universe. But I never lurked about. I'd go straight home and not give the matter another thought, until, some months later, I would be gripped by the impulse to hide another penny.
>
> There are lots of things to see, unwrapped gifts and free surprises. The world is fairly studded and strewn with pennies cast broadside from a generous hand. But—and this is the point—who gets excited by a mere penny? If you follow one arrow, if you crouch motionless on a bank to watch a tremulous ripple thrill on the water, and are rewarded by the sight of a muskrat kit paddling from its den, will you count that sight a chip of copper only, and go your rueful way? It is very dire poverty indeed for a man to be so malnourished and fatigued that he won't stoop to pick up a penny. But if you cultivate a healthy poverty and simplicity, so that finding a penny will make your day, then, since the world is in fact planted in pennies, you have with your poverty bought a lifetime of days. What you see is what you get.
>
> —Annie Dillard, "Pilgrim at Tinker Creek"

The first paragraph is nothing but narration, the personal story of what a little girl did with pennies. Only in the second paragraph does this personal story gain broader significance. Here the author guides us from the personal excitement of planting penny surprises to the universal idea that all of nature is planted with surprises. Thus she introduces the main point of her whole essay. Once again, notice the transitional word—*But*—early in the second paragraph. Can you see why it is there? Again there is a conflict, this time between the excitement of finding a surprise and the apparent worthlessness of a *mere penny*. The challenge of the essay is to resolve this conflict: to make readers see that what they often overlook in the world around them is decidedly worth looking at.

Here is another two-paragraph introduction:

The case *for* college has been accepted without question for more than a generation. All high school graduates ought to go, says Conventional Wisdom and statistical evidence, because college will help them earn more money, become "better" people, and learn to be more responsible citizens than those who don't go.

But college has never been able to work its magic for everyone. And now that close to half our high school graduates are attending, those who don't fit the pattern are becoming more numerous, and more obvious. College graduates are selling shoes and driving taxis; college students sabotage each other's experiments and forge letters of recommendation in the intense competition for admission to graduate school. Others find no stimulation in their studies, and drop out—often encouraged by college administrators.          —Caroline Bird, "Where College Fails Us"

The first paragraph briefly describes the reigning view of a college education. The main point here is not that college is good for everyone, but that everyone thinks it is. That is the starting point for the essay because in 1975, when it was written, that was the writer's estimate of what her readers thought. She did not need to spend time proving a point that her readers had long taken for granted.

The second paragraph—which begins with *But*—challenges the assumption described in the first. It turns our attention sharply from the popular view of college to a contrary view—the view that college is not good for everyone, that in fact it is bad for many. Note that the author has not changed *her* mind as she moves from the first paragraph to the second. She wants to change *our* minds, and the purpose of these two contrasting paragraphs is to guide us from one point to another, to move us from a comfortable assumption to an uncomfortable truth. If we believe that going to college is good for everybody, or nearly everybody, this introduction goads us to read on and find out why someone would say it is not.

What then, finally, do these introductions have in common? Besides catching the reader's attention and announcing a subject, they each turn on some kind of opposition. They challenge popular notions and vague ideas. They question. They probe. They expose. Whether revealing the simple excitement of a penny surprise, attacking the idea that college is good for everyone, or asking why intelligent people lose money in the stock market, a good introduction rumples the bed of our assumptions and wakes us up.

Now that you have seen what makes a good introduction, consider this opening sentence of a research paper written by a college freshman:

There were many reasons for dropping the atomic bomb on Japan in World War II.

As the beginning of a paper on the atomic bomb, this sentence has one great virtue: it points directly to the writer's topic. But the writer has failed to consider the feelings that the topic may arouse in many of her readers—readers who may regard the atomic bomb as a weapon of pure horror. How could she reach those readers? Instead of calmly starting with the reasons for dropping the bomb, she might begin by acknowledging its destructiveness:

> More than thirty years after the event, many people are still appalled by the fact that the United States dropped the atomic bomb on Japan in World War II. Even now, it is hard to fully justify the destruction of two cities, the death of thousands of men, women, and children, the suffering and permanent disfigurement of thousands more, and the generation of countless birth-defective children. Perhaps *no* reason can ever justify such devastation. Yet if only to prevent a second atomic bombing, we do well to consider the reasons that prompted the first one.

By describing the way many people feel about the destructiveness of the bomb, this paragraph prepares the reader for a discussion of the reasons that prompted its use. (For more on the technique used here—making concessions—see section 5.6, pp. 92–94.)

Now consider the whole of the student's original opening paragraph:

> There were many reasons for dropping the atomic bomb on Japan in World War II. Among them was the idea of the tremendous postwar diplomatic leverage the bomb might provide, especially in dealings with the Soviet Union. Though such motivation was of far less importance than the major desires to save American lives and to end the war sooner, it was still quite influential among many of the policy-makers of the war years. Its force was felt not so much in the actual decision to use the bomb as in some of the aspects that surrounded that use. Through the recognition of the situations that made this influence possible, as well as of its effect, comes an awareness of the American attitudes of which it was an indication. In these attitudes it is possible to see one of the basic causes of the arms race and our involvement in it, as well as a possible reason for our failure to end that involvement.

This introduction has one major weakness: it gradually leads the reader away from the topic instead of toward it. A good introduction ends with a statement or question that clearly forecasts what is to come. This introduction begins sharply, but it ends with a sentence that vaguely locates one cause of the arms race in *these attitudes.* To identify *these attitudes* we have to look in the previous sentence, where the word *attitudes* is connected with *it,* and *it* in turns refers to *this influence.* To identify *this influence,* we have to go back two more sentences to the statement that *it was still quite influ-*

*ential,* with *it* now referring to *motivation.* Moving back one more sentence, almost to the beginning of the paragraph, we at last discover that the motivation was *the idea of the tremendous postwar diplomatic leverage the bomb might provide.* This crucial point is stated just once, and then buried beneath layers of indirect reference. The reader has to be an excavator to find it.

How do you get the main point out into the open and keep it there, before the reader's eyes? One good way is to use the technique illustrated in the introductions previously quoted—the technique of opposition. The new concessive opening about the destructiveness of the bomb could be followed by this revised version of the student's opening paragraph:

> There were many reasons. The one most often cited was the desire to end the war and thus save American lives. But also important was the idea of the tremendous postwar diplomatic leverage the bomb might provide, especially in dealings with the Soviet Union. The idea of diplomatic leverage not only influenced our decision to bomb Japan in 1945; it is also one of the basic causes for our continuing involvement in the arms race now.

This version stresses the main point by setting it off against another point, by repeating it, and by keeping it in plain view to the end of the paragraph. Words that cover up the main point—words like *attitudes*—have been stripped away. What is left clearly announces the subject of the paper.

### Exercise 5   Composing an Introduction to an Argument

For a group of readers that includes people opposed to your position, introduce an argument for or against one of the following propositions.

> The federal government should underwrite the cost of an abortion for any woman who wants one but cannot afford to pay for it.
>
> The sale of marijuana should be legalized throughout the United States.
>
> Anyone eighteen years of age or older who is not certifiably insane should be allowed to own a handgun.
>
> All grade-school children in America should be taught to speak at least one foreign language.

### Exercise 6   Composing an Introduction Leading to a General Point

Beginning with the following sentence, write an introductory paragraph that leads to a general point about the relation between human beings and modern cities.

> In New York City a few years ago, a twenty-seven-year-old man named George Willig broke the law and yet became a hero when he managed to scale the 1,350-foot-high World Trade Center.

EXERCISE 7   Using a Personal Example in an Introduction

Use a personal example from your own childhood to introduce a general point about human nature or growing up.

EXERCISE 8   Citing a Popular Attitude in an Introduction

Write a paragraph to introduce an essay on a subject you know well. Begin by describing the popular attitude toward this subject; then set your attitude against the popular one.

## 3.7   Shaping the Body of Your Essay

If you have come up with a good introduction, you are well launched. If you have decided to put off writing the introduction until later, that's fine too. In either case, you should now start work on the body of the essay, the largest and most important part.

### Using Your Outline

Shaping the body of your essay calls for both invention and control. You need to follow your outline, but you should not be tyrannized by it. As you write, you will not only generate words, phrases, clauses, and sentences; you will think of new evidence, new strategies, even new points to be supported in their own right. If you write down everything that comes to mind, you will simply have some more raw material. But if you close your mind to new ideas, you may be putting the body of your essay into a straitjacket. You need to do your shaping with a flexible hand.

So what do you do with a brand-new idea that comes to you as you write? Is it a gift or a distraction? Will it be an asset to the essay or a digression that will waste your time and energy? Sometimes it can be hard to decide which. If the idea obviously supports the point you are making in the paragraph you are working on, you can take it up right away. If it doesn't, see whether it can be grafted onto a branch of your tree diagram, for use later on.

Some new ideas may not seem to fit anywhere. Suppose you are writing about television commercials, and suddenly your mind presents you with this: "What a terrible finish the Sox had last year!" What on earth can you do with something like that? Maybe your mind is just chafing at the discipline of creating to order, and is declaring its independence. But maybe your mind has also made some useful association and just isn't quite able to communicate it to you. To be safe, you might jot this stray thought down somewhere—"poor Sox finish"—and then go on with your draft. Later you might look again at the jotting and see whether it pulls something else out into the open. Sports on television is a fertile subject.

Athletes make commercials, and like the quarterback who posed in pantyhose, they sometimes make fools of themselves in the process. TV producers force the inclusion of enough time-outs to get in the required number of commercials, and a time-out can actually change the course of a game. (In broadcasts of some continuous sports, such as soccer, the game goes on invisibly while the commercials run; is that practice better or worse than introducing time-outs?) So if you're writing about TV commercials, you may decide to go back and tie in the subject of sports on television with your discussion of the link between commercials and programs.

Your outline, then, should be a guide but not a dictator. If you are using a tree diagram, remember that it is a tree and should grow. If you discover an entirely new branch to be added as you proceed, that may be just what the whole tree needs.

**Thinking in Paragraphs**

To write a sentence is to work with words, phrases, and clauses; to write a paragraph is to work with sentences. Paragraphing is a deliberate act, the act of thinking about the connections and the differences between one sentence and another. To think this way is to think in paragraph form—the form that all good writing customarily assumes.

One way to think in paragraphs is to use each of the subheadings in your outline as a paragraph starter. If you are writing from the tree diagram on p. 29, for instance, you can use the subheadings to start four paragraphs: one on the quick-solution formula in TV commercials, another on their music, a third on their settings, and a fourth on the way they present various characters. Moving from left to right across the tree diagram, you will thus get each of your points into paragraph form, supporting it with facts and ideas drawn from your raw material.

But of course this is only one way of translating your outline into paragraphs. Looking at your outline, you may decide that you would rather start with the characters portrayed in TV commercials and only then go to the quick-solution formula—the formula that the characters are created to fill. Furthermore, you may find as you think about your points that you need more than four paragraphs to develop them; you may need a whole paragraph, for instance, just to consider the way TV commercials present housewives or children. If you have enough supporting detail, you may give a paragraph to each of the sub-subheadings in your tree diagram, and your essay will then have a body of at least ten paragraphs.

If your outline makes sense and each of your paragraphs comes from one of its headings or branches, you will be on your way to a well-organized essay. To keep it well-organized, make sure that the main point of each paragraph is tied to the main point of the essay as a whole. If your main point is that TV commercials offer quick solutions to every problem, each of your paragraphs should deal with TV solutions to specific problems. If a new idea for a paragraph comes along as you write, you should try to connect it to your main point. Suppose that in the midst of an essay on the quick-solution formula you suddenly find yourself thinking about sex and music in TV commercials. Can these be related to the quick-solution formula? Do sex and music help to create a feeling of escape from real-life problems? If so, write a paragraph on this point; you can thus explain how sex and music reinforce the impact of the quick-solution formula.

(Since the organization of individual paragraphs is just as important as the organization of the essay as a whole, we give an entire chapter to the writing of paragraphs. See chapter 6, pp. 97–125.)

## 3.8 Ending Your Essay

The ending of your essay is your last chance to clarify and emphasize your main point, or to specify its implications. A good ending can take any of the following forms:

**1.** An answer to the question posed by the introduction. The complete introduction to Norman Cousins's essay "The Right to Die" (quoted in part on p. 41) leads up to a question: "Does an individual have the obligation to go on living even when the beauty and meaning and power of life are gone?" Here is the final paragraph of Cousins's essay:

> Death is not the greatest loss in life. The greatest loss is what dies inside us while we live. The unbearable tragedy is to live without dignity or sensitivity.

This is Cousins's final answer to the question he originally posed.

**2.** A recommendation of a specific course of action. The introduction to Nancy Weinberg's essay "Disability Isn't Beautiful" (quoted in part on p. 41) charges that handicapped people have been subject to discrimination "while the Government acts as if they were different from other minorities." Here is the final paragraph of her essay:

> The physically handicapped have the liabilities of a minority group. Shouldn't they be given the rights of a minority group? The answer is affirmative. It is time the action was also.

This final paragraph makes a specific recommendation. Note that the question here is rhetorical; it assumes and provokes the answer "Yes." It is designed not to generate an inquiry, but to conclude one—with a positive call for action.

**3.** A restatement of the main point, making its implications clear. Here is the concluding paragraph of an essay that sets out to show that violence on television makes the heavy viewer unusually frightened of the real world:

> We have found that violence on prime-time network TV cultivates exaggerated assumptions about the threat of danger in the real world. Fear is a universal emotion, and easy to exploit. The exaggerated sense of risk and insecurity may lead to increasing demands for protection, and to increasing pressure for the use of force by established authority. Instead of threatening the social order, television may have become our chief instrument of social control. —George Gerbner and Larry Gross, "The Scary World of TV's Heavy Viewer"

This ending is spare. It does not retrace all the steps of the argument that came before it, or cite all the evidence supporting the authors' main point. It simply restates that point, and then connects it with the increased demand for protection against danger—for the use of force by established authority. This point in turn leads to the final point, the explicit statement of what has already been said implicitly: television may have become our chief instrument of social control.

**4.** A final telling example to emphasize the main point. To end an essay on the amount of garbage produced by New York City, Katie Kelley has this paragraph about Fresh Kills, a Staten Island dumping site:

> "It sure has changed out here," one worker, who has been at Fresh Kills for years, told me. "Why, there used to be fresh natural springs over there." He gestured out over the hundreds of acres of garbage. Natural crab beds once flourished in the area. Now they, too, are gone, buried under tons of garbage.
> —"Garbage"

The final paragraph thus clinches the point of the whole essay. Instead of summarizing her principal points or restating her main one, the writer makes us see the quantity of garbage we produce and its smothering effect. The picture of the springs and crab beds buried under tons of garbage is far more effective than any final abstract statement about garbage could be.

As these examples show, you can end an essay in a variety of ways. You can give the answer to a question, recommend a course of action, restate the main point of your essay, or simply underscore the point with one final example. But in any case, your final paragraph is your final chance to drive your main point home. Whatever else it does, it should leave the reader with a clear understanding of what you have been trying to show or to do in the essay as a whole.

**EXERCISE 9   Composing an Ending**

Pick out one of the introductions you wrote for exercises 5–8, pp. 46–47, and write a final paragraph to go with it—a paragraph that could end the essay you introduced.

# 4

# STRATEGIES OF DEVELOPMENT
## Description, Narration, and Exposition

A writing strategy is a way of reaching the goal you set for yourself when you sit down to write. Suppose you want to re-create a frightening experience. How do you convey the feeling of that experience? Do you **describe** what you saw and heard at a particular moment? Do you **tell the story** of the events that led up to it? Description and storytelling (narration) are strategies of development, and you can use them both together to achieve your goal. Or suppose you want to show why America should fully revive its railroads. To make this point, you might **explain** such things as the "piggyback" railroading of long-distance freight, and you might try to **persuade** your readers that trains are better than cars for long-distance passenger travel. Like narration and description, explanation and persuasion are strategies of development, ways of reaching your goal.

This chapter and the next consider in turn each of the four major writing strategies. This chapter treats description, narration, and exposition (the art of explaining). Chapter 5, pp. 75–96, treats persuasion, which includes argumentation. Most writing combines at least two of these strategies, and we will show you some ways of combining them as we proceed. But first we explain each strategy by itself.

## 4.1   Description

**Description** is writing about the external features of people or things. To describe a thing is to say how it looks, feels, sounds, smells, or tastes. Some description can be given in a single sentence:

> The coyote is a long, slim, sick, and sorry-looking skeleton, with a
> grey wolf-skin stretched over it, a tolerably bushy tail that forever
> sags down with a despairing expression of forsakenness and mis-
> ery, a furtive and evil eye, and a long, sharp face, with slightly lifted
> lip and exposed teeth.                                   —Samuel L. Clemens

This lengthy, cumulative sentence is full of descriptive detail. After
the opening adjectives (*long, slim, sick, sorry-looking*) and the vivid
reference to the coyote as a *skeleton*, Clemens writes of the skin, the
tail, the eye, the face, the lip, and the teeth. His descriptions of all
these specific features help us to see the whole coyote clearly.

Now consider an extended description:

> Situated on the banks of the St. Johns River, Palatka was
> surrounded by dense tropical foliage in limitless swamps. It was
> always hot, and it rained daily. The town's main street, made of
> bricks, was called Lemon Street. Weeds grew out of the spaces
> between the bricks and out of the cracks in the sidewalks and at the
> bottom of the concrete buildings, so that to a stranger the vegeta-
> tion appeared to be strangling the town. There was a paper mill in
> town. It supplied most of the blacks and poorer whites with
> employment. Each morning at six they were summoned to work by
> a whistle that woke the entire area. Shortly thereafter Palatka was
> blanketed by a lavender haze and filled with a terrible stench.
> —Pat Jordan, *A False Spring*

The writer begins with a general statement about the surroundings
of the town (*dense tropical foliage in limitless swamps*), then turns to
the main street, and then to a close-up look at the weeds poking up
between the bricks and through the cracks in the sidewalks. He
goes on to appeal to the ear with *a whistle*, to the eye with *a lavender
haze*, and to the nose with *a terrible stench*. All of these descriptive
details work together to convey a general impression of Palatka.
Nowhere does the writer say that Palatka is a dreary and decaying
town, but every one of his details shows us that it is.

All good descriptive writing re-creates an impression. It presents the thing itself, not merely the author's feelings about the
thing. Suppose instead of Jordan's paragraph you had read:

> I couldn't stand Palatka. It was poor, seedy, smelly, and ugly,
> and the weather was always bad. I couldn't relate to the people
> either. My stay there was a nightmare.

Here the writer gets between us and the town. Instead of showing
us how and why the town affected him as it did, he simply talks
about his own feelings. He doesn't let us share his experience.

*dev/dne*

4.2

EXERCISE 1   Describing

In a single sentence, describe a person or animal you know. Follow the form of Clemens's sentence, using *with* phrases to add as many details as possible.

EXERCISE 2   Describing

Using Jordan's description of Palatka as a model, briefly describe the neighborhood in which you grew up. If you lived in several places while growing up, describe the one you remember most vividly. Include as many specific sights, sounds, and smells as possible, but tie them together with at least one statement about the general effect of the place. And assume that your reader has never visited it.

## 4.2   Narration

### Narrating Events in Sequence

**Narration** is writing about things that happened, and it normally shows the order in which they happened. To narrate is to tell how one event followed another:

> I got up early on Wednesday morning, jogged two miles, and then ate a breakfast of ham and eggs.

This is narration in just one sentence. But usually narration takes more than one sentence, as in this account of an incident that helped to provoke the Boston Massacre in 1770:

> On Friday, March 2, a Boston ropemaker named William Green, busy with his fellows braiding fibers on an outdoor "rope-walk" or ropemaking machine, called to Patrick Walker, a soldier of the Twenty-ninth [Regiment] who was passing by, and asked if he wanted work. "Yes," Walker replied. "Then go and clean my shithouse," was Green's response. The soldier answered him in similar terms, and when Green threatened him, he departed, swearing to return with some of his regimental mates. Return he did with no less than forty soldiers, led by a big Negro drummer.
> —Page Smith, *A New Age Now Begins*

Here the writer reports a sequence of actions and statements: Green called to Walker and asked him something, Walker replied, Green responded, the soldier answered, Green threatened, the soldier departed and then returned. The writer reports these events as they followed one another in time, and his use of dialogue—of Green's actual words—makes this moment in American history come vividly alive.

EXERCISE 3   Narrating

Using chronological order, give a brief narration of a fight or quarrel you have seen or been involved in. Concentrate on how the fight or quarrel got started.

## Narrating Events Out of Sequence

In the simplest kind of narration, the writer preserves the original sequence of events: *I got up early . . . , jogged two miles, and then ate a breakfast of ham and eggs.* But for various reasons, the writer may need to change the original sequence, moving backward and forward in time. For example:

> In June 1964 . . . two Italian fishing boats, working in tandem with a crew of 18, were dragging their nets along the bottom of the Adriatic. Toward dawn, as they pulled up the nets after a long trawl, the fishermen realized their catch was unusually heavy. . . . When they finally swung the nets inboard they saw an ungainly, prehistoric-looking figure missing both feet. It was, in fact, a 500-pound Greek statue covered with nearly 2,000 years of sea encrustations.
>
> In November 1977, this life-size bronze fetched the highest known price ever paid for a statue—$3.9 million. The work is attributed to the fourth century B.C. Greek artist Lysippus. . . . Professor Paolo Moreno of Rome University, author of two books on Lysippus, identifies the statue as the portrait of a young athlete after victory and suggests that it may have been plundered by ancient Romans from Mount Olympus. The ship bearing the statue was probably sunk in a storm and there may well have been other treasures on board. Pliny the Elder tells us Lysippus made more than 1,500 works, all of them bronze, but it was doubted that any of the originals had survived—until this one surfaced.
>
> The fishermen stealthily unloaded the barnacle-covered masterpiece in Fano, near Rimini, and took it to the captain's house, where it was put on a kitchen table and propped up against a wall.          —Bryan Rosten, "Smuggled!"

The first paragraph tells the story of how a statue was discovered in June 1964. To explain what makes the story important, the writer flashes forward to 1977, when the statue was sold for nearly four million dollars. Then he flashes back to ancient times, when the statue was lost. After these forward and backward flashes, he returns to the original story in the third paragraph.

EXERCISE 4   Using Flashbacks and Flash-forwards

Using at least one flashback and one flash-forward, tell the story of one of the following:

your first day on a full-time job

your first day in college

your first meeting with someone who later became important in your life

the first time you felt that you were doing something wrong

### Combining Narration and Description

Description is writing about people or things in space; narration is writing about events in time. But since events involve people and things, narration is often combined with description. For instance, in his description of Palatka (p. 53), Pat Jordan tells what happened every day (*it rained*) and what happened every morning (the workers *were summoned to work by a whistle that woke the entire area*, and then *Palatka was blanketed by a lavender haze and filled with a terrible stench*).

#### EXERCISE 5    Using Narration in Describing

Use narration to expand the description you wrote for exercise 2, p. 54.

#### EXERCISE 6    Using Description in Narrating

Use description to expand the narration you wrote for exercise 3, p. 55.

#### EXERCISE 7    Using Description and Narration Together

Using narration and description, tell how you were once asked to do something you did not want to do.

## 4.3   Exposition

### Using Narration and Description to Explain

**Exposition** is explanatory writing. Its purpose is to explain or clarify a certain point. And just as you can use narration and description to enrich each other, so you can use either one or both of them to help explain something. Suppose, for instance, you wanted to explain the relation between American colonists and the British army in the years before the outbreak of revolution. The story of the British soldier and the Boston ropemaker would help you to show how strained the relation was.

Of course you may not happen to know many stories about the American Revolution. But you do know something about your own experience, and telling the story of a personal experience can be an effective way of launching an expository essay. Consider this example:

When I was a little girl, my mother told me to wait for the light to turn green before I crossed the street and to cross always at the corner. This I did. Indeed, I was positive as a very young child that I would get mashed like a potato if I even so much as stepped a foot off the sidewalk while the light burned red. I followed my mother's advice until I realized that she herself jaywalked constantly, dodging in and out of moving traffic—and pulling me with her. So after a while I followed her example and not her advice.

My father told me never to cheat or steal and I remember my intense humiliation the day, only 6 years old, I received a public spanking for swiping three dimes from the windowsill where they had been left by a visiting uncle. Yet my father pushed me under the turnstile to get into the subway and got me into the movies for half fare, way after I was old enough to pay full price. And my mother continually brought home reams of stationery and other supplies lifted from the offices where she worked.

Both my parents exacted severe punishment for lying and yet I knew, in time, that they lied to me and to each other and to others when, presumably, they felt the occasion warranted it.

And this was just part of the story. But hypocrisy about sex, about race relations, about religion, took me a longer time to see. I was out of high school before that picture began to pull together. Understanding didn't devastate me because I had begun to absorb the knowledge little by little, through the years. By the time I was 18 or 19 I guess I was both old enough to understand and strong enough to face what I saw. And [I] could face it because I learned my parents were not unusual. Most everybody's parents were the same. And we, my friends and I, did come to take it for granted. Parents were that way. Older people were that way. The word for what we found out about our parents' generation was hypocrisy. And most of us accepted it as part of life—as the way things were.
—Lynn Minton, "Double Vision"

The writer starts with personal experience and guides us from there to the main point of her essay. The first paragraph shows how the mother ignored her own advice about jaywalking, the second how both parents ignored the father's advice about stealing, the third how both ignored their own rule against lying. Successively, these personal experiences lead to the main point of the essay: hypocrisy is a fact of life.

You can use personal experience anywhere in an essay—not just at the beginning. See how a story of personal experience enters this editorial essay:

Gun legislation is dead for another year. As a result, if statistics are any guide, there's every likelihood that a lot of people now living will also be dead before the year is over.

There's no point in citing those statistics again; they may

prove something, but they're not likely to prompt any concrete action. There is nothing very moving about statistics.

What is needed to produce results is passion—and that's where the anti-gun-control lobby has it all over the rest of us. Those who favor stronger gun legislation—a solid majority of Americans—can't hold a candle to the lovers of guns when it comes to zeal.

I had a taste of that passion recently, and I begin to understand something of what it is that fosters in gun libbers such dedicated resolve. Thanks to a bunch of Cub Scouts and an absurd little creature that went bump in the night, I've begun to realize why cold, unemotional tabulations of gun deaths will never lead to effective gun control.

The writer then tells the story of how he bought a pump gun so that the boys in his Cub Scout den could practice target shooting, how he used the gun one night on a possum that had been wreaking havoc in his garage, and how he was seized with the sense of absolute power that a gun gives its possessor. The main point of his essay grows directly out of the story:

No wonder, I thought, that people become hooked on guns. This is the feeling that explains their passion, their religious fervor, their refusal to yield. It's rooted in the gut, not in the head. And in the recurrent struggle over gun legislation it is no wonder that their stamina exceeds mine.

I can understand that passion because I've felt it in my own gut. I've felt the gun in my hand punch psychic holes in my intellectual convictions. And having felt all that, I do not have much hope that private ownership of deadly weapons will be at all regulated or controlled in the foreseeable future.

—Roger Verhulst, "Being Prepared in Suburbia"

EXERCISE 8  **Using a Story to Make a Point**

State a general point about authority, obedience, or obligation that can be illustrated by the personal story you told in exercise 7, p. 56.

**Using Examples**

One of the simplest means of explaining anything is to give an example. You have seen how a story can be used to illustrate a point; the whole of the story is then an example. But examples can be shorter than an entire story, as in this passage:

Anyone who reads [ancient Greek stories] with attention discovers that even the most nonsensical take place in a world which is essentially rational and matter-of-fact. Hercules, whose life was one long combat against preposterous monsters, is always said to have had his home in the city of Thebes. The exact spot where Aphrodite was born of the foam could be visited by any ancient tourist; it was just offshore from the island of Cythera. The winged steed Pegasus, after skimming the air all day, went every night to a comfortable stable in Corinth. A familiar local habitation gave reality to all the mythical beings. —Edith Hamilton, *Mythology*

This passage makes the point that the heroes of Greek mythology were said to have lived in real places. The first and last sentences state this point plainly. Between those two sentences are three examples: Hercules lived in Thebes; Aphrodite was born near Cythera; Pegasus was stabled in Corinth.

### EXERCISE 9  Stating a Point

Each of the following passages offers one or more examples to explain or illustrate a point. State the point in a single short sentence.

 1. A hockey player rushing up ice travels at more than twenty-five miles an hour; a slap shot hurls a frozen rubber disc toward a goalie at one hundred miles an hour. Everything that happens in hockey—passing, stickhandling, checking, shooting—happens fast. —Jeff Greenfield, "The Iceman Arriveth"
 2. Curiosity is as clear and definite as any of our urges. We wonder what is in a sealed telegram or in a letter in which someone else is absorbed, or what is being said in the telephone booth or in low conversation. —James Harvey Robinson, *The Mind in the Making*

### EXERCISE 10  Using Examples

Develop the following point by adding a series of short examples to illustrate it.

Some of the most important things we need to know have to be learned outside a classroom.

## Using Comparison, Contrast, and Analogy

The first question we commonly ask about anything new and strange is, What's it like? We ask the question because the only way we can understand what we don't know is by seeing its relation to what we do know, by learning how it resembles and how it differs from other things. To show these resemblances and differences, the writer of exposition uses comparison, contrast, and analogy.

**1. A comparison** states the similarities and differences—or just the similarities—between two or more things of the same class, such as two schools, two cars, two cities, two games:

Like football, soccer is a ball game played on an outdoor field with a goal at each end. But unlike football, soccer has no ball carriers.

**2.** A **contrast** states the differences between two or more things of the same class:

> Unlike a football, the soccer ball is round. It is not passed or carried, as the football is, but rather is kicked along the ground or hit with the head.

Since the word *comparison* can be used to mean a noting of similarities alone, the phrase *comparison and contrast* is sometimes used to designate a noting of similarities and differences.

**3.** An **analogy** notes the similarities between two or more things of different classes:

> The surface of the earth is like the skin of an orange, which cannot be spread out flat unless it is torn into strips. That is why flat maps of the whole earth always distort its appearance.

With an analogy, the writer links a remote, abstract, or specialized subject with something concrete, ordinary, and familiar; he or she can thus explain the subject to average readers.

All three of the techniques—comparison, contrast, and analogy—can be used at length. See the way analogy is used in this explanation of how the universe expands:

> My nonmathematical friends often tell me that they find it difficult to picture this expansion. Short of using a lot of mathematics I cannot do better than use the analogy of a balloon with a large number of dots marked on its surface. If the balloon is blown up, the distances between the dots increase in the same way as the distances between the galaxies. Here I should give a warning that this analogy must not be taken too strictly. There are several important respects in which it is definitely misleading. For example, the dots on the surface of a balloon would themselves increase in size as the balloon was being blown up. This is not the case for the galaxies, for their internal gravitational fields are sufficiently strong to prevent any such expansion. A further weakness of our analogy is that the surface of an ordinary balloon is two dimensional—that is to say, the points of its surface can be described by two co-ordinates; for example, by latitude and longitude. In the case of the Universe we must think of the surface as possessing a third dimension. This is not as difficult as it may sound. We are all familiar with pictures in perspective—pictures in which artists have represented three-dimensional scenes on two-dimensional canvases. So it is not really a difficult conception to imagine the three dimensions of space as being confined to the surface of a balloon. But then what does the radius of the balloon represent, and what does it mean to say that the balloon is being blown up? The answer

to this is that the radius of the balloon is a measure of time, and the passage of time has the effect of blowing up the balloon. This will give you a very rough, but useful, idea of the sort of theory investigated by the mathematician.

—Fred Hoyle, *The Nature of the Universe*

If you have ever seen what happens to the design on a balloon when it is blown up, you should readily understand this analogy. It is not perfect—no analogy ever is—but it does give you a rough idea of how the universe expands, a way of picturing that expansion in your mind. For the explanation of any unfamiliar subject, analogy is an enormously useful tool.

However, you should beware of arguing by analogy, of assuming that because two things are alike in some respects they are also alike in others. In some ways the expansion of the universe resembles the blowing up of a balloon. But you cannot therefore argue that the universe will eventually reach a breaking point and pop. (For more on this point, see "Arguing by Analogy," pp. 89–90.)

EXERCISE 11 **Using Analogy**

Explain the problems of choosing and pursuing a career by noting the similarities between this process and the experience of driving on the interstate highway system.

Comparison can sometimes serve the same purpose as analogy, explaining the unknown by relating it to the known. Piccadilly Circus in London, for instance, can be likened to Times Square in New York; the troubadours of medieval Europe can be likened to the folk singers of our own time. But in a comparison the noting of similarities usually goes hand in hand with the noting of differences. Consider this passage:

> A thousand years ago in Europe acres of houses and shops were demolished and their inhabitants forced elsewhere so that great cathedrals could be built. For decades the building process soaked up all available skilled labor; for decades the townspeople stepped around pits in the streets, clambered over ropes and piles of timber, breathed mortar dust and slept and woke to the crashing noise of construction. The cathedrals, when finished, stood half-empty six days a week, but most of them at least had beauty. Today the ugly office skyscrapers go up, shops and graceful homes are obliterated, their inhabitants forced away and year after year New Yorkers step around the pits, stumble through the wooden catwalks, breathe the fine mist of dust, absorb the hammering noise night and day and telephone in vain for carpenter or plumber. And the skyscrapers stand empty two days and seven nights a week. This is progress. —Eric Sevareid, *This Is Eric Sevareid*

Sevareid compares two different construction projects. Like the building of a medieval cathedral, the building of a skyscraper drastically interferes with the lives of human beings, and in each case the finished product stands empty for much of the time. But while most medieval cathedrals were beautiful, the skyscraper is ugly. The point of this comparison is that what we call "progress" is actually regress—progress in reverse.

Sevareid's point governs his comparison. A writer with a different aim would use these materials in a different way. There is almost always more than one way of comparing particular persons or things. How they are compared depends on the writer's purpose.

Normally, writers use contrast rather than comparison when they want to stress the difference between two or more things. See if you can spot the writer's purpose in this contrast:

> You see things vacationing on a motorcycle in a way that is completely different from any other. In a car you're always in a compartment, and because you're used to it you don't realize that through that car window everything you see is just more TV. You're a passive observer and it is all moving by you boringly in a frame.
>
> On a cycle the frame is gone. You're completely in contact with it all. You're *in* the scene, not just watching it anymore, and the sense of presence is overwhelming. That concrete whizzing by five inches below your foot is the real thing, the same stuff you walk on, it's right there, so blurred you can't focus on it, yet you can put your foot down and touch it anytime, and the whole thing, the whole experience, is never removed from immediate consciousness.
>
> —Robert Pirsig, *Zen and the Art of Motorcycle Maintenance*

Here the writer explains what riding a motorcycle is like by explaining what it's not like. Since cars and motorcycles are both in the same class—motor vehicles—and since both are familiar, the writer need not point to their obvious similarities. Instead, he contrasts the two, and the contrast reveals what is distinctive about riding a motorcycle: the sense of direct, unframed, participatory contact with the outside world. Pirsig does note the similarity between looking through the window of a car and watching TV, but this resemblance simply exposes the passivity of riding in a car, and thus sharpens the contrast between that and the activity of riding on a motorcycle.

EXERCISE 12  **Comparing**

Taking one of the following pairs, explain the first item in the pair by comparing it with the second.

college / high school
good teaching / bad teaching
your present neighborhood / your old neighborhood
your town or city / any other town or city
your favorite sport / any other sport
a good roommate / a bad roommate

## Using Definition

A definition explains a word or phrase. The task of defining a word can take up an entire essay, as it does in the essay on photography (pp. 73–74). But more often a definition is used within an essay, to explain a word or phrase that the reader needs to know in order to understand the essay as a whole. A definition of this kind saves the reader the trouble of consulting a dictionary, of course, but it can also explain the word or phrase more fully and clearly than the dictionary usually does. And if you want to use a word in a special way, your own definition will let the reader understand just what you mean by it.

There are many ways of defining a word. The least effective is the one that students most commonly use: quoting the dictionary ("Webster defines *freedom* as . . ."). Instead of quoting the dictionary, you can use one or more of the methods listed next.

**1.** Defining by synonym. A synonym is a word or phrase that means approximately the same thing as the word you are defining:

> *Apathetic* means *indifferent.*
> To *prevaricate* is to *lie.*
> *Clandestinely* means *secretly.*

The form of the synonym must correspond to the form of the word being defined. *Apathetic* means not *indifference,* but *indifferent; to prevaricate* means not *lying,* but *to lie.*

**2.** Defining by comparison, contrast, or analogy. You can define a word by comparing, contrasting, or likening it to another word:

> The *plover* is a bird that lives on the shore, like the sandpiper. But the plover is usually fatter, and unlike the sandpiper, it has a short, hard-tipped bill.
>
> While burglary is the stealing of property from a place, *robbery* is the stealing of property from a person.
>
> A *lien* on a piece of property is like a leash on a dog. It's a way of legally attaching the property to someone who has a claim against the property owner.

**3.** Defining by function. If the word denotes a person or object, you can define it by saying what the person or object does:

An *orthopedist* treats bone diseases.
An *ombudsman* defends an individual in a conflict with an institution.

**4. Defining by analysis.** You can define a word by naming the class of the person or thing it denotes and then giving one or more distinctive features:

| | CLASS | FEATURE |
|---|---|---|
| An *orthopedist* is | a doctor | who specializes in bones. |
| A *plover* is | a bird | that lives on the shore. |
| A *skylight* is | a window | set in the roof of a building. |

**5. Defining by example.** You can define a word by giving examples after naming the class of the person or thing it denotes:

A *crustacean* is a shelled creature such as a lobster, a shrimp, or a crab.
A *planet* is a heavenly sphere such as Jupiter, Mercury, Mars, or Earth.

**6. Defining by etymology.** Etymology is the study of the roots of words. You can sometimes define a word by giving its root meaning and thus showing where it came from:

*Intuition* comes from the Latin words *in* (meaning "in" or "into") and *tueri* (meaning "look" or "gaze"). Literally, therefore, it means a "looking inward."

A definition may use more than one of these methods, especially if it runs to a paragraph or longer. Here, for instance, from a recent article on cancer research, is a definition of *interferon:*

Interferon is a large hormone-like protein produced by the cells of all vertebrate animals. It was discovered in 1957 in Britain by virologists Alick Isaacs and Jean Lindenmann during their investigation of a curious phenomenon: people are almost never infected by more than one virus at a time. Seeking an explanation, the researchers infected cells from chick embryos with influenza virus. What they found was a substance that protected the chick cells from both the flu and other viruses. Because it interfered with the infection process, it was dubbed interferon.
—*Time,* November 6, 1978

This definition combines analysis with comparison and with etymology of a sort—a little digging into the origin of the word. Interferon is a *protein;* that is its class. It is compared to hormones—described as *hormone-like*—and its name is said to have come from the word *interfere.*

You may want to use a word in a special or restricted sense. If so, you should clearly explain to your reader just what you mean by it. *Webster's New Collegiate Dictionary* defines *diagram* as "a line drawing made for mathematical or scientific purposes." But Kenneth Clark defines *diagram* somewhat differently—in order to explain how it functions in art:

> By "diagram" I mean a rational statement in a visible form, involving measurements, and usually done with an ulterior motive. The theorem of Pythagoras is proved by a diagram. Leonardo's drawings of light striking a sphere are diagrams; but the works of Mondrian, although made up of straight lines, are not diagrams, because they are not done in order to prove or measure some experience, but to please the eye.
> —Kenneth Clark, "The Blot and the Diagram"

Strikingly enough, Clark defines *diagram* not as a drawing but as a "statement in a visible form," a way of proving or showing something. Then he gives examples of what a diagram is and what it is not. This definition is more than an incidental piece of clarification. It turns out to be essential to Clark's essay.

There are limits, of course, to how special your definition may be. In Lewis Carroll's *Through the Looking Glass,* when Humpty Dumpty defines *glory* as "a nice knockdown argument," Alice rightly objects. If your definition departs drastically from the customary one, you will either baffle your reader, who will find it difficult or impossible to set aside the customary definition entirely, or cause suspicion about your motives. Your own definition, therefore, should be a restricted version of the customary one, not a new definition altogether.

**EXERCISE 13   Defining**

Using at least two of the methods just described, define one of the following words.

| | |
|---|---|
| conservative | feminist |
| amateur | jazz |
| suburbanite | ecology |

## Analyzing by Classification and Division

Probably you have been asked more than once to analyze a particular topic or problem. But just what does *analyze* mean? Essentially, analyzing a subject means breaking it into parts small enough to handle. If you are asked to analyze American democracy, for instance, you can start by defining it as a system of government in which the people rule. But in order to talk about "the people," you must separate them into categories or groups: voters and nonvoters, elected officials and appointed officials, presidents, governors, representatives, mayors, sheriffs, school-board members, and the like. In so doing, you are using classification and division.

**Classification** is the arrangement of objects, people, or ideas with shared characteristics into classes or groups. Whenever you speak of professors, sophomores, women, men, joggers, jocks, or grinds, you are grouping individuals together as a class because of one or more things they have in common. You can do the same with individual objects or ideas. You can classify motorcycles, cars, and trucks as "motor vehicles"; apples, pears, and oranges as "fruits"; monarchy, democracy, and dictatorship as "political systems." Classification is a way of imposing order on the hundreds of individual persons and things we have around us. We place these in general categories, just as we place ice cream, salt, coffee, chicken, cereal, milk, peanuts, tomatoes, eggs, lettuce, and Coke in one big shopping bag and speak of everything inside as "groceries."

**Division,** on the other hand, is the act of cutting up one big group into two or more smaller ones. The first thing you are likely to do when you get home with that shopping bag full of groceries is to take out the eggs, ice cream, milk, chicken, lettuce, and tomatoes and put them in the refrigerator. Then you will put the cereal, peanuts, coffee, and salt in a cupboard or on a shelf or counter. In so doing, you are dividing your groceries into two categories— those that need refrigeration and those that don't. You will put the Coke in the refrigerator if you want to keep or get it cold; otherwise you won't.

There are many other ways of dividing up groceries. Which system you choose depends on your purpose. If you want to be sure of your nutritional balance, you will take stock of your "meat group" foods (chicken and eggs), vegetables (lettuce and tomatoes), dairy products (milk and ice cream), and fiber foods (cereal). If you are giving a party, you will get out party foods, such as Coke and peanuts. If you are dieting, you will separate fattening foods (Coke, ice cream) from nonfattening foods (lettuce, tomatoes, chicken).

In everyday living, then, everyone has to classify and divide in order to cope with a world of individual objects and people. And what is true in everyday living is also true in writing. It is hard to get very far into any subject without classifying and dividing its parts. Suppose you are writing an essay on why students go to college. Classification is inherent in your topic; you are writing about the class of individuals called "college students," or perhaps about the class of ideas called "reasons why students go to college." And to discuss the reasons in this class adequately, you will soon have to divide them according to one or more systems. You may decide to separate internal reasons from external ones, with internal reasons including the desire to grow intellectually, the desire to meet new people, and the desire to prepare for a profession, and external reasons including the expectations of parents, friends, and society at large. This system of division will enable you to discuss the interplay of internal and external reasons in particular students, and then to classify these students as primarily inner-directed or primarily outer-directed.

In any case, whenever you write about a group of people, objects, or ideas, you will need a system of classifying and dividing them. Complicated subjects may call for more than one system. Consider this analysis of the way certain study programs now treat the history of minority groups in America:

> . . . Most of the study programs today emphasize the goodness that is inherent in the different minority communities, instead of trying to present a balanced story. There are basically two schools of interpretation running through all of these efforts as the demand for black, red, and brown pride dominates the programs.
>
> One theory derives from the "All-American Platoon" concept of a decade ago. Under this theory members of the respective racial minority groups had an important role in the great events of American history. Crispus Attucks, a black, almost single-handedly started the Revolutionary War, while Eli Parker, the Seneca Indian general, won the Civil War and would have concluded it sooner had not there been so many stupid whites abroad in those days. This is the "cameo" theory of history. . . .
>
> The cameo school smothers any differences that existed historically by presenting a history in which all groups have participated through representatives. Regardless of Crispus Attucks' valiant behavior during the Revolution, it is doubtful that he envisioned another century of slavery for blacks as a cause worth defending.
>
> The other basic school of interpretation is a projection backward of the material blessings of the white middle class. It seeks to identify where all the material wealth originated and finds that each minority group *contributed* something. It can therefore be called the contribution school. Under this conception we should all love Indians because they contributed corn, squash, potatoes, tobacco, coffee, rubber, and other agricultural products. In like manner, blacks and Mexicans are credited with Carver's work on the peanut, blood transfusion, and tacos and tamales. . . .
>
> The danger with both of these types of ethnic studies theories is that they present an unrealistic account of the role of minority groups in American history. Certainly there is more to the story of the American Indian than providing cocoa and popcorn for Columbus' landing party. When the clashes of history are smoothed over in favor of a mushy togetherness feeling, people

begin to wonder what has happened in the recent past that has created the conditions of today.

—Vine Deloria, Jr., *We Talk, You Listen*

There are two systems of classification here for two different classes of things: "minority groups" on the one hand, and, on the other, study programs that emphasize the good in the history of those groups. Three races—black, red (Indian), and brown (Mexican)—are classified as "minority groups," and the programs that emphasize the goodness of those groups are divided into two schools of interpretation—the "cameo school" and the "contribution school."

Now, what is the purpose of this classifying and dividing? Deloria puts the three races into a single classification because, despite their differences, it is what they have in common that the study programs emphasize. On the other hand, he divides the study programs into two schools of interpretation so that he can distinguish between their approaches. Ironically, seeing the difference between these two approaches makes us recognize more clearly how similar are their results. Both schools of interpretation seek to blur distinctive racial identities into the single class "minority groups," and even to swallow up that class in a still larger class—"Americans." For the "cameo school" of interpretation, the Indian, the Mexican, and the black are just three more soldiers fighting for the good American cause; for the "contribution school," they are just three more wholesalers delivering their goods to the great American supermarket. Either way, indiscriminate classification blurs the lines of racial division and distinctiveness.

America has been called the melting pot, a vast caldron in which racial identities dissolve. Yet in recent years, various racial groups in America have reasserted their distinctive identities. What happens to those identities when we classify all blacks, Mexicans, and Indians simply as "minority groups," or as "Americans"? Deloria does not clearly answer this question. He simply raises it—and forces us to think about it.

Here is one more example of classification and division:

> There are 435 members of the House of Representatives and 417 are white males. Ten of the others are women and nine are black. I belong to both of these minorities, which makes it add up right. That makes me a celebrity, a kind of side show attraction. I was the first American citizen to be elected to Congress in spite of the double drawbacks of being female and having skin darkened by melanin.
>
> When you put it that way, it sounds like a foolish reason for fame. In a just and free society it would be foolish. That I am a national figure because I was the first person in 192 years to be at

once a congressman, black, and a woman proves, I would think, that our society is not yet either just or free.
—Shirley Chisholm, *Unbought and Unbossed*

The author classifies the members of Congress by two systems at the same time—by sex and by color. If she had classified them by these two systems separately, she would have had confusingly overlapping categories: 425 males, 426 whites. By using these two systems together, she makes you see that an overwhelming majority of the members of Congress—417 out of 435—are both white and male.

But she does classify women and blacks separately. Can you see why? She wants to dramatize a striking point: while the overlap between "white" and "male" in Congress is 417 individuals, the overlap between "black" and "female" in Congress is precisely 1— Shirley Chisholm herself. At the time she wrote, she was the only person in Congress who was both black and female. Classification and division here help to show just how whiteness and maleness together dominate Congress. The purpose of the classification governs its method.

**EXERCISE 14   Classifying and Dividing**

Write an account of yourself in which you do the following: (1) Identify one of the racial, religious, ethnic, or sexual groups you belong to. (2) Explain whether or not your group can be classified with other groups of people. (3) Explain the divisions that exist within your group. (4) Explain just where you place yourself. And finally (5) explain what this exercise teaches you about yourself.

## Explaining a Process

A **process** is a sequence of actions or events that lead or are supposed to lead to a predictable result. The transformation of a caterpillar into a butterfly is a process; so is fixing a flat tire, removing an appendix, frying an egg, knitting a sweater, or writing an essay.

Explaining a process is very much like narrating a series of happenings. In both kinds of writing the events of a sequence are usually recorded in order of time. The main difference is that narration records a sequence of events occurring just once, and since that sequence is past, it is usually recorded in the past tense:

> She *got up* early Sunday morning, *jogged* two miles, and then *took* a shower.

By contrast, a process is a sequence of events that happens again and again, with the same result each time. It is therefore explained in the present tense.

The way you explain a process depends on your purpose. If you want to teach someone else how to do it, you must be careful to give every step, as in this explanation of how to patch a punctured bicycle tube:

> With the cap from your tire-repair kit, or with a pocketknife, make a rough spot around the hole—a spot slightly bigger than the patch. Then put a small amount of special cement on the spot and spread it around evenly with your finger. Give the cement about thirty seconds to dry. When it feels tacky, remove the backing from the patch, but be careful not to touch the part newly exposed. Center the patch over the hole, and hold it in place for about thirty seconds, until the cement sets. Then sprinkle talcum powder on the patched area to keep it from being sticky.

This explanation does take a few things for granted. It assumes that you have removed the tube from the wheel and found the puncture—two processes that might require additional explanations. It also assumes that you have a repair kit (or a pocketknife, a patch, a bit of special cement, and a bit of talcum powder). But once you have removed the tube, assembled these items, and found the puncture, you can learn from this explanation all you need to know in order to patch the tube. It moves step by step, taking nothing for granted, and even anticipates possible missteps: *be careful not to touch the part newly exposed.* It is plainly designed as a **teaching** explanation.

If you wish only to help your reader understand a process rather than perform it, your explanation need not cover all the steps. For example, here is an explanation of how a caterpillar becomes a butterfly:

> In contact with the proper food on leaving the egg, the caterpillar begins to eat immediately and continues until it has increased its weight hundreds of times. On each of the first three segments of the body is a pair of short legs ending in a sharp claw. These legs correspond to the six legs of the adult insect. In addition, the caterpillar has up to ten short, fleshy feet called prolegs, which are shed before it changes form. The insect passes its pupal stage incased in comparatively rigid integuments [layers] that form a chrysalis.
>
> Most butterfly chrysalides remain naked, unlike those of the moth, which have a protective cocoon. Breathing goes on through an air opening while the complete adult, or imago, develops. Wings, legs, proboscis, even the pigment in the scales, form in the tight prison of the chrysalis.
>
> At maturity, the chrysalis splits its covering and wriggles out as an imago, or perfect insect. Hanging from a leaf or rock, it forces blood, or haemolymph, into the veins of its wet wings,

straightening them to their normal span. Soon the wings are dry, and the insect flies into a life of nectar drinking and courtship.
—"Butterfly," *Funk & Wagnalls New Encyclopedia*

This is a **reporting** explanation. The writer describes the stages through which the insect passes, but does not explain everything about its transformation. We are not told, for instance, how the wings, legs, and proboscis form, only when and where they form. The writer is trying to help us understand an overall process—not to teach us how to become butterflies ourselves.

These two kinds of explanation differ in form as well as in purpose. The teaching explanation uses the imperative mood to give a series of commands: *make, put, spread,* and so on. The reporting explanation uses the indicative mood to describe a series of actions: *the chrysalis splits its covering and wriggles out,* the imago *forces blood . . . into the veins of its wet wings,* and *the insect flies.* The consistent use of the imperative tells the reader that an explanation is designed to teach; the consistent use of the indicative tells the reader that an explanation is meant to report. (For a full discussion of the imperative and indicative moods, see sections 23.1–23.2, pp. 373–74.)

EXERCISE 15　**Composing a Teaching Explanation**

Write a teaching explanation of any simple process that you know well and that can be taught in writing—such as changing a tire, making a bed, frying an egg, or getting from one place to another. When you have finished, see if someone else can actually perform the process by following your instructions.

EXERCISE 16　**Composing a Reporting Explanation**

Write a reporting explanation of any process you know well, such as climbing a cliff, painting a picture, making a clay pot, taking or developing a good photograph. If you use any specialized terms, be sure to define them as you go along.

## Explaining Cause and Effect

A natural human response to a situation or event is to consider its causes, its effects, or both, and this is also one of the most useful ways of developing an essay. A cause is simply an answer to the question "Why?" Why do so many parents want their children to get a college education? Why did the Germans accept Hitler as their leader? Why did hundreds of American men, women, and children commit suicide in Guyana in November 1978? You can develop an essay by considering the answer to a question of this kind. Or you can consider the effects of a situation or event. What would happen if an atomic bomb were dropped on New York City? What would you do if you were placed in solitary confinement for thirty days? What is the effect of coeducation on college life?

When you attempt to determine the cause of a situation or event, you often construct a **hypothesis**—that is, a possible explanation of why it happened. Finding a baseball bat in your bed, for instance, you might hypothesize that your room had been visited by a practical joker while you were out, and you might even be able to guess who the joker was. In writing, you can likewise construct a hypothesis to explain a situation or event.

But whether or not you construct a hypothesis, questions about why something happens—or has happened—can often generate a flow of ideas. Consider this explanation of why we so often suppress the subject of death:

> I think there are many reasons for this flight away from facing death calmly. One of the most important facts is that dying nowadays is more gruesome in many ways, namely, more lonely, mechanical, and dehumanized; at times it is even difficult to determine technically when the time of death has occurred.
>
> Dying becomes lonely and impersonal because the patient is often taken out of his familiar environment and rushed to an emergency room. Whoever has been very sick and has required rest and comfort especially may recall his experience of being put on a stretcher and enduring the noise of the ambulance siren and hectic rush until the hospital gates open. Only those who have lived through this may appreciate the discomfort and cold necessity of such transportation which is only the beginning of a long ordeal— hard to endure when you are well, difficult to express in words when noise, light, pumps, and voices are all too much to put up with.                     —Elisabeth Kübler-Ross, *On Death and Dying*

One reason leads to another in these two paragraphs. The first says that we refuse to face death calmly because it has become lonely and dehumanized; the second shows that this cause is itself an effect, with a cause of its own: the removal of the patient from "his familiar environment."

**EXERCISE 17   Explaining Cause and Effect**

Explain why star college athletes are usually better known and more popular than top students, and show what effects this situation has on college life.

### Combining Methods of Exposition

When you are learning to write, you will find it useful to practice the various methods of exposition separately. But good writing usually combines several of them, as in the following essay:

# WHAT IS PHOTOGRAPHY?

[1] Most of us think of the camera as an instrument of preci-
sion. It catches a scene in an instant, a gesture in a second, an expression in a moment, recording these with absolute fidelity for
ever and ever—or so the advertisements would have us believe. But
if the camera takes the picture, we have reason to ask whether
photography can be an art, whether it actually requires anything
more creative than the clicking of a shutter. Such questions bring
us to the fundamental query: What is photography?

[2] The answer has as many sides as a professional photographer can find in a face. To the beginner, it is simple and pedes-
trian: photography is a succession of petty details. First, he or she
must choose and buy a camera from the seemingly infinite variety
of models available; then decide on film, whether color or black
and white; then learn how to load and wind, how to set the shutter,
the exposure meter, and the lens for proper light and focus in each
photograph; then snap the pictures, one by one, have them developed, and *finally* see the results. Some of the more ingenious new
cameras have eliminated one or more of these steps, but for most
beginners, this succession of petty, troublesome details is what photography is all about.

[3] For all this trouble, in fact, the beginner and the ordinary
amateur see the purpose of photography as primarily a matter of
record. More observant than the human eye, they think, more
tenacious than the human memory, the camera remembers baby as
mother never could, meticulously transcribing every wrinkle of his
little jowls and every bubble of his drool for the doubtful immor-
tality of a family album. In this seizing of an instant, there seems to
be scarcely more creativity (and possibly less) than is required of a
Xerox machine. The beginner seldom thinks that photography is
an art.

[4] And yet an art is precisely what photography can be—an
art with its own rules, distinct from photo-copying and equally distinct from movie-making. For movie-making is an art compounded
of many arts: writing, acting, and most especially editing—what
Alfred Hitchcock simply calls "the putting together of pieces of
film." But what Lessing said of poetry and painting may also be
said of cinema and photography. Cinema is the movement of many
pictures, and like poetry is essentially temporal, recreating the flow
of time. Photography is the freezing of movement, and like painting is essentially spatial. It stops time.

[5] I speak therefore only of the individual picture—of the
movement captured in time. And here we must remember that the
camera is an instrument. The camera will not take a picture for us,
any more than the carpenter's hammer will nail up a house for
him. It is nothing more or less than a tool. When I was in Europe
during the past summer, I bought in Paris a camera that functioned beautifully. But I was something less than a master of my
newly acquired device. When I expected to get the facade of the
Paris Opera House I caught a piece of fire hydrant; when I

expected to capture the unforgettable brilliance of the Côte d'Azur I got a patch of gray and unidentifiable coastline; when I sought to record the lights of Florence reflected one evening on the River Arno I got nothing.

[6] In part these were the blunders of a beginner, untutored in the technical subtleties of focus and exposure. But fundamentally they were failures in the discipline of form, shape, and arrangement that only a carefully ordered perspective can produce. Immanuel Kant is unintelligible to me most of the time, but I know what he means when he says that the eye creates what it sees. There is no such thing as a purely objective scene or landscape; there is only an odd collection of colors and forms, blended into a unified whole by the cohesive vision of the observer. It is he or she who creates the scene from his or her particular viewpoint, who fixes the relation between light and shadow, background and foreground, angle and curve.

[7] It is this, and only this, that makes of photography a creative art. Its instruments are admittedly more precise and more sophisticated than those of the painter, and they save a good deal of labor. But they can render no more than is actually seen or felt through the eye of the photographer himself, who catches with creative vision a moment of pain, fear, hatred, comedy, or pure beauty of form and light. Such captures are the products not of luck but of design, and in this the photographer is one with the artist of canvas and brush.

To begin with, the whole essay is a piece of definition—an attempt to define *photography*. But the writer uses a variety of methods to develop the definition. In paragraph 2, he explains the process of taking a photograph; in paragraph 3, he compares the camera to the human eye and memory; in paragraph 4, he classifies photography and painting as spatial arts, distinguishing them from the temporal arts, such as movie-making and poetry; in paragraph 5, he cites personal experience and several examples to show that the camera is only a tool; in paragraph 6, using cause and effect, he explains why the pictures he took were failures; and in paragraph 7, he uses comparison again to clinch the point that photography is a creative art.

### Exercise 18  Combining Methods of Exposition

Using at least three of the methods of exposition we have discussed, explain a subject you know well—surfboarding, stamp collecting, auto repairing, rock climbing, jazz, fishing, architecture, or whatever.

# 5

# STRATEGIES OF DEVELOPMENT
## Persuasion

**Persuasion** is the art of getting other people to do something or to believe something without being compelled to do so. You cannot persuade with violence or with threats—with a knife, a club, a gun, a bomb, or a fist; those are the weapons of compulsion. But you can persuade with a speech, a picture, a tone of voice, a pat on the back, a tear, or a piece of writing.

Only the last of these, of course, is normally available to the writer. Magazine ads often combine picture and text to persuade us that a certain kind of toothpaste will make the teeth sexier or that a certain kind of soap will get the body cleaner, but unless you are an advertising copywriter, you normally have to persuade your readers with the written word alone. You must therefore be more than usually sensitive to their needs.

One of the first things those readers will want to know is what it is that you want them to do or to believe. You may have good reason for not telling them immediately, especially if your topic is controversial. You may not even be sure, as you plunge into a topic, just what your own point of view is. But sooner or later you must declare it: you must state a definite opinion or recommend a specific course of action. And to win approval of that opinion or recommendation, you must appeal to the feelings of your readers, to their reason, or to both.

Advertising often makes a simple, straightforward appeal to the feelings. Over a big color picture of a New England farming family gathered around a tractor, a recent insurance ad proclaims:

**There are people more famous we insure.
But none more important.**

Under the picture the ad continues:

> For over a hundred years, we've tried to keep personal insurance from becoming too impersonal.
>
> When you do business with ———, it's with one of our independent agents. So when you have a question about auto, health, home or life insurance, you deal with someone who is close to you and your situation.
>
> You can easily find an independent ——— agent in the Yellow Pages.
>
> ——— is one of the world's largest insurance companies, a size that doesn't diminish our big concern for the individual.

As in many ads, picture and text together seek to persuade readers that the advertiser cares about each of them. The means of persuasion are essentially emotional. With the family picture reinforcing the point, the reader is told that the company deals in "personal insurance," that the company agent will be "someone who is close to you and your situation." The tone is warm and reassuring; the statement is the verbal equivalent of a friendly handshake. The ad offers no evidence that the company cares about individuals. It simply tries to make you feel that the company cares.

Since feelings play a part in the formation of almost every opinion, you need to understand as well as you can the feelings of your readers. But you can seldom persuade readers by appealing to their feelings alone. If you respect their intelligence, you will also appeal to their minds. And to do that, you must construct an argument.

## 5.1    What Is an Argument?

We commonly think of an argument as a quarrel—a shouting match in which tempers flare and necks turn red. But strictly speaking, an argument is not a quarrel at all. It is simply a rational means of persuasion. It differs from exposition in that it seeks to convince, not just to explain, and it differs from emotional persuasion in that it seeks to convince by appealing to the mind. To see these differences more clearly, consider the following three passages:

> 1.    The bear population of Maine is 7,000 to 10,000 animals, and the annual "harvest," or kill, averages 930. State wildlife biologists estimate that the number killed falls short by 120 of the "allowable harvest," i.e., "the harvest level that takes only the annual increase and does not affect the population size."
> —Jonathan Evan Maslow, "Stalking the Black Bear"

2.       Every year, bloodthirsty hunters go into the Maine woods and ruthlessly shoot to death hundreds of bears. The hunters care nothing for the suffering they cause, for the blood they spill, or for the harm they do to creatures who have done no harm to them. Hunters kill for a thrill, and that is all they care about. No one seems to care anything for the bears.

3.       Though some people may think hunting is nothing more than wholesale and wanton destruction of living creatures, hunters actually help to ensure the health and survival of wildlife. Take bear hunting in Maine as a case in point. Out of the 7,000 to 10,000 bears that roam the Maine woods, hunters kill an average of 930 a year. State wildlife biologists estimate that this is 120 fewer than the annual population increase. If the bear population were allowed to grow unchecked, it would increase by well over 1,000 a year, and the food available for any one bear would correspondingly decrease. By killing an average of 930 bears a year, hunters keep the annual increase down, and therefore help to ensure an adequate food supply for the bear population as a whole.

These three passages concern the same topic, but they treat it in fundamentally different ways. The first is **exposition;** it calmly explains the relation between the number of bears born and the number killed in Maine each year. The second is **emotional persuasion;** it tries to make the reader feel outrage at hunters and pity for bears. The third is **argument;** it tries to prove that hunting is beneficial to wildlife.

Consider first the difference between passage 2 and passage 3. Passage 2 relies on words like *bloodthirsty* to stir the reader's feelings; passage 3 relies on facts, figures, and authoritative estimates to gain the reader's agreement. Side by side, the two passages reveal the fundamental difference between emotional persuasion and argument. Purely emotional persuasion may well appeal to a reader who already tends to feel the way the writer does, but it is unlikely to change an opponent's mind. Words like *bloodthirsty* will simply antagonize the reader who likes to hunt. On the other hand, the argument of passage 3 is thought-provoking rather than antagonizing. It won't persuade all readers, but it will give even fervent conservationists something to think about.

Just as argument differs from emotional persuasion, so also does it differ from exposition. In exposition, every statement is offered as a matter of accepted fact. In argument, only some statements are offered as matters of fact, and these are given as reasons to make us believe other statements or claims, which are not self-evident matters of fact. For example, the assertion in passage 3 that "hunters actually help to ensure the health and survival of wildlife" is disputable and needs defending. Instead of assuming that we will believe it, the writer must give us reasons for doing so.

In argument, then, one or more statements are claims in need of defending, and statements of fact are introduced to defend them. The claims to be defended may concern what is happening ("Hunters help wildlife"), or what should happen ("Hunters should be appreciated").

In practice, writers often straddle the line between exposition and argument. The essay on photography (pp. 73–74), for instance, stands somewhere between defining photography and arguing that it should be considered an art. Likewise, the argument for bear hunting includes an explanation of what the bear population is and how it grows each year. But the distinction between exposition and argument is nonetheless important. In your own writing, you need to know when to explain, when to argue, and when to move from one to the other.

Whether or not a given statement needs defending depends on what readers will accept as a matter of fact. If you are writing for an audience of hunters, you can probably expect all of them to agree that hunting is good for wildlife—though some of them may want arguments for this point simply to use as ammunition against wildlife conservationists. If you are writing for general readers, you cannot expect all or even most of them to believe immediately that hunting is good for wildlife. You can much more reasonably expect them to believe that 930 bears a year are killed in Maine, or that the number of bears killed each year is smaller than the number born. For an antihunting audience, you may have to defend those statements too, showing how the number of kills is calculated, how the number of births is estimated, and who gathers the data. If you are writing a research paper, you will have to cite the sources of your information. But of course you cannot defend every statement you make, or you will go on forever. Eventually, you must present one or more statements as matters of fact, or direct your reader to one or more sources.

## 5.2 Combining General Claims and Specific Evidence *ev*

Effective arguments combine general claims with specific evidence. The general claim or proposition is essential because it tells the reader what you are arguing for, what you want him or her to believe: solar power can solve the energy crisis; presidents should have longer terms; parents should share equally the responsibility for raising their children. But unless the reader is ready to accept your general claim at once, you will need to support it with specific facts. Compare these three arguments—all written by first-term college freshmen:

1.     My feeling is that all people are equal. Neither sex is superior to the other. In the times of today, men and women both have an equal opportunity for education. They can pursue any career that they are qualified for. Schools are now getting away from trying to make certain things for boys and vice versa. Children are growing up as equals.

2.     Male athletes are stronger, faster, and tougher than their female counterparts. The men's record for the hundred-yard dash is about a full second faster than the women's. World records for the mile, marathon, high jump, discus, and all other track and field sports are much better on the male side than the female side. In tennis, a top male pro will always beat a top woman pro, and the same applies to swimming, skiing, basketball, hockey, and countless other sports.

3.     There are differences between men and women, but none that make either sex inferior. Athletic performance is a case in point. A major study by a West German doctor has shown that because of different skeletal leverage in men and women, muscles of identical strength will produce about 5 percent greater apparent strength in men. In sports such as running and mountaineering, however, women show greater endurance and resistance to stress. Several years ago, when I assisted a friend running the Boston marathon, I noticed that although many of the male runners were literally collapsing at the finish or at least in need of help, the women rarely needed any help at all.

These three arguments reveal opposing points of view. While writers 1 and 3 claim that the sexes are equal, writer 2 claims that they are not. But these three writers differ in more than their objectives. They differ also in their argumentative methods.

Writer 1 makes general claims that are not supported by specific and relevant facts. The statement about equal opportunity in education—even if the reader accepts it as fact—does not necessarily support the claim that "all people are equal." The fact that women *may* attend colleges and professional schools does not prove that they do indeed attend such schools in the same numbers as men do or that they perform as well as men once they get there. Writer 2 is considerably more effective because, to begin with, his objective is much more specific. Instead of saying simply that men and women are equal or unequal, he limits the argument to athletics; and instead of saying simply that men are better athletes than women, he contends that they are "stronger, faster, and tougher," and then proceeds to cite specific evidence for this point.

Of course, the evidence is not entirely convincing. By itself, the fact that the fastest male can outrun the fastest female does not really prove that men are generally faster than women, nor do the other world records cited answer this objection. Nevertheless, this writer does give the reader something to chew on. Instead of dealing in unsupported claims, he offers specific facts as evidence.

The writer of passage 3 does likewise. Though there is hardly enough evidence here to prove that the sexes are equal, this claim for their equality is much better supported—and hence more convincing—than that of the first passage.

## 5.3  Induction and Deduction  *reas*

Though all effective arguments combine one or more general claims with one or more specific facts, the combination may take one of two basic forms: induction and deduction. To see the difference between the two, compare the following passages:

1.  Nuclear power plants are fundamentally unsafe. The history of nuclear power is a list of major accidents and near catastrophes. At Windscale, England, in 1957, a fire and a partial meltdown of a nuclear core spread radioactivity across miles of pastureland, and thousands of gallons of contaminated cows' milk had to be dumped. In 1966 another partial meltdown occurred at Unit One of the Fermi plant near Detroit. In 1970 fifty thousand gallons of radioactive water and steam escaped from the reactor vessel of the huge Commonwealth Edison plant near Chicago. At Browns Ferry, Alabama, in 1975, a single candle started a fire at a nuclear power plant that burned for seven hours, caused 150 million dollars' worth of damage and loss to the plant, and—according to some experts—very nearly caused a catastrophic release of radiation. Even after the Rasmussen report supposedly analyzed everything that could go wrong with a nuclear reactor, a malfunctioning water gauge led to yet another near meltdown, at Three Mile Island, Pennsylvania, in 1979. Taken together, all of these accidents show that the risks we run in operating nuclear power plants are intolerably high.

2.  In spite of the widespread fear and resistance they often generate, nuclear power plants are fundamentally safe. From 1972 to 1975, a thorough study of nuclear power plants was made at a cost of four million dollars under the supervision of Norman Rasmussen, professor of nuclear engineering at M.I.T. Given the time, money, and expertise devoted to this study, its results must be reliable. And in fact they are not only reliable; they are also reassuring. After examining, identifying, and—with computer analysis—establishing the risk of every possible

accident that could release radiation from a nuclear power plant, the Rasmussen study concluded that in any given year the odds against a single death from a nuclear plant accident are five billion to one. Obviously, therefore, nuclear power plants are at least as safe as anything on earth can be.†

These two arguments not only represent different sides in the current debate about nuclear power; they also illustrate different methods of argumentation. The method of the first argument is inductive; the method of the second is deductive. We consider each method in turn.

### Induction—Using Examples

An inductive argument is based on examples. To prove that nuclear power plants are fundamentally unsafe, the writer of argument 1 cites five major accidents that have occurred at them since 1957. These examples do not necessarily prove that all nuclear power plants are unsafe; they show only that major accidents can occur at such plants. But taken together, the various examples support the conclusion that nuclear power plants are accident prone.

Now consider this argument:

> There seems to be a general feeling that country people never steal, whereas in the city the time that your neighbors have left from ripping off your apartment they devote to stealing your car. The second part of this statement may be true. The first is city myth. It is true that there are few spectacular robberies in this little town [Thetford, Vermont]—but that's only because there is nothing spectacular to steal. What we do have, people take, including stuff a city thief just wouldn't bother with. A couple of years ago, for example, some men came with a large truck and stole about 50 feet of stone wall from in front of a house just up the road. This past winter someone stole nearly all the chains that summer people like to put across their driveways before they leave in September. Weathervanes off barns are another popular item. . . . But the regular business, the bread-and-butter thievery around here, is breaking into summer people's houses, which is always done in the winter when the residents are away.
> —Noel Perrin, *First Person Rural*

Here the writer argues—or at least plainly implies—that robbery in the country is widespread. To prove the point, he cites a number of examples: thefts of a stone wall, of chains, of weathervanes, and of household belongings. These examples do not prove that rob-

† All the information used in these two arguments comes from the unofficial public transcript of a television program entitled "Incident at Browns Ferry," produced by WGBH, Boston, for NOVA, printed in Robert Fogelin, *Understanding Arguments* (New York: Harcourt Brace Jovanovich, 1978), pp. 191–208.

bery in the country is widespread, but they nevertheless invite that conclusion. Once again the argument is inductive.

### Deduction—Using Assumptions

A deductive argument is based on one or more assumptions, one or more points that the writer takes for granted and does not try to prove. Argument 2 is based on the assumption that a three-year, four-million-dollar study led by an M.I.T. professor of nuclear engineering is fully capable of determining just how dangerous nuclear power plants are. The statement of this assumption is followed by a statement of fact—namely, that the study reached a certain conclusion. Taken together, the assumption and the statement of fact constitute the premises of the argument—the statements from which the conclusion is drawn. If you assume that the study is reliable and you accept as a fact the statement about its results, you have to accept the writer's conclusion. In simplified form, the argument looks like this:

> ASSUMPTION: The study is reliable.
> STATEMENT OF FACT: The study found that nuclear power plants are fundamentally safe.
> CONCLUSION: Therefore such plants are fundamentally safe.

A deductive argument, then, is one in which the conclusion necessarily follows from the premises—from the combination of one or more assumptions with one or more statements of fact.

### Placing Your Conclusion

Whether the argument is inductive or deductive, the conclusion may sometimes be stated right at the beginning. If you want to prove inductively that nuclear power plants are unsafe, you can start by saying so, and then cite examples to support the point. If you want to prove deductively that nuclear power plants are safe, you can start by saying so, and then show how this conclusion is deduced. You may think that a conclusion should always come at the end of an argument, but in practice, a writer usually has some notion of the conclusion before he or she finds the examples or constructs the premises that are meant to prove it. In inductive reasoning especially, the conclusion often comes first. The writer begins with a claim and then gives examples to back it up.

However you reach your conclusion, where you put it is finally a matter of rhetorical choice. When you put it at the beginning, you tell the reader clearly what you intend to prove. When you put it at the end, you underscore the point that your assertion is a conclusion—the consequence of the facts or assumptions previously set out. In an inductive argument about current academic standards (exercise 1, pp. 175–76), Alston Chase gives a number of examples before he sets out his conclusion, and because of the way the examples build up to it, the conclusion strikes with telling effect. But in any case, an argument that runs to more than a paragraph should normally end with a conclusion, even if it also starts with one. Otherwise the reader may forget the point you are trying to prove.

Wherever the conclusion is placed, the argument behind it should be effective. And to argue effectively, you must understand the advantages and disadvantages of both induction and deduction.

### Induction—Advantages and Disadvantages

The chief advantage of an inductive argument lies in the cumulative impact of successive examples. Because of this impact, an inductive argument can sometimes feel powerfully persuasive, and argument 1 may feel that way to you. But would it persuade anyone who is not already opposed to nuclear power plants? Would it bring any new supporters to the no-nuke side, or merely bolster the morale of the old ones? To answer questions like these about an inductive argument, you must not only weigh the impact of its examples but also consider their number and their relevance to the conclusion.

Consider first the number of examples cited in argument 1. Given all the nuclear power plants throughout the world, is a record of five accidents in twenty-two years really intolerable? One problem with induction is that whenever you use it, you are playing a numbers game. Unless your examples add up to a majority of the members of a given class (the class of all nuclear power plants in this instance), any generalization you make about the whole class will be vulnerable. The skeptic will always be able to say something like, "These are only isolated cases. How can you say that all or even most nuclear power plants are accident prone?"

Another problem with induction is that its effectiveness depends on the relevance of the examples cited. The accidents mentioned in argument 1 were costly, but since none of them killed or even injured anyone, why must we conclude that nuclear power plants are fatally dangerous? To justify that conclusion, the writer would have to show that each accident was nearly fatal to one or more persons. Just saying they were nearly fatal does not make them so, and if we are asked to believe that a particular accident was nearly fatal because unnamed experts say it was, then argument 1 is making the same kind of assumption made by argument

2. So the relevance of the examples cited in an inductive argument may not always be obvious or easy to establish.

### Deduction—Advantages and Disadvantages

At this point you may begin to see the special advantages of deductive argument, which depends not on the accumulation of examples but rather on the strength of one or more basic assumptions. Of course, you may be wary of using assumptions. On the face of it, facts look much more convincing. But at least one assumption underlies every argument—even an argument that seems to be based entirely on fact. If you say that an accident occurred at Windscale, England, in 1957, you are assuming—unless you saw the accident yourself—that this piece of information is true. If you say that a particular accident was nearly fatal, and you cite unnamed experts in support of this point, you are assuming that the experts are right. And even if they are right, even if you can show that a large number of accidents at nuclear power plants were nearly fatal, the step from there to a conclusion about the danger of the plants requires a further assumption—that "nearly fatal" is essentially equivalent to "actually fatal." Arguing from the opposite assumption, a defender of the plants could point out that their emergency systems have in every case prevented actual fatality, and could then conclude that the plants are fundamentally safe.

To argue persuasively, therefore, you must know how to use deduction as well as induction. You must know how to formulate the assumptions without which it is virtually impossible to prove anything at all. And to the extent that you use deduction, you must understand what is needed to make a deductive argument sound.

### Making Deductive Arguments Sound— Truth, Credibility, Validity

The soundness of a deductive argument depends on three things: the truth of its one or more statements of fact, the credibility of its one or more assumptions, and the validity of its conclusion.

The first requisite of any argument—deductive or inductive—is that its statement or statements of fact be **true.** If you think the reader may doubt the truth of a particular statement, you may have to substantiate it with others, but for obvious reasons, you cannot substantiate every statement; you have to stop somewhere. What you can and should do is be sure that your statements of fact are true. If you are arguing against nuclear power plants and you state that people were killed in the 1979 accident at Three Mile Island, your argument will be unsound because the statement is false. To make the argument sound, you must state the truth about what the accident did and did not do.

Second, the one or more assumptions made by a deductive argument must be reasonably **credible.** Consider the assumption made in argument 2—that we can rely on a three-year study of nuclear power plants led by an M.I.T. professor of nuclear engineering. Can we rely on such a study? Is the assumption credible? These questions have no easy answers, but clearly, whether or not the study is wholly reliable, it deserves some respect. Unlike truth, credibility varies by degrees, and the assumption made about the Rasmussen study may be just as credible as the assumption that an elevator inspected within the past six months will not suddenly drop you to your death. Unless you like climbing stairs, you regularly accept that assumption—in part because the authority of an inspector stands behind it. Likewise, the authority of a nuclear specialist and a prolonged inspection stands behind the Rasmussen report. So the assumption that we can rely on the report will be credible enough to satisfy some readers—though certainly not all.

Credibility is something to be carefully weighed. If you think an assumption is not sufficiently credible to stand on its own, you should add an argument to defend it. If you aren't sure whether it needs defending, you should try it out on some listeners before you make it the basis of a written argument. In any case, the soundness of a deductive argument will heavily depend on the credibility of its one or more assumptions—on the plausibility of what you are asking the reader to believe.

Third, a deductive argument must have a validly drawn conclusion. A conclusion is **valid** when it follows necessarily from the premises—the one or more assumptions and the one or more statements of fact that the argument makes. Argument 2 assumes that the Rasmussen study is reliable and states what the study found: odds of five billion to one against a single death from a nuclear plant accident in any one year. If the assumption is credible and the statement of fact true, it necessarily follows that the annual odds against a fatal accident in a nuclear power plant are in fact five billion to one. That is a valid conclusion because it remains within the scope of the premises. If you tried to conclude that the annual odds against *any* accident in a nuclear power plant are five billion to one, your conclusion would be invalid because it would go beyond the scope of the premises, moving from one kind of accident to all kinds of accidents. A valid conclusion is one that stays within the boundaries defined by the premises. (For more on invalid conclusions, see "Arguing by Association," p. 88.)

Since validity involves merely the internal consistency of an argument, a conclusion that is validly drawn is not necessarily true.

To be true it must be validly drawn from one or more credible assumptions and one or more true statements of fact. A conclusion validly drawn from premises that are questionable or false is like a route carefully followed in strict obedience to a faulty compass. The route is only as good as the compass that determines it, and the conclusion is only as true as the premises that stand behind it.

### Combining Induction and Deduction

The main advantage of a deductive argument is that if its assumptions are credible, its statements of fact true, and its conclusion validly drawn, it must be accepted by any reasonable person. But meeting those three conditions can be hard. Just how do you establish a credible assumption about any subject worth arguing over? You may have to defend your assumption by using induction. To show that the Rasmussen study is reliable, for instance, you may have to cite other studies that confirm its findings. Alternatively, you may choose to work from a different assumption—the assumption, for example, that any large-scale enterprise which has functioned for more than twenty years without causing a single fatal accident is fundamentally safe. But to build a convincing argument from this assumption, you will probably have to show that nuclear power plants have caused neither fatal nor nearly fatal accidents. And here you will have to cite examples; you will have to show that accidents like those at Browns Ferry and Three Mile Island have posed no real threat to human life and—on the contrary—have demonstrated the effectiveness of safety systems.

Or consider again the inductive argument. If you want to convince your reader that nuclear power plants are fundamentally dangerous, you must do more than cite a list of nearly fatal accidents. You must also use deduction. You have to define what you mean by "nearly fatal," and in this case, to define is to assume. Also, you have to assume that anything which has caused an accident nearly fatal to thousands (though not actually fatal to anyone) is intolerably dangerous. From those two assumptions, and from the list of facts you can cite about particular accidents, you may then deduce that nuclear power plants are intolerably dangerous.

Assumptions and examples are equally important for almost any argument you may want to make. There is probably no such thing as a perfectly convincing argument on any controversial subject; if there were, the controversy would end. But even on controversial subjects, some arguments are more effective than others. We have already said that effective arguments combine general claims and specific evidence. Another way of putting this is to say that effective arguments usually combine deduction and induction, carefully stated assumptions and apt examples. Consider these two arguments:

1.     Whenever an American company helps to create a better standard of living for the poorer people of a foreign country, it should be allowed to stay there. In South Africa, American companies *are* improving the conditions of black people. Therefore, American business should be allowed to stay in South Africa.

2.     Whenever an American company helps the people of a foreign country to achieve a better standard of living, it should be allowed and encouraged to do so. In South Africa, American companies *are* improving the conditions of black people. In Tubatse, for instance, 175 miles northeast of Johannesburg, Union Carbide employs about four hundred blacks, pays them well above the government's minimum wage, has put many of them in supervisory jobs, and provides housing, school, and recreational facilities far superior to those provided by a local South African company. In Port Elizabeth, on the southeastern coast, the Ford Motor Company has actually encouraged black unionism in defiance of South African law, and is now training blacks for a wide variety of supervisory posts—including jobs in which they will supervise whites. Altogether, more than a hundred American firms operating in South Africa now subscribe to the so-called Sullivan principles, which call for increased pay and opportunities for blacks, integration of black and white workers, recognition of black unions, and general improvement of the workers' lives. For all these reasons, American business should be allowed to stay in South Africa.†

Here both writers take the same side, arguing that American business should be allowed to stay in South Africa. But while argument 1 is purely deductive, argument 2 combines deduction with induction. You will accept the conclusion to the first argument if—and only if—you accept the premises: the assumption made by the first sentence and the statement of fact made by the second. But many readers may not immediately believe that American companies really are improving the lives of South African blacks. So argument 2 uses induction to defend that point, giving specific examples before presenting the conclusion. And since the examples strongly support the point in question, the second argument is more convincing than the first.

It would be more convincing still if it also defended its assumption—that American companies should be allowed to stay wherever they are helping to create a better standard of living.

---

† All the information used in this paragraph comes from Roger M. Williams, "American Business Should Stay in South Africa," *Saturday Review,* Sept. 30, 1978, pp. 14–18.

This assumption is not self-evident; some would argue that if American companies in South Africa support a government that makes the black a second-class citizen, the companies should not be allowed to stay there—even if they are creating a better standard of living for some blacks. To be fully effective with all reasonable readers, then, the argument would have to include a defense of its assumption as well as a defense of its statement of fact.

## 5.4   Arguing Unsoundly—Fallacies   *fal*

In explaining what is required to make an argument sound, we have already noted some of the things that can make it unsound. They include not only false statements of fact, which we have already discussed, but also *fallacies*—that is, unsound or illogical ways of arguing. To help you avoid the most common fallacies, we describe them here.

### Arguing by Association

> It is well known that Senator Blank is a critic of the Chilean government. We also know that Latin American Marxists are critics of the Chilean government. It is clear, therefore, that Senator Blank has Marxist tendencies.

Here a deductive argument is misused to promote guilt by association. Because deductive argument leads to a necessary conclusion, politicians and other public figures sometimes use it to compel belief, to make you think that what they say must be true. But the conclusion to this argument does not follow from its premises and is therefore invalid. Only if we assume that *all* critics of the Chilean government are Marxist must we conclude that any one critic of that government is. It may well be true that Senator Blank and Latin American Marxists share an opposition to the Chilean government, but this does not mean that they share anything else. (In formal logic, this kind of error is called the fallacy of the "undistributed middle.")

### Assuming What Is to Be Proved

> Women and men make up the human race. In this sense they are alike. They have feelings, expressed and unexpressed, due to their various upbringings in our society. People have challenged men's superiority because women have begun to fend for themselves and to seek a larger role in society. They are better able to cope with the difficulties of social acceptance and equality than men are because they have been allowed to express their feelings

in the past. Men have it a bit harder. They have to learn to accept themselves as feeling human beings and to deal openly with their emotions instead of repressing them.

Men and women are emotional and intellectual equals. Neither sex is superior to the other. —College freshman

The writer clearly wants us to believe that men and women are equal. Yet nowhere does the passage give us reasons for believing this statement. On the contrary, the passage seems to say that men and women differ, that women are much more willing to release their feelings than men are. It is fairly obvious that equality of status can exist between people who do different things—carpentry and plumbing, for instance—but that is not the kind of difference in question here. The emotional and intellectual equality that concerns the writer is not at all self-evident, and it is not proved by the statement that men and women both "make up the human race." On the whole, then, the writer takes for granted what needs to be defended, or assumes what is to be proved.

**Arguing by Analogy**

Newspapers should be forbidden to criticize the president of the United States. The only one who can fairly judge the performance of a president is a former president, for he alone knows the burdens of the office from his own experience. When a newspaper reporter attacks the president, or tries to give him advice, it's like a nurse telling a doctor how to perform an operation. Nurses often watch operations, but without surgical training or experience they have no right to give advice about them. And a reporter has no more right to criticize the president.

This passage is an example of arguing by analogy: criticism of the president by a reporter is likened to criticism of a doctor by a nurse. But the two cases are not really the same. A doctor is specially trained to perform certain operations, and no one who has not been similarly trained can adequately judge his or her operative technique. But the president is not a specialist, nor is he obligated to undergo special training. He is a public official—a man elected by the people and accountable to them. Furthermore, newspaper reporters do not simply attend the president the way nurses attend an operating doctor. They study the world in which the president does his job, and by this means they train themselves to judge his performance. The argument is faulty and unconvincing, then, because it is based on analogy.

Now here you may have a question. Since we have already said (pp. 60–61) that you can use analogy to explain, why are we now saying that you can't use it to argue? The answer is that explanation and argument are two different things—even though they may sometimes look very much alike.

If you wanted to explain the special burdens of the presidency, you might well use the analogy of the doctor: like a doctor in the operating room, the president is watched and attended by others, but is alone in his responsibility for certain crucial actions and fateful decisions. Thus the analogy would help you explain the loneliness of the presidency, or the acute sense of responsibility that it entails. But we have already said that no analogy presents a perfect likeness. If you use analogy to argue, you are assuming that two things alike in one respect will also be alike in others. That is not a credible assumption, and any argument based on it is suspect.

### Arguing *Ad Hominem*

A furor about the American funeral customs . . . has been created by Jessica Mitford's book *The American Way of Death.* [Pertinent here] are some facts about Jessica Mitford Treuhaft, which were reported in the November 5, 1963 issue of *National Review.* Several people "under oath before legally constituted agencies of both federal and state governments" have identified Jessica Mitford as a member of the Communist party. In fact, according to the *National Review,* both Mr. and Mrs. Treuhaft have a long record of Communist activities.

Jessica Mitford's Communist connections are pertinent because they place her book in perspective as part of the left-wing drive against private enterprise in general and—in this case— against Christian funeral customs in particular.

—Rev. Irving E. Howard, review of Jessica Mitford's
*The American Way of Death.*

Jessica Mitford's book argues that funeral directors are greedy and exploitative. But instead of answering the argument itself, Irving Howard attacks the maker of the argument, labeling her a Communist and hence an enemy of free enterprise and Christianity. This is an example of argument *ad hominem* ("to the man,"—i.e., "to the person"), argument focused not on a point but on the person who made the point. It will convince those who believe that all evil in America is traceable to Communists, but it will not convince many others. The only rational way to prove that funeral directors are not exploitative is to cite evidence to the contrary.

### Arguing *Post Hoc, Ergo Propter Hoc*

Up until 1976, when Republican Gerald Ford left the White House, the U.S. enjoyed the friendship and support of Iran. Many Americans lived and worked there, and Iran supplied us with much of our oil. But scarcely two years after Democrat Jimmy

Carter became president, the Shah of Iran was driven out of his own country, and Americans were driven out after him. Clearly, then, the Democrats caused us to lose one of our most valuable allies in the Middle East.

This is the kind of argument you read and hear during political campaigns. It is based on the assumption called *post hoc, ergo propter hoc* ("after this, therefore because of it"): if X happened after Y, it must have happened because of Y. But *after* does not necessarily mean *because of*. If it did, the revolution in Iran could just as well be seen as the result of the Watergate scandal, the making of *Star Wars,* or your own birth—all of which occurred before the change in Iran.

## 5.5  Using Argumentative Words

Certain words signal an argument. *Therefore,* for instance, tells the reader that you are drawing a conclusion, that you are offering one statement as a reason for believing another:

> Hunters keep the growth of the bear population down, and *therefore* help to ensure an adequate food supply for the bear population as a whole.

When you use a word like *therefore,* you are making an argumentative connection, and the reader will hold you responsible for it. If you introduce the word simply to fill the gap between two sentences, you are using it irresponsibly:

> Many college students have serious problems during their freshman year. *Therefore* high school graduates should work for a year or two before starting college.

The word *Therefore* asks us to take one statement as a reason for believing another. But is the first statement in this passage a reason for believing the second? Would the problems of freshmen be eliminated if they came to college with a year or two of work behind them? There is no clear connection between these two statements, and filling the gap with *Therefore* is like bridging a river with a six-inch stick. Before you connect two statements with an argumentative word, be sure that one statement actually does follow from the other.

Argumentative words include *for, since, because, so, consequently, therefore, hence,* and *accordingly.* Some of these words, such as *since, for,* and *because,* may be used not only to argue but also to explain:

To ARGUE: American businesses should be allowed to stay in South Africa *because* they help to raise the standard of living for black people there.

To EXPLAIN: President Carter opposed U.S. participation in the Moscow Olympics *because* he wanted to protest the Soviet invasion of Afghanistan.

### EXERCISE 1  Composing an Argument

Following is a description of a nuclear power plant proposed for construction in New Hampshire. Using all of the facts given in this description, develop an argument for or against the building of the new plant.

> In 1976 the Nuclear Regulatory Commission (NRC) gave the Public Service Company of New Hampshire permission to build a nuclear power plant in the town of Seabrook, forty miles north of Boston, on New Hampshire's seacoast. The proposed
> 5  plant would house twin reactors with a total capacity of 2300 megawatts, which is enough electricity for a city of 2 million. In the new generation of nuclear plants, Seabrook would be of merely average size. It would cost, by the latest estimates, $2.6 billion, and it would occupy some forty acres about a mile and a half from the ocean.
> 10  The reactors would be cooled by seawater, approximately a billion gallons of it a day. The water would be taken in and then discharged, with its temperature elevated some 30 or 40 degrees, through two long, deep tunnels running under salt marsh and clamflats out to a point nearly a mile offshore. Biologists have
> 15  expressed considerable uncertainty about the effects of this heated water on marine life. In addition, the plant would lie in an area where a significant earthquake could occur, and within five miles of some very popular beaches.
> —Tracy Kidder, "The Nonviolent War against Nuclear Power"

## 5.6  Making Concessions

Compare these two arguments:

1.  No one should be admitted to college without a personal interview. What can admissions people tell from a piece of paper? They can't really tell anything. Only when they see a student face to face can they decide what kind of a person he is.
    —College freshman

2.  An admissions officer can tell some things from a piece of paper. He can tell how well a person writes and what he is interested in, factors which go a long way toward determining if a student is capable of using the college resources to the fullest extent possible. However, there are things that an application

cannot bring forth, things that can only be seen in a personal meeting. The way a person talks, the way he thinks about and answers questions on the spot, the way he reacts to certain pieces of information, are all important aspects of a person which cannot be found on a written piece of paper.

—College freshman

Both of these writers are arguing in support of the same point, that no one should be admitted to college without a personal interview by an admissions officer. But the first writer makes no concessions to the other side. He simply dismisses the idea that anything can be learned about an applicant from a piece of paper. The second writer concedes or admits that certain things can be learned from a written application, and then proceeds to show that certain other things can be learned only from an interview. The transitional word *However* marks the shift from concession to assertion. (For more on transitional words, see pp. 114–15.) Starting with concession is a good way to overcome the reader's resistance to an unpopular argument. Any issue worth examining has at least two sides, and if you refuse to grant either sympathy or respect to the views you oppose, you will antagonize many of your readers. But if you begin with one or more concessions, you may gain a hearing for even the most controversial point of view. Consider, for instance, how this writer opens an argument for test-tube babies:

> The mere mention of "test-tube babies" triggers instant repugnance in most of us. Visions arise, from Aldous Huxley's *Brave New World,* of moving assembly lines of glassware out of which babies are decanted at each terminus by a detached and impersonal technician. Procreation thus becomes reproduction in the full factory-like connotation of that word. And as we conjure up the distasteful (at the least) scene, words like *mechanization* and *dehumanization* reverberate through our neuronal networks.
>
> Nevertheless, despite the offense to our sensibilities provoked by even the thought of artificial wombs, there is a valid case to be made for test-tube babies in the full Huxleyan image—not mass-produced on an assembly line, perhaps, but nevertheless wholly and "artificially" grown in a scientifically monitored environment without ever being carried in the uterus of a human mother. Such a case can be made (which does not mean that I personally advocate it) on the basis not merely of bizarre and exotic speculations but of purely humane, down-to-earth considerations having to do with the health of individual babies.
>
> —Albert Rosenfeld, "The Case for Test-Tube Babies"

Here the writer begins with a whole paragraph of concession. Before he can effectively defend the growing of babies outside the womb, he must recognize that many people are horrified at the idea. Only then can he hope to gain a reasonable hearing for it. Once more a transitional word—*Nevertheless*—marks the shift from concession to assertion.

Be warned, however, that if you want to move from concession to assertion in one paragraph, you must be sure that concession does not take over the paragraph completely. See what happens in this one:

> It is true that men and women were made for different purposes physically. A man cannot be expected to bear a child and a woman was not built for doing strenuous outdoor labor (some women can do this and it is great for them). But the physical differences between men and women do not mean that they must differ mentally also. Throughout the years men have associated the women's weak physical structure with a weak mind. The men have always assumed that because they are strong, tough, and big, they can make decisions better than the "weak" women. Many people today do not believe that there is any correlation between the physical and mental structures and therefore that old theory is now being destroyed. —College freshman

The opening words—*It is true that*—label the first sentence as a concession, so we are properly notified that the writer's point of view will be different. But the second sentence extends the concession, and concedes so much that a qualification has to be added, in parentheses. The third sentence then announces what is apparently the main point of the paragraph: "physical differences between men and women do not mean that they must differ mentally also." But immediately after making this statement, the writer turns to more concession in the next two sentences, which describe the opposite view. Only in the last sentence does she return to her main point, and even there it fails to stand out as the expression of her own conviction, based on objective evidence. It looks instead like her description of what someone else believes. In the paragraph as a whole, then, the writer's many concessions to the views of others threaten to smother her statement of what she herself is trying to affirm.

### EXERCISE 2   Using Concession

Rewrite the following argument in one of two ways: (1) support the writer's point of view but add one or more concessive sentences at the beginning, or (2) argue against the writer's point of view by first making a concession to it and then defending the other side. Whichever you choose to do, be sure to use a transitional word between your concession and the main point you are making.

> Regional expressions are a hindrance to communication. Each part of the country has adopted many which cannot be found

anywhere else. For instance, New England is the only part of the U.S. where you can order a "frappe" in a drugstore or ice cream parlor. Try ordering a frappe in Nebraska and see what kind of reaction you will get. The purpose of language is to make communication possible. By separating regions of the country from each other, nonstandardized forms of expression defeat this purpose.                                                        —College freshman

## 5.7   Appealing to the Emotions

A working knowledge of argumentative technique is an indispensable tool for the writer who wants to persuade. But readers are seldom persuaded by rational arguments alone. For this reason the writer should try to understand the reader's feelings and appeal to them.

This does not mean that arguments should speak to feelings alone. It means only that an appeal to feeling can reinforce an argument that is fundamentally rational. To see the difference between a purely emotional appeal and a rational argument reinforced by emotional appeal, compare these two passages:

1.    Chemical sprays and insecticides are gradually destroying every living thing on earth—every flower, every bird, every tree, every animal, every man, woman and child. They are worse than the ovens in which Hitler burned little children, worse than the atomic bomb which obliterated Hiroshima, worse than any flood, fire, or earthquake ever recorded. Those disasters merely killed a limited number of people. But insecticides are slowly killing everyone and everything that lives.

2.    . . . The chemicals to which life is asked to make its adjustment are no longer merely the calcium and silica and copper and all the rest of the minerals washed out of the rocks and carried in rivers to the sea; they are the synthetic creations of man's inventive mind, brewed in his laboratories, and having no counterparts in nature.

      To adjust to these chemicals would require time on the scale that is nature's; it would require not merely the years of a man's life but the life of generations. And even this, were it by some miracle possible, would be futile, for the new chemicals come from our laboratories in an endless stream; almost five hundred annually find their way into actual use in the United States alone. The figure is staggering and its implications are not easily grasped—500 new chemicals to which the bodies of men and animals are required somehow to adapt each year, chemicals totally outside the limits of biologic experience.

      Among them are many that are used in man's war against nature. Since the mid-1940's over 200 basic chemicals have been

created for use in killing insects, weeds, rodents, and other orga-
nisms described in the modern vernacular as "pests"; and they
are sold under several thousand different brand names.

These sprays, dusts, and aerosols are now applied almost
universally to farms, gardens, forests, and homes—nonselective
chemicals that have the power to kill every insect, the "good"
and the "bad," to still the song of birds and the leaping of fish in
the streams, to coat the leaves with a deadly film, and to linger
on in soil—all this though the intended target may be only a few
weeds or insects. Can anyone believe it is possible to lay down
such a barrage of poisons on the surface of the earth without
making it unfit for all life? They should not be called "insecticides," but "biocides." . . .             —Rachel Carson, *Silent Spring*

Both passages maintain that insecticides may be fatally harmful to
all living things, and both use emotive language to make the antic-
ipated harm more vivid. In passage 1, for instance, we find *worse
than the ovens in which Hitler burned little children;* in passage 2, *a
barrage of poisons.* But passage 1 is nothing but an emotional, almost
hysterical, appeal. When the passage claims—without evidence—
that chemicals are worse than any disaster ever recorded, it invites
disbelief. By contrast, passage 2 begins with specific evidence about
the number of new chemicals introduced each year, the difficulty
of adjusting to them, and the danger posed by their "nonselective"
power to kill. Only after presenting this evidence does the passage
appeal to the reader's feelings—by summoning up the song of
birds and the leaping of fish, and by asking a stinging rhetorical
question: *Can anyone believe it is possible to lay down such a barrage of
poisons on the surface of the earth without making it unfit for all life?* Here
the emotional appeal simply intensifies a point that has already
been made by means of reason.

### EXERCISE 3   Combining Argument and Emotional Appeal

Using a combination of rational argument and emotional appeal, defend
or attack one of the following:

> legalization of marijuana
> government funding of abortion for the poor
> laws banning discrimination against homosexuals
> "quotas" for minority-group applicants to professional schools
> the Equal Rights Amendment
> scholarships for athletes
> the system of rating movies
> reciting the pledge of allegiance in public schools

# 6

# WRITING PARAGRAPHS

Effective essays are made with paragraphs, blocks of sentences that help the reader follow the stages of the writer's thought. Though a paragraph is commonly part of an essay, it can and sometimes does serve as an essay in its own right, and the writing of one-paragraph essays will give you small-scale practice in organization. You can sometimes learn a good deal about organization by writing a single sentence, and you can learn even more by writing a single paragraph. What you learn is the complex art of separating and connecting at the same time, of dividing groups of words into sentences and yet relating those sentences to one another, of drawing a continuous line of thought through a succession of full stops. For that reason, much of this chapter deals with the single paragraph as a self-contained unit.

But just as you learn how to relate the separate sentences of a paragraph, so also you should learn how to relate the separate paragraphs of an essay. Since most essays consist of more than one paragraph, you must know how to move from one paragraph to another. This chapter therefore shows you methods of connecting paragraphs as well as methods of constructing them.

## 6.1  Why Use Paragraphs?  ¶

Everyone who reads and writes has some idea of what a paragraph usually is: a set of sentences set off from preceding sentences by an indentation at the beginning. Paragraphs come in many shapes and sizes—from the slim one-sentence model made to fit the narrow columns of a newspaper, to the wide, many-sentenced model made for the pages of a book. What do they all have in common? Perhaps we could better begin by asking what paragraphs are for. Why do writers break up essays into blocks of sentences instead of just running all the sentences together?

Part of the answer is that an essay is like a long stairway. Unless it is interrupted now and then as if by a landing, a place to stop before continuing, the reader may get confused. New paragraphs usually begin where the writer's thought turns, just as landings often come where a stairway turns. Without such turning points clearly marked by new paragraphs, here is what you have:

> [At one time the migrants] had set forth in tribes. They wandered across the steppe or edged out of the forests down to the plains with wives and children and cattle in the long columns of all their possessions. Home was where they were and movement did not disrupt the usual order of their ways. It was quite otherwise in human experience when some among the Europeans of the sixteenth and seventeenth centuries migrated. Often it was a man alone, an individual, who went, one who in going left home, that is, cut himself apart from the associations and attachments that until then had given meaning to his life. Some inner restlessness or external compulsion sent such wanderers away solitary on a personal quest to which they gave various names, such as fortune or salvation. They were a diverse group. There were priests who had brooded over the problem of a world in eternity and made the startling discovery that a holy mission summoned them away. There were noblemen in the great courts who stared out beyond the formal lines of the garden and saw the vision of new empires to be won. There were young men without places who depended on daring and their swords and were willing to soldier for their fortunes. There were clerks in the countinghouses, impatient of the endless rows of digits, who thought why should they not reach out for the wealth that set their masters high? There were journeymen without employment and servants without situations and peasants without land and many others whom war or pestilence displaced who dreamed in desperation of an alternative to home. Through the eighteenth century their numbers grew and, even more, through the nineteenth. They had various destinations. The receding ships left them at the edge of an impenetrable wilderness; they moved up the river and the dark jungle closed in behind them; they came over the pass and the jagged forest shut off the sight of the land they had left behind. They had wandered indeed alone into the strangeness.

This passage is taxing to read. Because no indentations signal the end of one sequence of thought and the beginning of another, we have trouble following the progression of thought in the passage as a whole. But see what happens when it is broken up into paragraphs, as it actually was by the author:

> [At one time the migrants] had set forth in tribes. They wandered across the steppe or edged out of the forests down to the plains with wives and children and cattle in the long columns of all their possessions. Home was where they were and movement did not disrupt the usual order of their ways.
>
> It was quite otherwise in human experience when some among the Europeans of the sixteenth and seventeenth centuries migrated. Often it was a man alone, an individual, who went, one who in going left home, that is, cut himself apart from the associations and attachments that until then had given meaning to his life. Some inner restlessness or external compulsion sent such wanderers away solitary on a personal quest to which they gave various names, such as fortune or salvation.
>
> They were a diverse group. There were priests who had brooded over the problem of a world in eternity and made the startling discovery that a holy mission summoned them away. There were noblemen in the great courts who stared out beyond the formal lines of the garden and saw the vision of new empires to be won. There were young men without places who depended on daring and their swords and were willing to soldier for their fortunes. There were clerks in the countinghouses, impatient of the endless rows of digits, who thought why should they not reach out for the wealth that set their masters high? There were journeymen without employment and servants without situations and peasants without land and many others whom war or pestilence displaced who dreamed in desperation of an alternative to home. Through the eighteenth century their numbers grew and, even more, through the nineteenth.
>
> They had various destinations. The receding ships left them at the edge of an impenetrable wilderness; they moved up the river and the dark jungle closed in behind them; they came over the pass and the jagged forest shut off the sight of the land they had left behind. They had wandered indeed alone into the strangeness.
> —Oscar Handlin, *Race and Nationality in American Life*

Now the turns of thought are clearly marked. The first paragraph describes the movement of tribes, who carried their "home" with them. In contrast ("It was quite otherwise"), the second describes the movement of individuals, who cut themselves off from "home." The third paragraph then describes the various kinds of individuals who moved away ("They were a diverse group"), and the fourth describes their destinations. Each new paragraph marks a new stage in the development of the writer's thought and the reader's understanding.

### Exercise 1    Dividing a Passage into Paragraphs

In the following passage from Loren Eiseley's "Man of the Future," we have deliberately run the author's original three paragraphs into one. Divide the passage into what you think were Eiseley's original three paragraphs, and state the main point of each.

There are days when I find myself unduly pessimistic about the future of man. Indeed, I will confess that there have been occasions when I swore I would never again make the study of time a profession. My walls are lined with books expounding its mysteries; 5 my hands have been split and rubbed raw with grubbing into the quicklime of its waste bins and hidden crevices. I have stared so much at death that I can recognize the lingering personalities in the faces of skulls and feel accompanying affinities and repulsions. One such skull lies in the lockers of a great metropolitan museum. 10 It is labeled simply: Strandlooper, South Africa. I have never looked longer into any human face than I have upon the features of that skull. I come there often, drawn in spite of myself. It is a face that would lend reality to the fantastic tales of our childhood. There is a hint of Wells' *Time Machine* folk in it—those pathetic, 15 childlike people whom Wells pictures as haunting earth's autumnal cities in the far future of the dying planet. Yet this skull has not been spirited back to us through future eras by a time machine. It is a thing, instead, of the millennial past. It is a caricature of modern man, not by reason of its primitiveness but, startlingly, because 20 of a modernity outreaching his own. It constitutes, in fact, a mysterious prophecy and warning. For at the very moment in which students of humanity have been sketching their concept of the man of the future, that being has already come, and lived, and passed away.

### Exercise 2    Building Paragraphs

In the following passage from a student's essay about a character in a short story, some of the paragraphs are too short. Combine them so that each new paragraph marks a turn in the writer's thought.

Humble Jewett reveals his love of natural beauty in several ways.

When he and Amarantha reach the crest of the hill, he kneels down and prays to the Creator. He is moved to worship by 5 the sight of the sunlight lining the distant treetops.

He has a similar reaction later in the story as he is walking to Wyker's house. He is so awestruck by the splendor of the sunset that he doesn't notice the wound in his leg.

The sight of human beauty also casts a spell. He wants to 10 kiss Amarantha, yet he holds back, restrained by her loveliness. It's as if he chooses to keep such radiant beauty pure, within his sight but beyond his reach.

You have seen that paragraphing helps to mark the turns in a writer's thought. What else does it do? What other purpose does paragraph structure have? One way of answering these questions is to consider a set of sentences desperately in need of paragraph structure:

> My life has been a very satisfying one so far. I've faced many challenges and attained some of the goals I've set. I am one of five children. I have two older sisters and two younger brothers. My father was a successful chef. He had a college degree in electrical engineering, but chose to study cooking instead. He traveled in Europe and worked with many different chefs. He had a great influence on all of our lives. He showed me what determination and hard work could do for a person. My mother was a good mother. She guided me in a very practical way. I was able to learn and grow under their supervision. At times, it's hard to attain confidence in some situations, but I think of my parents and continue on. I enjoy knitting and making things for others and I also love to cook. Preparing economical meals is a constant challenge. I like to read a lot. I also enjoy watching my son grow up. Children are a tremendous challenge. I read to him and try to let him be as creative as possible. I have also helped my husband go through his last year of college. It was a proud moment for me to watch him walk up and get his degree. I enjoyed working with him and learning as he did. You really get a good feeling when you've helped someone. Your rewards are twofold. Helping others is my main goal in life. I enjoy people. So far, my life has been satisfactory to me. I've got future goals set to attain. I've got lots of hard work ahead of me. I just look forward to going day by day and getting further toward my one goal of a college education with a challenging job.
>
> —College freshman

The only thing that makes this set of sentences a "paragraph" is the indentation at the beginning. Every sentence here makes sense in itself, but reading these sentences one after the other is like trying to keep up with a kangaroo. The writer moves in short, sudden leaps, and the reader never knows where she will land next. She goes from goals and challenges to sisters and brothers, from parents to knitting and cooking, from helping others to helping herself. What point is she trying to make? She herself seems unsure. To reorganize a jumble like this, she must think about the connections and the differences between her sentences. Only then can she write a paragraph that makes sense.

We will return to this paragraph and go to work on it after we have examined the three basic elements of paragraph structure: unity, emphasis, and coherence.

## 6.2 Unity ¶ *u*

In general, a unified paragraph is a sequence of sentences that are all clearly related to a topic sentence. The **topic sentence** states the main point of the paragraph. At times this sentence may be simply implicit rather than openly stated, but usually it is explicit. It often appears at the beginning of the paragraph.

There are two basic ways of relating the other sentences of the paragraph to the topic sentence. The first is by treating the other sentences as items in a list; the second is by treating them as links in a chain.

### Using List Structure

Consider the following paragraph:

> This is the essence of the religious spirit—the sense of power, beauty, greatness, truth infinitely beyond one's own reach, but infinitely to be aspired to. It invests men with a pride in a purpose and with humility in accomplishment. It is the source of all true tolerance, for in its light all men see other men as they see themselves, as being capable of being more than they are, and yet falling short, inevitably, of what they can imagine human opportunities to be. It is the supporter of human dignity and pride and the dissolver of vanity. And it is the very creator of the scientific spirit; for without the aspiration to understand and control the miracle of life, no man would have sweated in a laboratory or tortured his brain in the exquisite search after truth.
> —Dorothy Thompson, "The Education of the Heart"

This paragraph opens with a topic sentence about the religious spirit. Then comes a list of sentences, each beginning with *It* and all referring to *the religious spirit,* defining and commenting on it. You can clearly see the list structure of the paragraph when the sentences beginning with *It* are separated and printed one below the other:

> TOPIC SENTENCE: This is the essence of the religious spirit—the sense of power, beauty, greatness, truth infinitely beyond one's own reach, but infinitely to be aspired to.
>
> SUPPORTING SENTENCES:
> 1. It invests men with a pride in a purpose and with humility in accomplishment.
> 2. It is the source of all true tolerance, for in its light all men see other men as they see themselves, as being capable of being more than they are, and yet falling short, inevitably, of what they can imagine human opportunities to be.
> 3. It is the supporter of human dignity and pride and the dissolver of vanity.

4. And it is the very creator of the scientific spirit; for without the aspiration to understand and control the miracle of life, no man would have sweated in a laboratory or tortured his brain in the exquisite search after truth.

The word *It* clearly attaches each supporting sentence to the topic sentence. Yet even though the writer repeats *It,* she avoids monotony by varying the length and pattern of her sentences. Compare, for instance, the length of the second sentence with that of the third, and compare the pattern of *It invests men* with the pattern of *It is the source.* While the repetition of *It* lends unity, the variety of the sentences helps to make the paragraph more interesting.

Another example of list structure is one of the paragraphs by Oscar Handlin quoted on p. 99:

TOPIC SENTENCE: They were a diverse group.

SUPPORTING SENTENCES:

1. There were priests who had brooded over the problem of a world in eternity and made the startling discovery that a holy mission summoned them away.
2. There were noblemen in the great courts who stared out beyond the formal lines of the garden and saw the vision of new empires to be won.
3. There were young men without places who depended on daring and their swords and were willing to soldier for their fortunes.
4. There were clerks in the countinghouses, impatient of the endless rows of digits, who thought why should they not reach out for the wealth that set their masters high?
5. There were journeymen without employment and servants without situations and peasants without land and many others whom war or pestilence displaced who dreamed in desperation of an alternative to home.

Here the topic sentence about the *diverse group* is followed by a list of sentences identifying the members of the group. Once again, all the sentences in the list follow the same basic pattern, this time taking the form *There were . . . who . . .* Only the last sentence in the paragraph (*Through the eighteenth century their numbers grew and, even more, through the nineteenth*) departs from the pattern to make a statement about all of the migrants. The pattern itself admits variety, with different constructions between *There were* and *who.* But the pattern also ensures that every sentence up to the last marches in step with the paragraph as a whole.

You can also use list structure in a paragraph of comparison and contrast. In the next example, a topic sentence about law and medicine is followed by a list of contrasts between them:

TOPIC SENTENCE: Though law and medicine are both demanding professions, medicine is more demanding than law.

SUPPORTING SENTENCES:

1. For one thing, it takes three years to earn a law degree, but four to earn an M.D., and still more years to become a fully qualified practitioner.
2. [Sentence pair] Second, lawyers always know in advance when they are scheduled to appear in court. But a doctor may be suddenly called upon at any hour of the day or night.
3. Finally, while a lawyer's mistake can mean the loss of a case, a doctor's mistake can mean the loss of a life.

Here again, all the sentences in the list refer to the key terms in the topic sentence: *medicine* and *law*. As long as every sentence or sentence pair describes a contrast between these two, and as long as the contrast shows that medicine is more demanding than law, the paragraph will be unified. Note too that in a list-structure paragraph, you can strengthen the order of sentences by using sequence tags: *For one thing, Second*, and *Finally*.

**EXERCISE 3    Using List Structure**

Using list structure, develop the following paragraph by adding at least three more sentences.

TOPIC SENTENCE: Some students are infuriatingly well-organized.

SUPPORTING SENTENCES:

1. They always get their assignments done on time.
2. When the professor calls on them, they always have the right answer.

**EXERCISE 4    Using List Structure**

Using list structure and sequence tags, develop one of the following paragraphs by adding at least three more contrasts. The contrasts may be presented in single sentences or sentence pairs.

TOPIC SENTENCE: It is better for students to work for a year between high school and college than to go directly from one to the other.

SUPPORTING SENTENCES:

1. For one thing, a year's earnings will pay much more of a student's college expenses than a summer's earnings will.

TOPIC SENTENCE: It is better for students to go from high school to college directly than to interrupt their education with a year of work.

SUPPORTING SENTENCES:

1. For one thing, students who drop out of school for a year often forget how to study. But students who stay in

school can improve in their studies from one year to the next.

## Using Chain Structure

Another way of unifying the sentences in a paragraph is to use chain structure. As long as the meaning of each new sentence is linked to that of the sentence before it, the paragraph will hold together. Consider this one:

> The process of learning is essential to our lives. All higher animals seek it deliberately. They are inquisitive and they experiment. An experiment is a sort of harmless trial run of some action which we shall have to make in the real world; and this, whether it is made in the laboratory by scientists or by fox-cubs outside their earth. The scientist experiments and the cub plays; both are learning to correct their errors of judgment in a setting in which errors are not fatal. Perhaps this is what gives them both their air of happiness and freedom in these activities.
>
> —Jacob Bronowski, *The Common Sense of Science*

The sentences in this paragraph are like the links in a chain:

TOPIC SENTENCE: The process of learning is essential to our lives.

A. All higher animals seek it deliberately.

 B. They are inquisitive and they experiment.

  C. An experiment is a sort of harmless trial run of some action which we shall have to make in the real world; and this, whether it is made in the laboratory by scientists or by fox-cubs outside their earth.

   D. The scientist experiments and the cub plays; both are learning to correct their errors of judgment in a setting in which errors are not fatal.

    E. Perhaps this is what gives them both their air of happiness and freedom in these activities.

As the lines in the diagram indicate, only the second sentence is directly linked to the topic sentence; each of the others is linked to the one just before it, and would make no sense if it came right after the topic sentence. There are no connecting lines between sentence B and the topic sentence, for example. The link between the first and last sentences of this paragraph is indirect, a result of all the direct links between the intermediate sentences.

For the writer, the advantage of chain structure is that each sentence tends to suggest or generate the next one. The idea of the process of learning leads to the idea of learners (*All higher animals*); *animals* leads to a comment on what they do (*experiment*); *experiment* leads to a definition of that term. While a list-structure paragraph stands still, piling up detail to describe its subject or support its point, the chain-structure paragraph shows thought in motion, making associations and discoveries. When you use chain structure, you are not free to forget about the topic sentence entirely, but you are free to experiment, to pursue the trail opened up by your own sentences, and even to discover something you did not foresee when you wrote the topic sentence. When Bronowski started this paragraph with a sentence about the process of learning, did he expect to end it with a sentence about happiness and freedom?

Note too how the sentences are linked together. In sentence A, the pronoun *it* refers to *The process of learning* in the sentence just before. In sentence B, *They* refers to *All higher animals* in sentence A. In sentence C, *experiment* is repeated from sentence B, but has been turned from a verb into a noun, to serve as the subject of the new sentence. Thus the sentences move with both continuity and progression.

EXERCISE 5    **Using Chain Structure**

Using chain structure, develop the following paragraph by adding at least three more sentences to it. Be sure that each new sentence is linked to the one before it.

> TOPIC SENTENCE: In the next hundred years, the exploration of outer space will undoubtedly change man's relation to the earth.
> A. Earth will be just one of many places where man may choose to live.

**Combining List Structure and Chain Structure**

List structure and chain structure can be used effectively together. Consider this paragraph by a college freshman:

> I have very vivid memories of the hours I spent waiting to leave the bottom of an eighty-foot pit cave. All the walls and formations in the cave were coated with a slimy film of mud moisture. But after crawling on my belly through hundreds of feet of ancient passageways, I no longer even attempted to avoid the filth. I didn't clean my hands when I scratched my face, and I can recall that my eyelids felt strange when I blinked because of the residue on them. Of the six cavers I was the last one to go up the shaft. Several of my friends had already reached the top, but it had taken them two hours, which is a very long time, especially if you are waiting to get out of a cave.

This paragraph is organized by list structure. The first sentence prepares us for a list of memories, and the other sentences supply it. But within the list structure, the writer creates some chains:

TOPIC SENTENCE: I have very vivid memories of the hours I spent waiting to | leave the bottom | of an eighty-foot pit | cave. |

1. A. All the walls and formations in the (cave) were coated with a slimy film of | mud moisture. |
    B. But after crawling on my belly through hundreds of feet of ancient passageways, I no longer even attempted to avoid the (filth.)
    C. I didn't clean my hands when I scratched my face, and I can recall that my eyelids felt strange when I blinked because of the (residue) on them.
2. A. Of the six | cavers | I was the last one to (go up the shaft.)
    B. Several of my (friends) had already (reached the top,) but it had taken them two hours, which is a very long time, especially if you are waiting to get out of a cave.

Here the items in the list are shown by numbers, and the links in the chain are shown by letters. After the topic sentence, three sentences form a chain. *Cave* in the topic sentence is linked to *cave* in sentence 1A, which adds the detail about *mud moisture; filth* in sentence 1B is a synonym for *mud moisture;* and *residue* in sentence 1C clearly refers to *filth* in sentence 1B. Note that you need not repeat a word or phrase in order to refer to it; a synonym or a closely associated phrase will do just as well. In sentence 2A, the phrase *go up the shaft* takes us back to *leave the bottom* in the topic sentence. Sentences 1A and 2A, both referring directly to the topic sentence, together form a list of "vivid memories." But sentence 2A, like sentence 1A, is also part of a chain. In sentence 2B, the phrase *reached the top* is linked to *go up the shaft* in sentence 2A, and *friends* is linked to *cavers*. Finally, though this is not shown diagrammatically, the phrase *waiting to get out of a cave* repeats key words from the topic sentence, and thus ties the whole paragraph together.

Our explanation of list and chain structure does not apply to all paragraphs, or even all effective paragraphs. A one-sentence paragraph obviously has neither list nor chain structure, and even in paragraphs of many sentences, it is sometimes hard to see either one. But while you will occasionally need to use other ways of organizing paragraphs, the great advantage of these two kinds of structure is that they can help you to generate sentences as well as to keep them together.

EXERCISE 6    **Using List and Chain Structure Together**

Expand one of the following paragraphs by using a combination of list and chain structure.

TOPIC SENTENCE: Co-ed colleges are better than single-sex colleges.

1. A. For one thing, they promote day-to-day contact between sexes.
   B. This helps young men and women to see each other as human beings—not simply as dates.
2. A. Second, . . .

TOPIC SENTENCE: Single-sex colleges are better than co-ed colleges.

1. A. First of all, they are much more likely to promote a serious atmosphere for work.
   B. It is hard for students to work seriously with members of the opposite sex around.
2. A. Second, . . .

## 6.3    Emphasis    ¶ *em*

Whether you are using list structure, chain structure, or a combination of both, you need to emphasize the main point of your paragraph. A paragraph without emphasis is baffling: we don't know how to look at it or what to make of it. Emphasis darkens certain lines, makes certain features stand out, and thus helps to define the character of a paragraph as a whole.

How do you emphasize your main point? You can of course underline or italicize it, but aside from these typographical methods (which should be used sparingly), the two most important ways of emphasizing a point are repetition and arrangement.

### Using Repetition for Emphasis

You may have been told that you should never repeat a word or phrase when you write, that you should scour your brain or your thesaurus for synonyms to avoid using a word or phrase again. That is nonsense. If repetition gets out of control, it will soon become monotonous and boring. But selective repetition can be highly useful.

What is selective repetition? Consider the following paragraphs:

> As a student begins his last year of high school, he may start to wonder what college or university is right for him. He will usually apply to several schools for admission. At ——— College, the student actually exchanges information on himself through his application and other forms and interviews for information about

the school. It is through a fair admissions process that ——— College and her candidates for entrance learn a lot about each other. This fair exchange of ideas and insight in the admissions process can be seen through the college's application for admission, the guidance counselor forms, and the alumni interview.

—College freshman

To me the interview comes as close as possible to being the quintessence of proper admissions procedure. It is a well-known secret (to use a paradox) that one can study for the achievement tests and the S.A.T. From personal experience I know that schools "pad" grades and that students can receive marvelous grades without one iota of knowledge in a subject. One cannot, however, "fudge" an interview. One can buy a new suit and put on false airs, but 999 times out of 1,000 the interviewer can easily unmask the fraud and can thus reveal the true person.

—College freshman

Both of these paragraphs use repetition, but only one of them uses it selectively. In the first paragraph, repetition gets out of control. The writer uses *admission* twice, *admissions process* twice, *information* twice, *application* twice, *fair* twice, *exchanges* and *exchange*, *interviews* and *interview*. We can understand that the paragraph concerns the process of applying for admission to a college, but with so many words repeated, we cannot tell which word is more important than the others, or what particular point about the admissions process is being made. Using too much repetition is like underlining every word in a sentence or shouting every word of a speech. When everything is emphasized, nothing is.

The other writer makes repetition work by using it sparingly. *Grades* appears once too often, but the only other word conspicuously repeated is the key term *interview*, which appears twice, along with *interviewer*, used once. This selective repetition keeps the eye of the reader on the writer's main point.

EXERCISE 7 **Using Selective Repetition**

Write a paragraph based on the topic sentence "Clothes tell more about the wearer than most people realize." Use selective repetition to emphasize the main point.

## Using Arrangement for Emphasis

You can emphasize a word by putting it at the beginning or the end of a sentence. Likewise, you can emphasize a point by putting it at the beginning or the end of a paragraph. That is why the first sentence of a paragraph is a good place to state your main point and the last sentence a good place to restate it.

The opening sentence of a paragraph always draws special attention. If you open with a topic sentence that clearly signals where the paragraph is headed, you have already begun to emphasize your main point. After the first sentence, the reader's attention moves toward the ends of the sentences and the end of the paragraph as a whole. In the paragraph on law and medicine (pp. 103–4) the writer emphasizes the main point—that medicine is more demanding than law—by placing it at the end of each sentence or sentence pair:

> TOPIC SENTENCE: Though law and medicine are both demanding professions, medicine is more demanding than law.
> 1. For one thing, it takes three years to earn a law degree, but four to earn an M.D., and still more years to become a fully qualified practitioner.

To see what a difference arrangement makes, consider these two ways to arrange the pair of sentences coming next in the paragraph on law and medicine:

> A doctor may be suddenly called upon at any hour of the day or night. But lawyers always know in advance when they are scheduled to appear in court.

> Lawyers always know in advance when they are scheduled to appear in court. But a doctor may be suddenly called upon at any hour of the day or night.

In any pair of sentences linked by a transitional *But,* the second sentence has the emphasis. The first arrangement of this pair of sentences stresses the predictability of a lawyer's life; the second stresses the unpredictability of a doctor's life, and thus reinforces the point of the topic sentence.

Still another way of emphasizing a point is to repeat it at the end of the paragraph:

> . . . a doctor's mistake can mean the loss of a life. All things considered, therefore, medicine is a more demanding profession than law.

## 6.4   Coherence   ¶ *coh*

Coherence is connection. When a paragraph is coherent, every sentence after the first is connected to the one before it, to the topic sentence, or to both, and readers can readily follow the writer's train of thought. When a paragraph is incoherent, the sentences are badly connected or not connected at all, and readers are likely to lose their way. To see the difference between coherence and incoherence, compare the following passages, both from paragraphs quoted previously:

1. The process of learning is essential to our lives. All higher animals seek it deliberately. They are inquisitive and they experiment. An experiment is a sort of harmless trial run of some action which we shall have to make in the real world; . . .

2. I enjoy knitting and making things for others and I also love to cook. Preparing economical meals is a constant challenge. I like to read a lot. I also enjoy watching my son grow up. Children are a tremendous challenge. I read to him and try to let him be as creative as possible.

In passage 1, as we have seen (pp. 105–6), every sentence is connected to the one after it, to the one before it, or to both. In passage 2, some connections are missing. We can see the link between *love to cook* and *Preparing economical meals,* but what is the link between the second sentence and the third, between *Preparing economical meals* and *I like to read?* Nothing in the third sentence refers, even indirectly, to anything in the one before it. Further on, *Children* in the fifth sentence clearly grows out of *my son* in the fourth, with the writer moving from the particular to the universal term, but then in the last sentence she returns to the particular. To understand what *him* refers to, we have to jump back over the general sentence about *Children* to the previous sentence about *my son.* The line of connection has been broken.

How can you ensure that your sentences will be connected? You can use one or more of three basic methods.

## Using List Structure for Coherence

In a paragraph with list structure, two or more sentences within the paragraph refer to a head-of-the-list sentence. Consider this passage:

[1] Vocationalism is the new look on campus because of the discouraging job market faced by the generalists. [2] Students have been opting for medicine and law in droves. [3] If all those who check "doctor" as their career goal succeed in getting their MDs, we'll immediately have ten times the target ratio of doctors for the population of the United States. [4] Law schools are already graduating twice as many new lawyers every year as the Department of Labor thinks we will need, and the oversupply grows annually.
—Caroline Bird, "Where College Fails Us"

In this paragraph sentence 2 is connected to sentence 1 by chain structure: the word *Students* recalls the word *campus.* Sentence 2, in turn, serves as the head of a list of sentences referring to *medicine* and *law:* in sentence 3, *"doctor"*, *MDs,* and *doctors* recall *medicine;* in sentence 4, *Law schools* and *lawyers* recall *law.* Note that nothing in sentence 4 refers to anything in sentence 3, but each of these sentences refers to the head of the list—sentence 2.

**EXERCISE 8 Using List Structure**

Write a head-of-the-list sentence to introduce the following sentences.

> Husbands are doing a good deal of the cooking and housecleaning. Children are spending their preschool years in day-care centers. More wives than ever before are holding full-time jobs outside the home.

## Using Chain Structure for Coherence

In a paragraph with chain-structure coherence, every sentence after the first refers to the one before it. It does so by repeating a key term, phrase, or clause; by recalling the key expression with a pronoun (such as *it*), a synonym, a paraphrase, or one or more words related to it; by moving from a general term to a particular instance, or vice versa. Consider again the paragraph by Richard Ney that was discussed on pp. 42–43:

> There are more than thirty-three million investors in the United States today. Most of them are losers. Not only do they lose their money; they lose their self-confidence, their security, and the chance they had at one time to use their money to make a killing in the market. Yet the fact is that to get the money needed to invest in the market, most of these people had to be fairly successful in their chosen career. As doctors or lawyers, for example, many of them had demonstrated an ability to think clearly, to make plans for the future, and to carry them out. Why then, employing the same intelligence, do they go wrong when they try to make money in the market?

Ney's chain-structure coherence is powerful. We move from *investors* in the first sentence to *them* in the second, from *losers* in the second to *lose* in the third, from *money to make a killing in the market* to *money needed to invest in the market,* from *these people* to *many of them,* from *an ability to think clearly* to *the same intelligence.* By an unbroken chain of repetition and reference, the writer takes us with him from the very first sentence to the question at the end.

**EXERCISE 9 Recognizing Chain Structure**

In the following paragraphs, pick out the words that connect each sentence with the one just before it and with any others before it as well.

1.      Whatever college graduates want to do, most of them are going to wind up doing what there is to do. During the next few years, according to the Labor Department, the biggest demand will be for stenographers and secretaries, followed by retail-trade salesworkers, hospital attendants, bookkeepers, building custodians, registered nurses, foremen, kindergarten and elementary-school teachers, receptionists, cooks, cosmetologists, private-household workers, manufacturing inspectors, and industrial machinery repairmen. These are the jobs which will eventually absorb the surplus archaeologists, urban planners, oceanographers, sociologists, editors and college professors.

—Caroline Bird, "Where College Fails Us"

2.      Much is said about the pain of growing up in poverty, but not much about the pain of growing up rich. My wealthy family never had to worry about a lack of material possessions. Growing up in this environment, especially as a woman, was a deadening experience. Because she had money, Mom hired other people to live for her: to take care of her children, to wash the clothes, to clean the house. She hated herself. There was nothing for her to be except a social ornament for Dad to introduce to his business friends. She never had a job—didn't know how to go about getting a job, didn't even consider that she was capable of working or of supporting herself.

—Anonymous letter to *Ms.* magazine

3.      All games are peculiar, one to the other, and defy the comprehension of nonplayers, but none is so bizarre as the game of dunking the ball through the basket. Until basketball, boys seven feet tall ran off and hid in the woods or joined a circus. Now the woods are combed in search of them. If they can dribble and dunk a ball, they've got it made. Rules are rules, and all the rules say is that the ball has to enter the basket at the top. The tall boys dunk it.      —Wright Morris, "Odd Balls"

**EXERCISE 10   Recognizing List and Chain Structure**

The following paragraph combines chain structure with list structure. Pick out the words that connect each sentence with a previous one (not necessarily the one just before), and identify the head-of-the-list sentence.

It's a rare Vermont winter that doesn't have one stretch of weather when it's twenty below every night, and not much above zero even at midday. Keeping warm during such a spell is either difficult or expensive—sometimes both. If you're living in a big old house in the country, and if you have an oil furnace, you've got roughly three choices. You can keep the thermostat up at 70 and go broke. You can turn it down to 55, put your family in long underwear, and shiver. Or you can heat two or three rooms with wood stoves, and move in, relying on the furnace only to keep the pipes in the rest of the house from freezing. That's what most of us do.      —Noel Perrin, *First Person Rural*

EXERCISE 11   **Providing Coherence**

Rearrange the following sentences to make a coherent passage.

> I enjoy watching my son grow up. Children are a tremendous challenge. I read to him and try to let him be as creative as possible.

## Using Transitional Words and Phrases

Transitional words and phrases enhance the coherence of a paragraph by signaling one of the following relations between one sentence and another:

### 1. Time

> *Until* basketball, boys seven feet tall ran off and hid in the woods or joined a circus. *Now* the woods are combed in search of them.
> —Wright Morris

> Technology makes life easier for everyone. *A hundred years ago* a man would have to take a horse-drawn carriage to deliver his produce to market. *Now* he can drive a truck.
> —College freshman

Other words that signal time are *previously, earlier, in the past, before, at present, nowadays, meanwhile, later, in the future, eventually.*

### 2. Addition

> Different as they were—in background, in personality, in underlying aspiration—[Grant and Lee] had much in common. Under everything else, they were marvelous fighters. *Furthermore,* their fighting qualities were really very much alike.
> —Bruce Catton, *A Stillness at Appomattox*

Other words that signal addition are *besides, moreover, in addition.*

### 3. Contrast or conflict

> At many universities across the country, more than half the students in each entering class plan on entering "med" school. *But* there just aren't enough spaces for them.
> —College freshman

Other words that indicate contrast or conflict are *nevertheless, however, conversely, on the other hand, still, otherwise, in contrast, unfortunately.*

### 4. Cause and effect

> The world of religion and philosophy was shocked recently when Henry P. Van Dusen and his wife ended their lives by their own hands. Dr. Van Dusen had been president of Union Theological Seminary; for more than a quarter-century he had been one of the luminous names in Protestant theology. He enjoyed world sta-

tus as a spiritual leader. News of the self-inflicted deaths of the Van Dusens, *therefore,* was profoundly disturbing to all those who attach a moral stigma to suicide and regard it as a violation of God's laws.
—Norman Cousins, "The Right to Die"

Other words that indicate cause and effect are *hence, as a result, consequently, accordingly.* Don't use *thus* to mean *therefore; thus* means *in that manner.*

## 5. Comparison

Geniuses have an uncanny power to defy physical handicaps. John Milton was blind when he wrote the greatest of English epics, *Paradise Lost. Likewise,* Beethoven was deaf when he composed some of his greatest symphonies.

Another word that indicates comparison is *similarly.*

## 6. Numerical order

Churchill had many reasons for cooperating with Stalin during the Second World War. *For one,* Stalin was battling the Germans on the Eastern front and thus reducing German pressure on England. *Second,* Russia had power, and in the face of German aggression, England needed powerful allies. *Finally,* Churchill's hatred of Hitler consumed all other feelings. Though Stalin made him uneasy, Churchill said once that to destroy Hitler, he would have made a pact with the devil himself.

Among words that indicate numerical order are *first, second, third; in the first place, in the second place, in the third place; to begin with, next, finally.* But use these words and phrases sparingly. A succession of numbered sentences soon becomes boring.

## 7. Spatial order

The once-a-year sale had apparently drawn just about everyone in town to Gerry's department store. *At left,* the three-acre parking lot was jammed with cars, motorcycles, and pickup trucks. *At right,* a line of people stretched down Main Street for six blocks.

Other words that indicate spatial order are *nearby, in the distance, below, above, in back, in front.*

### Exercise 12   Making Transitions

At one or more points in each of the following passages a transitional word or phrase is missing. Find the points and insert suitable transitions.

1. The group that led the campaign against "gay rights" in Florida held the belief that homosexuality is immoral and that, once allowed in an area, it would lead to a breakdown of the values of a society. Homosexuality has existed throughout the past. Some

of the world's greatest geniuses have professed to be homosexuals. These men have made great contributions to society. Whether one agrees that their practices were immoral or not, one must respect the contributions of men such as Michelangelo and Tchaikovsky.                    —College freshman

2. Higher education in America has recently hit a new low. In liberal-arts colleges, the abolition of many or even all specific requirements for graduation has left students to find their own way, which is too often a closed alley. Allowed to take any courses they want, many students concentrate on just one subject or specialized skill. They graduate with narrow minds.

3. Revolution and moderation seldom go hand in hand. In the early years of the French revolution, the moderate Girondists were outmaneuvered by the bloodthirsty Jacobins, who launched a reign of terror. Within months after the moderate Mensheviks launched the Russian revolution of 1917, the radical Bolsheviks seized power and established a government of ruthless repression.

4. In the seventeenth century, a voyage across the Atlantic took more than two months. A supersonic plane does the trip in three hours.

## 6.5 Paragraphing in Action—Rearranging Sentences

Now that you have seen how good paragraphs are put together, let's return to the one that needs major reconstruction—the one by the college freshman who is also a wife and mother:

[1] My life has been a very satisfying one so far. [2] I've faced many challenges and attained some of the goals I've set. [3] I am one of five children. [4] I have two older sisters and two younger brothers. [5] My father was a successful chef. [6] He had a college degree in electrical engineering, but chose to study cooking instead. [7] He traveled in Europe and worked with many different chefs. [8] He had a great influence on all of our lives. [9] He showed me what determination and hard work could do for a person. [10] My mother was a good mother. [11] She guided me in a very practical way. [12] I was able to learn and grow under their supervision. [13] At times, it's hard to attain confidence in some situations, but I think of my parents and continue on. [14] I enjoy knitting and making things for others and I also love to cook. [15] Preparing economical meals is a constant challenge. [16] I like to read a lot. [17] I also enjoy watching my son grow up. [18] Children are a tremendous challenge. [19] I read to him and try to let him be as creative as possible. [20] I have also helped my husband go through his last year of college. [21] It was a proud moment for me to watch him walk up and get his degree. [22] I enjoyed working with him and learning as he did. [23] You really get a good feeling

when you've helped someone. [24] Your rewards are twofold. [25] Helping others is my main goal in life. [26] I enjoy people. [27] So far, my life has been satisfactory to me. [28] I've got future goals set to attain. [29] I've got lots of hard work ahead of me. [30] I just look forward to going day by day and getting further toward my one goal of a college education with a challenging job.

Rereading these sentences in the light of what you know about paragraph structure, you may see that there is matter here for at least two paragraphs: one on the writer's childhood and the influence of her parents, the other on her life and goals as a wife, mother, and college student. This division in the material becomes obvious if you examine the links between the sentences. The first sentence looks like a topic sentence, and the second is connected to it, but the third sentence has nothing to do with *challenges* and *goals,* and not until sentence 15 does either of those words appear again. Sentences 3–13 are really a detour from the road that the first two sentences open up, and therefore need to be taken out and reorganized under a topic sentence of their own.

Sentences 3–13 can be used to make a paragraph because they all concern the same topic—the writer's childhood and her parents. But to develop a paragraph from these sentences, the writer will first have to identify one of them as a topic sentence, a sentence that states the main point of the whole group. A likely candidate is sentence 12: *I was able to learn and grow under their supervision.* To make this sentence work at the beginning of the paragraph, the writer will have to change *their* to *my parents'.* She will then have the start of a paragraph:

I was able to learn and grow under my parents' supervision.

Now see how this topic sentence can help the writer organize the other sentences in the 3–13 group:

TOPIC SENTENCE: I was able to learn and grow under my parents' supervision.

3. I am one of five children.
4. I have two older sisters and two younger brothers.
5. My father was a successful chef.
6. He had a college degree in electrical engineering, but chose to study cooking instead.
7. He traveled in Europe and worked with many different chefs.
8. He had a great influence on all of our lives.
9. He showed me what determination and hard work could do for a person.
10. My mother was a good mother.
11. She guided me in a very practical way.
13. At times, it's hard to attain confidence in some situations, but I think of my parents and continue on.

There are still some problems here. The topic sentence forecasts a discussion of the writer's parents, but sentences 3 and 4 concern her brothers and sisters. Though the brothers and sisters are obviously related to the writer's parents, they are not connected with her parents' supervision of her, or—except in the phrase *our lives* (sentence 8)—with their influence on her. When sentences 3 and 4 are cut out, you actually begin to see a paragraph taking shape:

> I was able to learn and grow under my parents' supervision.
>
> 5. My father was a successful chef.

The writer now has a definite link between the topic sentence and the one that follows it. In fact, she has the beginnings of a paragraph combining list structure and chain structure:

> TOPIC SENTENCE: I was able to learn and grow under my parents' supervision. [formerly sentence 12]
>
> 1. A. My father had a great influence on my life. [8, with *all of our lives* changed to *my life*]
>    B. He showed me what determination and hard work could do for a person. [9]
>    C. He had a college degree in electrical engineering, but chose to study cooking instead. [6]
>    D. He traveled in Europe and worked with many different chefs. [7]
>    E. He was a successful chef. [5]
> 2. A. My mother was a good mother. [10]
>    B. She guided me in a very practical way. [11]
>
> CONCLUDING SENTENCE: At times, it's hard to attain confidence in some situations, but I think of my parents and continue on. [13]

This is now a paragraph: a sequence of sentences that are all related to the topic sentence. The word *parents'* in the topic sentence leads to a list of two basic sentences, one about the father and one about the mother, and each of the two sentences in the list leads to its own chain of related sentences. *My father* in sentence 1A is linked to *He* in sentence 1B, and *hard work* in sentence 1B is linked to *study cooking* in sentence 1C. In turn, *study cooking* leads to *worked with many different chefs* in sentence 1D, which then leads to *successful chef* in sentence 1E. The second sentence in the list, the one about the mother, leads to just one other sentence (2B), and the paragraph concludes with an echo of its topic sentence, a restatement of its main idea.

With the basic structure of the paragraph established, the writer can improve it further by adding transitional words and combining some of the sentences. Both of these steps will strengthen the connections between the sentences, and in addition, the sentence combining will break the monotony of too many short, simple constructions. In the following revision, the new words are italicized:

> TOPIC SENTENCE: I was able to learn and grow under my parents' supervision.
> 1. A. My father had a great influence on me *because* he showed me what determination and hard work could do for a person.
>    B. He had a college degree in electrical engineering, but chose to study cooking instead, traveling in Europe and working with many different chefs.
>    C. He *thus became* a successful chef *himself.*
> 2. A. My mother was a good mother *who* guided me in a very practical way.
> CONCLUDING SENTENCE: At times, it's hard to attain confidence in some situations, but I think of my parents and continue on.

There is still room for development in this paragraph. To balance the chain of sentences about the father, the writer might say more about the mother, explaining how she gave guidance and what she taught. Specific statements here would enrich the paragraph and clarify the meaning of the topic sentence.

Shaping the rest of the original passage into paragraph form is harder. For one thing, there is no obvious topic sentence. Nearly all of the other sentences concern the writer's challenges and goals, but no one sentence on this subject covers the rest in the way that sentence 12 covers sentences 5–13. The writer speaks of past goals in sentences 1–2, 20–24, and 27, of present challenges and satisfactions in sentences 14–19 and 26, and of future goals in sentences 28–30. Most revealingly, she does not seem to know whether her main goal is helping others (sentence 25) or helping herself (sentence 30), or what the relation between those two goals might be. Before she can write a coherent paragraph on her goals, she will have to do some more thinking and decide just what they are.

For paragraphing is inseparable from thinking. You can study the way other writers put sentences together, and you can learn some of the ways by which sentences are connected, but you cannot get from someone else a knowledge of your own thoughts and attitudes—a sense of your own direction. The principles of paragraph structure cannot lead you to that. But they can help you to see whether you yourself have found your direction, and to compose unified, coherent paragraphs once you have clarified your thoughts.

EXERCISE 13    **Expanding a Paragraph**

Expand the final version of the paragraph given on p. 119 by inserting at least two sentences about the mother after sentence 2A.

EXERCISE 14    **Forming a Paragraph**

Choose a topic sentence from the following list and rearrange the remaining sentences to complete a paragraph, combining them and adding words where necessary.

1. The burglary was discovered.
2. The Watergate scandal showed how extensive political corruption can be.
3. High officials at the White House tried to block a full investigation of the burglary and thereby incriminated themselves.
4. In the presidential campaign of 1972, men working for the reelection of the president tried to burglarize a building in order to get information about their political rivals.
5. For the first time in history, the president of the United States was forced to resign in disgrace.
6. Investigators discovered wrongdoing by the president himself.

EXERCISE 15    **Forming a Paragraph**

Choose a topic sentence from the following list and rearrange the remaining sentences to complete a paragraph, combining them and adding words where necessary.

1. The announcement of this principle led scientists in the United States and Great Britain to test and prove it by various devices.
2. The zoetrope was a cylinder covered with images.
3. According to this principle, the human eye retains an image for a fraction of a second longer than the image is present.
4. The principle was announced in 1824 by a British scholar named Peter Mark Roget.
5. One of these was a toy known as a zoetrope.
6. These simple applications of Roget's principle eventually led to the development of the motion picture.
7. Motion pictures originated from the discovery of the principle known as the persistence of vision.
8. Another device was a small book of drawings that seemed to move when flipped by the thumb.
9. The motion picture is actually a rapid succession of still pictures put together by the persistence of vision in the eye.
10. The images merged into a single picture when the cylinder was rapidly spun.

EXERCISE 16    **Tightening a Paragraph**

Following is the introductory paragraph from the first draft of an essay about Samuel Beckett. Tighten the paragraph by cutting it down to no more than eight sentences.

> Lots of people suffer because nothing they do seems to make any sense. History shows men and women looking for meaning in their lives. Without it, life does not seem worthwhile, as we all know. Thus most people try to find a reason for existence, an
> 5 explanation for their being. They have believed the center of their being lay outside themselves. Throughout the ages many have looked to their religion, their gods, for an answer. Others have disagreed. They have said man must look to himself, not to nonexistent gods. Samuel Beckett is one of these. In his writings he
> 10 cries out against idealism. He says it is futile to search for meaning in an external force which does not exist. He says the truth is to be found in the individual. Men and women will learn the reason for their existence if they acquire self-knowledge.

## 6.6    Leading Up to the Main Point

We have so far been looking at the paragraph that states its main point in the opening sentence. But there are often good reasons for delaying the main point, holding it back until after the first sentence or even saving it to the very end. Here are two alternatives to the "main point" opening.

### The Concessive Opening

If you are writing an argumentative paragraph on a controversial topic, any position you take will probably meet resistance from some of your readers. You cannot defend or attack such things as abortion, capital punishment, gun control, the legalization of pot, or the lowering of the drinking age without stirring objections. In an argumentative paragraph, therefore, it is good strategy to begin by recognizing those objections, by letting readers on the other side know that you understand their point of view. You thus increase the chances that they will come to understand yours. (For a full discussion of this point, see section 5.6, pp. 92–94.)

### Putting the Main Point at the End

Put the main point at the end if you want to present it as a conclusion to the paragraph as a whole:

> Comparisons of men and women often involve physical ability. Why can't a woman lift as much as Vassily Alexyov? Where is

the woman who can throw a ball like Joe Namath? But women too can tell of their superstars. Didn't Billy Jean King beat Bobby Riggs in a game of tennis? Does anyone skate more beautifully than Peggy Fleming? When all games have been played and all contests completed, a standoff appears. Men excel in some sports and women in others. There seem to be no superiorities in the battle of the sexes.                                              —College freshman

The writer begins with a general indication of what the paragraph will do—compare men and women physically. But not until the last three sentences does he plainly state his main point: men and women are equally successful in athletics. By saving this point to the end of the paragraph, the writer clearly indicates that it is a conclusion.

EXERCISE 17   Ending a Paragraph with a Conclusion

The final sentence of this paragraph has been deleted. In place of the missing sentence, write a sentence of your own that could serve as a conclusion.

> Although Oberlin admitted women in 1837, and Elmira Female College was founded in 1855, American higher education remained a virtually all-male affair until after the Civil War. Not only were women thought generally incapable of intellectual self-discipline and rigor, but the attempt to impose it on them was thought debilitating to both mind and body. (This may not have been wholly delusory, given the character of nineteenth-century academic life.) The men who controlled job opportunities had no interest in hiring women in any but menial roles, and men looking for wives were also unlikely to be impressed by a girl's educational qualifications. . . .
> —Christopher Jencks and David Riesman, *The Academic Revolution*

## 6.7   Making Transitions between Paragraphs   *trans*

A good essay is more than a collection of separate paragraphs. It is made up of connected paragraphs, paragraphs linked to each other not only by the logic of what they have to say but by transitions between them. Much of what you already know about linking sentences within paragraphs can also be used to link paragraphs to each other. Here are three ways to do so.

**1.** Use a transitional word or phrase:

> Boston today can still provide a fairly stimulating atmosphere for the banker, the broker, for doctors and lawyers. "Open end" investments prosper, the fish come in at the dock, the wool market continues, and workers are employed in the shoe factories

in the nearby towns. For the engineer, the physicist, the industrial designer, for all the highly trained specialists of the electronic age, Boston and its area are of seemingly unlimited promise. Sleek, well-designed factories and research centers pop up everywhere; the companies plead, in the Sunday papers, for more chemists, more engineers, and humbly relate the executive benefits of salary and pension and advancement they are prepared to offer.

But otherwise, for the artist, the architect, the composer, the writer, the philosopher, the historian, for those humane pursuits for which the town was once noted and even for the delights of entertainment, for dancing, acting, cooking, Boston is a bewildering place. . . .
—Elizabeth Hardwick, "Boston: The Lost Ideal"

The single word *But* nicely marks the transition from a paragraph about the attractions of Boston to one about what it lacks. (Transitional words and phrases are listed and discussed on pp. 114–15.)

**2.** Start a new paragraph by answering one or more questions raised in the one before:

Married or single, working or not working today, women must begin to think in terms of a basic choice: Public role and private role—which is the more important? In an emergency which would you sacrifice? If your child was sick or unhappy, would you leave him in someone else's care, as a man must do? If your husband's job took him to another country, would you give up a promising career to go with him? Would you go far away from friends and relatives for your career?

However important, responsible and fulfilling a woman's work may be, the answer is quite predictable. Most women put their families first. And few will think them wrong. This is the choice women have been brought up to make and men have been taught to expect. It is the unusual woman, the woman wholly committed to her career or an impersonal goal, on whom criticism descends.          —Margaret Mead, "Women: A House Divided"

The first paragraph poses several questions stating choices women must make, and the second paragraph supplies an answer to those questions: *Most women put their families first.* The question-and-answer form makes the transition automatically, with no need for transitional words.

**3.** Start a new paragraph by echoing a key word or recalling a key idea from the one before:

There are days when I find myself unduly pessimistic about the future of man. Indeed, I will confess that there have been occasions when I swore I would never again make the study of time a profession. My walls are lined with books expounding its mysteries;

*Making Transitions between Paragraphs*   **123**

my hands have been split and rubbed raw with grubbing into the quicklime of its waste bins and hidden crevices. I have stared so much at death that I can recognize the lingering personalities in the faces of skulls and feel accompanying affinities and repulsions.

One such skull lies in the lockers of a great metropolitan museum. It is labeled simply: Strandlooper, South Africa. I have never looked longer into any human face than I have upon the features of that skull. I come there often, drawn in spite of myself. It is a face that would lend reality to the fantastic tales of our childhood. There is a hint of Wells' *Time Machine* folk in it—those pathetic, childlike people whom Wells pictures as haunting earth's autumnal cities in the far future of the dying planet.

—Loren Eiseley, "Man of the Future"

Here the repetition of *skull* at the beginning of the second paragraph links the two paragraphs together, and marks the transition from a general discussion of death to some thoughts about a particular skull.

You can also link paragraphs by means of a key idea, as Margaret Mead does in her essay "Women: A House Divided":

. . . This is the choice women have been brought up to make and men have been taught to expect. It is the unusual woman, the woman wholly committed to her career or an impersonal goal, on whom criticism descends.

Up to the present the dilemma is one most women have managed to avoid. One way of doing it has been by defining their work as an adjunct to their personal lives. Even today, when over one third of the women living in husband-wife homes—about 15 million married women—are working, this remains true. The kinds of positions women hold and the money they are paid are, at least in part, a reflection of women's own definitions of the place of work in their lives and of the reciprocal belief among men that giving a woman a career job is a high risk.

A *dilemma* is a difficult choice, and though *dilemma* itself does not appear in the previous paragraph, it echoes the sense of the key word *choice*, which does. More, it supplies a shade of meaning that is important to Mead's discussion and that the neutral word *choice* does not have.

An effective paragraph, then, is a group of sentences that usually has both internal and external connections. Internally, the paragraph must be unified and coherent, with sentences that have some topic in common, and with a line of thought leading from one sentence to the next. Externally, a paragraph that is part of an essay should look back to what has preceded it even as it breaks new ground. Thus it will serve to guide the reader from one point to another.

# 7

# CHOOSING WORDS

| |
|---|
| **7.1** |

*d*

Speaking and writing are both processes of choosing words. Words never choose themselves. In speaking and in the early stages of writing, the choosing of words is often an unconscious act. But to write effectively, you must make it a conscious one. You need to think about the words you are using, the shades of meaning they convey, and the effect they have on your readers. That is what this chapter aims to help you do.

## 7.1 Finding the Right Level of Diction  *d*

Most people do not talk the same way on every subject from peanut butter to politics. Nor do most people talk the same way to a six-year-old and to a policeman, to a close friend and to a complete stranger, to a teacher and to a fellow student. In speaking, people commonly choose their words to suit the things they are talking about and the people they are talking to. In writing, you should do the same.

Good writing is made of words that suit its subject and its expected audience. As you write, you constantly need to make choices among words that have similar meanings but different effects on people. The words you choose are called your **diction,** and the total effect of those words is your **level of diction**—that is, your level of formality or informality.

To see how a particular level of diction is set and maintained, consider this passage from an essay written for a college course:

Fears based on ignorance can sometimes be conquered by scientific fact. In 1938 a radio program called *War of the Worlds* actually terrified large numbers of Americans by pretending to report that the earth was being invaded by men from Mars. But as we now know from unmanned exploration of Mars itself, the idea that "Martians" could invade the earth is ——————.

As is right for a piece on a serious subject aimed at an intelligent and somewhat critical audience (the instructor), this passage is formal rather than casual in tone. But it is not too formal; it is only a term paper, not a State of the Union address. It is written at the middle level of diction, the normal level for most college and professional writing.

What, then, should the last word be? Here are some words that would fit the meaning of the passage. Choose one:

insupportable
preposterous
incredible
ludicrous
groundless
absurd
silly
false
crazy
looney
bull

A quick glance down the list should make you see that these eleven words descend through several levels of diction, from the stately, many-syllabled formality of *insupportable* through the informality of *crazy* to the outright slanginess of *bull*. If you chose a word from the middle of the list—*ludicrous, groundless, absurd, silly*, or *false*—you chose sensibly, for these words are all at the middle level of diction, and can fit into most contexts without seeming either coarse or pretentious, too low or too high. Slang words like *looney* and *bull* may be all right in conversation, but they do not suit a formal discussion of human fears, and the odds are they will not suit the audience either. So why not *insupportable*, from the top of the list? This word is impressively long, but its very length makes it carry more weight than most sentences can bear, and seasoned writers do not use long words just to impress their readers. In this case, the meaning of *insupportable* can readily be conveyed by a shorter word, such as *groundless*.

As you move toward the middle of the list, choosing becomes harder. The words from *ludicrous* to *false*, all from the middle level of diction, differ not so much in formality as in the shades of their meaning. Do you want to ridicule those who believed in Martians? Then you should say *ludicrous, absurd,* or *silly.* Do you simply want to reject their belief? Then you should describe it as *groundless* or *false.* (For a full discussion of the meanings of these words, see p. 136.) But in any case, all of these words belong to the middle level of diction. Choosing that level in the first place will help to make the final choice a little easier.

Though the middle level of diction is the one to use in most of your college and professional writing, some occasions call for high formality. Consider this passage:

> We dare not forget today that we are the heirs of that first revolution. Let the word go forth from this time and place, to friend and foe alike, that the torch has been passed to a new generation of Americans—born in this century, tempered by war, disciplined by a hard and bitter peace, proud of our ancient heritage, and unwilling to witness or permit the slow undoing of those human rights to which this Nation has always been committed, and to which we are committed today at home and around the world.
> —John F. Kennedy, Inaugural Address

Kennedy's language is marked by stately words: *heirs, generation, heritage, witness.* He is delivering a presidential speech on a ceremonial occasion, and that requires language of high formality.

On the other hand, readers sometimes expect a writer to use slang—in sports reporting, for example:

> Baker led off the ninth with a scorcher into the right-field corner, and took second when Bailey bobbled the ball. Muzio caught Lehmann looking at a slider on the outside corner, but Tetrazzini clouted the next delivery into the upper deck. In the bottom of the inning, Tom Stewart retired the Sox in order to ice the win.

These two passages show the extremes. Ordinarily, you should steer a middle course. But even when you are choosing most of your words from the middle level of diction, you may occasionally need a highly formal word, or—on the other hand—a piece of slang:

> In Moulmein, in Lower Burma, I was hated by large numbers of people—the only time in my life that I have been important enough for this to happen to me. I was sub-divisional police officer of the town, and in an aimless, petty kind of way anti-European feeling was very bitter. No one had the guts to raise a riot, but if a European woman went through the bazaars alone somebody would probably spit betel juice over her dress.
> —George Orwell, "Shooting an Elephant"

*Guts* is slang, but it is not hard to see why Orwell chose to use it in this passage of otherwise middle-level diction. Unlike the passage on the Martians, this one involves violent feelings. *Guts* therefore seems right here; it has bite and pungency. These qualities are reinforced by the word *spit,* which is not quite slang, but works together with *guts* to define and vivify the abstract phrase *anti-European feeling.*

One reason the slang is effective here is that Orwell has used it sparingly and with a specific purpose in mind. If you overuse slang, your writing will begin to sound like this:

> When I got out of high school, I figured I wouldn't start college right off because books were giving me bad vibes at the time and I wanted to get my head together first.

Just as bad is a sentence that suddenly lurches into slang with no good reason for doing so:

> When I finished high school, I decided not to enter college immediately because academic work was giving me bad vibes.

In formal writing, therefore, use slang sparingly, or not at all:

> When I finished high school, I decided not to enter college immediately because I just couldn't stomach any more academic work.

The verb *stomach* has plenty of force; you could also use *swallow* or simply *take.* None of these words is slang, but each of them gives most readers a stronger and more specific sense of the writer's feelings than does *bad vibes.* The more you write, the more you will find variety and power within the middle range of diction.

### EXERCISE 1   Making Diction Consistent

Some of the following sentences are marred by slang. Rewrite each sentence in which you think the diction is not consistently what it should be. If an entry is acceptable as it stands, write *No change needed.*

> EXAMPLE
> After learning that she had caught pneumonia, Emily decided not to make the scene at David's party.
> REVISED: After learning that she had caught pneumonia, Emily decided not to attend [or "not to go to"] David's party.

1. My sister wants to become a commercial-airline pilot because she is hung up on planes.
2. Because I fouled up on the midterm examination in history, I am now in danger of failing the entire course.
3. The variety of courses available at Wintergreen University provides ample opportunity for all students to do their own thing.
4. The best thing about taking a long run on a hot day is the feel of a cool shower afterward.
5. Since Jack's driving is sometimes reckless, I feel uptight whenever he gives me a ride.

6. If Jennifer designed that building all by herself, she must be really far out.
7. To leave school before you have learned how to read and write is to cop out on your duty to yourself.
8. Ticked off by his insults, she poured a glass of orange juice over his head.

**Exercise 2   Making Diction Consistent**

Revise the following passage to eliminate any unjustified slang or excessive formality in its diction.

> While I'm complaining, let me mention another gripe about New York. It's impossible to get a haircut here! When I inhabited a house in the town of Rye, I had a terrific barber, a person who, every month or so, would give me a straightforward trim for $3.50,
> 5  a price which was reasonable in my opinion. He always cut my tresses exactly as I wanted him to, and he never suggested that a different style would be more beneficial. I like simple haircuts but have yet to get one in the five months I've been attending Columbia University, which is right here in New York City. It is my consid-
> 10  ered opinion that all of the barbers left town years ago, to be replaced by hair stylists, as they label themselves, men who use scissors on a man's locks in the way bad sculptors use their mitts to put soft clay into some kind of shape. If I present a request for a simple trim, these bums spray my head with water, comb my hair in every
> 15  direction but the right one, grab tufts, and start hacking. They try to layer it in ways only a high-priced fashion model could ever want; and they leave the sideburns raw, claiming that's how men of taste want them. Then they plug in their damned hair dryers and blow up the mess they've made. In conclusion, they have the
> 20  effrontery to submit a bill for a monetary sum in excess of $10. You can't win.

## 7.2   Using General and Technical Diction   *jarg*

Most words above the level of informal diction and slang are appropriate when you are addressing adult readers, but of course you must be sure that your words will be understood. If, for instance, you are writing about skiing for an audience of skiers, you can safely use such words as *schuss* and *mogul;* these are technical terms skiers understand and use freely among themselves. Likewise, sociologists speak of *upward mobility;* computer programmers and electrical engineers speak of *feedback;* doctors speak of *blood counts;* and stockbrokers speak of *puts, calls, straddles,* and any number of other strange transactions. But if you are writing for a general audience, you cannot expect your readers to understand technical terms. Certain terms are so specialized that even the dictionary definitions will not help most readers. Faced with this problem, you can replace technical terms with standard English words, or you can define the terms as you go along. Better still, since both of these approaches can be awkward, you can sometimes use a technical term in a way that makes its meaning reasonably clear to a general reader, as in this passage:

> If we became free of disease, we would make a much better run of it for the last decade or so, but might still terminate on about the same schedule as now. We may be like the genetically different lines of mice . . . programmed to die after a predetermined number of days clocked by their genomes. If this is the way it is, some of us will continue to wear out and come unhinged in the sixth decade, and some much later, depending on genetic timetables.
> —Lewis Thomas, "The Long Habit"

The technical term *genomes* is surrounded by words and phrases anyone would know: *die, clocked, wear out, come unhinged.* Even if you have never seen the word *genomes* before, you can figure out roughly what it means here: something inside you, probably having to do with your genes, that may determine how long you are going to live.

However, while technical terms may and often should be used in writings on specialized subjects, they are otherwise out of place, especially when plain English substitutes are available. Writing needlessly filled with scientific and pseudoscientific terms is often called **jargon.** Many readers find it pretentious, hard to understand, or both. Here are two examples:

> When I asked my parents if I could use the car, the *feedback* was *negative.*
> TRANSLATION: When I asked my parents if I could use the car, the answer was "No." [or] When I asked my parents if I could use the car, they said, "No."

> The student-faculty *interface* has deteriorated since last year.
> TRANSLATION: Student-faculty relations have deteriorated since last year.

## 7.3 Avoiding Pretentious Words and Euphemisms *euph*

### Pretentious Words

The pretentious word or phrase is too long and high-flown for the meaning it actually delivers. You should substitute a simpler word wherever possible:

Were it not for the *lucrative financial rewards,* she would have quit the job.

TRANSLATION: Were it not for the money, she would have quit the job.

Big cars utilize excessive quantities of fuel.

TRANSLATION: Big cars use too much gas.

**Euphemisms**

A **euphemism** is a word or expression that takes the sting out of an unpleasant reality. A euphemism for *dead* is *departed;* a euphemism for *kill* is *eliminate.* Since euphemisms veil the truth instead of stating it openly, you should use them only when plainer words would needlessly hurt the feelings of those you are writing for or about.

If you are writing about people with physical defects, for instance, you may wish to call them *disabled* or *handicapped* rather than *crippled, maimed,* or *club-footed.* A word like *disabled* shows consideration for the feelings of the disabled people themselves. But euphemisms should never be used to hide the truth or to spare the feelings of those who have done wrong. George Orwell gives some telling examples:

> Defenseless villages are bombarded from the air, the inhabitants driven out into the countryside, the cattle machine-gunned, the huts set on fire with incendiary bullets: this is called *pacification.* Millions of peasants are robbed of their farms and sent trudging along the roads with no more than they can carry: this is called *transfer of population* or *rectification of frontiers.* People are imprisoned for years without trial, or shot in the back of the neck or sent to die of scurvy in Arctic lumber camps: this is called *elimination of unreliable elements.*          —"Politics and the English Language"

*Pacification* means "bringing peace," but the words that tell what really happened speak of war and destruction. The greater the outrage, the greater the need to hide it with a euphemism.

No absolute rule can tell you that a particular euphemism is right or wrong. You must exercise your own judgment. Irresponsible writers make free use of euphemisms to withhold vital but unpleasant facts. Honest and responsible writers use euphemisms only when plain words might needlessly offend or upset the reader. Good writing is the art of being at once truthful and tactful.

EXERCISE 3   **Using Plain English**

The following sentences are disfigured by jargon, euphemisms, or pretentious words. Using your dictionary if necessary, translate each sentence into plain English.

EXAMPLE
Big cars utilize excessive quantities of fuel.
TRANSLATION: Big cars use too much gas.

1. When I asked her to come to the party, the feedback was positive.
2. She was so surprised that she could not verbalize anything.
3. His utilization of the telephone was continual.
4. The motivation factor for his joining the navy was his desire to go to sea.
5. Responding to a call for help, the police went to the liquor store and arrested the perpetrator of a robbery.
6. The closing of the factory impacted negatively on the whole town.

## 7.4 Using the Dictionary

A good dictionary is the indispensable tool of a good writer. Words are useless, even dangerous, if you don't know what they mean. To show you just what a dictionary can tell you about a word—even about a word you use often—here is a sample entry from *The American Heritage Dictionary:*

Spelling    Pronunciation    Definition    Comparative and
                             as adjective   superlative forms

General usage

Slang usage

Informal or
colloquial usage

Definition as verb

Verb forms

Definition as
intransitive verb

Definition
as noun

History of
the word

Related forms

Distinctions in
meaning between
the word and
others like it

**cool** (kōōl) *adj.* *cooler, coolest.* 1. Moderately cold; neither warm nor very cold. 2. Reducing discomfort in hot weather; allowing a feeling of coolness: *a cool blouse.* 3. Not excited; calm; controlled. 4. Showing dislike, disdain, or indifference; unenthusiastic; not cordial: *a cool greeting.* 5. Calmly audacious or bold; impudent. 6. Designating or characteristic of colors, such as blue and green, that produce the impression of coolness. 7. *Slang.* Having a quiet, indifferent, and aloof attitude. 8. *Slang.* Excellent; first-rate; superior. 9. *Informal.* Without exaggeration; entire; full: *He lost a cool million.* —*v.* cooled, cooling, cools. —*tr.* 1. To make less warm. 2. To make less ardent, intense, or zealous. —*intr.* 1. To become less warm. 2. To become calm. —cool it. *Slang.* To calm down, slow down, or relax. —cool one's heels. *Informal.* To be kept waiting for a long time. —*n.* 1. Anything that is cool or moderately cold: *the cool of early morning.* 2. The state or quality of being cool. 3. *Slang.* Composure: *recover one's cool.* [Middle English *col,* Old English *cōl.* See gel-³ in Appendix.*] —cool′ly *adv.* —cool′ness *n.*

**Synonyms:** *cool, composed, collected, unruffled, nonchalant, imperturbable, detached.* These adjectives apply to persons to indicate calmness, especially in time of stress. *Cool* has the widest application. Usually it implies merely a high degree of self-control, though it may also indicate aloofness. *Composed* and *collected* more strongly imply conscious display of self-discipline and absence of agitation. *Composed* also often suggests serenity or sedateness, and *collected,* mental concentration. *Unruffled* emphasizes calmness in the face of severe provocation that may have produced agitation in others present. *Nonchalant* describes a casual exterior manner that suggests, sometimes misleadingly, a lack of interest or concern. *Imperturbable* stresses unshakable calmness considered usually as an inherent trait rather than as a product of self-discipline. *Detached* implies aloofness and either lack of active concern or resistance to emotional involvement.

**1.** Spelling, syllable division, pronunciation. You already know how to spell and pronounce a one-syllable word like *cool,* but what about a longer word, such as *government?* The definition of this word begins "**gov-ern-ment** (gŭv′ərn-mənt)." With the word broken into three syllables, you can tell where to divide it when you need to hyphenate it at the end of a line. The version of the word in parentheses tells you to pronounce it with the accent on the first syllable (*gŭv′*). Here the word is spelled phonetically—that is, according to the way it sounds. The pronunciation key at the beginning of the dictionary (and at the bottom of each page) explains that *ŭ* sounds like the *u* in *cut* and ə sounds like the *e* in *item.*

**2.** Parts of speech. Like many other words, *cool* can be used in various ways. The abbreviation *adj.* tells you that it is being defined first as an adjective; the entry then goes on to explain what it means when used as a verb (—*v.*) and as a noun (—*n.*). The definition of *cool* as an adjective is given first because that is the way the word is most often used.

**3.** Forms. For certain parts of speech several forms of the word are given. For example, *adj.* is followed by *cooler* and *coolest,* the comparative and superlative forms of the adjective *cool.* Similarly, —*v.* is followed by the main forms of the verb *cool:* the past participle, *cooled;* the present participle, *cooling;* and the third-person singular for the present tense, *cools.*

**4.** Definitions. When a word can function in various ways (as adjective or verb, for instance), a separate set of numbered definitions is given for each. Some dictionaries begin with the earliest meaning of the word and then proceed in order to the latest ones, but most dictionaries—like the *American Heritage*—simply begin with the central, commonest meaning of the word, whether or not it is also the earliest. Some definitions are accompanied by examples: *a cool blouse, a cool greeting.*

**5.** Usage labels. Usage labels help you decide whether the word is suitable for the level of diction you have chosen. Here are the most common of the many possibilities:

| WORD | LABEL | MEANING |
|---|---|---|
| cool | Informal *or* Colloquial | entire, full |
| cool | Slang | composure |
| yclept | Archaic *or* Obsolete | named, called |
| calculate | Regional *or* Dialect | think, suppose |
| nowheres | Nonstandard | nowhere |

All of these labels identify words or uses of words that are not part of current Standard American English. You will also find labels indicating words that are ethnically or technically specialized and will therefore have to be explained for most readers:

| WORD | LABEL | MEANING |
|------|-------|---------|
| ganef | Yiddish | thief, rascal |
| gamophylous | Botany | having united leaves |

Most of the time you need usage labels to find out not whether a word is specialized but rather what its level of diction is. As the preceding examples show, the level of diction is often set by the sense in which a word is used. *Cool* is informal only when used to mean "full" ("a cool million"), and slang only when used to mean certain other things, such as "first-rate" ("Jack is a cool guy") or "composure" ("Don't blow your cool").

**6.** Transitive and intransitive use of the verb. A verb may be transitive (*tr.*), intransitive (*intr.*), or both. After —*tr.* in the sample entry are definitions for *cool* as a transitive verb, one that acts on a direct object (as in "The icy stream cooled the beer"). Under —*intr.* are definitions of *cool* as an intransitive verb, a verb without a direct object (as in "The beer cooled slowly"). Sometimes the abbreviations *v.t.* and *v.i.* are used instead.

**7.** Etymology. The etymology of the word being defined—its history or derivation—is given in brackets: [ ]. Some dictionaries put it at the beginning of the entry. In our sample it comes near the end of the first part; there we learn that *cool* can be traced to the Old English word *cōl.* "See **gel-**[3] in Appendix" means that under the heading **gel-**[3] in an appendix to the dictionary, you can find still older roots for the word *cool* in a prehistoric group of languages known as Indo-European. The etymology of a word sometimes includes definitions of its roots. If you look up *calculate,* for instance, you will find that it comes from the Latin word *calculus,* which means "a small stone." (The ancient Romans used small stones for reckoning.)

**8.** Related forms. A related form is a variation on the form of the word being defined. For *cool,* the related forms include the adverb *coolly* (note the spelling) and the noun *coolness.* Sometimes these related forms have separate entries of their own.

**9.** Synonyms. To write well, you must know the exact meanings of the words you use so that you can distinguish between those that have similar meanings. In a standard dictionary, entries for some words include definitions of synonyms. To find more synonyms, consult a book like *Webster's New Dictionary of Synonyms.* (A thesaurus provides lists of synonyms, but does not usually define them.)

EXERCISE 4  Using New Words

Look up each of the following words in your dictionary, and then write a sentence in which you use it.

1. ingenuous
2. clandestine
3. diffident
4. flagrant
5. assiduous
6. slake
7. mordant
8. salacious
9. spry
10. venal

## 7.5  Choosing the Right Word  $ww$

To use a word effectively, you must know exactly what it means, its denotation, and also what it suggests, its connotation.

### Denotation

Here again is the final sentence from that passage about fear of an invasion from outer space:

> But as we now know from unmanned exploration of Mars itself, the idea that "Martians" could invade the earth is —————.

The blank should be filled with a word from the middle level of diction—from the group of words falling between high formality on the one hand and raw slang on the other. Within this category are to be found all of the following: *ludicrous, groundless, absurd, silly, false.* How do you know which of these synonyms to choose? Just as there are different shades of blue in the sky, so there are different shades of meaning in synonyms. To choose the right word for your purposes, you must know the exact **denotation** of each: the specific person, object, sensation, idea, action, or condition it signifies or names. With the help of your dictionary, you can discover the following:

*Ludicrous* means "worthy of scornful laughter."

*Groundless* means "unsupported by evidence." A *groundless* belief is not necessarily *silly, absurd,* or *ludicrous,* or even *false.* It simply has no basis in what is known.

*Absurd* means "irrational" or "nonsensical" but not "frivolous"; deadly serious people can sometimes have absurd ideas.

*Silly* means "frivolous," "foolish," or "thoughtless."

*False* means "not true." A statement may be *false* without being either *silly, ludicrous,* or *absurd.* It would be *absurd* to say that the first president of the United States was King George III, but merely *false* to say that the first president was Thomas Jefferson. Jefferson could have been the first president, though he was not; King George III could not have been the first president.

Learning just what every word denotes is not easy. A good dictionary will give you some help; beyond the dictionary, you must rely on your own experience of the way different words are used in what you read. Whatever else you do, you should develop the habit of discriminating between words, of looking for the shades of difference between words with similar meanings. Then you will know exactly how you want to describe the idea that Martians could invade the earth. Only you can make that final choice. No one else can do it for you.

## Connotation

Much of the time a knowledge of exact denotation will help you choose the one word that best suits your needs. But some words are so close in denotation that you can scarcely tell them apart. So you also need to think about the **connotation** of each word: the feeling, attitude, or set of associations it conveys.

Take for instance *house* and *home.* Both of these denote the same thing: a dwelling place or residence. But their connotations differ sharply. *House* connotes little more than it denotes—a place where people can live—while *home* normally connotes family affection, memories of childhood, and a reassuring sense of welcome. It is probably for this reason that people speak of putting elderly or mentally disturbed people into a *home;* that term sounds much warmer and pleasanter than *sanatorium.*

Precisely because they involve feelings, the connotations of a word are sometimes too personal and variable to be defined. The connotations of *steak,* for instance, will be different for a vegetarian and for a Texas cattleman. Yet many words do have widely accepted connotations, and more often than not it is these that determine the electrical charge of a word—positive or negative, favorable or unfavorable, generous or harsh. In fact, advertisers and propagandists often use connotations to win buyers or converts while making the competition look bad. And the same qualities in men and women are often described by adjectives with very different connotations:

He is ambitious; she is pushy.
He is tough-minded; she is ruthless.
He is foresighted; she is calculating.
He is firm; she is stubborn.

He is self-respecting; she is egotistical.
He is persistent; she is nagging.

The adjectives in each pair in this list are joined by denotation but split by connotation. The words describing "him" are generous, making him seem ideally suited for high responsibility in business or government. The words describing "her" are loaded with negative connotations, making her seem all but disqualified for any responsibility at all. Loaded language appeals only to readers who themselves are already loaded with the prejudices of the writer. If you want to persuade readers who have various views, you should try to choose words with connotations that are fair to your subject. This does not mean that you must never describe anyone in terms like *pushy, stubborn,* or *ruthless;* it means only that before you use such words, you must be sure your subject deserves them.

**EXERCISE 5   Recognizing Connotations**

Following are groups of three words alike in denotation but unlike in connotation. Arrange the words so that the one with the most favorable connotation is first and the one with the least favorable connotation is last. If you have trouble arranging them, your dictionary may help you.

EXAMPLE
pushy   ambitious   aggressive
ambitious, aggressive, pushy

1. frugal   stingy   thrifty
2. scent   stench   odor
3. corpulent   fat   plump
4. call   scream   yell
5. firmly   harshly   sternly
6. prejudiced   partial   bigoted
7. slender   emaciated   skinny
8. retreat   flee   depart
9. mistake   blunder   error
10. dull   stupid   unintelligent
11. question   interrogate   ask

**EXERCISE 6   Choosing Words by Connotation**

Replace the italicized word in each sentence with a word of similar denotation but more favorable connotation.

EXAMPLE
After I showed him my receipt, the store owner admitted his *blunder.*
error

1. Joe's decision to go skydiving reflects his *foolhardy* nature.
2. My uncle *reviled* me for treading on the flowers in his garden.

3. He has a *perverse* way of holding an umbrella.
4. The manager's *timidity* in discussing wages with employees is well known.
5. Professor Branch likes to *ridicule* his lab assistants about their rate of work.

## 7.6   Choosing Specific and Concrete Words   *vag*

Words range in meaning from the most general to the most specific. If you want to identify something named Fido that runs, barks, and wags its tail, you can call it a *creature,* an *animal,* a *dog,* a *hound,* or a *basset.* Each of the words in this series is more specific than the one before, and each of them has its use:

> Fido is the most lovable *creature* I know.
> Fido is the only *animal* I have ever liked.
> Fido is one of our three *dogs.*
> Fido is the fastest *hound* I've ever seen.
> We have three hounds: a dachshund named Willy, a greyhound named Mick, and a *basset* named Fido.

Almost everything can be described in several different ways, with words ranging from the very general to the very specific. If someone moves, for instance, you can write that she *moves,* or more specifically that she *walks,* or still more specifically that she *struts.* The range from general to specific may be illustrated as follows:

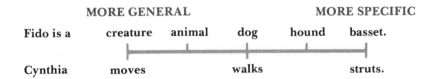

|  | **MORE GENERAL** | | | | **MORE SPECIFIC** |
|---|---|---|---|---|---|
| **Fido is a** | creature | animal | dog | hound | basset. |
| **Cynthia** | moves | | walks | | struts. |

A **concrete** word names something you can see, touch, taste, smell, or hear. Examples are *fingernail, strawberry, sandpaper, smoke, whisper,* or *scream.* An **abstract** word names a feeling (*love*), a state of being (*misery*), an idea (*democracy*), a theory (*evolution*), a field of study (*biology*), or a class of things too broad to be visualized (*creature, plant, organism*). Abstract words sum up the total effect of many particular, concrete things. If you see two people smiling, kissing, and hugging, for instance, you may sum up those concrete actions in the abstract word *love.*

More than once, you have probably been told not to use "vague" words. But there is no such thing as a vague word. There are only words used vaguely: general or abstract words floating free, unconnected with anything specific or concrete. Consider this passage:

> The party was fun. There was lots of excitement. Everything was great. I had a wonderful time.

In spite of the word *excitement,* this passage fails to excite the reader. It offers nothing concrete or specific, nothing to be seen or heard or touched, nothing to make the excitement felt and real. The word *excitement* here is used vaguely.

But consider the way *excitement* is used in this opening paragraph of an essay by Wallace Stegner:

> The town dump of Whitemud, Saskatchewan, could only have been a few years old when I knew it, for the village was born in 1913 and I left there in 1919. But I remember the dump better than I remember most things in that town, better than I remember most of the people. I spent more time with it, for one thing; it has more poetry and excitement in it than people did. . . .

Stegner has already given a very specific idea of where he found excitement in Whitemud—in the town dump. Soon he goes on to tell what made the dump exciting:

> We hunted old bottles in the dump, bottles caked with dirt and filth, half buried, full of cobwebs, and we washed them out at the horse trough by the elevator, putting in a handful of shot along with the water to knock the dirt loose; and when we had shaken them until our arms were tired, we hauled them off in somebody's coaster wagon and turned them in at Bill Anderson's pool hall, where the smell of lemon pop was so sweet on the dark pool-hall air that I am sometimes awakened by it in the night, even yet.
> —"The Town Dump"

This passage is rich in concrete and specific words: *bottles, cobwebs, horse trough, elevator, shot, knock, shaken, arms, hauled, wagon, pool hall, lemon pop.* These words not only show what the writer means by *excitement;* they also help to create the same kind of excitement in the reader. In contrast, reading the vague, limp sentences about the party is about as exciting as listening to party noises through a wall.

Almost any kind of writing benefits from the power of concrete, specific words. Notice how they are used in this paragraph written by a first-term college freshman:

> She spent several summer segments of her life waitressing at the Wharf by the Madison Beach Hotel, which had a commanding view of Long Island Sound. The restaurant, known for its fine food and friendly service, was a magnet for townies and summer tourists alike. This clientele included the regulars, elderly who

vacationed at the hotel, golfers from the club just up the street, day-trippers, and summer residents. Their common possession was the ability to try the patience of even the most efficient waitress, and she was no exception. Were it not for the lucrative financial rewards, personal challenge, and a chance to gain perspective on the business world and a range of people and problems, she would have stayed only one season. Waitressing was exhausting both mentally and physically for her. She succumbed to the pressure of time and had difficulty retaining her poise. Even so, she did manage to find humor in the sometimes slapstick disasters and near disasters which occur in every restaurant: spilled drinks, broken dishware, and head-on collisions.

This is certainly not a perfect paragraph. Aside from wordy phrases like *summer segments* instead of *summers* and *lucrative financial rewards* instead of *money,* it uses too many abstract or general words—words like *life, challenge, world, people, problems, mentally,* and *physically.* But there are many specific words here as well, beginning with the name of a specific restaurant and ending with a list of specific disasters. Indeed, the final sentence is perhaps the most effective of all. It connects the general word *humor* with the specific word *disasters,* and in turn connects *disasters* with a series of words that are vividly concrete: *spilled drinks, broken dishware,* and *head-on collisions.*

EXERCISE 7   **Recognizing General and Specific Words**

Following are groups of three words. Arrange the words in order, from the most general to the most specific.

> EXAMPLE
> walk   go   strut
> go, walk, strut

1. sofa   property   furniture
2. poodle   animal   dog
3. whale   creature   mammal
4. dwelling   shelter   cottage
5. pitcher   athlete   ballplayer
6. automobile   Chevrolet   vehicle
7. run   move   sprint
8. meat   pork   food
9. literature   novel   book
10. pain   problem   toothache

EXERCISE 8   **Using Concrete Words**

For each of the following abstract words, give three concrete words that might be connected with it.

EXAMPLE
love
kiss, smile, hug

1. anger
2. suffering
3. friendship
4. fear
5. contact

EXERCISE 9   Using Specific and Concrete Words

Replace the italicized word in each sentence with a word or phrase that is more specific, more concrete, or both.

EXAMPLE
Janet *spoke* to Tom.
whispered

1. Believing she could win with a strong finish, Harriet *ran* to the finish line.
2. In that climate people who fail to wear hats on a sunny day soon feel *uncomfortable.*
3. Soccer is becoming a popular *activity* in the United States.
4. After George III read a copy of the *paper,* he ordered his generals to suppress the rebellion.
5. I *looked* at the wad of five-dollar bills lying in the gutter.
6. During the race there were three *accidents.*
7. *Defects* in the pavement make driving difficult.
8. On a steaming hot day, nothing tastes so good as a *drink.*
9. On my first day of highway jogging, I stumbled over an *obstruction* and fell flat on my face.
10. Eight hours of heavy lifting made my *body* ache.

## 7.7   Using Words Figuratively— Simile and Metaphor   *fig*

An ordinary comparison involves two similar things: two cities, two people, two families, two houses, two books, two bathing suits, two abstract ideas. But you can also compare two dissimilar things: a poem and a tree, a woman and a rose, love and a duel. This kind of comparison is called **figurative.** Its purpose is to make you see a striking similarity beneath the surface of a contrast. Consider the following sentences:

1. Boston is like Philadelphia; it lives on its past.
2. My grandmother's house is older than my parents' house.

3. After the mole devoured its prey, it sank into the earth as a submarine sinks into the water.      —Konrad Z. Lorenz, adapted

4. I was put into the game and stuck to my man like glue.
—College freshman

5. A sleeping child gives me the impression of a traveler in a very far country.      —Ralph Waldo Emerson

6. What does education often do? It makes a straight-cut ditch of a free, meandering brook.      —Henry David Thoreau

7. Every muscle in my body ached and cried for mercy.
—College freshman

The first two sentences make ordinary comparisons between two things of the same kind: two cities, two houses. The rest of the sentences make figurative comparisons between two dissimilar things, such as a mole and a submarine.

Figurative comparisons bring unfamiliar things home to your reader and make abstractions come to life. By comparing a mole to a submarine, Lorenz shows readers who may never have seen a mole how quickly and effortlessly it can burrow into the ground. Likewise, by comparing education to ditch-digging, Thoreau makes us see what this abstract process often does. Figurative language gives the reader something to look at, touch, or listen to: a submarine, a traveler, a ditch, a cry.

Sentences 3–7 all make figurative comparisons. But you may have noticed a difference in the way those comparisons are made. In sentences 3–5, the writer says that one thing is like another, acts as another does, or gives the impression of another. This type of comparison is called a **simile.** In sentences 6 and 7, the writer says or implies that one thing is another: that education is a ditch-digger, a child's mind is a meandering brook, a muscle is a crying victim. Such a comparison, which is a compressed or intensified version of the simile, is called a **metaphor.**

How do you know when to use a simile and when to use a metaphor? The preceding examples can help to show you. See what happens, for instance, when sentence 3 is changed from a simile to a metaphor:

SIMILE: After the mole devoured its prey, it sank into the earth as a submarine sinks into the water.
METAPHOR: After the mole devoured its prey, it was a submarine sinking into the water.

Here the metaphor doesn't work because the earth is not mentioned. The reader cannot readily imagine what the mole was actually doing, and therefore cannot make sense out of the comparison. Now see what happens when sentence 7 is changed from a metaphor to a simile:

> METAPHOR: Every muscle in my body ached and cried for mercy.
> SIMILE: Every muscle in my body ached and was like a victim crying for mercy.

Here the simile breaks the flow of the sentence. Since the reader can easily imagine who might be crying for mercy, you don't need to specify *victim.* Using the shortcut of the metaphor, you can go straight to *cried.* When the reader cannot imagine a missing element, you have to mention it, and you will probably need a simile. But when the reader can supply the missing element, there is no need to mention it, and you can take full advantage of the intensity and compression that a metaphor provides.

**EXERCISE 10   Using Figurative Language**

In each of the following sentences, an abstract word or phrase is italicized. Change it to a simile or metaphor.

> EXAMPLE
> Life is *something to be organized.*
> REVISED: Life is like a lump of clay; it is our task to mold it.

> 1. Travel books are *descriptions* of far-off places
> 2. Entering a roomful of strange people is *frightening.*
> 3. The first week of college is *confusing.*
> 4. The fat man *moved awkwardly* across the street.
> 5. The child accepted the story *trustingly.*

## 7.8   Avoiding Wordiness   *wdy*

Good writing does not waste words. A good sentence may sometimes be long and detailed, but it carries no dead weight. Every one of its words helps to make the sentence go. For instance, consider this sentence:

> When I was six or seven years old, growing up in Pittsburgh, I used to take a penny of my own and hide it for someone else to find.
> —Annie Dillard

This is a long sentence, but none of its words is wasted. Every one of them adds its own bit of meaning: the speaker's remembered age, the place she grew up in, the taking of the penny, the fact that it was her own, the fact that she hid it, and the fact that it was hidden for someone to find. Of course she might have said *six or seven* instead of *six or seven years old,* but even *years old* serves a purpose, helping to emphasize the speaker's remembered age. To cut out any part of this sentence would be to cut out a part of its meaning. Now consider this sentence:

> Of all the different topics of controversy, from politics to religion to environmental questions, nothing appears to get people so inflamed as those questions dealing with sex.
>
> —College freshman

This sentence is cluttered with wasted words. *Questions,* itself used twice, merely repeats the meaning conveyed by *topics; those* is dead weight; and *dealing with* is a wordy way of saying *of* or *about.*

A first draft will usually be wordy. In writing it, you are preoccupied with stating and developing your ideas, organizing what you have to say into paragraphs, and showing the direction and connections in your line of thought. If you try at the same time to make your sentences perfectly tight, you will almost certainly get bogged down. The time to get the wordiness out of your writing is when you revise. Then you should reread what you have written with a critical eye, cutting out any needless words that may dull your readers' interest in what you have to say.

But how can you decide what to cut from your sentences? How can you tell the difference between the words you need and the words you don't? Learning the difference takes practice, but here is one general suggestion, followed by some specific techniques for eliminating unnecessary words.

### Identify the Most Important Words

If you can't figure out how to improve a sentence that sounds wordy, do these two things: (1) Underline the most important words. (2) Make a sentence out of them, using a minimum of linking words. Here is an example:

> It is a matter of the gravest possible importance to the health of anyone with a history of a problem with disease of the heart that he or she should avoid the sort of foods with a high percentage of saturated fats.

> 1. It is a matter of the gravest possible importance to the health of <u>anyone</u> with a <u>history</u> of a problem with <u>disease</u> of the <u>heart</u> that he or she should <u>avoid</u> the sort of <u>foods</u> with a high percentage of <u>saturated fats.</u>
> 2. <u>Anyone</u> with a <u>history of heart</u> disease should <u>avoid saturated</u> fats.

### Cut Out Words You Don't Need

Besides this general method, here are specific ways of cutting out or avoiding words you don't need.

**7.8**

*wdy*

**1.** Do not repeat a word unless you need it again for clarity or emphasis:

> During their tour of Washington, *they saw* the White House and *they saw* the Lincoln Memorial.

Here the sentence would go better without repetition:

> During their tour of Washington, *they saw* the White House and the Lincoln Memorial.

> Of all the different *topics* of controversy, from politics to religion to environmental *questions,* nothing appears to get people so inflamed as those *questions* dealing with sex.
> REVISED: Of all the different *topics* of controversy, from politics to religion to the environment, nothing appears to get people so inflamed as the *topic* of sex.

The revised version cuts out the repetition of *questions,* a word that—as already stated—merely repeats the meaning of *topics.* But for clarity, *topic* is repeated just once, at the end of the sentence.

> A college experience that piles *option* on *option* and *stimulation* on *stimulation* merely adds to the contemporary nightmare.
> —Caroline Bird

Here repetition emphasizes the sheer bewildering quantity of things that the college experience may offer. (See also "Using Repetition for Emphasis," pp. 108–9.)

**2.** Do not use two or more words that mean essentially the same thing:

> The defendant was accused of six *illegal crimes.*
> REVISED: The defendant was accused of six *crimes.*

Since a crime is an illegal act, there is no need for the word *illegal.*

> The purpose of this report is to *clarify, to explain, and to make clear* the reasons for the new Panama Canal treaty.
> REVISED: The purpose of this report is to *explain* the reasons for the new Panama Canal treaty.

> The fall of Othello is caused by three related *occurrences that happen throughout the play.* —First-term college freshman
> REVISED: The fall of Othello is caused by three related *occurrences.*

> She spent several *summer segments of her life* waitressing at the Wharf by the Madison Beach Hotel. —First-term college freshman
> REVISED: She spent several *summers* waitressing at the Wharf by the Madison Beach Hotel.

Since a summer is a segment of a lifetime, the phrase *segments of her life* is unnecessary.

**3.** In general, avoid starting sentences with *There is, There are,* or *There were:*

> *There are* two things which are necessary here.
> REVISED: Two things are necessary here.

This revision eliminates not only *There are* but also *which.*

> *There are* many women who want to work.
> REVISED: Many women want to work.

> *There were* repeated interruptions of the meeting.
> REVISED: The meeting was repeatedly interrupted.

Occasionally, however, *There is, There are,* or *There were* can be used with good effect to open a paragraph ("There are two reasons for acting now") or to line up the sentences in a list-structure paragraph (see p. 103).

**4.** Avoid cluttering sentences with nouns:

> The *contribution* of the *alumni* to the *college* will be in *relation* to their *understanding* of its *goals.*
> REVISED: The *alumni* will contribute to the *college* if they understand its *goals.*

The nouns *contribution* and *understanding* have been turned into the verbs *contribute* and *understand.*

> The *reason* for his *decision* to visit *Spain* was his *desire* to see a *bullfight.*
> REVISED: He decided to visit *Spain* because he wanted to see a *bullfight.* [or] He went to *Spain* to see a *bullfight.*

**5.** Wherever possible, get rid of adjective clauses like *who are, which was,* and *that had been:*

> Students *who are* in the band have to practice four times a week.
> REVISED: Students in the band have to practice four times a week.

> At the flea market she bought a jewel box *which was* made with tiny seashells.
> REVISED: At the flea market she bought a jewel box made with tiny seashells.

> For many years the country was ruled by a man *who had been* appointed by himself as dictator of the country.
> REVISED: For many years the country was ruled by a self-appointed dictator.

*Self-appointed* does all the work of *man who had been appointed by himself as.* Also, there is no need to repeat the word *country.*

**6.** Replace prepositional phrases with single adjectives or adverbs:

> She answered *in an angry way.*
> REVISED: She answered *angrily.*

He is a leader *of honesty and ability.*
REVISED: He is an *able, honest leader.*

### 7. Avoid *to be* in sentences like the following:

Tired from the long day of paddling, Ken found the portage *to be* burdensome.                    —First-term college freshman
REVISED: Tired from the long day of paddling, Ken found the portage burdensome.

Shakespeare is considered *to be* the greatest of all English playwrights.
REVISED: Shakespeare is considered the greatest of all English playwrights.

### 8. When possible, avoid *the fact that:*

*The fact that* Namath appeared in the stands nearly caused a riot.
REVISED: Namath's appearance in the stands nearly caused a riot.

### 9. Avoid verbal detours:

*It is very important for* a speaker *to have the ability to* hold the attention of the people *that he or she is speaking to.*
REVISED: A speaker must be able to hold the attention of his or her listeners. [or] Speakers must be able to hold the attention of their listeners.

When we try to understand what God is, our first problem is *that of non-encounter at the level of vision.*
REVISED: When we try to understand God, our first problem is that we cannot see him.

**EXERCISE 11   Making Sentences Concise**

The following sentences are wordy. Without dropping anything essential to their meaning, make each of them more concise.

EXAMPLE
The chipmunk who was hiding in the stone wall put his head out warily.
REVISED: The chipmunk hiding in the stone wall put his head out warily.

1. The kitchen in the old farmhouse has a stove that is wood-burning.
2. In Homer's *Odyssey,* the hero is threatened by a giant who has only one eye.
3. There are two reasons that I have for not going to St. Louis: the first is that I have to write an essay for my English class; the second is that I cannot afford a bus ticket.
4. There is one good trait which Mary has and that is generosity.
5. The fact that the president arrived in Moscow was reported today in the *New York Times.*

6. The only differences between the two cars are those of size and weight.
7. The reason for her attack on the book is her hatred of obscenity.
8. Carpenters are working to replace the shingles that have been damaged by fire.
9. The general ordered his troops to advance forward quickly.
10. I have never read a biography of the life of George Washington.
11. She sang in a charming way.
12. The teacher tried without any success to bring her students around to accepting the proposition that the moon was made of green cheese.

## 7.9   Spelling  *sp*

Careful writers spell their words correctly. Misspelled words not only mark you as a careless writer; they may also confuse your reader. The difference between *steel* and *steal,* for instance, is a difference in meaning as well as in spelling.

How can you learn to spell all of your words correctly? No one simple formula will guarantee that you will do so, but here are some steps that may help.

**1.** Keep a list of all the words misspelled in your essays. After an essay has been marked by your teacher, make a list of all the words you have misspelled in it. Beside each of the words, write out the correct spelling, as shown in your dictionary. (If you can't find the word in the dictionary, ask your teacher for help.) Then, beside the correct spelling of the word, write out the letter or letters involved in the error. Your list will look like this:

| MISSPELLED | CORRECTLY SPELLED | ERROR |
|---|---|---|
| neather | neither | ea/ei |
| cuting | cutting | t/tt |
| goverment | government | er/ern |
| silense | silence | se/ce |
| defensable | defensible | able/ible |
| imovable | immovable | im/imm |
| famuos | famous | uo/ou |
| feet | feat | ee/ea |
| boxs | boxes | s/es |

**2.** Learn how to add suffixes—extra letters at the end of a word. Here are the rules.

1. Change final *y* to *i*. If the *y* at the end of a word follows a consonant, change it to *i* before adding a suffix:

| | | |
|---|---|---|
| beauty | + ful | = beautiful |
| bury | + ed | = buried |
| tricky | + est | = trickiest |
| carry | + es | = carries |

EXCEPTION: If the suffix is *-ing,* keep the *y:*

| | | |
|---|---|---|
| carry | + ing | = carrying |
| bury | + ing | = burying |

2. Drop silent *e.* If a word ends in a silent (unpronounced) *e,* drop the *e* before adding *-able* or *-ing:*

| | | |
|---|---|---|
| love | + able | = lovable |
| care | + ing | = caring |

If any other suffix is added, keep the *e:*

| | | |
|---|---|---|
| care | + ful | = careful |

EXCEPTION: If the silent *e* follows *c* or *g,* keep the *e* before *-able:*

| | | |
|---|---|---|
| change | + able | = changeable |
| peace | + able | = peaceable |

3. Double a single consonant. If the word ends in a single consonant after a single vowel (*forget*) and the accent is on the last syllable (*for get'*), double the consonant before adding *-ing, -ed, -or,* or *-er:*

| | | |
|---|---|---|
| for get' | + ing | = forgetting |
| re fer' | + ed | = referred |
| bet' | + or | = bettor |
| win' | + er | = winner |

If the accent is not on the last syllable of the word, do not double the consonant:

| | | |
|---|---|---|
| ham' mer | + ing | = hammering |
| clat' ter | + ing | = clattering |

**3.** Know when to use *ie* and when to use *ei.* Remember the jingle:

Put *i* before *e*
Except after *c*
Or when pronounced *a*
As in *neighbor* and *weigh.*

Other examples are *believe* and *achieve, receive* and *deceive.* Exceptions include *either* and *neither, leisure, seize,* and *weird.*

**4.** Check plural forms in the dictionary. Though you form the plural of most nouns simply by adding *-s*, some nouns have special plurals:

> business, businesses; church, churches
> vacancy, vacancies; authority, authorities
> hero, heroes; potato, potatoes (*but* piano, pianos)
> leaf, leaves; life, lives
> foot, feet; woman, women

**5.** Control the apostrophe. To master this pesky punctuation mark, see section 25.14, pp. 410–11. Learn how to write correctly words like *won't* and *they've*, and how to make the proper choice from pairs like *its* and *it's, girl's* and *girls, society's* and *societies.*

**6.** Learn to distinguish between homonyms. Homonyms are words that sound alike but have different meanings and different spellings. Examples are *to* and *too; bear* and *bare; there, their,* and *they're.* If you have trouble with the last three words, which are often confused, look them up in the Glossary of Usage, p. 538.

**7.** Master your problem words. Each of us has problem words, words we find hard to spell. Many writers have trouble with words like *separate, definitely, existence,* and *dissatisfaction.* Some of these will appear in your own list of errors; many others are listed in the next section. The best way to master them is to write out your own usual spelling, then the correct spelling, and then the letters involved in the misspellings, as recommended on p. 149.

## 7.10 Words Frequently Misspelled

| | | | |
|---|---|---|---|
| absence | aerial | answer | athlete |
| absorption | affect | antiseptic | athletic |
| accessible | against | apparatus | author |
| accidentally | all right | apparent | auxiliary |
| accommodate | almost | appear | awful |
| accompanied | already | appearance | |
| accomplish | although | appetite | balloon |
| accustomed | altogether | appropriate | basically |
| achieve | always | argue | beginning |
| achievement | amateur | arguing | believe |
| acquire | among | argument | believed |
| across | analysis | arrangement | benefit |
| address | analyze | article | benefited |
| advice | angel | ascend | breath |
| advise | annual | assistance | breathe |
| adviser | anoint | assistant | brilliant |

burial
buried
bury
business
busy

cafeteria
calculator
calendar
capital
captain
careful
carrying
categorical
category
cede
ceiling
cemetery
certain
changeable
characteristic
characteristically
chief
choose
choosing
chose
climbed
clothes
coarse
column
coming
commitment
committed
committee
common
comparatively
competition
complement
compliment
conceivable
conceive
concentration
concern
connoisseur
conquer
conscience
conscientious
conscious
considerable

consistency
consistent
continually
continuous
control
controlled
convenience
conveniently
conversation
coolly
corporal
corroborate
council
counsel
countries
course
courteous
criticism
criticize
crowd
crystal
curiosity
cylinder

deceive
deception
decide
decision
decisively
definite
degree
dependent
derelict
describe
desperate
dessert
destroy
determine
develop
development
device
devise
difference
different
dilemma
dilettante
dining
disappear
disappoint

disapproval
disapprove
disastrous
discipline
discoveries
discriminate
discussion
disease
dissatisfaction
dissatisfied
dissection
dissipate
dissipation
distinction
divide
divine
division
drunkenness

easily
ecstasy
ecstatic
efficiency
efficient
eight
eighth
either
eligible
eliminate
embarrassed
embarrassment
emphasis
emphasize
enemies
enemy
engineer
environment
equipment
equipped
especially
essential
exaggerate
exaggeration
exceed
excel
excellent
except
exceptional
exercise

exhausted
exhaustion
exhilaration
existence
expense
experience
experiment
explanation
extremely

familiar
fascinate
fascinating
February
finally
financial
financier
flourish
forcibly
foreign
foresee
formally
formerly
forth
forty
forward
fourth
friend
frightening
fundamental
fundamentally
further

gardener
generally
government
governor
grammar
grateful
grievous
guarantee
guard
guidance

handle
height
heroes
heroine
hideous

hoping
humorous
hurriedly
hurrying

identification
identity
imaginary
imagination
imbecile
imitation
immediately
immigrant
incidentally
increase
independence
independent
indispensable
inevitably
influential
initiate
inoculate
insistent
intellectual
intelligence
intelligent
interest
interfere
interference
interpreted
invitation
irrelevant
irresistible
irritable
island
it's
its

jealous
judgment

kindergarten
knew
know
knowledge

laboratory
later
latter

led
leisure
length
library
license
lightning
likelihood
likely
literally
literary
literature
livelihood
loneliness
loose
lose
losing
loyally
loyalty
lying

magazine
maintenance
maneuver
marriage
married
mathematics
medicine
miniature
minutes
mischief
mischievous
misspelled
misspelling
morale
mournful
muscle
mysterious

naturally
necessary
necessity
neighbor
neither
newsstand
nickel
niece
ninety
ninth
noticeable

obstacle
occasion
occasionally
occur
occurred
occurrence
o'clock
official
omission
omit
omitted
omniscient
opportune
opportunity
optimism
optimist
optimistic
origin
original
oscillate

paid
panicky
parallel
parallelism
particular
particularly
partner
pastime
peaceable
peculiar
peculiarity
perceive
perception
perform
permanence
permanent
perseverance
persevere
persistent
personality
personally
personnel
perspiration
persuade
persuasion
pertain
piece

plain
planning
playwright
pleasant
pleasure
poison
political
politician
populace
portrayal
possess
possession
possessive
possible
practical
practically
prairie
precede
preceding
predictable
prefer
preference
preferential
preferred
prejudice
preparation
prepare
presence
prevalent
primitive
principal
principle
privilege
probably
procedure
proceed
professional
professor
profitable
prominent
pronunciation
proof
propeller
prophecy
prophesied
prophesy
prophet
prove
psychology

pursue
pursuit

quantity
quarter
quiet

realistically
realize
really
rebellion
recede
receipt
receive
recognize
recommend
referred
relieve
religious
repetition
representative
resemblance
resistance
respectability
restaurant
rhythm
rhythmical
ridiculous
roommate

sacrifice
sacrilegious
safety
satire

scarcely
scene
schedule
science
scientific
secretary
seize
seminar
sense
separate
sergeant
several
severely
shepherd
sheriff
shining
shoulder
signal
significance
significant
similar
similarity
simile
sincerely
sophomore
source
specimen
speech
stationary
stationery
stopping
straight
strength
strenuous
stretch

striking
studying
succeed
successful
successfully
suddenness
superintendent
supersede
suppress
surely
surprise
syllable
symmetrical

tariff
temperament
temperature
tendency
than
their
then
there
therefore
they're
thorough
through
title
together
toward
tragedy
transferred
tries
truly
twelfth

tyrannical
tyrannize
tyranny

undoubtedly
university
unnecessarily
unnecessary
until
unusual
using
usually

vacillate
vacuum
vengeance
versatile
vicious
village
villain

weather
Wednesday
weird
whereabouts
whether
whimsical
wholly
woman
women
wretched
writing
written

# 8

# REVISING YOUR ESSAY

If you have taken the steps explained in the previous chapters, you have produced the raw material for an essay and you have shaped that material into a first draft: a piece of writing with an introduction, a body, and a conclusion. But you have one further step to take. What remains is **revision,** which literally means "looking again."

Of course it can be hard to look again. Tired, pressed for time, or bored with writing your essay, you may want just to be rid of it—to get it to your reader as a way of getting it off your desk and off your mind. But you should try to keep it on your mind a little longer. If you don't take another look at your essay, you cannot clearly see what its effect on the reader will be. An unrevised piece of writing is like an uninspected machine. Neither one is likely to work very well.

Revision gives you the chance to enliven your sentences, to strengthen your organization, and to clarify or eliminate confusing words, phrases, or constructions. And since second looks often lead to second thoughts, it also lets you find new ways of making a point—or even new points to make.

## 8.1   Invigorating Your Style   *style*

Revision should first of all invigorate your style. Too many people write the way they jog, never changing the pace or skipping a beat, never leaping, zigzagging, or stopping to scratch the reader's mind. Does this mean that in order to be lively, you have to write like an acrobat? No, it doesn't. Different subjects call for different styles, and you shouldn't write about a problem in economics or history the same way you would write about a beach party or a New Year's Day parade. In most college writing you are expected to sound thoughtful and judicious. But no reader wants you to sound dull. To enliven your writing on any subject, here are three things you can do.

### Vary Your Sentences

Vary the length and construction of your sentences. Nothing animates prose like variety, and the sentence is infinitely variable. It can stop short after a couple of words. Or it can stretch luxuriously, reaching up over hills of thought and down into valleys of speculation, glancing to this side and that, moving along for as long as the writer cares to keep it going. You can vary its structure as well as its length. You can make it passive or active; you can arrange and rearrange its parts. Opening with a modifier, as we do in this sentence, you can hold your subject back. Or you can start with your subject and thus sound forthright and decisive. In structure and length as well as in meaning, English sentences admit of infinite variety.

How can you get some of that variety into your writing? Take a hard look at one of your paragraphs—or at a whole essay. Do all of your sentences sound about the same? If most are short and simple, combine some of them to make longer ones. If most are lengthened out with modifiers and dependent clauses, break some of them up. Be bold. Be unpredictable. Use a short sentence to set off a long one, a simple structure to set off a complicated one. Do anything to break the monotony of assembly-line sentences.

### EXERCISE 1   Using Short Sentences after Long Ones

One way to get variety into your writing is to use a very short sentence after one or more long ones. To see the effect this can have, add a suitable two-word sentence to each of the following entries.

> EXAMPLE
> Crossing the goal after a spectacular display of broken-field running, the halfback waved to the thousands of spectators in the stands. *They roared.*

1. Whenever I am asked to sit absolutely still and keep perfectly quiet, something awkward happens.
2. After cursing all automobile manufacturers for the stalling of his sedan on a deserted country road, Henry once again turned the ignition key. "This time," he muttered to himself, "the engine must turn over."

3. The two prisoners stared intently at the foreman of the jury. They felt sure his expression would reveal the verdict. If he frowned, they would be found guilty; if he smiled, they would be acquitted.
4. The startled customer could not believe his eyes as he stared at the lobster on his plate.
5. Concealing his nervousness behind a fixed smile, Jonathan approached Jennifer and asked her to dance.

## Use Verbs of Action

Use verbs of action as much as possible. Verbs of action show the subject not just being something but doing something. At times, of course, you need to say what your subject *is* or *was* or *has been*. But verbs of action can often replace verbs of being:

> Sheila *was the winner of* the race.
> Sheila *won* the race.

> Mr. and Mrs. Ault of Baltimore *were once owners of* Frederick Douglass.
> Mr. and Mrs. Ault of Baltimore *once owned* Frederick Douglass.

> Frederick's desire to learn reading *would have been a shock to* other slaveholders.
> Frederick's desire to learn reading *would have shocked* other slaveholders.

> It *was not a shock to* Mrs. Ault.
> It *did not shock* Mrs. Ault.

> Mr. Ault believed that learning *would be the ruin of* Frederick as a slave.
> Mr. Ault believed that learning *would ruin* Frederick as a slave.

The first sentence in each pair tells what the subject was, would have been, or would be; the second sentence tells what the subject did, would have done, or would do. In each case the verb of action tightens and invigorates the sentence. So whenever you can turn a verb of being into a verb of action, do so.

Does this mean that you should never use the passive voice? Since the passive requires *is, was, be, has been,* or *had been,* should you banish it forever from your prose? No, you shouldn't. Your subject can *generate* controversy or *demand* attention; but he, she, or it can also *be investigated, be ridiculed,* or *be misunderstood.* A verb that tells of a subject acted upon need not be lifeless.

But if you don't keep the passive voice under control, it can paralyze your writing. This is a problem to be seriously considered by anyone who has ever been asked to write an essay in which a subject of some sort is to be analyzed, to be explained, or to be commented upon by him or her. That sentence shows what overuse of the passive will do to your sentences; it will make them wordy, stagnant, boring, dead. Whenever you start to use the passive, ask yourself whether the sentence might sound better in the active. Often it will.

(For a full discussion of the active and passive voice, see chapter 22, pp. 365–72.)

### Ask Questions

Break the forward march of your statements with an occasional question. For example:

> One technical definition of a system is as follows: a system is a structure of interacting, intercommunicating components that, as a group, act or operate individually and jointly to achieve a common goal through the concerted activity of the individual parts. That is, of course, a completely satisfactory definition of the earth, except maybe for that last part about a common goal. What on earth is *our* common goal? How did we ever get mixed up in a place like this?
>
> This is the greatest discomfort for our species. Some of us simply write it off by announcing that our situation is ridiculous, that the whole place is ungovernable, and that our responsibilities are therefore to ourselves alone. And yet, there it is; we are components in a dense, fantastically complicated system of life, we are enmeshed in the interliving, and we really don't know what we're up to.                    —Lewis Thomas, *The Medusa and the Snail*

Thomas doesn't pretend to have all the answers; what he does have are questions about the common goal of mankind on earth. You can ask questions too. Don't feel bound to make every sentence a statement, to write as if you knew all there is to know about your subject. Get your curiosity out front. Make it generate questions, and get the questions into your writing. Questions let you speculate out loud, let you wonder what other people are thinking—or may have thought:

> He falls back upon the bed awkwardly. His stumps, unweighted by legs and feet, rise in the air, presenting themselves. I unwrap the bandages from the stumps, and begin to cut away the black scabs and the dead, glazed fat with scissors and forceps. A shard of white bone comes loose. I pick it away. I wash the wounds with disinfectant and redress the stumps. All this while, he does not speak. What is he thinking behind those lids that do not blink? Is he remembering a time when he was whole? Does he dream of feet?                    —Richard Selzer, "The Discus Thrower"

Questions like these can draw the reader into the very heart of your subject. And questions can do more than advertise your curiosity. They can also voice your conviction. In conversation you sometimes ask a question that assumes a particular answer—don't you? Such a question is called **rhetorical,** and you can use it in writing as well as in speech. It will challenge your readers, prompting them either to agree with you or to explain to themselves why they do not. And why shouldn't you challenge your readers now and then?

### EXERCISE 2    Revising to Invigorate Style

Doing this exercise requires knowledge of how to use coordination and subordination in connecting sentences. If you don't yet know how to use these methods, see chapter 16, pp. 290–95.

Following are three sets of sentences. The first has been put together for you as an example. Turn each of the other two sets into a short essay in which you (1) vary sentence length and structure, (2) use verbs of action as much as possible, and (3) ask at least one question. For a clear idea of what is to be done, study the example carefully before you begin.

> EXAMPLE
> Mr. and Mrs. Ault were once owners of Frederick Douglass.
> They were residents of Baltimore.
> At this time Frederick learned to read.
> He asked Mrs. Ault to help him.
> He felt safe in doing so.
> She thought of him more as a child than as a slave.
> Those of course were not the only alternatives.
> She could have seen him as a man.
> But at least he was more in her eyes than a piece of property.
> His request would have been a shock to other slaveholders.
> They would have thrashed him just for making it.
> But it was not a shock to Mrs. Ault.
> She was willing to help.
> Frederick learned the alphabet under her care.
> He began to read simple verses in the Bible.
> Then Mr. Ault intervened.
> He forbade his wife to continue the lessons.
> He believed that learning would be the ruin of Frederick as a slave.
> But fortunately Frederick had learned enough to teach himself more.
> Soon he became an excellent reader.

> ESSAY: Frederick Douglass learned to read while he was owned by Mr. and Mrs. Ault of Baltimore. He felt safe in asking Mrs. Ault to help him learn, for she thought of him more as a child than as a slave. Those of course were not the only alternatives. Couldn't she have seen him as a man? But at least he meant more in her eyes than a piece of property. Though his request would have shocked other slaveholders, who would have thrashed him just for making

it, it did not shock Mrs. Ault; she wanted to help him. Under her care Frederick learned the alphabet and began to read simple verses in the Bible. Then Mr. Ault intervened. He forbade his wife to continue the lessons because he believed that learning would ruin Frederick as a slave. But fortunately Frederick had learned enough to teach himself more, and he soon became an excellent reader.

SET A

1. Scott's mother took him to the Palace courtyard once a week.
2. They stayed there for half an hour.
3. They watched the Palace Guards.
4. Scott loved the Guards.
5. They each wore bright-red boots.
6. They each wore dark-blue stockings.
7. The stockings were knee-high.
8. They each wore white kilts.
9. They each wore a stiff white shirt.
10. The shirt had a closed collar.
11. They each wore a magnificent jacket.
12. The jacket was like a blazing fire.
13. It had silver sparkles.
14. It had shining gold epaulets.
15. It had red embroidery.
16. The whole uniform was topped by a black beret.
17. The black beret had a long tassle.
18. The tassle hung down below the jaw.
19. The Guards marched in this uniform.
20. They marched back and forth across the Palace courtyard.
21. They were all over six feet tall.
22. They held their rifles firmly against their right shoulders.
23. No boy could watch all of this without wishing.
24. Scott wished something.
25. He could someday be with them.

SET B

1. He had been running on level ground for half an hour.
2. Then suddenly the hill was ahead of him.
3. It rose up.
4. It looked as steep as a wall.
5. He didn't know whether he could get up that wall without stopping.
6. But he would damn well try.
7. He breathed heavily.
8. He relaxed his arms and shoulders.
9. His stride was shortened.
10. He started landing on his toes instead of his heels.
11. Then his whole body was pushed forward into the hill.
12. There was a push back made by the hill.

13. He pumped his arms against the hill.
14. His knees rose upward one after the other.
15. They came up almost to his chest.
16. The balls of his feet bounded off the solid ground.
17. He was a watcher of the ground ahead.
18. He wanted to be sure of his footing.
19. He couldn't afford to slip on pine needles.
20. He couldn't afford to slide on a loose bit of stone.
21. He kept moving.
22. He took quick, deep breaths.
23. He lengthened his stride at a certain point.
24. He was nearing the top of the hill.
25. Finally the ground leveled off.
26. He could ease his pace.
27. He had reached the top.

## 8.2   Checking the Parts of Your Essay

Besides giving you the chance to invigorate your style, revision lets you make sure that each part of the essay goes well with the others, and that all of them work together toward your purpose.

When you reread what you have written in light of your purpose, you may find that one or more sentences are out of place, that you have started a new paragraph too soon or too late, that a would-be paragraph is really just a string of disconnected sentences, that the main point of a paragraph does not support the main point of the essay, or that a key word is carelessly used. Revision is a kind of double focusing. It's a process in which you shift your eye back and forth between the whole and the part, the essay and the paragraph, the paragraph and the sentence, the sentence and the word.

We offer a checklist of steps that will help you to see the parts of your essay in relation to the whole, to recognize what kind of whole they form, and to decide where and how to make changes. The steps in the checklist move from the structure of the whole essay to the fine points of sentence structure and word choice. But at every step we invite you to think of revising as a continual process of adjusting all the parts of your essay to one another. You can locate advice on specific points by consulting the endpapers or the Index.

### Step 1. Check for Unity

Check the organization, content, and tone of the essay as a whole. Look for a line of thought from beginning to end, reliable generalizations supported by specific details, and a consistent point of view. Consider these questions:

1. What is the essay about? What is its main point?
2. Does the introduction clearly focus on that point?
3. Does each paragraph help to advance the main line of your thought?
4. Does any paragraph digress from that line of thought, or work against it?
5. Is your tone consistent, or does it suddenly change?
6. Does the conclusion show that the essay has reached its goal?

If one or more parts of your essay digress from the main line of your thought, identify the point they do develop. Should you write a new paper with this as the controlling idea? Should you redefine the main point of the present paper so that your digression will fit? Or should you simply cut out the digression entirely? You will have to do one of these things if you want a unified paper.

If you find a sudden shift in tone, you should reexamine your attitude toward your topic. How exactly do you feel about it now? Does the change in tone reflect a new insight that affects your view of the whole? In that case, you will need to recast the first part of your essay to make its tone consistent with that of the remainder. On the other hand, if the shift in tone is just an accident, you will need to revise the essay so that the tone you started with prevails throughout.

EXERCISE 3    Checking Essays for Unity

Following are brief accounts of three student essays. Read each account and then answer the question that follows it.

1. Carl wrote a 1,500-word essay about two kinds of dueling practiced in sixteenth-century England. The main point of the essay
   was to show how dueling enabled the participants to settle their
   quarrels. Along with the discussion of sixteenth-century duels,
   the draft included a 200-word description of the fight between
   David and Goliath.

   Should Carl keep, cut, or revise the part about David and
   Goliath? Give your reasons.

2. Beth wrote a 1,000-word essay about human intelligence and
   artificial intelligence. After defining artificial intelligence, she set
   out to argue that we ought not to develop computers that sur-
   pass us in intelligence. First she explained how the intelligence
   of computers could be made to exceed ours; then she explained
   why—in her opinion—this should not be allowed to happen.
   Finally, she outlined ways in which we could use the machines as
   partners.

Should Beth keep, cut, or revise the final section about using computers as partners? Give your reasons.

3. Kevin wrote a 1,000-word essay about a visit to a large city on the East Coast. His thesis was that visitors were lucky if they escaped bodily injury, robbery, and ridicule. For about half of the paper the writer's tone was lightly satirical. He described several close calls amusingly, exposing not just the aggressiveness of the city dwellers but also his own gullibility. Then, in the second half of the essay, he angrily denounced the city's inhabitants and praised country dwellers like himself. At the end he warned his readers not to visit any city.

Should this essay be changed in any way, or does it work well as it stands? Give your reasons.

## Step 2. Check the Effectiveness of the Rhetorical Strategy

1. If the paper is descriptive or uses description, what senses does it appeal to? How many details does it supply? And how vividly does it recreate the general impression given by what it describes?

2. If the paper is a narrative or uses narration, does it just recount a succession of separate events ("and then . . . , and then . . . , and then . . ."), or are the events clearly connected by some general point? If you do not follow chronological order in telling the story, are the back-and-forth movements clear?

3. If the paper is expository, have you combined generalization with specific detail? Is your explanation clear?

4. If the paper is partly or wholly written to persuade, do you support your generalizations with specific and relevant facts? Do you appeal to the feelings of your reader with specific images? Is your argument logically valid? Does it rely on any fallacies? Do you sound reasonable? Do you recognize objections to your argument, or do you consider only the facts that support your side? If you were a reader with an opposite point of view, how persuasive would you find the essay?

## Step 3. Check for Coherence and Proportion

1. Does the main point of each paragraph follow from the main point developed in the preceding one?

2. Are the shifts in topic from one paragraph to the next marked by clear transitions?

3. Are there gaps? Is more information needed anywhere?

4. Are there bulges? Are any points discussed at much greater length than others of equal importance? Is any of the commentary redundant?

5. Does the break between one paragraph and the next always mark the turn in the thought? Or are there places where one or more sentences should be moved from one side of the break to the other?

## Step 4. Check the Paragraphs

Once you are satisfied with the shape of the whole theme, look closely at each individual paragraph and consider these questions:

1. Is the main point of each paragraph within the body of the paper plainly stated or clearly implied?

2. Does each sentence follow clearly from the one before it, or from the topic sentence?

3. Are any of the paragraphs noticeably short? If so, is the brevity justified, or should the short paragraphs be combined to make a longer one?

4. Is any paragraph so long that a reader may get lost in it? Should it be broken up into two or three paragraphs?

5. Is there needless repetition or padding in any paragraph? Can any of the sentences be cut or combined to tighten the paragraph and sharpen its point?

## Step 5. Check Sentence Style

1. Are your sentences varied in length and structure, or do they generally sound alike?

2. Are any sentences tangled and hard to understand?

3. Have you overused the passive voice? Do you use it only with good reason, or would some of your passive-voice sentences work better in the active voice?

## Step 6. Check for Sentence Errors

1. Are all your sentences complete, or have you written some sentence fragments?

2. Does every modifier point clearly to its headword?

3. Does every pronoun refer clearly to its antecedent?

4. Are your pronoun forms correct? Are you unsure at any point about whether to use *he* or *him, she* or *her, they* or *them?*

5. Does any sentence contain faulty predication?

6. Is the parallelism in any sentence faulty?

7. Do you shift tense anywhere without a good reason? Are you unsure about the sequence of tenses in any of your sentences?

8. Does every verb agree with its subject?

9. Have you created a fused sentence by running two sentences together without any conjunction or punctuation between them?

10. Have you created a comma splice by joining two sentences with nothing but a comma?

11. If you have used quotations, are you sure that you have punctuated them correctly?

## Step 7. Check the Choice of Words

1. Is the level of diction right for your subject and your audience?

2. Do you suddenly switch from one level to another? If so, is the switch justified by your subject matter?

3. Does any word have the wrong denotation for its context? Can you substitute a word that states your meaning precisely?

4. Does any word have the wrong connotation for its context?

5. Is your language predominantly general and abstract? Can you make it more specific and concrete?

6. Can you make your language more figurative?

7. Are any of your sentences cluttered with words they don't need?

## Step 8. Check Spelling and Capitalization

Most writers misspell from two to five words in a five-hundred-word draft. To spot mistakes, first review our discussion of spelling (section 7.9, pp. 149–51). Then ask yourself the following questions:

1. Are the word endings -*es*, -*s*, -*'s*, and -*s'* used correctly?

2. Is the apostrophe misused anywhere, or mistakenly omitted?

3. Have you confused any homonyms, such as *there, their,* and *they're?*

4. Are your own spelling demons now spelled correctly?

5. Have you checked in the dictionary whenever you aren't sure of a spelling?

6. Are you unsure about whether or not to capitalize certain words?

EXERCISE 4    Proofreading

Correct the spelling and add, move, or delete apostrophes as necessary in the following passage.

EXAMPLE
line 2: sports editor

My job hunt took me to Boston for an interview with Ernie Roberts, the senior sports editer of the *Boston Globe.* At 11 oclock Wensday morning I walked into the Sports Department, wide-eyed

with excitment. I was hopeing to spot the writer's who's faces were
5 familiar to me from the pictures printed beside there bylines. I
wasn't disapointed. Both Ray Fitzgerald and Bud Collins were in
site. Ernie was'nt in his office, but another man who shared the
space told me to grab a seat and wait. After about ten minites, Ernie
bustled in. He apoligized for being late and explained we would
10 have to talk fast because he had an apointment in Cambridge.
Then he asked me to tell him about myself. As I spoke, he grabed
a cigar from his desk and began pufing. He looked happy smoking.
Evry so often he would take the cigar out of his mouth, study the
burning end, smile, and then take another puff. After I finished
15 speaking, they're was a long silense. He explained, firmly and
finaly, that my inexperience was going to be more of a handicap
than I had realised. He advised me to get a job with a small local
paper and possibly register for night course's in journalism. It was
sound advise and helpfull to hear. I thanked him for seeing me
20 and left. Maybe someday I'll have the experance and the creden-
tials to apply their for a job.

## Step 9. Check Quotations and Citations

If you are writing a paper in which you cite one or more sources,
ask yourself the following questions:

1. Are there too many quotations? Do they crowd out your
own statements, or substitute for them? Could you summarize or
paraphrase any of them instead of quoting directly?

2. Is each quotation accurate? Did you copy it correctly? If
you omitted words, did you mark the omissions properly, with
ellipsis dots?

3. Have you introduced each quotation clearly and with correct punctuation?

4. Have you clearly acknowledged every written source that
you have used in any way?

(For a full discussion of quoting and citing, see sections
27.3–27.8, pp. 455–83.)

## Step 10. Read the Essay Aloud

As a final check, read the entire draft aloud. If anything sounds
wrong, see whether you have overlooked part or all of a previous
step.

## 8.3   Preparing Your Final Copy   *ms*

If your teacher has special instructions about the format of your
final copy, you should of course respect those instructions. But oth-

erwise observe the following guidelines, which will help you produce a good-looking manuscript:

1. Use the right paper. If you type, use clean sheets of unlined, medium-weight typing paper of standard size (8½ by 11 inches). If you write by hand, use standard-size white paper with lines at least ⅜ of an inch apart. Do not use sheets torn from a spiral binder.

2. Use a typewriter or pen. If you type, use a fresh, black ribbon. Be sure the type is clean. If you write by hand, use a pen with dark ink. Write legibly, without splotches. For safety's sake, make a carbon copy or photocopy of your paper and keep it until the original is returned to you.

3. Give your paper a title. If you are not required to use a separate title page, type or write the title, your name, and other necessary information as shown in the first example on p. 168. If you do use a separate title page, follow the second example on p. 168, and repeat the title on the first page of text, as shown on p. 169.

4. Number your pages. After the first page of text, number each page in the upper right corner. Use arabic numerals; do not add a period, a circle, or any other mark. Directly below the page number write your name, and directly below that, the course number, as shown on p. 169.

5. Leave adequate margins. Leave a margin of 1 inch on each side and at the bottom of the page. When beginning a paragraph, indent the first word five spaces from the left margin.

6. Leave spaces between the lines. Double-space if you type; write on every other line if you use a pen.

## 8.4 Proofreading and Submitting Your Essay

Before submitting your essay, you should check the manuscript to be sure everything looks and reads as it should. You must see exactly what is there—nothing more, nothing less. This is not so easy as it seems. The mind has a way of making us believe something is on a page when it isn't, and you may find it hard to look at words and phrases as collections of letters rather than units of meaning. Yet you must proofread if you are to spot mistakes in spelling and punctuation, omissions, and unwanted repetition. Here's what to do:

1. Reread the final copy early on the day it is due. You may spot something you overlooked when writing it out.

2. Pause to examine the spelling of words that could be trou-

*Format with title on first page of text*

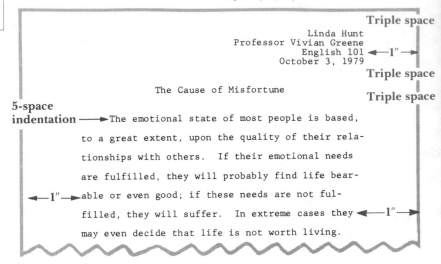

Triple space

Linda Hunt
Professor Vivian Greene
English 101 ←—1"—→
October 3, 1979

Triple space

The Cause of Misfortune

Triple space

5-space
indentation ——→The emotional state of most people is based,

to a great extent, upon the quality of their rela-

tionships with others.  If their emotional needs

are fulfilled, they will probably find life bear-

←—1"—→able or even good; if these needs are not ful-

filled, they will suffer.  In extreme cases they ←—1"—→

may even decide that life is not worth living.

*Format with separate title page*

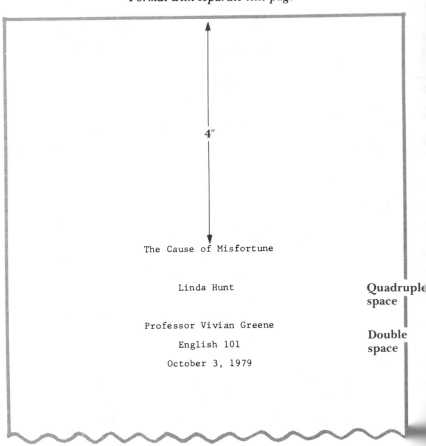

4"

The Cause of Misfortune

Linda Hunt

Quadruple
space

Professor Vivian Greene

English 101

Double
space

October 3, 1979

*First page of text following separate title page—note repetition of title*

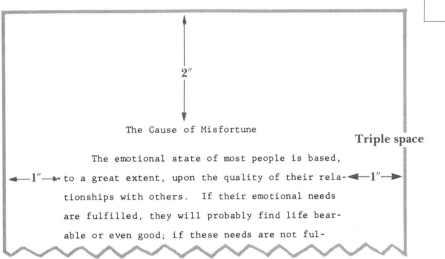

2"

The Cause of Misfortune

Triple space

The emotional state of most people is based,

◄—1"—► to a great extent, upon the quality of their rela- ◄—1"—►

tionships with others.  If their emotional needs

are fulfilled, they will probably find life bear-

able or even good; if these needs are not ful-

*Second and succeeding pages of text*

Page no.

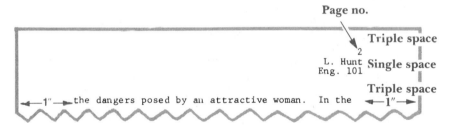

Triple space

2

L. Hunt  Single space
Eng. 101

Triple space

◄—1"—► the dangers posed by an attractive woman.  In the  ◄—1"—►

blesome, making yourself see the letters and checking in your dictionary when you have the slightest doubt.

3. Check the hyphenation of divided words, again using your dictionary if necessary.

4. Make corrections neatly. If there are more than five on a page, redo the entire page.

When you have finished the proofreading, staple the pages together, if permitted; otherwise use a paper clip or, if your teacher wishes, a plastic folder. To protect yourself in case some pages become separated or lost after you submit the paper, file your copy in a safe place. Also keep all your rough drafts. If any question should arise about whether your paper was your own work, they would provide strong evidence that it was.

**EXERCISE 5  Proofreading**

To find out how well you can see what is written on a page, compare the items in each of the following entries. If any item in a series is different from the others, describe the difference.

1. xxxxxx    xxxxxx    xxxxxx    xxxxxx    xxxxxxx
2. ++++ooo++    ++++ooo++    ++−+ooo++
3. /////,,,xyxxy    /////,,xyxxy    /////,,,xyxxy    /////,,,xyxxy
4. 777000066611    77700006666*l* 1    777000066611

**EXERCISE 6  Proofreading**

Check your ability to spot a misspelling. The first word in each entry is spelled correctly. If all of the others in the series are spelled correctly, write *Correct.* If any of the others is misspelled, describe the error.

1. description    description    description    description    description
2. ambivalence    ambivalence    ambivalance    ambivalence
3. rigidity    rigidity    rigidity    rigidity    rigididy
4. occurred    occured    occurred    occurred    occurred
5. refractory    refractory    refractory    refactory    refractory

**EXERCISE 7  Proofreading**

We have deliberately mutilated this passage from Samuel L. Clemens's "Advice to Youth" so that it contains three misspellings, a sentence fragment, and a comma splice. Find the errors and correct them.

> You want to be very careful about lying, otherwise you are nearly sure to get caught. Once caught, you can never again be, in the eyes of the good and the pure, what you were before. Many a young person has injured himself pernamently through a single
> 5 clumsy and ill-finished lie. The result of carelessness born of incomplete training. Some authorities hold that the young ought not to lie at all. That, of course, is puting it rather stronger than necessary; still, while I cannot go quite so far as that, I do maintane, and I believe I am right, that the young ought to be temperate in
> 10 the use of this great art until practice and experience shall give them that confidence, elegance, and precision which alone can make the accomplishment graceful and profitable.

# 9

# READING IN ORDER
# TO WRITE

Up to this point, we have shown you various ways of writing from your own knowledge and experience. We have shown you how to make the most of your inner resources, how to develop what you know or what you remember into a finished essay. But no one can write for long on the strength of inner resources alone. Here and there, we have already suggested that one of the best ways to get an idea for an essay or to enrich the ideas you already have is to read. This chapter is designed to amplify those earlier suggestions by showing you how to make the most of your reading when you sit down to write.

Reading generates writing in three basic ways. For a start, anything you read can stimulate a reaction—fascination, outrage, sympathy, bafflement, even just plain boredom. And as soon as you begin to **react** to a piece of writing, you can begin to think and write about that reaction. In turn, the act of thinking and writing about your reaction can lead you to think and write about what prompted it: to **analyze** what you have read, to explain, amplify, attack, defend, or evaluate the writer's facts, ideas, opinions, or arguments. Finally, any piece of writing that you enjoy reading can show you something about how to write. It can give you something to **imitate.**

This chapter will consider each of these ways of reading in order to write. We concentrate on the reading of nonfictional prose rather than literature, and we focus sharply on the reading of argumentative prose, but much of what we say can be applied to anything you read.

## 9.1 Subjective Response—Getting Down Your First Reaction

One way to get started writing about anything you read is to write about the way it feels to *you*. Do you like or dislike it? Why? Is it easy to understand or hard? Does it answer a question you've sometimes wondered about, or tell you something you've never thought about before? Does it leave you with further questions? And how do you feel about the author?

These are all questions that call for personal, subjective answers. As soon as you get the answers down on paper, you are beginning to write as well as to think about what you have read. You don't have to justify or explain your reactions to anyone else, or even use complete sentences. At this point, you're writing only for yourself.

As an example, here is a short passage from Carl L. Becker's *Modern History,* followed by one student's subjective reaction:

> Students often say to me: "I don't know any history; I think it would be a good thing to learn some." What they seem to mean is that they have never had a "course" in history, or have never read Gibbon's *Decline and Fall of the Roman Empire,* or Mr. Rhodes's *History of the United States from the Compromise of 1850,* or other books similar to these. But they are greatly mistaken if they think they "don't know any history." Every man, woman, and child knows some history, enough at least to stumble along in the world.
>
> Suppose, for example, that you had awakened this morning totally unable to remember anything—all your other faculties working properly, but memory entirely gone. You would be in a bad way indeed! You wouldn't know who you were, or where; what you had done yesterday, or what you intended or other people expected you to do today. What could you do in that case? Wander about helplessly, seeing and hearing things, taking them in as altogether new, not at all knowing what they might mean in relation either to the past or the future. You would have to discover your little world all over again, much as you discovered it in childhood; you would have to "re-orient" yourself and get a new running start. In short, you would be a lost soul because you had ceased to have any knowledge of history, the history of your personal doings and associations in the past.
>
> For history is no more than things said and done in the past. It is as simple as that; and we might as well omit the word "past," since everything said and done is already in the past as soon as it is said or done. Done, but not done *with.* We have to remember many things said and done in order to live our lives intelligently; and so far as we remember things said and done we have a knowledge of history, for that is what historical knowledge is—*memory of things said and done.* Thus everyone has some knowledge of history, and

it is quite essential that everyone should have, since it is only by remembering something of the past that we can anticipate something of the future. Please note that I do not say *predict* the future. We cannot predict the future, but we can *anticipate* it—we can look forward to it and in some sense prepare for it. Now if memory of some things said and done is necessary, it seems that memory of more things ought to be better. The more we remember of things said and done (if they be the right things for our purpose), the better we can manage our affairs today, and the more intelligently we can prepare for what is coming to us tomorrow and next year and all our lives.

Student reaction:

OK, OK. Knowledge and understanding of history is helpful and important. But not all *that* important. True it would be hard living every day without knowing what was said and done in the past but this could be an advantage.

We've learned a great deal socially through history that has proved beneficial but at times it seems history has not proved helpful. So maybe *no* knowledge of history could be an advantage. If we suddenly awakened and had no memory at all I believe many problems could be solved in social relations. We wouldn't have knowledge of some of the evil or great things one minority had done, and so we wouldn't look at any one group above or below the others. We would have no knowledge of the feuds and wars that may have existed and possibly still exist between nations and minorities. Present and past discrimination and prejudice would be forgotten. Now I'm not saying this would make the world one giant, laughing, and incredibly happy place but I believe it would make the value of life much greater. Doubtless that people would still become angered with each other, but it would be for a reason of their own, not because of some hate he or his ancestors may have for that person's minority. The world would now not be divided among nations and minorities but by the quality of the people.

Something exciting happens here. Carl Becker's argument that we cannot live without history has prompted this student to take the opposite view: that we could live better without it because we would then be free of the prejudices and racial hostilities that our knowledge of the past gives us. The student does not have the whole truth, but neither does Becker. The point is that a few minutes of reading, and perhaps fifteen minutes of writing, have given the student a topic to think further about. Without Becker's essay, this student might never have thought and written about history as he did. Reading Becker has put him in touch with his own ideas.

If he wants to state those ideas persuasively, of course, he will need to do more work. He will not only have to smooth out his sentences; he may also have to sharpen his main point. Does he really want to say that *all* history is better forgotten? Or does he believe that we should not let our knowledge of the past tie our hands as we try to shape the future? Can he find examples to support his belief? Thinking about his point may bring him to a more persuasive as well as more polished formulation of it.

But polishing a personal reaction does not mean depersonalizing it. Here is the first part of a published essay in which the writer states her personal reaction to a book:

> There's a book out called *Is There Life after High School?* It's a fairly silly book, maybe because the subject matter is the kind that only hurts when you think. Its thesis—that most people never get over the social triumphs or humiliations of high school—is not novel. Still, I read it with the respectful attention a serious hypochondriac accords the lowliest "dear doctor" column. I don't know about most people, but for me, forgiving my parents for real and imagined derelictions has been easy compared to forgiving myself for being a teenage reject.
>
> Victims of high school trauma—which seems to have afflicted a disproportionate number of writers, including Ralph Keyes, the author of this book—tend to embrace the ugly duckling myth of adolescent social relations: the "innies" (Keyes's term) are good-looking, athletic mediocrities who will never amount to much, while the "outies" are intelligent, sensitive, creative individuals who will do great things in an effort to make up for their early defeats. . . . In contrast, the ex-prom queens and kings he interviews slink through life, hiding their pasts lest someone call them "dumb jock" or "cheerleader type," perpetually wondering what to do for an encore.
>
> If only it were that simple. There may really be high schools where life approximates an Archie comic, but even in the Fifties, my large (5000 students), semisuburban (Queens, New York), heterogeneous high school was not one of them. The students' social life was fragmented along ethnic and class lines; there was no universally recognized, schoolwide social hierarchy. Being an athlete or a cheerleader or a student officer didn't mean much. Belonging to an illegal sorority or fraternity meant more, at least in some circles, but many socially active students chose not to join. The most popular kids were not necessarily the best looking or the best dressed or the most snobbish or the least studious. In retrospect, it seems to me that they were popular for much more honorable reasons. They were attuned to other people, aware of subtle social nuances. They projected an inviting sexual warmth. Far from being slavish followers of fashion, they were self-confident enough to set fashions. They suggested, initiated, led. Above all—this was their main appeal for me—they knew how to have a good time.
>
> —Ellen Willis, "Memoirs of a Non-Prom Queen"

This writer's account of a book she has read is both objective and subjective. Objectively, she mentions its thesis—its main point—in her first paragraph, and she goes on in the next one to describe its contents. But the rest of her discussion is personal. She is judging this book about the effects of high school in the light of what she personally observed when *she* was in high school, of what she saw not just in herself but in others—especially in those who were popular.

She does not contend that her Queens, New York, high school is typical of all high schools, or that her experience is universal. She simply sets her view of high school next to the one presented in the book, and invites her reader to compare the two. That is what you should do if you want to write a finished version of a personal reaction. You should fairly and honestly state the argument of what you have read, and then go on to state your own view.

EXERCISE 1    **Expressing a Subjective Response**

Read the following and then express your immediate personal reaction to it. Feel free to say anything that comes to mind, and do not worry about sentence structure or form.

> During the last ten years most colleges have dropped mandatory courses in essay writing and foreign languages and have weakened distribution requirements in the three basic areas of social science, natural science, and the humanities. During this
> 5 period the number of electives taken at the major private liberal arts colleges has increased from 29 to 35 percent.
> Curriculum committees, often with students on them, and college faculties routinely add new courses to the curriculum regardless of academic value, including courses in wood shop, pho-
> 10 tography, soap opera, roller coasting, political internship, and backpacking! Thus, each year the course catalogues become thicker with fashionable offerings of little or no academic value. Even the Harvard catalogue has doubled in thickness in the last twenty years and now contains over 2600 listings. And it is still
> 15 growing.
> Giving "extensions" on papers and "incompletes" in courses has become a national epidemic. At Yale, according to a recent report by Associate Dean Martin Griffin, 22 percent of all students took at least one "incomplete" in the fall term of 1977. Most dis-
> 20 turbing is the trend: while only 6 percent of the freshmen took "incompletes" that term, 20 percent of the sophomores, 33 percent of the juniors, and 31 percent of the seniors took at least one. Evidently the Yale experience teaches the rewards of procrastination.
> Grade inflation is also epidemic. At Harvard, where one
> 25 must assume resistance to this is greater than average, 85 percent

of the class of 1977 graduated with honors, as compared with 39 percent for the class of 1957. Also, according to a recent report of the Harvard administration, 85 percent of all grades given there last year were B-minus or higher (compared with 70 percent in
30  1965–1966). . . .

Many colleges delete from a student's transcript any failing grade. At Unity College in Maine, for instance, this is known as "non-punitive grading." The idea is that successes, not failures, be recorded.

35  Many colleges have committees, or "courts," often with students on them and sometimes without any faculty, that are empowered to overrule a professor on matters relating to giving grades, changing grades, granting extensions, incompletes, or dropping courses. Often these committees automatically find in favor of the
40  student.

Minority programs have affected academic quality. At some schools the average SAT score of the disadvantaged students is nearly 200 points lower than that of other students (the national average for minorities is 100 points lower than that for non-minor-
45  ity students). Faced with that disparity of achievement in the classroom, the professor, feeling pressure from the minorities and suffering from white guilt, usually gives passing grades to minority students even if they are failing. But if failing students are given C's, those students who would normally have earned D's and C's
50  will have to be given B's and A's, or else . . . the professor [will] simply throw up his hands and give all students A's.

As these examples suggest, America's colleges and universities have grievously failed to maintain minimum academic standards. For surely such standards require colleges to certify that
55  students have taken courses in a range of subjects which a consensus of scholars believes are important and intellectually respectable; that the work done is of a certain quality and students have been sufficiently challenged to gain new confidence in their abilities and awareness of their weaknesses; that course policies recognize
60  learning as a function of time, where taking twice as long to master a subject means learning half as much; and that students have mastered certain fundamental skills such as reading, writing, computation, and speaking a foreign language.

—Alston Chase, "Skipping through College"

## 9.2  Analytical Response

### Catching the Tone

Earlier, we discussed the ways in which you can convey a particular tone of voice in your own writing. (See section 3.4, pp. 34–36.) But tone is also part of what you experience when you read the writing of someone else. It affects the way you "take" what you read—the way you feel about it and hence the way you interpret it. When Carl Becker writes "Students often say to me," he reveals that he is probably a teacher, but we might also guess that from his lecture-room tone: "Please note that I do not say *predict* the future." Politely but firmly, he is treating us as students, carefully guiding us through his explanation. The tone tells us that he straightforwardly means what he says, so that we can take his words at face value.

But now consider this passage by Jonathan Swift:

### A MODEST PROPOSAL

#### For Preventing the Children of Poor People in Ireland from Being a Burden to Their Parents or Country, and for Making Them Beneficial to the Public

It is a melancholy object to those who walk through this great town or travel in the country, when they see the streets, the roads, and cabin doors, crowded with beggars of the female-sex, followed by three, four, or six children, all in rags and importuning every passenger for an alms. These mothers, instead of being able to work for their honest livelihood, are forced to employ all their time in strolling to beg sustenance for their helpless infants, who, as they grow up, either turn thieves for want of work, or leave their dear native country to fight for the Pretender in Spain, or sell themselves to the Barbadoes.

I think it is agreed by all parties that this prodigious number of children in the arms, or on the backs, or at the heels of their mothers, and frequently of their fathers, is in the present deplorable state of the kingdom a very great additional grievance; and therefore whoever could find out a fair, cheap, and easy method of making these children sound, useful members of the commonwealth would deserve so well of the public as to have his statue set up for a preserver of the nation. . . .

I shall now therefore humbly propose my own thoughts, which I hope will not be liable to the least objection.

I have been assured by a very knowing American of my acquaintance in London, that a young healthy child well nursed is at a year old a most delicious, nourishing, and wholesome food, whether stewed, roasted, baked, or boiled; and I make no doubt that it will equally serve in a fricassee or a ragout.

I do therefore humbly offer it to public consideration that of the hundred and twenty thousand children, already computed, twenty thousand may be reserved for breed, whereof only one fourth part to be males, which is more than we allow to sheep, black cattle, or swine; and my reason is that these children are seldom the fruits of marriage, a circumstance not much regarded by our savages, therefore one male will be sufficient to serve four females. That the remaining hundred thousand may at a year old be offered in sale to the persons of quality and fortune through the kingdom, always advising the mother to let them suck plentifully in the last month, so as to render them plump and fat for a good table. A child will make two dishes at an entertainment for friends; and when the family dines alone, the fore or hind quarter will make a reasonable dish, and seasoned with a little pepper or salt will be very good boiled on the fourth day, especially in winter. . . .

On the surface, the writer's tone is formal, reasonable, sympathetic, and self-effacing. He seeks and expects the agreement of "all parties" to his "modest" proposal. After sympathetically describing the "melancholy" plight of poor children in Ireland, he writes, "I shall now therefore humbly propose my own thoughts," and the word "humbly" is repeated two paragraphs later. Can we, then, take Swift's proposal seriously? Is he in earnest when he says that infants should be killed and eaten? The only way we can answer this question is to compare the tone of his writing, which is formal and reasonable, with the content of his proposal, which is—by ordinary moral standards—barbarous and insane. The huge gap between the seemingly reasonable tone and the barbarous content tells us that Swift is probably using the reasonable tone ironically, that he actually means the opposite of what he seems to be saying.

When someone tells you in the middle of a raging downpour that the weather is "beautiful," you know the word is ironic; the speaker really means the weather is horrible. Likewise, when Swift pretends that cannibalism is a reasonable solution to the problem of overpopulation, you can figure out that he means the opposite, that he wants to expose the ruthlessness of all supposedly "reasonable" policies that would treat the poor as less than fully human.

Catching the irony with which a writer uses a certain tone is obviously essential to understanding his or her meaning. But without special knowledge, you may not always be able to tell whether a writer is being ironic. When Hitler proposed the wholesale extermination of the Jews as the "final solution to the Jewish problem," he was *not* being ironic; he was displaying precisely the cold, "reasonable" ruthlessness that Swift attacks. On the other hand, when in 1702 Daniel Defoe published an essay that seemed to recommend the brutal suppression of religious dissent, he *was* being ironic; he was exposing the viciousness of antidissenters. But at a time of bitter religious controversy, only those who knew that Defoe was himself a dissenter could have clearly seen that he was being ironic.

So there is no foolproof way to detect irony. But whenever you read, you should be on the alert for a gap between tone and content, or for sheer implausibility. Even with a free press, most publishers will not gladly risk their reputations (and their money) on essays advocating cannibalism as a solution to the population explosion. Whenever you read something that strikes you as inhuman, crazy, silly, or wildly inconsistent, you may at least strongly suspect that the writer is being ironic.

The lecture-room tone of Becker and the ironically used "reasonable" tone of Swift exemplify just two of the many tones you will find in what you read. Now consider the tone in this passage:

> Home for Christmas my first year in college, I spoke to my best friend from high school. Elizabeth and I stayed on the phone for 45 minutes, but we had nothing very much to say to each other. After the conversation, I was upset. I remember wanting to tell my mother, who asked what the matter was, about the weirdness of discovering that this woman and I, who had talked every school day for five years, no longer had anything in common. All I could do was cry.
>
> Except for a brief, awkward visit to my house a month later when my father died, a church wedding where Elizabeth married a man I'd gone out with in seventh grade, and two short stopovers in southern New Jersey, I don't remember ever seeing or speaking to her again.
>
> We used to spend hours talking about our relationships with boys. We never discussed our relationship with each other. Except for the few minutes with my mother, who told me she thought Elizabeth and I never had anything in common, and my once making a distinction between acquaintances and friends, I'd never spoken about what I considered a real friendship.
>
> Many people have expressed agreement with Cicero that "friendship can only exist between good men." I'm not one of them. As a 30-year-old woman who has had friends since grade school, I have been very concerned with those friendships. Yet only in the last few years have such relationships been acknowledged as being as important as they've always been.
>
> It was always commonplace for girls in my high school to spend a great deal of time together. It was also commonplace for a girl to spend Saturdays with another girl listening to Johnny Mathis albums, trying on clothes to find something that fit right, or babysitting and then having the evening that was planned together usurped by some boy calling up for a date. When this happened to me, I felt betrayed. I never said anything. It didn't occur to me that this wasn't the natural order of things. I didn't know anyone who complained, nor do I remember anyone who ever turned down a boy because she'd already made plans with a girl.
> —Susan Lee, "Friendship, Feminism, and Betrayal"

Here the tone is neither didactic nor ironically "reasonable." The writer is neither telling us plainly what we ought to think ("Please note . . .") nor saying the opposite of what is really meant.

Instead, her tone is personal. As honestly as possible, she is striving to recall the conflicts she experienced in her adolescent friendships with other women.

EXERCISE 2  **Recognizing Tone**

Read the following passage and then briefly describe (1) the author's attitude toward his audience, (2) his tone, and (3) his intention.

> Being told I would be expected to talk here, I inquired what sort of a talk I ought to make. They said it should be something suitable to youth—something didactic, instructive, or something in the nature of good advice. Very well. I have a few things in my
> 5  mind which I have often longed to say for the instruction of the young; for it is in one's tender early years that such things will best take root and be most enduring and most valuable. First, then, I will say to you, my young friends—and I say it beseechingly, urgingly—
> 10  Always obey your parents, when they are present. This is the best policy in the long run, because if you don't they will make you. Most parents think they know better than you do, and you can generally make more by humoring that superstition than you can by acting on your own better judgment.
> 15  Be respectful to your superiors, if you have any, also to strangers, and sometimes to others. If a person offend you, and you are in doubt as to whether it was intentional or not, do not resort to extreme measures; simply watch your chance and hit him with a brick. That will be sufficient. If you shall find that he had
> 20  not intended any offense, come out frankly and confess yourself in the wrong when you struck him; acknowledge it like a man and say you didn't mean to. Yes, always avoid violence; in this age of charity and kindliness, the time has gone by for such things. Leave dynamite to the low and unrefined.
> —Samuel L. Clemens, "Advice to Youth"

## Finding the Writer's Main Point

The first place to look for a writer's main point is the first sentence you read. Consider this paragraph:

> People feel safer behind some kind of physical barrier. If a social situation is in any way threatening, then there is an immediate urge to set up such a barricade. For a tiny child faced with a stranger, the problem is usually solved by hiding behind its mother's body and peeping out at the intruder to see what he or she will do next. If the mother's body is not available, then a chair or some other piece of solid furniture will do. If the stranger insists on coming closer, then the peeping face must be hidden too. If the insensitive intruder continues to approach despite these obvious signals of fear, then there is nothing for it but to scream or flee.
> —Desmond Morris, *Manwatching: A Field Guide to Human Behavior*

The first sentence of this paragraph states its thesis, or main point: "People feel safer behind some kind of physical barrier." Every other sentence is a specific illustration of this general point. The behavior of "people" is illustrated by the actions of the tiny child; the "physical barrier" is illustrated by the mother's body and the chair or other piece of solid furniture.

Though the first sentence is the first place to look for the writer's main point, you will often have to look further. For example:

> The movement has many faces: from sweet ladies handing out red roses and right-to-life cookbooks, to demonstrators brandishing bottled fetuses and hoodlums attacking medical clinics. It has many voices as well: from righteous ministers preaching the sanctity of unborn souls, to editorials raising the specter of the holocaust, to crowds screaming "murderer" at elected officials who take a different position.
>
> This is the anti-abortion movement, a cause that refuses to yield. Six years ago, the U.S. Supreme Court ruled that the right to have an abortion is beyond the reach of government. Since then, public-opinion polls have consistently shown that a majority of Americans favor making abortion a matter for patient and doctor to decide. Despite these developments, the subject is more politically explosive today than ever before. Opposition to abortion has become the most implacable, and perhaps the nastiest, public-issue campaign in at least a half century.
>
> —Roger M. Williams, "The Power of Fetal Politics"

The first paragraph speaks of a "movement." But since no sentence in this paragraph tells us openly what the movement is, we are driven onward to the next paragraph. Here we find out what the movement is, and here also we find the writer's main point about it: "Opposition to abortion has become the most implacable, and perhaps the nastiest, public-issue campaign in at least a half century."

So how do you know this is the main point? How do you know the writer isn't mainly interested in the Supreme Court ruling or the results of public-opinion polls—both of which are mentioned in the second paragraph? The answer is that only the last sentence in the second paragraph contains, so to speak, all the other sentences in both paragraphs. Each of the other sentences specifically shows that the anti-abortion movement is either nasty or implacable. The Supreme Court ruling and the public-opinion polls are cited simply to show how implacable the movement is, how stubbornly it resists the judgments of both the Supreme Court and the court of public opinion.

Sometimes no one single sentence states the writer's main point. Consider this passage:

I once choked a chicken to death. It was my only barefaced, not to say barehanded, confrontation with death and the killer in me and happened on my grandparents' farm. I couldn't have been more than nine or ten and no firearms were included or necessary. I was on my knees and the chicken fluttered its outstretched wings with the last of the outraged protest. I gripped, beyond release, above its swollen crop, its beak gaping, translucent eyelids sliding up and down. . . . My grandfather, who was widely traveled and world-wise, in his eighties then, and had just started using a cane from earlier times, came tapping at that moment around the corner of the chicken coop and saw what I was doing and started gagging at the hideousness of it, did a quick assisted spin away and never again, hours later nor for the rest of his life, for that matter, ever mentioned the homicidal incident to me. Keeping his silence, he seemed to understand; and yet whenever I'm invaded by the incident, the point of it seems to be his turning away from me.

—Larry Woiwode, "Guns"

The last sentence tells us that the point of the incident was the grandfather's turning away. But this sentence merely implies the real point of the paragraph: the grandfather's turning away made the writer recognize himself as a killer.

Also implied rather than stated is the main point of an ironic passage. In "A Modest Proposal" (pp. 177–78), Swift nowhere states his main point openly; you have to figure out what it is. The same is true of Clemens's "Advice to Youth" (exercise 2, p. 180). While Clemens seems to be saying that young people should be obedient, respectful, and nonviolent, he is ironically showing the difference between the way people are normally told to behave and the way they actually do.

In an extended piece of writing, the main point of the whole may not be immediately apparent. That is, a point developed in the early paragraphs may lead up to another, more important point. Consider again an essay that you have already read in part:

## WALLS AND BARRIERS

My father's reaction to the bank building at 43rd Street and Fifth Avenue in New York City was immediate and definite: "You won't catch me putting my money in *there!*" he declared. "Not in that glass box!"

Of course, my father is a gentleman of the old school, a member of the generation to whom a good deal of modern architecture is unnerving; but I suspect—I more than suspect, I am convinced—that his negative response was not so much to the architecture as to a violation of his concept of the nature of money.

In his generation money was thought of as a tangible commodity—bullion, bank notes, coins—that could be hefted, carried, or stolen. Consequently, to attract the custom of a sensible man, a bank had to have heavy walls, barred windows, and bronze doors, to affirm the fact, however untrue, that money would be safe inside. If a building's design made it appear impregnable, the institution was necessarily sound, and the meaning of the heavy wall as an architectural symbol dwelt in the prevailing attitude toward money, rather than in any aesthetic theory.

But that attitude toward money has of course changed. Excepting pocket money, cash of any kind is now rarely used; money as a tangible commodity has largely been replaced by credit: a bookkeeping-banking matter. A deficit economy, accompanied by huge expansion, has led us to think of money as a product of the creative imagination. The banker no longer offers us a *safe;* he offers us a *service*—a service in which the most valuable elements are dash and a creative flair for the invention of large numbers. It is in no way surprising, in view of this change in attitude, that we are witnessing the disappearance of the heavy-walled bank. The Manufacturers Trust, which my father distrusted so heartily, is a great cubical cage of glass whose brilliantly lighted interior challenges even the brightness of a sunny day, while the door to the vault, far from being secluded and guarded, is set out as a window display.

Just as the older bank asserted its invulnerability, this bank *by its architecture* boasts of its imaginative powers. From this point of view it is hard to say where architecture ends and human assertion begins. In fact, there is no such division; the two are one and the same.

It is in the understanding of architecture as a medium for the expression of human attitudes, prejudices, taboos, and ideals that the new architectural criticism departs from classical aesthetics. The latter relied upon pure proportion, composition, etc., as bases for artistic judgment. In the age of sociology and psychology, walls are not simply walls but physical symbols of the barriers in men's minds.

In a primitive society, for example, men pictured the world as large, fearsome, hostile, and beyond human control. Therefore they built heavy walls of huge boulders, behind which they could feel themselves to be in a delimited space that was controllable and safe; these heavy walls expressed man's fear of the outer world and his need to find protection, however illusory. It might be argued that the undeveloped technology of the period precluded the construction of more delicate walls. This is of course true. Still, it was not technology, but a fearful attitude toward the world, which made people want to build walls in the first place. The greater the fear, the heavier the wall, until in the tombs of ancient kings we find structures that are practically all wall, the fear of dissolution being the ultimate fear.

And then there is the question of privacy—for it *has* become questionable. In some Mediterranean cultures it was not so much the world of nature that was feared, but the world of men. Men were dirty, prying, vile, and dangerous. One went about, if one could afford it, in guarded litters; women went about heavily veiled, if they went about at all. One's house was surrounded by a wall, and the rooms faced not out, but in, toward a patio, expressing the prevalent conviction that the beauties and values of life were to be found by looking inward, and by engaging in the intimate activities of a personal as against a public life. The rich intricacies of the decorative arts of the period, as well as its contemplative philosophies, are as illustrative of this attitude as the walls themselves.

We feel different today. For one thing, we place greater reliance upon the control of human hostility, not so much by physical barriers, as by the conventions of law and social practice—as well as the availability of motorized police. We do not cherish privacy as much as did our ancestors. We are proud to have our women seen and admired, and the same goes for our homes. We do not seek solitude; in fact, if we find ourselves alone for once, we flick a switch and invite the whole world in through the television screen. Small wonder, then, that the heavy surrounding wall is obsolete, and we build, instead, membranes of thin sheet metal or glass.

The principal function of today's wall is to separate possibly undesirable outside air from the controlled conditions of temperature and humidity which we have created inside. Glass may accomplish this function, though there are apparently a good many people who still have qualms about eating, sleeping, and dressing under conditions of high visibility; they demand walls that will at least give them a sense of adequate screening. But these shy ones are a vanishing breed. The Philip Johnson house in Connecticut, which is much admired and widely imitated, has glass walls all the way around, and the only real privacy is to be found in the bathroom, the toilette taboo being still unbroken, at least in Connecticut.

To repeat, it is not our advanced technology, but our changing conceptions of ourselves in relation to the world that determine how we shall build our walls. The glass wall expresses man's conviction that he can and does master nature and society. The "open plan" and the unobstructed view are consistent with his faith in the eventual solution of all problems through the expanding efforts of science. This is perhaps why it is the most "advanced" and "forward-looking" among us who live and work in glass houses. Even the fear of the cast stone has been analyzed out of us.

—Eugene Raskin

This essay begins by talking about banks, and the main point of the first four paragraphs is that since tangible money has been largely replaced by credit, the banker now offers not a heavy-walled safe, but a bright, open, inviting service. This point is a kind of landing place to which the first three paragraphs lead, step by step:

1. My father won't put his money in a glass-walled bank.
2. A glass-walled bank violates his concept of money.
3. People of his generation think of money as a tangible commodity that must be heavily protected.
4. However, since tangible money has been largely replaced by credit, the banker now offers not a heavy-walled safe, but a bright, open, inviting service.

The fourth point is the main point of the first four paragraphs, but not of the whole essay. In the fifth paragraph, the point about bank design gives way to a more general point about architecture as a whole, which is the subject of the rest of the essay. The contrast between old banks and new ones illustrates the contrast between traditional and modern architecture, and that contrast in turn supports the main point of the whole essay: architecture reflects the way we think about our relation to the outside world.

EXERCISE 3   **Identifying the Main Point**

In each of the following passages, one sentence expresses the main point. Identify that sentence.

1.      The history of Florida is measured in freezes. Severe ones, for example, occurred in 1747, 1766, and 1774. The freeze of February, 1835, was probably the worst one in the state's history. But, because more growers were affected, the Great Freeze of 1895 seems to enjoy the same sort of status in Florida that the Blizzard of '88 once held in the North. Temperatures on the Ridge on February 8, 1895, went into the teens for much of the night. It is said that some orange growers, on being told what was happening out in the groves, got up from their dinner tables and left the state. In the morning, it was apparent that the Florida citrus industry had been virtually wiped out.
—John McPhee, *Oranges*

2.      In early human history a Stone Age, a Bronze Age, or an Iron Age came into unhurried gestation and endured for centuries or even millennia; and as one technology gradually displaced or merged with another, the changes wrought in any single lifetime were easily absorbed, if noticed at all. But a transformation has come about in our own time. A centenarian born in 1879 has seen, in the years of his own life, scientific and technological advances more sweeping and radical than those that took place in all the accumulated past. He has witnessed—and felt the personal impact of—the Age of Electricity, the Automobile Age, the Aviation Age, the Electronic Age, the Atomic Age,

the Space Age, and the Computer Age, to name but a few of the "ages" that have been crowding in upon us at such an unprecedented rate, sometimes arriving virtually side by side. Let us use the shortcut designation the "Age of Science" to encompass them all.
— Albert Rosenfeld, "How Anxious Should Science Make Us?"

EXERCISE 4   **Identifying the Main Point**

Reread the passage on college standards given in exercise 1, pp. 175–76, and identify the main point of the selection.

## Summarizing

Summarizing a piece of writing is a good way to test and show your understanding of it. How you summarize will partly depend on whether you are dealing with a narrative or with an essay.

The summary of a narrative or a drama is usually called a plot summary; it may be sequential or comprehensive. A **sequential** plot summary follows the order in which the main events of a narrative or drama are presented in the original work. A sequential plot summary of *Moby-Dick,* for instance, would begin as follows:

> Bored with his life on land, a young schoolteacher who calls himself Ishmael decides to go to sea on a whaling ship. He travels to New Bedford, where he meets and strikes up a friendship with a harpooner named Queequeg. Then the two men go to Nantucket and sign on board a ship named the *Pequod.* . . .

Like all summaries, this one reduces each event to its bare essentials. It says that Ishmael meets Queequeg, for instance, but does not mention the startling conditions under which they meet. And because this is a sequential plot summary, it starts with chapter 1 and follows the order of the original in retelling the events.

But that is not always the order that best expresses what happens. Instead of starting with the first chapter of a book or the first scene of a play, you can start with a **comprehensive** statement about the chief action of the book or play, and then give the chain of events making up that action:

> *Moby-Dick* is the story of Ahab's relentless quest for revenge against a white whale that has taken his leg and that eventually takes his life. Ahab is the captain of a whaling ship named the *Pequod,* and the story of his quest is told by one of the seamen who serve on his ship—a man who calls himself Ishmael. Bored with his life on land, Ishmael decides to go to sea on a whaling voyage, so he signs on the *Pequod* along with a new-found friend named Queequeg. Shortly after the ship embarks, Ahab announces that

the sole purpose of the voyage is to catch and kill Moby-Dick, the great white whale that has cut off Ahab's leg. . . .

A comprehensive summary such as this gives a clearer account of the book as a whole than a sequential summary does. While a sequential summary simply recounts one event after another without saying which is the most important, a comprehensive summary immediately identifies the central action to which all other actions must be referred.

The summary of an essay should begin by stating the main point of the essay as a whole, and then proceed to the chief supporting points—all of the points used to explain or prove the main point. Here, for instance, is a summary of Eugene Raskin's "Walls and Barriers" (pp. 182–84):

> Architecture reveals the way we think about our relation to the outside world. While the heavy walls of traditional architecture express a fear of that world, the glass walls of modern architecture express confidence that human beings can master the outside world and eventually solve all of its problems.

This summary begins with the main point of the whole essay, and the second sentence states the chief supporting point. In the essay itself, the author uses banks and houses to show the difference between traditional and modern architecture, but such examples don't belong in a summary, which should consist of general facts and ideas, not specific illustrations. And this summary does not set down the main point of each paragraph in the essay; it simply goes to the final paragraph, which clearly states the essay's main point. The final paragraph of an essay, in fact, is often the best place to look for such a statement.

EXERCISE 5  **Summarizing**

Summarize the passage on college standards given in exercise 1, pp. 175–76.

## Judging the Supporting Points in an Essay

To summarize an essay, you must be able to identify its main point and its chief supporting points. To analyze an essay, you must also be able to judge the relevance and strength of each supporting point. You should therefore try to answer these questions:

**1.** Are the supporting points facts or opinions? A fact is a statement that can be indisputably verified. An opinion is a statement that may be impossible to verify absolutely but can be supported by facts—and usually must be.

Normally you can accept as a fact any statement that can be

verified—that is, established as true. If you read that the Great Freeze struck Florida in 1895, you can accept that statement as a fact because you can normally expect a writer to tell the truth about matters that can be decisively checked. But not all statements presented as facts actually are facts. Writers and printers sometimes make mistakes, and dishonest writers sometimes invent "facts" to strengthen their arguments. So if any particular statement is crucial to the writer's argument, and especially if you would like to use it in your own writing, you should look for the source that is cited to verify it, or ask yourself whether it can be verified.

An opinion may be impossible to verify as absolutely true, but it can be supported by facts, and it usually needs such support in order to make an impression on the reader. In the passage in exercise 1, pp. 175–76, Alston Chase expresses an opinion when he says that "America's colleges and universities have grievously failed to maintain minimum academic standards." He supports this opinion with statements we can take as facts—such as the statement that "many colleges delete from a student's transcript any failing grade." This statement does not prove absolutely that Chase's opinion is true, but it helps to show that his opinion is probably true. Anyone who wishes to combat that opinion will have to show that Chase's supporting statements (facts) are false, that he has ignored an opposing point (see p. 191), or that his reasoning is faulty (see section 5.4, pp. 88–91).

Since an opinion cannot stand on its own feet, you should take a hard look at what is said to support it. Sometimes there is no supporting statement at all, and sometimes the supporting statement turns out to be nothing but another opinion. When a writer says that "young people no longer work seriously" to persuade us that the nation is declining, the supporting statement is mere opinion. It cannot be verified until we know who the "young people" are, what their "work" is, and how to measure their seriousness. When a writer says that there is life outside the solar system, that too is an opinion; it remains to be verified—though it may one day become an established fact. (The established fact that the earth is round was once merely the opinion of daring thinkers.) Likewise, when a writer says that the United States must spend more on weapons because Russia is "winning the arms race," that too is opinion; it cannot be verified until we agree on what "winning" means here. Does it mean producing more nuclear weapons than the other nation, or producing more conventional weapons, or developing better antimissile missiles? Vague opinions must be made specific before they can be adequately supported by facts, and no opinion can serve by itself to support another opinion.

Between fact and opinion stands another kind of statement:

the questionable claim. Suppose you read that there are eight million rats in New York City. This looks like a statement that can be checked and verified—a fact. But who can actually count the number of rats in New York? Contrary to popular belief, numbers have no special authority over words. The figures a writer cites are only as reliable as the methods used to get them.

Arguments that rest on statistics must therefore be read with special care. In 1950 *Time* magazine reported that the average Yale graduate of the class of 1924 was earning $25,111 a year. Would this statement support the contention that Yale is (or was) the gateway to prosperity for all its graduates? Not necessarily, because an "average" income of $25,111 a year can be earned by one multimillionaire and two hundred paupers. So even if the figures themselves are reliable, what is done with them in an argument may not be. You as the reader must be the final judge of what the figures can legitimately be made to mean.

Questionable assertions take a variety of other forms, and no definition of them can replace common sense and healthy skepticism. In general, you should read with a question mark between you and the page. Be on the watch for deceptive exaggeration, "figures" that come out of thin air, and editorial opinion masquerading as reportorial fact ("The president has lost the confidence of the American people"). Life is too short for you to check out every unsupported claim or surprising new "fact" for yourself; usually you must trust the writer. But you can reasonably ask that a writer earn your trust—by respecting the difference between fact and opinion.

**2.** Are the supporting points relevant to the main point? A main point "supported" by irrelevant points is like a house at number 32 Main Street supported by a foundation laid at number 31. Consider this passage:

> It would be foolish and dangerous for the United States to make any further agreement with Russia that would limit the production or deployment of strategic weapons. Russia is a communist country that tyrannizes her citizens. She crushes personal initiative. She demands unquestioning obedience to the Communist party line. She persecutes any who disagree. Some of her most brilliant writers have been subjected to prolonged imprisonment and even torture, and most of her citizens are virtual prisoners all of the time, forbidden to leave the country. The U.S. should have nothing whatsoever to do with such a ruthlessly totalitarian regime.

The first sentence states the writer's main point, and the rest of the sentences are offered to support it. But they fail to support it because they are beside the point. Even if we accept as matters of common belief the statements made about Russia's treatment of her citizens, Russia's domestic policies are not clearly relevant to the arms race, any more than American domestic policies are. In a persuasive argument against an arms-limitation agreement, the main point would have to be supported by relevant supporting points—such as the fact that the agreement fails to provide for U.S. inspection of Soviet weapons factories.

**3.** Do all the supporting points really work for the thesis—not against it? Consider the following passage:

> [1] The Watergate scandal of the early 1970s clearly showed how extensive political corruption can be. [2] In the first place, men working in a presidential campaign tried to burglarize a building in order to get information about their political rivals. [3] In the second place, after this burglary was discovered, high officials at the White House tried to block a full investigation of it, and thereby incriminated themselves. [4] Finally, investigators discovered wrongdoing by the chief executive himself, and for the first time in history, a president of the United States was forced to resign his office in disgrace. [5] As a result of the Watergate scandal, the Senate has established rules to ensure that political campaigns will be honestly run in the future.

Sentence 1 states the main point, and sentences 2, 3, and 4 all support it by showing just how far the Watergate scandal reached. Furthermore, sentence 5 seems to follow sentence 4 nicely, for it begins with the phrase *As a result.* But in fact sentence 5 does not support the main point of the passage, which is that the Watergate scandal showed how widespread political corruption can be. Instead, sentence 5 says that the Watergate scandal led to high-minded political reform. If the writer wanted to end the paragraph with the sentence on reform, he or she should have started with a different point about the scandal as a whole.

**4.** Are there enough supporting points? In the paragraph on barriers (p. 180), Desmond Morris's main point is that "people feel safer behind some kind of physical barrier," and he supports this point by describing what a child does when confronted by a stranger. Can you see what is missing? Clearly, Morris does not adequately support his point about "people" by simply describing the actions of a "tiny child." But Morris's paragraph on the child is merely the opening of a chapter in which he describes the barrier signals that grownups use, the subtle movements and postures with which adults continue to shield themselves in unfamiliar company. By citing specific examples of adult as well as child behavior, Morris convincingly supports his point in the chapter as a whole.

Supporting points, then, should cover a representative sample of the people or objects that the main point refers to. If a writer wants to show that blacks have become increasingly successful in American politics, his or her argument need not cite examples from all fifty states, but it should certainly cite examples from more than one state, and from states in different parts of the country. The greater the variety as well as the number of the examples, the more convincing the argument will be.

**5.** Is the writer deliberately ignoring an opposing point? To be wholly convincing, an argument must recognize the major points that can be set against it. A convincing argument about the evils of the Watergate scandal would somehow have to recognize the reforms that grew out of it, just as a convincing argument about the success of black politicians would have to recognize the defeat of Senator Edward Brooke of Massachusetts in his 1978 campaign for reelection, and the defeat of Congresswoman Shirley Chisholm of New York in her 1972 campaign for the Democratic presidential nomination. Of course, you do not expect political reforms to be cited in support of an argument about political evils, or black political losses to be cited in support of an argument about black successes. But when you read a completely one-sided essay on a subject you know has at least two sides, you may be sure that the argument is slanted.

### Judging an Argument as a Whole

To judge a whole argument, you must identify its main point, identify and judge its supporting points, and then determine how well all of these points work together. Try your hand with this passage:

> [1] The free exit of people from the Soviet Union is prohibited. The Soviet Union has a problem with people leaving the country, which it calls "defection."
> [2] The free entry of opiates into the United States is prohibited. The United States has a problem with opiates coming into the country, which it calls "trafficking in dope."
> [3] The United States recognizes that its citizens have an inalienable right to leave their country. The United States therefore has no such problem as "defection."
> [4] Similarly, if the United States recognized that its citizens also have an inalienable right to self-medication (a right of which they were deprived in 1914), there would be no illegal inflow of heroin into the country. The United States would therefore have no such problem as "trafficking in dope."
> [5] Of course, some people would still take drugs some other people did not want them to take. But this would no more constitute "drug abuse" than leaving the country constitutes "border abuse."

[6] In short, if a government believes that its citizens have no right to leave their country, it will generate policies which, in turn, will create the "problem of defection." Similarly, if a government believes that its citizens have no right to use "dangerous drugs," it will generate policies which, in turn, will create the "problem of drug abuse." Many national and social "problems" are thus created not by what people do, but by the way governments *define* what they do and by the policies which such definitions impose on rulers and ruled alike.

[7] Confronted with such totalitarian laws, most people in the "free" world assert that the prohibitions are criminal and that the victims are the citizens whose freedom they curtail. Yet, confronted with similar therapeutic laws—which prohibit certain movements in the chemical and sexual, rather than in the geographical, sphere—most people in the "free" world assert that the prohibitions are merely unfortunate or unwise because they create "crimes without victims." This is self-deception of the worst sort: it is the unwillingness to see and acknowledge the malevolent tyranny of one's own rulers, and, where it applies, of one's own conscience, on whose behest a "free" people deprive themselves of a liberty whose burden they are too weak to bear.

—Thomas Szasz, *Heresies*

The first five paragraphs of this selection concern drugs and "defection," but when we get to the sixth paragraph we learn that neither of these is what the essay is really about. Like the bank buildings described in Eugene Raskin's essay on architecture, "defection" and the "problem of drug abuse" are simply two examples offered to illustrate a general point: "Many national and social 'problems' are . . . created not by what people do, but by the way governments *define* what they do and by the policies which such definitions impose on rulers and ruled alike." In turn, this point supports the writer's main point, which appears in the seventh paragraph: the so-called "problems" created by law make us unwilling to see how government and conscience together deprive us of our freedom.

This main point is supported by the examples of "defection" and "trafficking in dope." But since the word "problem" is crucial to the whole argument, we must understand what the writer means by it. By "problem" he seems to mean a conflict between what people do and what the law tells them to do or not to do. In other words, a "problem" is something created by a law, and therefore when the law disappears, so does the "problem."

The example of emigration is cited to illustrate this definition. But while comparison of the Soviet Union and the United States seems to show that the law alone determines whether or not emigration is a "problem," other examples could be cited to show that emigration causes problems that are independent of the law. For instance, England has no law against emigration, but in the 1950s the departure of many of its best scientists and doctors was regarded as a problem—that is, an obstacle to scientific research and a threat to the quality of life in that country.

A similar objection can be made to the example of "trafficking in dope." If all of the problems connected with "drug abuse" were created by antidrug laws, the repeal of those laws would remove the problems. But the writer does not show that all of the problems connected with "drug abuse" are created by the laws. Federal laws against trafficking in liquor ended long ago, but "alcohol abuse" is still a problem—that is, a cause of distress for the abuser and of death on the roads for thousands of people every year.

Szasz therefore fails to provide convincing support for his main point: that "problems" created purely by law make us unwilling to see how government and conscience deprive us of our freedom. It may be argued, of course, that a particular problem is not serious enough to justify a law, or that the law dealing with it is ineffective. But those are other arguments altogether.

EXERCISE 6   **Analyzing a Paragraph**

Read the following paragraph and answer these questions: (1) What is the main point? (2) What are the supporting points? (3) Are any of the supporting points not strictly relevant to the main point? (4) Which are the facts and which are the opinions?

> Today Japan is the world's foremost economic power. Last year the Japanese manufactured one and a half times as much per capita as Americans. While for the first time in decades our exports of industrial goods fell behind our imports, Japan exported $75
> 5  billion more of industrial goods than it imported. Japan's investment rate, as well as its GNP growth rate, is more than twice ours and its research and development efforts are growing much more rapidly than our own. Its workers, contrary to our old stereotype, are effectively better paid than our own. And its performance in
> 10  educating the population, minimizing disparities of income, reducing the crime rate, and increasing the length of human life is substantially ahead of America's. These differences will have far more profound consequences than we have begun to imagine.
>
> —Ezra Vogel, "The Miracle of Japan: How the Post-War Was Won"

EXERCISE 7   **Analyzing and Judging an Argument**

Analyze and judge Carl Becker's argument about history (pp. 172–73) or Eugene Raskin's argument about modern architecture (pp. 182–84).

EXERCISE 8    Using Facts in an Argument

Explain whether or not the facts stated by Alston Chase (exercise 1, pp. 175–76) could be used to support a positive conclusion about the state of American colleges.

## 9.3    Imitative Response—Reading for Style

Reading is to writing what hearing is to talking. Just as you cannot learn to talk without hearing other people speak, so you cannot learn to write without reading what others have written, without seeing and absorbing the huge variety of ways in which sentences, paragraphs, essays, stories, and poems have been put together. No guidelines for good writing can ever take the place of good writing itself, used as a model. If you like tennis, you don't watch John McEnroe play Bjorn Borg just to find out what the final score will be. You watch the game to see how McEnroe serves and Borg returns, to study the lobs, drop shots, passing shots, forehands, backhands, overhead smashes, and putaways, to see why one man finally wins and the other loses. In the same way, you should read good writing for more than its content. You should watch the way good writers make their points.

Style is often thought to be a mysterious ingredient. But the more you study the styles of good writers, the more tangible style becomes. Compare these two paragraphs:

> It is surprising, perhaps even embarrassing, to consider the ways in which ants resemble human beings. Fungi, for example, are grown by ants, and in this respect the ants are like human farmers. Furthermore, aphids are raised by ants, just as pigs are raised by farmers. Other activities include fighting in large numbers, just as human armies fight. Also, chemical sprays are sometimes used in those battles to disturb and confuse enemies. In addition, ants are taken to work for other ants as slaves. Moreover, in families of weaver ants, the larvae, or "children," are used for work; they are held like shuttles to spin out the thread with which leaves are sewn together for fungus gardens. Finally, information is continually passed back and forth among ants. Altogether, they do a considerable number of things that human beings do.

> Ants are so much like human beings as to be an embarrassment. They farm fungi, raise aphids as livestock, launch armies into wars, use chemical sprays to alarm and confuse enemies, capture slaves. The families of weaver ants engage in child labor, holding their larvae like shuttles to spin out the thread that sews the leaves together for their fungus gardens. They exchange information ceaselessly. They do everything but watch television.
> —Lewis Thomas, *Lives of a Cell*

These two paragraphs say essentially the same thing, but their styles are drastically different. The first is plodding, wordy, and ponderous; the second leaps and sings. Why?

Part of the answer is compression. The second version says the same things as the first in about half as many words. Instead of starting out by zigzagging around the main point ("It is surprising, perhaps even embarrassing, to consider the ways . . ."), Thomas goes directly to it: "Ants are so much like human beings as to be an embarrassment." The second sentence of the first paragraph takes seventeen words to say what Thomas says in three: "They farm fungi." In Thomas's version, these are merely the first three words of a single sentence that does the work of five sentences in the first version.

One thing that makes this compression possible is the use of the active voice. The first version is cluttered with passives: *are grown, are raised, are . . . used, are taken, are held, are sewn, is . . . passed.* In Thomas's version, the wordy passive constructions give way to short active ones, and the active verbs bring the ants to life: they *farm, launch, use, capture, engage, exchange*—in sum, do everything that humans do.

Besides compression and life, Thomas's version also has variety. The sentences of the first version are nearly all of the same length and construction, with openings hung up on commas (*It is surprising, . . . ; Fungi, for example, . . . ; Furthermore, . . . ; Also, . . . ; In addition, . . . ; Moreover, . . . ; Finally, . . . ; Altogether, . . .*). Thomas varies the length of his sentences, and the shorter ones have no commas at all. What is constant about Thomas's sentences is that they all have *Ants* (or *They* or *The families of . . . ants*) as the subject. Keeping his eye on this subject, Thomas varies the construction as well as the length of his sentences to show what a variety of things ants do.

Thomas also keeps his audience awake with an occasional joke, as when he says that ants do everything but watch television. Of course he is exaggerating. He doesn't expect us to believe that ants drill oil wells, write novels, or play basketball. But he does expect us to make the implied comparison with human beings, many of whom do little *but* watch television. What he mischievously implies is that ants are much more lively and interesting than we are.

In writing, as in any other art, you learn by studying and imitating styles you admire. If you read a sentence or a paragraph that knocks your eye out, make it your own. Write it down or memorize it. Then quote it when you get the chance, or imitate its style in a sentence of your own. Nobody can tell you whose style is the best model for you. But there must be at least one writer whom you love to read, whose words make you want to applaud. Whether or not you set out to imitate that writer consciously, the study of his or her style will almost certainly invigorate yours.

Conscious and formal imitation of a writer you like can be an excellent exercise. To feel the full force of a style you might like to imitate, read aloud to yourself this passage from Samuel L. Clemens's *Autobiography:*

> As I have said, I spent some part of every year at the farm until I was twelve or thirteen years old. The life which I led there with my cousins was full of charm and so is the memory of it yet. I can call back the solemn twilight and the mystery of the deep woods, the earthy smells, the faint odors of the wild flowers, the sheen of rain-washed foliage, the rattling clatter of drops when the wind shook the trees, the far-off hammering of woodpeckers and the muffled drumming of wood-pheasants in the remoteness of the forest, the snapshot glimpses of disturbed wild creatures scurrying through the grass—I can call it all back and make it as real as it ever was, and as blessed. I can call back the prairie, and its loneliness and peace, and a vast hawk hanging motionless in the sky with his wings spread wide and the blue of the vault showing through the fringe of their end-feathers. I can see the woods in their autumn dress, the oaks purple, the hickories washed with gold, the maples and the sumachs luminous with crimson fires, and I can hear the rustle made by the fallen leaves as we plowed through them. I can see the blue clusters of wild grapes hanging amongst the foliage of the saplings, and I remember the taste of them and the smell. I know how the wild blackberries looked and how they tasted; and the same with the pawpaws, the hazelnuts, and the persimmons; and I can feel the thumping rain upon my head of hickory-nuts and walnuts when we were out in the frosty dawn to scramble for them with the pigs, and the gusts of wind loosed them and sent them down.

Clemens organizes this long passage by means of two simple techniques. First, except in his short introduction, he begins every sentence and independent clause with a statement that he is calling back specific memories, things that can be seen or heard or smelled or felt: *I can call back, I can see, I can hear, I can feel.* He is not afraid to repeat, to turn back again and again for more sights and sounds and smells and feelings. Second, he fills each sentence with lists of the memories, getting as particular as possible: *I can see the woods in their autumn dress, the oaks purple, the hickories washed with gold, the maples and the sumachs luminous with crimson fires.*

You may not think you could ever write like this. But you can—right now. In your own descriptive writing you can immediately use the two simple techniques illustrated here; the very words *I remember* and *I can see* may help you to rediscover things long buried in your own memory. Here, for instance, is a description of working on an asparagus farm written by a student who was deliberately imitating Clemens:

> I can still remember changing pipe in nothing but gym shorts and tennis shoes, with swarms of bees humming all around me in the fern and never once was I stung. I remember disturbing countless quail and pheasants, and once in a while catching a brief glimpse of a coyote or jackrabbit. I remember freezing hands in early spring, when frost covered the pipes in the early morning, and burning hands in late summer, when a line had lain in the hot sun for a day or so. I know the sweet taste of grapes liberated from the next field, and the bitter taste of raw potato from another neighboring unit. I know how to grab a handful of wheat and rub off the chaff, leaving only the crunchy grain, and how good it tastes after a hard day's work. I can call back the ringing in my ears after driving a tractor all day, nonstop, and how good it would have felt to have had some earplugs. I remember the shimmering sun baking us to a golden brown as we lay snoozing on the ground after the pipes were changed, and how once in a while the boss would find us in that position. He never appreciated our attitude towards work.

You can easily recognize the two basic techniques used by Clemens: starting each sentence with a memory statement (*I remember, I know, I can call back*) and listing specific memories (*freezing hands in early spring, burning hands in late summer*). And this is a creative imitation. The student writer is not copying Clemens's words; he is using the techniques to summon up personal memories, to generate a description of his own experience.

A passage of any length can be a model for you to imitate. Here, for instance, is a single long sentence:

> For four years this lovely college life lasted, and I simply survived in a happy somnambulistic state, blowsy, disheveled, dropping hairpins, tennis balls, and notebooks wherever I went, drinking tea with Dr. Lily Campbell and the professors, lapping up talk of books and history, drinking tea with classmates and Elizabeth Boynton, the librarian, having dated or nearly dated with the two M's on either side of me, Macon and Morgan, having dates with Leonard Keller, who was working out campus thefts and misdemeanors with the first lie detector, falling asleep in all afternoon lectures, late for every appointment, smiling sheepishly on the rare occasions when I arrived in class on time, and, always and ever, dreaming. —Agnes De Mille, *Dance to the Piper*

The writer begins with two simple statements: *For four years this lovely college life lasted, and I simply survived in a happy somnambulistic state.* Then she adds a string of adjectives and modifying phrases:

*blowsy, disheveled, dropping hairpins, drinking tea, falling asleep, late for every appointment, smiling sheepishly.* This type of sentence is open-ended: once you have started it off with a statement or two, you can go on adding adjectives and modifiers as they come to mind.

### Exercise 9  Imitating the Style of a Sentence

Imitating Agnes De Mille, describe your four years of high school in a single sentence. You can start the sentence with just one simple statement if you wish.

### Exercise 10  Imitating the Style of a Passage

Drawing on your own memories of a specific period or experience in your life, write an imitation of Clemens's passage. Begin at least one of your sentences with *I can still see,* at least one with *I can still hear,* and at least one with *I can still feel.*

### Exercise 11  Explaining and Imitating the Style of a Passage

Copy out a brief passage by any writer whose work you admire, and then (1) explain why you admire its style, and (2) imitate its style in a passage of your own.

# II

# WRITING
# SENTENCES

# 10

# THE SIMPLE SENTENCE— SUBJECT AND PREDICATE

The sentence is a fundamentally human creation. Like the human beings who write them, sentences come in a seemingly endless variety of shapes and sizes: some stretch out for line upon line; others stop short after two or three words. Yet the sentence has a basic structure, just as the body does. Despite the variety in the human race, there are certain things we can say about all human bodies, or about *the* human body, the structure that all of us share as long as we live. And despite the variety in sentences, there are certain things we can say about the structure of *the* sentence, the structure that most of us use whenever we write.

## 10.1  The Subject and the Predicate

A sentence normally has a subject and a predicate. The **subject** is the word or word group that tells who or what the sentence is about. The **predicate** is the word or word group that tells what the subject does, has, or is, or what is done to it. Consider the sentence *Jack scowled:*

SUBJECT     PREDICATE
Jack    /    scowled.

The subject is *Jack,* a noun. The predicate is *scowled,* a verb; it tells what Jack did.

201

## 10.2 The Sentence and the Clause

Every sentence normally has at least one combination of subject and predicate; such a combination is called a **clause.** A sentence may have more than one clause:

CLAUSE 1                CLAUSE 2
[s] Jack / [p] scowled, and [s] Penny / [p] laughed.

CLAUSE 1             CLAUSE 2
[s] Jack / [p] scowled, [s] Penny / [p] laughed,
CLAUSE 3
and [s] I / [p] grinned.

In later chapters we consider sentences such as these—sentences with two or more clauses. In this chapter we consider the one-clause sentence, usually called the **simple sentence.** The simple sentence can in fact get highly complicated; it is called "simple" because it consists of a single clause, one combination of subject and predicate.

## 10.3 About the Predicate

### Verbs and Verb Phrases

The predicate always includes a verb or verb phrase. The verb in a sentence is one of three types: transitive, intransitive, or linking.

A **transitive verb** names an action that directly affects a person or thing mentioned in the predicate. The word or word group naming this person or thing is the direct object of the verb. In each of the following sentences the direct object comes right after the verb:

> Janet *drove* a bulldozer.
> David *writes* songs.
> Harry *gives* lectures.
> Gamblers *lose* money.

An **intransitive verb** names an action that has no direct impact on anyone or anything named in the predicate:

> Frank *scowled.*
> Gail *won.*
> Children *giggle.*
> Whales *sing.*
> Frank *disappeared.*

A **linking verb** (often a form of *be,* such as *is, are, was,* or *were*) is followed by a word or word group that identifies or describes the subject:

> Whales *are* mammals.
> Caterpillars *become* butterflies.
> Stephen Sondheim *is* a songwriter.
> Susan *felt* sleepy.
> Aspirin *tastes* bitter.
> The alligator *looked* hungry.

Linking verbs include *seem, become, feel, look, sound,* and *taste,* as well as *be*—the most common of all.

A word that follows a linking verb and identifies the subject is called a **predicate noun.** In the preceding examples *mammals, butterflies,* and *songwriter* are predicate nouns. A word that follows a linking verb and describes the subject is called a **predicate adjective.** In the preceding examples *sleepy, bitter,* and *hungry* are predicate adjectives.

A **verb phrase** consists of two or more verbs—a base verb and at least one "helping" verb, called an **auxiliary:**

> Gail *can win.*
> Gail *did win.*
> Gail *could have lost.*

As these examples show, auxiliaries include *can, did, could,* and *have.* Other auxiliaries are *is, are, was, were, has, had, do, does, may, might, would,* and *should.*

In many questions the sentence begins with an auxiliary:

> *Can* Gail *win?*
> *Did* Gail *win?*
> *Could* Gail *have lost?*

## Voice—Active and Passive

A transitive verb can be in either the active or the passive voice. A verb is in the **active voice** when the subject performs the action named by the verb:

> Bees *make* honey.

A verb is in the **passive voice** when the subject undergoes the action named by the verb:

> Honey *is made* by bees.

The performer of the action can be specified in a *by* phrase after the verb. But the performer need not be specified:

Four presidents *have been* assassinated.

(For a full discussion of the active and passive voice, see chapter 22, pp. 365–72.)

### Objects—Direct and Indirect

A transitive verb can have two objects: a direct object, as already shown, and an indirect object. The **direct object** names the person or thing directly affected by the action that the verb specifies:

> Keith bought *a necklace.*
> The professor gave *a makeup exam.*

The **indirect object** names the person or thing indirectly affected by the action:

> Keith bought a necklace for *Janet.*
> The professor gave *me* a makeup exam.

The indirect object may go after the direct object or immediately after the verb. When it goes immediately after a verb like *send, give, show, offer, write,* or *told,* it can be used without *to* or *for.*

### Object Complements

An **object complement** is a word or word group that immediately follows a direct object and identifies or describes it:

> Stafford considers Alice *the best runner on the team.*
> Critics thought the lyrics *meaningless.*
> Employers found North *lazy.*
> Reagan named Haig *secretary of state.*

Object complements follow such verbs as *name, elect, appoint, think, consider, judge, find* (in the sense of "judge"), and *make* (as in "What makes some people stars?").

## 10.4   About the Subject—
## Nouns, Pronouns, Verbal Nouns,
## and Noun Phrases

The subject of a sentence can be a single **noun,** a word that names a person, creature, place, thing, activity, condition, or idea. The subjects in the preceding examples—*Stafford, Critics, Employers,* and *Reagan*—are of this type. The subject can also be a single **pronoun,** a word that takes the place of a noun:

He was speaking.
*Everyone* laughed.
*That* annoyed him.

(For a full discussion of pronouns, see chapter 18, pp. 305–19.)

Sometimes the subject is a **verbal noun,** a word or phrase that is formed from a verb and used as a noun:

*Hunting* can be dangerous.
*To err* is human.

(For a full discussion of verbal nouns, see chapter 12, pp. 240–46.)

Frequently the subject is a **noun phrase,** a group of words consisting of a noun and the words that describe, limit, or qualify it:

*The price* soared.
*The price of gold* soared.

In each of these sentences the simple subject is *price.* The complete subject of the first is *The price;* the complete subject of the second is *The price of gold.* The complete subject consists of the simple subject and the modifiers that accompany it. Modifiers are more fully explained in the next section.


## 10.5 Modifiers

A word or phrase that describes, limits, or qualifies another word or phrase is called a **modifier.** In the preceding examples *The* and *of gold* are modifiers of the noun *price* and are part of the subject. In each of the following sentences the italicized word is a modifier of the verb or verb phrase and is part of the predicate:

Janet can drive a bulldozer *anywhere.*
Harry *seldom* gives lectures.
Frank disappeared *suddenly.*
Setbacks can be instructive *sometimes.*

Since modifiers include even such words as *the* and *a,* nearly all sentences have at least one, and most sentences have them in both the subject and the predicate. In the following examples the modifiers are italicized:

        S                  P
*The* boy *inside the closet*  |  was yelling *desperately.*

        S                  P
*The heavy packing* case  |  fell *to the floor.*

S                               P

*The clumsy* workmen   /   dropped *the heavy* crate *to the floor.*

S                               P

*Raised in Wyoming,* David   /   *sometimes* writes songs *about sad cowboys.*

S                               P

*Shivering in the icy wind,* Steve   /   pounded *the heavy oak* door *of the old house.*

(For a full discussion of modifiers, see chapter 11, pp. 211–39.)

### Exercise 1   Composing: Recognizing Subjects and Predicates

In each of the following sentences, identify the subject and the predicate. Then write a new sentence that follows the form of the original.

EXAMPLE
Foam from the liquid soap covered the water's surface.

S                               P

Foam from the liquid soap   /   covered the water's surface.

S                               P

Smoke from the burning schoolhouse   /   blackened the midday sky.

1. The hills across the valley of the Ebro were long and white.
                                   —Ernest Hemingway
2. Civilizations decay.
3. Will the Protestants of Northern Ireland ever make peace with the Catholics?
4. Man without writing cannot long retain his history in his head.
                                     —Loren Eiseley
5. At once a black fin slit the pink cloud on the water, shearing it in two.                       —Annie Dillard

### Exercise 2   Sentence Expanding with Modifiers

Expand each of the following sentences by adding modifiers to both the subject and the predicate.

EXAMPLE
I fidgeted.
EXPANDED: Sitting in the back row, I fidgeted restlessly during the long lecture.

1. Sylvester [a cat] hissed.
2. Boys shouted.
3. Birds sang.
4. John grinned.
5. Claude mumbled.

# 10.6   Compounds

By means of a conjunction, such as *and,* any part of a simple sentence may be turned into a **compound phrase:**

> s        P
> Steve *and* Cynthia   /   yelled.

> s         P
> Steve *and* Cynthia   /   yelled *and* pounded.

> s          P
> Steve *and* Cynthia   /   yelled at the top of their lungs *and* pounded
> the heavy oak door.

>                   s
> Soaked to the bone *and* shivering in the wind, Steve *and* Cynthia   /
>       P
> yelled at the top of their lungs *and* pounded the heavy oak door.

> s            P
> Karen   /   is the captain of the soccer team *and* the president of
> her class.

(For a full discussion of compound phrases, see section 13.2, pp. 247–49.)

### EXERCISE 3   Sentence Expanding with Compounds

Expand each of the sentences in exercise 2, p. 206, by using compounds wherever possible.

> EXAMPLE
> I fidgeted.
> EXPANDED: Craig and I yawned and fidgeted.

### EXERCISE 4   Sentence Expanding with Compounds and Modifiers

Expand each of the sentences in exercise 2, p. 206, by using compounds and modifiers wherever possible.

> EXAMPLE
> I fidgeted.
> EXPANDED: Sitting in the back row and shuffling our feet, Craig and I yawned and fidgeted restlessly during the long and boring lecture.

### EXERCISE 5   Composing: Subjects and Objects

Add a subject and direct object to each of the following verbs to make a simple sentence. Also add any modifiers that come to mind.

> EXAMPLE
> devastated
> A savage tornado devastated the town of Wichita Falls, Texas, in 1979.

1. hugged
2. tackled
3. created
4. stung
5. splashed

### EXERCISE 6 Composing: Objects

Some verbs can be intransitive in one sentence and transitive in another. For each of the following verbs, write one sentence in which the verb does not have a direct object and another in which it does have one. Add any modifiers that come to mind.

> EXAMPLE
> cheered
> The crowd cheered.
> The crowd cheered Henniker's spectacular catch.

1. sang
2. painted
3. stretched

## 10.7 Faulty Predication  *pred*

**Faulty predication** is the use of a linking verb between two expressions that are not equivalent. Consider this example:

> *Another kind of flying is a glider.

The sentence says that an activity—*flying*—is equivalent to an object—*a glider*. But an activity and an object are not equivalent. When you declare equivalence between two things that are not equivalent, your predication is faulty. To correct the sentence, you must make them equivalent:

> Another kind of flying is gliding. [or] Another type of aircraft is a glider.

Here is another sentence with faulty predication:

> *The reason for the evacuation of the building was because a bomb threat had been made.

This sentence tries to say that a *reason* is *because*. Those two words seem to go together, but they are not equivalent; *reason* is a noun, and *because* is not. To correct the sentence, use *that* instead of *because:*

> The reason for the evacuation of the building was that a bomb threat had been made.

*That a bomb threat had been made* is a noun clause, the equivalent of a noun. (For a full discussion of noun clauses, see section 15.3, pp. 271–73.)

Here is another example of faulty predication:

*One unanswered question is the author of the play.

This sentence tries to say that a question is a person. It is not. If you are going to say what the question is, you need to write it out:

One unanswered question is "Who wrote the play?"

Alternatively, you can say:

The author of the play is unknown.

Here is one more example:

*A picnic is when you eat outdoors.

This sentence tries to say that a picnic is a particular time, a *when*. It is not a particular time, but an event or occasion that may occur at different times. Here is one way of rewriting the sentence:

A picnic is an outdoor meal.

Use *when* only to define a particular time or season:

Autumn is when leaves turn red, birds fly south, and classes start.

### Exercise 7  Recognizing Correct Predication

Each of the following consists of two sentences with linking verbs. In one sentence the predication is correct; in the other it is faulty. Copy out the sentence with correct predication, and underline the two equivalent words or word groups.

EXAMPLE
(a) Another kind of flying is gliding.
(b) Another kind of flying is a glider.
a. Another kind of <u>flying</u> is <u>gliding.</u>

1. (a) Running a political campaign is where you have to sell a personality.
   (b) Running a political campaign is a process of selling a personality.
2. (a) The main fault of Claghorn's speeches was the offense they gave to voters over sixty.
   (b) The main fault of Claghorn's speeches was how they offended voters over sixty.
3. (a) Sean's greatest achievement was when he predicted the scores of ten straight games correctly.
   (b) Sean's greatest achievement was predicting the scores of ten straight games correctly.

4. (a) An effective way to promote self-confidence in children is to encourage them to do things for themselves.
   (b) An effective way to promote self-confidence in children is doing things for themselves.
5. (a) A funny moment in the show is when the villain falls into a pile of wet cement.
   (b) A funny moment in the show is the villain falling into a pile of wet cement.
6. (a) The reason for the lawsuit was because the paper had published a lie.
   (b) The reason for the lawsuit was that the paper had published a lie.

### EXERCISE 8   Composing: Using Correct Predication

Each of the following consists of one whole sentence and the first part of another. Complete the second sentence with a phrase like the one italicized in the first.

> EXAMPLE
> Religion is *the opium of the people*. —Karl Marx
> Television is   the junk food of the mind.

1. The best way to shed weight is *to change your eating habits*.
   The quickest way to lose money is —————.
2. My father's favorite summertime activity is *barbecuing steak*.
   My own favorite summertime activity is —————.
3. My father's favorite wintertime activity is *watching hockey on TV*.
   My own favorite wintertime activity is —————.
4. A graduating high school senior is *a nervous diver standing on a very high board*.
   A first-term college freshman is —————.
5. To play football for Vince Lombardi was *to become part of a goal-scoring machine*.
   To run a marathon is —————.
6. The big car has lately become *a big headache*.
   The small car has lately become —————.

# 11

# MODIFIERS

## 11.1 What Modifiers Do

A **modifier** is a word or word group that describes, limits, or qualifies another word or word group in a sentence. Consider what modifiers can do for this sentence:

The balloons rose.

This is a bare-bones sentence. It has a subject (*balloons*) and a predicate (*rose*), but no modifiers (except *The*), no words to tell us what the balloons looked like or how they rose. Modifiers can show the reader the size, color, and shape of a thing, or the way an action is performed. Thus they can help to make a sentence vivid, specific, emphatic, and lively:

The balloons rose *slowly, big, red, and round, bobbing and weaving toward the fluffy white clouds.*

Modifiers also let you add information without adding more sentences. If you had to start a new sentence for every new piece of detail, you would soon begin to sound monotonous:

The balloons rose.
They rose *slowly.*
They were *big.*
They were *red.*
They were *round.*

Instead of serving up information in bite-size pieces like these, you can arrange the pieces in one simple sentence, putting each piece where it belongs:

The *big, red, round* balloons rose *slowly*.

There is often more than one place in a sentence where a modifier can go. You can add the word *slowly* to either end of a base sentence, or you can drop it into the middle:

The balloons rose *slowly*.
*Slowly* the balloons rose.
The balloons *slowly* rose.

(For a full discussion of how to place modifiers, see sections 11.10–11.11, pp. 229–32.)

Anything from a single word to an entire clause can be used as a modifier. In chapter 15, pp. 292–32, we treat modifying clauses; here we treat modifying words and phrases. They include adjectives, adverbs, participles, infinitives, appositives, and absolute phrases. We consider each of these in turn.

## 11.2 Adjectives and Adjective Phrases

An **adjective** is a word that modifies a noun, specifying such things as how many, what kind, and which one:

*Three big* balloons exploded.
In the *cool green* shade I licked an *orange* Popsicle.
Martha drove the *shiny new* Buick down the *long dusty* road.

As shown in the preceding chapter (p. 203), an adjective that modifies the subject of a sentence can appear in the predicate after a linking verb, and is then called a predicate adjective:

[s] The kick / [p] was *good*.

An **adjective phrase** is a group of words modifying a noun; it usually tells more about the noun than a single adjective can:

She grew up in a *large* house. [adjective]
She grew up in a house *with twenty-five rooms*. [adjective phrase]

Like a single adjective, an adjective phrase that modifies the subject of a sentence can appear in the predicate after a linking verb:

[s] The city / [p] was *in debt*.

A phrase that starts with a preposition—a word like *with, under, by, of,* or *at*—is called a **prepositional phrase.** Phrases of this type are often used as adjectives, to modify nouns. Here are further examples:

It was Seymour, *with a bottle*.
Twenty-dollar bills sprouted from the pockets *of his coat*.

The grin *on his face* lit up the street.
The gleam *in his eye* was triumphant.
His day *at the racetrack* had made him rich.

Since adjective phrases contain nouns, you can add adjectives and other adjective phrases to them:

It was Seymour, *with a big bottle.*
It was Seymour, *with a big bottle of champagne.*
It was Seymour, *with a big bottle of champagne in his hand.*
Twenty-dollar bills sprouted from the pockets *of his red plaid coat.*

Like other modifiers, two or more adjective phrases can be made into a compound:

It was Seymour, *with a big bottle of champagne in his hand, a mile-wide grin on his jolly fat face, and a triumphant gleam in his eye.*

Adjectives and adjective phrases can modify any noun in a sentence. See what they do for this sentence:

Mike kicked the ball through the window.
Mike kicked the *hard white* ball through the window.
Mike kicked the *hard white* ball through the *big, new, expensive* window.
Mike kicked the *hard white* ball through the *big, new, expensive* window *of the restaurant.*
Mike kicked the *hard white* ball through the *big, new, expensive* window *of the Italian restaurant.*
Mike kicked the *hard white* ball through the *big, new, expensive* window *of the Italian restaurant on the corner of Main Street and Shearing Boulevard.*

You can enrich any sentence by adding adjectives to its nouns in this way. And whenever you add an adjective phrase that contains a noun, you can modify that noun with still another adjective or adjective phrase. Thus the window *of the restaurant* becomes the window *of the Italian restaurant* and then the window *of the Italian restaurant on the corner of Main Street and Shearing Boulevard.*

## 11.3   Nouns in Place of Adjectives

A noun used before another noun often serves as an adjective. Like an adjective, it modifies the word that comes next:

Cars may not travel in the *bus* lane.
A *stone* wall surrounded the farm.
An orthopedist is a *bone* doctor.
Mike kicked the hard white *soccer* ball through the window.

*mod*

| 11.4 |
|------|

It is perfectly all right to use a single noun in place of an adjective, but you should avoid overusing nouns in this way. Too many nouns run together make a sentence confusing:

> The fund drive completion target date postponement gave the finance committee extension time to raise contributions.

In this sentence the nouns are simply thrown together, and the reader is left to figure out how they relate to one another. To clarify the sentence, turn some of the nouns into ordinary adjectives or adjective phrases:

> The postponement of the target date for completion of the fund drive gave the finance committee additional time to raise contributions.

## 11.4   Adverbs and Adverb Phrases

An **adverb** is a word that modifies a verb, an adjective, another adverb, or a whole sentence. It tells such things as how, when, where, why, and for what purpose. Consider first an adverb modifying a verb:

> The balloons rose *slowly*.

*Slowly* is an adverb that tells something about how the balloons rose. Like most adverbs, it consists of an adjective (*slow*) plus the ending *-ly*. In speech we often neglect the distinction between adverbs and adjectives, saying things like "We stopped quick"; but in formal writing most adjectives need *-ly* before they can be used as adverbs.

Even in formal writing, however, some words are the same whether they are used as adjectives or as adverbs. Compare:

1. We made a *quick* stop. [adjective]
   We stopped *quickly*. [adverb]

2. We made a *fast* stop. [adjective]
   We stopped *fast*. [adverb]

If you aren't sure whether a particular word needs *-ly* when used as an adverb, look it up in a dictionary.

Just as you can modify a noun with an adjective phrase, you can modify a verb with an **adverb phrase:**

> The balloons rose *at noon.*
> The balloons rose *in the distance.*
> The balloons rose *with the wind.*
> The balloons rose *against the blue sky.*
> The balloons rose *in a great red cluster.*

**214   Modifiers**

Each of the italicized phrases modifies the verb *rose,* telling when, where, or how the balloons rose. (Within some of the phrases, the nouns have adjectives: *blue* modifies *sky; great* and *red* modify *cluster.*) *At, in, with,* and *against* are all prepositions; as these examples show, an adverb phrase is often a prepositional phrase used as an adverb. An adverb phrase can also start with *like:*

> Holmes used his right fist *like a sledgehammer.*
> Missing the beat completely, Elmer danced *like an elephant.*

Besides modifying a verb, an adverb or adverb phrase can modify an adjective, another adverb or adverb phrase, or a whole sentence.

**1.** Modifying an adjective:

> The bolt was *dangerously* loose.
> Joan gasped, wide-eyed and red *to the roots of her hair.*

**2.** Modifying another adverb:

> Light travels *amazingly* fast.
> He spoke haltingly *at first.*

**3.** Modifying a whole sentence:

> The bolt was loose.
> That was unfortunate.
> COMBINED: *Unfortunately,* the bolt was loose.

> The bolt was loose.
> That was its condition at the start of the flight.
> COMBINED: *At the start of the flight* the bolt was loose.

**EXERCISE 1   Sentence Combining**

Combine the sentences in each of the following sets by using the first sentence as a base and adding modifiers (shown in italics) from the others. Combine the sentences of each set in at least two different ways. Then, if you prefer one of the combinations, put a check next to it.

> EXAMPLE
> The balloons hung.
> They were *in the air.*
> They were *big.*
> They were *red.*
> They were *round.*
> They were *like apples.*
> The apples were *oversized.*
> The apples were *enormously* so.
> COMBINATION 1: The balloons hung in the air, big, red, and round, like enormously oversized apples.

COMBINATION 2: Big, red, and round, the balloons hung in the air like enormously oversized apples.

1. The trumpeter blew.
   He was *fat*.
   He was *sweaty*.
   He was *red*.
   The redness was *in his face*.
   He blew *stridently*.
   He was *like an archangel*.
   The archangel was *mad*.
   The archangel was *hopelessly* so.
   The archangel was *drunken*.
   The archangel was *outrageously* so.

2. The president spoke.
   His speech was *in a certain kind of voice*.
   The voice was *low*.
   It was *chillingly* so.
   He was *stiff*.
   He was *somber*.
   He was *grim*.
   The grimness was *at the mouth*.
   He was *like a captain*.
   The captain was *in charge of a ship*.
   The ship was *sinking*.
   It was doing that *steadily*.

3. Ellen stood.
   She did so *during most of the evening*.
   She did so *elegantly*.
   She was *against a column*.
   The column was *fluted*.
   The column was *white*.
   The column was *on the terrace*.
   The terrace was *flagstone*.

## 11.5   Comparatives and Superlatives

The comparative and the superlative are forms of the adjective and the adverb. The **comparative** is used to compare one thing with another; the **superlative** is used to compare one thing with all others in a group of three or more:

> Jake is *tall*.
> Jake is *taller* than Steve. [comparative]
> Jake is the *tallest* man on the basketball team. [superlative]

All three of the italicized words—*tall, taller,* and *tallest*—modify *Jake,* but each does so in a different way.

## Comparatives

When you add *-er* to some adjectives, you make them comparative. A **comparative adjective** starts a comparison between two different things or sets of things. Normally the comparison must be completed by *than* plus a noun or noun equivalent:

> Marilyn is *taller* than her brother.
> Dolphins are *smarter* than sharks.
> Skiing is *riskier* than skating.

With a long adjective, you form the comparative by using *more* rather than *-er:*

> Jake is *more aggressive* than Steve.

You can use *less* with an adjective of any length:

> Harrigan is *less experienced* than Rosenberg.

Do not use *-er* and *more* at the same time:

> *Marilyn is more taller than her brother

To form a **comparative adverb** use *more* before an adverb ending in *-ly;* otherwise, add *-er:*

> The north star shines *more brightly* than any other star.
> Corrigan runs *faster* than Pelz.

Use *less* before any adverb:

> Wood heats *less expensively* than oil.

(For more on comparisons, see section 15.6, pp. 286–87.)

## Superlatives

When you add *-est* to some adjectives, you make them superlative. A **superlative adjective** normally compares one thing with all others in its class:

> Jake is the *tallest* man on the basketball team.
> St. Petersburg is the *oldest* city in Florida.
> The blue whale is the *largest* of all living creatures.

With a long adjective, you form the superlative by using *most* rather than *-est:*

> Jake is the *most aggressive* player on the team.

You can use *least* with an adjective of any length:

> Harrigan is the *least experienced* man on the job.

Do not use *-est* and *most* at the same time:

> *St. Petersburg is the most oldest city in Florida.

Normally, you also use *most* or *least* to form a **superlative adverb:**

> Everybody said that ours was the *most lavishly* decorated float in the whole parade.
> Of all grammatical forms, the superlative adverb is perhaps the one *least commonly* used.

### Special Forms

Some modifiers have special forms for the comparative and superlative:

| POSITIVE | COMPARATIVE | SUPERLATIVE |
|---|---|---|
| good [adjective] <br> well [adverb] | better | best |
| bad [adjective] <br> badly [adverb] | worse | worst |
| little [adjective and adverb, for quantity] | less | least |
| much [adjective and adverb] | more | most |
| far [adjective and adverb] | farther | farthest |

## 11.6  Participles and Participle Phrases

Another way to modify nouns is to use a **participle,** a word you normally make by adding *-ing, -d,* or *-ed* to the bare form (present tense) of a verb. You make a present participle by adding *-ing;* you normally make a past participle by adding *-d* or *-ed;* you form other participles by using *having* or *having been* with the past participle. Participles of all of these types can be used as modifiers. (The present participle can also be used as a noun, as shown in chapter 12, pp. 240–46.)

### Present Participles

The **present participle** modifies a noun by describing it as acting:

> Sullivan stood up on his chair.
> He was shouting.
> COMBINED: Sullivan stood up on his chair, *shouting.*

*Shouting* is a present participle. In the second sentence it is part of the verb phrase *was shouting;* in the combined sentence, it is used as a modifier of the noun *Sullivan.* Because it is based on a transitive verb (*shout*), this present participle can take a direct object. The group of words thus formed is a **participle phrase:**

> Sullivan stood up on his chair, *shouting insults.*

Nearly all present participles can be modified by adverbs and adverb phrases. The result is again a participle phrase:

> Ruth doubled over.
> She was laughing uncontrollably at the sight of Frank.
> COMBINED: Ruth doubled over, *laughing uncontrollably at the sight of Frank.*
>
> Sullivan stood up on his chair.
> He was furiously shouting insults at the startled speaker.
> COMBINED: Sullivan stood up on his chair, *furiously shouting insults at the startled speaker.*

A present participle or participle phrase can modify any noun in a sentence—not just the subject:

> The prospector studied the gold dust *shining brightly in his hand.*
> I backed away from the *barking* dogs.
> Ruth doubled over, laughing uncontrollably at the sight of Frank *wearing a bright red wig.*

## Past Participles

The **past participle** modifies a noun by describing it as acted upon:

> The heavyweight sank.
> He was exhausted.
> He was battered.
> He was beaten.
> COMBINED: The heavyweight sank, *exhausted, battered,* and *beaten.*

*Exhausted, battered,* and *beaten* are all past participles modifying *heavyweight.* When used in this way, the past participle is like a verb in the passive voice. It cannot take a direct object, but it can take a *by* phrase:

> The heavyweight sank, *exhausted, battered,* and *beaten by his relentless opponent.*

Like the present participle, the past participle can usually be modified, and the result is a participle phrase:

> The heavyweight sank, *thoroughly exhausted and beaten in every way.*

Also like the present participle, the past participle or participle phrase can modify any noun in a sentence:

> My grandfather gave me a whalebone figure *carved by a sailor before the Civil War.*

My sister and I found an *injured* hawk.

Politicians *influenced by flattery* talk of victory at receptions *given by self-serving backers.*

*Watched by thirty thousand fascinated fans,* Tom Seaver pitched a shut-out *marked by sixteen strikeouts and no walks.*

Most past participles are formed by the addition of *-d* or *-ed* to the present form of the verb, so that *dare* becomes *dared,* *work* becomes *worked,* and *praise* becomes *praised.* But a few have special or "irregular" forms. For example, the past participle of *buy* is *bought;* that of *swim* is *swum;* that of *fly* is *flown.* (For a full list of irregular past participles, see section 20.5, pp. 349–53.)

The past participle has a progressive form:

*By being tortured,* he was finally made to give up his secret.

But since this construction often sounds awkward and wordy, you do well to avoid it when you can:

Torture finally made him give up his secret.

*By being defeated,* I had my self-confidence shaken.
REVISED: Defeat shook my self-confidence.

**Perfect Participles**

The **perfect participle** modifies a noun by describing it as having acted:

Baker dropped out of the presidential race.
He had lost four straight primaries.
COMBINED: *Having lost* four straight primaries, Baker dropped out of the presidential race.

*Having lost* is a perfect participle. It denotes action already complete. Here is another example:

*Having completed* his mission for the day, the astronaut reentered the spaceship.

Instead of using the perfect participle, you can use *after* with the present participle:

*After losing* four straight primaries, Baker dropped out of the presidential race.

*After completing* his mission for the day, the astronaut reentered the spaceship.

The passive form of the perfect participle modifies a noun by describing it as having been acted upon:

*Having been denounced* as a traitor, the famous singer could not appear at the benefit performance.

But instead of this construction you can use *after being* with the past participle, or—to cut out needless words—you can use the past participle all by itself:

> The famous singer could not appear at the benefit performance *after being denounced* as a traitor. [or] *Denounced* as a traitor, the famous singer could not appear at the benefit performance.

### Participles and Commas

Normally a participle or participle phrase should be set off by one or more commas from the word or phrase it modifies:

> *Stalking her prey noiselessly,* the cat crept up to the mouse.
> The mouse, *frightened,* darted off into a hole.
> The cat squealed, *clawing the hole in vain.*

In some cases, however, you should omit the commas.

**1.** Don't use commas to set off a single participle when it is part of a noun phrase:

> A *raging* wind fanned the flames.
> The *exhausted* fighter sank to his knees.
> Let *sleeping* dogs lie.

**2.** Don't use commas to set off a single participle when it immediately follows a verb:

> The cat lay *sleeping* on the floor.
> The fighter sank *exhausted* to his knees.
> Steve walked *muttering* out of the room.

**3.** Don't use commas to set off a participle phrase when it restricts—that is, specifies—the meaning of the word or phrase it modifies:

> The prospector studied the gold dust *shining brightly in his hand.*
> Students *majoring in economics* must take at least one course in statistics.

In both of these sentences the participle phrase is essential to the meaning of the word it modifies. (For more on restrictive and non-restrictive modifiers, see p. 391.)

EXERCISE 2   **Sentence Combining**

Combine the sentences in each of the following sets by using the first sentence as a base and turning each of the others into a modifying participle or participle phrase. Combine the sentences of each set in at least two different ways. Then, if you prefer one of the combinations, put a check next to it.

EXAMPLE

Ruth doubled over.

She was laughing uncontrollably.

She was laughing at the sight of Frank.

Frank was wearing a bright red wig.

COMBINATION 1: Ruth doubled over, laughing uncontrollably at the sight of Frank wearing a bright red wig.

COMBINATION 2: Laughing uncontrollably at the sight of Frank wearing a bright red wig, Ruth doubled over.

1. The man looked at the sky.
   The man was startled.

2. The baby amused onlookers.
   The baby was laughing.

3. Corporal Grey stared straight ahead during inspection.
   Corporal Grey was trained to show no emotion.

4. The spaniel hid under the big easy chair.
   The spaniel was frightened by crashes of thunder.
   The crashes of thunder were resounding above the cabin.

5. The apartment building will house tenants.
   The apartment building is now being constructed on Ocean Drive.
   The tenants will be earning under fifteen thousand dollars a year.

6. At the track we watched a driver.
   The driver was practicing starts in a new car.
   The car was designed by Fenmore Wheel.

7. I could not get out of my chair.
   I had eaten five éclairs.
   The éclairs were filled with custard.
   The éclairs were coated with Danish chocolate.

8. The combination included a manager, a team of veterans, and a rookie.
   The combination was a winning one.
   The manager was jesting.
   The veterans were aiming for their first pennant.
   The rookie was yearning to make his name.

### EXERCISE 3   Sentence Combining

Combine the sentences in each of the following sets by using the first sentence as a base and adding modifiers from the others. Some modifiers may have to be combined with each other before they can be joined to the base sentence. Combine the sentences of each set in at least two different ways. Then, if you prefer one of the combinations, put a check next to it.

EXAMPLE
The bird sailed.
He did so for hours.
He was searching the grasses.
The grasses were blanched.
The grasses were below him.
He was searching with his eyes.
The eyes were telescopic.
He was gaining height.
He was gaining it against the wind.
He was descending in swoops.
The swoops were mile-long.
The swoops were gently declining.

—Deliberately altered from a sentence by
Walter Van Tilburg Clark

COMBINATION 1: The bird sailed for hours, searching the blanched grasses below him with his telescopic eyes, gaining height against the wind, descending in mile-long, gently declining swoops.

COMBINATION 2: Searching the blanched grasses below him with his telescopic eyes, gaining height against the wind, descending in mile-long, gently declining swoops, the bird sailed for hours.

1. Wally sang.
   He was soulful.
   He was swaying.
   He was sensuous.
   He was dressed in a skinsuit.
   The skinsuit was glittering.
   The skinsuit was white.
   The skinsuit was satin.
   He was stroking his guitar.
   The guitar was electric.
   He stroked with fingers.
   The fingers were long.
   The fingers were pink.
   The fingers were nimble.
   The fingers were well manicured.

2. The quarterback lay.
   He was on the yard line.
   It was the fortieth.
   He was panting.
   He was still clutching the ball.
   He was nearly smothered.
   The smothering was done by the linebackers.
   There were two linebackers.
   They were burly.
   They were sprawled.
   They were on top of him.

Exercise 4  Sentence Expanding with Modifiers

Expand each of the following sentences by adding as many modifiers as possible. Let your imagination go.

1. The gorilla roared.
2. The flames crackled.
3. The clown danced.
4. The rock-climber slipped.
5. The building shook.

(Keep the sentences you write for this exercise. You will need them again for exercise 14, p. 235.)

## 11.7  Infinitives and Infinitive Phrases

Still another way to modify a word or word group is to use an **infinitive,** a form usually made by the placing of *to* before the bare form of a verb. (The infinitive can also be used as a noun, as shown in chapter 12, pp. 240–46.) An infinitive can modify almost any part of a sentence:

Chichester set out *to sail.*

The infinitive modifies *set out,* a verb phrase.

After years away from the bullring, the legendary El Cordobes was eager *to return.*

The infinitive modifies *eager,* an adjective.

Asked *to dance,* she smiled and nodded.

The infinitive modifies *Asked,* a participle.

Civilization has never eradicated the urge *to hunt.*

The infinitive modifies *urge,* a noun.

Like some verbs, some infinitives can take a direct object. The group of words thus formed is an **infinitive phrase:**

Chichester set out *to sail a boat.*
Desperate *to find the key,* we looked everywhere.
The timekeeper fired his gun *to start the race.*

Whether or not they take a direct object, most infinitives can be expanded with modifiers. In either case the result is again an infinitive phrase:

*To write effectively,* you must know something about sentence structure.
On August 27, 1966, Sir Francis Chichester set out *to sail a 53-foot boat singlehandedly around the world.*

Jan shuffled off, dismayed *to find the old house empty.*
Madame Curie did many experiments *to prove the existence of radium.*

An infinitive or infinitive phrase that modifies a verb usually expresses purpose. You can emphasize the purpose by putting *in order* before the infinitive:

Some men will do anything *in order to win.*
The actors rehearsed twice a day *in order to be ready for the October 3 opening.*

Use *in order for* when an introductory infinitive is preceded by a noun:

*In order for the plan to work,* everybody had to be on time.

Do not start with *for* alone:

*\*For the plan to work,* everybody had to be on time.

Infinitives occasionally include *be, have,* or *have been;* these infinitives are made with the past participle:

The work *to be done* that morning seemed enormous. Sandra was glad *to have slept* a full eight hours the night before. But she was annoyed *to have been told* nothing of this work earlier.

(For a full discussion of infinitives of this type, see section 20.4, p. 348.)

## Split Infinitives

When one or more adverbs are wedged between *to* and the rest of an infinitive, the infinitive is said to be **split:**

Detectives needed special equipment *to thoroughly and accurately investigate the mystery.*

This sentence is weakened by the cumbersome splitting. The adverbs should go at the end of the infinitive phrase:

Detectives needed special equipment *to investigate the mystery thoroughly and accurately.*

Sometimes an infinitive may be split by a one-word modifier that would be awkward in any other position:

The mayors convened in order *to fully* explore and discuss the problems of managing large cities.

A construction of this type is acceptable nowadays to most readers. (A generation ago, adherence to so-called grammatical rules was stricter than it is today, and the split infinitive was an especially sore point.) But even now, unless you are sure there is no other suitable place in the sentence for the adverb or adverb phrase, do not split the infinitive with it.

EXERCISE 5  **Supplying Infinitives**

Complete each of the following sentences with a suitable infinitive or infinitive phrase.

> EXAMPLE
> The sheer will __to live__ brought him through the operation.

1. A starving prisoner will do almost anything _____ .
2. Man's desire _____ has already taken him to the moon, and may someday take him beyond the solar system.
3. The cheerleader jumped a good three feet off the ground, overjoyed _____ .
4. After thirty-six hours of practically nonstop driving, I was desperate _____ .
5. Columbus sailed west _____ .
6. _____, Brent stopped eating rich desserts.

## 11.8  Appositives

An **appositive** is a noun or noun phrase that is used to identify another noun or noun phrase, or a pronoun:

> Robert Strauss, *the chairman of the Democratic party during Carter's presidency,* resigned after Carter lost the election of 1980.
> Robert Earl Hughes, *the heaviest man ever known,* reached a weight over a thousand pounds before he died of uremia in 1958.
> Michelle bought a new toy, *a Triumph Spitfire.*
> Could I, *a knock-kneed beginner,* ever hope to ski down that icy slope without breaking a leg?

In the first sentence the appositive identifies Robert Strauss; in the second, it identifies Robert Earl Hughes; in the third, it identifies the new toy; in the fourth, it identifies *I.*

### Punctuating Appositives

Normally an appositive is set off by commas, as it is in each of the preceding examples. But you can sometimes set off an appositive with dashes instead, and you should use dashes if it consists of three or more nouns in a series:

> The dog—a big gray German shepherd—went straight for my throat.
> Ninety-foot statues of three Confederate leaders—Jefferson Davis,

<br>

Robert E. Lee, and Stonewall Jackson—have been carved on the face of Stone Mountain in Georgia.

## Placing Appositives

An appositive is usually placed right after the word or phrase it identifies. But it may sometimes come just before:

*A chronic complainer,* he was never satisfied.

### EXERCISE 6   Sentence Combining

Combine the sentences in each of the following pairs by turning the second sentence into an appositive.

EXAMPLE
Could I ever hope to ski down that icy slope without breaking a leg?
I was a knock-kneed beginner.
COMBINED: Could I, a knock-kneed beginner, ever hope to ski down that icy slope without breaking a leg?

1. Mount Everest was first conquered in 1953 by two members of a British expedition.
   Mount Everest is the highest mountain in the world.

2. One of the two was Edmund Hillary.
   He was a New Zealander.

3. The other was Tenzing Norkay.
   He was a Nepalese guide.

4. Hillary and Colonel John Hunt were knighted for their achievement.
   Hunt was the leader of the expedition.

5. Since the British conquest of Everest, several other countries have sent climbers to the summit.
   Those other countries are Switzerland, America, India, and Japan.

6. Could I ever get to the summit of Everest?
   I am a weekend backpacker.

7. She stole the show.
   She was a born actress.

## 11.9   Absolute Phrases

An **absolute phrase** is a modifier usually made from a noun or noun phrase and a participle. It modifies the whole of the base sentence to which it is attached:

Donna laughed.
Her eyes were flashing.
COMBINED: Donna laughed, *her eyes flashing.*

*Her eyes flashing* modifies the whole of the base sentence, *Donna laughed,* telling how Donna looked when she laughed. Absolute phrases often start with a pronoun like *his* or *her,* but just as often they start with a noun alone:

*Eyes flashing,* Donna laughed.

The participle in an absolute phrase can be expanded into a participle phrase:

Donna laughed, *eyes flashing with mischief.*

You can also make an absolute phrase with certain other combinations.

**1.** Noun and adverb:

*Head down,* the bull charged straight at the man.

**2.** Noun and adverb phrase:

*Nose in the air,* she walked right past me.

**3.** Noun and adjective:

*Eyes bright,* Peg shot up her hand.

**4.** Noun and adjective phrase:

*Eyes bright as new pennies,* Peg shot up her hand.

Finally, you can compound absolute phrases, and you can use them in succession:

*Eyes bright and flashing with mischief,* Donna laughed.

The Texan turned to the nearest gatepost and climbed to the top of it, *his alternate thighs thick and bulging in the tight jeans, the butt of his pistol catching and losing the sun in pearly gleams.*
—William Faulkner

The skaters are quick-silvering around the frosty rink, *the girls gliding and spinning, the boys swooping, their arms flailing like wings.*
—College student

He stood at the top of the stairs and watched me, *I waiting for him to call me up, he hesitating to come down, his lips nervous with the suggestion of a smile, mine asking whether the smile meant come, or go away.*
—College student

EXERCISE 7    **Sentence Combining**

Combine the sentences in each of the following sets by using the first sentence as a base and turning the others into absolute phrases.

EXAMPLE
Donna laughed.
Her eyes were flashing.
COMBINED: Donna laughed, her eyes flashing. [or] Eyes flashing, Donna laughed.

1. Finch dozed.
   His chin was on his chest.

2. I gripped the wheel of the skidding car.
   My knuckles were white.
   My hair was standing on end.
   My stomach was heaving.

3. Janet rode the big wave.
   Her shoulders were hunched.
   Her hair was streaming in the wind.
   Her toes were curled over the edge of the board.

4. Traffic inched along.
   Horns were honking.
   Truck drivers were yelling.
   Policemen were whistling and flailing their arms.

5. Reese studied the board.
   His forehead was wrinkled.
   His mouth was pursed.
   His watch was ticking.

## 11.10   Placing Modifiers

One of the hardest things about writing an effective sentence is that unless you can plan it out completely in your head beforehand, you may not know at once the best way to arrange all of its parts. You know by habit, of course, that an adjective usually comes before the noun it modifies. You don't write *leaves green* or *fumes smelly* or *brass hot;* you write *green leaves, smelly fumes,* and *hot brass.* But the placing of other modifiers—especially modifying phrases— may call for some thought. Often, in fact, you will not be able to decide where to put a particular modifier until *after* you have written out the whole sentence in which it appears.

While you are writing a sentence, therefore, don't worry about where to place the modifiers. Just start with the base sentence and put the modifiers at the end, simply to get them down on paper. Thus, instead of having to plan out the whole sentence in advance, you can make it up as you write, adding modifiers as you think of them, using one modifier to lead you to another. Consider the way this sentence grows:

Mary traveled.

Where from?

> Mary traveled *from Denver.*

Where to?

> Mary traveled *from Denver to San Francisco.*

How?

> Mary traveled *from Denver to San Francisco by hitchhiking.*

Did she hitchhike all the way?

> Mary traveled *from Denver to San Francisco by hitchhiking to the house of a friend in Salt Lake City.*

And how did she finish the trip?

> Mary traveled *from Denver to San Francisco by hitchhiking to the house of a friend in Salt Lake City and then borrowing his motorcycle to make the rest of the trip.*

Now, having written your base sentence and added as many modifiers as you want, you can think about where to place those modifiers. You may decide, for instance, that you want to put most of them up front instead of at the end. In that case, bracket the words you want to move and use an arrow to show where they are to go:

> Mary traveled from Denver to San Francisco [by hitchhiking to the house of a friend in Salt Lake City and then borrowing his motorcycle to make the rest of the trip.]

When you rewrite the sentence, it will look like this:

> By hitchhiking to the house of a friend in Salt Lake City and then borrowing his motorcycle to make the rest of the trip, Mary traveled from Denver to San Francisco.

Do you like this version better than the other? That's the kind of question you will have to answer for yourself. If you want to state a simple point and then develop it, you will lead with that point and put the modifiers after it; you will first say where Mary went and then explain how she got there. But if you want to create suspense, if you want the reader to wait for a main point that is delivered at the end like a knockout punch, you will put all or most of your modifiers first. You will make the reader travel to the end of the sentence to discover Mary's destination.

So what does placing modifiers really mean in practice? Do you have to rearrange the words of every sentence just as soon as you've written it? No, you don't. *But you do have to develop the habit of considering various possibilities.* Good writers know that almost every sentence can be arranged in more than one way. As you develop your writing skill, you will learn how to place modifying phrases while you are composing a sentence instead of after you have completed it. But the longer and more complicated your sentences become, the more carefully you must consider how to arrange them. And the more you consciously study the art of placing your modifiers, the better you will write.

Placing a modifier well means not only creating a particular effect but also connecting the modifier to its **headword**—the word or phrase it modifies. If it doesn't clearly point to its headword, the modifier is *misplaced;* if it can't point to a headword because the headword is completely missing from the sentence, the modifier *dangles.* These problems are discussed in the next sections.

## 11.11   Misplaced Modifiers   *mm*

A **misplaced** modifier is one that does not clearly point to its headword— the word or phrase it modifies. Compare the following sentences:

1. The balloons rose slowly, big, red, and round, bobbing and weaving toward a fluffy white cloud.
2. The big, red, round balloons rose slowly, bobbing and weaving toward a fluffy white cloud.
3. *The balloons rose slowly, bobbing and weaving toward a fluffy white cloud, big, red, and round.

Sentences 1 and 2 are perfectly clear. Whether the adjectives *big, red,* and *round* come just before *balloons* or just after *slowly,* they clearly point to their headword, *balloons.* But something goes wrong in sentence 3. Because *big, red,* and *round* come right after *cloud,* the sentence seems to be saying that the cloud was big, red, and round. The word *cloud* gets between the modifiers and their true headword, *balloons.*

Here, then, the modifiers are misplaced. They do not clearly point to their true headword, the word they actually modify. To make them do so, you must see that no false headword gets between them and their true headword. The surest way is to put them right next to the true headword, as in sentence 2. But as long as no false headword comes between the two, a modifier and its true headword may be separated by one or more words, as in sentence 1.

Here is another example:

A letter was addressed to the house next door.
By mistake the mailman delivered it to us.

MISCOMBINED: *By mistake the mailman delivered a letter addressed to the house next door to us.

In this case, *the house next door* gets between the modifier, *to us*, and its headword, *delivered*. The result is a mystifying sentence. To clear up the mystery, put *to us* right after its headword:

By mistake the mailman delivered to us a letter addressed to the house next door.

Here is one more example:

A born crapshooter, Sadowski almost won five hundred dollars that night.

Did he win anything at all then? The headword of *almost* seems to be *won*, and a gambler who has *almost won* may actually have lost everything. If Sadowski did win, the true headword of *almost* is *five hundred dollars*, and *almost* belongs next to that:

A born crapshooter, Sadowski won almost five hundred dollars that night.

(Modifiers include not only words and phrases but also clauses. On these, see "Placing Adjective Clauses," pp. 278–79, and "Placing Adverb Clauses," pp. 284–85.)

EXERCISE 8   **Recognizing Headwords**

In each of the following sentences a modifier is italicized. Write down the headword of the modifier.

EXAMPLE
The armchair *near the fireplace* was an antique.
armchair

1. Many girls in the audience admired the leaps *of the ballerina*.
2. There is still some sign of life in the maple *struck by lightning last year*.
3. The navy provided *only* two helicopters instead of five.
4. *On reaching the podium*, the victorious candidate grinned and waved to the cheering delegates on the floor below him.
5. The sun will set *at eight o'clock*.

EXERCISE 9   **Recognizing Modifiers**

In each of the following sentences a headword is italicized. Write down the phrase modifying the headword.

EXAMPLE
Uncle Joe gave me *tickets* to the World Series.
to the World Series

1. A *craving* for chocolate ice cream got me out of bed at three o'clock in the morning.
2. Shakespeare's Macbeth speaks of life as "a *tale* told by an idiot."
3. Most of the younger people applying for visas to Australia are *graduates* disheartened by the high rate of unemployment in their countries.
4. Bent over his history text in the now deserted study hall, *Finzer* brooded over the sad lot of bookworms.
5. The fisherman *stared* at the lighthouse.

## EXERCISE 10    Recognizing Well-Placed Modifiers

Each of the following consists of two sentences, one with a misplaced modifier and the other correct. Say which sentence you think is clearer—and why.

EXAMPLE

(a) The restaurant only serves brunch on Sunday.
(b) The restaurant serves brunch on Sunday only.
Sentence *b* is clearer because there is just one possible headword; *only* modifies *on Sunday* and cannot modify anything else. In sentence *a, only* can modify either *serves brunch* or *on Sunday,* so the reader can't tell whether brunch is the only meal served on Sunday or Sunday is the only day on which brunch is served.

1. (a) A nineteenth-century French scientist named Paul Broca weighed hundreds of brains taken from human corpses trying to prove men smarter than women.
   (b) Trying to prove men smarter than women, a nineteenth-century French scientist named Paul Broca weighed hundreds of brains taken from human corpses.
2. (a) The female brains weighed by Broca were on average 14 percent lighter than the male brains.
   (b) The female brains weighed by Broca on average were 14 percent lighter than the male brains.
3. (a) In Broca's opinion this relative lightness proved the intellectual inferiority of women.
   (b) This relative lightness in Broca's opinion proved the intellectual inferiority of women.
4. (a) But Broca made no effort to measure the effect on the size of the brain of body size.
   (b) But Broca made no effort to measure the effect of body size on the size of the brain.
5. (a) Without such a measurement, Broca's findings cannot prove the intellectual superiority of men over women.
   (b) Broca's findings cannot prove the intellectual superiority of men over women without such a measurement.
6. (a) In spite of his claims to objectivity, then, Broca only measured brains to support his prejudices about male superiority.

(b) In spite of his claims to objectivity, then, Broca measured brains only to support his prejudices about male superiority.

EXERCISE 11 **Correcting Misplaced Modifiers**

Revise each of the following sentences that includes a misplaced modifier. If a sentence is correct as it stands, write *Correct*.

EXAMPLE

An article describes the way skunks eat in *Time* magazine.
REVISED: An article in *Time* magazine describes the way skunks eat.

1. We watched the gulls flying over the windswept waves and barren rocks with the aid of powerful binoculars.
2. Despite her inexperience and small size, Coach Jette has said that Sarah Wingate is the best goalie in the league.
3. When visiting the zoo, children should not put their hands between the bars of cages.
4. The detective advised the suspect of his right to consult a lawyer before booking him.
5. Circling steadily overhead, Seymour lay in a hammock and watched the vultures.
6. The pair of antique candlesticks attracted the admiring glances of many visitors shining brightly on the table.
7. She even puts ketchup on her ice cream.
8. After buying presents for my brother and my parents, I only could afford Christmas cards for my uncles and aunts.

EXERCISE 12 **Sentence Combining**

Combine the sentences in each of the following pairs by using the italicized word or phrase in the second sentence as a modifier in the first.

EXAMPLE

The president announced that he would not run for reelection.
He made the announcement *on Monday*.
COMBINED: The president announced on Monday that he would not run for reelection.

1. Meg wanted to see the restaurant owner.
   Meg was *annoyed by the slovenly service and bad food*.

2. Some students open their books on the night before exams.
   That is the *only* time they open their books.

3. The coach said that she was planning to quit her job at the end of the season.
   She made the statement *on Wednesday*.

4. Marianne showed her grandchildren the house where she was born.
   She showed it to them *last week*.

5. As a birthday present, Dawn gave a teddy bear to her little brother.
The teddy bear was colorful, *with green eyes and a big yellow nose.*

EXERCISE 13    Placing Modifiers

Each of the following sentences is followed by a phrase. Use the phrase as a modifier in the sentence and then underline the word or phrase that you want it to modify.

> EXAMPLE
> The senator announced that he would not run for reelection.
> in New York
> The senator <u>announced</u> in New York that he would not run for reelection. [or] The senator announced that he would not <u>run for reelection</u> in New York.

1. The emerald belongs to a family of minerals.
   known as beryl
2. The emerald gets its color from chromium.
   distinctively bright green
3. The emerald was known not only for its beauty but also for its supposed power to cure eye ailments.
   in ancient times
4. Flawless specimens of good color and size bring higher prices than diamonds.
   of equal weight
5. Emeralds are among the most precious of all stones.
   now chiefly mined in Colombia

EXERCISE 14    Correcting Misplaced Modifiers

Look at the sentences with added modifiers that you wrote for exercise 4, p. 224. If any of the modifiers you added do not clearly refer to their headwords, revise the sentences in which they appear.

## 11.12   Dangling Modifiers   *dg*

A modifier dangles when its headword is missing. A modifier always needs a headword, and will attach itself to a false headword if the true one is not in the sentence. For example:

> *Speaking before a crowd of people for the first time, my knees shook.

In this sentence, *Speaking before a crowd of people for the first time* is a modifier. After this modifier, the reader expects to find its headword, the word or phrase it modifies, but what turns up in the headword slot is *knees.* Thus the sentence seems to say that knees were speaking.

Such a mistake, called a **dangling modifier,** results from the miscombination of two sentences. In this instance they are:

I was speaking before a crowd of people for the first time.
My knees shook.

These two sentences have different subjects: *I* and *My knees.* When you combine two sentences like these by making one of them modify the other, you must normally keep both of their subjects:

When I was speaking before a crowd of people for the first time, my knees shook.

This combination turns the first sentence into a subordinate clause. (For a full discussion of subordinate clauses, see chapter 15, pp. 267–89.)

When you combine two sentences, you can normally drop one of the subjects only if it is the same as the other subject. Consider this combination:

I was speaking before a large audience for the first time.
I was nervous.
COMBINED: Speaking before a large audience for the first time, I was nervous.

Here both subjects are the same—*I* and *I*—so the writer can drop one of them. The *I* that is left identifies the speaker and thus serves as the headword of *Speaking before a large audience for the first time.*

Here is another example:

*Standing at fixed attention, the guardsman's bayonet glinted in the noonday sun.

Once again this is a miscombination of two sentences with different subjects:

The guardsman stood at fixed attention.
His bayonet glinted in the noonday sun.

The miscombination keeps both subjects, but turns *guardsman* into a modifier of *bayonet,* so the sentence seems to say that the guardsman's bayonet was standing at attention. To combine the two sentences correctly, you must not only keep the two different subjects, but keep them separate:

As the guardsman stood at fixed attention, his bayonet glinted in the noonday sun. [or] The guardsman stood at fixed attention, his bayonet glinting in the noonday sun.

Here is one more example:

\* Based on the gradual decline in College Board scores over the past twenty years, American high school education is less effective than it used to be.

This is a miscombination of two sentences:

American high school education is less effective than it used to be. This conclusion is based on the gradual decline of College Board scores over the past twenty years.

So how can you combine these two sentences and not leave *Based* dangling? Our advice is kick the *Based* habit altogether. To combine sentences like these, use *shows that, indicates that,* or *leads to the conclusion that:*

The gradual decline of College Board scores over the past twenty years indicates that American high school education is less effective than it used to be.

Now see if you can spot the error in this sentence:

\* By being dominated, men have made women dependent.

Because *men* comes right after *being dominated,* this sentence seems to say that men have been dominated. But the writer actually means to say that women have been dominated. That simple fact has been twisted by a miscombination of these two base sentences:

Women have been dominated.
Men have made women dependent.

Since these two sentences have different subjects, any combination of them must keep both of their subjects. For example:

Since women have been dominated, men have made them dependent.

But this sentence still doesn't tell us who has been dominating women. It fails to do so because the base sentence about domination is in the passive voice, and does not mention the agent—in this instance the person or persons *by whom* women are dominated. That agent should be named:

Women have been dominated by men.

Once the agent is named, this sentence can be changed from the passive to the active voice:

Men have dominated women.

Now see what happens when this version of the sentence is combined with the other base sentence:

Men have dominated women.
Men have made women dependent.
COMBINED: By dominating women, men have made them dependent. [or] Men have made women dependent by dominating them.

To correct your own dangling modifiers, you will often need to change a sentence from the passive to the active voice. (For a full discussion of the active and passive voice, see chapter 22, pp. 365–72. For more advice on how to avoid constructions like *By being dominated* and *having been dominated,* see pp. 220–21.)

### EXERCISE 15    Avoiding Dangling Modifiers

Each of the following consists of two sentences, one with a dangling modifier and the other correct. Say which sentence you think is clearer—and why.

EXAMPLE
(a) While waiting for a bus, a passing car splashed mud all over my skirt.
(b) While I was waiting for a bus, a passing car splashed mud all over my skirt.

Sentence *b* tells plainly who was waiting for a bus. In sentence *a*, *While waiting for a bus* is a dangling modifier, with no headword to support it; we are not clearly told who was waiting.

1. (a) By exploring this problem thoroughly, a solution will hopefully be found.
   (b) By exploring this problem thoroughly, I hope to find a solution.
2. (a) By being overtaxed, the government of California goaded property owners into rebellion.
   (b) By overtaxing property owners, the government of California goaded them into rebellion.
3. (a) While walking to my chemistry final, a dog nipped my leg.
   (b) While I was walking to my chemistry final, a dog nipped my leg.
4. (a) In studying the stars, we must calculate the time which their light takes to reach us.
   (b) In studying the stars, the time which their light takes to reach us must be calculated.

### EXERCISE 16    Correcting Dangling Modifiers

Revise each of the following sentences that includes a dangling modifier. Either supply a headword as best you can, or reconstruct the whole sentence. If a sentence is correct as it stands, write *Correct.*

EXAMPLE
After considering the offer carefully, it was refused.
REVISED: After considering the offer carefully, I refused it.

1. Peering into the fog, only a dim blue light shone in the distance.
2. Dancing to an old Beatles record, the thought of John Lennon's death suddenly ran through my mind.
3. The canoe tipped over while stepping into it.
4. After skipping lunch, I ate a big dinner.
5. Making our way slowly along the winding and bumpy road, a place to eat was finally found.
6. Insisting on her right to be heard, the microphone was seized.
7. Based on the growing number of women in all fields, women have more opportunities than ever before.
8. Looking first of all at the plot, it seems contrived.

## EXERCISE 17 Sentence Combining

Combine the sentences in each of the following pairs by using the italicized words in one sentence as a modifier in the other.

EXAMPLE
I was *painting our house last summer.*
I fell off a ladder and broke my arm
COMBINED: While painting our house last summer, I fell off a ladder and broke my arm.

1. I was *chopping wood last summer.*
   I cut my foot.

2. Harriet was *eager to see the sun rise.*
   She got up at 5:30 A.M.

3. The boats were loaded with refugees.
   The refugees had been *driven out to sea by the Malaysians.*

4. The child stood mute.
   The child was *too frightened to utter a sound.*

5. The plane dropped.
   *Its engines* were *failing.*

## EXERCISE 18 Composing with Modifiers

Each of the following is a phrase that can serve as a modifier. Write a suitable base sentence for each modifier, and attach the modifier to it.

EXAMPLE
upon hearing the news
Upon hearing the news, he let out a whoop.

1. after waiting at the hot, dusty, deserted gas station for an hour and a half
2. sounding the hours with solemn tones
3. ignoring the No Parking sign
4. bringing him down with a flying tackle
5. trying to change the tire with nothing but a jack and a pair of pliers

# 12

# VERBAL NOUNS

**12.1** A **verbal noun** is a present participle or an infinitive used as a noun; it can also be a participle phrase or an infinitive phrase used as a noun. Verbal nouns enable you to treat an action as if it were a thing, and thus to get more action into your sentences:

> The rockets burst.
> That lit up the sky.
> COMBINED: *The bursting of rockets* lit up the sky.

> She won the marathon.
> That took every ounce of her strength.
> COMBINED: *To win the marathon* took every ounce of her strength.

> The dog barked and howled.
> That kept me awake.
> COMBINED: *The barking and howling of the dog* kept me awake.

## 12.1   Types of Verbal Nouns

Verbal nouns are of four types.

**1.** Present participle used as a noun:

> *Singing* makes my head ache.
> *Smoking* can damage your lungs.
> My favorite sport is *swimming.*

(The present participle can also be used as a modifier, as shown in section 11.6, pp. 218–19. On the present participle as part of a verb phrase, see "Using Common and Progressive Forms," p. 337.)

**2.** Infinitive used as a noun:

> She wanted *to win.*
> *To quit* is *to lose.*

You normally form the infinitive by placing *to* before the bare form of the verb. (The infinitive can also be used as a modifier, as shown in section 11.7, pp. 224–26.)

**3.** Participle phrase used as a noun:

> *Smoking cigarettes* can damage your lungs.
> What do we gain by *standing passively on the sidelines?*
> The coach congratulated her for *leading the team to victory.*
> His hobby is *collecting mushrooms.*
> *Swimming every day* keeps me in shape.
> *Sky diving in cloudy weather* can be dangerous.
> My father relaxes by *puttering in his garden.*

**4.** Infinitive phrase used as a noun:

> They tried *to leave the building quietly.*
> *To see clearly* is sometimes hard.
> *To see yourself through the eyes of others* is *to be awakened.*

## 12.2 Using Verbal Nouns

You can use verbal nouns to combine sentences in any of the ways shown here:

> 1. Some photographers develop their own pictures.
>    They like that.
>    COMBINED: Some photographers like *to develop their own pictures.*
>    [or] Some photographers like *developing their own pictures.*

In each of the combined sentences the predicate *develop their own pictures* becomes a verbal noun, the direct object of *like.*

> 2. The young prince had only one ambition.
>    He would be king.
>    COMBINED: The young prince had only one ambition, *to be king.*

The predicate *would be king* here becomes a verbal noun, *to be king.* The verbal noun is used as an appositive modifying *ambition.*

> 3. He saw his father in a clown suit.
>    That tickled him.
>    COMBINED: *To see his father in a clown suit* tickled him. [or] It tickled him *to see his father in a clown suit.*

The predicate *saw his father in a clown suit* here becomes the subject of *tickled.* (In the second version *It* is an introductory filler word, and the subject follows *him.*)

*vn*

12.2

4. He saw his father in a clown suit.
   That was funny.
   COMBINED: It was funny for him *to see his father in a clown suit.*

Note the use of *for* in this example. Normally, a construction of this type should follow the main verb, not precede it. Otherwise your sentence will sound awkward:

For him *to see his father in a clown suit* was funny.

5. She was promoted after just six months on the job.
   That was a triumph.
   COMBINED: It was a triumph for her *to be promoted after just six months on the job.*

Here the passive verb *was promoted* becomes the passive infinitive *to be promoted.* Note again the phrase *for her.* You don't need the *for* phrase if the surrounding sentences make it clear who the infinitive refers to:

*She* was ecstatic. It was a triumph *to be promoted after just six months on the job.*

6. How do you write a research paper?
   Many college freshmen do not know.
   COMBINED: Many college freshmen do not know *how to write a research paper.*

Here the infinitive makes it possible to turn a whole question into a verbal noun, the object of *know.* You can turn a question into a verbal noun by using the infinitive after such words as *how, where, what, whom, whether,* and *when.* Examples of the resulting phrases are *where to go, what to write, whom to see, whether to leave or stay,* and *when to leave.*

7. The candidate had a weakness.
   He forgot people's names.
   That handicapped him at rallies.
   COMBINED: The candidate's weakness—*forgetting people's names*—handicapped him at rallies.

The changing of *forgot* to *forgetting* turns the second sentence into a verbal noun, which is then used as an appositive modifying the noun phrase *The candidate's weakness.* (That phrase is made from the first sentence. When the subject of a sentence is said to *have* something or to *own* something, you can often turn the sentence into an ordinary noun phrase by simply adding *-'s* to the subject and dropping the verb—in this case *had.*)

8. The man shouted.
   That scared me.
   COMBINED: *The man's shouting* scared me.

**242   Verbal Nouns**

To make a verbal noun out of the original sentence in a case like this, you add *-'s* to the subject and change the ending of the verb to *-ing*.

> 9. The man shouted threats.
>    That scared me.
>    COMBINED: *The man's shouting of threats* scared me.

Here again you add *-'s* to the subject and change the ending of the verb to *-ing*. But this time the verb that is changed has an object, *threats*. To keep that object in the combined version, you must normally put *of* in front of it.

> 10. Dylan sang "Blowin' in the Wind."
>     The crowd warmly applauded that.
>     COMBINED: The crowd warmly applauded *Dylan's singing of "Blowin' in the Wind."*

Here again you must add *-'s* to the subject of the original sentence, use the present participle of the verb, and follow it with *of* in order to turn the sentence into a verbal noun. If the subject is a pronoun, it must be changed to the possessive form; thus *He sang "Blowin' in the Wind"* would become *his singing of "Blowin' in the Wind."*

> 11. Samson was strong.
>     He was proud of that.
>     COMBINED: Samson was proud of *being strong*.

The predicate *was strong* becomes the verbal noun *being strong*.

## 12.3   Verbal Nouns and Ordinary Nouns

Sometimes you can turn a sentence into a noun phrase by turning the verb into an ordinary noun instead of a verbal noun. See how these sentences can be combined:

> Hitler invaded Poland.
> That started World War II.
> COMBINED: *Hitler's invading of Poland* started World War II. [or] *Hitler's invasion of Poland* started World War II.

The verb *invaded* can become the verbal noun *invading* or the ordinary noun *invasion*. With *invasion*, the original sentence about Hitler becomes the ordinary noun phrase *Hitler's invasion of Poland*.

## 12.4   Misusing Verbal Nouns   *mvn*

Normally a noun or pronoun used before a verbal noun should be in the possessive case. Otherwise the verbal noun is misused:

*Jack complaining irritated me.
REVISED: *Jack's complaining* irritated me.
*I got sick of him complaining.
REVISED: I got sick of *his complaining.*

(For a full discussion of case in pronouns, see section 18.5, pp 316–19.)

Normally a verbal noun that follows a possessive noun or pronoun should not, in turn, be directly followed by a noun or noun phrase:

*Simpson's winning the lottery made him a millionaire.

Add *of* after *winning:*

Simpson's *winning of the lottery* made him a millionaire.

However, when a preposition appears before the verbal noun, you can skip the *of* after it:

Congress disapproved of *Russia's invading Afghanistan.*
The minister disapproved of *my taking pictures* during the ceremony.

### EXERCISE 1    Recognizing Verbal Nouns

Write down the verbal nouns in each of the following sentences

EXAMPLE
The bursting of rockets lit up the sky.
The bursting of rockets

1. Winning isn't everything; it's the only thing.
                                        —Vince Lombardi
2. We needed to practice.
3. To know him was to loathe him.
4. She loved playing tennis in the morning, swimming in the afternoon, and dancing at night.
5. My notion of relaxing is to lie in a hammock all day long.
6. His tuneless whistling got on my nerves.
7. Everyone loved Samantha's trumpet playing.
8. Barbara's directing of the play was inspired.
9. As we cornered, his grinding of the gears made me think we would lose the transmission altogether.
10. I couldn't stand their arguing all the time.

### EXERCISE 2    Correcting Misused Verbal Nouns

Revise each of the following sentences in which the writer misuses a verbal noun. If a sentence is correct as it stands, write *Correct.*

EXAMPLE
Jack complaining irritated me.
REVISED: Jack's complaining irritated me.

1. Jan resented him seizing the initiative in her project.
2. Alan denying the accusation convinced no one.
3. Davy Crockett defending the Alamo is one of the greatest feats in American history.
4. Vivian yawned; she already knew all about his winning of the election.
5. From Tom wrecking my car to Barbara ditching me, this semester has been a disaster.
6. William gobbling his food annoyed his mother.
7. The Voyager transmitting pictures all the way from Saturn to earth was a technological triumph.


EXERCISE 3   **Sentence Combining**

Combine the sentences in each of the following pairs by turning one of them into a verbal noun or an ordinary noun phrase and joining it to the other. Where you find a set of three sentences, turn two of them into verbal nouns or ordinary noun phrases and join them to the third.

EXAMPLE
He kicked field goals.
That was his specialty.
COMBINED: His specialty was kicking field goals. [or] His specialty was to kick field goals.

1. He played football all day.
   That left him drained.

2. She would become an architect.
   That was her greatest ambition.

3. Motorists waited hours for gas.
   Motorists hated that.

4. The oil companies made huge profits during the oil shortage.
   Many people criticized the oil companies for that.

5. The baby screamed.
   That woke up everyone in the house.

6. He drove the truck through a roadblock.
   That put the police on his tail.

7. The president announced a new policy on the Middle East.
   That pleased the Arabs and disturbed the Israelis.

8. Fred had a fondness for something.
   He ate peanut butter straight out of the jar.

9. Fred had a fondness for something.
   He ate peanut butter straight out of the jar.
   That often amused his friends.

10. The governor worried about just one thing.
    He might lose his campaign for reelection.

11. The little boy rode the elevator all by himself.
    That was scary.

12. We sang.
    That drove the bus driver nuts.

13. Jake recited a spicy limerick.
    We all chuckled at that.

14. The general was saluted by everyone.
    He was accustomed to that.

# 13

# COORDINATION

## 13.1 Using Coordination

To **coordinate** two or more parts of a sentence is to give them the same rank and role by making them grammatically similar. You can coordinate words or phrases to make a compound phrase; likewise, you can coordinate simple sentences to make a compound sentence. The very fact that several ideas and actions of roughly equal weight are joined in one sentence indicates a connection among them, and the use of one conjunction rather than another shows just what the connection is. Further, when some sentences are compound and others are not, the variety of sentence length and structure helps to keep alive the reader's attention.

## 13.2 Compound Phrases

A **compound phrase** joins words or phrases to show such things as a contrast or a choice between them or simply the addition of one to the other. Compound phrasing also helps to tighten your writing by reducing wordiness. When you combine two or more sentences with the same subject or the same predicate, you can cut out the extra subject or predicate at the same time as you show one of the following relations:

**1.** Addition

> The quarterback was smart.
> The quarterback was fast.
> COMBINED: The quarterback was *smart and fast.*

The dancer was lean.
The dancer was acrobatic.
The dancer was bold.
COMBINED: The dancer was *lean, acrobatic, and bold.*

Squirrels scampered among the trees.
Chipmunks scampered among the trees.
Field mice scampered among the trees.
COMBINED: *Squirrels, chipmunks, and field mice* scampered among the trees.

Ants crawled over the floor.
Ants crawled up the wall.
Ants crawled onto the counter.
Ants crawled into the honey pot.
COMBINED: Ants crawled *over the floor, up the wall, onto the counter, and into the honey pot.*

McGreavy took the ball from center.
He stepped back.
He looked coolly for his receiver.
He threw a bullet pass right over the middle of the line.
COMBINED: McGreavy *took the ball from center, stepped back, looked coolly for his receiver, and threw a bullet pass right over the middle of the line.*

### 2. Contrast

The deer was dying.
But he was not yet dead.
COMBINED: The deer was *dying but not yet dead.*

### 3. Choice

Motorists must curb their demand for gas.
Otherwise they must face the prospect of gas rationing.
COMBINED: Motorists must *either curb their demand for gas or face the prospect of gas rationing.*

### Joining the Parts of a Compound Phrase

The parts of a compound phrase should normally be joined by one of the means listed here.

**1.** One or more conjunctions, such as *and, yet, or, but,* or *nor:*

Television commercials sell youth *and* glamor.
She spoke pleasantly *but* firmly.
He was fresh *and* eager to please *but* not gullible.

(For more on conjunctions, see pp. 252–53.)

**2.** A comma:

> The fat, sleek walrus slipped into the icy water.

**3.** A comma plus a conjunction:

> The dancer was lean, acrobatic, *and* bold.

When a compound phrase has three or more items, you normally need a comma plus a conjunction between the last two. Many writers also use a comma before *but* when it joins two phrases. Compare:

> She spoke pleasantly *but* firmly.
> She won the point, *but* lost the game.

**4.** A pair of correlatives, such as *both . . . and* or *either . . . or:*

> *Both* England *and* Russia fought Germany in World War II.
> Motorists must *either* curb their demand for gas *or* face the prospect of gas rationing.

Among other correlatives are *not only . . . but also, whether . . . or,* and *neither . . . nor.* (For more on correlatives, see p. 262.)

**EXERCISE 1   Sentence Combining**

Combine the sentences in each of the following sets by using compound phrases.

> EXAMPLE
> Martha is a tennis player.
> Martha is a gymnast.
> Martha is a member of the swimming team.
> COMBINED: Martha is a tennis player, a gymnast, and a member of the swimming team.

> 1. Proud nations have gradually fallen into the dust.
>    Great civilizations have gradually fallen into the dust.

> 2. The painting was savage.
>    The painting was sensuous.
>    The painting was brilliant.

> 3. The dog leaped.
>    The dog yelped.
>    The dog ran.

> 4. The Vietnam War cost millions of dollars.
>    It took thousands of American lives.
>    It left behind a legacy of national guilt.

> 5. The policeman whistled.
>    He signaled me to stop.
>    He strode grimly to the car.

He asked me to get out.
He demanded to see my driver's permit.

6. We looked under the sofa.
   We looked over the bookcase.
   We looked in the closet.
   We looked behind the television set.

7. He saw the truck coming out of the fog.
   He could not avoid hitting it.

8. The president must use his power.
   Otherwise he must lose it.

9. She spent the summer in Newport.
   She spent the winter in Haiti.
   She spent the rest of the year in debt.

10. He walked slowly.
    He walked awkwardly.
    He walked timidly.

## 13.3 Using Compound Sentences

A compound sentence joins two or more simple sentences to show one of the following relations between them:

**1.** Addition

> The sentencing of criminals often ignites controversy, and the death sentence sometimes causes a furor.

**2.** Contrast

> Art is long, but life is short.

**3.** Cause and effect

> The price of fuel oil has risen sharply in the Northeast; therefore, many homeowners are installing wood-burning stoves.

**4.** Choice

> We must conquer inflation, or it will conquer us.

## 13.4 Making Compound Sentences

As the preceding examples show, a **compound sentence** consists of two or more simple sentences joined together on the same level. When a simple sentence is thus joined to another simple sentence, each is called an **independent clause** because each could stand by itself as a complete sentence:

SIMPLE SENTENCES

S　　　P
Art　/　is long.

S　　　P
Life　/　is short.

COMPOUND SENTENCE

INDEPENDENT CLAUSE　　　　　　INDEPENDENT CLAUSE
[s] Art　/　[P] is long,　　but　　[s] life　/　[P] is short.

SIMPLE SENTENCES

　S　　　　P
Joggers　/　can use the trails provided by the Recreation Department.

　S　　　P
They　/　can battle motorists for control of the highways.

COMPOUND SENTENCE

INDEPENDENT CLAUSE
[s] Joggers　/　[P] can use the trails provided by the Recreation Department,

or

INDEPENDENT CLAUSE
[s] they　/　[P] can battle motorists for control of the highways.

SIMPLE SENTENCES

　　　　　　　S　　　　　　　　　　P
The sentencing of criminals　/　often ignites controversy.
　　　　　　S　　　　　　　　　P
The death sentence　/　sometimes causes a furor.

COMPOUND SENTENCE

INDEPENDENT CLAUSE
[s] The sentencing of criminals　/　[P] often ignites controversy

and

INDEPENDENT CLAUSE
[s] the death sentence　/　[P] sometimes causes a furor.

In each of these examples, the compound sentence preserves the whole of each simple sentence in an independent clause.

## 13.5 Joining Independent Clauses

You can join the independent clauses of a compound sentence in one of three ways: with a semicolon, with a conjunction, or with a conjunctive adverb.

### The Semicolon

A semicolon alone can join two independent clauses when the relation between them is obvious:

> Some books are undeservedly forgotten; none are undeservedly remembered. —W. H. Auden
>
> The house was empty; everyone had gone.

### Conjunctions

A **conjunction** can show a relation between words, phrases, or clauses. Conjunctions used between clauses include *for* and *so* as well as those listed earlier—*and, yet, or, but,* and *nor.* Each indicates one of the relations listed here.

**1.** Addition, shown by *and:*

> The whistle blew, *and* the big train chugged out of the station.

**2.** Addition of a negative point, shown by *nor:*

> Many of the settlers had never farmed before, *nor* were they ready for the brutal Dakota winters.

When *nor* introduces a clause, the subject is postponed. *They were ready* becomes *nor were they ready.*

**3.** Contrast, shown by *but* or *yet:*

> We are all in the gutter, *but* some of us are looking at the stars. —Oscar Wilde

**4.** Logical consequence, shown by *for* or *so:*

> My father never attended the military parades in the city, *for* he hated war.
>
> During World War II, Americans of Japanese descent were suspected of disloyalty, *so* they were placed in detention camps.

*For* introduces a reason; *so* introduces a consequence.

**5.** Choice, shown by *or:*

> Nelson could keep his ships near England, *or* he could order them out against the French in Egypt.

A conjunction used between clauses normally has a comma just before it, but there are two exceptions.

**1.** You can omit the comma when the clauses are particularly short:

> Many are called but few are chosen.

**2.** You can replace the comma with a semicolon when there are commas elsewhere in the sentence:

> On the morning of June 28, 1969, the weather finally cleared; but the climbers, wearied by their efforts of the previous days, could not attempt the summit.

You can use a comma without a conjunction when there are more than two clauses, but you should normally use a conjunction between the last two:

> The sun shone, a stiff breeze ruffled the bay, the sails bellied out, and the bow cut the water like a knife.

### Conjunctive Adverbs

A **conjunctive adverb** is a word or phrase that indicates the relation between the clauses it joins, as a conjunction does. But a conjunctive adverb is usually weightier and more emphatic than a conjunction:

> The Iron Duke had complete confidence in his soldiers' training and valor; *furthermore*, he considered his battle plan a work of genius.
> Chamberlain made an ill-considered peace treaty with Hitler after the German invasion of Czechoslovakia; *as a result*, England stood idly by during the German invasion of Poland.

While a conjunction is normally preceded by a comma, a conjunctive adverb is normally preceded by a semicolon and followed by a comma. Compare these two sentences:

> The price of oil has risen sharply, *so* wood stoves are popular again.
> The price of oil has risen sharply; *therefore*, wood stoves are popular again.

A conjunction always stands between the two clauses it joins. But you can move a conjunctive adverb around within the second clause until you find the position you like best:

> The price of oil has risen sharply; wood stoves, *therefore*, are popular again.
> The price of oil has risen sharply; wood stoves are *therefore* popular again.

In the next-to-last example the conjunctive adverb is set off by commas. In the last example there are no commas around the conjunctive adverb because it appears within the base predicate of the clause—*are popular.*

Like conjunctions, conjunctive adverbs specify a relation between one clause and another. Each indicates one of the relations listed here.

**1.** Addition, shown by *besides, furthermore, moreover,* or *in addition:*

> The Iron Duke had complete confidence in his soldiers' training and valor; *furthermore,* he considered his battle plan a work of genius.

**2.** Likeness, shown by *likewise, similarly,* or *in the same way:*

> Many young Englishmen condemned the English war against France in the 1790s; *likewise,* many young Americans condemned the American war against North Vietnam in the 1960s.

**3.** Contrast, shown by *however, nevertheless, still, nonetheless, conversely, otherwise, instead, in contrast,* or *on the other hand:*

> Einstein's theory of relativity was largely the product of speculation; experiments made within the past fifty years, *however,* have confirmed many of its basic points.

**4.** Cause and effect, shown by *accordingly, consequently, hence, therefore, as a result,* or *for this reason:*

> Chamberlain made an ill-considered peace treaty with Hitler after the German invasion of Czechoslovakia; *as a result,* England stood idly by during the German invasion of Poland.

**5.** A means-and-end relation, shown by *thus, thereby, by this means,* or *in this manner:*

> John F. Kennedy swept the 1960 presidential primaries; *thus* he cleared the way for his nomination at the Democratic convention.

Do not use *thus* to mean "therefore" or "for this reason."

**6.** Reinforcement, shown by *for example, for instance, in fact, in particular,* or *indeed:*

> Public transportation will also be vastly improved; a high-speed train, *for instance,* will take passengers from Montreal to Toronto in less than two hours.
> The repeal of the Stamp Act delighted the colonists; for a time, *in fact,* they actually regarded King George as the champion of their rights.

**7.** Time, shown by words like *meanwhile, then, subsequently, afterward, earlier,* and *later:*

> First the tree must be cut into logs; *then* the logs must be split.

**Summary**

The independent clauses (IC) of a compound sentence must normally be joined in one of the following three ways:

1. <u>  IC  </u> ; <u>  IC  </u> .
2. <u>  IC  </u> , conjunction<u>  IC  </u> .
3. <u>  IC  </u> ; conjunctive adverb<u>  IC  </u> .
   (placement optional)

Exceptions are discussed on p. 253.

**EXERCISE 2    Sentence Combining**

Combine the sentences in each of the following sets into a single compound sentence. Then in parentheses state the relation that your combination shows.

EXAMPLE
We are all in the gutter.
Some of us are looking at the stars.
COMBINED: We are all in the gutter, but some of us are looking at the stars. (contrast)

1. A college education may lead to a well-paying job.
   It cannot guarantee success.

2. Many students do little or no writing in high school.
   They must learn to write in college.

3. Every New Year's Day I make a set of resolutions.
   I have never managed to keep any of them.

4. On its very first voyage, the "unsinkable" *Titanic* hit an iceberg.
   It sank.

5. James Joyce was a painstaking writer.
   He once spent half a day on the composition of a single sentence.

6. President Carter brought the leaders of Israel and Egypt together at Camp David.
   He helped to negotiate a peace treaty between the two countries.

7. The discovery of gold in California created the gold rush.
   The discovery of oil in Alaska created an oil rush.

8. The safety of nuclear power plants can never be absolutely guaranteed.
   Many people demand a shutdown of all existing plants and a halt to the building of new ones.

9. The shutdown of all nuclear power plants would be a serious step.
   Nuclear power is a major source of our energy.

10. You can take a leisurely five days to cross the Atlantic by ship.
    You can cross it in three hours by supersonic plane.

11. There may be more oil within the shale of the Rocky Mountains
    than in all of Saudi Arabia.
    Extracting the oil from the shale is difficult and expensive.

12. The brakes failed.
    The car skidded out of control
    A brick wall loomed up suddenly before us.
    Then we crashed.

13. The wind died down.
    Night closed in.
    The moon came out.
    Lights came on in the scattered houses.

**Overusing *and***

Use *and* sparingly in compound sentences. A series of clauses strung together by *and* soon becomes boring:

> I was born in Illinois, and the first big city I ever saw was Chicago. I went there with my mother and father, and we stayed in a big hotel on the Loop. We spent a whole day just walking around the city, and I got a stiff neck from looking up at the skyscrapers.

To break the monotony of compounding with *and,* substitute other linking words—or other constructions:

> I was born in Illinois, so the first big city I ever saw was Chicago. My mother and father took me to a big hotel on the Loop. We spent a whole day just walking around the city, and I got a stiff neck from looking up at the skyscrapers.

Used sparingly, sentences like the last one can be relaxing to your style; overused, they become numbing. (For more on alternatives to the *and* construction, see the discussion of subordination, chapter 15, pp. 267–89.)

## 13.6 Comma Splices *cs*

The **comma splice,** also called the "comma fault," is the error of joining two independent clauses with nothing but a comma:

> *She wore huge dark glasses, no one recognized her.

The meaning calls for a full stop between *glasses* and *no,* but the comma doesn't provide one, so the sentence leaves the reader with a sense of something missing.
    To correct the error, you can do one of three things.

**1.** Put a conjunction after the comma:

> She wore huge dark glasses, so no one recognized her.

**2.** Replace the comma with a semicolon:

> She wore huge dark glasses; no one recognized her.

**3.** Replace the comma with a period, making two sentences:

> She wore huge dark glasses. No one recognized her.

Sometimes a comma splice occurs when the second clause in a sentence begins with a conjunctive adverb:

> *Most working people get at least one raise a year, nevertheless, inflation often leaves them with no increase in buying power.

*Nevertheless* is a conjunctive adverb, and a conjunctive adverb used between two clauses must be preceded by a semicolon:

> Most working people get at least one raise a year; nevertheless, inflation often leaves them with no increase in buying power.

Alternatively, you can use a period, making two sentences:

> Most working people get at least one raise a year. Nevertheless, inflation often leaves them with no increase in buying power.

EXERCISE 3  **Correcting Comma Splices**

Each of the following contains a comma splice. Correct it.

> EXAMPLE
> The holiday pleased the children, they welcomed the chance to play in the snow.
> REVISED: The holiday pleased the children; they welcomed the chance to play in the snow.

1. On moonlit nights some animals serenade all listeners, others scurry about looking for mates.
2. Cigarette smoking is no longer widely accepted, on the contrary, smokers have become an embattled minority.
3. The original settlers were short and dark, in contrast, the new colonists tend to be tall and fair.
4. Thoreau went to the woods in order to simplify his life, he also wanted to live close to nature.
5. Fairy tales end with the hero and heroine living happily together ever after, *A Doll's House* ends with the heroine leaving her husband.
6. A sense of humor is like fresh tonic water, it keeps bubbling to the surface.
7. Before the battle the king's forces had nine cannons, the peasants had none.

8. The high cost of gas makes life in the suburbs expensive, therefore some people are moving back to the cities.
9. To prevent another four-term presidency like that of Franklin D. Roosevelt, the law permits the president to succeed himself just once, nevertheless, no president is guaranteed reelection.
10. The price of serious illness has risen drastically in recent years, for example, some hospital rooms now cost over a hundred dollars a day.

## 13.7   Fused Sentences   *fus*

A **fused sentence** runs two independent clauses together with no punctuation or conjunction between them:

> *Emily listened to the lobster boats chugging out to sea from the cove she watched the gulls sailing overhead.

Here the first independent clause simply pushes into the second one. We cannot even tell for sure where the first ends. Is its last word *sea* or *cove?*

To correct the error, you can do one of three things.

**1.** Use a comma and a conjunction between the two clauses:

> Emily listened to the lobster boats chugging out to sea from the cove, and she watched the gulls sailing overhead.

**2.** Put a semicolon at the end of the first clause, in this case after *cove:*

> Emily listened to the lobster boats chugging out to sea from the cove; she watched the gulls sailing overhead.

**3.** Put a period at the end of the first clause. You will then have two sentences.

EXERCISE 4   **Correcting Comma Splices and Fused Sentences**

In some of the following, the punctuation is faulty. Correct any mistakes you find, adding words where necessary. If a sentence is correct as it stands, write *Correct.*

EXAMPLE
Cloudy days tend to make us gloomy, sunny days, in contrast, make us cheerful.
REVISED: Cloudy days tend to make us gloomy; sunny days, in contrast, make us cheerful.

1. Prejudice is like the bottom of a Coke bottle it shows you the world in a distorted light.
2. In the last act the collapse of Lady Macbeth is quite unexpected,

earlier in the play she seemed to have almost superhuman strength.

3. On other long walks I had sometimes lost my way without feeling worried this time I panicked.

4. Scientists have sought the secret of hibernation in the endocrine glands; these are reduced in size during the winter sleep.

5. The new president was supported by the peasants he was distrusted by the wealthy landowners.

6. John is short and silent his roommate is tall and talkative.

7. Reckless drivers should be severely penalized in fact they should lose their driver's permits for at least six months.

8. Most fraternities include only students of a certain type and social category, thus fraternities reinforce social barriers.

9. Macaulay was a child prodigy by the age of ten he was writing a world history.

10. Before Columbus, the Central American Mayans developed a remarkable civilization, they built elaborate temples, devised a highly accurate calendar, and invented a form of writing.

# 14

# PARALLEL CONSTRUCTION

## 14.1    Why Choose Parallelism?

**Parallel construction,** also called "parallelism," is a method of enhancing the coordination of words, phrases, or statements in a sentence by arranging two or more elements in gramatically equivalent patterns: noun lined up with noun, verb with verb, phrase with phrase, and clause with clause. Parallelism can lend clarity, elegance, and symmetry to what you say. For example:

> I came; I saw; I conquered.                    —Julius Caesar

Caesar uses three one-word verbs to list the three things he did.

> In many ways writing is the act of saying *I*, of imposing oneself upon other people, of saying *listen to me, see it my way, change your mind.*                    —Joan Didion

To reinforce her point about the assertiveness of writing, Didion uses three verbal nouns and three imperatives.

> To be or not to be: that is the question.
>
>                    —William Shakespeare

The choice Hamlet contemplates is memorably clear because the phrase *to be* is grammatically parallel with the phrase *not to be*.

> It is better to break sod as a serf than to lord it over all the exhausted dead.            —Homer, translated by Robert Fitzgerald

Here the phrase *to break sod* is grammatically parallel with the phrase *to lord it,* and the parallel structure sharpens the comparison between life and death.

260

Each must live within the isolation of his own senses, dreams and memories; each must die his own death.          —Ralph Ellison

The theme of man's loneliness is emphasized by the repetition of *each must* and *his own* as well as by the series of nouns: *senses, dreams, memories,* and *death.*

Most of the floggings and lynchings occur at harvest time, when fruit hangs heavy and ripe, when the leaves are red and gold, when nuts fall from the trees, when the earth offers its best.
          —Richard Wright

Wright's sentence swells, but he keeps it under firm control by repeating the word *when,* thereby lining up the clauses that follow the opening clause about floggings and lynchings. Layer on layer, Wright builds his sentence to the final irony of the last clause— *when the earth offers its best.*

You can do similar things in your own writing if you follow the basic guidelines presented here.

## 14.2  Using Parallelism

### Kinds of Parallelism

When you have two or more items in a list, a series, a contrast, a choice, a statement of equivalence, or a comparison, put all of the items into the same grammatical form.

**1.** List

I have nothing to offer but *blood, toil, tears,* and *sweat.* [four nouns]
          —Winston Churchill

**2.** Series

Let every nation know, whether it wishes us well or ill, that we shall *pay any price, bear any burden, meet any hardship, support any friend, oppose any foe* to assure the survival and the success of liberty. [five verb-object combinations]          —John F. Kennedy

**3.** Contrast

On all these shores there are echoes of past and future: of the flow of time, *obliterating* yet *containing* all that has gone before [two participles]          —Rachel Carson

**4.** Series plus contrast

Rather than *love,* than *money,* than *fame,* give me *truth.* [four nouns]
          —Henry David Thoreau

**5.** Choice

> *We must indeed all hang together,* or most assuredly, *we shall all hang separately.* [two clauses] —Benjamin Franklin

**6.** Statement of equivalence

> *An empty house* is *a lonely place.* [two noun phrases]

**7.** Comparison

> *A living dog* is better than *a dead lion.* [two noun phrases]
> —Ecclesiastes
> *Crawling down* a mountain is sometimes harder than *climbing up.* [two participle phrases]

## Parallelism with Correlatives

When using a pair of correlatives, be sure that the word or word group following the first member of the pair is parallel with the word or word group following the second. The principal correlatives are *both . . . and, not only . . . but also, either . . . or, neither . . . nor,* and *whether . . . or:*

> She not only *got the job* but also *won a promotion* after just three months. [two verb-object combinations]
> Before the Polish strikes of 1980, both *the Hungarians* and *the Czechs* tried in vain to defy Soviet authority. [two noun phrases]
> Sheila was sure to be either *at the office* or *on her way.* [two adverb phrases]

**EXERCISE 1   Recognizing Parallel Elements**

Each of the following sentences contains a parallel construction. Write down the parallel elements.

EXAMPLE
Crawling down a mountain is sometimes harder than climbing up.
Crawling down, climbing up

1. For me slipping on a piece of ice is as easy as falling off a log.
2. The more I read about tax reform, the less I understand about it.
3. The new method of photographing copies is less expensive than the old one.
4. We must either get control of inflation or lose control of the economy.
5. They were weak in numbers but strong in pride.
6. What is written without effort is in general read without pleasure. —Samuel Johnson

# 14.3   Faulty Parallelism   //

When two or more parts of a sentence are parallel in meaning, you should coordinate them fully by making them parallel in form. If you don't, your sentence will be marred by **faulty parallelism.** Here are some examples of this error and of ways to correct it.

> 1. *The Allies decided to invade Italy and then that they would launch a massive assault on the Normandy coast.

The two Allied decisions can and should be stated in parallel form, but they aren't. The infinitive phrase beginning with *to invade* does not line up with the clause beginning with *that they would launch.* You can fix the sentence by stating both decisions either in infinitive phrases or in *that* clauses. But infinitive phrases will give you a tighter sentence:

> The Allies decided *to invade Italy* and then *to launch a massive assault on the Normandy coast.*

> 2. *I like swimming, skiing, and to play ice hockey.

This sentence is awkward because *swimming* and *skiing,* both participles, do not line up with *to play ice hockey,* an infinitive phrase. You should use either infinitives or participles for all three activities:

> I like to *swim, ski,* and *play ice hockey.* [or] I like *swimming, skiing,* and *playing ice hockey.*

In a series like this, with three or more short items, you may put the key word *to* before the first item only. But you may sometimes need to repeat the key word for the sake of clarity, as shown in the revisions of sentences 4 and 5, below.

> 3. Chemistry used to be taught here from a textbook; now the lab method is followed.

Both clauses concern methods of teaching chemistry, so parallel construction can emphasize the correspondence between them:

> *Chemistry* used to be *taught* here *from a textbook;* now *it* is *taught in the lab.*

> 4. The Dean can force a student to attend class but not think.

Repetition of *to* will make the sentence clearer:

> The Dean can force a student *to attend class* but not *to think.*

> 5. Centuries ago many people believed that the earth was flat and one could fall off the edge of it.

Repetition of *that* will clarify the sentence:

*Faulty Parallelism*   263

Centuries ago many people believed *that* the earth was flat and *that* one could fall off the edge of it.

6. *Either we must make nuclear power safe or stop using it altogether.

The sentence will be better if its correlatives (*either . . . or*) are immediately followed by grammatically parallel items:

We must either *make* nuclear power safe or *stop* using it altogether. [or] Either *we must make* nuclear power safe or *we must stop* using it altogether.

### EXERCISE 2   Recognizing Correct Parallel Construction

Each of the following consists of two sentences, one with correct parallel construction and the other with faulty parallelism. Write down the letter of the sentence with correct parallel construction.

1. (a) Skateboarding is both exciting and there is danger in it too.
   (b) Skateboarding is both exciting and dangerous.
2. (a) The detective stories of Max Brand are not so hard-boiled as Mickey Spillane.
   (b) The detective stories of Max Brand are not so hard-boiled as those of Mickey Spillane
3. (a) The sentence is difficult to understand not because the vocabulary is technical but because the syntax is faulty.
   (b) The sentence is difficult to understand not because of the technical vocabulary but because the syntax is faulty.
4. (a) The actor was not only stunned by the noise of booing but also by the sight of flying tomatoes.
   (b) The actor was stunned not only by the noise of booing but also by the sight of flying tomatoes.
5. (a) Marian could not decide whether she should start college right after high school or to get a job first.
   (b) Marian could not decide whether to start college right after high school or to get a job first.

### EXERCISE 3   Correcting Faulty Parallelism

Revise each of the following sentences that is marred by faulty parallelism. If a sentence is correct as it stands, write *Correct.*

EXAMPLE
You can improve your performance if you master the fundamentals and by training diligently.
REVISED: You can improve your performance by mastering the fundamentals and by training diligently.

1. The captain ordered his men to dig foxholes, to post sentries, and their weapons were to be cleaned before dark.
2. Smoking cigarettes can be as dangerous as to play Russian roulette.

3. Some writers care only about wealth and becoming famous.
4. The more David says about the pleasures of popcorn, the more I want to stuff his mouth with bubble gum.
5. Rooming with Fred was like if you shared a telephone booth with a hippopotamus.

## EXERCISE 4 Sentence Combining

Combine the sentences in each of the following sets by means of coordination and parallel construction. Change the wording where necessary.

EXAMPLE
The old Chevy pickup had three major defects.
The brakes were bad.
There was a crack in the windshield.
Sometimes the starter failed to work.
COMBINED: The old Chevy pickup had three major defects: bad brakes, a cracked windshield, and an unreliable starter.

1. Professor Harvey made two main points.
   He said that modern painting is essentially personal.
   He saw impersonality as the essence of modern architecture.

2. In the summer I especially like three things.
   I like to swim.
   I like to read science fiction.
   I like lying in the sun.

3. Not only may the study of literature help you to understand other people.
   You may also be helped to understand yourself.

4. Most writers hate neglect.
   They love to be acclaimed.

5. Summer was at an end.
   Another school year began.

## EXERCISES 5 Sentence Combining

Combine the sentences in each of the following sets into a single compound sentence, using compound phrases if necessary. Be careful to join all items in your compounds correctly, and use parallel construction where possible.

EXAMPLE
Black people in American have been neglected for years.
Black people in America have been underestimated for years.
Their recent accomplishments in a variety of fields have made "black power" a reality.
Their recent accomplishments in a variety of fields have made black pride possible.
COMBINED: Black people in America have been neglected and underestimated for years, but their recent accomplishments in a

variety of fields have made "black power" real and black pride possible.

1. The hero in early cowboy movies was modest.
He was reticent.
He was shy with pretty women.
He rode hard.
He shot straight.
He survived a hundred dangers.
He always overcame the villain.

2. Much of the land was arid.
Much of the land was filled with rocks.
There was barrenness.
The Moabites loved their homeland.
The Moabites fought to keep their homeland.

3. People in the Northeast can spend more money on gasoline.
They can spend more money on heating oil.
They have alternatives.
They can organize car pools.
They can put more insulation in the walls of their houses.

4. Some theories about humor are interesting.
These theories are also surprising.
An example is George Orwell's theory.
According to Orwell, "a joke worth laughing at always has an idea behind it, and usually a subversive idea."

5. According to Marcel Pagnol, the cause of laughter is the same in all times.
According to Pagnol, the cause of laughter is the same in all countries.
Laughers feel momentarily superior to others.
Their laughter is "a song of triumph."

# 15

# SUBORDINATION

## 15.1   Using Subordination

Subordination enables you to show the relative importance of the parts of a sentence. To use **subordination** is to make one or more parts of a sentence depend on the part that is most important to you.

Suppose you want to describe what a dog did on a particular night, and you want your description to include the following points:

> The dog lived next door.
> The dog was scrawny.
> The dog barked.
> The dog was old.
> The dog howled.
> The dog kept me awake.
> I was awake all night.

What is the best way to arrange these isolated facts in a sentence? Part of the answer is to coordinate facts that belong on the same level. (For a full discussion of coordination, see chapter 13, pp. 247–59.) You can readily see that *scrawny* and *old* go together, and so do *barked* and *howled*. So here is one way of combining those sentences:

> The dog was scrawny and old, and he lived next door; he barked and howled and kept me awake all night.

Coordination has clearly begun the work of arranging the facts about the dog; it has brought some order and continuity to a collection of separate statements. Yet the sentence lacks something. It trots along without a jump or a leap. It never gets off the ground because it never tells us which of the many facts about the dog is most important to the writer.

Which *is* the most important? Only you as the writer can decide—in light of the context for which you are writing the sentence. If you are writing an essay on the people next door, the most important fact about the dog is that it belonged to them; if you are writing about yourself, the most important fact is that the dog kept you awake. Whichever the case, you can emphasize the key fact by subordinating all others to it.

You can begin with the simplest kind of subordination: using a word or phrase as the **modifier** of another word or phrase. (For a full discussion of modifiers, see chapter 11, pp. 211–39.) By using various words as modifiers, you can combine the seven original sentences in a number of different ways. For example, you can use *scrawny, old, next door,* and *all night* as modifiers without changing their form, and you can use *barked* and *howled* as modifiers when their endings are changed to *-ing.* The result will be a sentence like one of these:

> Barking and howling, the scrawny old dog next door kept me awake all night.
> The scrawny old dog next door kept me awake all night by barking and howling.

Both of these sentences are designed to emphasize one key statement: *the dog kept me awake.* All the other statements about the dog have been turned into modifiers of *dog* or *kept me awake,* and thus everything else has been subordinated to the one key statement.

But suppose the most important thing about that sleepless night was simply the noise. Here is one way of subordinating everything else to that:

> What kept me awake all night was the barking and howling of the scrawny old dog next door.

In this sentence, the fact that you were kept awake is presented in a **noun clause**—a complete clause, with its own subject and predicate, used as if it were a noun:

| | | LINKING | PREDICATE |
|---|---|---|---|
| | SUBJECT | VERB | NOUN |
| [s] *What* / | [p] *kept me awake all night* | was | the barking and howling of the scrawny old dog next door. |

The noun clause subordinates the fact of your wakefulness to a statement about the noise that kept you awake. The noise is now even more important than the dog who made it, for *barking* and *howling* are here used as **verbal nouns.** (For a full discussion of verbal nouns, see chapter 12, pp. 240–46.) No longer modifiers, *barking* and *howling* have joined to become a compound noun phrase, and *dog* is merely part of the attached modifier—*of the scrawny old dog.* So this construction indicates that the sound of the dog was more important than your wakefulness or even than the dog itself. The infernal racket is what you remember most vividly from that sleepless night.

Now suppose you want to emphasize the fact that the dog lived next door. Here is a way of doing so:

The dog that kept me awake lived next door.

*That kept me awake* is an **adjective clause,** sometimes called a "relative clause." An adjective clause has its own subject and predicate, but its first word (in this instance *that*) relates it to a word or phrase that comes before it (here *dog*) and thus makes the whole clause modify that word or phrase:

SUBJECT        PREDICATE

The dog  [s] *that*  /  [p] *kept me awake*  lived next door.

You can add other modifying words and phrases to this sentence without changing its basic structure:

SUBJECT        PREDICATE

The scrawny old dog  [s] *that*  /  [p] *kept me awake all night with its barking and howling*  lived next door.

Here *barking* and *howling* are still verbal nouns, but they have become part of a *with* phrase modifying *kept me awake*. In turn, *kept me awake* is part of an adjective clause modifying *dog*. So all the other facts about the dog are now subordinated to the fact that it lived next door.

Finally, suppose you want to subordinate that and all the other facts about the dog to a brand-new fact. Suppose you mainly want to tell what happened to you *as a result* of that sleepless night. Then you might write a sentence like this:

Because the barking and howling of the scrawny old dog next door had kept me awake all night, I fell asleep in the middle of the chemistry final.

*Because* introduces an **adverb clause**—an entire clause that modifies another clause, as ordinary adverbs can. In this instance it tells *why* the writer fell asleep.

Whether you want to stress this fact in your sentence will depend on what you want to emphasize in the paragraph containing the sentence. The various methods of subordination make it possible to control and adjust the emphasis of any sentence, no matter how simple or complicated it is. But you can use the methods effectively only if you know what you want to emphasize—and why. For different contexts, a sentence should be written to emphasize different things. Consider these paragraphs:

> For me, the one big problem with dogs is noise. On the night before I had to take a final exam in chemistry, "man's best friend" turned out to be my worst enemy. I got to bed at eleven, but I didn't sleep a wink. *What kept me awake all night* was *the barking and howling of the scrawny old dog next door.*

> The Bible tells us all to love our neighbors, but I have always had trouble even liking most of mine. When I was about six years old, I climbed over the fence in our backyard, wandered into Mr. O'Reilly's flower garden, and sat down in the middle of some big yellow daffodils. Mr. O'Reilly came up from behind and whacked me so hard I can still feel it now. We've moved a few times since then, but I have yet to find neighbors that I love. On the contrary, many of the things I don't love seem to come from across a fence. In El Paso, for instance, *a scrawny old dog that kept me awake all night with its barking and howling lived next door.*

> In the chemistry course I managed to do just about everything wrong. To begin with, I bought a used textbook at a bargain price, and then found out that I was supposed to buy the new edition. Trying to get along instead with the old one, I almost always wound up reading the wrong pages for the assignment and giving the wrong answers to quiz questions. I did no better with beakers and test tubes; the only thing my experiments showed is that I could have blown up the lab. But the worst came last. *Because the barking and howling of the scrawny old dog next door had kept me awake all night, I fell asleep in the middle of the final.*

The sentence about the dog is written three different ways to emphasize three different things: the noise it made, the fact that it lived next door, and the fact that something happened because of its noise. In each case, the methods of subordination make the sentence fit the particular context for which it is written. The three ways of writing the sentence illustrate three different kinds of subordinate clauses; we consider these in the next sections.

## 15.2   Subordinate Clauses

A **subordinate clause,** also called a "dependent clause," is a group of words that has its own subject and predicate but cannot stand alone as a sentence. It must be included in or connected to a **main clause**—a clause that can stand by itself as a sentence:

MAIN CLAUSE

SUBORDINATE CLAUSE
1. [s] What broke the window   /   [P] was a  baseball.

SUBORDINATE CLAUSE       MAIN CLAUSE
2. As he was being tackled,    he threw the ball.

MAIN CLAUSE                SUBORDINATE CLAUSE
3. Medical researchers have long        that takes thousands of
   been seeking a cure for a disease   lives each year.

SUBORDINATE       SUBORDINATE
MAIN CLAUSE       CLAUSE                CLAUSE
4. Keene was tackled    as he threw the pass   that might have
                                              saved the game.

A subordinate clause can be a noun clause, an adjective clause, or an adverb clause. Each of these will be discussed in turn.

## 15.3   Noun Clauses

A **noun clause** is a clause used as a noun within a sentence; it serves as subject, object, or predicate noun. A noun clause begins with a word like *whoever, whichever, whatever, who, that, what, how, why, when,* or *where.*

**1.** Noun clause as subject:

Sylvia did something.
It amazed me.
COMBINED: *What Sylvia did* amazed me.

Something kept me awake all night.
It was the barking and howling of the scrawny old dog.
COMBINED: *What kept me awake all night* was the barking and howling of the scrawny old dog.

Someone will win the nomination.
That person will be running against a popular incumbent.
COMBINED: *Whoever wins the nomination* will be running against a popular incumbent.

In a *whoever* clause the future is indicated by the present or present perfect tense. In this instance *Someone will win* becomes *Whoever wins.*

**2.** Noun clause as object:

> I feared something.
> We would never get out alive.
> Combined: I feared *that we would never get out alive.*

> Many voters will support any person of a certain kind.
> This kind of person promises lower taxes.
> Combined: Many voters will support *whoever promises lower taxes.*

> How did the prisoner escape?
> The police have not discovered that.
> Combined: The police have not discovered *how the prisoner escaped.*

Note the difference between the direct question and the noun clause based on it. The word order changes, the auxiliary *did* is dropped, and *escape* becomes *escaped.* Consider another example:

> Was the strange and moody explorer murdered on his last trip to the Arctic?
> No one knows for certain.
> Combined: No one knows for certain *whether (or not) the strange and moody explorer was murdered on his last trip to the Arctic.*

The use of *or not* after *whether* is optional.

> A prize will be given to some person.
> That person will solve the riddle.
> Combined: A prize will be given to *whoever solves the riddle.*

> The early bird gets indigestion along with the worm.
> My sister says that.
> Combined: My sister says *that the early bird gets indigestion along with the worm.*

> What would marriage do to her?
> Alexandra wondered that.
> Combined: Alexandra wondered *what marriage would do to her.*

The last two examples illustrate the use of noun clauses in the indirect reporting of discourse. (For a full discussion of indirect reporting, see sections 24.2, p. 382, and 24.4, pp. 383–84.)

**3.** Noun clause as predicate noun:

> My only hope was something.
> We might be rescued.
> Combined: My only hope was *that we might be rescued.*

How was Stonehenge built?
Archaeologists have tried to learn that.
COMBINED: Archaeologists have tried to learn *how Stonehenge was built.*

Gunslingers are people of a certain kind.
The founding fathers wanted to protect the American people against people of this kind.
COMBINED: Gunslingers are *what the founding fathers wanted to protect the American people against.*

Of course there is almost always more than one way of combining a pair or a set of sentences. For instance, you might combine the sentences in the preceding example by writing *The founding fathers wanted to protect the American people against gunslingers.* But suppose you want to make *gunslingers* important. Suppose you are attacking the notion that gunslinging is the essence of Americanism—in a paragraph like this:

> Such a definition of Americanism would come as a stark surprise to the men who were most directly involved in the making of the national undertaking that carries the name of the United States. For the one word that best expresses their purpose and their aspirations in founding this country is *law.* The U.S. Constitution is nothing if it is not a monument to law. It holds that anyone who takes the law into his own hands is to be treated as a criminal. It is based on the assumption that even the best men become dangerous when they substitute force for law. Gunslingers . . . are precisely what the founding fathers wanted to protect the American people against. —Norman Cousins, "In Praise of Famous Men"

The *what* construction lets you put a key word or phrase just where you want it to stress its importance. It also strengthens the link between one sentence and another by letting you start a new sentence with a reference to something already established in the one before.

EXERCISE 1   **Sentence Combining**

Combine the sentences in each of the following pairs by turning the first sentence into a noun clause and joining it to the second. Begin the noun clause with the word in parentheses. Where you find a set of three sentences, follow the accompanying special instructions.

EXAMPLE
Someone climbs all the way up a mountain. (whoever)
That person knows the thrill of reaching the top.
COMBINED: Whoever climbs all the way up a mountain knows the thrill of reaching the top.

*Noun Clauses*   **273**

*sub*

**15.4**

1. How do automatic elevators respond to conflicting signals? (how)
I have sometimes wondered.

2. Something solves one problem. (what)
The same thing often causes another.

3. Direct negotiations between Israel and the Palestine Liberation Organization would have required Israel's recognition of the PLO. [Leave this sentence as it stands, but combine the next two sentences so that they follow it effectively.]
But Israel would not grant something. (what)
That was recognition of the PLO.

4. We would win. (that)
The coach predicted that.

5. Is there intelligent life on some distant planet? (whether)
No one knows.

6. Someone goes into politics. (whoever)
That person discovers something quickly.
Nothing will please all of the voters all of the time. (that)
[Turn the first and third sentences into noun clauses and then join them to the second.]

7. The witness was lying. (that)
That soon became evident.

8. Something is hard to learn. (whatever)
It may prove easy to remember.

## 15.4   Adjective (Relative) Clauses

An **adjective clause,** sometimes called a "relative clause," normally begins with a relative pronoun (*which, that, who, whom,* or *whose*) and normally modifies the word or phrase that comes before it. An adjective clause can be used to combine two sentences that refer to the same person or thing:

> Amelia Earhart disappeared in 1937 during a round-the-world trip.
> She set new speed records for long-distance flying in the 1930s.
> COMBINATION 1: Amelia Earhart, who set new speed records for long-distance flying in the 1930s, disappeared in 1937 during a round-the-world trip.
> COMBINATION 2: Amelia Earhart, who disappeared in 1937 during a round-the-world trip, set new speed records for long-distance flying in the 1930s.

In each of these sentences the relative pronoun is *who.* Combination 1 subordinates Earhart's record setting to her disappearance;

combination 2 subordinates her disappearance to her record setting. In each, the subordinating word *who* marks the clause that the
writer thinks less important.

An adjective clause usually says more than a modifying word
or phrase does. Compare these two sentences:

> Medical researchers have long been seeking a cure for a *fatal* dis-
> ease.
> Medical researchers have long been seeking a cure for a disease
> *that takes thousands of lives every year.*

In each sentence the modifier describes *disease.* But the modifying
clause tells more about the extent and effect of the disease than the
one word *fatal* does.

**Relative Pronouns and Antecedents**

A **relative pronoun**—*which, that, who, whom,* or *whose*—introduces
an adjective clause. The word, phrase, or clause modified by the
adjective clause is called the **antecedent** of the pronoun. Which
relative pronoun you use in a sentence will depend on the antecedent.

**1.** Use *which* or *that* when the antecedent is one or more things:

> Hypocrisy is the tribute *that* vice pays to virtue.
> —La Rochefoucauld

The antecedent of *that* is *the tribute,* a thing.

> Medical researchers have long been seeking a cure for a disease
> *that* takes thousands of lives every year.

The antecedent of *that* is *a disease,* a thing.

> Historians cannot always tell the reasons for *which* wars are fought.

The antecedent of *which* is *the reasons,* a set of things. In a construction of this kind, a word like *for, to,* or *in* may come between the
pronoun and its antecedent.

> The crowd booed, *which* made the speaker angry.

The antecedent of *which* is *The crowd booed*—the whole clause taken
as a thing. But you must be careful when you use a whole clause as
an antecedent. If the clause ends with a noun, the sentence may be
confusing:

> The crowd booed the introduction, *which* made the speaker angry.

The antecedent of *which* could be either *The crowd booed the introduction* or just *the introduction,* so the sentence doesn't clearly tell us
what made the speaker angry.

**2.** Use *who, whom,* or *whose* when the antecedent is one or more persons:

> A cynic is a man *who* knows the price of everything and the value of nothing. —Oscar Wilde

The antecedent of *who* is *a man.* Relative pronouns that refer to persons have case (see section 18.5, pp. 316–19), and the case of the pronoun depends on how it is used. Here the pronoun is the subject of *knows,* so the subject case—*who*—is employed.

> Millard Fillmore is a president *whom* nobody remembers.

The antecedent of *whom* is *a president.* Here the pronoun is the direct object of *remembers.* You must therefore use *whom*—the object case. Or you can simply drop the pronoun and write *Millard Fillmore is a president nobody remembers.*

> Writers *whose* books turn into movies may suddenly find themselves rich.

The antecedent of *whose* is *Writers.* Since the adjective clause concerns the books of the writers, the relative pronoun, *whose,* is in the possessive case.

> There is no god in *whom* everyone believes.

The antecedent of *whom* is *god; whom* is in the object case because it is the object of the preposition *in.* Less formally, you could also write *There is no god everyone believes in.*

> I remember Mr. Spingold, short and fat, *who* carried an umbrella every day of the year.

Here the phrase *short and fat* comes between the pronoun *who* and its antecedent, *Mr. Spingold.*

You can sometimes use *that* for persons as well as things—especially when you want to avoid using *whom:*

> Barry Goldwater was the man *that* Lyndon Baines Johnson defeated in the presidential campaign of 1964.

**3.** In addition to the ordinary relative pronouns, you can use *where* or *when* as a relative pronoun, when the antecedent is a place or a time:

> That morning we drove to the town of Appomattox Court House, Virginia, *where* Lee surrendered to Grant at the end of the Civil War.

The antecedent of *where* is *the town of Appomattox Court House, Virginia.*

Her favorite season was spring, *when* the earth seemed born again.

The antecedent of *when* is *spring*.

## Adjective Clauses and Commas

Use commas to set off an adjective clause when and only when it is **nonrestrictive**—that is, when it neither identifies nor restricts the meaning of the antecedent:

> Phineas Q. Gradgrind, *who earned a cumulative grade-point average of 3.9999,* was graduated with highest honors.

This adjective clause does not identify or restrict the meaning of the antecedent, *Phineas Q. Gradgrind.* The proper name by itself completely identifies the individual meant, so the clause is nonrestrictive, not essential to the sentence. Without the adjective clause some details would be lacking, but the sentence would still provide basically the same information:

> Phineas Q. Gradgrind was graduated with highest honors.

Do *not* use commas to set off an adjective clause when it is **restrictive**—that is, when it does identify or restrict the meaning of the antecedent:

> Any student *who earns a cumulative grade-point average of 3.7 or more* will be graduated with highest honors.

This adjective clause restricts the meaning of the antecedent, *Any student.* Without the clause, the sentence would say something quite different:

> Any student will be graduated with highest honors.

Since a restrictive clause is essential to the meaning of the antecedent and of the sentence as a whole, it must not be set off or cut off from that antecedent by commas. (For more on restrictive and nonrestrictive modifiers, see p. 391.)

## Compound Adjective Clauses

You can sometimes turn an adjective clause into a compound by using a compound predicate:

>                    S                    P
> Ronald Reagan, *who* | *made his name in the movies and then became governor of California,* won the presidency by a landslide in 1980.

But if the clause gets long or complicated, you should repeat the relative pronoun:

In 1964 the Republicans nominated Barry Goldwater, *who* gained widespread support for his staunchly conservative views but *who* was nonetheless beaten by Lyndon Baines Johnson.

### Placing Adjective Clauses

The best place for an adjective clause is right after the antecedent of the relative pronoun:

> Students *who* cheat poison the atmosphere of a college.
> Newhouse made a proposal *that* nobody liked.

When the relative pronoun follows its antecedent immediately, the reader can tell at once what the antecedent is.

If you put any words between the relative pronoun and its antecedent, you must be sure that none of them can become a false antecedent. Compare these two sentences:

> I remember Mr. Spingold, short and fat, *who* always carried an umbrella.
> *I remember Mr. Spingold and his dog, *who* always carried an umbrella.

In the first sentence we have no trouble connecting *who* with *Mr. Spingold* because the intervening phrase, *short and fat,* does not include any words that could be the antecedent of *who.* In the second sentence we have trouble getting from *who* to *Mr. Spingold* because we trip over *his dog* on the way. *His dog* is a false antecedent of *who.*

Now consider this example—a sentence-combining problem:

> Leonardo da Vinci painted the *Mona Lisa.*
> He painted it about 1504 in Florence.
> Da Vinci's knowledge of sculpture, painting, architecture, engineering, and science made him the intellectual wonder of his time.

If you care more about the *Mona Lisa* than about da Vinci's other accomplishments, you will want to subordinate the third sentence to the first two. The problem is how to do it—how to get an adjective clause right after *da Vinci,* which comes at the beginning of the first sentence. Here is one way:

> Leonardo da Vinci, *whose* knowledge of sculpture, painting, architecture, engineering, and science made him the intellectual wonder of his time, painted the *Mona Lisa* about 1504 in Florence.

This is clear but cumbersome. It puts the relative pronoun right after its antecedent, but drives an enormous wedge between the subject and verb of the main clause, between *da Vinci* and *painted.*

You can make a smoother sentence by changing the verb in the main clause from the active to the passive voice:

> The *Mona Lisa* was painted about 1504 in Florence by Leonardo da Vinci, whose knowledge of sculpture, painting, architecture, engineering, and science made him the intellectual wonder of his time.

This change brings the parts of the main clause together and moves *da Vinci* from the beginning of the clause to the end, where it can still be immediately followed by *whose.* Note too that in order to get *da Vinci* at the very end of the opening clause, you have to put *about 1504* and *in Florence* right after the verb. (For more on this use of the passive voice, see pp. 370–71.)

**Overusing Adjective Clauses**

Do not use adjective clauses starting with phrases like *who is* and *which are* when you don't really need them. Sometimes the modifying can be done by a phrase alone:

> Amelia Earhart, *who was born in 1898,* was the first woman to fly the Atlantic.
> REVISED: Amelia Earhart, *born in 1898,* was the first woman to fly the Atlantic.

> Some of the compact cars *which are sold by American companies* are manufactured in Japan.
> REVISED: Some of the compact cars *sold by American companies* are manufactured in Japan.

> Joseph P. Kennedy, *who was the father of President John F. Kennedy,* was a financial wizard.
> REVISED: Joseph P. Kennedy, *father of President John F. Kennedy,* was a financial wizard.

In the last sentence you don't even need *the* before *father.* And note that getting rid of *who was* eliminates the repetition of *was,* just as getting rid of *which are* in the preceding example eliminates the repetition of *are.* (For more on this point, see p. 147.)

EXERCISE 2   **Sentence Combining**

Combine the sentences in each of the following pairs by turning one sentence into an adjective clause and using it in the other. Then underline the adjective clause and in parentheses state whether it is restrictive or nonrestrictive.

> EXAMPLE
> Students of a certain kind will be expelled.
> These students cheat.
> COMBINED: Students <u>who cheat</u> will be expelled. (restrictive)

1. Charles Gates Dawes wrote a hit song during his student days at Yale.
   He later became vice-president of the United States under Calvin Coolidge.

2. Women of a certain kind are a vanishing breed.
   These women just want to be housewives.

3. Helen Keller lost her sight and hearing in infancy.
   She nevertheless became a celebrated writer, lecturer, and scholar.

4. I wanted to buy a car of a certain kind.
   This car would last at least as long as the payments on it.

5. Colombia supplies the world with coffee and emeralds.
   It is also a leading source of the cocaine and marijuana smuggled into the United States.

6. It is often hard to find a certain kind of negotiator.
   Both sides will trust this negotiator.

7. Students of a certain kind are becoming rare.
   Their parents can afford the total cost of a college education.

8. The president's special emissary was sent to the Middle East for a purpose.
   He did not achieve the purpose.

### EXERCISE 3  Sentence Combining

Combine the sentences in each of the following sets by using one or more adjective clauses. Where possible, avoid clauses using the verb *be*—that is, starting with *who is, which are,* and the like. Combine the sentences of each set in at least two different ways. Then, if you prefer one of the combinations, put a check next to it.

EXAMPLE
Ronald Reagan won the presidency by a landslide in 1980.
Reagan made his name in the movies.
Then he became governor of California.
COMBINATION 1: Ronald Reagan, who won the presidency by a landslide in 1980, made his name in the movies and then became governor of California.
COMBINATION 2: Ronald Reagan, who made his name in the movies and then became governor of California, won the presidency by a landslide in 1980.

1. A fundamental belief guided the founding fathers.
   According to this belief, all men are created equal.

2. In 1848 men rushed to California.
   The men hoped to get rich quickly.
   Gold had just been discovered in California.

3. Pierre Charles L'Enfant laid out plans for the nation's capital in 1791.
   L'Enfant was a French architect.
   He had volunteered for service in the Continental Army.
   He had won the admiration of Washington for his heroism as an officer of engineers.

4. In 1978 a California medical school had to accept a man.
   The man was named Bakke.
   Bakke charged the school with reverse discrimination.
   Bakke won his case in the Supreme Court.

5. Space satellites are seeking the answer to a question.
   The space satellites are headed out beyond the solar system.
   The question has fascinated man for centuries.

6. Charlie Brown seems destined to remain forever a lovably bumbling little boy.
   He has been a national celebrity since the early fifties.
   That was when Charles M. Schulz invented him.

## 15.5 Adverb Clauses

Like an ordinary adverb, an **adverb clause** can modify a word, a phrase, or an entire clause. It begins with a subordinator, a word like *before* or *because:*

> To reach the store *before it closed,* I drove like a madman.

The adverb clause starting with *before* modifies the phrase *To reach the store.*

> Furious *because the door was locked,* I kicked and pounded on it.

The adverb clause starting with *because* modifies the adjective *furious.*

> *Even though I kicked and pounded on the door,* the storekeeper would not open it.

The adverb clause starting with *Even though* modifies the clause about the storekeeper.

### Adverb Clauses and Main Clauses

Directly or indirectly, an adverb clause is always subordinate to the main clause in a sentence:

ADVERB
CLAUSE          MAIN CLAUSE
*As he was being tackled,*   he threw the ball.

In this sentence the main point is that the player threw the ball; the subordinate point is that he was being tackled at the same time. The sentence is designed to fit into a particular kind of story, probably one in which the pass won the game:

> The line wavered, and Keene knew it would break in seconds. But he dropped back, dancing around until he spotted a receiver. *As he was being tackled, he threw the ball.* Polanski made a leaping catch at the twenty-five-yard line, came down running, zigzagged past the Iowa safety, and crossed the goal line. The crowd went wild.

But what if the story is different? Suppose the most important thing is not the pass but the tackle?

> Keene looked desperately for a receiver, sensing the seconds ticking away. Suddenly his blocking broke down and he was surrounded. *As he threw the ball, he was being tackled.* The pass went nearly straight up, then fell to earth behind him. The game was over.

Now the sentence highlights the tackle. In the structure of the sentence, as in the situation it describes, the tackle is more important than the pass that failed because of it. Once again, the adverb clause lets you indicate which of two actions is more important.

**Adverb Clauses and Adverbs**

An adverb clause normally tells more about what it modifies than an adverb does. Compare these two sentences:

> *Anxiously,* he threw the ball.
> *As he was being tackled,* he threw the ball.

The adverb and the adverb clause both modify *he threw the ball.* But the single word says much less than the clause. While the word suggests a state of mind, the clause conveys the tension and excitement of the action, the urgent sense that one action affects another, that one thing happens while or because or if or even though something else happens. An adverb clause lets the writer present the circumstances of an action as well as the action itself.

**Choosing Subordinators**

As noted earlier, an adverb clause starts with a **subordinator,** a word or phrase that subordinates the clause to whatever it modifies. A subordinator can be used to signal one of the following relations:

**1.** Time

> He threw the ball *as* he was being tackled.
> *Until* the power lines were restored, we had to read at night by candlelight.

You can also signal time with *after, as soon as, as long as, before, ever since, when,* and *while.*

**2.** Causality

> Kate was happy *because* she had just won her first case.
> *Since* he was being tackled, he threw the ball.

**3.** Concession and contrast

> Money cannot make you happy, *though* it can keep you comfortable.

The clause begun by *though* concedes a point that contrasts with the main point, which is that money cannot make you happy. If you attach *though* to the point about *money,* you can subordinate it to the point about comfort, and thus reverse the emphasis of the sentence:

> *Though* money cannot make you happy, it can keep you comfortable.

You can also signal concession and contrast with *although, even though,* and *whereas:*

> *Although* he was being tackled, he threw the ball.
> *Although* he threw the ball, he was being tackled.

*While* can signal concession and contrast as well as time:

> *While* Marian sang, Zachary played the piano. [time]
> *While* Finnegan himself never ran for any office, he managed many successful campaigns. [concession and contrast]

**4.** Condition

> *If* battery-powered cars become popular, the price of gas will drop.
> He ran *as if* he had a broken leg.

You can also signal condition with *provided that, unless,* and *as though.* (For more on conditional clauses, see section 23.4, pp. 377–78.)

**5.** Purpose

> I worked in a department store for a year *so that* I could earn money for college.

You can also signal purpose with *in order that* and *lest.*

**6.** Place

> Where federal funds go, federal regulations go with them.

**7.** Result

> We are *so* accustomed to adopting a mask before others *that* we end by being unable to recognize ourselves.          —William Hazlitt

Here *so* and *that* are separated. You can also use them together:

> She fixed the clock *so that* it worked.

**8.** General possibility

> *Whatever* the president wants, Congress has a will of its own.

You can also signal general possibility with *whenever, wherever, whoever, whichever,* and *however:*

> I can't pronounce the name *however* it is spelled.

**9.** Comparison

> The river is cleaner now *than* it was two years ago.

The clause begun by *than* completes the comparison initiated *cleaner.* (For more on writing comparisons see section 15.6, pp. 286–87.)

**Placing Adverb Clauses**

An adverb clause normally follows the word or phrase it modifies. But when it modifies a main clause, it can go either before or after that clause. To be clear-cut and straightforward, lead with your main clause and let the adverb clause follow:

> The colonel ordered an investigation as soon as he heard the complaint of the enlisted men.
> I worked in a department store for a year so that I could earn money for college.

That kind of order has a brisk, no-nonsense effect, and you will seldom go wrong with it. But it is not always the best order. To create suspense, or to build up to your main point, put the adverb clause at the beginning and save the main clause for the end. Consider these two versions of a sentence spoken by Winston Churchill in 1941, when the Germans had occupied most of Europe and were threatening to invade England:

> We shall not flag or fail even though large tracts of Europe and many old and famous states have fallen or may fall into the grip of the Gestapo and all the odious apparatus of Nazi rule.

Even though large tracts of Europe and many old and famous states have fallen or may fall into the grip of the Gestapo and all the odious apparatus of Nazi rule, we shall not flag or fail.

There is nothing grammatically wrong with the first sentence, which starts with a main clause and finishes with a long adverb clause. But this sentence has all the fire of a wet match. Because the crucial words *we shall not flag or fail* come first, they are virtually smothered by what follows them. By the time we reach the end of the sentence we may even have forgotten its main point. The arrangement of the second sentence—the one Churchill actually wrote—guarantees that we will remember. Precisely because we are made to wait until the end of the sentence for the main clause, it now strikes with telling effect.

**Shortened Adverb Clauses**

The adverb clause can sometimes be shortened:

Frank sings folk songs *while driving his car.*

The complete clause would be *while he is driving his car,* but the writer has dropped the subject *he* and the auxiliary verb *is.* You can do this with a few surbordinators, but only when the subject of the adverb clause is the same as the subject of the main clause it follows. If the two subjects are different, you may end up with a sentence like this:

*The gas tank exploded while driving the car.

Here is another example:

The pies should be left in the oven *until cooked.*

The complete clause would have been *until they* [or *the pies*] *are cooked.*

EXERCISE 4   **Sentence Combining**

Combine the sentences in each of the following pairs by turning one sentence into an adverb clause and attaching it to the other. Be sure to begin the adverb clause with a suitable subordinator, and in parentheses state the relation that the subordinator shows.

EXAMPLE
I see roses.
Then my nose starts to itch.
COMBINED: Whenever I see roses, my nose starts to itch. (time)

1. I had studied my notes for hours.
   I could not remember a thing.

2. The bell in the steeple tolled midnight.
   A shrouded figure appeared at the entrance to the cemetery.

3. Scientists will continue to investigate the universe.
   They may never discover life on another planet.

4. Assume that commercial airlines will offer regular flights to the moon by the year 2000.
   The moon may become the new playground of the super-rich.

5. The general saw that all his troops were ready.
   He ordered the invasion.

6. Many young wives are postponing motherhood indefinitely.
   Babies interfere with career plans.

7. I ran all the way to school in a downpour.
   I was drenched.

8. Tickets to professional football games get steadily more expensive.
   Each year the players demand higher salaries.

9. Wigglesworth lost the election.
   She had pledged to cut property taxes in half.

10. One clown took a huge, ungainly swing at the other and wound up punching himself in the nose.
    The children burst out laughing.


## 15.6   Making Comparisons Complete   *comp*

To be complete a comparison may require an adverb clause, as in the following examples:

> Most Americans are probably tested more *than they are taught.*
> —Thomas C. Wheeler
> The more I eat Blotto Flakes, *the less I like them.*
> The river is as clean now *as it was two years ago.*

Often you need the full clause; if you leave out *it was* in the last of these examples, the sentence will not be clear. But certain words can sometimes be omitted from the adverb clause—provided the comparison is perfectly clear without them. Such words are shown in parentheses here:

> The new exhaust system emits less sulphur dioxide *than the original system (did).*
> The new method of photographing a manuscript is not so [or "not as"] costly *as the old method (was).*
> Some writers think more about plot *than (they do) about characters.*

When you compare two versions of the same activity (two kinds of thinking, for instance), you don't need a full adverb clause after *than:*

> Many forces have contributed to the decline of American students' writing ability, but none has been more effective *than the widespread use of multiple choice tests.*   —Thomas C. Wheeler

A second *has been* is unnecessary because it would merely repeat the first one.

> Roger moves faster *than any other player on the team* (*does*).

*Does* may be omitted, but if Roger himself is a player on the team, the word *other* is essential. If you merely compare him with *any player*, you are comparing him with himself as well as with others, and doing that makes no sense.

> Tokyo's population is larger *than New York's* (*is*).

The *is* may be omitted, but the *-'s* on *New York* is essential. Without it the sentence is comparing a population to a city. You could also write:

> Tokyo's population is larger *than that of New York.*

### Exercise 5   Correcting Faulty Comparisons

Each of the following sentences makes a comparison. Revise any sentence in which the comparison is not clear and complete. If a sentence is correct as it stands, write *Correct*.

> EXAMPLE
> The river is as clean now as two years ago.
> REVISED: The river is as clean now as it was two years ago.

1. Gas and oil cost much more now than ten years ago.
2. Hardwoods such as maple and oak burn more slowly.
3. Jack tackles harder than anyone on the team. [Jack is a member of the team.]
4. The old house on the bay looks just as good as it did five years ago.
5. Some students care more about grades than learning.
6. Many teachers talk more than listen.
7. In 1970, Mexico's recorded murder rate was higher than any other country in the world.

## 15.7   Using Two or More Subordinate Clauses

A sentence can have more than one subordinate clause. Sometimes two or more subordinate clauses are directly attached to a main clause; sometimes one subordinate clause is attached to or contained within another. Consider the following examples:

1. When the alarm sounded, no one could leave the room because the door was bolted.

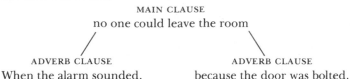

MAIN CLAUSE
no one could leave the room

ADVERB CLAUSE
When the alarm sounded,

ADVERB CLAUSE
because the door was bolted.

2. Before an applicant can have an interview, he or she must fill out a questionnaire that would baffle an Einstein.

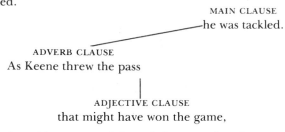

MAIN CLAUSE
he or she must fill out a questionnaire

ADVERB CLAUSE
Before an applicant can have an interview,

ADJECTIVE CLAUSE
that would baffle an Einstein.

3. As Keene threw the pass that might have won the game, he was tackled.

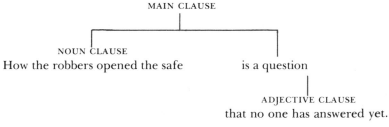

MAIN CLAUSE
he was tackled.

ADVERB CLAUSE
As Keene threw the pass

ADJECTIVE CLAUSE
that might have won the game,

4. How the robbers opened the safe is a question that no one has answered yet.

MAIN CLAUSE

NOUN CLAUSE
How the robbers opened the safe

is a question

ADJECTIVE CLAUSE
that no one has answered yet.

5. Historians believe that no one will ever discover what happened to the members of the 1902 polar expedition.

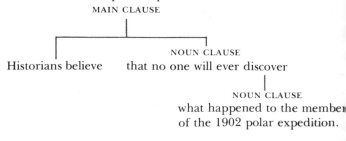

MAIN CLAUSE

Historians believe

NOUN CLAUSE
that no one will ever discover

NOUN CLAUSE
what happened to the member
of the 1902 polar expedition.

**EXERCISE 6  Sentence Combining: Review of Subordination**

Combine the sentences in each of the following sets by using at least two of the three different kinds of subordinate clauses—noun clauses, adjective clauses, and adverb clauses. Then in parentheses state which kinds of clauses you have used; if one of them is an adverb clause, state also what relation it shows. Note that the sentences of each set may be combined in more than one way.

EXAMPLE
Frank Waters was a powerful man.
He could not lift the big stove.
It weighed over four hundred pounds.
COMBINED: Though Frank Waters was a powerful man, he could not lift the big stove, which weighed over four hundred pounds. (adverb clause of contrast, adjective clause)

1. The Sioux Indians settled down near the Black Hills.
   The Black Hills were invaded by white men.
   The white men were searching for gold.

2. A U.S. treaty forbade white men to enter the Black Hills.
   Army cavalrymen entered the Black Hills in 1874 under General George Custer.
   Custer had led the slaughter of the Southern Cheyenne in 1868.

3. Red Cloud led the Sioux.
   Red Cloud denounced Custer's invasion.
   The invasion violated the treaty.

4. I had not seen the movie.
   Everyone else was talking about it.
   I felt left out of the conversation.

5. In the Bakke case, the Supreme Court ruled something.
   Bakke had to be accepted by a California medical school.
   The medical school had rejected him.

6. Suppose my rich uncle dies and leaves me all his money.
   I will buy a Rolls-Royce Silver Cloud.
   I can drive around in a certain style.
   Such a style will suit me.

# 16

# USING COORDINATION AND SUBORDINATION TOGETHER

## 16.1 Coordination and Subordination

Using coordination and subordination together, you can arrange all the parts of a sentence according to their relative importance. Almost every sentence calls for some subordination, some indication that one part is more important than another. But in some sentences you also want to put two or more parts on the same level of importance; you want to coordinate as well as subordinate. For example:

1. I remember Mr. Spingold.
2. He was short.
3. He was fat.
4. He always carried a black umbrella.
5. He always predicted rain.
   COMBINED: I remember Mr. Spingold, short and fat, who always carried a black umbrella and who always predicted rain.

The combined sentence is the product of coordination and subordination. Sentence 1 becomes the main clause. Sentences 2 and 3 turn into adjectives modifying *Mr. Spingold;* they are subordinated to *Mr. Spingold* and coordinated with each other in a compound phrase. Sentences 4 and 5 turn into adjective clauses modifying *Mr. Spingold,* the antecedent of both *who*'s, so they too are subordinated to *Mr. Spingold* and coordinated with each other.

This example shows how coordination and subordination work together in a sentence with just one main clause. But they can also work together in a sentence with two or more main clauses. For example:

1. No one had the guts to raise a riot.
2. But suppose a European woman went through the bazaars alone.
3. Somebody would probably spit betel juice over her dress.
   COMBINED: No one had the guts to raise a riot, but if a European woman went through the bazaars alone somebody would probably spit betel juice over her dress. —George Orwell

In the combined sentence, both sentence 1 and sentence 3 have become main clauses; they are on the same level of importance, coordinated with each other and joined by *but*. The result is a compound sentence. Within it, sentence 2 becomes a subordinate clause. The word *if* subordinates it to the main clause that used to be sentence 3.

When you can manipulate entire clauses in this way, you have the power to express a highly complicated idea in a single sentence. Here are further examples:

Thus the essence of freedom of opinion is not in mere toleration as such, but in the debate which toleration provides; it is not in the venting of opinion, but in the confrontation of opinion.
—Walter Lippmann

Lippmann reinforces the coordination between two main clauses by using parallel construction, with a total of four *in* phrases. At the same time, the sentence is enriched and varied by the adjective clause *which toleration provides;* it modifies *debate,* explaining what makes the debate possible.

Galileo and Shakespeare, who were born in the same year, grew into greatness in the same age; when Galileo was looking through his telescope at the moon, Shakespeare was writing *The Tempest* and all Europe was in ferment, from Johannes Kepler to Peter Paul Rubens, and from the first table of logarithms by John Napier to the Authorized Version of the Bible. —Jacob Bronowski

Here again coordination and subordination are skillfully used. The sentence conveys a powerful sense of simultaneous action, of many things happening at once. The ferment Bronowski talks about is packed into the very structure of his sentence, yet coordination and subordination work together to keep that ferment under control.

EXERCISE 1    **Sentence Combining**

This exercise tests your ability to use coordination and subordination together. If you feel uncertain about how to use coordination and subordination separately, review chapters 13, pp. 247–59, and 15, pp. 267–89, before you begin this exercise. Using coordination and subordination together, make one sentence from each of the following sets of sentences. Include all the information given, but feel free to change the wording or arrangement of the sentences. Combine the sentences of each set in at least two different ways. Then, if you prefer one of the combinations, put a check next to it.

EXAMPLE
The snow melts in the spring.
The dirt roads in the region turn into muddy streams.
Certain people live in isolated houses.
Those people use old footpaths to reach Bridgeton.
Bridgeton has two grocery stores.
It has one gas pump.
COMBINATION 1: The snow melts in the spring, so the dirt roads in the region turn into muddy streams; certain people live in isolated houses, and those people use old footpaths to reach Bridgeton, which has two grocery stores and one gas pump.
COMBINATION 2: When the snow melts in the spring, the dirt roads in the region turn into muddy streams, so people who live in isolated houses use old footpaths to reach Bridgeton, which has two grocery stores and one gas pump.

1. He seldom got angry.
   His opponents often misrepresented the facts.
   He believed something about reason.
   Reason alone had power, in his view, to win an argument.

2. Only a few men and women remember the famine of 1943.
   Many recall certain celebrations.
   Those celebrations marked the coming of peace in 1952.

3. At graduation the seniors are happy.
   They have earned their diplomas.
   They are also sad.
   They are leaving friends.
   They may never see the friends again.

4. The treasurer of the company proposed something.
   Suppose the company made a profit.
   Every employee would get a pay raise.
   Suppose the company took a loss.
   Every employee would get a pay cut.

5. Charleston, South Carolina, sits at the mouths of two rivers.
   The rivers empty into the Atlantic.
   The people of Charleston like to say something about their city.
   Charleston is a certain kind of place, in their opinion.
   Two rivers meet in that place to form an ocean.

6. The senator admitted something.
   The admission was public.
   He was an alcoholic.
   He offended some of his supporters.
   He got many letters.

The letters were sympathetic.
The letters were from certain people.
Those people admired his willingness to speak out.
He spoke on a personal problem.
He spoke honestly.
He spoke openly.

EXERCISE 2    **Writing One-Sentence Summaries**

This exercise tests your ability to compress as well as combine a set of sentences by means of coordination and subordination. Using either one or both, write a one-sentence summary of each of the following passages.

EXAMPLE
More than ever before in American politics, language is used not as an instrument for forming and expressing thought. It is used to prevent, confuse and conceal thinking. Members of each branch and agency of government at every level, representing every hue of politicial opinion, habitually speak a language of nonresponsibility.             —Richard Gambino, "Through the Dark, Glassily"
ONE-SENTENCE SUMMARY: More than ever before, American politicians and government workers use language not to express thought but to prevent, confuse, and conceal it; they speak a language of nonresponsibility.

1. The average person has many worries, but there is one thing he does not generally worry about. He does not worry that somewhere, without his knowledge, a secret tribunal is about to order him seized, drugged, and imprisoned without the right of appeal. Indeed, anyone who worries overmuch about such a thing, and expresses that worry repeatedly and forcefully enough, would probably be classified as a paranoid schizophrenic.
   —Hendrik Hertzberg and David C. K. McClelland, "Paranoia"
2. Of all things banish the egotism out of your conversation, and never think of entertaining people with your own personal concerns or private affairs; though they are interesting to you, they are tedious and impertinent to everybody else; besides that, one cannot keep one's own private affairs too secret.
   —Lord Chesterfield, in a letter to his son
   [Summarize Chesterfield's long sentence in a sentence of not over twenty words.]
3. Nevertheless a prince should not be too ready to listen to talebearers nor to act on suspicion, nor should he allow himself to be easily frightened. He should proceed with a mixture of prudence and humanity in such a way as not to be made incautious by overconfidence nor yet intolerable by excessive mistrust.
   —Niccolò Machiavelli, *The Prince*
4. The need of securing success at the *outset* is imperative. Failure at first is apt to damp the energy of all future attempts, whereas

past experiences of success nerve one to future vigor. Goethe says to a man who consulted him about an enterprise but mistrusted his own powers: "Ach! you need only blow on your hands!" And the remark illustrates the effect on Goethe's spirits of his own habitually successful career.

—William James, "Habit"

## 16.2   Untangling Your Sentences   *tgl*

It is sometimes hard to put several ideas into a single sentence without getting them tangled up in the process. Here, for instance, is a sentence written by a college freshman:

> *Due to the progress in military weaponry over the years, there has been an increased passivity in mankind that such advancements bring as wars are easier to fight resulting in a total loss of honor in fighting.

What does this sentence mean? To answer that question clearly, the writer must first take the sentence apart and state each of its ideas in a simple sentence:

1. There has been progress in military weaponry over the years.
2. There has been increased passivity in mankind.
3. Such advancements bring passivity.
4. The passivity is due to the progress.
5. Wars are easier to fight.
6. This results in a total loss of honor in fighting.

The first four sentences can now be turned into one simple sentence that eliminates repetition and redundancy:

> Progress in military weaponry over the years has brought increased passivity in mankind. [or] Progress in military weaponry over the years has made mankind more passive.

By parallel construction, sentence 5 can then be coordinated with the predicate of the new sentence:

> Progress in military weaponry over the years has made mankind more passive and wars easier to fight.

Finally, if sentence 6 states the result of these conditions, that may be the most important point of all, and the coordinated sentence just formed can be subordinated to it:

> Since progress in military weaponry over the years has made mankind more passive and wars easier to fight, there has been a total loss of honor in fighting. [or] Since progress in military weaponry over the years has made mankind more passive and wars easier to fight, fighting has lost all honor.

The original sentence is thus untangled, and its meaning brought to light. If you find a tangled sentence in your own writing, or if your teacher points one out to you, treat it as shown here. Take it apart so that you can see its individual points; then use coordination and subordination to put it clearly back together.

EXERCISE 3  **Sentence Untangling: A Challenge**

This may well be the toughest exercise in the book. All of the following sentences were written by students who had a lot to say but who got into a tangle when they tried to say it. So you will probably have trouble even figuring out what the writers meant. But we're asking you to do just that—and more. We're asking you to untangle each sentence in the same way we untangled the sentence about weaponry in the preceding discussion. First, cut up each tangled sentence into a series of short, simple sentences; second, using coordination, subordination, or both, recombine these into one long sentence that makes sense. If you can untangle even half of the following sentences to your own satisfaction, you'll be doing very well.

1. As a youth Moses led a secure life because of the pharaoh's daughter's adoption of him, but one day he rashly murdered an Egyptian overseer, forcing him to flee from Egypt and change his life-style.
2. The author of "The Cold Equations" is saying, in effect, that the main difference of life on the frontier for the people living there is their lives are ruled by laws of nature rather than rules that people make.
3. For fifty years the people prospered under his rule; then feeling a personal responsibility for the welfare of his subjects and their safety, the old king fought another monster which he was severely injured and soon died.
4. If something in one of your paragraphs is marked as being "wrong," one possibility is the teacher making a mistake, not you, although the possibility is seldom admitted, teachers being mostly sure they are always right.
5. Since he spent so much time outdoors in nature which he loved so much, there was no reason to try and prevent it from entering his cabin, and he symbolized a doormat as a mistake of avoiding the sight of natural things like leaves and soil like his neighbors did.
6. The bean field made him self-sufficient, which was one of his beliefs, and he could also see it as an extension of himself, through the bean field, into nature in returning to a natural state.

# 17

# COMPLETE SENTENCES AND SENTENCE FRAGMENTS

**17.1**

Good writers usually make their sentences complete. They do so because complete sentences convey or help to convey what most readers expect to find in writing: complete thoughts. Sentence fragments often do just the opposite. Unless skillfully used, they convey the impression that the writer's thoughts are fragmentary or incomplete.

To make all of your sentences complete or even to use sentence fragments skillfully, you must know the difference between a complete sentence and a sentence fragment. This chapter explains the characteristics of sentence fragments, the risks of using them, and the ways of turning them into complete sentences.

## 17.1 What Is a Sentence Fragment?

A sentence fragment is a part of a sentence punctuated as if it were a whole one. Here are some examples:

1. Then went to bed.†
2. Charlie Chaplin.
3. To keep litterbugs from spoiling the beaches.
4. Because it gives you a superstar smile.
5. But always meeting ourselves.
6. Showing an ability to think quickly in tight spots.

† Normally in this book nonstandard constructions used for illustration are marked with a star. However, in this chapter sentence fragments are not starred because, as the text points out, they may be acceptable under certain special circumstances.

Each of these examples *looks* like a sentence. Each begins with a capital letter and ends with a period, and each gives information. But none of them is complete. Fragment 1 lacks a subject; it could be turned into a sentence like *Then I went to bed.* Fragment 2 lacks a predicate; it could be turned into something like *Charlie Chaplin was the great tramp comedian of silent films.* Many of the other examples appear to have been cut off by their punctuation from their rightful place in a sentence. Thus fragment 3 might be part of a sentence like this: *The selectmen in Wellfleet have been discussing ways to keep litterbugs from spoiling the beaches.*

## 17.2  What's Wrong with Sentence Fragments?

Rightly or wrongly, sentence fragments turn up often in both speech and writing. In conversation we use and hear them all the time. Fragment 2, for instance, could be the spoken answer to a spoken question, such as *Who was the great tramp comedian of silent films?* We also use fragments in informal letters—letters written to a reader who knows the writer well. Fragment 1, in fact, comes from a letter sent by J. R. R. Tolkien to his son Christopher—a letter in which he wrote:

> Spent part of day (and night) struggling with chapter. Gollum is playing up well on his return. A beautiful night with high moon. About 2 A.M. I was in the warm silver-lit garden, wishing we two could go for a walk. Then went to bed.

This passage contains several fragments, but the reader for whom it was written certainly had no trouble understanding it. Because Christopher knew the letter was from his father, he could take it for granted that the subject of *Spent* and *went* was *I.*

Sentence fragments appear not only in conversation and informal letters but also in print. Consider these passages:

> Buy Dazzle toothpaste. Today. Because it gives you a superstar smile.                                    —Advertising copy

> Every life is many days, day after day. We walk through ourselves, meeting robbers, ghosts, giants, old men, young men, wives, widows, brothers-in-love. But always meeting ourselves.
>
> —James Joyce

Each of these has one or more sentence fragments, but no problems result; the meaning of each fragment is perfectly clear in its context. In fact, these fragments serve to emphasize points that might not have been made so effectively with complete sentences.

So why should you not feel free to use sentence fragments

in your own essays? The answer is that until you learn how to use them sparingly and strategically, your writing will look disorganized. Consider the two sentence fragments in this piece of student writing:

> In conclusion I feel Falstaff proves to be a most likable and interesting character. Showing an ability to think quickly in tight spots. But above all he lends a comical light to the play. Which I feel makes it all the more enjoyable.

This passage is not much longer than the one by Joyce, but it is harder to read. Joyce's passage has just one fragment, and coming as it does at the end, after a long, abundantly complete sentence, the four-word tailpiece snaps the reader to attention. But the student's two fragments are simply confusing. Alternating with sentences of about equal length, they seem improvised and arbitrary—as if the writer could only now and then form a complete thought.

Though sentence fragments can sometimes enhance a passage, they are just as likely to break it into disconnected pieces. For that reason, they are generally not accepted in college essays, and you should avoid them. If you do use a sentence fragment, be sure that the surrounding text reveals your ability to write complete sentences, and be prepared to say why you have written the fragment.

## 17.3 Spotting and Correcting Sentence Fragments *frag*

To correct sentence fragments, you have to be able to spot them. How can you tell whether a particular word group is a sentence fragment? Here are some useful questions to ask if you aren't sure.

**1.** Does the "sentence" sound like a sentence?

Before you submit your essay, read the whole thing aloud, exaggerating the fall of your voice whenever you come to a period. Often when you read a sentence fragment, the sound of your voice contrasting with the sense of your words will tell you that something is missing from the "sentence" you have just read.

**2.** Does the "sentence" have a subject and a predicate?

A sentence has both a subject and a predicate; a word group lacking either one is a sentence fragment. (If you aren't sure you can identify subject and predicate, see chapter 10, pp. 201–10.) Consider this example:

> Entertained tens of thousands with an outdoor concert every Fourth of July.

This word group has no subject; we are not told who did the entertaining. To make a complete sentence, you must supply a subject:

> Arthur Fiedler entertained tens of thousands with an outdoor concert every Fourth of July.

Here is another example:

> All of the officials with jobs at the Kennedy Space Center.

This word group has no verb; it could be a subject lacking a predicate—in which case you must supply one:

> All of the officials with jobs at the Kennedy Space Center were worried about the fall of Skylab.

Or perhaps this word group is meant to be not a subject but part of a predicate. Then you must supply both a subject and a verb:

> The director summoned all of the officials with jobs at the Kennedy Space Center.

Here is one more example:

> With a panoramic view of the Rockies.

Here both subject and predicate are missing; the word group is a modifier floating without a headword. Often in such a case the headword can be found in the sentence just before the fragment:

> They went to a ski lodge. With a panoramic view of the Rockies.

To fix a fragment of this type, combine it with the preceding sentence:

> They went to a ski lodge with a panoramic view of the Rockies.

And here is a final example:

> After inventing the telephone.

As before, both subject and predicate are missing. *Inventing*, a participle, cannot be the verb of a sentence; it is a modifier of some missing word. Again, in such a case the missing word is often found in the sentence just before or after the fragment:

> After inventing the telephone. Alexander Graham Bell turned his attention to the phonograph.

To fix a fragment of this type, combine it with the adjacent sentence:

After inventing the telephone, Alexander Graham Bell turned his attention to the phonograph.

**3.** If the "sentence" has both a subject and a predicate, does it start with a subordinator?

Because political success often calls for compromise.

This word group is a clause, for it has its own subject and predicate. In conversation it could be the answer to a question:

Why is it hard to find perfect consistency in a politician? Because political success often calls for compromise.

In conversation we often answer a *Why* question with a *Because* statement. *Because* is a subordinator. It makes the whole clause subordinate, and in formal written English a subordinate clause cannot stand alone. Directly or indirectly, it must be connected to a main clause:

Perfect consistency in a politician is rare because political success often calls for compromise. [or] Because political success often calls for compromise, perfect consistency in a politician is rare.

Subordinators include such words as *since, because, although, when, if, after,* and *whoever.* (For a full discussion of clauses introduced by subordinators, see section 15.5, pp. 281–85.)

**4.** If the "sentence" has both a subject and a predicate, does it start with a relative pronoun, such as *who* or *which?*

Which can fly from New York to London in three hours.

This word group is a clause, but it begins with a relative pronoun, *which.* (For more on relative pronouns, see pp. 275–77.) A pronoun of this type makes the whole clause modify something else—an antecedent. To complete the sentence, you must supply an antecedent, and the antecedent must be either connected to or included in a main clause:

The British and French together developed a supersonic plane called the Concorde, which can fly from New York to London in three hours.

**5.** If the "sentence" has both a subject and a predicate, does it start with a noun and an adjective clause?

The Ohio senator who sought the Republican presidential nomination in 1952.

The word group beginning with *who* is a clause, and *who* makes it an adjective clause, with *The Ohio senator* as the antecedent. (For more on adjective clauses, see section 15.4, pp. 274–79.) Once

again, the antecedent must be either connected to or included in a
main clause:

> General Dwight D. Eisenhower easily beat Robert A. Taft, the Ohio
> senator who sought the Republican presidential nomination in
> 1952. [or] Robert A. Taft, the Ohio senator who sought the Repub-
> lican presidential nomination in 1952, was beaten by General
> Dwight D. Eisenhower.

**EXERCISE 1   Recognizing Sentence Fragments**

Identify each of the following word groups as either a sentence or a sentence fragment.

1. The gunman stood behind the gatehouse at the main entrance
   to the palace.
2. Forgot to put a stamp on the envelope.
3. But the Egyptians rejected the proposal when it was first made.
4. To make abortion once again illegal throughout the United
   States.
5. The people who want to abolish all nuclear power plants.
6. I had no time to correct the essay before submitting it.
7. After crawling for three hours in pitch darkness.
8. Under the welcome mat at the front door.
9. Which goes a hundred miles on a gallon of gas.
10. Whenever I see a thick, juicy steak sizzling on a barbecue.

## 17.4   Avoiding Sentence Fragments

To avoid fragments, you need to know how they happen. Here are
some common ways.

**1.** The writer breaks up a single sentence by using a period where
there should be either a comma or no punctuation at all:

> On Halloween night some years ago, a full-grown man with a sick
> sense of humor disguised himself as a ghost. *So that he could terrify
> little children.*

Because *So that* is a subordinator, the italicized word group is a
fragment—cut off by a period from the sentence about the man in
disguise. Such an error can easily occur if you finish a sentence and
then decide to expand it. To add the fragment to the sentence,
change the period before it to a comma or simply remove the
period, and write the first word without a capital letter:

> On Halloween night some years ago, a full-grown man with a sick
> sense of humor disguised himself as a ghost so that he could terrify
> little children.

Now look at this passage:

> I cut my hand on the first day of the trip while trying to open a can of spaghetti. *With a hatchet.*

A period cuts off the phrase *With a hatchet* from the clause about cutting the hand. Perhaps the writer was trying for an effect—a kind of verbal double take—but the result is still a fragment. It would be better to write:

> I cut my hand on the first day of the trip while trying to open a can of spaghetti with a hatchet.

**2.** The writer skips the subject in the belief that a previous sentence has already provided it:

> Lancelot won fame as a knight because of his prowess in battle. *Defeated the other great warriors in the kingdom.*
>
> —College freshman

This passage appeared in an examination bluebook, and the writer may have been pressed for time. In any case, he forgot to provide a subject for the second word group. If you budget your time for a writing assignment so that you can reread what you have written before turning it in, you will probably be able to catch any error of this type and correct it by supplying the missing subject:

> Lancelot won fame as a knight because of his prowess in battle. He defeated the other great warriors in the kingdom.

**3.** The writer omits the verb and instead provides it in the next sentence:

> *Staying up all night to finish a paper.* That left me red-eyed in the morning.

The first word group is a subject without a predicate. Perhaps the writer began with one idea about how to write the sentence, and then switched to another idea without revising what was already on paper. There are two ways of eliminating the fragment. You can combine it with the sentence that comes next:

> Staying up all night to finish a paper left me red-eyed in the morning.

Or you can rewrite it as a separate sentence:

> I stayed up all night to finish a paper. That left me red-eyed in the morning.

**EXERCISE 2  Eliminating Sentence Fragments**

Each of the following consists of a sentence and a sentence fragment—not necessarily in that order. Make whatever changes are necessary to eliminate the fragment.

EXAMPLE
I cut my hand on the first day of the trip while trying to open a can of spaghetti. With a hatchet.
REVISED: I cut my hand on the first day of the trip while trying to open a can of spaghetti with a hatchet.

1. The farmers welcomed the evening breeze. Because they had sweltered all day.
2. When the temperature falls below zero and a north wind blows across the pasture. A pair of long johns will keep you warm.
3. To keep the cabin from slipping into the pond. We had to put a jack under the front porch and raise the frame eight inches.
4. I followed the buck for three tough miles. Running hard to keep up with him.
5. After a long search I found the ignition key. In a little box magnetically attached to the inside of the front bumper.
6. Gathering your own firewood takes plenty of hard work. But saves you money.
7. One reason for this punishment could have been the people's sullen behavior. Their constant complaining about their burdens.
8. Some dream of leaving the city and finding better conditions in the country. Such as uncrowded neighborhoods, peaceful streets, and clean air.
9. The people of America should develop their country's natural resources. In order to be free of foreign domination.
10. Carts were handy for pioneers winding their way over mountains. Whereas families crossing the Great Plains needed wagons.
11. According to one historian, Julius Caesar suffered from dizzy spells. Even fell to the ground sometimes.
12. A construction crew has started work on the foundation of the new library. Which will be paid for by donations from the alumni.
13. The sight of approximately five hundred people waiting to enter the store. It made the manager beam with pride.
14. The affluent nations are not meeting their obligations to the millions living in the Third World. And suffering from malnutrition, inadequate health programs, and widespread unemployment.
15. Astronomers at the Mount Flume observatory have been disappointed by the performance of the new telescope. Supposed to have been the most powerful of its kind.

## EXERCISE 3 Eliminating Sentence Fragments

The following paragraph is a rewritten version of a paragraph in Erich Fromm's *The Heart of Man.* In rewriting Fromm's paragraph, we have deliberately introduced several sentence fragments. Make whatever changes are necessary to remove them.

line 2: manipulated so

     In a bureaucratically organized and centralized industrial-
ism, tastes are manipulated. So that people consume maximally
and in predictable and profitable directions. Their intelligence and
character become standardized. By the ever increasing role of tests
5  which select the mediocre and unadventurous. In preference to
the original and daring. Indeed, the bureaucratic-industrial civilization which has been victorious in Europe and North America has
created a new type of man; he can be described as the *organizational
man.* As the *automaton man,* and as *homo consumens.* He is, in addi-
10  tion, *homo mechanicus;* by this I mean a gadget man. Deeply attracted by all that is mechanical. And inclined against that which is
alive. It is true that man's biological and physiological equipment
provides him with such strong sexual impulses. That even *homo
mechanicus* still has sexual desires and looks for women. But there is
15  no doubt that the gadget man's interest in women is diminishing.
A *New Yorker* cartoon pointed to this very amusingly; a salesgirl
trying to sell a certain brand of perfume to a young female customer recommends it by remarking: "It smells like a new sports-
car." Indeed, any observer of male behavior today will confirm
20  that this cartoon is more than a clever joke. There are apparently
a great number of men. Who are more interested in sports cars,
television and radio sets, space travel, and any number of gadgets.
Than they are in women, love, nature, food; who are more stim-
ulated by the manipulation of nonorganic, mechanical things than
25  by life.

# 18

# USING
# PRONOUNS

A **pronoun** is a word that commonly takes the place of a noun or noun phrase that has already been used:

> Brenda thought that she had passed the exam.
> The old man smiled as he listened to the band.

*She* takes the place of *Brenda,* a noun; *he* takes the place of *the old man,* a noun phrase. Pronouns thus eliminate the need for awkward repetition. Without them, you would have to write sentences like these:

> Brenda thought that Brenda had passed the exam.
> The old man smiled as the old man listened to the band.

A pronoun can also take the place of a whole clause or a sentence:

> On June 28, 1914, the archduke of Austria was assassinated by Serbian nationalists. That precipitated World War I.

## 18.1   Pronouns and Antecedents

As already stated in "Relative Pronouns and Antecedents," pp. 275–77, the word or word group that a pronoun refers to is called the **antecedent** of the pronoun. In the sentence about Brenda, the antecedent of *she* is *Brenda;* in the sentence about the old man, the antecedent of *he* is *The old man;* in the passage about the archduke, the antecedent of *That* is the whole first sentence. Now consider this example:

The victors in the ancient Olympic games enjoyed dazzling prestige. They were idolized for their achievement.

There are two pronouns here, *They* and *their*. Both refer to the same antecedent, *The victors.*

> Shortly before the war of 1914, an assassin whose crime was particularly repulsive (he had slaughtered a family of farmers, including the children) was condemned to death in Algiers. He was a farm worker who had killed in a sort of bloodthirsty frenzy but had aggravated his case by robbing his victims.　　—Albert Camus

The pronouns here are *whose, he, He, who, his,* and *his.* The antecedent of *he* and *He* is *an assassin;* the antecedent of *his* and *his* is *a farm worker.* You may have recognized *whose* and *who* as relative pronouns, words that normally come right after their antecedents and that introduce adjective clauses. The antecedent of *whose* is *an assassin,* and the antecedent of *who* is *a farm worker.*

> To build city districts that are custom-made for easy crime is idiotic.

*That* is a relative pronoun; its antecedent is *city districts.*

> To build city districts that are custom-made for easy crime is idiotic. Yet that is what we do.　　—Jane Jacobs

Here the second *that* refers to a whole word group: *To build city districts that are custom-made for easy crime.*

### EXERCISE 1　Recognizing Pronouns and Antecedents

Each of the following includes one or more pronouns. Write down each pronoun and its antecedent, using an arrow to identify the antecedent.

> EXAMPLE
> Sharon was surprised to find a frog in her mailbox.
> her ——→ Sharon

1. One of Jeff's hobbies is restoring old cars. He is now working on a 1955 Thunderbird that his father bought in Indianapolis.
2. Senator Black has assured his closest associates he will confer with them before deciding whether or not to seek reelection. Concerned about his failing health, they hope he will retire.
3. The children felt uneasy when the waiter served them cold bean soup. This was something that they had never seen before, and they were suspicious. It looked strange in the small bowls.
4. In the midst of the argument Sally said that she had never lost her temper. This amazed Mick, who saw her turning purple even as she said it.
5. When several children in the audience shouted that the magician was hiding something, she invited two of them to join her on the stage so that they could observe the next trick at close range.

## 18.2  Pronouns That Have No Antecedent

Although a pronoun is usually preceded by its antecedent, some pronouns have no antecedent, and others may sometimes be used without one.

**1.** Certain pronouns, such as *everyone* and *anything*, normally have no antecedent. Compare these two sentences:

> *She* needs some privacy.
> *Everyone* needs some privacy.

*She* is a **definite** pronoun. It refers to a particular person, and its meaning is clear only if its antecedent has been provided—that is, if the person has already been identified. But *Everyone* is an **indefinite** pronoun. Because it refers to unspecified persons, it has no antecedent. Other widely used indefinite pronouns include *everybody, no one, each, many,* and *some.* (For a complete list of indefinite pronouns, see p. 314.)

**2.** The pronouns *I* and *you* normally have no antecedent because they are understood to refer to the writer and the reader or to the speaker and the listener.

**3.** A definite pronoun needs no antecedent when it is immediately followed by a relative pronoun, such as *who:*

> Those who cannot remember the past are condemned to repeat it.
> —George Santayana

*Those* has no antecedent; it is explained by what comes after it rather than by what comes before.

**4.** The pronoun *we* sometimes appears without an antecedent, for example in newspaper editorials, where the writer clearly speaks for a group of people. But do not use *we* when you mean simply *I.* That is a privilege limited to royalty and the pope. If you use *we,* you should let your reader know just whom *we* refers to. That is what we have done on the title page of this book.

## 18.3  Pronoun Reference  *pn ref*

### Clear Reference

The meaning of a definite pronoun is clear when readers can identify the antecedent with certainty. Here are some examples of clear reference:

> The selectmen recommend a tax on public parking. They believe it would give the city approximately $10,000 annually.

The antecedent of each pronoun is obvious. *They* clearly stands for *The selectmen,* and *it* stands for *a tax on public parking.*

> People who saw the Tall Ships sail up the Hudson River in 1976 will long remember the experience. It gave them a handsome image of a bygone era.

Again, the antecedent of each pronoun is obvious. *Who* clearly refers to *People; It* refers to *the experience; them* refers to *People who saw the Tall Ships.*

> The attorney stated that his client, Mary White, had been hospitalized for seven weeks. This, he claimed, was the reason for her prolonged absence from her job.

The meaning is clear because we can tell that *his* and *he* refer to *The attorney, This* refers to the fact that *his client . . . had been hospitalized for seven weeks,* and *her* refers to *Mary White.*

**Unclear Reference**

The meaning of a definite pronoun is unclear when readers cannot identify the antecedent with certainty:

> The detective studied the manuscript with the aid of a powerful magnifying glass. Then he put it in his pocket and left the library.

The meaning of *he* is clear, but the meaning of *it* is ambiguous: is the antecedent *the manuscript* or *a powerful magnifying glass*? You can't be sure. Sometimes you may have to replace the pronoun with a noun in order to be clear:

> Then he put the magnifying glass in his pocket and left the library.

Here is another example of unclear reference:

> George Orwell's *1984* contains vivid descriptions of the way political prisoners are tortured in a police state. They put you in a special room and confront you with whatever you fear most of all.

The second sentence here has two faults. First, the writer uses the pronoun *they* vaguely, as people often do when they say or write such things as "In some states they don't really enforce the speed limits" or "In high school they made me take three years of algebra." In the sentence about *1984,* the reader has no way of knowing who is meant by *They.* The only possible antecedent in this context is *prisoners,* but this hardly makes sense, since the prisoners are in no position to put anyone in a special room. So *They* has no antecedent. Second, the writer uses the pronoun *you* vaguely. Strictly speaking, the pronoun *you* can refer only to the person directly addressed by the writer—in other words, the reader. But here it is made to stand for *prisoners.*

With the first sentence left unchanged, the second may be improved in either of two ways. One is to replace the initial *They* by *A guard* (*A torturer* would be equally suitable) and the confusing *you*'s by *them* and *they*—both of which would clearly refer to *prisoners:*

> A guard puts them in a special room and confronts them with whatever they fear most of all.

The other is to turn *put* and *confront* into passive-voice verbs:

> They are put in a special room and confronted with whatever they fear most of all.

*They* now clearly refers to *prisoners.* The prisoners are indeed the ones who are put in a special room and confronted with what they fear.

Here is one more example of unclear reference:

> A recent editorial contained an attack on the medical profession. The writer accused them of charging excessively high fees.

Who is meant by the pronoun *them?* From the phrase *medical profession* you may guess that the writer is referring to doctors. But *profession* cannot be the antecedent of *them,* for *them* is plural and *profession* is singular. Before using *them,* the writer should clearly establish its antecedent:

> A recent editorial contained an attack on hospital administrators and doctors. The writer accused them of charging excessively high fees.

Finally, the reference of a pronoun will be unclear if the pronoun gets too far from its antecedent:

> Bankers have said that another increase in the prime lending rate during the current quarter would seriously hurt their major customers: homeowners, small business personnel, and self-employed contractors using heavy equipment. It would keep all of these borrowers from getting needed capital.

The definite pronoun *It* is so far from its antecedent that we cannot readily put the two together. To clarify the second sentence, the writer should repeat the antecedent:

> Such an increase would keep all of these borrowers from getting needed capital.

EXERCISE 2  **Supplying Pronouns**

Complete each of the following with one or more pronouns referring to the word or phrase shown in italics.

EXAMPLE
Harriet viewed *her car* with disgust. Noticeably rusty, __it__ looked out of place between the new Cadillac and the gleaming Lincoln Continental.

1. After hearing *Roger* praise the appearance of the ugliest statue in the museum, Wanda was tempted to turn her back on _____ and leave.
2. *Today's dollar* buys about one-fifth of what _____ bought forty years ago.
3. The patient's back was covered with *sores*. According to his doctor, _____ might have been caused by malnutrition.
4. The police said they have found no evidence to suggest *the door* was forced open. _____ bore no marks of rough handling.
5. *Warts* are wonderful structures. _____ can appear overnight on any part of the skin, like mushrooms on a damp lawn, full grown and splendid in the complexity of _____ architecture.          —Lewis Thomas, with words deliberately omitted

EXERCISE 3  **Correcting Unclear Pronouns**

In each of the following, the italicized pronoun has been used confusingly. Briefly diagnose what is wrong, and then provide a cure, in the shape of a revised sentence.

EXAMPLE
The boy and the old man both knew that *he* had not much longer to live.
DIAGNOSIS: *He* is ambiguous; it can refer to either the boy or the old man.
CURE: The boy and the old man both knew that the old man had not much longer to live. [The ambiguous pronoun is simply replaced by its antecedent.]

1. The tracker fired at the cave from which the cry had come. He was directly on target, for *it* struck Coyotito in the head.
2. Hanging on a wall to the right of the entrance was a huge map showing the floor plan of the modern edifice. *It* was painted in six different colors.
3. Johnny kept throwing his cup to the floor. Finally, his mother decided to break him of *it*.
4. The job was tough. *They* made me work seventy-two hours a week.
5. The new robots work twenty-four hours a day without making a mistake, whereas human workers normally operate on eight-

hour shifts and make mistakes periodically. Thus *they* have substantially increased production.

## 18.4 Making Pronouns and Antecedents Agree *pn agr*

Wherever possible, a pronoun should agree with its antecedent in gender and number.

### Gender

In English, gender affects only the singular definite pronoun, which is masculine (for example, *he*), feminine (*she*), or neuter (*it*), depending on the gender of its antecedent. Consider this passage:

> The men of our civilization have stripped themselves of the fineries of the earth so that they might work more freely to plunder the universe for treasures to deck my lady in. New raw materials, new processes, new machines are all brought into her service. My lady must therefore be the chief spender as well as the chief symbol of spending ability and monetary success. While her mate toils in his factory, she totters about the smartest streets and plushiest hotels with his fortune upon her back and bosom, fingers and wrists, continuing that essential expenditure in his house which is her frame and her setting, enjoying that silken idleness which is the necessary condition of maintaining her mate's prestige and her qualification to demonstrate it.
> —Germaine Greer, *The Female Eunuch*

The feminine pronouns *her* and *she* refer to *my lady*, a woman; the masculine pronoun *his* refers to *her mate*, a man; the neuter pronoun *it* refers to a thing, *her mate's prestige*. The distinctions among *his* and *her*, *she* and *it*, help to make the meaning of the passage clear.

### Pronouns with Antecedents of Unspecified Gender

When the antecedent of a pronoun is clearly singular and masculine, you use *he, his,* or *him;* when the antecedent is clearly singular and feminine, you use *she* or *her.* But what do you use when the gender of the antecedent is not clear—when it could be either masculine or feminine? What do you do with words like *everyone, student, doctor,* and *lawyer?* Not long ago, it was considered all right to say:

> Everyone has his own story to tell.
> A doctor needs years of training before he is fully qualified to operate.

But sentences like these are unfair to women. Saying *his* or *he* seems to imply that *Everyone* is exclusively male or that all doctors are men. To be fair to women, you must recognize that words like *everyone* usually refer to both sexes. Here is one way of using pronouns fairly:

> Everyone has his or her own problems.
> A doctor needs years of training before he or she is fully qualified to operate.

This double-pronoun construction is now widely used. But there is a problem with it. If repeated, the double pronouns soon become tedious and distracting:

> A doctor needs years of training before he or she is fully qualified to operate on his or her patients by himself or herself.

One alternative to *he or she* is *s/he*. But *s/he* cannot be read aloud, and even if it could be, it could not take the place of *his or her*. Another alternative is *he/she, her/his,* and *himself/herself,* but repetition of these soon becomes just as tedious as the repetition of a phrase like *he or she*. Still another alternative is the following:

> *Everyone has their own story to tell.

*Their* can refer to both women and men, so its use eliminates the need for *his or her;* the problem is that *their* is plural, and does not match *Everyone,* which should be treated as singular in formal writing. When the antecedent is a specific word, such as *doctor,* the mismatch becomes even more glaring:

> *A doctor needs years of training before they are fully qualified to operate.

Fortunately, there are better ways of avoiding sexism in the use of pronouns. One way is to make the antecedent plural, so that it does match the plural pronoun:

> Doctors need years of training before they are fully qualified to operate.

Another way is to avoid specifically masculine and feminine pronouns altogether—when you can:

> To become fully qualified to operate, a doctor needs years of training.
> Everyone has a story to tell.
> Everyone has personal problems.

## Number

A pronoun is singular if it refers to one person or thing, and plural if it refers to more than one.

A singular antecedent calls for a singular pronoun; a plural antecedent calls for a plural pronoun:

> The boy saw that he had cut his hand.
> The Oilers thought they would win their first game.

Antecedents of the following kinds are problem cases—hard to classify as either singular or plural. We suggest that you treat them as indicated.

**1.** Two or more nouns or pronouns joined by *and* are usually plural:

> Orville and Wilbur Wright are best known for their invention of the airplane.
> He and I left our coats in the hall.

Nouns joined by *and* are singular only if they refer to one person or thing:

> The chief cook and bottle-washer demanded his pay.

**2.** When two nouns are joined by *or* or *nor,* the pronoun normally agrees with the second:

> A squirrel or a chipmunk has left its tracks in the new-fallen snow.
> Neither Pierre LaCroix nor his boldest followers wanted to expose themselves to danger.

*Its* matches *chipmunk,* and *themselves* matches *his boldest followers.*

**3.** A noun or pronoun followed by a prepositional phrase is treated as if it stood by itself:

> In 1980 the United States, together with Canada and several other countries, kept its athletes from participating in the Moscow Olympics.

The antecedent of *its* is simply *United States.* Unlike the conjunction *and,* a phrase like *together with* or *along with* does not make a compound antecedent. The antecedent is what comes before the phrase.

> The leader of the strikers said that he would negotiate.

The pronoun agrees with *leader,* just as if *of the strikers* were omitted and *leader* stood by itself, with the sentence reading *The leader said that he would negotiate.*

**4.** Collective nouns can be either singular or plural, depending on the context:

> The team chooses its captain in the spring.

Since the captain is a symbol of unity, the writer treats *The team* as singular, using the singular pronoun *its.*

The audience shouted and stamped their feet.

Since each person in the audience was acting independently, the writer treats *The audience* as plural, using the plural pronoun *their*.

**5.** Some indefinite pronouns are singular, some are plural, and some can be either singular or plural:

ALWAYS SINGULAR

| | | |
|---|---|---|
| anybody | either | one |
| anyone | neither | another |
| anything | nobody | somebody |
| each | none | someone |
| each one | no one | something |
| everybody | nothing | |
| everyone | | whatever |
| everything | | whichever |
| | | whoever |

ALWAYS PLURAL

both    few    others    several

SOMETIMES SINGULAR AND SOMETIMES PLURAL

| | | |
|---|---|---|
| all | many | some |
| any | most | |

As this list indicates, *each* is always singular:

Each of the men brought his own tools.

Here *each* serves as the antecedent of the possessive pronoun, which is therefore singular—*his*. But when *each* follows a plural noun, the pronoun agrees with the noun:

The men each brought their own tools.

The antecedent of *their* is *men,* not *each.*

Though some writers treat *everybody* and *everyone* as plural, we recommend that you treat them as singular, or simply avoid using them as antecedents:

Everyone in the cast had to furnish his or her own costume.
The cast members each had to furnish their own costumes.

The number of a pronoun in the third group depends on the number of the word or phrase to which it refers:

Some of the salad dressing left *its* mark on my shirt.

Some of the students earn *their* tuition by working part time.

Many of the customers do not pay *their* bills on time.

Many a man owes *his* success to *his* first wife, and *his* second wife to *his* success. —Sean Connery

**6.** The number of a relative pronoun depends on the number of its antecedent:

> Marcia is one of those independent women who want to work for *themselves*.

> Marilyn is the only one of the graduating women who wants to start *her* own business.

**EXERCISE 4   Recognizing Correct Pronoun Agreement**

Each of the following consists of two sentences. In one sentence the number of each pronoun matches that of its antecedent; in the other there is a faulty shift in number. Say which sentence is correct—and why.

EXAMPLE
(a) A squirrel or a chipmunk had left its tracks in the new-fallen snow.
(b) A squirrel or a chipmunk had left their tracks in the new-fallen snow.
Sentence *a* is correct because the singular pronoun *its* matches the singular noun *chipmunk*—which is the second of two antecedents joined by *or*.

1. (a) Steve liked playing soccer, but not the warm-ups they had to do before a game.
   (b) Steve liked playing soccer, but not the warm-ups he had to do before a game.
2. (a) Gritch, together with many of his fiercest followers, wanted to vent their rage in a ferocious counterattack.
   (b) Gritch, together with many of his fiercest followers, wanted to vent his rage in a ferocious counterattack.
3. (a) As the ambulance sped off with the injured man, the crowd broke up and shuffled back to their cars.
   (b) As the ambulance sped off with the injured man, the crowd broke up and shuffled back to its cars.
4. (a) Neither of the two men has openly declared their candidacy.
   (b) Neither of the two men has openly declared his candidacy.
5. (a) Everyone carried their own provisions.
   (b) Everyone carried his or her own provisions.
6. (a) Twenty years ago, a woman who kept her own name after marriage was hardly considered married at all.
   (b) Twenty years ago, a woman who kept their own name after marriage was hardly considered married at all.
7. (a) Groucho is the only one of the Marx brothers who went from fame in the movies to a television show of their own.

*Making Pronouns and Antecedents Agree* 315

(b) Groucho is the only one of the Marx brothers who went from fame in the movies to a television show of his own.

8. (a) As usual, the orchestra will give their final performance of the year on December 30.

(b) As usual, the orchestra will give its final performance of the year on December 30.

## 18.5  Pronoun Case  *pn ca*

The **case** of a pronoun is the form it takes as determined by its role in a sentence. An essay about Paul McCartney, for instance, might include the following statements:

> *He* sings soulfully.
> Teen-agers love *him*.
> *He* likes to polish *his* Rolls-Royce.

The pronouns *He, him,* and *his* all have the same antecedent, Paul McCartney. They are different because they have different functions in the sentences: the first serves as a subject, the second serves as an object, and the third indicates possession. In English only a few pronouns have case forms.

CASE FORMS OF PRONOUNS

PERSONAL PRONOUNS

|  | I | He | She | It | We | You | They |
|---|---|---|---|---|---|---|---|
| *Subject case* | I | he | she | it | we | you | they |
| *Object case* | me | him | her | it | us | you | them |
| *Possessive case* | my, mine | his | her, hers | its | our, ours | your, yours | their, theirs |
| *Reflexive / emphatic case* | myself | him-self | her-self | itself | our-selves | yourself, your-selves | them-selves |

PRONOUNS USED IN QUESTIONS AND ADJECTIVE CLAUSES

|  | Who | Whoever |
|---|---|---|
| *Subject case* | who | whoever |
| *Object case* | whom | whomever |
| *Possessive case* | whose |  |

## Subject Case

Use the subject case when the pronoun is the subject of a verb:

> *Who* knows anyone else perfectly?
>
> When Adam and Eve were accused of eating the forbidden fruit, *they* each excused themselves; *he* blamed Eve for tempting him, and *she* blamed the serpent for tempting her.
>
> My best friend in the first grade was a boy named Nate, *who* moved away just before *I* started the second grade. After *he* moved away, *he* and *I* drew comic books for each other about some characters *we* invented, and *we* sent them back and forth in the mail.

Do not use an expression like *him and I* or *me and him* as the subject of a verb.

## Object Case

**1.** Use the object case when the pronoun is the direct or indirect object of a verb:

> Rolls-Royces are so expensive that only millionaires can afford *them.*
>
> After several weeks of silence, Janet finally sent *us* a postcard.
>
> The earliest thing I can remember is the day that my father took my sister and *me* to the circus.

Do not use an expression like *my sister and I* as the object of a verb.

**2.** Use the object case when the pronoun is the object of a preposition, a word such as *to* or *against:*

> When John F. Kennedy was assassinated, people from all over the world paid tribute to *him.*
>
> Where can the voters find an honest and effective leader? To *whom* can they turn?
>
> From the start of the tournament, I figured that Southwick was the man to beat, and that if I could get through the semifinals, I would end up playing against *him.*

**3.** Use the object case when the pronoun comes immediately before an infinitive:

> The teacher asked *me* to recite the Gettysburg Address in front of the whole school.
>
> The coach told Rosenberg and *me* to run eight laps before practice began.
>
> Just to be sure, he watched *us* run.

### Possessive Case

**1.** Use the possessive case of the pronoun to indicate ownership of an object or close connection with it:

> Jill's trip went smoothly until she reached Santa Fe, where an accident wrecked *her* motorcycle and broke *her* leg in three places.
> *Whose* right is greater—the mother's or the unborn child's?
> On summer nights everyone sat outside, we on *our* front porch and the neighbors on *theirs*.

*Theirs* here means *their porch;* this type of possessive has a possessed thing as its antecedent. Other examples are as follows:

> The house is *mine.*
> The car is *yours.*
> The ring is *hers.*

**2.** Use the possessive case of the pronoun to indicate responsibility for an action:

> The pollsters predicted that Senator Blank would lose. *His* winning of the New Hampshire primary surprised almost everyone, and for the first time, commentators began to speak of *his* gaining the nomination.
> Because I had already studied calculus in high school, the math department approved *my* taking of advanced calculus.

Do not write *\*approved me taking.* When you use an *-ing* word as a verbal noun—as the name of an action—the pronoun before it must be in the possessive case. Use the object case only if the pronoun is an object and the *-ing* word is a modifier of it:

> She caught *me* taking a piece of cake.

(For more on this point, see section 12.4, pp. 243–44.)

**3.** Use the possessive case of the pronoun to indicate experience of an action:

> Senator Stump's campaign was badly shaken by *his* defeat in the New Hampshire primary.

By itself, *his defeat* refers to the defeat experienced by Senator Stump. To refer to his defeat of someone else, the term must be followed by *of* and an object:

> Senator Stump gained national attention by *his* defeat of Senator Claghorn in the New Hampshire primary.

**4.** Do not confuse *its* and *it's* or *their, there,* and *they're*. If you are unsure about which of these words to use in a sentence, look them up in the Glossary of Usage, pp. 529 and 538.

## Reflexive/Emphatic Case

**1.** Use the reflexive/emphatic case of the pronoun to indicate a reflexive action—an action affecting the one who performs it:

> While sharpening a knife, the butcher cut *himself.*
> I groaned when I saw *myself* in the mirror.

**2.** Use the reflexive/emphatic case of the pronoun to indicate emphasis:

> The Alaskans *themselves* had mixed feelings about the new pipeline.
> The governor *herself* was opposed to the bill.

**3.** The forms *\*hisself* and *\*theirselves* are not used in Standard American English.

EXERCISE 5   **Choosing Correct Case**

Choose the correct form for the pronoun or pronouns in each of the following sentences, and explain the reason for each choice.

> EXAMPLE
> The coach watched Rosenberg and (I, me) run.
> *Me* (object case) is correct because the pronoun is the direct object of the verb *watched.*

1. (Me, My) father wants (me, my) to become an engineer.
2. Ruth's favorite sport is tennis; (my, mine) is hockey.
3. (Me, My) mother was smart; whenever (she, her) had just one chocolate bar to split between (me, my) sister and (I, me), she asked (I, me) to cut the candy in half and gave (me, my) sister first choice.
4. The Israelis believe that (they, their) country will always be subject to attack.
5. (She, Her) and (I, me) always get into arguments about politics.
6. To (who, whom) are we sending messages in outer space?
7. Sometimes children (who, whom, whose) parents are both working have to look after (them, themselves).
8. Harrigan wanted to run the club like a marine platoon. He hated (me, my) raising of objections.
9. The teacher asked Harriet and (I, me) to give a report on Greenland.
10. An experienced stunt man can fall down a whole flight of stairs without hurting (him, hisself, himself).

# 19

# SUBJECT-VERB
# AGREEMENT

## 19.1 What Is Agreement?

To say that a verb **agrees** in form with its subject is to say that a verb has more than one form, and that each form matches up with a particular kind of subject. Here are three parallel sets of examples based on a verb in the common present tense:

|  | STANDARD AMERICAN ENGLISH | FRENCH | SPANISH |
|---|---|---|---|
| *Singular* | I live | je vis | (yo) † vivo |
|  | you live | tu vis | (tú) vives |
|  | he lives | il vit | (él) vive |
|  | she lives | elle vit | (ella) vive |
| *Plural* | we live | nous vivons | vivimos |
|  | you live | vous vivez | vivis |
|  | they live | ils vivent [masc.] | (ellos) viven [masc.] |
|  |  | elles vivent [fem.] | (ellas) viven [fem.] |

† In Spanish, when the subject is a pronoun, it is sometimes omitted.

In this example, Spanish has six different verb forms, French has five, and Standard American English has just two: *live* and *lives*. When a verb changes its form to agree with its subject, the verb is said to be inflected. The English verbs are much less inflected than the Spanish and French verbs.

# 19.2 Choosing the Verb Form— Rules of Agreement  *sv agr*

Here are the rules governing agreement of subject and verb.

**1.** In most cases, the subject affects the form of the verb only when the verb is in the present tense. When the tense is present and the subject is a singular noun, add *-s* or *-es* to the bare form of the verb:

> Peggy *wants* to study economics.
> The bank *gives* 6 percent interest.
> Seymour *polishes* the car once a week.

Add *-s* or *-es* also when the tense is present and the subject is a third-person singular pronoun, such as *she, it, this, each,* or *everyone:*

> It *serves* over two thousand depositors.
> Each of them *holds* a passbook.
> He *does* the dishes once a month.

**2.** When the tense is present and the subject is not a singular noun or a third-person singular pronoun, use the bare form of the verb:

> Economists *study* the rise and fall of prices.
> Reporters and novelists both *write* for a living.
> We *polish* silver.
> Most of O'Henry's stories *have* surprise endings.
> I *do* very little work on Sundays.

In speaking certain dialects of English, you may use such forms as *He live* and *They goes.* But in writing Standard American English, you must follow the rules just given, which require *He lives* and *They go.*

**3.** Whatever the subject, do not add *-s* or *-es* to a verb accompanied by an auxiliary, such as *does, can,* or *may:*

> Does he *play* the sax?
> Can she *sing?*
> He can *run.*
> She may *dance.*
> The plane should *fly.*

**4.** Do not add *-s* or *-es* to the infinitive—whether or not it is preceded by *to:*

> Gail expects Jack to *wash* the dishes. [infinitive with *to*]
> Gail makes Jack *wash* the dishes. [infinitive without *to*]

Do not write *\*Gail makes Jack washes the dishes.*

**5.** Use the forms of *be* as shown here. This is the only verb in English with more than two forms in the present tense and more than one in the past:

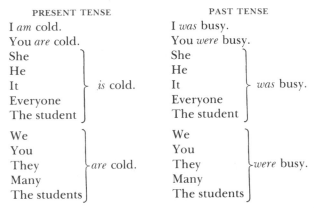

PRESENT TENSE

I *am* cold.
You *are* cold.

She
He
It      } *is* cold.
Everyone
The student

We
You
They    } *are* cold.
Many
The students

PAST TENSE

I *was* busy.
You *were* busy.

She
He
It      } *was* busy.
Everyone
The student

We
You
They    } *were* busy.
Many
The students

In speaking certain dialects of English, you may use such forms as *She be cold* and *They be cold.* But in writing Standard American English, you must use the forms shown here.

**6.** Use the forms shown here when *be* serves as an auxiliary:

I *am* confused by tax forms.
The building *is* painted every two years.
Supposedly, prisoners of war *are* protected by the Geneva Convention.
Jane *is* learning to speak Russian.
Several doctors *are* attending the meeting.
Last night I *was* awakened by a scream.
My roommates *were* awakened too.
Architects *were* examining a house erected in 1703.
One architect *was* explaining its construction.
Naomi *was* completing an experiment in physics.
Each of the diamonds *was* shining.

**7.** When the verb is *have,* whether by itself or as an auxiliary, use *has* if the subject is a singular noun or a third-person singular pronoun. With all other subjects, use the bare form, *have:*

I *have* a headache.
My dog *has* fleas.
Many students *have* jobs.
I *have* worked on a tobacco farm.
Strong men *have* failed to lift that carton.
She *has* finished plowing the wheat field.
The bank *has* closed for the holiday.
Two suspects *have* been questioned by the police.
Many of the athletes *have* been exercising for two hours.
Everyone *has* been waiting for the parade to start.

EXERCISE 1   **Using Correct Verb Forms**

For each verb in parentheses, write down a verb form that agrees with the subject. The correct form will sometimes be the same as the one in parentheses.

EXAMPLE
A nice cold drink (taste) good on a hot day.
tastes

1. Whenever Frank (sing), Ellen (dance).
2. Whenever Ellen (hear) Frank (sing), she (dance).
3. Many men (fix) cars for a living; Jack (fix) bicycles.
4. Can he (reach) Indianapolis by six?
5. If he (catch) the 4:05 bus, he can (reach) Indianapolis by six.
6. I (have) three courses this term; she (have) four.
7. They (have) failed the courses; he (have) passed.
8. The workers (be) angry; the manager (be) frightened.
9. The workers (be) complaining; the manager (be) refusing to listen.
10. While they (was *or* were) throwing rocks at his office window, he (was *or* were) escaping by the back door.
11. Most people (do)n't work on Sundays, but Father Francis (do).
12. Money (do)n't grow on trees.

## 19.3   Finding the Subject

To make a verb form agree with the subject of the verb, you must know where to find the subject. This is easy to do when the subject comes right before the verb, as it does in many sentences:

s
Alan Paton   /   has written movingly about life in South Africa.

s
Many readers   /   consider *Cry, the Beloved Country* a classic.

s
The theme of the novel   /   is an ancient one, the struggle between people who hate and people who love.

However, a subject sometimes follows its verb, as in the kinds of sentences listed next.

**1.** Sentences starting with *There* or *Here:*

s
There was once   /   a thriving civilization in the jungles of the Yucatán.

s
Here comes   /   trouble.

**2.** Sentences with inverted word order:

                                                                    s
Visible alongside millions of U.S. roadways is  /  evidence of
                                                   widespread
                                                   littering.

For this example, the customary word order would be:

                        s
Evidence of widespread littering  /  is visible alongside millions of
                                     U.S. roadways.

**3.** Some questions:

                        s
Does  /  the course in astronomy  /  require homework?

                        s
Have  /  recent decisions of the Supreme Court  /  clarified
                                                    matters?

EXERCISE 2    **Recognizing Subjects and Verbs**

Write down the complete subject and the verb of each of the following
sentences.

EXAMPLE
During the rainy season few farmers labor in the fields.
SUBJECT: few farmers
VERB: labor

1. Darwin, on the other hand, extended his revolution in thought
   consistently throughout the entire animal kingdom.
                                          —Stephen Jay Gould
2. In the area between Spokane and the Snake and Columbia rivers to the south and west, many spectacular, elongate, subpar-
   allel channelways are gouged through the loess and deeply into
   the hard basalt itself.            —Stephen Jay Gould
3. How could we ever convert an adult rhinoceros or a mosquito
   into something fundamentally different?
                                          —Stephen Jay Gould
4. There is no gene "for" such unambiguous bits of morphology
   as your left kneecap or your fingernail.
                                          —Stephen Jay Gould
5. During the past fifteen years, however, challenges to Darwin's
   focus on individuals have sparked some lively debates among
   evolutionists.                     —Stephen Jay Gould
6. Disappearing into the hugeness of system is not unattractive.
                                          —Richard Hugo
7. With single-syllable words we can show rigidity, honesty,
   toughness, relentlessness, the world of harm unvarnished.
                                          —Richard Hugo

8. Behind the company's present fiscal policies lies a record of broken agreements and inept management.

9. Both the unemployment rate and the inflation rate are determined by the total level of spending on the goods and services produced by the economy.　　　　　—Edwin Mansfield

10. How does monetary policy affect our national output and the price level?　　　　　—Edwin Mansfield

## 19.4　Recognizing the Number of the Subject

A subject is considered singular when it means one, and plural when it means more than one. Some subjects are made with words or word groups that are **fixed** in number, clearly marked by their spelling or by some inherent feature; other subjects are made with words that are **variable** in number, changing with the contexts in which they are used. We treat each category in turn.

## 19.5　Recognizing Number—Words and Word Groups Fixed in Number

Words and word groups fixed in number include most nouns and pronouns (whether modified or not), verbal nouns, and noun clauses.

### Nouns

**1.** The number of most nouns is indicated by their spelling. A final -*s* or -*es* usually indicates the plural:

| Singular | Plural |
|---|---|
| boy | boys |
| automobile | automobiles |
| sandwich | sandwiches |
| cassette | cassettes |
| boss | bosses |
| lens | lenses |

If you don't know whether to add -*s* or -*es*—to a word like *poncho,* for example, or *portico*—see your dictionary. Some nouns form the plural by changing their spelling in other ways:

| Singular | Plural |
|---|---|
| tooth | teeth |
| child | children |
| man | men |
| woman | women |
| datum | data |
| criterion | criteria |

Again, see your dictionary if you don't know the plural of a particular word, or if you don't know whether a word is singular or plural.

**2.** A noun ending in *-s* but referring to just one thing is treated as singular:

> The news *is* largely created by those who report it.
> *The Grapes of Wrath was* written by John Steinbeck.
> Economics *touches* almost every aspect of our lives.
> *Sixty Minutes is* one of my favorite TV shows.
> Politics *is* the science of how who gets what, when and why.
> —Sidney Hillman
> Robotics *is* the study of robots—machines designed to work like human beings.

**3.** Some nouns have no plural form:

> patience
> courage
> paternalism
> frigidity

**Pronouns**

Some pronouns used as subjects are always treated as singular; some are always treated as plural:

ALWAYS SINGULAR

| | | |
|---|---|---|
| I | each | one |
| he | each one | another |
| she | | |
| it | everybody | somebody |
| | everyone | someone |
| this | everything | something |
| that | | |
| | either | whatever |
| anybody | neither | whichever |
| anyone | | whoever |
| anything | nobody | |
| | none | |
| | no one | |
| | nothing | |

ALWAYS PLURAL

| | | | |
|---|---|---|---|
| we | these | both | others |
| they | those | few | several |

**Modified Nouns and Pronouns**

The number of a modified noun or pronoun usually depends on the noun or pronoun itself—not on any of the modifiers attached to it. Normally, therefore, the verb should agree with the noun or pronoun—not with any of the modifiers.

A ship *enters* the harbor every Friday.
A ship carrying hundreds of tourists *enters* the harbor every Friday.
The girls *swim* fifty laps every day.
The girls that Sally Benson is coaching for an Olympic medal *swim* fifty laps every day.
*Each* of the candidates *has* published a list of contributors to his or her campaign.
I suspect that none of the candidates *is* telling the whole truth.
Every one of the Catholics and Protestants in Northern Ireland *knows* what political violence is.
Neither of the finalists *was* well-known before the tournament began.
The leader of the abolitionists *was* John Brown.
The leaders of the expedition *were* Meriwether Lewis and William Clark.

## Verbal Nouns

A subject based on a verbal noun is treated as singular:

Reassembling the broken pieces of a china bowl *takes* steady hands and patience.

The simple subject is *Reassembling*, a verbal noun.

To raise two million dollars for the hospital *is* our goal for the year.

The simple subject is the verbal noun *to raise*.

## Noun Clauses

A subject consisting of a single noun clause is treated as singular:

That they got the letter *was* by no means certain.

But a compound noun clause is treated as plural:

What Karen said and what she meant *were* two different things.

EXERCISE 3   Recognizing Number

Each of the following consists of a word, phrase, or clause that could be used as a noun and therefore as the subject of a verb. With this use in mind, classify each as singular or plural. You may want to refer to your dictionary.

EXAMPLE
the texture of the woolen goods
singular

1. oxen
2. comparing last year's prices with the present ones
3. everybody
4. women who seek a high position in the federal government
5. data
6. an apparatus for recording the sounds made by whales
7. few
8. to reduce the incidence of heart disease among people under forty
9. whoever examines the town's financial reports
10. *The Three Musketeers* [a novel]

## 19.6 Recognizing Number— Words Variable in Number

When the subject is made with a word that is variable in number, the number of the subject depends on the context in which the word is used—that is, on the words used with it. Several kinds of nouns and certain pronouns are variable in number. They are described next.

**Nouns**

**1.** A noun that is spelled the same in the plural as in the singular usually depends for its number on the words used with it:

> A deer *is* nibbling the lettuce in our garden.
> Two deer *were* spotted in the south pasture last night.

In the first sentence *A* makes *deer* singular; in the second sentence *two* makes the same word plural. Its form does not change.

> In Japan, one means of transportation *is* a two-wheeled cart known as a rickshaw.
> Three other means of transportation used there *are* cars, bicycles, and trains.

In the first sentence *one* makes *means* singular; in the second sentence *Three other* makes the same word plural. Again, its form does not change. Other nouns of this type are *species, sheep,* and *moose.*

**2.** A collective noun is singular when it refers to a unit, and plural when it refers to the individuals that make up the unit:

> To an actor, the audience *is* a big dark animal waiting to be fed.
> The audience *were* coughing and shuffling their feet.

Other collective nouns are *board, class, committee, crowd, faculty, group, jury, majority, minority, public,* and *team.*

**3.** A noun of whole measurement is singular when it means a unit, and plural when it refers to separate items:

> Fifty pounds *is* a lot to lose in one month.
> Ten miles *was* the length of the race.
> Miles of railroad track in America *need* repair.

Other nouns of whole measurement are *quarts, dollars,* and *kilometers.*

**4.** A noun of partial measurement depends for its number on what is being measured:

> Half of her jewels *were* stolen.
> Half of the cake *was* eaten.

*Half of her jewels* is plural because *jewels* is plural. *Half of the cake* is singular because *cake* is singular.

**5.** Certain nouns ending in *-s* may refer either to a single field of study or to items in a collection. Treat them as singular when they refer to a field, and as plural when they refer to the items in a collection:

> Statistics *is* the study and analysis of numerical information about the world.
> Recent statistics *show* a marked decline in the birthrate during the past twenty years.

**Pronouns**

Pronouns that are variable in number include *all, any, many, more, most, some, who, that,* and *which.* The number of such a pronoun depends on the number of the word or phrase to which it refers:

> Most of the sand *is* washed by the tide.
> Most of the sandpipers *are* white.
> All of the money *was* gone.
> All of the ships *were* lost.
> Some of the oil *has* been cleaned up.
> Some of the problems *have* been solved.
> A woman who *wants* complete financial independence starts her own business.
> Women who *want* complete financial independence start their own businesses.
> Titan is one of the fifteen known satellites that *revolve* around Saturn.

Titan is the only one of those satellites that *has* an atmosphere.

*Many* is singular only when used with *a:*

Many of the men *underestimate* women.

Many a man *underestimates* women.

### EXERCISE 4  Recognizing Number

Write down the complete subject of the italicized verb in each of the following sentences. Then say whether the subject is treated as singular or as plural—and why.

EXAMPLE
Most of the pies *were* stale.
Most of the pies
The subject is treated as plural because the number of *Most* depends on the number of the word it refers to—*pies.*

1. The team *practices* six days a week.
2. Some of the coloring *looks* unfinished.
3. Billions *are* needed by undeveloped nations.
4. Fifty dollars *was* a lot to pay for a sun visor.
5. The public *are* welcome at all of the meetings.
6. People who *live* in glass houses may have a heating problem.
7. None of the furniture *was* in place for the grand opening.
8. George is the only one of the hikers who *has* climbed above twenty thousand feet.
9. The crowd *was* noisy before the game.
10. Bert likes to spend his vacation in an old mining town that *defies* description.

### EXERCISE 5  Composing with Correct Agreement

Use each of the following nouns and pronouns as the subject in two sentences, adding modifiers as necessary. Treat the noun or pronoun as singular in the first sentence and as plural in the second. Use verb *a* in the first sentence, verb *b* in the second.

EXAMPLE
some   a. was   b. have
Some of the oil was cleaned up.
Some of the problems have been solved.

1. sheep   a. shivers   b. gather
2. dollars   a. is   b. buy
3. third   a. was   b. were
4. most   a. has   b. have
5. who   a. hates   b. dance

# 19.7 Recognizing Number—Compound Subjects

**1.** When items joined by *and* or *both . . . and* refer to more than one person or thing, treat the subject as plural:

> Both Jupiter and Saturn *have* now been photographed at close range.
> The lion and the tiger *belong* to the cat family.
> The lion, the tiger, and the cougar *belong* to the cat family.

When items joined by *and* refer to one person or thing, treat the subject as singular:

> The chief executive of the United States and the commander in chief of its armed forces *is* the president.
> Ham and eggs *is* one of my favorite dishes.

**2.** When items are joined by *or, either . . . or, neither . . . nor, not . . . but,* or *not only . . . but also,* the verb should agree with the second item, no matter what the first is. Treat the subject as singular if the second item is singular, and as plural if the second item is plural:

> Neither steel nor glass *cuts* a diamond.
> Not only Alaska but also Mexico *has* major oil reserves.
> Not only the Arab states but also Mexico *has* major oil reserves.
> Not a new machine but new workers *are* needed for the job.

**3.** When a noun or pronoun is followed by a phrase like *together with* or *but not,* the result looks like a compound, but it isn't one. The verb should agree with what comes before such a phrase, not with what comes after it:

> Edmund, together with Goneril and Regan, *meets* disgrace and death at the end of the play.
> Many senators, but not the senator from Wyoming, *support* the bill.

### EXERCISE 6  Recognizing Number

Write down the complete subject and the verb of each of the following sentences. Then say whether the subject is treated as singular or as plural—and why.

> EXAMPLE
> Both a carpenter and a painter are working on the new wing.
> SUBJECT: Both a carpenter and a painter
> VERB: are working
> The subject is plural because the items joined by *and* refer to two persons.

1. Not stars but planets are visible on a night like this.
2. Either our dog or the neighbor's cat has taken the suet.

3. Neither a pile of sandbags nor a heavy-duty pump is able to prevent water from seeping into the basement.
4. The town manager, along with five selectmen, has approved the proposed budget.
5. Not only Mexico but the Arab states have major oil reserves.
6. Brad's aunt and uncle capture poisonous snakes for a living.

## 19.8   Recognizing Number—Special Cases

**1.** When a subject begins with *every,* treat it as singular:

Every cat and dog in the neighborhood *was* on the street fighting.

**2.** When a subject consists of a plural noun followed by *each,* treat it as plural:

Big cities each *have* their own special problems.

**3.** Treat *the number of* as always singular, *a number of* as always plural:

*The* number of applications *was* huge.
*A* number of women now *hold* full-time jobs.

**4.** When the subject is a foreign word or expression, use a dictionary to find out whether it is singular or plural:

The *coup d'état* just completed *has caught* diplomats by surprise.
The *Carbonari* of the early nineteeth century *were* members of a secret political organization in Italy.

**5.** When the sentence begins with *It* and a linking verb, make the verb singular:

It *has been* many years since man first landed on the moon.

**6.** When the sentence begins with *There* and a linking verb, make the verb agree with the noun immediately after it:

There *were* seagulls resting on the beach.
There *was* a desk and two chairs in the room.
There *were* two chairs and a desk in the room.

**7.** When the subject is followed by a linking verb and a predicate noun, make the verb agree with the subject:

His business *was* newspapers.
Newspapers *were* his business.

EXERCISE 7   **Recognizing Number**

Write down the complete subject and the verb of each of the following sentences. Then say whether the verb is singular or plural—and why.

EXAMPLE

There are mounds of dirt in the backyard.

SUBJECT: mounds of dirt

VERB: are

The verb is plural to match the plural of *mounds*.

1. The cargo on the boat was bananas.
2. It is ten miles from Lexington to Boston.
3. Directly under the label are two pictures.
4. Many a prisoner has tried to escape.
5. Every manager, foreman, and worker on the line is working to keep the company solvent.
6. The Smith sisters each have a tractor.

## EXERCISE 8  Correcting Faulty Agreement

In some of the following sentences, the verb does not agree with its subject. Correct every verb you consider wrong and then explain the correction. If a sentence is correct as it stands, write *Correct*.

EXAMPLE

One of the insurance agents arc a graduate of my university.

The verb should be *is* because the subject is *One,* a singular pronoun.

1. The members of the transportation committee have agreed on a solution to the parking problem on Main Street.
2. There has been many thunderstorms this summer.
3. A lawyer for the insurance company is reviewing my case.
4. Each of the spectators are bringing a pair of field glasses.
5. *Twenty Thousand Leagues under the Sea* have thrilled thousands of readers.
6. A number of bird watchers is gathering at Stony Point this Sunday.
7. Both the players and the owners want to negotiate new contracts.
8. Two-thirds of the room have been painted.
9. No one in the two buildings was injured in the fire.
10. Does everybody in the four towns want a fair?
11. Ten cents are little to pay for a large glass of cold lemonade.
12. Half of the apartments in the building is without heat.
13. Half of the furniture in the office was rented.
14. Physics are an important course for engineering students.
15. An additional means of support need to be found.

## EXERCISE 9  Choosing Correct Verb Forms

In some of the following sentences the subject is singular; in some it is plural. Write down the subject of each sentence, and choose the verb form that agrees with it.

SV

19.8

EXAMPLE
One of the candidates (was, were) a seventy-five-year-old woman.
SUBJECT: One
VERB: was

1. The only thing he loved (was, were) the cheers of the audience.
2. Two hundred dollars (was, were) all I could pay for the car.
3. Mumps (is, are) painful to many adults.
4. Neither the Arab nations nor Israel (wants, want) yet another all-out war.
5. There (was, were) thirteen colonies when America declared its independence of Great Britain.

EXERCISE 10   Correcting Faulty Agreement

It is one thing to deal with subject-verb agreement in individual sentences; it is another to deal with it in paragraphs and essays, as you will have to do when you revise your own essays before you turn them in. To give you practice in this kind of revising, we have deliberately inserted some mistakes of subject-verb agreement in the following passage from Juanita H. Williams's *Psychology of Women.* We hope you can spot and correct them.

EXAMPLE
lines 3–5: efficiency and level . . . are usually measured

Cognition is the process by which the individual acquires knowledge about an object or an event. It includes perceiving, recognizing, judging, and sensing—the ways of knowing. The efficiency and level of the acquisition of knowledge is usually
5 measured in older children and adults by the use of tests which requires language. Studies of infant cognition, of what and how babies "know," have begun to appear only in the last decade, with the development of new techniques which provides insights into what and how babies learn.
10 In spite of the persistent belief that babies differ along sex lines—for example, that girl babies vocalize more and boy babies are more active—sex differences in cognitive functions in the first two years of life has not been demonstrated (Maccoby and Jacklin, 1974). Measurements of intellectual ability, learning, and memory
15 does not differ on the average for boys and girls. However, patterns of performances are different for the two sexes, as are the consistency (thus the predictability) of the measures as the infants get older. A longitudinal study of 180 white, first-born infants, 91 boys and 89 girls, each of whom were tested in the laboratory at
20 four, eight, thirteen, and twenty-seven months, offers some evidence concerning these patterns (Kagan, 1971). One of the behaviors for which different patterns were observed for boys and girls were vocalization, the infant's response when aroused or excited by an unusual or discrepant stimulus.

# 20

# VERBS
# Tense

If English is your native language, you probably have a good work-ing knowledge of tenses. You know how to describe what someone or something did in the past, is doing in the present, or will do in the future. But you may not know just how to describe an action that doesn't fall neatly into one time slot. For instance, how do you describe the action of a character in a novel or a play? How do you describe an action that started in the past but is still going on now? How do you write about an action that will be completed at some time in the future? This chapter is chiefly meant to answer ques-tions like those.

The chapter is limited to verbs in the indicative mood (the mood of fact or matters close to the fact) and in the active voice (in which the subject performs the action, as in "Harry *drives* an old jalopy"). For a full discussion of mood, see chapter 23, pp. 373–79; for a full discussion of voice, see chapter 22, pp. 365–72.

## 20.1 Tense and Time

The **tense** of a verb helps to indicate the time of an action or con-dition:

> PAST: The sun *rose* at 6:03 this morning.
> PRESENT: As I *write* these words, the sun *is setting*.
> FUTURE: The sun *will rise* tomorrow at 6:04.

But tense is not the same as time. A verb in the present tense, for instance, may be used in a statement about the future:

The bus *leaves* tomorrow at 7:30 A.M.

As in this example, the time of an action or state is often indicated by a word or phrase like *tomorrow, next week,* or *last week.*

## 20.2   Forming the Tenses   *tf*

**Forming the Principal Parts of Verbs**

The tenses of all but a few verbs are made from the four **principal parts:** the present (also called the "bare" form), the present participle, the past, and the past participle. The principal parts of most verbs are formed as shown here, with *-ing* or *-ed* added to the bare form as indicated. Such verbs are called **regular.**

| PRESENT (BARE FORM) | PRESENT PARTICIPLE | PAST | PAST PARTICIPLE |
|---|---|---|---|
| cook | cook*ing* | cook*ed* | cook*ed* |
| lift | lift*ing* | lift*ed* | lift*ed* |
| polish | polish*ing* | polish*ed* | polish*ed* |

Verbs with some principal parts formed in other ways are called **irregular.** Here are some examples:

| eat | eating | ate | eaten |
|---|---|---|---|
| write | writing | wrote | written |
| go | going | went | gone |
| speak | speaking | spoke | spoken |

(For the principal parts of commonly used irregular verbs, see section 20.5, pp. 349–53.)

**Forming the Present**

With most subjects, the form of a verb in the present tense is simply the bare form:

> I *drive* a cab.
> I *polish* it once a week.

But after a singular noun or a third-person singular pronoun, such as *she, it, this, each,* or *everyone,* you must add *-s* or *-es* to the bare form of the verb:

> Helen *likes* her work.
> Helen *drives* a cab.
> She *polishes* it once a week.

(For more on this point, see section 19.2, pp. 321–22.)

## Forming the Past

The past tense of regular verbs is formed by the addition of *-d* or *-ed* to the bare form:

> Helen *liked* her work.
> She *polished* her cab regularly.

(For the past tense of commonly used irregular verbs, see section 20.5, pp. 349–53.)

## Forming Tenses with Auxiliaries

Besides the present and the past, there are four other tenses. You form these by using auxiliary verbs, such as *will, has,* and *had:*

|  | REGULAR VERB | IRREGULAR VERB |
|---|---|---|
| FUTURE: | She will work. | She will speak. |
| PRESENT PERFECT: | She has worked. | She has spoken. |
| PAST PERFECT: | She had worked. | She had spoken. |
| FUTURE PERFECT: | She will have worked. | She will have spoken. |

## Using Common and Progressive Forms

The **common** forms discussed so far indicate a momentary, habitual, or completed action. Ths **progressive** forms indicate that the action named by the verb phrase is viewed as continuing:

> PRESENT: You are speaking.
> PAST: You were speaking.
> FUTURE: You will be speaking.
> PRESENT PERFECT: You have been speaking.
> PAST PERFECT: You had been speaking.
> FUTURE PERFECT: You will have been speaking.

The progressive consists of some form of the auxiliary *be* followed by a present participle—a verb with *-ing* on the end.

## Using *have, be,* and *do*

Three auxiliaries have major roles in forming tenses. As we have seen, *have* is used in forming the perfect tenses, and *be* in forming the progressive. The third auxiliary is *do*, used in forming some negatives, some questions, and emphatic statements:

> I do not jog.
> Do you jog?
> I do lift weights.

*Have, be,* and *do* are used to form tenses as follows:

### 1. *Have*

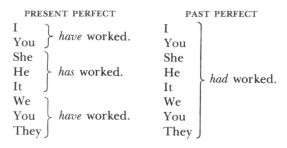

PRESENT PERFECT

I
You } *have* worked.

She
He } *has* worked.
It

We
You } *have* worked.
They

PAST PERFECT

I
You
She
He } *had* worked.
It
We
You
They

### 2. *Be*

PRESENT PROGRESSIVE

I *am* slipping.
You *are* slipping.
She
He } *is* slipping.
It

We
You } *are* slipping.
They

PAST PROGRESSIVE

I *was* slipping.
You *were* slipping.
She
He } *was* slipping.
It

We
You } *were* slipping.
They

### 3. *Do*

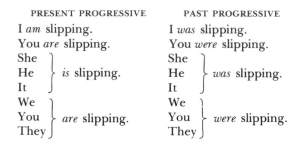

PRESENT

I
You } *do* fly.

She
He } *does* fly.
It

We
You } *do* fly.
They

PAST

I
You
She
He } *did* fly.
It
We
You
They

### EXERCISE 1   Writing Principal Parts

For each of the following sentences write out the principal parts of the italicized verb, listing in sequence the present, the present participle, the past, and the past participle. Whenever you are unsure of a form, refer to your dictionary or to the list of irregular verbs in section 20.5, pp. 349–53.

EXAMPLE
The concert *begins* at 8 P.M.
begin, beginning, began, begun

1. The sun *rose* at 6:32 this morning.
2. Your spaghetti sauce always *smells* good.

3. The mayor *laid* the cornerstone for the new town hall.
4. Some tourists *lie* on the beach for hours. [For a full discussion of the verbs *lie* and *lay*, see the Glossary of Usage, pp. 530–31.]
5. *Have* you ever *flown* in a balloon?
6. Old age *is creeping* up on us.
7. She never *finished* her painting of Mount Flume.
8. *Did* you *break* your watch?
9. Bob *has been visiting* his grandparents.
10. *Do* you *swim* every day?
11. The plane *flies* over Newfoundland on its way to New York.
12. He *has forbidden* the use of calculators in his classroom.
13. *Are* you *leading* a good life?
14. Customers *hurry* in and out of the shop at lunchtime.
15. She *bears* her responsibilities calmly.

## 20.3 Using the Tenses *tu*

### The Present

**1.** Use the common present—

1. To report what a person or thing does regularly:

   Helen *drives* a cab.
   I *run* two miles every day.
   Leaves *change* color in autumn.

2. To state a fact or widely held belief:

   Water *freezes* at 32° F.
   Opposites *attract.*

3. To describe characters, events, or other matters in an aesthetic work, such as a painting, a piece of music, a work of literature, a movie, or a television show:

   In *Jaws,* a man-eating shark *attacks* and *terrifies* swimmers until he is finally killed.

4. To describe an opinion or idea:

   In the Marxist vision of history, the ruling classes ceaselessly *oppress* the working class.

5. To say what a writer or a creative artist does in his or her work:

   Shakespeare *exposes* the ruinous effects of "vaulting ambition" in many of his plays.
   In *The Wealth of Nations* (1776), Adam Smith *argues* that an "invisible hand" regulates individual enterprise for the good of society as a whole.

In his famous Fifth Symphony, Beethoven *reveals* the power and fury of his imagination.

6. To indicate that a condition or situation is likely to last:

My sister *loves* chocolate ice cream.
After one course with Professor Vickers, students *speak* French like natives.

7. To describe a future action that is definitely predictable:

The sun *rises* tomorrow at 6:04.

8. To report a statement of lasting significance:

"All art," *says* Oscar Wilde, "is quite useless."

2. Use the present progressive—

1. To indicate that an action or state is occurring at the time of the writing:

The sun *is setting* now, and the birches *are bending* in the wind.

2. To indicate that an action is in progress—even though it may not be taking place at the exact moment of the writing:

Suburban life *is losing* its appeal. Many young couples *are moving* out of the suburbs and into the cities.

EXERCISE 2    Using the Present—Common and Progressive Forms

Each of the following consists of a pair of sentences, one complete and one with a verb omitted but the bare form supplied in parentheses. For each pair, complete the second sentence by using the parenthesized verb in the same form as the italicized verb in the first sentence. Then make up a new sentence in which you use another verb in the same form.

EXAMPLE
Joanne *is writing* a play.
Martha _____ a house. (build)
Martha ___is building___ a house.
I am taking astronomy.

1. A ghost *haunts* the old house every Halloween.
   The mayor _____ a speech every Fourth of July. (deliver)
2. *Are* the Russians *planning* for World War III?
   _____world  population  _____  to  unmanageable size? (grow)
3. Jack *designs* board games for Parker Brothers.
   Alice _____ the news for radio station WTSL. (broadcast)
4. As I write these words, the white birch *is bending* in the wind.
   As I write these words, the withered leaves _____ to the ground. (fall)

5. In the first scene of *King Lear,* the old king *disowns* his daughter Cordelia.
   In the last scene, he _____ her dead body in his arms. (hold)
6. In the mind of the liberal, the federal government *saves* us all from poverty and prejudice.
   In the mind of the conservative, the federal government _____ free enterprise. (suffocate)
7. In *Star Wars,* Luke Skywalker *destroys* the Death Star.
   In *The Empire Strikes Back,* Darth Vader _____ Admiral Ozzel. (strangle)
8. Normally, heat *stimulates* molecular movement.
   Normally, cold _____ molecular movement. (reduce)

## The Present Perfect

**1.** Use the common present perfect—

    1. To report a past action or state that touches in some way on the present:

        I *have* just *finished* reading *Gone with the Wind.*
        A presidential commission *has* already *investigated* the causes of one nuclear accident.

        The words *just* and *already* are often used with the present perfect.

    2. To report an action or state begun in the past but extending into the present:

        Engineers *have begun* to explore the possibility of harnessing the tides.
        Medical researchers *have known* about interferon since 1960.
        An old buffalo nickel *has* always *brought* me good luck.
        Since the invention of the automobile, traffic accidents *have taken* many thousands of lives.

    3. To report an action performed at some unspecified time in the past:

        *Have* you ever *seen* the Statue of Liberty?
        I *have read* all of Judy Blume's books.

**2.** Use the progressive form of the present perfect when you want to emphasize the continuity of an action from the past into the present, and the likelihood of its continuing into the future:

        Some man-made satellites *have been traveling* through space for years.
        The cost of medical care in America *has been growing* at a staggering rate.

A cost that *has been growing* is still growing, while a cost that *has grown* may have stopped doing so.

EXERCISE 3  **Using the Present Perfect—Common and Progressive Forms**

Each of the following consists of a pair of sentences, one complete and one with a verb omitted but the bare form supplied in parentheses. For each pair, complete the second sentence by using the parenthesized verb in the same form as the italicized verb in the first sentence. Then make up a new sentence in which you use another verb in the same form.

EXAMPLE

An old buffalo nickel *has* always *brought* me good luck.
My uncle Fred ——————— always ——————— me a ten-dollar bill for my birthday. (send)
My uncle Fred __has__ always __sent__ me a ten-dollar bill for my birthday.
I have always wanted to own a motorcycle.

1. Descendants of Ezra Brown *have worked* that farm for five generations.
   Farmer Fuller ——————— chickens for the past ten years. (raise)
2. The mayor *has been planning* a town celebration.
   The townspeople ——————— about it for weeks. (talk)
3. The elevators *have* not *been working* since yesterday morning.
   The clock ——————— not ——————— for days. (tick)
4. Frank *has* just *returned* from Colorado.
   Vivian ——————— just ——————— for Mexico. (leave)
5. The chairman of the Finance Committee *has* already *rejected* the president's proposal to cut taxes next year.
   The president ——————— already ——————— the chairman to reconsider his decision. (ask)

## The Past

**1.** Use the <u>common past</u>—

1. To report an action or state definitely completed in the past:

   The robbers *dropped* their weapons and *surrendered.*
   I *saw* the Statue of Liberty three years ago.
   I *did* not *see* the World Series last year.
   Thomas Edison *invented* the phonograph in 1877.
   The city *became* calm after the cease-fire.

2. To report actions repeated in the past but no longer occurring at the time of the writing:

   The family always *went* to church on Sundays.
   He *hiked* up and down mountains every summer.

**2.** Use the past progressive—

1. To emphasize the continuity of a past action:

The engine *was* slowly *dying.*
His insults *were becoming* unbearable.

2. To say that one action was being performed when another occurred:

I *was pouring* a glass of water when the pitcher suddenly cracked.
The secretaries *were polishing* their fingernails as the manager entered the office.

EXERCISE 4   **Using the Past—Common and Progressive Forms**

Each of the following consists of a pair of sentences, one complete and one with a verb omitted but the bare form supplied in parentheses. For each pair, complete the second sentence by using the parenthesized verb in the same form as the italicized verb in the first sentence. Then make up a new sentence in which you use another verb in the same form.

EXAMPLE
A bolt of lightning *struck* the elm.
A tongue of fire ⎯⎯⎯⎯⎯ the leaves. (lick)
A tongue of fire ⎯licked⎯ the leaves.
In November 1980, an earthquake in southern Italy killed over three thousand people.

1. Harold Stassen *ran* for president many times.
   Every summer I ⎯⎯⎯⎯⎯ to camp. (go)
2. Jefferson *wrote* the Declaration of Independence.
   Thomas Edison ⎯⎯⎯⎯⎯ the light bulb. (invent)
3. In spite of his soul-stirring speeches, William Jennings Bryan *did* not *win* any presidential elections.
   In spite of his prolonged searching, Ponce de León ⎯⎯⎯⎯⎯
   not ⎯⎯⎯⎯⎯ the legendary Fountain of Youth. (find)
4. Nobody *was jogging* in the park yesterday.
   Heather and I ⎯⎯⎯⎯⎯ in the pool yesterday. (swim)
5. Joe *was talking* on the phone when the office caught on fire.
   We ⎯⎯⎯⎯⎯ to Houston when the right front tire blew out. (drive)

**The Past Perfect**

**1.** Use the common past perfect

1. To say that an action or state was completed by a specified time in the past:

By noon we *had gathered* three hundred bushels.

2. To indicate that one past action or state was completed by the time another past action or state occurred:

By the time Hitler sent reinforcements, the Allies *had* already *taken* much of France.

I suddenly realized that I *had left* my keys at home.

3. To report an unfulfilled hope or intention:

The Greens *had hoped* to see the World Series, but they could not get tickets.

Mary *had planned* to travel as far as Denver, but her money ran out while she was still in Chicago.

**2.** Use the <u>progressive</u> form of the <u>past perfect</u> to say that the first of two past actions or states went on until the second occurred:

Before Gloria entered Mark's life, he *had been spending* most of his time with books.

**EXERCISE 5   Using the Past Perfect—Common and Progressive Forms**

Each of the following consists of a pair of sentences, one complete and one with a verb omitted but the bare form supplied in parentheses. For each pair, complete the second sentence by using the parenthesized verb in the same form as the italicized verb in the first sentence. Then make up a new sentence in which you use another verb in the same form.

EXAMPLE
By the time Hitler sent reinforcements, the Allies *had* already *taken* much of France.

By the time I finished the first assignment, the other students _____ already _____ the second. (do)

By the time I finished the first assignment, the other students <u>had</u> <u>already</u> <u>done</u> the second.

By the time we left the carnival, I had spent all of my money.

1. As soon as I saw her, I knew that I *had met* her before.
   With our first bite of the jellied clams, we realized that we _____ a mistake in ordering them. (make)

2. Carl *had hoped* to watch the late movie, but a short circuit ruined the picture tube.
   Sally _____ to take the day off, but one of her patients needed an emergency operation. (plan)

3. By the time we arrived, everyone else *had left* the party.
   By the time the rain came, the drought _____ the farmland into a desert. (turn)

4. By sunset we *had driven* five hundred miles.
   By the age of three Coleridge _____ to read. (learn)

5. Before she broke her leg, she *had been running* fifty miles a week.
   Before I gave up cigarettes, I _____ two packs a day. (smoke)

6. She thought she *had lost* the point.
   But the judge ruled that she _____ it. (win)

7. By the end of the play I *had fallen* asleep.
By the age of twenty-five she _____ stardom. (achieve)

## The Future

There are many ways to say that something will happen in the future. Here are some examples:

> We see Harold Murphy in the morning.
> We are seeing Harold Murphy in the morning.
> We are to see Harold Murphy in the morning.
> We are going to see Harold Murphy in the morning.
> We are sure to see Harold Murphy in the morning.
> We expect to see Harold Murphy in the morning.
> We have a date to see Harold Murphy in the morning.
> We shall see Harold Murphy in the morning.
> We shall be seeing Harold Murphy in the morning.
> We will see Harold Murphy in the morning.
> We will be seeing Harold Murphy in the morning.
> We shall have seen Harold Murphy by eleven in the morning.

Each of the constructions illustrated here can be used to indicate future action. But in the discussion that follows, we use only the verb forms that serve this purpose alone.

**1.** Use the <u>common future</u>—

1. To report a future event or state that will occur regardless of human intent:

   > The sun *will rise* at 6:35 tomorrow morning.
   > I *will be* nineteen on my next birthday.

2. To indicate willingness or determination to do something:

   > The president has declared that he *will veto* the bill.

3. To report what will happen under certain conditions:

   > If a player misses more than three practices the coach *will drop* him from the team.
   > If you get up early enough, you *will see* the sunrise.

4. To indicate future probability:

   > The cost of a college education *will increase.*

   (In reality, the cost may not increase, and you could therefore add a qualifier like *probably.* But as every parent and student knows, the probability that it will increase is a virtual certainty.)

In the preceding examples, the auxiliary *will* is used. Another auxiliary for the future tense is *shall,* with its negative contraction *shan't.* Years ago, *will* was used only with *you, they, he, she, it, t*

20.3

*tu*

and noun subjects, and *shall* was used with *I* and *we* to express the simple future. When *will* was used with *I* and *we,* it signified the speaker's (or writer's) determination: "We will stop the enemy." (The speaker of that sentence would have stressed *will.*) The use of *shall* with *you, they, he, she, it,* or a noun subject had the same function: "You shall pay the tax." This useful distinction was invented by an eighteenth-century English grammarian. However, in current American usage *shall* and *will* mean about the same thing, and most writers use *will* with all subjects to express the simple future. Some writers substitute *shall,* again with all subjects, to express determination or certainty: "We shall overcome."

**2.** Use the <u>future progressive</u>—

1. To say that an action or state will be continuing for a period of time in the future:

   Economists *will be* closely *watching* fluctuations in the price of gold.

2. To say what the subject will be doing at a given time in the future:

   Next summer I *will be teaching* tennis.

EXERCISE 6   **Using the Future—Common and Progressive Forms**

Each of the following consists of a pair of sentences, one complete and one with a verb omitted but the bare form supplied in parentheses. For each pair, complete the second sentence by using the parenthesized verb in the same form as the italicized verb in the first sentence. Then make up a new sentence in which you use another verb in the same form.

EXAMPLE
The cost of a college education *will increase.*
In years to come, many cars ——————— on batteries. (run)
In years to come, many cars   will run   on batteries.
Battery-powered cars will provide short-distance transportation.

1. I *will be* twenty-one next month.
   My grandfather ——————— retirement age on his next birthday. (reach)
2. The school committee *will propose* a new building.
   The taxpayers ——————— its cost. (resent)
3. At this time tomorrow shoppers *will be crowding* into the new mall.
   Next week the president ——————— on his State of the Union message. (work)
4. Congresswoman Kowalski says that she *will run* for reelection.
   Senator Tomkins says that he ——————— on her behalf. (campaign)

5. If you sleep on a sagging mattress, your back *will ache.*
   If you try to stop suddenly on an icy road, your car _____.
   (skid)

## The Future Perfect

**1.** Use the common future perfect—

1. To say that an action or state will be completed by a specified time in the future:

   At the rate I'm living, I *will have spent* all my summer earnings by the end of October.

2. To say that an action or state will be completed by the time something else happens:

   By the time an efficient engine is produced, we *will have exhausted* our supplies of fuel.

**2.** Use the progressive form of the future perfect to say that an activity or state will continue until a specified time in the future:

   By 1985 the *Pioneer 10* probe *will have been traveling* through space for more than ten years.

### EXERCISE 7    Using the Future Perfect—Common and Progressive Forms

Each of the following consists of a pair of sentences, one complete and one with a verb omitted but the bare form supplied in parentheses. For each pair, complete the second sentence by using the parenthesized verb in the same form as the italicized verb in the first sentence. Then make up a new sentence in which you use another verb in the same form.

> EXAMPLE
> By the end of the year I *will have saved* $750.
> By Sunday night I _____ the assignment. (finish)
> By Sunday night I __will have finished__ the assignment.
> By graduation I will have taken eight chemistry courses.

1. By opening night the actors *will have been rehearsing* for ten weeks.
   By 6:00 P.M., the long-winded filibustering senator _____ nonstop for seventeen hours. (speak)
2. If they are lucky, the farmers *will have harvested* the wheat before the storm breaks.
   If oil spills in the Gulf of Mexico continue, they _____ most of the beaches there by 1990. (foul)
3. When George Argos leaves the cast of *Barefoot in the Park* next week, over five thousand people *will have seen* him perform.
   By the time the colossal new movie is finished, the producers _____ more than ten million dollars to make it. (spend)

## 20.4 Tense and Time with Participles and Infinitives

Participles and infinitives have two tenses: the present and the perfect. The present consists of the present participle or the infinitive by itself. The perfect participle consists of *having* and the past participle; the perfect infinitive requires *have* between *to* and the past participle.

**1.** Use the present tense when the action or state named by the participle or infinitive occurs at or after the time of the main verb:

> We spend hours in conference with individual students, hours *meeting* together and with counselors, *trying* to teach ourselves how to teach and *asking* ourselves what we ought to be teaching.
> ——Adrienne Rich
>
> The speaker used the chalkboard *to outline* his main points.
> Many undergraduates take biology *to prepare* for medical school.
> By sunset the trapped animal had ceased *to struggle*.

**2.** Use the perfect tense when the action or state named by the participle or infinitive occurred before the time of the main verb:

> *Having lost* his cargo during the hurricane, the captain faced bankruptcy when his vessel finally reached port.
> Several reporters are sorry *to have missed* the president's impromptu press conference.

#### EXERCISE 8  Using Tenses: Review

This exercise tests your ability to use the various tenses treated in this chapter. Each of the following consists of a pair of sentences, one complete and one with a verb omitted but the bare form supplied in parentheses. For each pair, complete the second sentence by using the parenthesized verb in the same tense and form as the italicized verb in the first sentence. Then make up a new sentence in which you use another verb in the same tense and form.

> EXAMPLE
> Four quarts *make* a gallon.
> The earth _____ on its axis. (rotate)
> The earth <u>rotates</u> on its axis.
> Water freezes at 32° F.

1. She *was standing* on the corner when a passing truck splashed mud on her brand-new jeans.
   She _____ an operation when the lights failed. (perform)
2. By the time he reached the store, looters *had taken* everything of value.
   By the time I found the cheese, the mice _____ most of it. (eat)

3. White paper exposed to light for a long time *will turn* yellow.
   Fish left unrefrigerated for more than a day or two
   _____. (rot)

4. In recent years, many women *have been demanding* rights equal
   to those of men.
   Some men _____ women's demands. (resist)

5. In the final episode of the novel, the hero *risks* his life in a blizzard.
   In the last scene of the movie, the great ship _____. (sink)

6. We always *spent* Thanksgiving Day with my grandmother.
   Every Saturday I _____ stickball in a vacant lot behind
   the supermarket. (play)

7. By the end of the day we *had cut* five cords of wood.
   By the end of the sixties, the United States _____ a man
   on the moon. (put)

8. Next semester I *will be taking* physics.
   Next summer I _____ houses. (paint)

9. In 1894 Hugh Duffy *set* the all-time major-league batting
   record with an average of .438.
   During a career of more than sixteen seasons, he _____
   almost six hundred bases. (steal)

10. For years we *have dumped* chemical wastes into our rivers, lakes,
    and oceans.
    We _____ many of our waterways. (pollute)

## 20.5 Principal Parts of Commonly Used Irregular Verbs

Following is a partial list of irregular verbs, those with special forms
for the past, the past participle, or both. When more than one form
is shown, the first is more commonly used. For verbs not listed
here, see your dictionary.

| PRESENT (BARE FORM) | PRESENT PARTICIPLE | PAST | PAST PARTICIPLE |
|---|---|---|---|
| arise | arising | arose | arisen |
| awake | awaking | awoke, awaked | awoke, awaked, awoken |
| be † | being | was/were | been |
| bear [bring forth] | bearing | bore | born, borne |
| bear [carry] | bearing | bore | borne |
| beat | beating | beat | beaten, beat |
| begin | beginning | began | begun |

† In this one case the bare form (*be*) is not the same as the present (*am, is, are*).

*t*

| PRESENT (BARE FORM) | PRESENT PARTICIPLE | PAST | PAST PARTICIPLE |
|---|---|---|---|
| bend | bending | bent | bent |
| bet | betting | bet, betted | bet |
| bid [command] | bidding | bade | bid, bidden |
| bid [offer to pay] | bidding | bid | bid |
| bind | binding | bound | bound |
| bite | biting | bit | bitten |
| bleed | bleeding | bled | bled |
| blend | blending | blended, blent | blended, blent |
| blow | blowing | blew | blown |
| break | breaking | broke | broken |
| breed | breeding | bred | bred |
| bring | bringing | brought | brought |
| build | building | built | built |
| burn | burning | burned, burnt | burned, burnt |
| burst | bursting | burst | burst |
| buy | buying | bought | bought |
| cast | casting | cast | cast |
| catch | catching | caught | caught |
| choose | choosing | chose | chosen |
| cling | clinging | clung | clung |
| clothe | clothing | clothed, clad | clothed, clad |
| come | coming | came | come |
| cost | costing | cost | cost |
| creep | creeping | crept | crept |
| crow | crowing | crowed, crew | crowed |
| cut | cutting | cut | cut |
| deal | dealing | dealt | dealt |
| dig | digging | dug | dug |
| dive | diving | dived, dove | dived |
| do | doing | did | done |
| draw | drawing | drew | drawn |
| drink | drinking | drank | drunk, drunken |
| drive | driving | drove | driven |
| eat | eating | ate | eaten |
| fall | falling | fell | fallen |
| feed | feeding | fed | fed |
| feel | feeling | felt | felt |
| fight | fighting | fought | fought |
| find | finding | found | found |
| fling | flinging | flung | flung |
| fly | flying | flew | flown |
| forbid | forbidding | forbade, forbad | forbidden, forbid |
| forget | forgetting | forgot | forgotten, forgot |
| freeze | freezing | froze | frozen |

| PRESENT (BARE FORM) | PRESENT PARTICIPLE | PAST | PAST PARTICIPLE |
|---|---|---|---|
| get | getting | got | got, gotten |
| give | giving | gave | given |
| go | going | went | gone |
| grind | grinding | ground | ground |
| grow | growing | grew | grown |
| hang [execute] | hanging | hanged | hanged |
| hang [suspend] | hanging | hung | hung |
| have | having | had | had |
| hear | hearing | heard | heard |
| heave | heaving | heaved, hove | heaved, hove |
| hide | hiding | hid | hidden, hid |
| hit | hitting | hit | hit |
| hold | holding | held | held |
| hurt | hurting | hurt | hurt |
| keep | keeping | kept | kept |
| kneel | kneeling | knelt, kneeled | knelt, kneeled |
| knit | knitting | knitted, knit | knitted, knit |
| know | knowing | knew | known |
| lay | laying | laid | laid |
| lead | leading | led | led |
| lean | leaning | leaned, leant | leaned, leant |
| leap | leaping | leaped, leapt | leaped, leapt |
| learn | learning | learned, learnt | learned, learnt |
| leave | leaving | left | left |
| lend | lending | lent | lent |
| let | letting | let | let |
| lie [recline] | lying | lay | lain |
| lie [tell a falsehood] | lying | lied | lied |
| light | lighting | lighted, lit | lighted, lit |
| lose | losing | lost | lost |
| make | making | made | made |
| mean | meaning | meant | meant |
| meet | meeting | met | met |
| mow | mowing | mowed | mowed, mown |
| pay | paying | paid | paid |
| plead | pleading | pleaded, pled | pleaded, pled |
| prove | proving | proved | proved, proven |
| put | putting | put | put |
| quit | quitting | quit, quitted | quit, quitted |
| read | reading | read | read |
| rend | rending | rent | rent |
| rid | ridding | rid, ridded | rid, ridded |

*Principal Parts of Commonly Used Irregular Verbs* 351

| PRESENT (BARE FORM) | PRESENT PARTICIPLE | PAST | PAST PARTICIPLE |
|---|---|---|---|
| ride | riding | rode | ridden |
| ring | ringing | rang | rung |
| rise | rising | rose | risen |
| run | running | ran | run |
| saw | sawing | sawed | sawed, sawn |
| say | saying | said | said |
| see | seeing | saw | seen |
| seek | seeking | sought | sought |
| sell | selling | sold | sold |
| send | sending | sent | sent |
| sew | sewing | sewed | sewed, sewn |
| shake | shaking | shook | shaken |
| shave | shaving | shaved | shaved, shaven |
| shed | shedding | shed | shed |
| shine | shining | shone | shone |
| shoe | shoeing | shod, shoed | shod, shoed |
| show | showing | showed | shown, showed |
| shred | shredding | shredded, shred | shredded, shred |
| shrink | shrinking | shrank, shrunk | shrunk, shrunken |
| shoot | shooting | shot | shot |
| shut | shutting | shut | shut |
| sing | singing | sang | sung |
| sink | sinking | sank, sunk | sunk, sunken |
| sit | sitting | sat | sat |
| slay | slaying | slew | slain |
| sleep | sleeping | slept | slept |
| slide | sliding | slid | slid |
| sling | slinging | slung | slung |
| slink | slinking | slunk | slunk |
| slit | slitting | slit | slit |
| smell | smelling | smelled, smelt | smelled, smelt |
| sow | sowing | sowed | sown, sowed |
| speak | speaking | spoke | spoken |
| speed | speeding | sped, speeded | sped, speeded |
| spin | spinning | spun, span | spun |
| spit | spitting | spit, spat | spit, spat |
| split | splitting | split | split |
| spoil | spoiling | spoiled, spoilt | spoiled, spoilt |
| spread | spreading | spread | spread |
| spring | springing | sprang | sprung |
| stand | standing | stood | stood |
| steal | stealing | stole | stolen |
| stick | sticking | stuck | stuck |
| sting | stinging | stung | stung |
| stink | stinking | stank, stunk | stunk |
| stride | striding | strode | stridden |

| PRESENT (BARE FORM) | PRESENT PARTICIPLE | PAST | PAST PARTICIPLE |
|---|---|---|---|
| strike | striking | struck | struck, stricken |
| string | stringing | strung | strung |
| strive | striving | strove | striven |
| swear | swearing | swore | sworn |
| sweat | sweating | sweat, sweated | sweat, sweated |
| sweep | sweeping | swept | swept |
| swell | swelling | swelled | swelled, swollen |
| swim | swimming | swam | swum |
| swing | swinging | swung | swung |
| take | taking | took | taken |
| teach | teaching | taught | taught |
| tear | tearing | tore | torn |
| tell | telling | told | told |
| think | thinking | thought | thought |
| throw | throwing | threw | thrown |
| thrust | thrusting | thrust | thrust |
| toss | tossing | tossed, tost | tossed, tost |
| tread | treading | trod | trodden, trod |
| wake | waking | woke, waked | woke, waked, woken |
| wear | wearing | wore | worn |
| weave | weaving | wove | woven |
| wed | wedding | wed, wedded | wed, wedded |
| weep | weeping | wept | wept |
| wet | wetting | wet, wetted | wet, wetted |
| win | winning | won | won |
| wind | winding | wound | wound |
| work | working | worked, wrought | worked, wrought |
| wring | wringing | wrung | wrung |
| write | writing | wrote | written |

# 21

# VERBS
## Sequence of Tenses

When a passage has more than one verb, the relation between the tenses of the verbs is called the **sequence of tenses.** Various sequences are possible.

### 21.1 Sequence of Tenses in a Sentence

When all the verbs in a sentence describe actions or states that occur at or about the same time, their tenses should be the same:

> Whenever the alarm clock *rings,* I *yawn, stretch,* and *roll* over for another fifteen minutes of sleep. [all present tense]
> The batter *cocked* his arms, *stepped* into the pitch, and *took* a round-house swing. [all past tense]
> My parents *will pay* for my tuition, but I *will pay* for all my other college expenses. [both future tense]

But of course actions do not always happen at the same time, even if they are described in the same sentence. A sentence may describe actions that happen at different times, and it will then have verbs in different tenses. In other words, the tense in the sentence will shift. The nature of the shift will depend on the kind of clauses in which the verbs appear.

When the clauses are **independent,** the tenses of the verbs in those clauses may be entirely independent of each other:

> In the past, most consumers *wanted* big cars; now they *want* small cars. [past and present tense]
> The accident *broke* her spinal column; as a result, she *will* never *walk* again. [past and future tense]

When one or more of the clauses are **subordinate**, the tense of the subordinate verb depends on the tense of the main verb, as shown in the examples that follow.

## Main Verb in the Present

When the main verb is in the present tense, the subordinate verb is commonly in the present also:

| MAIN VERB | SUBORDINATE VERB |
|---|---|
| | PRESENT |
| Some Americans *are* so poor | that they *suffer* from malnutrition. |
| | PRESENT |
| Monetarists *think* | that federal interference with the economy *does* more harm than good. |

The subordinate verb is in the present perfect or the past only when it refers to action that occurred before the time of the main verb:

| MAIN VERB | SUBORDINATE VERB |
|---|---|
| | PRESENT PERFECT |
| Most children *learn* to talk | after they *have learned* to walk |
| | PAST |
| Greg *likes* to boast about the marlin | that he *caught* last summer. |

The subordinate verb is in the future when it refers to action in the future:

| MAIN VERB | SUBORDINATE VERB |
|---|---|
| | FUTURE |
| Astronomers *predict* | that the sun *will die* in about ten billion years. |

## Main Verb in the Present Perfect

When the main verb is in the present perfect tense, the subordinate verb is normally in the past tense:

| MAIN VERB | SUBORDINATE VERB |
|---|---|
| | PAST |
| Scientists *have studied* the rings of Saturn | ever since Galileo *discovered* them. |

## Main Verb in the Past

When the main verb is in the past tense, the subordinate verb is normally in the past or past perfect tense. (For an exception, in the indirect reporting of discourse, see section 24.2, p. 382.) An auxiliary verb in the subordinate clause should also be in the past tense, taking a form like *was, were, had, did, could, might, should, used to,* or *would:*

| MAIN VERB | SUBORDINATE VERB |
|---|---|
| Centuries ago most people *believed* | PAST<br>that the sun *revolved* around the earth. |
| Stacy *thought* | PAST<br>that she *could win* the match<br>PAST PERFECT<br>even though she *had lost* the first set. |
| In 1969 the Cuyahoga River in Cleveland *was* so full of wastes | PAST<br>that it *caught* fire. |
| After the presidential election of 1948, some newspapers mistakenly *reported* | PAST PERFECT<br>that Dewey *had beaten* Truman. |

## Main Verb in the Past Perfect

When the main verb is in the past perfect tense, the subordinate verb is normally in the past tense:

| SUBORDINATE VERB | MAIN VERB |
|---|---|
| PAST<br>By the time the fire engine *arrived,* | the blaze *had* already *gutted* the house. |

## Main Verb Indicating Future

When the main verb refers to action in the future, the subordinate verb is normally in the present or the present perfect tense—but not in the future tense:

| MAIN VERB | SUBORDINATE VERB |
|---|---|
| I *start* [or *will start*] my summer job | PRESENT<br>just as soon as I *finish* my final exams. |
| I *start* [or *will start*] my summer job | PRESENT PERFECT<br>just as soon as I *have finished* my final exams. |

Do not write:

   *I *start* [or *will start*] my summer job just as soon as I *will finish* my final exams.

## Main Verb in the Future Perfect

When the main verb is in the future perfect tense, the subordinate verb is normally in the present or present perfect tense—but not in the future tense:

| MAIN VERB | SUBORDINATE VERB |
|---|---|
| | PRESENT |
| Workmen *will have completed* their repairs | by the time the airport *is* reopened. |

| SUBORDINATE VERB | MAIN VERB |
|---|---|
| PRESENT PERFECT | |
| Before a new SALT agreement *has been* signed, | the United States and Russia *will have spent* billions on the development of new weapons systems. |

### EXERCISE 1   Using Tenses

Complete each of the following sentences by inserting, in a suitable tense, the appropriate form of each verb shown in parentheses.

EXAMPLE
Brenda cheered when she ——————— the news. (hear)
Brenda cheered when she ___heard___ the news.

1. Keynesian economists believe that federal action often ——————— to stabilize the economy. (help)
2. Conservatives think that the welfare system ——————— millions of dollars. (waste)
3. In the summer of 1980, Polish workers went on strike so that they ——————— the right to run their own unions. (can win)
4. At the start of the race Fran wondered if she ——————— the turn where the snow ——————— during the night. (can make, freeze)
5. The director interviewed over two hundred applicants before she ——————— one of them. (choose)
6. When I ——————— college, I will go to law school. (finish)
7. By the time I saw the ad, the company ——————— someone else. (hire)
8. In the seventy-five years since the Wright brothers ——————— the airplane, it has drastically changed the way we live. (invent)

### EXERCISE 2   Transforming Tenses

This exercise should help you understand how the tense of a subordinate verb is related to the tense of the main verb. In each of the following, change the main verb to the past tense if it is in the present, and to the present tense if it is in the past. Then make whatever other tense changes have become necessary.

EXAMPLE
We want to take a walk before it starts raining.
TRANSFORMED: We wanted to take a walk before it started raining.

1. The office manager was looking for a machine that would print fifty copies a minute.
2. The ducks circle above the pond until all humans have left the area.
3. The children hope they can see the circus at least once before it leaves town.
4. When the stock market crashes, millions of workers lose their jobs.
5. Most students did not start learning a foreign language until after they had finished grade school.

## 21.2 Sequence of Tenses in a Paragraph

A single sentence can often include more than one verb and more than one tense. A paragraph normally includes many verbs and often several different tenses. But you should shift tenses in a paragraph only when you have good reason for doing so.

A well-written paragraph is normally dominated by just one tense. Consider the following paragraph:

> Before I set my world record, I was a great fan of *The Guinness Book of World Records* and read each new edition from cover to cover. I liked knowing and being able to tell others that the world's chug-a-lug champ consumed 2.58 pints of beer in 10 seconds, that the world's lightest adult person weighed only 13 pounds, that the largest vocabulary for a talking bird was 531 words, spoken by a brown-beaked budgerigar named Sparky. There is, of course, only a fine line between admiration and envy, and for awhile I had been secretly desiring to be in that book myself—to astonish others just as I had been astonished. But it seemed hopeless. How could a nervous college sophomore, an anonymous bookworm, perform any of those wonderful feats? The open-throat technique necessary for chug-a-lugging was incomprehensible to my trachea—and I thought my head alone must weigh close to 13 pounds.
> —William Allen, "How to Set a World Record"

The author is describing a past condition, so the dominant tense here is the simple past. That is the tense, for example, of *was, read, liked, consumed, weighed,* and *seemed.* About the middle of the paragraph the author shifts out of the simple past, saying that there *is* a fine line between admiration and envy, and that he *had been* secretly *desiring* to be in the *Guinness* book. He has good reasons for both of these shifts; *is* describes a general truth and *had been desiring* describes a condition that existed before the simple past, before the time described in the rest of the paragraph. Then the author returns to the simple past with *seemed, was,* and *thought.*

Now consider this paragraph:

> February 2, 1975. Wasps begin to appear in country houses about now, and even in some suburban houses. One sees them dart uncertainly about, hears them buzz and bang on window panes, and one wonders where they came from. They probably came from the attic, where they spent the early part of the winter hibernating. Now, with longer hours of daylight, the wasps begin to rouse and start exploring.
>
> —Hal Borland, "Those Attic Wasps"

This passage describes not a past condition but a recurrent one—something that happens every year. The dominant tense of the verbs is therefore the present: *begin, sees, hears, wonders, begin, start.* Since the presence of the wasps calls for some explanation, the writer shifts tense in the middle of the paragraph to tell us where they *came* from and where they *spent* the early part of the winter. But in the final sentence, *Now* brings us back to the present, and the verbs of this sentence, *begin* and *start,* are in the present tense.

Here is another example:

> As a first gain from the sale of the heroin, the simple motorbikes on which Wyatt and Billy were riding at the start of the picture are replaced by a pair of the biggest, flashiest, most expensive motorcycles ever to fill the male American heart with envy. It is on these splendid vehicles—Fonda-Wyatt's is decorated with a splash of American flag—that the two men now begin their beautiful journey from California to near New Orleans, where their trip will be suddenly and violently cut off.
>
> —Diana Trilling, "*Easy Rider* and Its Critics"

Since this passage tells what happened at a certain point in a film, the prevailing tense of the verbs is the present: *are replaced, is, is decorated,* and *begin.* But the first sentence compares the motorcycles which are seen "now" with the motorbikes on which Wyatt and Billy *were riding* earlier, and the end of the second sentence anticipates what *will* happen later in the film. Normally, the present tense should predominate when you describe an aesthetic work of any kind, such as a film, a play, a symphony, a painting, a photograph, a recording, or a piece of sculpture.

The present tense should also predominate in any explanation of a repeatable process or a function—of what someone or something regularly does. Consider this passage:

> Commercial banks have two primary functions. First, banks hold demand deposits and permit checks to be drawn on these deposits. This function is familiar to practically everyone. Most

people have a checking account in some commercial bank, and draw checks on this account. Second, banks lend money to industrialists, merchants, homeowners, and other individuals and firms. At one time or another, you will probably apply for a loan to finance some project for your business or home. Indeed, it is quite possible that some of the costs of your college education are being covered by a loan to you or your parents from a commercial bank.

—Edwin Mansfield, *Economics: Principles, Problems, Decisions*

Since the writer's subject is the functions of commercial banks, the tense of all but one of the verbs in this passage is the present: *have, hold, permit, is, have, draw, lend, is, are being covered.* The writer departs from the present just once—to say what business you will probably do with a bank in the future.

## 21.3 Faulty Tense Shifts *shift*

The shift of tenses in a sentence or passage is faulty when the tense of one verb does not correspond properly to the tense of another.

### Faulty Tense Shifts in a Sentence

The shift of tenses in a sentence is faulty when the tense of any verb differs without good reason from the tense of another, or when the tense of a subordinate verb is inconsistent with the tense of the main verb:

> *I *turned* the key, but the engine *fails* to start.

The shift from the past tense (*turned*) to the present (*fails*) is faulty. Both verbs refer to actions that occurred at about the same time. If the first verb is in the past, the second should also be in the past:

> I *turned* the key, but the engine *failed* to start.

Now consider this example:

> *The novel *describes* the adventures of two families of immigrants who *enter* the United States at New York, *withstand* the stresses of culture shock, and *traveled* to the Dakota Territory to make their fortune.

The shift to the past (*traveled*) is faulty. The time of the action should be reported in the present—the tense of the main verb (*describes*) and of the other subordinate verbs:

> The novel *describes* the adventures of two families of immigrants who *enter* the United States at New York, *withstand* the stresses of culture shock, and *travel* to the Dakota Territory to make their fortune.

Here is another example:

> *General Lee *informed* his staff that he *would* not *order* a retreat unless General Stuart *advises* him to.

The shift to the present (*advises*) is faulty. All of the actions reported in the sentence occurred at about the same time in the past—the time of the main verb (*informed*):

> General Lee *informed* his staff that he *would* not *order* a retreat unless General Stuart *advised* him to.

Here is one more example:

> *Marthe *likes* to display the miniature spoons she *had collected* since her marriage to an antique dealer.

A subordinate verb in the past perfect (*had collected*) is inconsistent with a main verb in the present (*likes*). In this sentence the tense of the subordinate verb should be present perfect:

> Marthe *likes* to display the miniature spoons she *has collected* since her marriage to an antique dealer.

And here is a final example:

> *The president *insists* he *would campaign* in Michigan next week.

The main verb in the present (*insists*) should in this instance be followed by a subordinate verb in the future:

> The president *insists* he *will campaign* in Michigan next week.

**EXERCISE 3  Correcting Faulty Shifts in a Sentence**

In some of the following sentences, the tense of one or more verbs does not properly correspond to the tense of the italicized verb. Correct those sentences. If a sentence is correct as it stands, write *Correct*.

EXAMPLE
A roll of thunder *announced* the coming of the storm; then drops of rain begin to pelt the earth.
REVISED: A roll of thunder announced the coming of the storm; then drops of rain began to pelt the earth.

1. Filters *are being installed* in water systems that had been threatened by pollutants from industrial wastes.
2. Many of the American soldiers who serve in Korea *enroll* in language classes to learn the Korean language.
3. My grandfather always *tooted* the horn of his Model A as he drives past the police station.
4. Caroline *is* excited; she had just received a fellowship which enables her to do research in chemistry.
5. When the rain came, the streets *are flooded*.

6. Every Saturday morning the station *broadcasted* music that listeners have requested.

7. The circulation of the regional newspaper *has been climbing* ever since the editors begin printing feature stories about local characters.

8. In "The Tell-Tale Heart" Edgar Allan Poe *creates* suspense until it was almost unbearable in the final scene.

9. The appearance of gray streaks in the paint *stumped* the chemist; he has no idea what causes them.

10. Magicians *delight* us partly because they seemed superior to the laws of nature.

**Faulty Tense Shifts in a Paragraph**

The shift of tenses in a paragraph is faulty when the tense of any verb differs without good reason from the dominant tense of the paragraph. Consider this passage, a commentary on *Green Mansions,* a novel by W. H. Hudson:

> [1] On his return to the once peaceful woods, Abel is horrified to learn that his beloved Rima has been slain by savages. [2] Rage and grief swell within him as Kua-kó tells how Rima was forced to seek refuge in a lofty tree and how the tree became a trap when the savages sent searing flames and choking smoke high into the branches. [3] As Abel hears of her final cry—"Abel! Abel!"—and fatal plunge to earth, he fought against a wild impulse to leap upon the triumphant Indian and tear his heart out.

Since this is a description of a literary work, the dominant tense is the present (*swell, tells,* and *hears*). There is one shift to the present perfect (*has been slain* in sentence 1) and four shifts to the past (*was forced, became,* and *sent* in sentence 2, and *fought* in sentence 3). The shifts in sentences 1 and 2 are correct; the shift in sentence 3 is not. In sentence 1, *has been slain* tells what happened before Abel is horrified to learn about it. In sentence 2, the past-tense verbs describe what happened shortly before Kua-kó *tells* about it. But in sentence 3, the verb *fought* tells what Abel does just at the time that he *hears* of Rima's death. *Fought* should therefore be *fights*.

EXERCISE 4   **Correcting Faulty Tense Shifts in a Paragraph**

Each of the following paragraphs is a rewritten version of a paragraph from the source cited after it. In rewriting each paragraph, we have deliberately introduced one or more faulty shifts in tense. Correct them.

EXAMPLE
line 3: manfully thrashes

1.        However violent his acts, Kong remains a gentleman. Whenever a fresh boa constrictor threatens Fay, Kong first sees

that the lady is safely parked, then manfully thrashed her attacker.
(And she, the ingrate, runs away every time his back was turned.)
5 Atop the Empire State Building, ignoring his pursuers, Kong
places Fay on a ledge as tenderly as if she were a dozen eggs. He
fondled her, then turned to face the Army Air Force. And Kong is
perhaps the most disinterested lover since Cyrano: his attentions to
the lady were utterly without hope of reward. After all, between a
10 five-foot blonde and a fifty-foot ape, love can hardly be more than
an intellectual flirtation. His forced exit from his jungle, in chains,
results directly from his single-minded pursuit of Fay. He smashes
a Broadway theater when the notion entered his dull brain that the
flashbulbs of photographers somehow endanger the lady. His
15 perilous shinnying up a skyscraper to have plucked Fay from her
boudoir is an act of the kindliest of hearts. He was impossible to
discourage even though the love of his life can't lay eyes on him
without shrieking murder.

—Deliberately altered from X. J. Kennedy,
"Who Killed King Kong?"

2.     To understand Marx, we need to know something about
the times in which he lived. The period was characterized by revolutionary pressures against the ruling classes. In most of the
countries of Europe, there was little democracy, as we know it. The
5 masses participated little, if at all, in the world of political affairs,
and very fully in the world of drudgery. For example, at one factory in Manchester, England, in 1862, people work an average of
80 hours per week. For these long hours of toil, the workers generally receive small wages. They often can do little more than feed
10 and clothe themselves. Given these circumstances, it is little wonder
that revolutionary pressures were manifest.

—Deliberately altered from Edwin Mansfield,
*Economics: Principles, Problems, Decisions*

## Exercise 5   Supplying Verbs

In the following passage from Alex Haley's *Roots*, we have deliberately
omitted some of the author's verbs. For each of the blanks, supply a suitable verb or verb phrase.

Example
line 2: told

In Banjul, the capital of Gambia, I met with a group of Gambians. They _____ me how for centuries the history of Africa
has been preserved. In the older villages of the back country there
are old men, called *griots*, who _____ in effect living archives.
5 Such men _____ and, on special occasions, _____ the
cumulative histories of clans, or families, or villages, as those histories _____ long been told. Since my forefather _____
said his name was Kin-tay (properly spelled Kinte), and since the

Kinte clan _____ known in Gambia, the group of Gambians
10   would see what they could do to help me.
      I was back in New York when a registered letter _____
from Gambia. Word had been passed in the back country, and a
*griot* of the Kinte clan _____, indeed, _____ found. His
name, the letter said, _____ Kebba Kanga Fofana. I returned
15   to Gambia and _____ a safari to locate him.

# 22

# VERBS
## Active and
## Passive Voice

The word "voice" generally refers to the sound of someone speaking. But as applied to sentences, "voice" has to do with verbs. When the subject of a verb acts, the verb is in the **active voice;** when the subject is acted upon, the verb is in the **passive voice.**

The active voice stresses the activity of the subject and helps to make a sentence direct, concise, and vigorous:

> Babe Ruth *hit* sixty home runs in one season.
> Each man *kills* the thing he *loves.* —Oscar Wilde

The passive voice enables you to do several things.

**1.** You can keep the focus on someone or something important that is acted upon:

> The barn *was struck* by a bolt of lightning.
> In Moulmein, in Lower Burma, I *was hated* by large numbers of people—the only time in my life that I have been important enough for this to happen to me. —George Orwell

**2.** You can describe an action when you do not know or do not care to say who or what performed it:

> The great French cathedral of Notre Dame *was designed* in the twelfth century.
> Fragments of a Russian spy satellite *were discovered* in Canada.

**3.** You can put the person or thing acting at the end of a clause, where you can easily attach a long modifier:

> On October 2, 1980, Muhammad Ali *was beaten* by Larry Holmes, who won the fight with a technical knockout after just ten rounds.

## 22.1 Changing from Active to Passive

If a verb has a direct object, you can change it from active to passive. Compare the following sentences:

> Heavy waves pounded the seacoast. [active]
> The seacoast was pounded by heavy waves. [passive]

In the first sentence, the subject—*waves*—is what performs the pounding, what acts. In the second sentence, the subject—*seacoast*—is what receives the pounding, what is acted upon. When you change the voice of a verb from active to passive, you must rearrange the rest of the sentence:

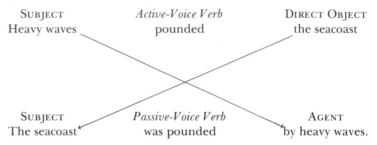

| SUBJECT | *Active-Voice Verb* | DIRECT OBJECT |
|---|---|---|
| Heavy waves | pounded | the seacoast |

| SUBJECT | *Passive-Voice Verb* | AGENT |
|---|---|---|
| The seacoast | was pounded | by heavy waves. |

The direct object of the active verb becomes the subject of the passive verb, and the subject of the active verb becomes the **agent** of the passive verb—the one by whom the action is said to be performed. The word *by* goes before the agent.

When the verb in a clause changes from active to passive, phrases and clauses that modify the whole clause can stay where they are. But modifiers of particular words in the clause must follow those words to their new positions:

> After the tanker capsized in the hurricane, heavy waves covered with oil slick pounded the rocky New England seacoast.
> After the tanker capsized in the hurricane, the rocky New England seacoast was pounded by heavy waves covered with oil slick.

If you want the passive verb to have no agent, you may drop the subject of the active verb when you change it to the passive:

> Years ago in Plymouth, Massachusetts, bandits robbed a U.S. Mail truck of nearly a million dollars.
> Years ago in Plymouth, Massachusetts, a U.S. Mail truck was robbed of nearly a million dollars.

You can change a verb from active to passive only if it has a direct object. If the active verb has no direct object, there is nothing to become the subject of the passive verb:

John cheered.

_____?_____was cheered by John.

**EXERCISE 1   Transforming Verbs**

Change the main verb in each of the following sentences from active to passive, and rearrange the other words as necessary.

EXAMPLE

Heavy waves covered with oil slick pounded the rocky New England seacoast.

TRANSFORMED: The rocky New England seacoast was pounded by heavy waves covered with oil slick.

1. Leonardo da Vinci painted the *Mona Lisa.*
2. People found traces of the oil spill as far away as Newfoundland.
3. In years to come, unmanned space satellites will explore planets beyond the solar system.
4. Voters elected Ronald Reagan president of the United States in 1980.
5. Her colored shawl, which caught in the wheel of a moving car, strangled the famous dancer.
6. Thomas Jefferson, who later became president of the United States, wrote the Declaration of Independence.
7. The Revenue Act of 1978 made important changes in the tax law.
8. Some people built the pyramids at Teotihuacán, Mexico, during the second and third centuries A.D.
9. Some people sharply attacked Lincoln for his opposition to slavery.
10. Father Robert L. Charlesbois, a forty-eight-year-old Catholic priest from Gary, Indiana, with twelve years of experience in the Vietnam war zone, organized a secret mission to help thousands of starving Cambodians in the summer of 1979.

## 22.2   Changing from Passive to Active

Consider these sentences:

Pearl Harbor was bombed by the Japanese. [passive]
The Japanese bombed Pearl Harbor. [active]

In the first sentence, the subject—*Pearl Harbor*—is acted upon. In the second sentence, the subject—*The Japanese*—acts. When you change the voice of a verb from passive to active, you must again rearrange the rest of the sentence:

*Changing from Passive to Active*   **367**

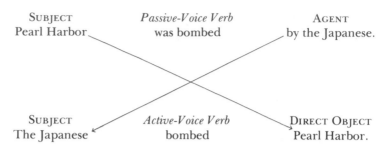

The subject of the passive verb becomes the direct object of the active verb. The agent of the passive verb—the one by whom the action is performed—becomes the subject of the active verb. The word *by* drops out.

When the verb in a clause changes from passive to active, phrases and clauses that modify the whole clause can stay where they are. But modifiers of particular words in the clause must follow those words to their new positions:

> On December 7, 1941, Pearl Harbor, an American base in the Hawaiian Islands, was bombed without warning by the Japanese. [passive]
> On December 7, 1941, the Japanese without warning bombed Pearl Harbor, an American base in the Hawaiian Islands. [active]

Normally you can change a verb from passive to active only if it is followed by a *by* phrase naming an agent. If no agent is named, you must either keep the passive or supply the agent yourself before changing to the active.

> The city of Washington was planned in 1791. [passive, no agent]
> The city of Washington was planned in 1791 by Pierre Charles L'Enfant. [passive, agent supplied]
> Pierre Charles L'Enfant planned the city of Washington in 1791. [active]

If you didn't know about L'Enfant, you could still write this:

> Someone planned the city of Washington in 1791.

But why bother?

### EXERCISE 2  Transforming Verbs

Change the verb or verbs in each of the following sentences from passive to active, and rearrange the other words as necessary.

> EXAMPLE
> On December 7, 1941, Pearl Harbor, an American base in the Hawaiian Islands, was bombed without warning by the Japanese.
> TRANSFORMED: On December 7, 1941, the Japanese without warn-

ing bombed Pearl Harbor, an American base in the Hawaiian Islands.

1. Karate lessons are being taken by Roberta.
2. Permanent settlements in the new land were never established by the Vikings.
3. A solution to the problems of inflation and high unemployment is being urgently sought by the president.
4. No bribes are taken by Death.
5. A novel about the stormy years of the French Revolution was written by Charles Dickens.
6. Weekly meetings are held by the company commander so that the questions of the recruits can be answered by him.
7. No tales are told by dead men.
8. A play about the hardships which were suffered by her during a canoe trip down the Amazon River in 1972 has been written by Jane Stowe.
9. In every work of genius our own rejected thoughts are recognized by us.

## 22.3   Choosing the Active Voice

Frequent use of the active voice will help to make your writing vigorous, direct, and concise. If you have done the preceding exercise, you have seen what can happen to a sentence when the verb is changed from passive to active:

> Karate lessons are being taken by Roberta. [passive]
> Roberta takes karate lessons. [active]

The active version ditches the excess verbal baggage—*are being* and *by*. Further, because it makes *Roberta* the subject, the active version makes her more important and stresses her activity. To a great extent, the life and energy of your writing will depend on what the subjects of your sentences do.

## 22.4   Choosing the Passive Voice

You may have read or heard that you should avoid the passive voice because it is "weak." But is the passive weak in the Declaration of Independence, where we read that "all men are created equal"? Some sentences actually work better in the passive voice than they do in the active. Thinking you should never use the passive is like thinking you should never back up a car. A good driver knows when to shift into reverse; a good writer knows when to shift into the passive. We therefore suggest that you use the passive for the purposes described next.

**1.** Use the passive when you want to keep the focus on someone or something important that is acted upon:

> Ronald Reagan *was elected* president of the United States in 1980.

We don't need *by the voters;* everyone knows who did the electing. What's important here is the identity of the person elected.

> On August 13, 1927, while driving on the Promenade des Anglais at Nice, Isadora Duncan met her death. She *was strangled* by her colored shawl, which became tangled in the wheel of the automobile. —Janet Flanner

Here the writer shifts from the active (*met*) in the first sentence to the passive (*was strangled*) in the second sentence. The shift from active to passsive enables the writer to keep the focus on a subject who is shown first acting, and then acted upon.

> Frederick Douglass learned to read while he *was owned* by Mr. and Mrs. Ault of Baltimore.

Here the writer moves from active to passive in one sentence. The shift keeps the focus on Douglass, who is shown at once acting (he *learned*) and acted upon (he *was owned*).

**2.** Use the passive when you do not know or do not care to say who or what performed the action shown by the verb:

> Traces of the oil spill *were found* as far away as Newfoundland.

There is no need to say who found the traces of the oil spill.

> The pyramids at Teotihuacán, Mexico, *were built* during the second and third centuries A.D.

The writer may not know who built these pyramids, and we hardly need to be told that they were built *by some people.*

**3.** Use the passive when you want to put the person or thing acting at the end of a clause, where you can easily attach a long modifier:

> A secret mission to help thousands of starving Cambodians *was organized* in the summer of 1979 by Father Robert L. Charlesbois, a forty-eight-year-old Catholic priest from Gary, Indiana, with twelve years of experience in the Vietnam war zone.
> A secret mission to help thousands of starving Cambodians *was organized* in the summer of 1979 by Father Robert L. Charlesbois, who sent truck convoys loaded with food, medicine, and other emergency supplies to a remote part of southern Thailand near the Cambodian border.

The person shown acting in each of these sentences is Father Robert L. Charlesbois. Use of the passive voice enables the writer to name him at the end of the main clause, where a lengthy modifier can be attached without any awkward separation of subject and verb, such as you find in sentence 10 of exercise 1, p. 367.

EXERCISE 3   **Choosing the Appropriate Voice**

Select five sentences from exercise 1, p. 367, and five from exercise 2, pp. 368–69. Indicate for each whether the passive or active version is better, and explain the reason for your choice.

> EXAMPLE
> In exercise 1, sentence 10, the passive version is better because it puts the agent, Father Robert L. Charlesbois, at the end of the clause, where the long modifier can easily follow.

## 22.5   Misusing the Passive Voice  *pass*

Do not switch from active to passive in midsentence or midparagraph without a good reason:

> Usually I run two miles in the morning, but that morning it *was decided* that a four-mile run *should be taken.*

The passive voice turns the second part of the sentence into a pretzel, and since there is no *by* phrase, we can't be sure just who made the decision. Keep the active voice as long as the person or thing you are writing about is acting rather than acted upon:

> Usually I run two miles in the morning, but that morning I decided to run four.

The active voice makes the sentence snap into shape. You should switch to the passive only if the person or thing you are writing about is acted upon:

> Usually I run two miles in the morning, but that morning I *was kept* in bed by the flu.

EXERCISE 4   **Sentence Combining**

Following is a group of simple sentences, some with verbs in the active voice, others with verbs in the passive. Make one continuous passage out of these sentences by combining some of them and changing the voice of the verbs where necessary.

> EXAMPLE
> 1. As prime minister of England from 1940 to 1945, Churchill led his country through World War II.
> 2. But immediately after the war people voted him out of office.
> 3. Later his position as prime minister was regained by him.

4. That office was left by him.
5. Great popularity for the rest of his life was enjoyed by him.
6. He died in 1965.
7. People acclaimed him as a national hero.

COMBINED: As prime minister of England from 1940 to 1945, Churchill led his country through World War II, but immediately after the war he was voted out of office. Later he regained his position as prime minister. After he left that office, he enjoyed great popularity for the rest of his life, and when he died in 1965, he was acclaimed as a national hero.

1. The political structure of modern China was largely created by Mao Zedong.
2. Mao led the Chinese Communist revolution.
3. The theory behind it was formulated by him.
4. China was virtually ruled by him from 1949 to his death in 1976.
5. Mao worked for revolution throughout much of his early life.
6. In 1911 the Nationalist armed forces of Hunan Province were joined by him in their revolt against the Manchu dynasty.
7. He was then eighteen.
8. In 1921 he helped to found the Chinese Communist party.
9. In the spring of 1928, the Fourth Chinese Red Army was organized by him and a fellow revolutionary named Zhu De.
10. In 1934–35, he and Zhu De led a six-thousand-mile march of Chinese Communist forces to northwest China.
11. There a new base of operations was established by the two leaders.
12. The new base was established against the Kuomintang.
13. That was the Nationalist political organization.
14. Generalissimo Chiang Kai-shek headed it.
15. Mao and Chiang joined forces during World War II in order to fight their common enemy, the Japanese.
16. But in the summer of 1946 full-scale civil war against the Nationalists was resumed by Mao.
17. Mao's forces won the war in three years.
18. On September 21, 1949, the establishment of the People's Republic of China was proclaimed by Mao.
19. A succession of increasingly powerful posts was then assumed by him.
20. The posts included chairmanship of the Government Council, chairmanship of the Republic, and most important, chairmanship of the Chinese Communist party.
21. In effect, China was ruled by Mao for nearly thirty years.
22. For better or worse, a lasting change in that country was made by Mao.
23. People will long remember him as one of the most important revolutionaries of the twentieth century.

# 23

# VERBS
## Mood

The **mood** of a verb or verb phrase indicates your attitude toward a particular statement as you are making it. Do you think of it as a statement of fact? Then you will use the indicative mood. Do you think of it as a command? Then you will use the imperative. Do you think of it as a wish, a recommendation, or a hypothetical condition? Then you will use the subjunctive.

The mood of a verb is sometimes shown by a special form or an auxiliary. We treat each mood in turn.

## 23.1 The Indicative

The **indicative** is the mood in most writing.

**1.** Use the indicative in statements of actuality or strong probability:

> Diane Peters *is writing* a play.
> Bruce Rogers *runs* ten miles a day.
> George McGovern *ran* for president in 1972.
> Erich Segal *has run* in the Boston Marathon.

**2.** Use *do*, *does*, or *did* with the indicative for emphasis:

> Fred is no Olympic star, but he *does run* ten miles a day.
> Small cars are often short on leg room, but they *do save* gas.
> The blizzard of '78 was not the worst in history, but it *did paralyze* Boston for several days.

## 23.2   The Imperative

The **imperative** is the mood of commands and requests made directly.

**1.** Use the bare form of the verb for commands addressed entirely to others:

> *Vote* for Harrington.
> *Fight* pollution.
> *Be* yourself.
> Kindly *send* me your latest catalog.

**2.** When a command or suggestion includes yourself as well as others, use *let us* or *let's* before the bare form of the verb:

> *Let us negotiate* our differences in a spirit of mutual trust and respect.
> *Let's cooperate.*

## 23.3   The Subjunctive

The **subjunctive** is the mood in statements of hypothetical conditions or of wishes, recommendations, requirements, or suggestions. Normally the subjunctive requires either a modal auxiliary or a subjunctive verb form.

**Using Modal Auxiliaries**

**Modal auxiliaries** are helping verbs that indicate the subjunctive mood. Here is a list of the meanings they can express.

**1.** A <u>wish</u>, shown by *would* or *could:*

> Some people wish the federal government *would* support them for the rest of their lives.
> I wish I *could* climb Mount Everest.

When the thing wished for is impossible or contrary to fact, use *could.*

**2.** <u>Probability</u>, shown by *should:*

> The increased production of oil in the United States *should* reduce our dependence on foreign oil.

**3.** <u>Possibility</u>, shown by *may, might, can,* or *could:*

> The next president of the United States *may* be a woman.
> A third world war *might* lead to the death of every living thing on earth.

When Cal turns up at a party, anything *can* happen.
A major earthquake *could* strike California within the next ten years.

**4.** Capability, shown by *can:*

> *Can* the Israelis and the Palestinians ever make peace?

**5.** Permission, shown by *may* or *can:*

> Students who cannot afford tuition *may* apply for loans.
> Americans *can* visit China now.

Some writers believe that *can* may be used only for capability, and that permission always calls for *may.* But *can* is now commonly used for both purposes.

**6.** A requirement, shown by *must:*

> Firemen *must* be ready for action at any hour of the day or night.

**7.** A recommendation or suggestion, shown by *should* or *ought:*

> Students who hope to get into medical school *should* take biology.
> The government *ought* to cut taxes.

*Ought* is normally followed by an infinitive.

**8.** A conclusion, shown by *must:*

> Jimmy Hoffa *must* have been murdered.

**9.** A contrary-to-fact condition, shown by *could:*

> If I *could* run a mile in three minutes, I would be famous.

(For a full discussion of conditional sentences, see section 23.4, pp. 377–78.)

Do not use more than one of these modal auxiliaries at a time. You can write *I might go* or *I could go* but not *\*I might could go.*

---

EXERCISE 1 **Supplying Modal Auxiliaries**

Complete each of the following sentences with a suitable modal auxiliary. Then in parentheses identify the meaning it expresses.

> EXAMPLE
> Students who hope to get into medical school _____ take biology.
> Students who hope to get into medical school <u>should</u> take biology. (recommendation)
>
> 1. In the volcanic world of the Middle East, open warfare _____ erupt at any time.

2. After weeks of training with the barbells, Doug White ——————— lift 350 pounds.
3. To become an actor, you ——————— learn how to manage your body as well as your voice.
4. If I ——————— speak Italian, I would spend the summer in Rome.
5. To help the poor effectively, we ——————— understand the causes of poverty.
6. If there were no limit on the supply of money in our economy, the dollar ——————— soon lose all its value.

## Using Subjunctive Verb Forms

The subjunctive mood is sometimes indicated by a special verb form instead of by a modal auxiliary.

**1.** The present subjunctive is the same in form as the bare form of the verb. Use it to express a hope, a requirement, a recommendation, or a suggestion:

| INDICATIVE | SUBJUNCTIVE |
|---|---|
| God *has* mercy on us. | God *have* mercy on us! |
| The queen *lives*. | Long *live* the queen! |
| A premed student normally *takes* biology. | The college requires that every student *take* freshman English. |
| The trustees' meetings *are* closed. | The students demand that those meetings *be* open. |

**2.** The past subjunctive is the same in form as the common past, except that the past subjunctive of *be* is *were* with every subject. Use the past subjunctive to express a wish for something in the present:

| INDICATIVE (FACT) | SUBJUNCTIVE (WISH) |
|---|---|
| I *have* five dollars. | I wish (that) I *had* a million dollars. |
| I *am* a pauper. | I wish (that) I *were* a millionaire. |
| I *am taking* Math 36. | I wish (that) I *were taking* Math 23. |
| I *live* in Illinois. | I wish (that) I *lived* in Florida. |

**3.** The past perfect subjunctive is the same in form as the common past perfect. Use it to express a wish for something in the past:

| INDICATIVE (FACT) | SUBJUNCTIVE (WISH) |
|---|---|
| I *saw* the second half of the game. | I wish (that) I *had seen* the first. [or] I wished (that) I *had seen* the first. |
| I *was* there for the second half. | I wish (that) I *had been* there for the first. |

EXERCISE 2    Using Subjunctive Verb Forms

Complete each of the following sentences by inserting the appropriate form of the verb shown in parentheses. The appropriate form will sometimes be the same as the one in parentheses.

EXAMPLE

I saw the second half of the game, but I wish I _____ all of it. (see)

I saw the second half of the game, but I wish I __had seen__ all of it.

1. I took History 34 last term, but I wish that I _____ History 32. (take)
2. Some students demand that the university _____ all of its stocks in companies that do business in South Africa. (sell)
3. Since Sally is the best player on the team, the other players insist that she _____ the captain. (be)
4. The Social Security system requires that every worker _____ a fixed percentage of his or her earnings to a government-sponsored retirement fund. (contribute)
5. Sal felt out of place at the meeting and wished that he _____ someplace else. (be)
6. Since the old ambulance was no longer reliable, the townspeople voted to recommend that the fire department _____ a new one. (buy)

## 23.4   Forming Conditional Sentences

A conditional sentence normally consists of an *if* clause, which states a condition, and a result clause, which states the result of that condition. The mood of the verb in the *if* clause depends on the likelihood of the condition.

### The Possible Condition

If the condition is likely or even barely possible, the mood is indicative:

[condition] If wages *are* increased, [result] prices will rise.

An increase in wages is more than likely, so the mood is indicative; the verb is *are*.

### The Impossible or Contrary-to-Fact Condition

If the condition is impossible or contrary to fact, the mood of the verb in the *if* clause is subjunctive, and the result clause usually includes a modal auxiliary, such as *would:*

[condition] If oil *were* plentiful, [result] there would be no energy crisis.

Since oil is not plentiful, the condition is contrary to fact, and the mood is subjunctive; the verb is *were.* In formal writing *was* would be incorrect here. As this example shows, a condition that is contrary to present fact must be stated in the past subjunctive. When a condition is contrary to past fact, it must be stated in the past perfect subjunctive:

[condition] If Jimmy Carter *had obtained* the release of the Iranian hostages before November 1980, [result] he might have been reelected to the presidency.
[condition] If the Watergate scandal *had* not *occurred,* [result] Gerald Ford would never have become president.

A condition introduced by *as if* is always contrary to fact and therefore always requires the subjunctive:

Atop the Empire State Building, ignoring his pursuers, Kong places Fay on a ledge as tenderly as if she *were* a dozen eggs.
—X. J. Kennedy

The verb is *were* because the condition is contrary to present fact—to what Fay is at the time Kong places her on the ledge.

After the fight he looked as if he *had been* through a meat grinder.

The verb is *had been* because the condition is contrary to past fact.

EXERCISE 3   **Supplying Verbs**

Using the facts in brackets as a guide, complete each of the following sentences by supplying a suitable verb or verb phrase.

EXAMPLE
If Jimmy Carter _____ the release of the Iranian hostages before November 1980, he might have been reelected to the presidency. [Carter did not obtain the release of the hostages before November 1980.]
If Jimmy Carter had obtained the release of the Iranian hostages before November 1980, he might have been reelected to the presidency.

1. If high-speed trains _____ all major cities in the United States, Americans could travel much more often without their cars. [High-speed trains serve hardly any cities in the United States.]
2. If my father _____ five hundred shares of IBM in 1950, he would be a millionaire today. [Alas, my father never bought any shares of IBM.]

3. If the prime rate _____, unemployment may go up also. [The prime rate goes up and down regularly.]
4. After winning the match, Joan felt as if she _____ the world. [She did not actually conquer the world.]
5. If the Continental Army _____ to the British at Yorktown, George Washington might never have become president of the United States. [The Continental Army did not lose to the British at Yorktown.]

EXERCISE 4  **Supplying Verbs**

For each of the blanks in the following passage supply a suitable verb or verb phrase.

EXAMPLE
line 2: were

Many students wish that the Thanksgiving recess _____ one week long, or that the fall term _____ completely before Thanksgiving, so that they could stay home between Thanksgiving and Christmas. But the students have not asked for
5  either of those things. They have asked only that the Thanksgiving recess _____ on the Wednesday before Thanksgiving. If the recess _____ on Wednesday, students would have one full day to travel home before Thanksgiving Day itself. Many students need that time. If every student _____ rich, he or she could
10  fly home in an hour or two. But most students are not rich. They wish the college year _____ longer breaks. By the end of November, in fact, they often wish the fall term _____ early enough so that it could be all over by Thanksgiving.

# 24

# DIRECT AND INDIRECT REPORTING OF DISCOURSE

| |
|---|
| 24.1 |

Any statement, whether written or spoken, can be reported directly—by quotation of the actual words—or indirectly. But some statements deserve direct reporting while others do not.

Use **direct** reporting when the exact words of the original statement are memorable or otherwise important:

> Emerson wrote, "In every work of genius we recognize our own rejected thoughts."
> There are five strong stresses in Robert Frost's line, "Something there is that doesn't love a wall."

Use **indirect** reporting when the exact words of the original statement are less important than their content:

> My father said that he wanted me to get a college education.
> The new governor says he will cut property taxes.

## 24.1 Direct Reporting of Statements— Using Quotation Marks

Most discourse consists of statements rather than questions. Here is a statement that might be made in a conversation or a letter:

> You should go to law school.

To report this statement directly, the writer must keep the words exactly as they are and enclose them in quotation marks:

> "You should go to law school."

By using quotation marks the writer tells the reader that the words were originally spoken or written by someone else. But in addition, the writer should normally say who that someone is, and should explain the reference of any pronouns in the quotation, such as *You* in the example. A quotation therefore needs an explanatory tag:

> "You should go to law school," said the judge to his daughter.

(For a full discussion of how to punctuate quotations, see pp. 404–6.)

## Using Tenses in Tags

Since no statement can be reported until after it has been made, you should normally use the past tense for the verb in the tag:

> "I want to go to law school," she *said.*
>
> In 1782 Thomas Jefferson *wrote:* "There must doubtless be an unhappy influence on the manners of our people produced by the existence of slavery among us."

But use the present when you are quoting a statement of lasting significance or a statement made by a literary character:

> "In every work of genius," *observes* Emerson, "we recognize our own rejected thoughts."
>
> In the first chapter of *Huckleberry Finn,* Huck *says,* "I don't take no stock in dead people."

## Quoting Dialogue

In reporting an exchange between two speakers, you should first indicate clearly who is speaking and in what order. You can then omit tags until the dialogue ends or is interrupted. The speakers' remarks should be set off from each other with quotation marks, and you should normally begin a new paragraph whenever one speaker gives way to another:

> "Our market surveys indicate," Hurts said, "that there are also a lot of kids who claim their parents don't listen to them. If they could rent a gun, they feel they could arrive at an understanding with their folks in no time."
>
> "There's no end to the business," I said. "How would you charge for Hurts Rent-A-Gun?"
>
> "There would be hourly rates, day rates, and weekly rates, plus ten cents for each bullet fired. Our guns would be the latest models, and we would guarantee clean barrels and the latest safety

devices. If a gun malfunctions through no fault of the user, we will give him another gun absolutely free." . . .

"Why didn't you start this before?"

"We wanted to see what happened with the gun-control legislation. . . ." —Art Buchwald, "Hurts Rent-A-Gun"

When you quote more than four lines of prose or two lines of poetry, you should indent instead of using quotation marks, as described in "Quoting Long Passages," pp. 405–6.

## 24.2 Indirect Reporting of Statements

When a statement is reported indirectly, no quotation marks are used:

> ORIGINAL STATEMENT: I want you to get a college education.
> DIRECT REPORT (QUOTATION): My father said to me, "I want you to get a college education."
> INDIRECT REPORT: My father said that he wanted me to get a college education.

As this example shows, an indirect report does the following:

**1.** It refers to the speaker or writer.

**2.** It often puts *that* just before the reported statement. But *that* may be omitted:

> My father said he wanted me to get a college education.

**3.** It changes the pronouns in the reported statement where necessary. In this example, *I* becomes *he,* and *you* becomes *me.*

**4.** It may change the tense of the verb in the reported statement. If the introductory verb is in the past tense, the verb in the reported statement may be in the past tense also—even if the verb in the original was not. Thus, after *My father said,* which includes a past-tense verb, *I want you* may become *he wanted me.* But if the original statement was recently made or has lasting significance, the original tense may be kept in the reported statement:

> My father said that he wants me to get a college education.
> Ben Franklin once said that the sting of a reproach is the truth of it.

**EXERCISE 1  Transforming Reports of Statements**

Each of the following consists of a statement, with the speaker and listener identified in brackets. Write a direct and an indirect report of the statement. Then put a check next to the version you think is more suitable, and say why you prefer it.

EXAMPLE

I want you to go to college. [*Speaker:* my father; *listener:* me]
DIRECT: "I want you to go to college," said my father.
√ INDIRECT: My father said that he wanted me to go to college.
The content is more important than the exact words.

1. You will have to earn your own spending money. [*Speaker:* my father; *listener:* me]
2. I do not mind lying, but I hate inaccuracy. [*Writer:* Samuel Butler]
3. I will pay you $3.50 an hour. [*Speaker:* the manager; *listener:* me]
4. You have been baptized in fire and blood and have come out steel. [*Speaker:* General Patton; *listeners:* the battle survivors]
5. Nothing in education is so astonishing as the amount of ignorance it accumulates in the form of inert facts. [*Writer:* Henry Adams]
6. Fanaticism consists in redoubling your efforts when you have forgotten your aim. [*Writer:* George Santayana]

## 24.3   Direct Reporting of Questions

To report a question directly, you normally use a verb of asking in the past tense:

> The Sphinx asked, "What walks on four legs in the morning, two legs at noon, and three legs in the evening?"
> "Have you thought about college?" my father asked.

Use the present tense when you are reporting a question of standing importance or a question asked by a literary character:

> The consumer advocate asks, "How can we have safe and effective products without government regulation?"
> The businessman asks, "How can we have free enterprise with government interference?"
> When Tom Sawyer proposes to form a gang that will rob and kill people, Huck asks, "Must we always kill the people?"

## 24.4   Indirect Reporting of Questions

In many respects the indirect reporting of questions resembles the indirect reporting of statements. But to report a question indirectly, you must normally introduce it with a verb of asking and a word like *who, what, whether, how, when, where, why,* or *if*:

> ORIGINAL QUESTION: Do you want to go to college?
> INDIRECT REPORT: My father asked me if I wanted to go to college.

As this example shows, you must change the word order and the wording of the question: *Do you want* becomes *if I wanted.* Also, the question mark at the end of the original question becomes a period. Do not write:

> *My father asked me did I want to go to college?

As in the direct reporting of questions, use the present tense for the introductory verb when reporting a question of continuing importance or a question asked by a literary character:

> The consumer advocate asks how we can have safe and effective products without government regulation.
> The businessman asks how we can have free enterprise with government interference.
> When Tom Sawyer proposes to form a gang that will rob and kill people, Huck asks whether they must always kill the people.

After a past-tense verb of asking, you must normally use the past tense in the reported question. But you may use the present tense if the reported question is essentially timeless:

> The Sphinx asked what walks on four legs in the morning, two legs at noon, and three legs in the evening.

### EXERCISE 2    Transforming Reports of Questions

Each of the following sentences contains either a direct or an indirect question. If the question is direct, make it indirect; if it is indirect, make it direct. Then say which version you think is more suitable, and why you prefer it.

> EXAMPLE
> "Do you plan to seek reelection, Ms. Greene?" a reporter for Channel 31 asked.
> TRANSFORMED: A reporter for Channel 31 asked Ms. Greene whether she was planning to seek reelection.
> The indirect question is preferable because the content is more important than the exact words.

1. The waitress asked us, "What would you like?"
2. Many economists are asking themselves how the rate of inflation can keep rising during a period of high unemployment.
3. At one point in *Leaves of Grass*, Whitman asks us, "What do you suppose will satisfy the soul, except to walk free and own no superior?"
4. Early in *The Republic* one of Socrates' friends asks him if he wants to prove that justice is always better than injustice.
5. "But how shall we expect charity towards others, when we are uncharitable to ourselves?" asks Sir Thomas Browne.
6. One citizen asked the selectmen how they proposed to pay for the new addition to the high school.
7. "Do you expect to increase the tax on personal property?" she asked the selectmen.

# 25

# PUNCTUATION
# AND MECHANICS

This chapter explains how to use punctuation marks and how to follow certain mechanical conventions. You need punctuation marks to separate sentences, to set off parts of sentences, and to clarify the meaning or increase the effect of individual words. You need to follow mechanical conventions so that your writing will look the way formal writing is expected to look. We treat punctuation marks first and then mechanical conventions.

•

## 25.1  The Period   •

**1.** Use a period to mark the end of a declarative sentence, a mild command, or an indirect question:

> The days are growing shorter, and the nights are becoming cool.
> Please send me the report.
> The taxi driver asked us where we wanted to go.

**2.** Use a period to mark the end of some abbreviations:

| | |
|---|---|
| Dr. Boyle | Mr. G. H. Johnson |
| 500 Fifth Ave. | Mrs. L. S. Allingham |
| N.Y., N.Y. | Ms. N. A. Stephens |
| Kate Fansler, Ph.D. | 3 P.M. |
| | 350 B.C. |

Generally, you don't need periods with acronyms (words formed from the initials of a multiword title) or with capital-letter abbreviations of technical terms, names of agencies, or names of organizations:

| CBS | ROTC | IBM |
|------|------|------|
| NATO | TVA | IQ |
| FM | ID | KP |
| | CIA | VISTA |

● But you do need periods with B.C. and A.D., and with abbreviations standing for the names of political entities:

U.S.A.　　U.K.　　U.S.S.R.

For guidance, see your dictionary.

**3.** In general, do not use a period to make a sentence fragment:

Customers should be treated courteously. *Even if they are rude.

The *even if* clause should not be separated from its base sentence. To correct the error, either drop the period or change it to a comma, and do not capitalize *even:*

Customers should be treated courteously even if they are rude.

Here is another example:

What motorists want is a well-made automobile. *That they can drive without going to the poorhouse.

The adjective clause should not be separated from the word it modifies—*automobile.* To correct the error, drop the period and do not capitalize *that:*

What motorists want is a well-made automobile that they can drive without going to the poorhouse.

(For more on sentence fragments, see chapter 17, pp. 296–304.)

EXERCISE 1　**Using Periods**

Each of the following may require the addition or removal of one or more periods. Make any necessary change; also make any accompanying change in capitalization that may be required. If an entry is correct as it stands, write *Correct.*

EXAMPLE
Dr Brenda Lange is scheduled to present a paper on kinesics at Friday's meeting.
REVISED: Dr. Brenda Lange is scheduled to present a paper on kinesics at Friday's meeting.

1. Please remove all litter. Before leaving the picnic area
2. Mr and Mrs Frank L Thomas will ask the mayor why the town has failed to install street lights in their neighborhood
3. No one wants to rent an apartment at 10 South Main Street. Because the incessant traffic is both noisy and dangerous
4. Delegates to the A.F.L.-C.I.O. convention in Chicago are asking when the secretary of labor will address them

5. I wonder how many peanut butter and jelly sandwiches are consumed in one day

## 25.2 The Question Mark ?

**1.** Use a question mark at the end of a direct question:

Must the problems of the small farmer be ignored?

**2.** Use a question mark to indicate uncertainty within a statement:

Some animal—a skunk?—is boring holes in the lawn at night.
They must have paid a lot of money ($50?) for that meal.

**3.** Do not use a question mark at the end of an indirect question:

*I wonder who wrote this song?
REVISED: I wonder who wrote this song.

## 25.3 The Exclamation Point !

**1.** Use an exclamation point to mark the end of an exclamatory sentence:

What a trip it was!

**2.** Use an exclamation point to mark the end of an exclamatory phrase:

What a beautiful view!

Use exclamation points sparingly; too many of them will dull your effect:

We got there! We thought we'd never make it!! But we were there at last!!!

Be especially cautious about using them as an easy method of indicating sarcasm or your own disagreement with a reported statement:

He said he was the best (!) singer in the club.

EXERCISE 2 **Using Question Marks and Exclamation Points**

Each of the following may require a question mark or an exclamation point. Add any necessary punctuation. If an entry is correct as it stands, write *Correct*.

EXAMPLE
What is the weather forecast for Saturday
REVISED: What is the weather forecast for Saturday?

*The Exclamation Point* 387

1. A lion was loose in the park
2. One vehicle—was it a jeep—finished the whole three-thousand-mile course without a single breakdown.
3. What a shock
4. Customers often ask us where their typewriters can be repaired.
5. After giving me a written estimate for $175, why have you sent me a bill for $300

EXERCISE 3   **Using Periods and Question Marks**

Improve the punctuation in the following paragraph by adding a period or question mark wherever necessary; also make any accompanying change in capitalization that may be required. As you make these corrections, write out the entire paragraph.

How do historians rate the contributions of Gen Gordon to his country their opinions differ some consider him a military genius, one of the greatest soldiers in British history others criticize him severely in their opinion C G Gordon, or "Chinese" Gordon as he was popularly known, acted impulsively he was rash he was dangerous he was not fit to hold a command did he seek death on Jan 26, 1885 historians give conflicting answers

## 25.4   The Comma  ,

### Using Commas

**1.** Use a comma to set off an introductory clause, phrase, or conjunctive adverb from the rest of the sentence:

*Whenever it rains hard,* the roof leaks. [clause]
*To prepare for the bar exam,* Jan attended a tutoring school after work. [phrase]
*As a result,* sales declined. [conjunctive adverb]
*Nevertheless,* some of the problems caused by automation remain unsolved. [conjunctive adverb.]

You may omit the comma after an introductory phrase if the phrase is short:

*By jogging daily* Bob has improved his health.

Do not use a comma after an introductory conjunction:

*But* he still wears a spare tire around his waist.

EXERCISE 4   **Using Commas after Introductory Elements**

Each of the following may require a comma after an introductory clause, phrase, or conjunctive adverb. Add any needed comma. If an entry is correct as it stands, write *Correct.*

EXAMPLE

Furthermore an increase in property taxes would severely limit the number of young adults who could live in the area.

REVISED: Furthermore, an increase in property taxes would severely limit the number of young adults who could live in the area.

1. To cope with the heavy fogs many fishermen have installed radar equipment in their boats.
2. Nevertheless, left-handed pitchers have an advantage over most left-handed batters.
3. Unable to think of a topic the student stared glumly at his pencil.
4. Frightened by the jangling of the fire alarm a child began crying.
5. If we ate less food we would have fewer dishes to wash.

**2. Use a comma before a conjunction that links two independent clauses:**

The prospectors hoped to find gold on the rocky slopes of the towering Sierra Madre, so they set out eagerly.

Do not use a comma when both of the clauses are short:

Many are called but few are chosen.

EXERCISE 5   **Using Commas before Conjunctions**

Each of the following may require a comma before a conjunction. Add any needed comma. If an entry is correct as it stands, write *Correct.*

EXAMPLE

We can stop for the night in Port Arthur or we can push on to Houston.

REVISED: We can stop for the night in Port Arthur, or we can push on to Houston.

1. Grant may have lost the battle but he left the enemy weakened beyond recovery.
2. My grandfather never carried his gun into the woods above Southport for he loved the sight and sound of the wildlife there.
3. The captured sailors received no message from Admiral Walker nor had they expected to receive one.
4. Bob gave two quarts of maple syrup to Helen and Betty and Ruth mailed one gallon to her mother.
5. All of the seats in the stadium have been painted and a new scoreboard has been erected atop the center-field bleachers.
6. The traditional approach to landscape painting bored him so he experimented with radically new ways to depict form and light.
7. We had been driving for six hours without a break, but Rob refused to stop for lunch.
8. Columbus wanted to find a new way of reaching the Indies and he also hoped to prove a new theory about the shape of the earth.

**3.** Use a comma in a series—

    1. To join three or more coordinate items:

> Sally, Beth, and Cathy were reading in the library.
> The cat purred, stretched, and leaped from the chair.
> The sentry asked us why we had entered a restricted zone, where we had come from, and what we were planning to do.

When a series includes three or more items, you normally need a conjunction between the last two. Use a comma before this conjunction, but not after it:

> *The speaker coughed, studied his notes, and, frowned in dismay.
> REVISED: The speaker coughed, studied his notes, and frowned in dismay.

When items in a series are long or internally punctuated, use semicolons between them. (See p. 397.)

    2. To join two or more adjectives preceding a noun:

> The old man spoke in a low, mysterious voice.
> A big, old, dilapidated house stood on the corner.

You do not need a conjunction between adjectives preceding a noun, and you can sometimes omit the comma between two adjectives, especially when the first is a modifier of the second:

> His deep blue eyes stared at me furiously.
> A rusty iron gate blocked our way.

EXERCISE 6   **Punctuating Parallel and Coordinate Items**

Each of the following may require the addition or removal of commas or semicolons. Make any necessary change. If an entry is correct as it stands, write *Correct*.

    EXAMPLE
    The carpenter's chest contained a tape measure two chisels some nails and a hammer.
    REVISED: The carpenter's chest contained a tape measure, two chisels, some nails, and a hammer.

    1. The motor coughed wheezed sputtered and died.
    2. Strands of thick heavy rope were strewn about the freshly varnished deck of the old ship.
    3. The deer bounded swiftly gracefully and, beautifully through the meadow.
    4. On hand to greet the freshmen were Margaret Smith, the new dean of students, Frank Blunt, the registrar, and Barbara Fisk, director of buildings and grounds.
    5. Our guide was slow to rise in the morning slow to work during the day but quick to eat at night.

**4.** Use a pair of commas to set off a **nonrestrictive** modifier—a phrase or clause that does not restrict the meaning of the head-word or antecedent:

> Richard M. Nixon, *who tried to obstruct justice,* was forced to resign from the presidency.

In this sentence the *who* clause does not restrict the meaning of the antecedent, *Richard M. Nixon.* It merely adds information about a man who has already been identified by name; if the clause were omitted, the sentence would still say basically the same thing—that Nixon was forced to resign. But compare that sentence with this one:

> All presidents *who try to obstruct justice* should be forced to resign.

Here the *who* clause is **restrictive;** it restricts, or limits, the meaning of the antecedent, *presidents,* by identifying exactly which presidents should resign. If the clause were removed, the meaning of the sentence would change significantly: it would say that all presidents, not just certain ones, should be forced to resign. That is not what the original sentence asserts. The *who* clause is therefore essential to the meaning of *presidents* in this sentence and must not be set off from *presidents* by commas. Here are further examples:

> A wood-burning stove *that can be used with the doors open or closed* gives you the pleasure of an open fire whenever you want it. [restrictive clause]
> The Vigilant stove, *which can be used with the doors open or closed,* gives you the pleasure of an open fire whenever you want it. [nonrestrictive clause]
>
> The windows *facing north* will be boarded up during the winter. [restrictive phrase]
> In our living room the picture window, *facing north,* gives us a splendid view of Mount Morris. [nonrestrictive phrase]

Use just one comma to set off a nonrestrictive phrase or clause that comes at the end of a sentence:

> On Friday we reached Tucson, where Carrie was waiting for us.

### EXERCISE 7  Using Commas with Nonrestrictive Phrases and Clauses

Each of the following contains a phrase or clause that modifies a preceding noun. Write down the phrase or clause and in parentheses state whether it is restrictive or nonrestrictive. Then rewrite the sentence if it needs commas added or removed. If an entry is correct as it stands, write *Correct.*

> EXAMPLE
> Motorists are required to replace any tire, with tread less than $^3/_{16}$ of an inch thick.

with tread less than $3/16$ of an inch thick (restrictive)
Motorists are required to replace any tire with tread less than $3/16$ of an inch thick.

1. The management never refunds the purchase price of any items, which are sold below cost.
2. The newly formed chamber ensemble will be conducted by Harriet Brown onetime first violinist with the Hartford Symphony Orchestra.
3. Three of the men, who have applied for the job, have had extensive experience working in foreign countries.
4. Muriel had to jump from the boat to retrieve the rudder which had slipped out of its clamp.
5. Students who earn a grade of B or higher on the weekly quizzes need not take the final examination.
6. The president of the university who for many years had taught classics began his speech in Latin.
7. Young couples trying to buy houses nowadays are faced with frightening interest rates.
8. A man, in a crisp white coat, answered the door.
9. At the zoo we saw toucans which I had never even heard of before.
10. Anyone, who thinks the depression is a thing of the past, should consider what has lately been happening to the American automobile industry.

**5.** Use a comma or a pair of commas to set off nonessential words and phrases, specifically—

1. To set off an absolute phrase:

Eyes flashing, Gretta stood up and denounced the speaker.
José stood helpless, his arms hanging limp at his sides.

2. To set off a phrase of contrast:

Fearful, not confident, they set out for the West.

3. To set off an appositive:

Southwick, the quarterback, was injured in the third quarter.

(For a full discussion of the punctuation of appositives, see section 11.8, pp. 226–27.)

4. To set off a conjunctive adverb when it is used in the middle of a clause:

In the seventh inning, *however,* the pitcher suddenly lost his control.

You may omit the commas when a conjunctive adverb is next to a verb:

The chairman did not bother to count the votes. I therefore protested.

When a conjunctive adverb is used between two clauses of a compound sentence, it is set off by a semicolon on one side and a comma on the other:

Money cannot find happiness for you; nevertheless, it can keep you comfortable while you are looking.

EXERCISE 8    **Punctuating Nonessential Words and Phrases**

Each of the following contains an absolute phrase, a phrase of contrast, an appositive, or a conjunctive adverb. Add any necessary punctuation. If an entry is correct as it stands, write *Correct.*

EXAMPLE
This toy rocket for example costs only $9.98.
REVISED: This toy rocket, for example, costs only $9.98.

1. The new seats in the auditorium are more comfortable than the old ones were. The acoustics however, are worse.
2. She has all the necessary experience; furthermore she is ambitious.
3. Workers at Plant A have refused to consider any delay in setting the new pay scale; workers at Plant C on the other hand will agree to a sixty-day extension of the deadline.
4. The size of the crowds visiting the wildlife preserve has disturbed the mating cycle of the cranes. Next season therefore fewer visitors will be admitted.
5. Laughter is good for the soul; it may also be good for the lungs.
6. Before the sixteenth century nearly everyone believed that the earth not the sun was the fixed center of the universe.
7. In the sixteenth century Nicolaus Copernicus a Polish astronomer startled his contemporaries by declaring that the earth revolves around the sun.
8. A man dressed up to look like Santa Claus bounded into the auditorium his eyes flashing merrily.
9. The storm having passed the cyclists resumed their journey through the ravine.
10. The shark was beached, its voracious heart finally still.
11. A faint smirk twisting his lips the teller put the day's deposits in his Thermos and left the bank.
12. Their crests rising to fearsome heights, the huge waves moved shoreward.

**6.** Use a comma as needed with names, letter greetings and closings, dates, and addresses—

1. To separate the name of a person from any titles or degrees shown after it:

George Dean, M.A.
Barbara Kane, M.D.

2. To separate the parts of a proper name when the last name is given first:

Lunt, George D., Jr.

3. To follow the greeting in a friendly or informal letter, and to follow the closing in a letter of any kind:

Dear Mary,
Sincerely,
Cordially,
Very truly yours,

4. To set off successive items in a date or an address:

On the afternoon of July 1, 1863, the fighting began.
The return address on the letter was 23 Hockney Street, Lexington, Kentucky 40502.

Do not put a comma between the name of a month and the day, between a street number and the name of the street, or between the name of a state and the zip code:

\*15, Amsterdam Avenue
REVISED: 15 Amsterdam Avenue

\*October, 22
REVISED: October 22

\*Lebanon, N.H., 03766
REVISED: Lebanon, N.H. 03766

EXERCISE 9   **Using Commas with Names, Letter Greetings and Closings, Dates, and Addresses**

Each of the following may require one or more commas. Add any needed comma. If an entry is correct as it stands, write *Correct.*

EXAMPLE
The convoy reached Brussels Belgium on November 8 1942.
REVISED: The convoy reached Brussels, Belgium, on November 8, 1942.

1. Mail should be forwarded to Ms. Jane Flynt 22 Wheeler Avenue Wiscutt Massachusetts 08566.
2. The parade will start promptly at 11 A.M. November 26 1982.
3. A crowd gathered outside 10 Downing Street to catch a glimpse of the prime minister.
4. The fireworks display on July 4 may be viewed from the roof of the Marine Terminal at 55 Shore Drive Rockport Oregon.

5. The Smiths arrived in Montreal Canada on March 3 1978 and departed for Mexico City on April 15 of the following year.
6. After finishing business school, she proudly signed all of her letters like this:

Yours truly
Janet Mason M.B.A.

**7.** Use a comma in punctuating some quotations, as described on p. 404.

## Misusing Commas

As has been shown, there are many ways of misusing commas. The two most common ways require special notice.

**1.** Do not use a comma to join two independent clauses:

> *Gray's Peak is one of the highest peaks in the Rocky Mountains, it rises 14,274 feet above sea level.

This sentence illustrates the comma splice. To correct the error, add a conjunction after the comma or replace the comma with a semicolon or a period:

> Gray's Peak is one of the highest peaks in the Rocky Mountains; it rises 14,274 feet above sea level.

Here is another example:

> *The accident left Helen's right hand crippled, nevertheless, she continued her piano lessons.

Once again there is a comma splice. The comma before *nevertheless* should be replaced with a semicolon or a period:

> The accident left Helen's right hand crippled; nevertheless, she continued her piano lessons.

(For a full discussion of the comma splice, see section 13.6, pp. 256–57.)

**2.** Do not use a comma between a subject and its predicate:

> *Voters with no understanding of the issue, should learn the facts before the next town meeting.

The comma after *issue* should be dropped because it separates the whole subject of the sentence—*Voters with no understanding of the issue*—from the predicate:

> Voters with no understanding of the issue should learn the facts before the next town meeting.

## EXERCISE 10    Eliminating Misused Commas

Each of the following may contain a comma incorrectly used between two independent clauses or between a subject and its predicate. Remove any misused comma, substitute another punctuation mark if necessary, and make any accompanying change in capitalization that may be required. If an entry is correct as it stands, write *Correct.*

EXAMPLE
*The Count of Monte Cristo* was written by Alexandre Dumas, it is one of the most exciting historical novels ever published.
REVISED: *The Count of Monte Cristo* was written by Alexandre Dumas. It is one of the most exciting historical novels ever published.

1. Every snowflake swirling about in the sky, has a unique design.
2. The leaves of the magnificent maple trees, gradually fluttered to the ground.
3. The first message that came from the spacecraft, indicated trouble.
4. She writes first drafts quickly, she revises slowly.
5. Stinson Library opened in 1975, it has an entire room reserved for readers under thirteen.

## EXERCISE 11    Using Commas: Review

In the following passage from Peter M. Lincoln's "Documentary Wallpapers," we have deliberately introduced some errors in punctuation. Add a comma wherever one is needed, and remove any comma that is misused.

EXAMPLE
line 2: France,

Many early American homes were decorated with block-printed wallpapers. Imported from England and France the papers made the arrival of ships from abroad an exciting event for Colonial homemakers. Merchants looking for sales, advertised that
5　papering was cheaper than whitewashing and they urged would-be customers to examine the endless variety of brightly colored patterns. Indeed by today's standards the colors in many Colonial papers seem vibrant intense and even gaudy. One wonders whether the citizens of Boston Massachusetts and Providence
10　Rhode Island yearned for bright reds greens and blues because of the grey New England winters.
　　　The process of reproducing historic wallpapers, requires the finesse of a craftsman. To establish a particular paper's full pattern the expert may have to fit together the fragments of surviving sam-
15　ples which he finds in museums in the attics of old houses and even under layers of other papers. He determines the original hue of the colors in various ways: he runs chemical tests or he matches a fragment to a fresh original in some museum. Even then he must be careful before proceeding to the next step printing the design.
20　As a final precaution therefore he makes a blacklight examination

knowing it may reveal otherwise indistinguishable elements of the pattern.

One of the leading experts in America is Dorothy Waterhouse cofounder of Waterhouse Hangings. She first became interested in historic wallpapers in 1932 when she was restoring an old house on Cape Cod Massachusetts. While stripping the walls in one room she got down to the eighth and bottom layer of paper. She became very excited; she knew it had to be over 140 years old. That discovery was the first of many. Today she has a collection of some three hundred historic wallpapers all carefully stored in her Boston home.

## 25.5    The Semicolon    ;

**1.** Use a semicolon to join two independent clauses that are closely related in meaning:

> Insist on yourself; never imitate.        —Ralph Waldo Emerson
> During the summer the resort is crowded with tourists; during the winter only sea gulls perch on the benches or walk the beach.

**2.** Use a semicolon to join two independent clauses when the second begins with or includes a conjunctive adverb:

> Shakespeare's plays are nearly four hundred years old; nevertheless, they still speak to us.
> The voters have rejected a plan to widen Main Street; truckers, therefore, will have to find an alternate route through town.

**3.** Use a semicolon between items in a series when one or more of the items include commas:

> There were three new delegates at the meeting: Ms. Barbara Smith from Red Bank, New Jersey; Ms. Beth Waters from Pocumtuck, Massachusetts; and Mr. James Papson from Freeport, Maine.

**4.** Do not use a semicolon between a phrase and the clause to which it belongs:

> *The climbers carried an extra nylon rope with them; to ensure their safe descent from the cliff.
> REVISED: The climbers carried an extra nylon rope with them to ensure their safe descent from the cliff.

**5.** Do not use a semicolon between a subordinate clause and the main clause:

> *Most of the crowd had left; before the concert ended.
> REVISED: Most of the crowd had left before the concert ended.

**6.** Do not use a semicolon to introduce a list:

*The prophets denounced three types of wrongdoing; idolatry, injustice, and neglect of the needy.

Use a colon (as discussed in the next section) for this purpose:

The prophets denounced three types of wrongdoing: idolatry, injustice, and neglect of the needy.

EXERCISE 12   **Using Semicolons**

Each of the following requires the addition or removal of one or more semicolons. Make any necessary change, adding other punctuation if appropriate.

EXAMPLE
Some people give others take.
REVISED: Some people give; others take.

1. The company increased its sales by over 20 percent in the third and fourth quarters, however, the directors have voted not to declare a dividend.
2. Weary fire fighters see no way of extinguishing the flames; unless the strong winds subside.
3. The newcomers brought needed manpower and supplies to the small community, on the other hand, they also brought unwanted customs and ideas.
4. The Gateway Arch in St. Louis symbolizes the soaring aspirations of the pioneers; who ventured forth into unknown lands.
5. The old reception center lacks office space, a comfortable lounge, and adequate restrooms, nevertheless, many people like it.
6. During the first stage of the trip, tourists visit London, the capital of Great Britain, Paris, the capital of France, Madrid, the capital of Spain, and Rome, Italy, the oldest capital of them all.
7. Winter brings skiers to the region, summer brings mosquitoes.
8. A basketball team has five players; a center, two forwards, and two guards.

## 25.6  The Colon   :

**1.** Use a colon to introduce a list, an example, or an explanation directly related to something just mentioned:

Passengers may have one of four beverages: coffee, tea, milk, or soda.
The plan had three advantages: no one would have to remain at the base camp, we could turn back whenever we needed to, and we would have a good chance of reaching the summit.

Do not use a colon before a list when the items follow a preposition, such as *of,* or a form of the verb *be:*

*John's sentence consists of: a subject, a verb, two complements, and four modifiers.
REVISED: John's sentence consists of a subject, a verb, two complements, and four modifiers.

*Three ways of traveling are: flying, driving, and walking.
REVISED: Three ways of traveling are flying, driving, and walking.

**2.** Use a colon to introduce a quotation (usually of more than one line) in an essay:

> In the opening sentence of his novel *Scaramouche,* Rafael Sabatini says of his hero: "He was born with the gift of laughter, and a sense that the world was mad."

**3.** Use a colon to follow the salutation in a formal letter:

> Dear Mayor:
> Dear Mr. Watson:
> To Whom It May Concern:

**4.** Use a colon to separate hours from minutes when the time of day is shown in numerals:

> 8:40    6:30    11:15

### EXERCISE 13   Using Colons

Each of the following requires the addition or removal of one or more colons. Make any necessary change.

EXAMPLE
The Council has received recommendations from: seniors, juniors, and freshmen.
REVISED: The Council has received recommendations from seniors, juniors, and freshmen.

1. The plane should arrive in Montreal at 4 30 P.M.
2. La Rochefoucauld punctures the illusions of many in a maxim about pity "We are all strong enough to endure the misfortunes of others."
3. On display were: a diamond necklace, a pair of gold earrings, a pin with four rubies, and a diamond engagement ring.
4. The 12 30 broadcast will offer music by the following composers Bach, Mozart, Debussy, and Copeland.
5. To Whom It May Concern We, the undersigned, hereby declare our unyielding support of the Union. Long may it stand!

### EXERCISE 14   Using Semicolons and Colons

In the following passage from Ismene Phylactopoulou's "Greek Easter," we have deliberately removed some of the author's punctuation. Add a semicolon or a colon wherever necessary.

EXAMPLE

line 1: 10:00

The events on Good Friday are tragic. At 10 00 a grim-looking priest conducts a solemn service Christ is removed from the Cross and placed in a tomb. All work ceases flags fly at half mast. Soldiers carry their rifles reversed as they do during funeral
5 processions. Offices and shops close everyone goes to church. The church bells will toll all day long. After the service the young girls of the parish perform a bitter-sweet task they decorate the bier of Jesus with flowers from 11 00 to 1 00. By that time it is a mass of flowers.
10 Lunch consists of simple fare boiled lentils, which represent the tears of the Virgin, and vinegar, which represents the vinegar given to Christ on the Cross.
On Friday evening the church is filled to overflowing. All in the city are present old men and women, officials, husbands and
15 wives, children. The songs of mourning are lovely in their sadness for example, in one of them Mary refers to her dead son as a child who was as sweet as spring. After the service, which usually ends at 9 00, a kind of funeral procession takes place. It follows a definite order first comes a band playing a funeral march next comes a
20 priest carrying the Cross then comes the bier accompanied by girls in white, the Boy Scouts, and a detachment of soldiers then come the other priests. The people follow, each carrying a brown candle. The gathering has spiritual meaning it is also deeply human.

## 25.7 The Dash —

**1.** Use a dash to introduce a word, phrase, or clause that summarizes the words preceding it:

The strikers included plumbers, electricians, carpenters, truck drivers, miners—all kinds of workers.

**2.** Use a dash to set off an interruption that is closely relevant to the sentence but not grammatically part of it:

Al's slight acquaintance with Linda—he had met her just once—made him hesitate to phone her.

Less relevant interruptions may be set off by parentheses (as discussed in the next section). Use dashes sparingly; too many can make your writing seem breathless.

In typing, make a dash with two hyphens (--) and leave no space on either side.

## 25.8  Parentheses  ( )

**1.** Use parentheses to enclose words, phrases, or complete sentences that offer a side comment or help to clarify a point:

> During last month's meeting at City Hall, opponents of the proposed leash law (they are certainly a vocal group) dominated the discussion.

A parenthesized sentence that appears within another sentence does not need a capital or a period.

> Among those attending the concert were Peter Mengis, Roberta Green (the composer), and Reginald Grant.

A comma may follow the closing parenthesis, but should not precede the opening parenthesis.

**2.** Use parentheses to enclose numerals or letters introducing the items of a list:

> One of the selectmen supports the proposed change in traffic patterns for three reasons: (1) more customers would be attracted to the shopping area, (2) the hospital zone would become quieter, and (3) fire engines would be able to move more quickly than they now can.

**3.** Use parentheses to enclose numerals clarifying or confirming a spelled-out number:

> The law permits individuals to give no more than one thousand dollars ($1,000.00) to any one candidate in a campaign.

## 25.9  Brackets  [ ]

**1.** Use brackets to insert a clarifying detail, comment, or correction of your own into a passage written by someone else:

> "DeCato's bid [$850] sounds reasonable to me," declared Robert Grant, chairman of the school board.
> "When we last see Lady Macbeth [in the sleepwalking scene], she is obviously distraught."
> "The Allied invasion of Brittany [Normandy] began on June 6, 1944."
> "Only three other senators were present to hear the speech—Senators Brown, Stilmore, and Wiggins. [In reality, Senator Stilmore was in a hospital.] To a man, they called it the most eloquent attack on slavery they had ever heard."

25.9

[ ]

When a misspelling occurs in quoted material, the Latin word *sic* ("thus") may be used to call attention to it, or the correct spelling may be given within the brackets:

> "There were no pieces of strong [*sic*] around the boxes," one witness wrote. [or] "There were no pieces of strong [string] around the boxes," one witness wrote.

Typewriters do not normally include keys for brackets. You may either put the brackets in by hand or construct them using the slash and underlining keys: ⌐ ⌐

**2.** Do not use brackets when inserting comments into your own writing. Use parentheses or dashes.

### EXERCISE 15   Using Dashes, Parentheses, and Brackets

Each of the following requires dashes, parentheses, or brackets. Using the comment in brackets as a guide, add the appropriate punctuation.

> EXAMPLE
> The asking price for the clock a whopping $500,000 has not deterred some collectors from attending the auction. [The explanatory phrase is relevant and important.]
> REVISED: The asking price for the clock—a whopping $500,000— has not deterred some collectors from attending the auction.

1. The number of acres allotted to one family may not be less than twenty-five 25 nor more than fifty 50. [The numerals clarify the spelled-out numbers.]
2. The pioneers celebrated Thanksgiving in the new settlement the exact location is unknown and then returned to Springfield for the winter. [The aside is relatively unimportant to the discussion.]
3. They eloped to Paris is there any better city for lovers? and had five glorious days before emerging to pay the piper. [The question is closely relevant to the narrative.]
4. "This song, which was composed by Bailey in 1928 1930, reflects the influences of his five years in New Orleans." [The second date represents your correction of a mistake in a sentence written by someone else.]
5. "The most popular recording of the song featured Bix Dandy on the trumpit trumpet." [The second spelling represents your correction of a misspelling in a passage written by someone else.]
6. The neighborhood needs three things: 1 paved roads, 2 traffic lights at every major intersection, and 3 a committee consisting of homeowners who would welcome and orient newcomers. [The numerals introduce the items in a list.]

# 25.10 Quotation Marks and Quoting " "

## Double Quotation Marks

**1.** Use double quotation marks (" ") to enclose any words, phrases, or short passages quoted from speech, writing, or printed matter:

> After the murder of the old king in Shakespeare's *Macbeth*, Lady Macbeth imagines there is blood on her hand and cries, "Out, damned spot!"
>
> "An agnostic," writes Clarence Darrow, "is a doubter."
>
> At his press conference yesterday, the president said that his talk with the Russian ambassador had been "fruitful."

**2.** Use double quotation marks to set off common words and phrases that you don't take at face value:

> When a man and woman decide to live together without being married, are they "living in sin"?
>
> In what sense is the German Democratic Republic "democratic"?

But use underlining (as discussed in section 25.16, pp. 413–14) to set off a word you refer to as a word:

> The word *freedom* means different things to different people.

**3.** Use double quotation marks to set off certain titles (as specified in section 25.17, pp. 414–15).

**4.** Do not use quotation marks for emphasis. Quotation marks can actually weaken a statement. For example:

> Joe's restaurant serves "good" pie. [TRANSLATION: They say it's good, but I know better.]

## Single Quotation Marks

**1.** Use single quotation marks (' ') to enclose a quotation within a quotation:

> At the beginning of the class, Professor Baker asked, "Where does Thoreau speak of 'quiet desperation' and what does he mean by this phrase?"

**2.** Use single quotation marks to enclose a title requiring quotation marks when it is part of another title requiring quotation marks or is mentioned within a quotation:

> "Fences and Neighbors in Frost's 'Mending Wall' " [title of an essay on the poem]
>
> "Frost's 'Mending Wall,' " said Professor Ainsley, "is a gently disarming poem."

*p/mech*

25.10

" "

## Punctuating Quotations

To punctuate quotations, you must often use quotation marks with other punctuation. Here are guidelines.

**1.** Use a comma or a colon to introduce a quotation:

> Frank said, "Let's buy some beer and a pizza."
> Carl Jung writes: "Ideas spring from something greater than the personal human being."

Most writers use a comma to introduce quoted speech and a colon to introduce quoted writing. But you need neither a comma nor a colon to introduce a quoted word or phrase:

> The doctor said that Fenster "might not live."
> The president said the talks were "encouraging."

**2.** Use a comma to mark the end of a quoted sentence that is followed by an identifying tag:

> "It's time to eat," said John.
> "I'm leaving tomorrow," said Nancy. "We can clean up when I get back."

But do not use the comma if the quoted sentence ends in a question mark or an exclamation point:

> "What's the evidence?" the scientist asks.
> "Get out!" he screamed.

As these examples show, even after a full stop the tag begins with a lower-case letter, not a capital.

**3.** Use a pair of commas to set off a tag that interrupts a quoted sentence, whether spoken or written:

> "I have noticed," Benwick Branch declared, "that no one else arrives at work on time."
> "Ideas," writes Carl Jung, "spring from something greater than the personal human being."

The second part of the quotation does not begin with a capital letter because it does not begin a new sentence. It completes the sentence that was interrupted by the tag.

**4.** Use a period to mark the end of a quoted statement that is not followed by a tag:

> John said, "I'm hungry."

**5.** When you use a comma or a period at the end of a quotation, put it inside the closing quotation mark:

Though Thoreau wrote that most men "lead lives of quiet desperation," much of his book about Walden Pond expresses joy.
One of the astronauts said, "The earth looked unbelievably beautiful from the spaceship."

**6.** When you use a semicolon or a colon at the end of a quotation, put it outside the closing quotation mark:

The senator announced, "I will not seek reelection"; then he left the room.
The new contract has "new benefits for women": payment for overtime, maternity leave, and seniority privileges.

**7.** When you use a question mark or an exclamation point at the end of a quotation, put it inside the closing quotation mark only if it belongs to the quotation; otherwise, put it outside:

Who wrote, "What's in a name?"
A new idea about the universe always prompts the scientist to ask, "What's the evidence for it?"
Should the United States support Latin American governments that it considers "moderately repressive"?
Suddenly he screamed, "Get out!"
Yet the congressman simply dismissed the charge as "unimportant"!

Wherever you put the question mark or the exclamation point, do not use a period with it.

### Quoting Poetry

If you quote more than a single line of poetry, you must show where one line ends and another begins. Use a slash (/), with a space on each side, to mark the division:

Dylan Thomas wrote: "The force that through the green fuse drives the flower / Drives my green age."

If you quote more than two lines of poetry, use indentation instead of quotation marks, as described next in "Quoting Long Passages."

### Quoting Long Passages

**1.** To quote more than four lines of prose or more than two lines of poetry, use indentation instead of quotation marks. Introduce the quotation with a colon, leave a double space, indent the whole quotation at least five spaces, and double-space the quotation itself:

```
In "Civil Disobedience," Thoreau states:
    I was not born to be forced. I will breathe
```

```
after my own fashion. Let us see who is the
strongest. What force has a multitude? They
only can force me who obey a higher law than
I. They force me to become like themselves. I
do not hear of men being forced to live this
way or that by masses of men. What sort of
life were that to live? When I meet a gov-
ernment which says to me, "Your money or your
life," why should I be in a haste to give it
my money?
```

**2.** When a passage you indent contains quoted matter of its own; preserve the double quotations marks around that, as shown in the preceding example.

**3.** When the lines of poetry are short, center them on the page:

```
William Blake's "The Tyger" begins with the lines:
            Tyger! Tyger! burning bright
            In the forests of the night,
            What immortal hand or eye
            Could frame thy fearful symmetry?
```

EXERCISE 16   **Punctuating Quotations**

Punctuate the quotations in each of the following sentences.

EXAMPLE:
We are all strong enough wrote La Rochefoucauld to endure the misfortunes of others.
REVISED: "We are all strong enough," wrote La Rochefoucauld, "to endure the misfortunes of others."

1. What writer asked, Who has deceived thee so oft as thyself
2. The professor concluded her lecture by saying, I hope each of you will read a few poems by Hopkins, especially one called The Windhover
3. Then the singer said, I wish I could remember the name of the person who wrote Brother, Can You Spare a Dime
4. Did Ambrose Bierce define a bore as a person who talks when you wish him to listen
5. Alexander Pope wrote, True wit is nature to advantage dressed, What oft was thought, but ne'er so well expressed
6. The history of life on earth says Rachel Carson has been a history of interaction between living things and their surroundings.

EXERCISE 17   **Punctuating Dialogue**

Punctuate the quotations in the following passage. As you add the punctuation, write out the entire passage.

Everything in Texas is big said the Texan to the Alaskan.

Tell me about it said the Alaskan.

Well, for one thing the Texan said we have the biggest jackrabbits in the world and the biggest cowboy hats.

5    That's impressive said the visitor. Anything else?

The smallest of our ranches is larger than most states, and we serve the biggest mint julep in the entire South. It takes the average person an entire week to finish one the Texan said. What have you-all got in Alaska?

10    The Alaskan smiled. Then he said That must seem like a mighty big drink to you folks. He paused, shaking his head. But I guess you couldn't know any better he said if you haven't seen the icebergs in Alaska. We use them for ice cubes.

## 25.11   Ellipsis Dots   . . .

**1.** Use three spaced dots—

1. To signal the omission of a word or words from the middle of a quoted sentence:

Thoreau wrote, "We must learn to reawaken and keep ourselves awake . . . by an infinite expectation of the dawn, which does not forsake us in our soundest sleep."

In all cases, the material left out should be nonessential to the meaning of what is quoted. Here, for example, the words omitted are "not by mechanical aids, but."

2. To signal hesitation or halting speech in dialogue:

"I . . . don't know what to say," he whispered.

**2.** Use four spaced dots—

1. To show that you are omitting the end of a quoted sentence:

Thoreau wrote, "We must learn to reawaken and keep ourselves awake, not by mechanical aids, but by an infinite expectation of the dawn. . . ."

Like all periods, the fourth dot comes before the closing quotation mark. Normally you may cut off the end of a quoted sentence in this way only if what remains makes a complete sentence.

2. To show that you have omitted one or more whole sentences:

"In other words," as Percy Marks says, "the spirit of football is wrong. 'Win at any cost' is the slogan of most teams, and the methods used to win are often abominable. . . . In nearly every scrimmage the roughest kind of unsportsmanlike play is indulged in, and the broken arms and ankles are often intentional rather than accidental."

**3.** Use an entire line of spaced dots to signal that a line (or more) of poetry has been omitted:

> In the beginning was the word, the word
>
> . . . . . . . . . . . . . . . . . . . . . . . .
>
> And from the cloudy bases of the breath
> The word flowed up, translating to the heart
> First characters of birth and death.　　　　　—Dylan Thomas

EXERCISE 18　**Quoting with Ellipses**

Select a passage of expository prose in a book or magazine. In three separate quotations from it, use ellipsis dots to signal omissions of (1) part of the middle of a sentence, (2) the end of a sentence, and (3) a complete sentence or more. Be careful to avoid distorting the meaning and tone of the original passage. Also, be sure to space the dots properly.

## 25.12　**The Slash**　/

**1.** Use a slash, or virgule, to indicate alternative words:

> Every writer needs to know at least something about his/her audience.

**2.** Use a slash to mark off lines of poetry when you run them on as if they were prose, as described on p. 405.

**3.** Use a slash in typing a fraction that is not on one of your typewriter keys:

> $2\frac{1}{2}$　　5 7/8　　15/16

## 25.13　**The Hyphen**　–

**1.** Use a hyphen to divide a long word at the end of a line:

> The long, black centipede walked across the sand with an enormous limp.

The word should be divided at the end of a syllable. If you aren't sure what the syllables of a word are, see your dictionary.

**2.** Use a hyphen to show that two or three words are being used as a single grammatical unit:

a round-the-world voyage
beady-eyed poker players

**3.** Use a hyphen to form a compound noun or a compound modifier:

According to Plato, the ruler should be a philosopher-king.
The university welcomes scholar-athletes.
Enrico Caruso was a world-famous tenor.
A well-known economist has warned against a tax cut at this time.
The new translation of the Bible will be welcomed by all English-speaking peoples.

Not all compounds require a hyphen. Some are written as one word (*wildlife, storytelling, playhouse*), some as two separate words (*social security, police officer*). When you are in doubt, see your dictionary.

**4.** Use a hyphen to join a prefix to a proper noun or proper adjective:

un-American
post-Renaissance

Do not use a hyphen when you join a prefix to an uncapitalized word:

postwar
deemphasize
nonprofit

**5.** Use a hyphen in a number written as two words, provided it is below one hundred:

Thirty-five applicants have requested interviews.
Two-thirds of the trees had been cut.

Do not attach a hyphen to the word for any number over ninety-nine:

Some suits now cost over three hundred dollars.
Some of the new "economy" cars cost more than eight thousand dollars.
Thirty-five thousand spectators watched the game.

*Thirty-five*, which is below one hundred, is hyphenated, but no hyphen is attached to *thousand*.

EXERCISE 19    **Using Slashes and Hyphens**

Each of the following may require one or more slashes or hyphens. Add any necessary punctuation. If an entry is correct as it stands, write *Correct*.

EXAMPLE
One way to cut gas consumption in America is to run high speed trains between major cities.
REVISED: One way to cut gas consumption in America is to run high-speed trains between major cities.

1. The long distance runners looked buoyant as they passed the fifteen mile mark.
2. Auden's poem entitled "Lullaby" ends somewhat enigmatically: "Nights of insult let you pass Watched by every human love."
3. A world renowned biologist representing the well known organization Food Now will present a report to an all Russian audience.
4. Rescue workers have removed three-quarters of the debris.
5. Fifty five of the survivors had been able to salvage only one quarter of their personal belongings.
6. The town is medium sized, with a population of forty six thousand.

## 25.14   The Apostrophe   '

**1.** Use an apostrophe to mark the omission of letters in a contraction:

I've     isn't     doesn't     won't     it's cold

**2.** Use an apostrophe to help form the possessive of some nouns and pronouns.

1. If the noun is singular, add the apostrophe and -*s:*

    girl's     anyone's     James's

    The final -*s* may be omitted in a singular proper noun ending in -*s:*

    James'

2. If the noun is plural and ends in -*s*, add just the apostrophe:

    boys'     the Joneses'

3. If the noun is plural but does not end in -*s*, add the apostrophe and -*s:*

    men's

4. To indicate joint possession, add the apostrophe, and the -*s* if necessary, to the second of two nouns:

    Paul and Edith's wedding anniversary

5. When using a compound, add the apostrophe, and the -*s* if necessary, to the last word:

> mother-in-law's invitation
> commander in chief's report

**3.** In general, do not use an apostrophe with nouns naming inanimate things:

> the front door of the house
> NOT: *the house's front door

> the surface of the painting
> NOT: *the painting's surface

> the impact of the revolution
> NOT: *the revolution's impact

**4.** Do not use an apostrophe with a possessive pronoun:

> my, mine
> your, yours
> his
> her, hers
> its
> our, ours
> their, theirs

Many writers confuse the contraction *it's* with the possessive pronoun *its*. If you have trouble keeping them straight, try remembering this:

> Use *its* like *his;* use *it's* like *he's.*
> > his success     he's successful
> > its success     it's successful

**5.** Use an apostrophe to help form the plural of a figure, a letter, or a word treated as a word:

> three 7's     the 1920's     two *b*'s     five *but*'s

Some writers are beginning to drop the apostrophe when writing the plural of a figure or a letter:

> three 7s     the 1920s     two *b*s

Do not use an apostrophe when you spell out a date:

> the twenties

**EXERCISE 20   Using the Apostrophe**

Improve the punctuation in the following passage by adding or removing an apostrophe wherever necessary. As you make these corrections, write out the entire passage.

Everyones talking about Frank Smiths novel. Its plot seems to be based on something that happened to him during his freshman year. Its weird to read about characters youve seen in class or in the students lounge. I dont think there are many of his classmate's
5 who wont be annoyed when they discover theyve been depicted as thugs' and moron's. Its as if Frank thought that his experiences were the same as everyones—Johns, Marys, and Jims. That kind of thinking can be overlooked in someone whos in his early teen's, but it isnt all right for someone in his twenties'.

## 25.15 Capitalization *cap/lc*

**1.** Capitalize the first word of a sentence:

The quick brown fox jumps over the lazy dog.

**2.** Capitalize, with a few exceptions, the words in a proper noun, such as the name of a person, a specific place, a firm, or a special event:

| | | |
|---|---|---|
| Thomas Paine | Mount Everest | General Motors |
| John of Gaunt | Lake Michigan | International Business |
| Canada | Mars | Machines |
| Texas | the Milky Way | J. C. Penney |
| Chicago | the East [the | DuPont |
| Botetourt County | area, not the | Crilson and Sons |
| the Mississippi | direction] | Ice Capades |
| River | | |

As these examples show, a word like *County, River,* or *Lake* is capitalized when it forms part of the name of a particular place.

**3.** Capitalize the first word in a line of poetry—unless lower case is used in the original:

Whose woods these are I think I know.
His house is in the village, though;
He will not see me stopping here
To watch his woods fill up with snow.
—Robert Frost

somewhere i have never travelled, gladly beyond
any experience, your eyes have their silence
—e. e. cummings

(Note that some modern poets use no capitals at all.)

**4.** Capitalize certain words in titles (as specified in section 25.17, pp. 414–15).

**5.** Capitalize the pronoun *I* whenever it occurs:

When I heard the news, I laughed.

EXERCISE 21   **Using Capitals**

Improve each of the following by capitalizing where necessary.

1. multinational corporations have invested millions to extract minerals from the jungles along the amazon river in south america.
2. bruce jenner competed for the united states in the 1976 olympic games, which were held in montreal.
3. "i can't find my philosophy book," said frank. "has anyone seen it?"
4. lake george is one of the most popular vacation spots in the northeast. it has been praised in many poems, like the one that begins, "i love thy scented shores."
5. after graduation sally and sandy plan to work at the general motors plant in pontiac, michigan.

## 25.16   Italics and Underlining for Italics   *ital*

Most of this book is set in ordinary type (known as "roman"), but you've no doubt already noticed that we have been using *italic type* for distinction and emphasis (*this is an example of italic type*). You may need to use italics in your own writing, but if you are using a pen or pencil or a standard typewriter, you cannot readily produce words in italic lettering. You can, however, represent italics by underlining.

**1.** Use italics to emphasize a word or phrase in a statement:

There are <u>just</u> laws and there are <u>unjust</u> laws.
                    —Martin Luther King, Jr.

**2.** Use italics to identify a letter or a word treated as a word:

The word <u>suspense</u> has three <u>s</u>'s.
The poet uses <u>eyes</u> twice in the first stanza and once in the second.

**3.** Use italics to identify a foreign word or phrase not yet absorbed into English:

<u>au courant</u>   <u>Angst</u>   <u>Bildungsroman</u>   <u>carpe diem</u>

**4.** Use italics to identify the name of a ship, an airplane, or the like:

<u>Queen Elizabeth II</u> [ship]
<u>Spirit of St. Louis</u> [airplane]
<u>Apollo 2</u> [spaceship]

*Italics and Underlining for Italics*   413

**5.** Use italics to designate certain titles (as specified in the next section).

Exercise 22   **Using Italics**

Each of the following may require the addition or removal of italics. Make any necessary change, using underlining to indicate italics. If an entry is correct as it stands, write *Correct.*

1. They named their motorboat The Linda Ronstadt.
2. I can never remember how to spell harassment.
3. After their *yoga* and *karate* classes, Carol and Alex always went out for a *pizza.*
4. A drink known as a *frappe* in one part of the country may be called a *cabinet,* a *frost,* or a *milk shake* in another.
5. The English word mother derives from the Middle English word moder and is akin to the Latin word mater.

## 25.17   Titles   *title*

**1.** Capitalize the first and the last word of a title, whatever they are, and all the words in between except articles (such as *a* and *the*), prepositions (such as *for, among,* and *to*), and conjunctions (such as *and, but,* and *or*):

Zen and the Art of Motorcycle Maintenance [book]
"Ode on a Grecian Urn" [poem]
"What Americans Stand For" [essay]
Death of a Salesman [play]

**2.** Use italics for the title of a book, scholarly journal, magazine, newspaper, government report, play, musical, opera or other long musical composition, film, television show, radio program, or long poem:

The Grapes of Wrath [book]
The Collected Poems of Dylan Thomas [book]
The American Scholar [journal]
Newsweek [magazine]
New York Times [newspaper]
Uniform Crime Reports for the United States [government publication]
Hamlet [play]
Oklahoma [musical]
The Barber of Seville [opera]
Scheherazade [orchestral suite]
Star Wars [film]
All in the Family [television show]

<u>Morning Pro Musica</u> [radio program]
<u>Song of Myself</u> [long poem]

**3.** Use quotation marks for the title of an article in a magazine or newspaper, and for the title of an essay, short story, short poem, song or other short musical composition, speech, or chapter in a book:

"Seal Hunting in Alaska" [magazine article]
"The Hot Seat" [newspaper column]
"Bullfighting in Hemingway's Fiction" [essay]
"The Tell-Tale Heart" [short story]
"Mending Wall" [short poem]
"You Ain't Nothin' but a Hound Dog" [song]
"The American Scholar" [speech]
"Winning the West" [chapter in a book]

**4.** Do not use italics or quotation marks when you write the title at the head of your own essay or report, except where your title includes a reference to another title:

The Invasion of Hitler's Third Reich
Hemingway's Use of Symbols in <u>A Farewell to Arms</u>

EXERCISE 23   **Writing Titles**

Each of the following titles requires capitalization and may also require italics or quotation marks. Make the necessary changes.

1. carmen [opera]
2. spray [ship]
3. my old kentucky home [song]
4. washington post [newspaper]
5. what freud forgot [essay]
6. 60 minutes [television show]
7. the will of zeus [history book]
8. john brown's body [long poem]
9. the mismatch between school and children [editorial]
10. natural history [magazine]
11. solutions to the energy problem [your report]
12. the role of fate in shakespeare's romeo and juliet [your essay]
13. imagery in the battle hymn of the republic [your essay]
14. barefoot in the park [play]

## 25.18   Abbreviations   *ab*

Abbreviations occur often in informal writing, but in formal writing you should use them less often. We suggest you follow these guidelines.

**1.** Use abbreviations for most titles accompanying a name:

| | |
|---|---|
| Mrs. James Low | Dr. Martha Peters. |
| Mr. Peter Smith | Robert Greene, Jr. |
| Ms. Elizabeth Fish | Susan Flagg, D.D. |
| BUT: Miss Jenny Lind | Joseph Stevens, M.D. |

But use the full titles when referring to religious, governmental, and military leaders:

the Reverend Leonard Flischer
Senator Margaret Chase Smith
the Honorable Hugh Carey, governor of New York
General George C. Marshall

**2.** Use abbreviations for the terms that help to specify a date or a time of day:

| | |
|---|---|
| 350 B.C. | 8:30 A.M. |
| A.D. 1776 | 2:15 P.M. |

**3.** You may use abbreviations in referring to well-known firms and other organizations:

| | |
|---|---|
| NBC | YMCA |
| IBM | NAACP |

**4.** Use abbreviations to designate certain units of measurement when the accompanying amounts are given in numerals:

55 mph (or m.p.h.)     35 mpg (or m.p.g.)

**5.** If an abbreviation comes at the end of a declarative sentence, use the period marking the abbreviation as the period for the sentence:

The rocket was launched at 11:30 P.M.

If an abbreviation ends a question, add a question mark:

Was the rocket launched at 11:30 P.M.?

**6.** Do not use abbreviations in formal writing for the days of the week and the months of the year:

| | |
|---|---|
| Sunday | August |
| Saturday | December |

**7.** Do not use abbreviations in formal writing for the names of most geographical entities:

| | | |
|---|---|---|
| New England | Great Britain | Mulberry Street |
| Mississippi | the Snake River | Lake Avenue |
| Canada | the Rocky Mountains | |

Many writers do now use *U.S.* and *U.S.S.R.* You may also use *Mt.* before the name of a mountain, as in *Mt. McKinley,* and *St.* in the name of a place, as in *St. Louis.*

**8.** Do not use abbreviations in formal writing for the names of academic subjects:

| | |
|---|---|
| Old English poetry | European history |
| French 205 | biology |

If you aren't sure how to abbreviate a particular term, see your dictionary. If you don't know whether you should abbreviate a term at all, don't. In formal writing most terms should be spelled out in full.

## 25.19   Numbers   *num*

**1.** Spell out a number when it begins a sentence:

Eighty-five dignitaries attended the opening ceremony.
Five orchestras performed.

Rearrange the sentence if spelling out the number would require three or more words:

The opening ceremony was attended by 1,250 dignitaries.

**2.** Spell out a number that can be written in one or two words, except as noted in item 4, below:

A batter is out after three strikes.
The firemen worked without relief for twenty-two hours.
The stadium can hold eighty thousand spectators.

**3.** Use numerals if spelling out a number would require more than two words:

She has a herd of 350 cows.
The stadium can hold 85,600 spectators.

**4.** Use numerals for addresses, dates, exact times of day, exact sums of money, exact measurements such as miles per hour, scores of games, mathematical ratios, fractions, and page numbers:

| | |
|---|---|
| 22 East Main Street | 65 mph |
| October 7, 1981 | by a score of 5 to 4 |
| 44 B.C. | a ratio of 2 to 1 |
| 11:15 A.M. | 5⅞ |
| $4.36 | page 102 |
| $3.5 million | |

However, when a time of day or a sum of money is given as a round figure, spell it out:

> Uncle Ben always gets up at six.
> He used to earn two dollars for ten hours of work.
> With ten cents in his pocket, anything seemed possible.

### Exercise 24 Using Abbreviations and Numbers

Each of the following may include incorrectly handled abbreviations and numbers. Make any necessary change. If an entry is correct as it stands, write *Correct*.

1. "Why," said the White Queen to Alice, "sometimes I've believed as many as 6 impossible things before breakfast."
   —Adapted from Lewis Carroll
2. We plan to spend part of our vacation on a Miss. Riv. steamboat and the rest in the Adirondack Mts.
3. For my psych homework I have to review pages eighteen and 38.
4. 2 students were elected to the presidential search committee, which also included Doctor Laura Freeman, the Rev. David Proctor, and Professor Ann Kaufman, Doctor of Philosophy.
5. The Young Women's Christian Association will hold an art fair on Mon., Jul. twenty-third, beginning at ten-fifteen A.M.
6. In this town, if you exceed the speed limit of 30 mph, you will be fined fifty dollars.
7. The Star Trek Convention attracted a crowd of 25 hundred fans.
8. If we split the costs by a ratio of three to one, my contribution will be seven hundred dollars and seventy-two cents.
9. Ms. Emily Sutherland will speak tonight on behalf of ERA.
10. He has four hundred and twenty matchboxes in his collection.

# III

# THE
# RESEARCH
# PAPER
# AND OTHER
# WRITING
# TASKS

# 26

# PREPARING THE RESEARCH PAPER

Writing a library research paper is much like writing an ordinary essay. Both kinds of writing involve many of the same basic steps: choosing a topic, asking questions to define and develop it, gauging the audience, getting raw material to work with, outlining the paper, writing it, and revising it. What makes a research paper different is that much of your raw material comes not from your own head but from printed sources, chiefly books and periodicals. Collecting raw material—by reading and taking notes—corresponds to the process of prewriting an ordinary essay.

Since the prewriting of a research paper involves reading and note-taking, it requires much more time than the prewriting of an ordinary essay. Getting ready to tackle the first draft of a research paper normally takes at least two weeks of regular work. So it makes sense to start the research as soon as you can. If you give yourself adequate time and follow the steps explained in this chapter, you will find your task much more manageable than it would otherwise be.

You will also find—we hope—that research pays dividends. Locating sources, reading them, and taking notes on them can be hard work. But once you have done the work, once you have done the reading and taken your notes, you will have something substantial to make a paper from. When you write an ordinary essay, your own brain must supply most of the raw material; when you start to write the research paper, you have the raw material already at hand. Furthermore, because this paper grows out of specialized and concentrated reading, putting it together should be a genuine learning experience for you. When you finish the paper, you will feel—and rightly so—that you are beginning to become an expert on your topic.

A research paper may belong to one of two basic types. It may be a survey of facts and opinions available on a given topic, or it may be an analysis of them. Your teacher may tell you which type of paper you are expected to write; if the teacher does not, you yourself should eventually choose between surveying and analyzing. Then you will have a consistent way of dealing with your sources.

In a research paper that is a **survey** of facts and opinions, you make little attempt to interpret or evaluate what your sources say. You simply assemble quotations and write summaries of material about your topic. Selecting and arranging your material calls for a good deal of judgment, of course, but the main business of a survey paper is not to argue a position but to provide a representative sampling of facts and opinions, a noncommital report on what various writers have said about a particular topic.

In an **analysis** of facts and opinions, you do considerably more. You do not simply quote, paraphrase, and summarize. You interpret, question, compare, and judge the statements you cite. You explain why one opinion is sound and another is not, why one fact is relevant and another is not, why one writer is correct and another is mistaken. Your purpose may vary with your topic; you may seek to explain a situation, to recommend a course of action, to reveal the solution to a problem, or to present and defend a particular interpretation of a historical event or a work of art. But whether the topic is space travel or Shakespeare's *Hamlet,* an analysis deals actively with the statements it cites. It makes them work together in an argument that you create—an argument that leads to a conclusion of your own.

What follows will help you write either a survey or an analysis. Whichever you choose, we suggest you read everything that follows—along with our earlier section "Judging the Supporting Points in an Essay," pp. 187–91.

Our suggestions should help you with many kinds of research papers, but we do not promise to cover all the skills you need to handle any possible topic. Works of literature, music, cinema, art, and architecture sometimes call for specialized critical techniques that are not considered in our discussion. Likewise, research projects in the sciences often call for laboratory or field experiments, which we do not treat. What we do present in this chapter and the next are the basic methods of finding, reading, and noting down what has been written on a given topic, and turning the notes into a paper.

# 26.1 Choosing a Topic

Choosing a topic for a research paper is in some ways like choosing a topic for an ordinary essay—a process already considered (see section 1.2, p. 15). But there are some differences. As you weigh your topic, ask yourself these questions.

**1.** <u>Do you really want to know more about this topic?</u> You should ask this question even when you start work on an ordinary essay, but you should particularly ask it when you undertake a research paper. Research on any subject will keep you busy for weeks. You will do it well only if you expect to learn something interesting or important in the process.

**2.** <u>Are you likely to find many sources of information on this topic?</u> You cannot write a research paper without consulting a variety of sources. If only one source, or none at all, is readily available, you should rethink your topic or choose another. Suppose, for instance, that you came across a book called *Weird and Tragic Shores*, by Chauncey Loomis. Published in 1969, this is a biography of a nineteenth-century American explorer of the Arctic named Charles Francis Hall. Loomis's account of Hall's frustrating career and mysterious death might easily awaken your curiosity, but if you chose Hall as a research topic, you would soon find that little else has been written about him. Your research paper would be nothing more than a report on Loomis's book.

You should also be wary of topics that have just appeared in the news and are therefore likely to change their shape even as you try to write about them. You may like keeping up with the latest thing in clothes, music, and life-styles, but trying to catch up with it in a research paper is like trying to catch a plane in midair. You need not avoid subjects like solar power or population control or the Equal Rights Amendment—all of which are continually in the news—but you should hesitate to write about the latest earthquake or the latest cult. If you want a contemporary topic, choose one that has been around long enough to generate substantial articles and books.

**3.** <u>Can you get the topic down to manageable size?</u> Part of the process of choosing a research topic is whittling it down to a size you can work with. Be reasonable and realistic about what you can do in a period of two to four weeks. If your topic is "The Causes of the American Revolution," you will scarcely have time to make a list of books on your subject, let alone read and analyze them. Find something specific, such as "The Harassment of Loyalists after

Watertown" or "The Role of Patrick Henry in the American Revolution."

**4. What questions can you ask about the topic itself?** You should always ask questions about the topic you choose for a paper. Questions help you get the topic down to manageable size, discover its possibilities, and find the goal of your research—the specific problem you want to investigate. Suppose you want to write about oil spills, a topic very much in the news. You could ask at least two pointed questions: What is being done to reduce the risk of major spills on the world's oceans? How much damage does a major spill do to marine life? Either one of these could become the major question of your paper, and if you chose to concentrate on it from the beginning, your research would immediately gain a specific purpose.

**EXERCISE 1    Writing Questions about a Topic**

Choose five of the following topics, and write two questions on each of the five. Make the questions as pointed and specific as possible.

1. Solar energy
2. The explorations of the Vikings in North America
3. Eskimos in modern Alaska
4. Prohibition in the United States
5. Divorce
6. The Vietnam War
7. The circus in America
8. The meaning of dreams
9. Balloon flight
10. Reverse discrimination

**EXERCISE 2    Writing Questions about a Topic**

Think of a research topic that interests you, or take a topic you have been assigned, and write at least three specific questions about it.

## 26.2   Getting an Overview—Preliminary Reading

Once you have tentatively chosen a topic, you should do some exploratory reading to get an overview of your subject, a general idea of what the basic issues and problems are. The overview will help you decide just how to tackle the topic—or whether you definitely want to tackle it. You can get such an overview from one or more of the sources described here. Your teacher or a reference librarian may be able to direct you to additional sources for your particular topic, since here and elsewhere in this chapter we mention just some of the sources you might consult.

A textbook is the first place to look for an overview. Most likely it will be one of the books you are using in the course for which the research paper is assigned. Check the index and table of contents to see if any part of the book deals with your subject. Besides giving you information, the writer may mention other sources, which you could check later. Suppose you are thinking about a paper on meditation for a course in psychology, and one of the textbooks for the course is the second edition of *The Psychology of Consciousness,* by Robert E. Ornstein. Chapter 8 of Ornstein's book would give you both an overview of meditation and references to eight other sources.

26.2

Standard encyclopedias offer articles on a large number of subjects in language that a nonspecialist can understand. Furthermore, many of the articles conclude with a short list, or bibliography, of books recommended to anyone interested in learning more. If you don't own an encyclopedia, go to the reference section of your library and ask to see the thirty-volume *Britannica,* the thirty-volume *Americana,* or the big one-volume *Columbia.*

Specialized encyclopedias cover subjects in particular fields, such as art, music, psychology, and history. Ask the reference librarian to help you identify the encyclopedia you need, or see Eugene P. Sheehy's *Guide to Reference Books,* ninth edition, published in 1976. If you are studying dreams, for instance, you might be led to the *International Encyclopedia of the Social Sciences.* Here you would find a five-page article on dreams by Calvin Hill, a leading authority in the field, along with references to other appropriate articles and books.

Biographical sources give brief accounts of notable figures, and bibliographies are sometimes included. The following are widely used:

*Who's Who* has various volumes for different countries. Some of these are general (covering all living Americans, for example), some specific (limited, for example, to black Americans or American women). There are also *Who Was Who* volumes, with entries for the deceased.

The *Dictionary of American Biography* has entries for deceased Americans of note.

The *Dictionary of National Biography* has entries for deceased British figures.

The *Biography Index* directs you to books and magazine articles about various figures.

Magazines with a reputation for thoughtful essays and articles are another good source for preliminary reading. You will find solid articles on a variety of subjects in general magazines, such as *Harper's Magazine, Saturday Review,* and *The Atlantic,* but specialized magazines are more likely to treat the subject you are interested in. The December 1978 issue of *Psychology Today,* for instance, contains three articles giving overviews of current research about dreams.

To learn what magazines to use, ask a reference librarian for advice or consult the *Readers' Guide to Periodical Literature.* Issued every month and cumulated annually, this is an author and subject index to articles of general interest printed in over a hundred American periodicals. If you are looking for articles on oil pollution, for instance, here are the entries you will find for the period March 1978–February 1979.

OIL pollution of lakes. See Oil pollution of rivers, harbors, etc.

OIL pollution of rivers, harbors, etc.
Crankcase oils: are they a major mutagenic burden in the aquatic environment? J. F. Payne and others. bibl il Science 200:329-30 Ap 21 '78
Ingestion of crude oil: sublethal effects in herring gull chicks. D. S. Miller and others. bibl il Science 199:315-17 Ja 20 '78

**Conferences**
Conference program to assess ecological impacts of oil spills. BioScience 28:282 Ap '78

**Laws and legislation**
Oil spill superfund sets course for biologists. N. K. Eskridge. BioScience 28:537-8 Ag '78

OIL pollution of the sea
Oil in the sea: how little we know. F. Graham, Jr. Audubon 80:133-40+ N '78
Oil in the water. J. Mattill. Tech R 81:16 D '78
Oil spills: the causes and the cures. E. W. S. Hull. il Sea Front 24:360-9 N '78
Pollution & flags of convenience: the sea itself may die. P. J. Bernstein. Nation 227:242-4 S 16 '78
Separating oil from sea birds. J. Small. Oceans 11:59-61 Jl '78
Tanker vs. environment: failure of technology? il Tech R 81:84-5 D '78

**Conferences**
Two anti-pollution treaties adopted at Kuwait conference. il UN Chron 15:32-3 My '78

**Control**
Bantry Bay skimmer; oil recovery vessel. E. R. Cattallozzi. il Sea Front 24:237-9 Jl '78
Rising tide of oil spills; cleanup technology. M. Harwood. il N Y Times Mag p32-3+ Ap 9 '78
Supertankers and oil spills. I. Hargreaves. il Atlas 25:48 Je '78

**Atlantic Ocean**
Aftermath of the Amoco Cadiz: shoreline impact of the oil spill. E. D. Schneider. il Oceans 11:56-9 Jl '78
Amoco Cadiz: a lasting disaster; NOAA-EPA report. il Sci News 114:85 Ag 5 '78
Amoco Cadiz incident points up the elusive goal of tanker safety. L. J. Carter. il Science 200:514-16 My 5 '78; Discussion. 200:1218+; 201:398 Je 16, Ag 4 '78
Black day for Brittany; Amoco Cadiz wreck. N. Grove. il map Nat Geog 154:124-35 Jl '78
Black tide; wreck of the supertanker Amoco Cadiz along Brittany coast. il Time 111:55 Ap 10 '78
Brittany's black days; wreck of the Amoco Cádiz. F. Willey and C. Mitchelmore. il Newsweek 91:44 Ap 3 '78
Brittany's black tide; Amoco Cádiz wreck. E.

OIL pollution of the sea—Atlantic Ocean—*Cont.*
    Keerdoja and C. Mitchelmore. il Newsweek 92:
      11 Jl 24 '78
    Brittany's inky tide; Amoco Cádiz. il Newsweek
      91:71 Mr 27 '78
    Disaster off the Brittany coast. il Time 111:64
      Ap 3 '78
    In the wake of the Argo Merchant. il Sci News
      113:38 Ja 21 '78
    Oil and water; wreck of the Argo Merchant.
      M. Harwood. il maps Harpers 257:43-50+ S
      '78
    Oil spills and offshore drilling. bibl il Science
      199:125+ Ja 13 '78
    Toughening the rules after the Amoco Cadiz;
      Brittany coast oil spill. il Bus W p48 Ap 17 '78

    *Anecdotes, facetiae, satire, etc.*
Last page; Amoco Cadiz oil spill. J. G. Mitchell.
    Audubon 80:132 My '78

    **San Francisco Bay**
When oil blackened the Golden Gate; wreck of
    the tankers Lyman K. Stewart and the Frank
    H. Buck. J Zobel and L. Zobel. il Mankind
    6:34-7 My '78

To identify a source listed here, you must of course know how to read the entries. The first article cited, for instance, is entitled "Crankcase Oils: Are They a Major Mutagenic Burden in the Aquatic Environment?" Written by J. F. Payne and others, this article appears in the April 21, 1978, issue of the magazine *Science*, on pages 329–30 of volume 200. The abbreviation *il* means the article is illustrated, and *bibl* means it has a bibliography—a list of further sources.

The reference librarian can answer your questions about the abbreviations in the *Readers' Guide* and about any other aspect of finding sources. Helping researchers is an essential part of the reference librarian's job.

After you have gained an overview from one or more of these sources, you should rethink your topic and raise additional questions about it. If you've been reading about oil spills, have you found that the experts seem divided on the question of how much damage oil spills cause? If so, why are they divided? If you've been reading about dreams, can you tell how important is the Freudian theory that a dream is the fulfillment of a hidden wish? What are the arguments for competing theories? Do you see a way to get into this topic, a wedge to cut it open? Could you use for this purpose the question of why we need to dream at all? What's important at this stage is that you begin to read actively and interrogatively. Even if you are simply going to write a survey paper, you need to establish the boundaries of your territory and to get some idea of what it will contain.

EXERCISE 3   **Using a Standard Encyclopedia**

Read an article in a standard encyclopedia about the research topic you chose for exercise 2, p. 424. Jot down any questions that this article raises for you.

EXERCISE 4   Using a Specialized Encyclopedia

With the help of a reference librarian or Sheehy's *Guide to Reference Books*, find a specialized encyclopedia that contains an article on your topic. Read this article, and explain how it differs from the one in the standard encyclopedia.

EXERCISE 5   Using a Magazine

Go to the section of your library where the periodicals are kept, and pick a magazine for the nonprofessional reader, such as *American Heritage, Natural History,* or *Psychology Today.* Read one or two of the articles, and jot down any questions that come to mind.

EXERCISE 6   Using the *Readers' Guide*

Go to the reference section of your library, and find the latest issue of the *Readers' Guide to Periodical Literature.* Look up your topic, and copy out the information on three articles you would like to read.

## 26.3   Finding Sources— Primary and Secondary Sources

Once you have gained an overview of your topic and begun to define it, you need to identify and locate the sources on which your paper will be based. To do so effectively, you should know something about the difference between primary and secondary sources, and you must know how to use a library.

Books and other sources used in research may be classified as primary or secondary. *Primary* means "first," and a primary source is one on which later, or secondary, sources are based. Depending on the subject, primary sources may be more or less valuable than secondary ones.

There are two kinds of primary sources: informational and authorial. An informational primary source is any firsthand account of an experience or discovery—an Arctic explorer's diary of an expedition, a scientist's report on the results of an experiment, a news story on a disaster written by someone who has seen it. Writings of this kind give you firsthand information about a topic. One of the two men who discovered the molecular structure of DNA, for instance, told the story of the discovery in a book called *The Double Helix,* and published a scientific report of it in a professional journal, *Nature.* But informational primary sources are more likely to be letters, transcribed interviews, journals, diaries, and newspaper stories. Any or all of these may be used in a book, and the book will then be a secondary source, a piece of writing based on other writings.

Authorial primary sources are the writings of the individual you are studying. If you are investigating the life, works, or theories of a particular person, anything written by that person is a primary source for your purposes; anything written about that person's writings is a secondary source. If you are writing a paper on Herman Melville, for instance, *Moby-Dick* will be a primary source, and any critical study of *Moby-Dick* will be a secondary source. Likewise, if you are studying Freudian psychology, the writings of Freud himself will be primary sources, and commentaries on Freud's works will be secondary sources.

The line between primary and secondary sources is sometimes hard to draw. The works of the author you are studying may sometimes rest in part on the writings of others; an informational book or essay may be based on reading as well as on firsthand observation. But you need not always draw a line between primary and secondary sources, nor should you always feel obliged to start with primary ones. If you are investigating a particular author or thinker, you should normally start by reading at least some of what he or she has written and then see what has been written about that person's works. But if you are seeking information of an impersonal kind, you do best to start with secondary sources and let them lead you to the primary ones. Secondary sources are further than primary sources from what they describe, but for that very reason, they may give you a more detached, objective point of view. They can help you to see the relation between one primary source and another, and thus to understand the significance of each. As a rule, therefore, unless you are studying the works of a particular author, the best way to start research is to look at some secondary sources.

## 26.4 Using the Library

If the search for an overview of a topic has taken you into a library, you have already found the most important source of all. You cannot write a research paper without using a library, and if you don't yet know your way around one, now is the time to learn. What we say should help you find your way around any library, but once again, for the answers to questions about your library in particular, you will do best to go to the reference librarian. (If the library offers an orientation tour or a self-guided tour, by all means take it.)

### Using the Card Catalog

The card catalog tells you about all the books in the library. Each book is listed in three ways: by its author, by its title, and by its subject. Usually the author cards, title cards, and subject cards are alphabetized together; in some libraries, the subject cards are placed in a separate section. If you don't know where to find a particular card, ask a librarian to help you.

If you know the author of the book you want but aren't sure of the title, check the author card. The author card will give you the title—and a good deal more.

**Library call number indicates where you can find the book**

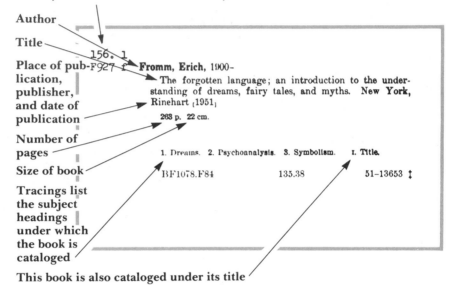

**Author**

**Title**

**Place of publication, publisher, and date of publication**

**Number of pages**

**Size of book**

**Tracings list the subject headings under which the book is cataloged**

156. 1
F927 f  **Fromm, Erich,** 1900–

The forgotten language; an introduction to the understanding of dreams, fairy tales, and myths. New York, Rinehart ₁1951₁

263 p.  22 cm.

1. Dreams.  2. Psychoanalysis.  3. Symbolism.    I. Title.

BF1078.F84                135.38                51–13653 ↕

**This book is also cataloged under its title**

If you know the title of the book you want but aren't sure of the author, check the title card.

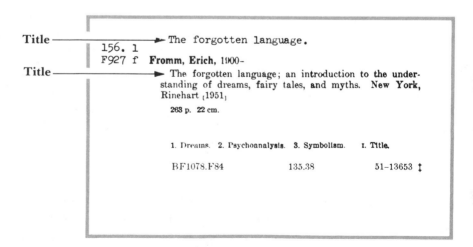

**Title**

156. 1
F927 f  **Fromm, Erich,** 1900–

**Title**

The forgotten language.

The forgotten language; an introduction to the understanding of dreams, fairy tales, and myths. New York, Rinehart ₁1951₁

263 p.  22 cm.

1. Dreams.  2. Psychoanalysis.  3. Symbolism.    I. Title.

BF1078.F84                135.38                51–13653 ↕

If you have only a subject, check the subject card.

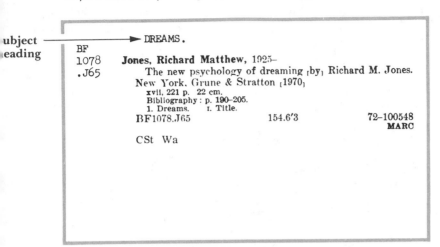

Subject heading →

    DREAMS.
    BF
    1078        Jones, Richard Matthew, 1925–
    .J65              The new psychology of dreaming [by] Richard M. Jones.
                  New York, Grune & Stratton [1970]
                      xvii, 221 p.  22 cm.
                      Bibliography : p. 190–205.
                      1. Dreams.     I. Title.
                  BF1078.J65                    154.6'3                    72–100548
                                                                                MARC

                  CSt  Wa

Subject cards tell what books a library has on a subject. But you may not readily find your subject among the headings in the card catalog. For instance, if your research topic is "Blacks in Business," you have to know that until 1976 the subject heading for books on blacks was "Negroes"; if you are doing research on computers, you may have to look under "Electronic Calculating Machines." Once again, if you can't readily find the subject heading for your topic, ask the reference librarian to help you.

If a card has tracings, check them for possible leads. Tracings tell you what subjects to look for in the library catalog in order to find more books on your topic. If you are doing research on dreams and you come upon the author card for Fromm's *The Forgotten Language* (p. 430), you will probably want to see what other books are cataloged under "Dreams"; you may also want to check the books cataloged under "Psychoanalysis" and "Symbolism."

Or take another example. After reading Herman Melville's *Moby-Dick,* a student wanted to find out about whaling in nineteenth-century America. Checking the subject cards for "Whaling," she found one for *Yankee Whalers in the South Seas,* by A. B. C. Whipple. The second tracing on this card was "Voyages and travels." On checking through the cards with this subject heading, she found one for the book *Whale Hunt,* by Nelson Cole Haley, a harpooner. Here was a book by someone with firsthand experience of whaling—an ideal source for anyone interested in that topic.

**Choosing the Most Useful Books**

You will probably find listings in the catalog for more books on your topic than you can possibly read in the time available to you.

**26.4**  You should not try to read them all, or even to get hold of them all. Instead, you should choose the books that seem likely to be most useful for your project. As you work your way through the catalog, look for the following:

**1.** Books with obvious relevance to your topic. The title of Fromm's book clearly indicates that it should be useful to anyone doing research on dreams, myths, or fairy tales. Likewise, a book with the title *Whale Hunt* should be irresistible to anyone doing research on whaling. But a student doing research on voyages of exploration should resist Haley's book—even though it is cataloged under the subject heading "Voyages and travels." Whaling and exploration are two different things, and the slim chance that Haley might have something to say about the latter doesn't really justify a search for his book. Your time is limited. Use it well.

**2.** Books published recently. As you go through the card catalog, you should check the publication date of each book relevant to your topic. The date is among the details of publication given just after the title. Recently published books will give you fairly up-to-date information, and even for a topic having to do with the past—the period of the American Revolution, for example—a recent book is likely to be more reliable and informative than one published in 1872 or even in 1924. (The paradox of research is that the further we get from the past, the more we learn about it.) Furthermore, a recent book is likely to cite several or even most of the important books on its subject that came before it.

How recent is "recent"? That depends on the field. If you are writing about computers or energy sources or television or the exploration of outer space, you will want books published within the past five or ten years, because these are technological fields, and technology changes fast. But if your topic is in a slower-moving field, such as history or psychology, you can regard anything published since 1960 as relatively recent.

**3.** Books that are classics in their fields. Some books stay alive long after they are published. Among "classic" books we find not just novels, such as *Moby-Dick,* but nonfiction works of lasting importance in various fields: in economics, for instance, Thorstein Veblen's *Theory of the Leisure Class* (1899); in political theory, Alexis de Tocqueville's *Democracy in America* (1835); in biology, Charles Darwin's *Origin of Species* (1859); in psychology, Sigmund Freud's *Interpretation of Dreams* (1900). Unfortunately, the card catalog won't tell you whether a particular book is a classic in its field. But if you start your research by reading an overview of your topic, or a recent book on it, you are almost certain to find out what the classics in the field are.

4. <u>Books with bibliographies.</u> The catalog card tells you whether the book includes a bibliography—a list of related books and articles. Because it focuses on a given topic, a bibliography can save you a lot of time—especially if it appears in a recent book.

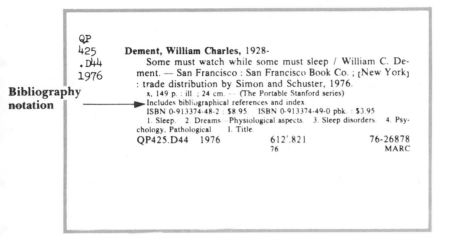

**Bibliography notation**

QP
425
.D44
1976

**Dement, William Charles,** 1928-
Some must watch while some must sleep / William C. Dement. — San Francisco : San Francisco Book Co. ; [New York] : trade distribution by Simon and Schuster, 1976.
x, 149 p. : ill. ; 24 cm. — (The Portable Stanford series)
Includes bibliographical references and index.
ISBN 0-913374-48-2 : $8.95.   ISBN 0-913374-49-0 pbk. : $3.95
1. Sleep.  2. Dreams - Physiological aspects.  3. Sleep disorders.  4. Psychology, Pathological   I. Title.
QP425.D44   1976          612'.821              76-26878
                          76                   MARC

Some bibliographies are annotated, supplying descriptions and evaluations of the works they list. And in place of a list, you will often find bibliographical notes—that is, a succession of paragraphs about various books. Here, for instance, is an excerpt from the bibliographical notes in William Charles Dement's *Some Must Watch While Some Must Sleep:*

DREAMS AND DREAMING

Although quite a bit of information on dreaming is sprinkled throughout the books listed above, perhaps the best book which deals with dreaming and takes the laboratory findings into account is *The Psychology of Sleep* by David Foulkes (New York: Charles Scribner's Sons, 1966). Another book, edited by Milton Kramer, is entitled *Dream Psychology and the New Biology of Dreaming* (Springfield, Ill.: C. C. Thomas, 1969). . . .

The granddaddy of them all with regard to the meaning of dreams is, of course, Sigmund Freud's *Interpretation of Dreams* (London: Allen & Unwin, 1954; first printing, 1900). By virtue of both his exceptionally clear exposition and excellent translation, this book is marvelously readable. It is the foundation of what is still the most important approach to the meaning (if any) of dreams. A companion volume to this, and one which is quite interesting, is *The New Psychology of Dreaming* by Richard M. Jones (New York:

Grune and Stratton, 1970), which deals with modern psychoanalytic theory of dreaming in light of laboratory findings. . . .

**Exercise 7  Using a Bibliography**

In the card catalog under a subject heading that interests you, find the title of a book with a bibliography. Then get the book, consult the bibliography, and write down the four sources you would most want to read if you were doing a research paper on the subject.

## Using Reference Books

The reference section of most libraries has a large collection of reference books, including atlases, dictionaries, encyclopedias, indexes, and bibliographies. Whatever your subject may be, a reference book is likely to give you both direct information and titles of relevant books and articles. Also, as you work, watch for leads provided by cross references. In some publications, for example, when you check for entries under "Oil Spills" you may be referred to "Oil Pollution of Water."

To locate the reference book you need, ask the reference librarian. We have already mentioned some reference books (see p. 425). Here are some others.

**1.** Books giving direct information

*Statistical Abstract of the United States,* published annually by the U.S. Department of Commerce. This offers statistics on many subjects.

*Facts on File.* Described by the publisher as a "weekly news digest with cumulative index," this provides up-to-date summaries of current events, with names, dates, and places.

*New York Times Index.* This indexes all news stories and articles printed in the *Times* for every year since 1851. Except for the current year, the index appears in bound volumes—one for each year.

**2.** Books giving information about other books

*Guide to Reference Books,* compiled by Eugene P. Sheehy, ninth edition, published in 1976. Already mentioned, this is the best place to look for the titles of guides to research in all subjects: specialized encyclopedias, dictionaries, bibliographies, and the like.

*Book Review Digest.* This contains summaries of book reviews. Reading them will tell you quickly what a book does and how good it is. If, for instance, you are writing on evolution and are thinking of using *The Dragons of Eden,* by Carl Sagan, published in 1977, you may want to look at the five summaries of reviews of this book in the 1977 edition of the *Digest;* these can help you to decide whether to examine the book or skip it.

*Book Review Index* and *Current Review Citations.* If you can't find entries for the books you want in *Book Review Digest,* you may find them in these volumes, which don't print digests of reviews but do tell you where to find the reviews themselves.

*Essay and General Literature Index.* This volume lists the titles and the authors of articles collected in books. Since other sources usually tell you just the title of the whole book and the name of the person who edited it, you'll need the *Essay and General Literature Index* to find out what such a book actually contains.

*Cumulative Book Index* (1898–present), *Books in Print* (1948–present), *Paperbound Books in Print* (1955–present), *Subject Guide to Books in Print* (1957–present). The *Cumulative Book Index* lists all books published in the United States from 1898 to the present; the guides to books in print list hardbound and paperback books currently in print (available from the publisher). They can tell you about new books which the library may not yet have, or may not yet have cataloged.

**3.** Indexes to articles in periodicals

1. For articles of general interest:

*Readers' Guide to Periodical Literature.* Already mentioned, this is an author and subject index to articles of general interest printed in over a hundred American periodicals.

*Magazine Index.* This is a microtext, made to be used with a special viewer. It indexes more than 350 periodicals, some presenting articles of general interest and others addressed to specialists.

2. For articles in special fields (a selection):

*Environment Index.* Entries are arranged under subject headings. In the 1978 edition, for instance, you will find the general heading "Oil Spills" and its several subheadings, among them "Oil Spill Analysis," "Oil Spill Incidents," and "Oil Spills—Tanker." Brief summaries of many of the articles cited are available in a companion volume, *Environment Abstracts.*

*General Science Index.* This is a subject index to articles in such fields as astronomy, botany, genetics, mathematics, physics, and oceanography.

*Humanities Index.* This is an author and subject index to 260 periodicals in such fields as archaeology, folklore, history, language and literature, the performing arts, and philosophy.

*MLA International Bibliography.* This lists articles and books on modern languages, literatures, folklore, and linguistics.

*Public Affairs Information Service: Cumulative Author Index.* This covers government documents and books as well as articles on public affairs and public policy.

*Social Sciences Index.* This is an author and subject index to over 250 periodicals in such fields as anthropology, economics, law and criminology, medical science, political science, and sociology.

**4.** Government publications. The United States government publishes a vast amount of information on a wide range of subjects. Here is a sample.

*ASI (American Statistics Index).* This work is in two volumes, *Index* and *Abstracts.* The first is a subject index to statistical documents produced by hundreds of government offices; the second describes the documents more fully.

*CIS.* This work too is in two volumes, *Index* and *Abstracts.* Published by the Congressional Information Service, it indexes the working papers of Congress, including hearings, prints, reports, documents, and other special publications of nearly three hundred House, Senate, and joint committees and subcommittees. A researcher investigating oil spills, for instance, would find in the 1977 *Abstracts* a summary of a congressional hearing on their effects.

*Monthly Catalog of United States Government Publications.* This is a subject index to a variety of sources.

EXERCISE 8   **Finding Facts**

Assume that you want to do research on oil spills at sea. Select a six-month period of a recent year, and see what you can learn about oil spills during this period from *Facts on File* and the *New York Times Index.*

EXERCISE 9   **Using Book Reviews**

Using the *Book Review Index* and the *Book Review Digest,* investigate reviews of *Time on the Cross,* by Robert William Fogel and Stanley L. Engerman, a book about slavery published in 1974. What impression of the book do you get from the reviews?

EXERCISE 10   **Using a Subject Index**

In the reference area of your library, locate a subject index to sources in a field of study that interests you—political science, education, astronomy, or the like. Find out what is listed under two subject headings, and make a note of the two most interesting sources you find under each one. If you come upon cross references, such as "see also Moon Landings" under "Space Exploration," check one of them and make a note of two of the sources listed under it.

EXERCISE 11 **Finding Government Publications**

With the aid of a reference librarian, learn what government publications the library has dealing with a topic you might do research on. List the titles of at least three.

## Finding Articles

Once you have found the authors and titles of articles on your topic, you need to find the articles themselves. Here is what to do.

If the article is in a book of essays, find the call number of the book by looking at its title card in the card catalog.

If the article appeared in a periodical more than a year ago, look up the name of the periodical in the card catalog. The card will direct you to bound volumes of the periodical; each volume usually covers a one- or two-year period, with the individual issues arranged chronologically.

If the article appeared within the past year, you will find it in the section of the library where the unbound periodicals are kept. Usually you will also find in this section a guide to where each periodical is.

(Since it always takes some time for the periodicals of the past year to be bound, the issue you want may be neither in the periodical section nor on the shelf, but at the bindery. If you can't find the issue you want, ask the reference librarian when and where it will be available.)

## Using Microtexts

Because of storage problems, libraries have increased their use of microtexts—printed material photographically reduced in size and readable only with the aid of mechanical viewers. The two most common forms are microfilm (on reels) and microfiche (in which the images are placed in rows on cards). On general principles you should probably familiarize yourself with your library's supply of microtexts and with the procedures for viewing them. Some excellent sources, such as complete files of major newspapers, may be available only in this form.

EXERCISE 12 **Finding Microtext Sources**

Find out whether any promising sources on your topic are printed on microfilm or microfiche. Make a list of at least three such sources.

## 26.5 Keeping Track of Your Sources

Once you start working your way through the card catalog and reference books, you will quickly find out about many books and articles on your topic. Fill out a 3-by-5-inch card on each source you mean to investigate. The card will enable you to keep track of the source from the beginning to the end of your research—from the time you find it in the library until you cite it in the notes and bibliography of your paper.

Here are two examples of source cards, the first for a book, the second for an article in a periodical.

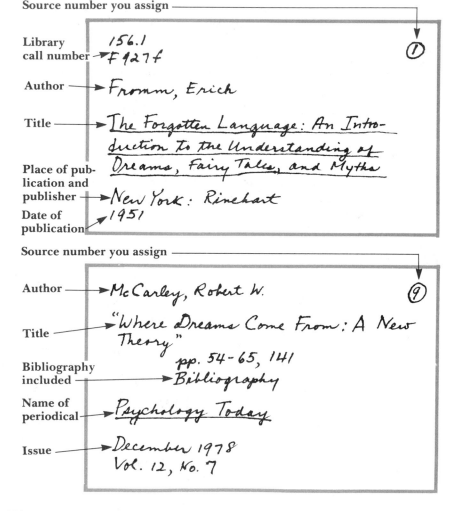

The call number at left enables you to locate the book in the stacks, or to fill out a call slip to give to the librarian at the circulation desk. The circled number at right is your number for the source; when you refer to the book or article in your notes, you can save space and time by citing this number rather than the title. You assign each new source a number of its own.

The full name of the author (last name first) will be needed if you cite this source in your paper. So will the title and, for a book, the place of publication and the name of the publisher. The punctuation of the title tells whether the item is a book or an entire journal (both underlined) or a chapter in a book or an article in a journal (both enclosed within quotation marks).

The date, of course, tells you when a book or article was published. This information can save you from some embarrassing mistakes—for example, from claiming that one book has influenced another that was actually published years earlier. You will also need the date for your notes and bibliography. For a recent reprint of an older book, record both the date of the original publication and the date of the reprint. For an article, record the month, year, volume, and number of the periodical in which the article appeared.

If the book or article has a bibliography, you should note that fact. The bibliography may well lead you to more sources.

EXERCISE 13   **Making Source Cards**

Fill out two 3-by-5-inch cards, one for a book and the other for an article. Using the sample cards shown in the text as models, record all the information you will need if you use these sources for your research paper.

## 26.6   Examining Your Sources

When you have decided which sources you want to read, have located them in the library, and have made up your cards, you are ready to examine the sources themselves. As you read, of course, you will probably learn about other sources, and you should keep a record of these for later investigation. But your chief task now is to examine the materials you have on hand. Here are some suggestions about how to do so.

**1.** Organize your reading time. List in order of importance the books and articles you plan to consult, and set up a reading schedule. Plan to do some reading every day and to finish all your reading and note-taking a week before the paper is due. You may not make that deadline, but if you come within a day or two of it, you will be much better off than if you are reading sources the night before the paper is due. After you have done your reading and note-taking, you will need time to assimilate your sources, to make coherent sense out of them.

**2.** Read selectively. You can often get what you want from a source without reading all of it. Since you may have to consult many sources in a very short time, you should learn to read them selectively.

If your source is a book, read the preface to get an idea of its scope and purpose. Then scan the table of contents and the index for specific discussions of your topic. If you are writing on slavery, for instance, and you are particularly interested in slave children, look for that subject in any source you consult. Then read any promising sections, watching for important facts and interpretations and taking notes. With practice, you may find that you can gather three or four useful quotations from a book in less than an hour.

**3.** Read responsibly. Respect the context of what you quote. Reading selectively doesn't mean reading carelessly or lifting statements out of context. To understand what you are quoting and to judge it adequately, you may have to read a good part of the section or chapter in which it appears—enough, at least, to familiarize yourself with the context. Suppose you read in a book about slavery in America that slaves sometimes did clerical and even managerial work. You should try to see if the author says when, where, and how often this occurred, and if that information is given, you should make it part of your note.

**4.** Read critically. Critical reading is more important for an analytical research paper than for a survey, but in either case, you need to decide whether what you are reading is worth citing at all. Beyond that, you need to decide how reliable its evidence and arguments are. If the writer gives opinions without facts to support them, or makes statements of "fact" without citing sources, you should be suspicious.

## 26.7   Taking Notes

Make each note clear, complete, and accurate. When you write the paper, you will rely chiefly on your notes, not on the sources themselves, which you probably will not have at hand. Take time now to put down all the information you will need later.

Use one whole card (4 by 6 or 5 by 7 inches) for each quotation, paraphrase, or summary. The larger size makes it easy to keep note cards separate from source cards and leaves room for notes of your own, which in the finished paper may become comments on your source. Also, the use of a separate card for each note enables you to rearrange your notes without difficulty when you are trying out different ways of organizing your paper. (If a note is long, continue it on a second card, which can be stapled to the first.) On each card, write down the source number you have assigned the item, and the page number or numbers of the text referred to in your note. You will need to give the page numbers in the final draft of your essay.

26.7

## Summarizing What You Read

You will need some quotations in your paper, but if there are too many of them, the reader will lose track of what you are trying to say. As you take notes, therefore, you should begin to put the writer's ideas into your own words by paraphrasing or summarizing them. Summarizing a writer's ideas is a particularly good way of making sure you understand them.

Suppose you have decided to do your research on dreams. One of your note cards could look like this:

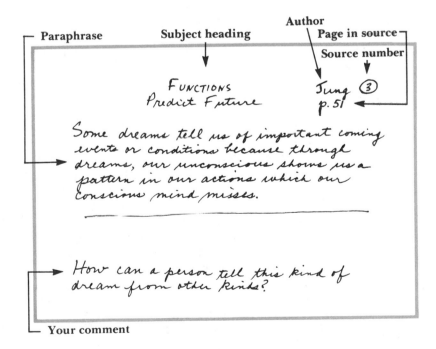

Paraphrase · Subject heading · Author · Page in source · Source number

FUNCTIONS
Predict Future

Jung ③
p. 51

Some dreams tell us of important coming events or conditions because through dreams, our unconscious shows us a pattern in our actions which our conscious mind misses.

How can a person tell this kind of dream from other kinds?

Your comment

This note was taken from p. 51 of an essay by Carl G. Jung that appears in a book entitled *Man and His Symbols* (Garden City, N.Y.: Doubleday, 1964). Here is what the source actually says:

> Thus dreams may sometimes announce certain situations long before they actually happen. This is not necessarily a miracle or a form of precognition. Many crises in our lives have a long unconscious history. We move toward them step by step, unaware of the dangers that are accumulating. But what we consciously fail to see is frequently perceived by our unconscious, which can pass the information on through dreams.

The note does four things with Jung's passage.

**1.** It gives the passage a subject heading. Using this kind of heading, you can easily identify and "place" each note when you write your paper. You can put this note with other notes about the functions of dreams, and you can also tell at a glance which function this note describes.

**2.** It gives all the information required for a note or parenthetical reference. To write such a note or reference, you need only turn to source card 3, which gives most of the necessary information, and then add the page number from the note card. Actually, you don't even have to write the author's name on your note cards, but doing so is easy enough and will save you trouble in various ways when you write the paper.

**3.** It sums up the passage in one sentence. The summary catches the essential point of Jung's words. You can often summarize a writer's words in less time than it would take to copy all of them out, and when you summarize a passage, you are getting a firm grip on its meaning.

**4.** It records the researcher's reaction. After summarizing a passage, you can draw a line and then write down one or more questions or comments. In this instance a question has occurred to the note-taker: If it is true that dreams can predict the future, can one ever know which dream will "come true"?

A summary may cover more than just a brief passage, of course. Three pages are summarized in the note at the top of p. 443. To be sure, it takes a little work and thought to summarize three pages in a single sentence. But once again, it takes much less time to write a summary than to copy all the pages out.

As you summarize, you should of course feel free to quote particular words or phrases that seem important, as shown in the note (p. 443) on David Foulkes's "Dreams of Innocence," an article in *Psychology Today*, 12 (December 1978). Notice that quotation

MEANING                    Fromm ①
                           pp. 36-8

To interpret the content of a dream, we must
know the dreamer, his or her emotional
state at the moment of going to sleep,
and the elements in the dream that
correspond with reality as he or she
ordinarily sees it.
_____

Is this always true? Is any content
universal rather than personal?


CONTENT                    Foulkes ②
Children                   p. 78

Research conducted over a period of five
years has led Foulkes to question the
belief of Freudians that the dreams of
children are marked by "irrational feelings in relatively bizarre imagery." He
has found the content of their dreams to
be "rather simple and unemotional."
_____

Does this mean that children themselves are
"rather simple and unemotional"? Seems unlikely.

marks are used around phrases taken directly from Foulkes's article, and also that the quotations are blended into the language of
the summary. (For more on summarizing, see pp. 186–87.)

EXERCISE 14   Note-taking

For a source that interests you, make a 3-by-5-inch source card. Then read
three or four pages in the source and summarize them on one side of a 4-
by-6-inch note card, adding your own comment or question. Be sure the

note card has a subject heading, the author's name, the source number, and the pages you have used.

## Quoting from Sources

You should quote rather than summarize a statement when it precisely and concisely expresses one of the author's fundamental views, when its language is notably vivid or eloquent, or when you expect to analyze it in detail. The note shown here, for instance, quotes a key statement about distortion in dreams from Sigmund Freud's *The Complete Introductory Lectures on Psychoanalysis*, translated and edited by James Strachey (New York: Norton, 1966).

> INTERPRETATION  Freud ②
> Censorship     p. 147
>
> "For the time being let us hold fast to this: dream-distortion is a result of the censorship which is exercised by recognized purposes of the ego against wishful impulses in any way objectionable that stir within us at night-time during our sleep."
>
> Was Freud dogmatic about his theories? He sounds like it.

Quote accurately. Be careful to avoid mistakes of any kind. After copying a passage, always proofread your version, comparing it with the original. Remember that you will be depending on your copy when you write your paper, and this will probably be your only chance to check the copy against the original.

Use quotation marks to indicate the beginning and the end of quoted material. You must always distinguish between quotation and paraphrase on the card. In the final draft of your paper, you may quote without quotation marks only if you indent the quoted material, as shown on pp. 405–6.

Use ellipsis dots (. . .) to indicate that you have deliberately omitted words in writing out the quotation. Be careful not to make an omission that distorts the original. You may leave out words only when they are not essential to the meaning of what you quote.

> ORIGINS     Jung ③
>        p. 52
>
> "One cannot afford to be naive in dealing
> with dreams. They originate in a spirit
> that is not quite human, but is rather
> a breath of nature. . . . If we want
> to characterize this spirit, we shall
> certainly get closer to it in the sphere of
> ancient mythologies, or the fables of the
> primeval forest, than in the con-
> sciousness of modern man."
>
> ─────────────────────────
>
> Compare Fromm. Is Fromm "naive"?

Compare the quotation on the note card above with the complete passage:

> One cannot afford to be naive in dealing with dreams. They originate in a spirit that is not quite human, but is rather a breath of nature—a spirit of the beautiful and generous as well as of the cruel goddess. If we want to characterize this spirit, we shall certainly get closer to it in the sphere of ancient mythologies, or the fables of the primeval forest, than in the consciousness of modern man.

The researcher uses three ellipsis dots to indicate that the last part of the second sentence has been omitted; the fourth dot is a period. If the words before the omission did not make a complete sentence, the researcher would use just the three ellipsis dots and then finish the sentence: "One cannot . . . be naive in dealing with dreams."

What the researcher has omitted in this note is not essential to the meaning of the passage quoted. But see what happens to the passage when a quotation does leave out something essential:

> One cannot afford to be naive in dealing with dreams. They originate in a spirit that is not quite human, but is rather a breath of nature. . . . If we want to characterize this spirit, we shall certainly get closer to it . . . in the consciousness of modern man.

Jung is now made to say just the opposite of what he actually said. This is the worst possible way of quoting a source.

Use brackets to mark explanatory words added within a

quotation. On the note card below, the brackets indicate an insertion made by the note-taker to indicate who *He* is. The first set of ellipsis dots marks the omission of a whole sentence; the second set marks an omission within a sentence.

FUNCTIONS                    Fromm    ①
                              p. 45

"Not only do insights into our relation to others or theirs to us, value judgments and predictions occur in our dreams, but also intellectual operations superior to those in the waking state.... The best known example of this kind of dream is the one of the discoverer of the Benzine ring. He [Friedrich Kekule] had been searching for the chemical formula for Benzine ... and one night the correct formula stood before his eyes in a dream. He was fortunate enough to remember it after he awoke."
So one function of dreams is problem solving.

### EXERCISE 15   Quoting a Source

On a note card quote a statement from one of your sources, being sure to use quotation marks. Then check your version against the original, word for word.

### EXERCISE 16   Using Ellipsis Dots

In one of your sources find a passage of four or five sentences from which words could be omitted without distortion of the original. Write a version in which you use ellipsis dots twice.

### EXERCISE 17   Summarizing and Quoting

Make a note that includes both summary of a source and quotation from it.

## 26.8   Choosing Your Writing Goal

By the time you feel that you have finished your research, you will have a substantial pile of note cards—perhaps thirty or more. The first step in turning the notes into a paper is to sort them according to their headings. If you are writing on dreams, for instance, you could make three separate piles: one for notes on the origin of dreams, one for notes on their function, and one for notes on their meaning.

When you have sorted the cards, you should reread them, one pile at a time. As you read, you may find that some cards are in the wrong pile, or that some of them belong in a new pile, with a subject heading such as "Structure of Dreams" or "Dreams and Myth" or "Dreams and Real Life." In other words, you may rethink your categories as you reread and sort the cards, for the process of sorting note cards is the beginning of thinking your way into the organization of the paper.

As you work with your cards, you should also be thinking about what your writing goal will be. Rereading the cards gives you a concentrated review of all of your research, and thus prepares you to decide or discover where your reading leads. What basic question will your paper attempt to answer? Will it concern the origin of dreams, their function, or their meaning? Or will it address a larger question—for example, What is the relation between dreams and waking life? Since many dreams originate from waking-life experiences, serve some function in our lives as a whole, and have a meaning that the waking mind can understand, all three of your original categories are related to this general question.

Asking a question of this sort is a way of stating the main goal of the paper. With the question in mind, you should look for relations among your notes. You should see how one idea reinforces, qualifies, or contradicts another. You must be patient at this point; you must be willing sometimes to stare at a card for five or ten minutes, wondering what to do with it. This is the crucial moment of organization, the moment when you begin to see how various individual notes can be made to work together.

Unless you have already done so, you must now also decide what kind of paper you will write. Will it be a survey or an analysis? The choice depends partly on your own preference and partly on your subject and the results of your research. At any rate, you will have to make the choice before you start to write your paper.

## 26.9 Filling Gaps in Your Research

While you are rereading and sorting your notes, or even after you have decided what kind of paper you will write and what its main goal will be, you may discover that you need to know more about one or two things. You may suddenly realize that you have failed

**26.9**

to consult an important source—one that several of your sources often refer to—or failed to answer an important question. What are the arguments against Freud's theory that a dream is the fulfillment of a wish? (A paper on dreams that doesn't even mention Freud is ignoring a major authority on the subject.) What have the most recent experiments shown about our need to dream, or about the predictive power of dreams? (A paper on dreams that makes no reference to modern sleep experiments is seriously out-of-date.) Before you start to write a first draft, you should try to fill such gaps in your research.

In one sense, of course, it is impossible to complete research on any topic. The number of older books and articles can be staggering, and new ones appear every month; there is never enough time to read them all. But at this stage, with extensive research already completed, you can distinguish between questions that are relevant and questions that are not, between necessary and optional further reading. Your objective now is to finish preparing yourself to write the paper that is already taking shape in your mind.

# 27

# WRITING THE
# RESEARCH PAPER

In every writing project there comes a time when you must shift from exploring your subject and gathering materials about it to writing a full first draft. For the research paper, this time comes when you are reasonably sure that there are no major gaps in your reading, and when you begin to find patterns of thought or argument as you sort through your note cards. For many writers, the logical next step is to make an outline.

27.1

## 27.1   Making an Outline

The outline of your research paper will grow directly from the arrangement of your note cards. If you have sorted them carefully, you have established the main subject categories of your paper, and the notes themselves, of course, contain the material you will consider under those headings. You must now decide the order in which you will arrange the headings and the order in which, under each heading, you will present your materials. Since by now you should know what your main goal is, you need to find the order that will best enable you to reach it.

Before you write out your outline, therefore, you should consider your cards once more, checking to see whether your categories are right. You can then consider which is the most effective order for the categories. Should you treat the origin of dreams before or after you consider their meaning? And when should you take up their function? If the main goal of the paper is to explain the relation between dreams and waking life, you might begin by showing how they originate from waking-life experience, then consider their meaning in light of that experience, and finally examine their function—the ways in which they may help us to live better or understand ourselves better in the waking world.

When you have decided on the order of your categories and have laid out your cards, you can outline your paper. Since you have the material of your paper before you, you don't need a preliminary session of free writing. And since you have on the cards almost all the points you will cover in your paper, you may find that a standard vertical list will serve you better than a tree diagram. (For a full discussion of vertical lists and tree diagrams, see section 3.1, pp. 26–30.) Here is a sample outline for the research paper on dreams:

WORKING TITLE: Dreams and Waking Life
Basic Question: What is the relation between dreams and waking life?
    I. Origin of dreams
        A. Inspiration
            1. Divine source
            2. Other mysterious sources
        B. Memory of things experienced in waking life
        C. Personality of dreamer
    II. Meaning of dreams
        A. Fulfill wishes
        B. Express physical condition of dreamer
        C. Express personality of dreamer
    III. Function of dreams
        A. Put us in touch with our instincts
        B. Solve problems
        C. Give us a general sense of competence
        D. Help us to deal with stressful situations
Tentative Conclusion: Dreams help us to make sense out of our waking lives.

One advantage of an outline is that it lets you see the major divisions of your paper. When you write the paper itself, you may wish to indicate these divisions by using roman numerals before each of them, as shown in the sample paper (see section 27.9, pp. 483–98).

An outline not only lets you see at a glance the ground your paper will cover; it also lets you see why you need to choose between writing a survey and writing an analysis. Under each of the three major headings in this outline are conflicting theories about the origin, meaning, and function of dreams. Before you could write a paper based on this outline, you would have to decide whether you were going to evaluate the conflicting views or simply describe them.

The conclusion in this outline is tentative because you do not need to be absolutely sure of your conclusion before you start. You need a question, but you do not immediately need the final answer. On the contrary, you should leave room for discovery as you write.

## 27.2 Writing the First Draft

Writing the first draft of a research paper is in many ways like writing the first draft of an ordinary essay. With raw material on your note cards and an outline at hand, you need to turn the material into a coherent explanation of a topic or a persuasive argument about it. You need to introduce your explanation or argument, to develop it with the aid of your notes, and to conclude it. Beyond these general requirements, the writing of a research paper makes its own special demands. To help you meet them we make these suggestions:

**1.** Introduce the paper by clearly announcing its subject, scope, method, and purpose. You can introduce an ordinary essay with a brief informal paragraph that simply points to a particular subject and gives some indication of how that subject will be treated. But the introduction to a research paper must be more formal, thorough, and rigorous. Now that you have studied your notes, sorted them into categories, formulated the question you intend to answer, decided whether you are going to write a survey or an analysis, and outlined your paper, you should have some grasp of what the paper is going to do. If the grasp is not yet firm, you don't have to write the introduction first. You can write it after you've written the rest of the paper—when you know exactly what you're introducing. But whenever you write it, the introduction should clearly announce the subject, scope, method, and purpose of the paper as a whole.

Like any good introduction, it should also take account of the reader. Here, for instance, is the way you might introduce the paper on dreams to a reader who does not specialize in the study of them:

> Dreams are universal. Though we sometimes forget our dreams, each of us has at least one dream virtually every time we sleep, and without much difficulty each of us could probably remember a dream in some detail. Over literally thousands of years, dreams have been treated by poets and studied by psychol-

ogists. Yet certain basic questions about dreams remain to be settled: Where do they come from? What do they mean? Do they serve any purpose? This paper will consider how those questions have been answered by a variety of psychologists and experimenters. By analyzing their statements on the origin, meaning, and function of dreams, it will attempt to explain the relation between dreams and waking life.

Notice what this introduction does. It first appeals to universal experience, describing dreams in language that any intelligent reader can understand. Then it lists the basic questions that motivate the study of dreams: questions about their origin, meaning, and function. Having introduced these questions, it then defines the scope, method, and purpose of the paper. Its scope—the range of material it will examine—is a body of statements by psychologists and experimenters about the origin, meaning, and function of dreams. Its method will be to analyze those statements. And the purpose of this analysis will be to explain the relation between dreams and waking life.

**2.** Make your sources work together. Writing the main part of a research paper is largely a process of weaving your sources into a coherent whole. That whole is made up of quotations and summaries from your notes, combined with your own commentary. You are responsible for showing your reader the relations among your sources, for explaining what they signify when taken together.

The trouble with many student research papers is that they are not much more than collections of quoted passages. It is tempting to quote at length, for long quotations fill up the page and save you the trouble of filling it with your own words. But you will not get much credit for a paper full of long quotations. You are much more likely to get a question from your instructor about what you have to say for yourself.

Whenever you quote anything, therefore, ask yourself why you are quoting it. Quote only as much as you need to make your point, and no more. Bear in mind that quoting a word or phrase is a way of emphasizing it—provided it is quoted all by itself. If you want to stress the point that Carl Jung sees dream symbols as "message carriers" from the unconscious to the conscious mind, the quotation marks do the emphasizing for you. But you will lose that emphasis if the phrase is buried in a quotation several paragraphs, or even several sentences, long.

In general, your commentary on anything you quote should be at least as long as the quotation itself. If a lengthy passage is important enough to be quoted in full, you ought to have some important thing to say about it. If you don't have much to say about a passage, don't quote it at length, or at all. A long quotation followed by a single sentence of commentary usually tells the reader that the writer is dozing his or her way through the paper.

27.2

Remember, too, that quoting is not the only way of using the material in your notes. If you have taken our advice and often written summaries instead of quotations, you already have at hand alternatives to quotation, restatements of your sources in your own words. You will find that when you use summaries instead of lengthy quotations, you can wield your sources much more effectively, that you can make them talk to each other instead of just stolidly filling up a page. Consider this passage from a first draft:

> Fromm and Jung represent two poles of thought in modern theorizing about the origin of dreams. While Fromm traces the dream to a specific occurrence, Jung seeks its origin in something mystical, something "not quite human," something outside the dreamer's personal experience. (Fromm, ①, pp. 156–57, Jung, ③, p. 52) But recent research on dreams—especially children's dreams—indicates that any search for their origin must at the very least begin with that experience. If dreams come from outside the dreamer's experience, children's dreams should be as Jung describes them: rich, complex, and full of strange, frightening archetypes. (Jung, ③, pp. 69–75) But after five years of study, David Foulkes has found that young children's dreams are in general "rather simple and unemotional," that the complexity of children's dreams grows as the child does, and therefore that the content of a dream is closely linked to the development of the dreamer in the waking world. (Foulkes, ⑧, pp. 78, 86–88) Clearly, then, the dreamer's waking experience must provide at least part of the answer to the question of where dreams originate.

Here the writer contrasts one source with another in a single paragraph. The use of brief summaries instead of long quotations allows the writer to keep the cited material under control, to frame it within a paragraph that has a point of its own to make. (The method of using numbered references in the first draft is explained on p. 455.)

**3.** Always explain the relation between the statements you cite, and in an analysis, also evaluate the statements. The very least you should normally do with the statements you quote or cite is to explain the relation between them. Unless it is immediately obvious, you should tell the reader how one statement reinforces, qualifies, or contradicts another. And you should do this whether or not you are writing an analysis. If, for instance, you are describing the views of Jung, Fromm, and Foulkes on the origin of dreams, you should at least point up the contrast between the views of Jung and those of Foulkes.

In an analysis, you should evaluate the statements you cite, especially when they represent conflicting points of view. If you don't evaluate the statements and choose between them, you will not make your own viewpoint clear, and you will fail to present an argument in the paper as a whole.

**4.** In a survey, end by summarizing the various viewpoints you have considered; in an analysis, end by stating your own viewpoint and the reasons for it.

If you set out to make a survey of various opinions about the nature of dreams, you should end by summarizing or broadly categorizing them:

> A survey of theories about dreams, then, shows that there is little agreement and much disagreement about where they come from, what they mean, and what purpose they serve. Jung locates their origin in the unconscious and in ancient archetypes; others, such as Fromm, regard them as the product of experiences in our waking life. Virtually all commentators on dreams agree that they mean something, but what they mean is disputed. While Freud says that a dream is the fulfillment of a wish, others see it as the result of a purely physical activity—of rapid eye movement during certain phases of sleep. Finally, while Jung regards dreams as "message carriers" from the instincts to the conscious mind, others argue that dreams solve specific problems and enable us to cope with the waking world. I can only conclude that dreams are—and will probably remain—a subject of debate and dispute.

By contrast, the writer of an analysis should end by making his or her own view explicit and by giving the reasons for it:

> What then is the overall relation between dreams and waking life? I believe that each is needed to help us understand the other. We cannot adequately explain dreams by saying that they come from God or some mysterious source beyond the dreamer—such as Jung's "breath of nature." But neither can we explain them by saying simply that they come from the body, like the dreamer's heartbeat and rapid eye movements. Researchers can measure those things while the dreamer sleeps, but the only way they can get to the dream itself is to wake the dreamer up, and in order to understand the dream, they must know something about the dreamer's waking life and waking mind. I do not think anyone can make sense out of a dream without some reference to the waking, walking, observable personality of the dreamer.
>
> Yet just as we need our lives to interpret our dreams, we

need dreams to make sense out of our lives. Though dreams seem to turn things topsy-turvy, they tell us things about ourselves that we may be able to learn in no other way. They may remind us of things long forgotten; they may expose us to things we repress; above all, they may reveal to us the naturally creative powers of our own minds. Perhaps, after all, that is the most important thing dreams do for us. More than fulfilling our wishes, predicting the future, or solving a specific problem, dreams show us what the mind can do with all that we experience in the waking world.

This is certainly not the last word on the subject of dreams, nor does the writer pretend it is. In any subject as disputable as dreams, all conclusions are provisional—subject to qualification or complete overthrow. But a conclusion like this one shows that the writer has thought through the material, not simply surveyed it.


## 27.3  Citing Sources As You Write

### Informal Documentation

In the final draft of your paper you must formally document each use of your sources (see sections 27.4–27.8, pp. 460–83). But while you are writing the first draft, you can document informally. After each use of a source, put the following information in parentheses:

> the author's name
> the circled number you have given to the source on your source card
> the page numbers in the source for the particular material used

Consider an example from the first draft of a survey paper about dreams:

> Psychologists disagree about the content and significance of children's dreams. Jung believed that children's dreams could be rich, complex, and full of archetypes. He cites the dreams of an eight-year-old girl as evidence, suggesting they put her in touch with primordial images foretelling her death. (Jung, ③, pp. 69–75) Foulkes questions this view. His own research has led him to conclude that children's dreams are "rather simple and unemotional." (Foulkes, ⑧, p. 78)

This passage illustrates various ways of using sources—summarizing, paraphrasing, and quoting. Whichever form your use of a source takes, you must put the documentation right after it, every time.

**27.3**

## Introducing Sources

Whenever you use a source in any way, you should introduce it smoothly, either naming the author or clearly indicating that you are about to use a source. If you begin summarizing or paraphrasing without referring to the author, the reader has no way of knowing where your comment ends and your source material begins. Compare these two passages:

> It is no easy matter to interpret a dream. We must know the dreamer, his or her emotional state at the moment of going to sleep, and the elements in the dream that correspond with reality as he or she ordinarily sees it. (Fromm, ①, 36–38)

> It is no easy matter to interpret a dream. Erich Fromm says that in order to do so, we must know the dreamer, his or her emotional state at the moment of going to sleep, and the elements in the dream that correspond with reality as he or she ordinarily sees it. (Fromm, ①, 36–38)

In the first passage, the reader has no way of knowing just where the writer's use of Fromm begins. In the second, the writer clearly indicates the beginning as well as the end of that use.

Quotation marks indicate the boundary between your own words and those of your source, but unless you have some special reason for doing so, you should not drop an anonymous quotation into the middle of your text. Compare these two passages:

> The mind in sleep is often more creative than the mind in waking hours. "Not only do insights . . . , value judgments and predictions occur in our dreams, but also intellectual operations superior to those in the waking state." (Fromm, ①, p. 45)

> The mind in sleep is often more creative than it is in waking hours. Erich Fromm writes: "Not only do insights . . . , value judgments and predictions occur in our dreams, but also intellectual operations superior to those in the waking state." (Fromm, ①, p. 45)

In the first version, the quotation marks indicate that the second sentence is a quotation, but the reader will have to consult a note just to find out who is being quoted. In the second version the reader learns the author's name at once. If you were the reader, which would you prefer?

Here are other examples of how to introduce a source.

> According to Fromm, dreams involve "intellectual operations superior to those in the waking state." (Fromm, ①, p. 45)

Freud believed that a dream was always the fulfillment of a wish. (Freud, ②, p. 154)

27.3

Foulkes questions this view. His own research has led him to conclude that children's dreams are "rather simple and unemotional." (Foulkes, ⑧, p. 78)

But recent studies cast serious doubt on the Jungian theory that children's dreams are full of frightening archetypes and primitive myths. After five years of research, David Foulkes has reported as follows:

> At no age was the typical child's REM [rapid eye movement] dream particularly frightening or overwhelming. Little direct evidence could be found, at any age, for a peremptive role of primitive impulses or fantasies in the organization of children's dreams. Little or no evidence could be found, at any age, for the hypothesis that children's dreams bring them into contact with a symbolically complex world of archetypal, primitive myths. (Foulkes, ⑧, p. 81)

In each of these examples, the writer introduces a source by naming the author. In addition, the last two examples mark a transition from one point of view to another.

## Managing Quotations

When you quote short passages of poetry or prose, you should put quotation marks around them and make them part of your own text. When you quote long passages, you should set them off from your text and omit the quotation marks—as is done in the last of the preceding examples. (For more on this point, see pp. 405–6.)

## Plagiarism

Plagiarism is the dishonest act of presenting the words or thoughts of another writer as if they were your own. You commit plagiarism whenever you use a source *in any way* without indicating that you have used it. If you quote anything at all, even a phrase, you must put quotation marks around it, or set it off from your text; if you summarize or paraphrase an author's words, you must clearly indicate where the summary or paraphrase begins and ends; if you use an author's idea, you must say that you are doing so. In every instance, you must also formally acknowledge the written source from which you took the material.

The only time you can use a source without formal acknowledgment is when you refer to a specific phrase, statement, or passage that you have used and acknowledged earlier in the same paper. In the conclusion to the sample paper on dreams, for instance, the writer mentions Jung's "breath of nature" (p. 493). Since the writer has already formally acknowledged the specific source of this phrase (p. 486), there is no need to acknowledge it again in the conclusion. Nor is there any need to enumerate the sources of a summary statement based on several different passages that have been used earlier in the paper and have already been acknowledged. But you are free to skip the acknowledgment only when you are referring a second time to exactly the same material. When you use new material from a source already cited, you must make a new acknowledgment.

Elsewhere in this chapter we show you how to use sources honestly, how to draw the line between what is your own and what you have taken from others. Now here are examples of various kinds of plagiarism. In each instance, the source is a passage from p. 102 of E. R. Dodds's *The Greeks and the Irrational* (Berkeley, 1951; rpt. Boston: Beacon, 1957). First, here is the original note, copied accurately from the book.

FUNCTIONS                    Dodds ⑫
                             p. 102

"If the waking world has certain advantages of solidity and continuity, its social opportunities are terribly restricted. In it we meet, as a rule, only the neighbors, whereas the dream-world offers the chance of intercourse, however fugitive, with our distant friends, our dead, and our gods. For normal men it is the sole experience in which they escape the offensive and incomprehensible bondage of time and space."

Fantasy — an obvious function, but nicely described.

And here are five ways of plagiarizing this source.

**1.** Word-for-word continuous copying without quotation marks or mention of the author's name:

> Dreams help us satisfy another important psychic need—our need to vary our social life. This need is regularly thwarted in our waking moments. If the waking world has certain advantages

of solidity and continuity, its social opportunities are terribly restricted. In it we meet, as a rule, only the neighbors, whereas the dream world offers us the chance of intercourse, however fugitive, with our distant friends. We awaken from such encounters feeling refreshed, the dream having liberated us from the here and now. . . .

**2.** Copying many words and phrases without quotation marks or mention of the author's name:

> Dreams help us satisfy another psychic need—our need to vary our social life. In the waking world our social opportunities, for example, are terribly restricted. As a rule, we usually encounter only the neighbors. In the dream world, on the other hand, we have the chance of meeting our distant friends. For most of us it is the sole experience in which we escape the bondage of time and space. . . .

**3.** Copying an occasional key word or phrase without quotation marks or mention of the author's name:

> Dreams help us satisfy another psychic need—our need to vary our social life. During our waking hours our social opportunities are terribly restricted. We see only the people next door and our business associates. In contrast, whenever we dream, we can see our distant friends. Even though the encounter is brief, we awaken refreshed, having freed ourselves from the bondage of the here and now. . . .

**4.** Paraphrasing without mention of the author's name:

> Dreams help us satisfy another important psychic need—our need to vary our social life. When awake, we are creatures of this time and this place. Those we meet are usually those we live near and work with. When dreaming, on the other hand, we can meet far-off friends. We awaken refreshed by our flight from the here and now. . . .

**5.** Taking the author's idea without acknowledging the source:

> Dreams help us to satisfy another important psychic need— the need for a change. They liberate us from the here and now, taking us out of the world we normally live in. . . .

A final note: if there is anything about plagiarism you do not understand, *ask your teacher.*


Exercise 1   **Recognizing Plagiarism**

Pick out the sentences, phrases, and key words that were taken from Dodds in examples 1–3.

EXERCISE 2    Recognizing Plagiarism

Read this two-paragraph passage. Then read the summary that follows, and indicate whether any part of the summary—aside from the word "motifs"—should be in quotation marks.

> And, speaking more generally, it is plain foolishness to believe in ready-made systematic guides to dream interpretation, as if one could simply buy a reference book and look up a particular symbol. No dream symbol can be separated from the individual
> 5 who dreams it, and there is no definite or straightforward interpretation of any dream. Each individual varies so much in the way that his unconscious complements or compensates his conscious mind that it is impossible to be sure how far dreams and their symbols can be classified at all.
> 10 It is true that there are dreams and single symbols (I should prefer to call them "motifs") that are typical and often occur. Among such motifs are falling, flying, being persecuted by dangerous animals or hostile men, being insufficiently or absurdly clothed in public places, being in a hurry or lost in a milling crowd, fighting
> 15 with useless weapons or being wholly defenseless, running hard yet getting nowhere. A typical infantile motif is the dream of growing infinitely small or infinitely big, or being transformed from one to the other—as you find it, for instance, in Lewis Carroll's *Alice in Wonderland.* But I must stress again that these are motifs that must
> 20 be considered in the context of the dream itself, not as self-explanatory ciphers.
> —Carl G. Jung, "Approaching the Unconscious," in *Man and His Symbols,* ed. Carl G. Jung and M.-L. von Franz (Garden City, N.Y.: Doubleday, 1964), p. 53

SUMMARY: According to Carl G. Jung in "Approaching the Unconscious," it would be just plain foolishness for anyone to think he or she could interpret dreams reliably by buying a ready-made reference book. No such guide has value because it is impossible to separate a dream symbol from the person who dreams it, and the unconscious of everyone is unique. Jung does admit that certain dreams and symbols come often to many. Calling these "motifs," he lists several, including falling, fighting with useless weapons, and running hard yet getting nowhere. But he emphasizes that even the motifs cannot be understood properly unless considered in the context of each dream itself.

## 27.4   Citing Sources in the Final Draft

In the final draft of a research paper you must clearly identify all of the sources you have quoted from, summarized, or paraphrased. You can do this in one of two ways: (1) by means of notes at the bottom of each page (footnotes) or at the end of the paper (endnotes), or (2) by means of parenthetical references within your own text. In papers on humanistic subjects, such as literature and art, you normally use notes for at least the first reference to each source, though you may use parentheses for later references; in papers on the sciences, you normally use parentheses for all references. Your teacher will tell you which method you are expected to use. If you are asked to use notes, at least in part, read sections 27.5–27.6, pp. 461–80. If you are asked to use parentheses for all references, read sections 27.7–27.8, pp. 480–83.

## 27.5   Citing with Notes   *cit/n*

### Footnotes and Endnotes

To cite a source by means of a note, put a slightly raised number in your text and, at the foot of the page or on a page of endnotes, a corresponding number followed by your identification of the source. Since careful measurements are needed to fit footnotes on the bottom of a page, endnotes are much easier to use. But footnotes are easier for the reader to find. Ask your teacher which format you are expected to follow.

*Placement of footnotes*

dreams.   Jung believed that children's dreams could be rich, complex, and full of symbolic archetypes.   He cites the dreams of an eight-year-old girl as evidence, suggesting they put her in touch with primordial images foretelling her own

**Raised numbers in text** death.² But Foulkes questions this view.   His own research has led him to conclude that children's dreams are "rather simple and unemotional."³

**Number indented 5 spaces and raised** ²Carl G. Jung, "Approaching the Unconscious," in <u>Man and His Symbols</u>, ed. Carl G. Jung and M.-L. von Franz (Garden City, N.Y.: Doubleday, 1964), pp. 69-75.

³David Foulkes, "Dreams of Innocence," <u>Psychology Today</u>, 12 (December 1978), 78.

**Quadruple space between text and first note**

**Double space between and within notes**

Whether you use footnotes or endnotes, you should number your notes consecutively throughout the paper. Do not start with number 1 on each new page of your text.

Put the note number at the end of the sentence or group of sentences in which you have used a source. Avoid the awkwardness of putting a number in the middle of a sentence:

```
While Jung says that children's dreams are com-
plex and frightening,2 Foulkes's research has led
him to conclude that children's dreams are
"rather simple and unemotional."3
```

Every number you insert draws the reader away from your text to a note, and no reader wants to be interrupted in the middle of a sentence. If you refer to two or more sources in one sentence, use one number at the end of the sentence and one note to identify them all; within the note, use a semicolon between one reference and another:

```
While Jung says that children's dreams are com-
plex and frightening, Foulkes's research has led
him to conclude that children's dreams are
"rather simple and unemotional."2


     2Carl G. Jung, "Approaching the Unconscious,"
in Man and His Symbols, ed. Carl G. Jung and M.-L.
von Franz (Garden City, N.Y.: Doubleday, 1964),
pp. 69-75; David Foulkes, "Dreams of Innocence,"
Psychology Today, 12 (December 1978), 78.
```

**Explanatory Notes**

Besides documenting a source, a note can give an explanation that cannot be easily fitted into the text:

```
Psychologists disagree about the content and sig-
nificance of children's dreams.1 Jung believed
that children's dreams could be rich, complex,


     1I refer to children old enough to talk
about their dreams. Though measurement of REM may
tell us how long and how often infants dream, we
have no way of knowing just what they dream about.
```

Explanatory notes are sometimes necessary, but before you write one, you should try to see whether you can fit the explanation into your text. Every note interrupts the reader, and the fewer the interruptions, the more readable your paper will be.

*Sample endnotes*

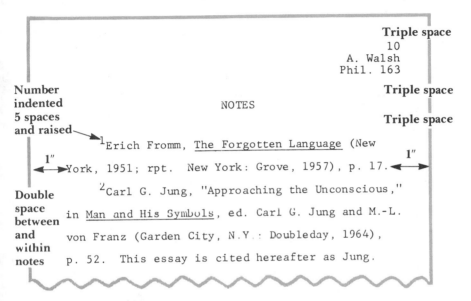

Triple space
10
A. Walsh
Phil. 163

**Number indented 5 spaces and raised**

NOTES
Triple space
Triple space

¹Erich Fromm, <u>The Forgotten Language</u> (New

*1"* ←→York, 1951; rpt. New York: Grove, 1957), p. 17. ←→ *1"*

**Double space between and within notes**

²Carl G. Jung, "Approaching the Unconscious," in <u>Man and His Symbols</u>, ed. Carl G. Jung and M.-L. von Franz (Garden City, N.Y.: Doubleday, 1964), p. 52. This essay is cited hereafter as Jung.

## Placing First and Later References

There are two ways of citing sources in a paper with notes; one way is used for the first reference to a source and another for all later references. The footnote or endnote for the first reference provides extensive information, as in this example:

²Erich Fromm, <u>The Forgotten Language</u> (New York, 1951; rpt. New York: Grove, 1957), p. 17. This book is cited hereafter as Fromm.

Thereafter, you need just a short, simple reminder. Unless your teacher requires that all references be made in notes, we suggest that you put the later references within parentheses in your text:

To interpret the content of a dream, says Fromm, we must know the dreamer, his or her emotional state at the moment of going to sleep, and the elements in the dream that correspond with real—

ity as he or she ordinarily sees it (Fromm, pp. 36-38).

As the preceding example indicates, a parenthetical reference following a paraphrase or summary goes between the last word of the sentence and the period. A reference following a short direct quotation of prose or verse goes between the closing quotation mark and the period:

> In "The Short Happy Life of Francis Macomber," for instance, Hemingway's account of the fatal shooting is deliberately understated and technical. Mrs. Macomber, he says, "hit her husband about two inches up and a little to one side of the base of his skull" (<u>Short Stories</u>, p. 36).

A reference following a prose extract set off from the text without quotation marks goes immediately after the final period:

> In <u>A Room of One's Own</u>, Virginia Woolf goes on to speak about women in literature and history:
>
>> A very queer, composite being thus emerges. Imaginatively she is of the highest importance; practically she is completely insignificant. She pervades poetry from cover to cover; she is all but absent from history. She dominates the lives of kings and conquerors in fiction; in fact she was the slave of any boy whose parents forced a ring upon her finger. Some of the most inspired words, some of the most profound thoughts in literature fall from her lips; in real life she could hardly read, could scarcely spell, and was the property of her husband. (Woolf, pp. 45-6)

A reference following verse set off from the text goes at the right-hand end of the last line of the quotation:

> Out, out, brief candle!
> Life's but a walking shadow, a poor player

That struts and frets his hour upon the stage

And then is heard no more. It is a tale

Told by an idiot, full of sound and fury,

Signifying nothing.           (<u>Macbeth</u> V.v.23–28)

If the reference doesn't fit there, it goes at the right-hand end of the next line.

## Writing Notes for Various Sources

Listed here are the kinds of sources you are most likely to use, with examples of the proper ways to cite them. You will notice that all the facts needed to cite any source should be contained on your source and note cards. For more information on citing, see the *MLA Handbook for Writers of Research Papers, Theses, and Dissertations* (New York: Modern Language Association of America, 1977).

**1.** <u>A book with one author</u>

FIRST REFERENCE

[1]Paul MacKendrick, <u>The Greek Stones Speak:</u> <u>The Story of Archaeology in Greek Lands</u> (New York: St. Martin's, 1962), p. 72.

This note illustrates the basic pattern to be followed in most of the notes you will write. Here the title in the example includes a subtitle, which follows a colon; the subtitle may be omitted from the notes if you prefer, but must be included in the bibliography. The title is followed by parentheses enclosing the place or places of publication, a colon, the name of the publisher, a comma, and the date of publication. After the parentheses come a comma, the page reference, and a period. If you give the author's full name in the text when introducing the source, you need not repeat the name in your note:

[1]<u>The Greek Stones Speak</u> (New York: St. Martin's, 1962), p. 72.

As in this example, you may use the short form of the name of a widely known publisher, such as St. Martin's Press. However, you always give the full name of a university press:

[2]Marion Clawson, <u>America's Land and Its Uses</u> (Baltimore: Johns Hopkins University Press, 1972), p. 52.

LATER REFERENCES

<sup>3</sup>MacKendrick, pp. 190–95.

If your paper cites more than one work by the same author, the later references should include a short title:

<sup>3</sup>MacKendrick, <u>Greek Stones Speak</u>, pp. 190–95.

As has been mentioned, later references can take the form of either short notes or parenthetical reminders within the text. In most of the examples in this section, we show the later references as short notes. To convert them to the parenthetical form, you omit the reference number at the beginning and the period at the end, substituting opening and closing parentheses:

(MacKendrick, pp. 190–95)

(MacKendrick, <u>Greek Stones Speak</u>, pp. 190–95)

**2.** A book with two or three authors

FIRST REFERENCE

<sup>4</sup>Milton Meltzer and Walter Harding, <u>A</u> <u>Thoreau Profile</u> (New York: Crowell, 1962), p. 150.

Give the names of the authors in the order in which they appear on the title page.

LATER REFERENCES

<sup>5</sup>Meltzer and Harding, p. 55.

**3.** A book with more than three authors

FIRST REFERENCE

<sup>6</sup>F. S. Scott et al., <u>English Grammar</u> (London: Heinemann, 1968), p. 22.

The abbreviation *et al.* stands for *et alii*, which means "and others." You may use it instead of writing out the names of all the other authors.

LATER REFERENCES

<sup>7</sup>Scott et al., pp. 115–20.

**4.** A book with a corporate author

FIRST REFERENCE

    8United States Capitol Society, <u>We, the
People</u> (Washington, D.C.: National Geographic
Society, 1964), p. 8.

LATER REFERENCES

    9U.S. Capitol Society, pp. 33–40.

Use these forms if the identity of the author is relevant to the discussion in your paper. Otherwise, put the title first in the first reference, and use the title alone in the later references:

FIRST REFERENCE

    8<u>We, the People</u>, by the United States Capitol Society (Washington, D.C.: National Geographic Society, 1964), p. 8.

You need *by* when the author's name follows the title.

LATER REFERENCES

    9<u>We, the People</u>, pp. 33–40.

### 5. A work in more than one volume

FIRST REFERENCE

    10Robert Graves, <u>The Greek Myths</u>
(Baltimore, Md.: Penguin, 1955), II, 250–55.

The roman numeral designates the volume number; in this format, with the volume number specified, you omit *pp.* before the page numbers.

LATER REFERENCES

    11Graves, I, 140.

### 6. A work with an editor

FIRST REFERENCE

    12Theodore Dreiser, <u>Sister Carrie</u>, ed. Kenneth S. Lynn (New York: Rinehart, 1959), p. 41.

LATER REFERENCES

    13Dreiser, p. 90.

If you refer in the text to the editor's preface or introduction, the editor's name goes first in the note:

FIRST REFERENCE

> [12]Kenneth S. Lynn, ed., <u>Sister Carrie</u>, by Theodore Dreiser (New York: Rinehart, 1959), p. ix.

LATER REFERENCES

> [13]Lynn, p. ix.

**7.** A work in a book with other selections by the same author

FIRST REFERENCE

> [14]Lewis Thomas, "The Long Habit," in <u>The Lives of a Cell: Notes of a Biology Watcher</u> (New York: Viking, 1974), p. 48.

First comes the title of the chapter, essay, or story, then the title of the book in which it appears.

LATER REFERENCES

> [15]Thomas, p. 51.

If your paper cites more than one of the selections in a book, you must mention the selection title each time, either in your text or in the note:

> [15]Thomas, "The Long Habit," p. 50.

**8.** A work in a book with selections by various authors

FIRST REFERENCE

> [16]George E. Dimock, Jr., "The Name of Odysseus," in <u>Essays on the Odyssey</u>, ed. Charles H. Taylor (Bloomington: Indiana University Press, 1963), pp. 56–57.

LATER REFERENCES

> [17]Dimock, p. 60.

**9.** A second or later edition

FIRST REFERENCE

18Robert E. Ornstein, <u>The Psychology of</u>
<u>Consciousness</u>, 2nd ed. (New York: Harcourt,
1977), pp. 82–86.

The abbreviation *2nd ed.* means "second edition."

LATER REFERENCES

19Ornstein, p. 90.

### 10. A modern reprint

FIRST REFERENCE

20Jessie L. Weston, <u>From Ritual to Romance</u>
(London, 1920; rpt. Garden City, N.Y.: Anchor-
Doubleday, 1957), pp. 65–80.

The abbreviation *rpt.* means "reprinted."

LATER REFERENCES

21Weston, p. 58.

### 11. A play without numbered lines

FIRST REFERENCE

22Tennessee Williams, <u>A Streetcar Named</u>
<u>Desire</u> (New York: New Directions, 1947), p. 35.

LATER REFERENCES

23Williams, p. 59.

### 12. A play with numbered lines

FIRST REFERENCE

24William Shakespeare, <u>Romeo and Juliet</u>,
ed. John E. Hankins (Baltimore, Md.: Penguin,
1960), I.i.79–83.

If the text of a play is given in acts, scenes, and numbered lines,
you cite these instead of page numbers, using upper-case roman
numerals for the act, lower-case roman numerals for the scene,
and arabic numerals for the lines. If the play has been edited, you
must of course mention the editor in the first reference.

LATER REFERENCES

25<u>Romeo and Juliet</u>, III.ii.65–66.

If the play has act, scene, and line numbers, later references to it give the title, not the author.

**13.** A long poem with numbered lines

FIRST REFERENCE

²⁶John Milton, <u>Paradise Lost</u>, ed. Scott Elledge (New York: Norton, 1975), I.1–3.

If a work is divided into "books" or cantos and has numbered lines, you cite these instead of page numbers, using upper-case roman numerals for the book or canto and arabic numerals for the lines.

LATER REFERENCES

²⁷<u>Paradise Lost</u> IV.797–800.

**14.** A translation

FIRST REFERENCE

²⁸Sigmund Freud, <u>Totem and Taboo</u>, trans. James Strachey (New York: Norton, 1950), p. 119.

LATER REFERENCES

²⁹Freud, p. 38.

Like the name of an editor, the name of a translator follows the title of the work. But if you want to cite the translator's introduction, you begin with his or her name, and put the author's name after the title:

FIRST REFERENCE

²⁸James Strachey, trans., <u>Totem and Taboo</u>, by Sigmund Freud (New York: Norton, 1950), p. vii.

LATER REFERENCES

²⁹Strachey, p. vii.

**15.** An article in an encyclopedia

FIRST REFERENCE

³⁰Athelstan Spilhaus and Jane J. Stein, "Pollution Control," <u>Encyclopaedia Britannica: Macropaedia</u>, 1974 ed.

        31Spilhaus and Stein.

The first reference starts with the author's name, if known. In the reference work cited in this example, the authors of each article are identified by their initials at the end of the article, and their names are listed in a guide to the work. In citing any well-known reference work, you need not give any details about publication except for the edition number, if any, and the year. The editions of some reference works are now identified by the year of publication. If you cite a reference work that lists entries alphabetically, you can skip the volume and page numbers, provided you refer to all of an article. But if you are citing a particular page of a multi-page article, you do have to give volume and page numbers:

FIRST REFERENCE

        32Edward S. Kilma, "Phonetics," Funk &
Wagnalls New Encyclopedia, 1973, 19, 59.

The volume number comes first, then the page number; this note refers to volume 19, p. 59.

LATER REFERENCES

        33Kilma, 19, 60.

If an article is unsigned, begin the note with the title:

FIRST REFERENCE

        34"Pollution," The Columbia Encyclopedia,
1963 ed.

LATER REFERENCES

        35"Pollution."

## 16. A publication that is part of a series

FIRST REFERENCE

        36Alan S. Downer, Recent American Drama,
University of Minnesota Pamphlets on American
Writers, No. 7 (Minneapolis: University of Minne-
sota Press, 1961), pp. 8–10.

LATER REFERENCES

        37Downer, p. 45.

**17.** An article in a journal or magazine with continuous pagination

FIRST REFERENCE

> ³⁸Max Delbrück, "Mind from Matter?" <u>The
> American Scholar</u>, 47 (1978), 340–43.

Use this form when the pagination is continuous throughout a volume—that is, when the numbering of an issue begins where that of the preceding one leaves off. The sequence of the items is author, title of article, name of journal, then volume number (in arabic numerals), year of issue (within parentheses), and page numbers. The abbreviation *pp.* is not used when the volume number is cited.

LATER REFERENCES

> ³⁹Delbrück, p. 344.

Here *p.* is used because the entry does not include the volume number.

**18.** An article in a periodical without continuous pagination

FIRST REFERENCE

> ⁴⁰Bill Nichols, "Style, Grammar, and the
> Movies," <u>Film Quarterly</u>, 28 (Spring 1975), 33.

Use this form when the pagination in each issue starts over from p. 1. Include within the parentheses not only the year but also the season, month, or date of issue.

LATER REFERENCES

> ⁴¹Nichols, p. 34.

For periodicals that do not have volume numbers, the date goes between commas instead of parentheses, and the abbreviation *p.* or *pp.* is used:

FIRST REFERENCE

> ⁴²Jane Stein, "The Bioethicists: Facing
> Matters of Life and Death," <u>Smithsonian</u>, Jan.
> 1979, p. 112.

LATER REFERENCES

> ⁴³Stein, p. 113.

FIRST REFERENCE

44"The Vietnam War: The Executioner,"
Newsweek, 13 Nov. 1978, p. 70.

Since the article is unsigned, the entry begins with the title. Note how the date is written.

LATER REFERENCES

45"The Vietnam War: The Executioner," p.
71.

## 19. An article in a newspaper

FIRST REFERENCE

46Richard L. Strout, "Another Bicentennial,"
Christian Science Monitor, 10 Nov. 1978, p. 27,
col. 1.

The abbreviation *col.* identifies the column on p. 27 in which the article is found.

LATER REFERENCES

47Strout.

Let the reader know when your source in a newspaper is an editorial rather than a news report:

FIRST REFERENCE

48"How to End Watergate," Editorial, New
York Times, City Ed., 10 Jan. 1979, Sec. A, p.
22, cols. 1-2.

The edition is specified because the content of different editions can vary, and the section is named because the pagination in each section starts over from p. 1. The sequence of the items is section, page, columns.

LATER REFERENCES

49"How to End Watergate."

## 20. A personal letter to the researcher

FIRST REFERENCE

50Letter to the author from George Savvides, 10 Jan. 1979.

LATER REFERENCES

⁵¹Savvides.

## 21. The Bible

FIRST AND LATER REFERENCES

In Genesis, the very first book of the Bible, we are told that Jacob went to sleep and dreamed of a ladder reaching up to heaven with angels climbing up and down it and the voice of God above it saying, "I am the Lord God of Abraham thy father, and the God of Isaac: the land whereon thou liest, to thee will I give it, and to thy seed" (Genesis 28.12–13). Jacob's dream clearly origi-

Regardless of the method used for other citations, a reference to the Bible is normally placed in parentheses in the text immediately following the quotation. Passages in the Bible are normally cited by book, chapter, and verse; no other documentation is needed.

EXERCISE 3  Writing Notes

Take the information given in each of the following and use it to write two notes—one for a first full reference and one for a later short reference. For the first reference, use the number of the problem as your note number. Write the second reference in either the note style or the parenthetical style—whichever your teacher prefers. If you use the note style, assign each of the later references its own number, starting with 11.

EXAMPLE

1. The source is a book by Edwin Way Teale entitled *The Strange Lives of Familiar Insects*. It was published in 1962 by Dodd, Mead & Company; the place of publication is listed as New York. Your first reference is to page 121; your second is to page 57.

FIRST REFERENCE

¹Edwin Way Teale, The Strange Lives of Familiar Insects (New York: Dodd, Mead, 1962), p. 121.

LATER REFERENCE, NOTE STYLE

¹¹Teale, p. 57.

LATER REFERENCE, PARENTHETICAL STYLE

(Teale, p. 57).

1. The source is a book by Bernard Gert. On the spine of the book the title is *The Moral Rules;* on the title page the title is *The Moral Rules: A New Rational Foundation for Morality.* The book was published in 1970 by Harper & Row of New York. Your first reference is to pages 32 through 36; your second is to page 73.

2. The source is a paperback edition of a book by Alfred Kazin entitled *A Walker in the City.* The book was originally published in 1951 by Harcourt, Brace & Company of New York. The modern paperback reprint was published by Grove Press of New York in 1958. Your first reference is to pages 52 through 55; your second is to pages 92 through 94.

3. The source is an essay entitled "Achieving Womanhood." It is included in a book by two authors, William H. Grier and Price M. Cobbs. Entitled *Black Rage,* the book was published by Basic Books of New York in 1968. Your first reference is to page 42 of the essay, which appears on pages 39 through 54; your second is to page 52 of the essay.

4. The source is F. N. Robinson, the editor of a book entitled *The Works of Geoffrey Chaucer.* Your copy is a second edition, published by Houghton Mifflin Company of Boston in 1957. Your first reference is to the editor's introduction, page xxv; your second is to page xii of that introduction.

5. The source is a passage in a book by Albert Camus. The book was translated from the French by Justin O'Brien, who called it *The Fall.* The publisher of the translation is Alfred A. Knopf of New York; the date, 1957. Your first reference is to pages 50 through 55; your second is to page 98.

6. The source is a pamphlet entitled *Health Effects of Air Pollutants.* Written by a corporate author, the United States Environmental Protection Agency, it was published in Washington, D.C., in 1976 by the Government Printing Office. Your first reference is to page 5; your second is to page 3. (Pamphlets are cited the same way as books are.)

7. The source is an article by Daniel Hoffman entitled "Edwin Muir: The Story and the Fable." The article appeared in the spring 1966 issue of volume 55 of the *Yale Review,* a journal. Your first reference is to pages 416 through 418 of the article, which is found on pages 403 through 426; your second is to page 425. The pagination in the volume is continuous.

8. The source is an article appearing on pages 27 and 28 of the January 8, 1979, issue of *Newsweek* magazine. The article, "Inside Cambodia," was written by Elizabeth Becker. Your first reference is to the entire article; your second is to page 28.

9. The source is a newspaper article entitled "Bakhtiar Maneuvers for Room," by Geoffrey Godsell. The article appeared in columns 1 and 2 on page 6 of the January 12, 1979, issue of the *Christian Science Monitor.* Your first reference is to the entire article, and so is your second.

10. The source is an unsigned article entitled "Hippocrates." It appears on page 953 of the 1963 edition of *The Columbia Ency-*

*clopedia.* Your first reference is to the entire article, and so is your second.

## 27.6 Writing the Bibliography for a Paper with Notes *bib*

The bibliography for a paper with notes is a list of all the sources you have used in writing the paper. Ordinarily, it should not include any works that are not cited in your notes, since every source you use should be cited in them. Arrange the entries alphabetically according to the authors' last names. Where you include several works by one author, list these alphabetically by title. Instead of repeating the author's name, use an eight-space line followed by a period, as shown on p. 497.

The bibliography goes at the end of your paper. It should be typed as shown in the sample.

*Sample bibliography*

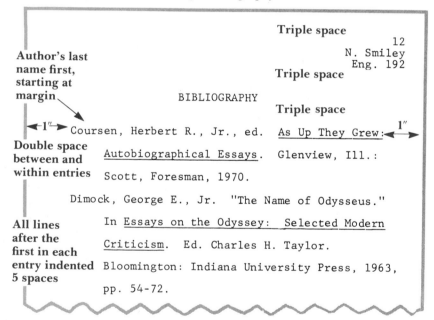

Here are the ways of citing various sources in a bibliography.

**1.** A book with one author

> MacKendrick, Paul. <u>The Greek Stones Speak: The</u>
> <u>Story of Archaeology in Greek Lands</u>. New
> York: St. Martin's Press, 1962.

The author's name is inverted and followed by a period. The title, given in full, is also followed by a period. Then the place of publication, publisher, and date of publication are given without parentheses.

**2.** A book with two or three authors

> Meltzer, Milton, and Walter Harding. A Thoreau
> Profile. New York: Crowell, 1962.

Only the first author's name is inverted.

**3.** A book with more than three authors

> Scott, F. S., et al. English Grammar: A
> Linguistic Study of Its Classes and
> Structures. London: Heinemann, 1968.

**4.** A book with a corporate author

BEGINNING WITH AUTHOR

> 'Inited States Capitol Society. We, the People:
> The Story of the United States Capitol.
> Washington, D.C.: National Geographic Soci-
> ety, 1964.

BEGINNING WITH TITLE

> We, the People: The Story of the United States
> Capitol. By the United States Capitol Soci-
> ety. Washington, D.C.: National Geographic
> Society, 1964.

**5.** A work in more than one volume

> Graves, Robert. The Greek Myths. 2 vols. Balti-
> more, Md.: Penguin, 1955.

Use this form when the material in your paper comes from both volumes of the work. If the material in your paper comes from only one volume, list the volume number at the end of the entry:

> Graves, Robert. The Greek Myths. Baltimore, Md.:
> Penguin, 1955. Vol. II.

**6.** A work with an editor

> Dreiser, Theodore. <u>Sister Carrie</u>. Ed. Kenneth S.
> Lynn. New York: Rinehart, 1959.

The editor's name goes first when his or her contribution (an introduction, for example) has been used as a source in the paper:

> Lynn, Kenneth S., ed. <u>Sister Carrie</u>. By Theodore
> Dreiser. New York: Rinehart, 1959.

**7.** A work in a book with other selections by the same author

> Thomas, Lewis. "The Long Habit." In <u>The Lives of
> a Cell: Notes of a Biology Watcher</u>. New
> York: Viking, 1974, pp. 47–52.

**8.** A work in a book with selections by various authors

> Dimock, George E., Jr. "The Name of Odysseus." In
> <u>Essays on the Odyssey: Selected Modern
> Criticism</u>. Ed. Charles H. Taylor. Blooming-
> ton: Indiana University Press, 1963, pp. 54–
> 72.

**9.** A second or later edition

> Ornstein, Robert E. <u>The Psychology of Con-
> sciousness</u>. 2nd ed. New York: Harcourt,
> 1977.

**10.** A modern reprint

> Weston, Jessie L. <u>From Ritual to Romance</u>. London,
> 1920; rpt. Garden City, N.Y.: Anchor-
> Doubleday, 1957.

**11.** A play without numbered lines

> Williams, Tennessee. <u>A Streetcar Named Desire</u>.
> New York: New Directions, 1947.

**12.** A play with numbered lines

> Shakespeare, William. <u>Romeo and Juliet</u>. Ed. John
> E. Hankins. Baltimore, Md.: Penguin, 1960.

**13.** A long poem with numbered lines

Milton, John. <u>Paradise Lost</u>. Ed. Scott Elledge.
New York: Norton, 1975.

**14.** A translation

Freud, Sigmund. <u>Totem and Taboo</u>. Trans. James
Strachey. New York: Norton, 1950.

The translator's name goes first when his or her contribution (an introduction, for example) has been used as a source in the paper:

Strachey, James, trans. <u>Totem and Taboo</u>. By Sigmund Freud. New York: Norton, 1950.

**15.** An article in an encyclopedia

Spilhaus, Athelstan, and Jane J. Stein. "Pollu-
tion Control." <u>Encyclopaedia Britannica:
Macropaedia</u>. 1974 ed.
Kilma, Edward S. "Phonetics." <u>Funk & Wagnalls
New Encyclopedia</u>. 1973.

Use this form when the authors are identified and the entries are listed alphabetically. As noted on p. 471, the editions of some reference works are now identified by the year of publication. If the author is not named and the entries are listed alphabetically, begin with the title of the article:

"Pollution." <u>The Columbia Encyclopedia</u>. 1963 ed.

**16.** A publication that is part of a series

Downer, Alan S. <u>Recent American Drama</u>. University
of Minnesota Pamphlets on American Writers,
No. 7. Minneapolis: University of Minnesota
Press, 1961.

**17.** An article in a journal or magazine with continuous pagination

Delbrück, Max. "Mind from Matter?" <u>The American
Scholar</u>, 47 (1978), 339-53.

As in the corresponding note, the abbreviation *pp.* is not used when the volume number is cited.

**18.** An article in a periodical without continuous pagination

> Nichols, Bill. "Style, Grammar, and the Movies."
> Film Quarterly, 28 (Spring 1975), 33–49.
>
> Stein, Jane. "The Bioethicists: Facing Matters of
> Life and Death." Smithsonian, Jan. 1979, pp.
> 107–15.
>
> "The Vietnam War: The Executioner." Newsweek, 13
> Nov. 1978, p. 70.

As in the corresponding note, when the pagination in each issue starts over from p. 1, you must include the season, month, or date of the issue as well as the year.

**19.** An article in a newspaper

> Strout, Richard L. "Another Bicentennial."
> Christian Science Monitor, 10 Nov. 1978, p.
> 27, col. 1.
>
> "How to End Watergate." Editorial. New York
> Times, City Ed., 10 Jan. 1979, Sec. A, p.
> 22, cols. 1–2.

**20.** A personal letter to the researcher

> Savvides, George. Letter to author. 10 Jan. 1979.

**EXERCISE 4   Writing a Bibliography**

Write a bibliography that includes all of the sources described in exercise 3, pp. 474–76, including the example. Be sure each source is given in correct bibliographical form, and arrange the entries in alphabetical order.

## 27.7   Citing with Parentheses in the Text   *cit/p*

When you are asked to use parentheses for all of your references, the form of each citation will depend on whether you have mentioned the author in your text.

   If you use a source without mentioning the author, your parenthetical reference will include the author's surname, the date of publication, and the relevant page or pages of the source. You can put this reference in one of two places. You can put it just before the material you are documenting:

```
Recent research (Foulkes, 1978, p. 78) has led to
the conclusion that young children's dreams are
in general "rather simple and unemotional."
```

Or you can put it just after the material you are documenting:

```
Recent research has led to the conclusion that
young children's dreams are in general "rather
simple and unemotional" (Foulkes, 1978, p. 78).
```

When the parenthetical reference follows a quotation that is part of your text, put it between the closing quotation mark and the period.

The use of a date in the reference allows you to cite two or more works by the same author without getting them confused:

```
Since some of these desires would offend us even
in sleep, the imagery of our dreams symbolizes
the fulfillment of them in disguised form
(Foulkes, 1966, pp. 182-84).
```

The date, 1966, distinguishes this source from the one hitherto cited, which was published in 1978.

If you have mentioned the author in your text, the date of the source must be shown in parentheses right after the name. But you can put the page number in one of two places. You can put it alongside the date:

```
But after five years of study, David Foulkes
(1978, p. 78) has found that young children's
dreams are in general "rather simple and unemo-
tional."
```

Or you can put it in parentheses after the material you are documenting:

```
But after five years of study, David Foulkes
(1978) has found that young children's dreams are
in general "rather simple and unemotional" (p.
78).
```

When the reference covers more than a single quotation, put the page numbers after the material you are documenting:

References

Cartwright, R. Problem solving: Waking and sleeping. Journal
   of Abnormal Psychology, 1974, 83, 451-455.

Cartwright, R. Happy endings for our dreams. Psychology Today,
   December 1978, pp. 66-76.

Dement, W. C. Some must watch while some must sleep. San
   Francisco: San Francisco Book Co., 1976.

Dodds, E. R. The Greeks and the irrational. Boston: Beacon,
   1957. (Originally published, 1951.)

Erikson, E. H. Insight and responsibility: Lectures on the ethical implications of psychoanalytic insight. New York:
   Norton, 1964.

Foulkes, D. The psychology of sleep. New York: Scribner, 1966.

Foulkes, D. Dreams of innocence. Psychology Today, December
   1978, pp. 78-88.

Freud, S. [The interpretation of dreams] (J. Strachey, Trans.).
   New York: Basic, 1972.

Fromm, E. The forgotten language: An introduction to the understanding of dreams, fairy tales, and myths. New York:
   Rinehart, 1951.

Hall, C. S., & Nordby, V. J. The individual and his dreams.
   New York: New American Library, 1972.

Jones, R. M. The new psychology of dreaming. New York: Grune
   and Stratton, 1970.

Jung, C. G. Approaching the unconscious. In C. G. Jung &
   M.-L. von Franz (Eds.), Man and his symbols. Garden City,
   N.Y.: Doubleday, 1964.

McCarley, R. W. Where dreams come from: A new theory. Psychology Today, December 1978, pp. 54-65; 141.

But after five years of study, David Foulkes
(1978) has found that young children's dreams are
in general "rather simple and unemotional," that
the complexity of children's dreams grows as the
child does, and therefore that the content of a
dream is closely linked to the development of the
dreamer in the waking world (pp. 78, 86–88).

When the page reference follows a quotation that is set off from
your text, put it after the period:

locates their origin outside experience. Carl G.
Jung (1964) writes:

One cannot afford to be naive in dealing
with dreams. They originate in a spirit that
is not quite human, but is rather a breath
of nature. . . . If we want to characterize
this spirit, we shall certainly get closer
to it in the sphere of ancient mythologies,
or the fables of the primeval forest, than
in the consciousness of modern man. (p. 52)

## 27.8  Writing the Reference List for a Paper with Parenthetical Citations  *list*

When you use parenthetical citations for all of your references, you
must give a reference list at the end of your paper—a list that
includes all the sources you have cited, but nothing else. Since the
formats for the several sciences vary in certain details, you should
ask your teacher which one you are expected to use. The reference
list opposite, for the sources cited in the sample research paper on
dreams (pp. 484–98), is based on the format required for papers
submitted to journals of the American Psychological Association.
You will note that this format differs in several respects from that
of the bibliography at the end of the research paper.

## 27.9  Sample Research Paper

The sample paper that follows has numbered notes for the first
references to sources. This format may be used in papers dealing
with a variety of subjects, but if you are writing on a scientific subject, your teacher may expect you to give all of your citations in
parentheses, as discussed in sections 27.7–27.8, pp. 480–83.

Dreams and Waking Life

Anthony Walsh

Professor Hoyt Shepherdson

Philosophy 163

May 4, 1980

Dreams and Waking Life

Dreams are universal. Though we sometimes forget our
dreams, each of us has at least one dream virtually every time
we sleep, and without much difficulty, each of us could probably remember a dream in some detail. Over literally thousands
of years, dreams have been treated by poets and studied by psychologists. Yet certain basic questions about dreams remain to
be settled: Where do they come from? What do they mean? Do
they serve any purpose? This paper will consider how those
questions have been answered by a variety of psychologists and
experimenters. By analyzing their statements on the origin,
meaning, and function of dreams, it will attempt to explain the
relation between dreams and waking life.

I

In ancient times, dreams were thought to come from God or
some mysterious source outside the dreamer. In modern times,
the search for their origin has focused much more on the mind
and natural experience of the dreamer than on anything super-
natural. Erich Fromm, for instance, says that nearly every
dream we have is prompted by our reaction to some occurrence of
the preceding day.[1] I suspect that each of us has had such
dreams. I myself have dreamed about driving a car across the
ocean soon after a day at the beach, and about getting

swallowed up by a lion after a visit to the zoo. But not every dream can be readily traced to an experience of the previous day, and even if it could, the memory of an experience cannot explain why and how a dream transformed it, why and how a day at the beach becomes a drive across the ocean. The gap between dreams and remembered experience is sometimes so wide, in fact, that at least one modern psychologist locates their origin in something outside of experience. Carl G. Jung writes:

> One cannot afford to be naive in dealing with dreams.
> They originate in a spirit that is not quite human, but
> is rather a breath of nature. . . . If we want to char-
> acterize this spirit, we shall certainly get closer to
> it in the sphere of ancient mythologies, or the fables
> of the primeval forest, than in the consciousness of
> modern man.[2]

Fromm and Jung represent two poles of thought in modern theorizing about the origin of dreams. While Fromm traces the dream to a specific occurrence, Jung seeks its origin in some-thing mystical, something "not quite human," something outside the dreamer's personal experience. But recent research on dreams--especially children's dreams--indicates that any search for their origin must at the very least begin with that experi-ence. If dreams come from outside the dreamer's experience, children's dreams should be as Jung describes them: rich, com-plex, and full of strange, frightening archetypes (Jung, pp. 69-75). But after five years of study, David Foulkes has found that young children's dreams are in general "rather simple and unemotional," that the complexity of children's dreams grows as the child does, and therefore that the content of a dream is closely linked to the development of the dreamer in the waking world.[3] Clearly, then, the dreamer's waking experience must provide at least part of the answer to the question of where dreams originate.

Yet the whole answer involves much more than the experience of the day which precedes the dream. For one thing, the memories reworked in a dream may come from any part of the dreamer's life. Citing evidence gathered by Rechtschaffen, William C. Dement says that dreams move backward in time as the night progresses, that they gradually turn from the contemporary world to childhood and "stored images."[4] Furthermore, dreams come not just from particular memories but from the whole personality of the dreamer. After analyzing thousands of dreams into their constituent elements, Calvin S. Hall and Vernon J. Nordby concluded that the dreams of individuals are "amazingly consistent in subject matter from one year to the next," that dreams originate from habitual ways of feeling and thinking, from "the wishes and fears that determine our actions and thoughts in everyday life."[5] Hall and Nordby thus emphasize the continuity between dreams and waking life. Yet even though they trace dreams to the personality of the dreamer, they also say that the source of a dream may lie far beneath the surface. The "wishes and fears" behind our dreams, they say, may have their roots not only in childhood but in "prenatal experiences and racial history" (Hall and Nordby, p. 146).

II

These contemporary findings about the deep-rooted origin
of dreams take us back to the single most important modern study
of their meaning--Sigmund Freud's Interpretation of Dreams,
first published in 1900.  Freud explains dreams as the expression of certain drives within the dreamer, and he specifically
states that "a dream is the fulfillment of a wish."[6]  A brief
paper such as this one can hardly do justice to Freud's theories,
but they may be summarized as follows:  Dreams gratify desires
that we repress in waking life, usually because of taboos
against them.  Since some of these desires would offend us even
in sleep, the imagery of our dreams symbolizes the fulfillment
of them in disguised form.[7]

Freud's theories about the meaning of dreams have been
widely influential.  According to Foulkes, modern dream researchers now accept the principle that dreams express "profound
aspects of personality" (Foulkes, Sleep, p. 184).  But the idea
that a dream is the disguised fulfillment of a wish has been
challenged by a number of writers in different ways.  Citing
dreams in which the wish to be free or to be alive is threatened, Fromm contends that such dreams express "not the fulfillment of the wish but the fear of its frustration" (Fromm,
pp. 185-88).  Other researchers have argued that dreams are
physiological as much as psychological.  According to Foulkes,
dreams vary as the sleeper moves from a state of rapid eye movement (REM), when the eyes move rapidly under the eyelids, to a
state of deep sleep (non-REM), in which the eyes do not move

5
A. Walsh
Phil. 163

(Foulkes, Sleep, pp. 1-40). The meaning of a dream may therefore depend on the state in which it occurs. Noting, for
instance, that nightmares occur primarily during non-REM sleep,
Foulkes speculates that a nightmare may be "a kind of unconscious 'panic' response to the slowing of life functions . . .
that occurs during the profound non-REM state" (Foulkes,
"Dreams," p. 88).

Yet the very fact that Foulkes is speculating here illustrates the difficulty of explaining dreams by means of the body
alone. If we cannot always interpret dreams as the fulfillment
of wishes, neither can we interpret them as simply the products
of physical stimulation. For all the research that has been
done on the physiology of dreaming, for all the monitoring of
dreamers' brain waves, eye movements, heartbeats, and breathing
patterns, researchers cannot fully explain dreams without some
reference to the dreamer's personality. Robert W. McCarley,
for instance, says that dreams originate from the activity of
the sensory system--especially the eyes--during REM sleep, and
that this activity sends messages to the higher levels of the
brain, where the messages are "synthesized . . . into a coherent story."[8] But to explain the story, McCarley has to move
beyond physiology. Contributions to "the ultimate synthesis,"
he says, may include the "motivational state, memories, drives,
and personality of the dreamer."[9]

To know what a dream means, then, we have to know something about the personality of the dreamer--which is to say,
something about the dreamer's waking life. In fact, as Dement

27.9

6
A. Walsh
Phil. 163

notes, one of the difficulties of understanding anyone else's
dream is that we can learn of it only after the dreamer has
waked up and reported on what he or she remembers of it (Dement,
pp. 59-65). Some knowledge of the dreamer's waking life is
therefore essential to any understanding of a dream, and no single formula will explain all dreams. To interpret the content
of a dream, says Fromm, we must know the dreamer, his or her
emotional state at the moment of going to sleep, and the elements in the dream that correspond with reality as he or she
ordinarily sees it (Fromm, pp. 36-38).

III

If the meaning of a dream depends on the personality of
the individual dreamer, then dreams must be individually interpreted, and any generalization about the meaning of all dreams
is suspect. We cannot say that every dream is a prophecy, or
a reincarnation of ancient myth, or--as Freud says--the fulfillment of a wish. But the problem of saying anything universal about the meaning of dreams should not keep us from asking
questions about their function, about what they contribute to
our lives. And the question I wish to raise now is simply
this: to what extent do dreams help us cope with the world we
live in when we are awake?

One answer is that dreams restore our psychological balance by putting us in touch with our instincts. According to
Jung, the world around us threatens our individuality by tend-
ing to make us lead "a more or less artificial life" (Jung,

**490   Writing the Research Paper**

7
A. Walsh
Phil. 163

p. 49). Dreams give us an alternative to this life: a world
of vivid, seemingly ridiculous images, of disrupted time, and
of commonplace things with a "fascinating or threatening aspect"
(Jung, p. 39). These strange images, says Jung, are "the essential message carriers from the instinctive to the rational
parts of the human mind, and their interpretation enriches the
poverty of consciousness so that it learns to understand once
again the forgotten language of the instincts" (Jung, p. 52).
For this reason some dreams may tell us of important coming
events. By putting us in touch with our instincts, they show
us a pattern in our actions which our conscious mind misses and
thus they indicate where our actions may be leading (Jung, p. 51).

Jung's account of what dreams do for us is suggestive but
vague, for it seems to presuppose that we know how to interpret
our dreams, how to understand the messages and predictions they
bring us from the unconscious. But without mysterious messages,
some dreams can help the dreamer solve a particular problem.
Fromm cites the example of Friedrich Kekule, who had been seeking the chemical formula for benzine and discovered it one
night in a dream (Fromm, p. 45). Dement cites other examples:
a dream led Hermann Hilprecht to the translation of the Stone
of Nebuchadnezzar, and Otto Loewi's dream of an experiment with
a frog heart led to research rewarded with a Nobel Prize
(Dement, p. 98). Dreams of this kind serve a clear and definite purpose. Unlike the mysterious messages that Jung speaks

of, they provide the dreamer with a specific solution to a specific problem.

Yet very few dreams serve so specific a purpose. Instead of solving particular problems, dreams more often leave the dreamer with a general sense of liberation and power. Dreams, says E. R. Dodds, allow us to "escape the offensive and incomprehensible bondage of time and space."[10] Such an escape invigorates the dreamer. Erik H. Erikson writes that in dreams, a mass of unfulfilled infantile wishes and present dangers can turn into something manageable. Instead of feeling helpless before the evidence of weakness and limitation, the dreamer's ego experiences a sense of power, an ability to produce and progress.[11] Likewise, Rosalind Cartwright says that dreaming "seems to provide the energy space for working out problems set aside through days filled with busy activity; and in general, it offers a kind of workshop for the repair of self-esteem and competence."[12]

Even dreams we regard as "bad" may help us to come to terms with threatening situations in the outside world. In a study cited by Cartwright, subjects who had dreamed after viewing a stress-producing film showed less strain on a second viewing than subjects who had not. According to Cartwright, such a study suggests that "dreaming helps to 'defuse' anxiety-provoking material so that it can be experienced in the waking state with less disruptive effect. This might be expected to lead to more rational and perhaps efficient handling of previously upsetting experiences."[13] Cartwright's conclusion is

9
A. Walsh
Phil. 163

tentative and limited. She does not say that all bad dreams have good effects, or that frightening dreams will necessarily prepare us to face frightening experiences. She merely opens our eyes to one of the ways in which dreams _may_ help us to cope with the waking world.

What then is the overall relation between dreams and waking life? I believe that each is needed to help us understand the other. We cannot adequately explain dreams by saying that they come from God or some mysterious source beyond the dreamer --such as Jung's "breath of nature." But neither can we explain them by saying simply that they come from the body, like the dreamer's heartbeat and rapid eye movements. Researchers can measure those things while the dreamer sleeps, but the only way they can get to the dream itself is to wake the dreamer up, and in order to understand the dream, they must know something about the dreamer's waking life and waking mind. I do not think anyone can make sense out of a dream without some reference to the waking, walking, observable personality of the dreamer.

Yet just as we need our lives to interpret our dreams, we need dreams to make sense out of our lives. Though dreams seem to turn things topsy-turvy, they tell us things about ourselves that we may be able to learn in no other way. They may remind us of things long forgotten; they may expose us to things we repress; above all, they may reveal to us the naturally creative powers of our own minds. Perhaps, after all, that is the

most important thing dreams do for us.  More than fulfilling
our wishes, predicting the future, or solving a specific problem, dreams show us what the mind can do with all that we
experience in the waking world.

NOTES

[1] The Forgotten Language (New York: Rinehart, 1951), pp. 156-57. This book is cited hereafter as Fromm.

[2] "Approaching the Unconscious," in Man and His Symbols, ed. Carl G. Jung and M.-L. von Franz (Garden City, N.Y.: Doubleday, 1964), p. 52. This essay is cited hereafter as Jung.

[3] "Dreams of Innocence," Psychology Today, 12 (December 1978), 78, 86-88. This article is cited hereafter as Foulkes, "Dreams."

[4] Some Must Watch While Some Must Sleep (San Francisco: San Francisco Book Co., 1976), p. 71. This book is cited hereafter as Dement.

[5] The Individual and His Dreams (New York: New American Library, 1972), pp. 82, 94, 102. This book is cited hereafter as Hall and Nordby.

[6] The Interpretation of Dreams, trans. James Strachey (New York: Basic, 1972), p. 154.

[7] I am here paraphrasing an account of Freud's theories given in David Foulkes, The Psychology of Sleep (New York: Scribner, 1966), pp. 182-84. This book is cited hereafter as Foulkes, Sleep.

[8] "Where Dreams Come From: A New Theory," Psychology Today, 12 (December 1978), 54-62. This article is cited hereafter as McCarley.

[9] McCarley, p. 54. Likewise, Richard M. Jones says that the cause of dreaming is not psychological but physiological-- the activity of REM sleep; yet what REM sleep activates, he

says, are wish-fulfilling dreams, and these cannot be understood without reference to the dreamer's mental life. See The
New Psychology of Dreaming (New York: Grune and Stratton, 1970),
pp. 120-21.

[10] The Greeks and the Irrational (Berkeley, 1951; rpt.
Boston: Beacon, 1957), p. 102.

[11] Insight and Responsibility: Lectures on the Ethical
Implications of Psychoanalytic Insight (New York: Norton, 1964),
pp. 185-201.

[12] "Happy Endings for Our Dreams," Psychology Today, 12
(December 1978), 76.

[13] "Problem Solving: Waking and Sleeping," Journal of
Abnormal Psychology, 83 (1974), 451.

13
A. Walsh
Phil. 163

BIBLIOGRAPHY

Cartwright, Rosalind. "Happy Endings for Our Dreams." Psychol-
    ogy Today, 12 (December 1978), 66-76.

_____. "Problem Solving: Waking and Sleeping." Journal of
    Abnormal Psychology, 83 (1974), 451-55.

Dement, William C. Some Must Watch While Some Must Sleep. San
    Francisco: San Francisco Book Co., 1976.

Dodds, E. R. The Greeks and the Irrational. Berkeley, 1951;
    rpt. Boston: Beacon, 1957.

Erikson, Erik H. Insight and Responsibility: Lectures on the
    Ethical Implications of Psychoanalytic Insight. New York:
    Norton, 1964.

Foulkes, David. "Dreams of Innocence." Psychology Today, 12
    (December 1978), 78-88.

_____. The Psychology of Sleep. New York: Scribner, 1966.

Freud, Sigmund. The Interpretation of Dreams. Trans. James
    Strachey. New York: Basic, 1972.

Fromm, Erich. The Forgotten Language: An Introduction to the
    Understanding of Dreams, Fairy Tales, and Myths. New York:
    Rinehart, 1951.

Hall, Calvin S., and Vernon J. Nordby. The Individual and His
    Dreams. New York: New American Library, 1972.

Jones, Richard M. The New Psychology of Dreaming. New York:
    Grune and Stratton, 1970.

Jung, Carl G. "Approaching the Unconscious." In Man and His
    Symbols. Ed. Carl G. Jung and M.-L. von Franz. Garden
    City, N.Y.: Doubleday, 1964, pp. 18-103.

McCarley, Robert W.   "Where Dreams Come From:  A New Theory."

Psychology Today, 12 (December 1978), 54-65, 141.

# 28

# BEYOND FRESHMAN ENGLISH
## Writing Examinations, Applications, and Letters

Freshman composition is like a course in body building or modern dance. Just as either of those courses can develop your muscles, so a composition course can develop your powers of expression. But the long-range value of any such course depends on what you do after you take it. If you stop exercising your muscles after completing the body-building course, you may lose your new-found strength; if you stop writing after completing the composition course, you may lose your hard-earned facility with words. So you should keep on writing. If you do, you will find yourself increasingly able to face a variety of writing tasks: to write effective examination essays, business letters, job applications, and applications to postgraduate programs.

28.1

    Anyone who writes well is likely to succeed in almost any writing task. But the requirements for various kinds of writing differ in some respects, and you should know what these differing requirements are. Also, you should know what good writing can do for you in the world beyond freshman composition. This chapter therefore aims to show you how to use your writing skills for a variety of purposes both in and out of the classroom.

## 28.1  Writing Examination Essays

Obviously, the first thing you need in order to write a good examination essay is a knowledge of the subject on which you are being examined. But knowledge alone is not enough. In an examination essay, as in any other kind of essay, you must be able to organize what you are saying and point it toward a specific end. In this case, you must focus your knowledge on a particular question.

The best way to start writing a good examination essay, therefore, is to read the question carefully. If you are asked to discuss the causes of the Great Depression, you will be expected to do just that—not simply to describe the depression itself. You should try to recall specifically what the causes were, and then make a list of them. With the list before you, you may find that you can explain and discuss each of the causes quickly—which is what you will have to do in the hour or two that is usually allowed. (On explaining and exposition in general, see section 4.3, pp. 56–74.)

Here is a question asked on a sociology examination:

> Goode, in Scanzoni and Scanzoni, speaks of four alternatives open in cases of family conflict. Identify and give an example of each. Discuss why each of the four might be chosen in particular situations.

This question is quite specific. It asks not for a general discussion of family conflict, but for a presentation of the alternatives open to those caught up in it, of the ways in which conflict can be ended or resolved. Here is one student's answer:

> The first of the 4 alternatives open in cases of family conflict is escape. This would be an easy solution to a family situation that is perceived as intolerable or suffocating. Probably the most common forms of escape are children running away from home (usually as a response to perceived parental injustice) and husbands deserting the family. Many husbands desert as a result of family disagreements, but among urban blacks there is an understanding that the man who earns no income cannot expect his wife to support him. In that situation, social norms dictate desertion.
>
> The second alternative is simply to yield. Thus, in a marriage defined as owner-property or head-complement, if the wife wants to work, for example, she must obtain her husband's consent. If he denies it, she must yield. In the owner-property marriage, a premium is placed on strict obedience; in the head-complement marriage, the wife may question, but is expected to eventually yield out of deference to the man's authority. In this case, where the wife yields of her own volition, the power is legitimate and can be called authority. In a situation where one is forced to comply against one's will, the power is nonlegitimate and can be called domination. Compliance in the family is very highly valued for children as well as wives. Around the age of 3–4 years, the child discovers that he has this resource of compliance. When instructed by his parents, he may yield (bestowing the resource) or he may disobey (withholding it).
>
> The third approach to conflict is to change the situation so that the conflict is resolved. (If the conflict is merely squelched or

regulated, it will very likely recur.) Conflicts may be seen as either personality-based or situational-based. The personality-based conflict is resolved by adjustment; an unhappy wife would be told to accept her husband's authority more freely. The situation-based conflict has to be resolved by actually changing an arrangement. For example, a wife who used to play the "complement" role and is now a "junior partner" would be accorded more decision-making power in the marriage. Conflicts can also be changed or resolved through either "diplomacy" or "statesmanship." Diplomacy involves clearing up misunderstandings and bettering communication, while statesmanship involves changing the situation.

The fourth alternative open in cases of conflict is violence, and this is not an uncommon response. 25% of all homicides in U.S. involve one family member killing another; half of these are spouse homicides. Less severe than homicide are beatings, also common. Although reports of child abuse are in the millions nationwide, these figures are considered vastly underreported. In one study of about 600 divorcing couples, spouse beatings were found to be a cause of dissatisfaction in about a third of the cases. Violence usually takes one of two forms: explosive or coercive. Explosive violence is not premeditated. When the teenage son totals the family car, the father may explode and break a window, hit the kid, etc. Coercive violence is pointed and intentional; it has the goal of producing compliance. Thus, a blow delivered with a threat not to repeat certain behavior would be coercive.

Like most examination essays, this one shows signs of haste, especially in the last paragraph. Rushing to finish, the writer lapses into slang expressions like *totals the family car* and *hit the kid*. But no one who is writing an examination essay has much time to worry about diction or other fine points of style. Aside from substance, the main thing that such an essay should have is organization, and this one has it. Each of its four paragraphs is organized under a topic sentence that identifies a specific alternative open in cases of family conflict. Within those paragraphs, you can see both list structure and chain structure. (For a full discussion of these two kinds of structure, see section 6.2, pp. 102–8.) In the first paragraph, for instance, the word *This* in the second sentence links that sentence to the first, and the writer then goes on to list *common forms of escape*.

Overall, this essay is written to fit the question, to furnish everything the question requires. Unlike an ordinary essay, an examination essay can begin without an introduction because the question itself has already provided one. That is why the writer of this essay simply starts right in with *The first of the 4 alternatives*. Normally, an examination essay should have a distinct conclusion, but in this instance the question simply asks the student to identify,

**28.1** illustrate, and discuss four alternatives. And that is exactly what the writer has done.

Here is another question from the same examination:

> In terms of Scanzoni and Scanzoni, define "economic-opportunity structure" and describe its relationship to the traditional nuclear family.

And here is an answer:

The "economic-opportunity structure" (EOS) refers to the "working world" and is most often associated with the practical aspect of marriage. Traditionally, males have had superior access to this structure and still do today.

In the traditional nuclear family, the male is the mediator between the family and the EOS. Such a position gives him considerable "power" within the family unit. If members of a family are totally dependent on the man for economic survival, they must concede all power and authority to him. He is the "king of the family." He brings home the fruits of the EOS, the production (usually monetary), and the family consumes these products, investing in various material possessions which in turn give them social status and prestige.

The man's degree of success in the EOS highly affects his relation to his wife and family. In the traditional family, if the man fulfills his "duty" as chief economic supporter, the wife "rewards" him with more attention to his needs and to her traditional duties—keeping a house and raising children. The husband then rewards her in various ways, with a car of her own, perhaps, or a fur coat, or a bigger house. It's an ongoing cycle. The higher-status wives are also more likely to concede that the husband should have the "upper hand" in the marriage.

This whole cycle works in reverse in lower-status families where the husband is unsuccessful as a breadwinner, causing resentment among the wives and unwillingness to submit to his authority.

If the wife in the traditional nuclear family decides to enter the EOS, her commitment to a career is usually far less than that of her husband. Her primary duty is still to her family and husband. The husband remains chief economic provider. But the woman gains more marital power because now she actually brings income into the house. Her occupation gives her self-esteem, and the marriage moves toward an egalitarian relation.

All of these cases show how economic power outside the family affects the balance of power within it. A successful breadwinner is rewarded with attention; an unsuccessful one has to put up with resentment; and the status of a wife within the family improves when she takes a job. Thus the power of any one member of a nuclear family seems to depend a lot on his or her performance in the "economic-opportunity structure"—the working world.

The question calls not for a listing of points, but for a definition of a phrase and an explanation of a relationship. The answer provides both. It defines the phrase and explains the relationship of the "EOS" to the traditional nuclear family, showing how the husband's power to make money affects his power within the family and how the status of the wife is affected by her decision to take a job. This essay has no introduction because it needs none; in effect, it is introduced by the question. But it does have a conclusion. Its final paragraph sums up its principal points, and its final sentence clearly states the essential point of the whole essay. (For more on conclusions, see section 3.8, pp. 49–51.)

To write a good examination essay, then, you should go directly to the point of the question. You should deal with the question as specifically as possible, and you should keep it continually in sight. Finally, unless you are asked simply to comment on separate points, as in the first example discussed, you should end your answer with a distinct conclusion.

## 28.2 Applying for Admission to a Postgraduate Program—The Personal Statement

Applying for admission to a postgraduate program takes more than simply filling out an application form. Most schools ask you to write a personal statement in which you explain why you plan to go into business, medicine, law, or an academic field. Your chances of getting admitted will of course depend considerably on your college grades, your letters of recommendation, and your performance on examinations like the LSAT. But a personal statement often tells more about you than anything else can. That is why it may well determine whether or not you are admitted to a particular school.

What kind of statement do admissions officers want? They want to know as specifically as possible what has led you to choose a particular career, what you hope to accomplish in it, and what you have already done to prepare yourself for it. The more specific you can be about your motivation, your experience, and your long-range plans, the more persuasive your statement will be. To see how this kind of information can be effectively presented, consider this statement made by an applicant to medical school:

> A major turning point in my life occurred following my second year in college, when I was hired as a research assistant in pediatric hematology at the New England Medical Center. During the sixteen months I spent in Boston, I gained valuable insights into the practice of medicine and found that I had a special apti-

tude for research. I returned to college determined to become a doctor and quite motivated in my academic work.

At New England Medical Center I worked with very little supervision and was expected to be resourceful and creative in carrying out my lab responsibilities. I found that I had a talent for working out technical problems and the intellectual ability to design my own procedures. In addition to my laboratory work, I took the initiative to learn about the diseases seen by the department and about the treatment programs that were employed.

I learned a great deal about terminal illness through my job, and also through the death, from leukemia, of the young son of close friends of mine. During the last months of this child's life, I spent a considerable amount of time with his family, helping them to cope with their impending loss. I found I was able to offer types of support other friends and family members could not. I matured and grew from this experience. I learned that I could be open and responsive when faced with difficult and painful situations. I also realized that a need existed for people who could assist the terminally ill and their families.

In January 1979 I joined Hospice of Santa Cruz, where I was trained as a volunteer visitor and was assigned to the family of a man with stomach cancer. I feel that my involvement with the family is of benefit both to them and to me. I can support them by serving as a catalyst to get feelings expressed, and from them I am learning to be a compassionate listener. I am convinced my experience with Hospice will help me, as a medical worker, to be understanding and open in dealing with death.

My academic work during the past two years, has, for the most part, been of outstanding quality. I chose to complete a chemistry major, with emphasis in biochemistry, and will be graduating in December 1979. I have worked for the past year and a half on a senior research project in cryoenzymology. Laboratory work presents numerous technical and intellectual challenges, and I have become quite skilled and competent in approaching these problems. I have been attracted to research because it serves to ground the theory one learns in the classroom in practical day-to-day applications. Whereas I do not expect to pursue a career in research, my laboratory experience has given me a good perspective into the nature of scientific study, has helped me develop critical thinking skills, and has offered the pleasure and satisfaction that comes with the successful completion of a project.

This past academic year I have encountered for the first time the challenge of teaching. I have been a tutor for organic chemistry, introductory chemistry, and biochemistry. To be a good tutor one not only needs to have a solid command of the subject matter but must also look at the material from the student's perspective and seek creative methods to convey information in a way that can be grasped by the student. I have found that I can do this quite effectively, both at the very basic introductory level and at the more sophisticated level of biochemistry. Through tutoring I have discovered that I love teaching. I now realize that one of the compelling attractions that medicine offers me is the opportunity to be a teacher of all kinds of people, from patients to other physicians.

I am grateful to have had in these past five years a rich variety of experiences that have prepared me for the diversity I expect to encounter in a medical career. Research, teaching, the direct care of people who are sick, and encounters with death are all part of the practice of medicine. I have gained insights, limited though they may be, into all of these. As a result I am confident that I know what I will be facing as a doctor and that I have the skills and ability to be a creative and supportive physician.

This statement is rich in detail. It tells exactly how the writer discovered her interest in medicine and what she has already done to prepare herself for a career in it. By specifically describing her experiences in laboratory research, college courses, teaching, and working with the families of the terminally ill, she convincingly shows that she has both the ability and the sensitivity to make a career in medicine. (For more on being specific, see sections 3.2, pp. 30–32, and 7.6, pp. 139–41.)

Furthermore, this statement is very well organized. Introduced with a paragraph on the particular experience that led the writer to a medical career, the statement concludes with a paragraph on the net effect of all her experiences. In between these two paragraphs, she tells in chronological order the story of her development, and each of her paragraphs is written to develop a point about what she learned. Altogether, it is not hard to see why she was admitted to medical school.

Obviously, this applicant had plenty of experience to write about. But if you take the time to recall the various kinds of work that you yourself have probably done, you may discover that you too have had a good deal of experience. In any case, the fact that you have had experience will not by itself make your statement effective. You have to organize your account of that experience, to present it in such a way that the reader can see how it led to a specific end. The statement just discussed is organized in exactly this way, clearly showing how the stages of the writer's experience led to her desire for admission to medical school. To see what a difference organization makes, compare her statement with one made by an applicant to a graduate school of business:

> Represented a Cable TV association in a twelve-million dollar public financing. Responsibilities included fostering a marketable image of our client and their objectives for the benifet of the underwriters and potential investors. This also involved making

numerous decisions and analyses in regard to our interface with FCC requirements.

The more significint factors impacting my long-range development from this experience include that I learned the coordination of financing needs and federal requirements. Throughly mastered quality control. Discovered how to identify areas of agreement and difference among the participants. Who eventually reached agreement through my involvement. Developed methods of meeting and turning around objections. And developed the ability to state my opinions in spite of intense pressure from various individules in a high-demand environment situation.

The writer has obviously had a good deal of experience in business, but he has failed to describe it in an organized way. Indeed, the first paragraph is barely coherent. It begins with a sentence fragment, a sentence without a subject (see chapter 17, pp. 296–304), and the clipped opening of the second sentence (*Responsibilities* rather than *My responsibilities*) reinforces the impression that he is more concerned with sounding terse and businesslike than with being clear. As a result of this cryptic presentation, the reader cannot tell what *This,* in the third sentence, stands for, or how that sentence connects with the other two. The statement is not an organized summary of the writer's experience; it is a string of disconnected remarks. (For a full discussion of coherence, see section 6.4, pp. 110–15.)

Furthermore, the language is at once pretentious and sloppy. On the one hand, the statement is cluttered with confusing jargon, in phrases like *fostering a marketable image, in regard to our interface,* and *impacting my long-range development.* On the other hand, it is marred by spelling errors, among them *objictives* for *objectives, benifet* for *benefit, significint* for *significant,* and *individules* for *individuals.* In the second paragraph the writer claims to have *throughly mastered quality control,* but he has not yet mastered the spelling of *thoroughly.* Worst of all, he can barely write a complete sentence. He not only starts with a sentence fragment but uses fragments repeatedly throughout. What kind of impression do you think such a statement leaves?

These two examples show what makes the difference between a bad statement and a good one, or—to put it bluntly— between rejection and acceptance. If you want to be rejected, put a lot of high-sounding words and phrases together without bothering to check your organization, sentence construction, or spelling, and without bothering to provide any clear and telling detail about what you have done. If you want to be accepted, write clearly, honestly, and specifically about your own experience and goals; take the time to see that your statement is well organized, that every sentence is complete and correct, and that every word is spelled right. Sloppy writing makes a bad impression; careful writing makes a good one. If you write carefully and explain specifically what has led you to choose a particular career, your statement will carry the kind of commitment and conviction that admissions officers want to see.

## 28.3 Applying for a Job—The Résumé and the Covering Letter

The most important thing you need when applying for a job is a résumé—a list of your achievements and qualifications. The résumé should give all the essential facts about the position you seek, the date of your availability, your education, your work experience (with informative details), your extracurricular activities, and your special interests. You may include personal data, but you do not have to. The résumé should also list the names and addresses of your references—persons who can write to a prospective employer on your behalf; before listing their names, of course, you should get their permission to do so. The sample résumé on p. 508 shows the format we recommend.

The résumé alone, however, will seldom get you a job or even an interview. With the résumé you must send what a hiring officer expects to see first: a covering letter. Since the résumé will list all the essential facts about you, the covering letter may be brief. But it should nonetheless be carefully written. If the letter makes a bad first impression, you will have one strike against you even before your résumé is seen. With some company offices getting over a thousand applications a month, you need to give yourself the best possible chance, and your covering letter can make a difference in the way your résumé is read.

What do hiring officers want in a covering letter? They look for a capsule summary of the résumé itself, and also for the things that résumés don't often tell them: how much you know about the company you hope to work for, what kind of work you hope to do, where you want to work, and what special skills you may have that need to be emphasized. The résumé defines your past; the covering letter can define your future, indicating what you hope to do for the company if you are hired.

To see what a difference a covering letter can make, compare these two, both sent to the same company:

Dear Mr. ———:
In January, 1980, you were interviewing at the ——— College campus. I was schedule to see you but I had just accepted a position with ——— Stores and canceled my interview.
At the present time I am working as assistant buyer in Tulsa, Oklahoma. I have been commuting every two weeks to see my fam-

*Sample résumé*

```
                        Harold B. Rivers
                         44 Buell Street
                    Faribault, Minnesota 55021
                        (507) 555-6789
```

Job Objective          Marketing or advertising trainee
                       (Date available:  July 1, 1982)


Education

    1978-82            Monmouth College, Monmouth, Illinois
                       Degree:  B.A. (expected in June 1982)
                       Major:  Business administration

    1974-78            Faribault Senior High School, Faribault, Minnesota
                       Academic degree


Work Experience

    Summer 1981        Acting Assistant Manager, Brown's Department Store,
                       Faribault, Minnesota.  Responsibilities included checking
                       inventory, handling complaints, and processing special
                       orders.

    Summer 1980        Salesclerk, Brown's Department Store, Faribault, Minnesota

    Summers 1978       Waiter, The Village Pub, Northfield, Minnesota
     and 1979


Extracurricular        Undergraduate Council, Monmouth College
   Activities          Debate Forum (President, 1981-82), Monmouth College
                       Drama Club (President, 1977-78), Faribault Senior High School


Special Interests      Photography, public speaking, drama


References             For academic references:
                       Office of Student Placement
                       Monmouth College
                       Monmouth, Illinois 61462

                       Mr. George C. Hazen
                       Manager, Brown's Department Store
                       300 Main Street
                       Faribault, Minnesota 55021

                       Mrs. Nancy Wright
                       Manager, The Village Pub
                       24 Harris Street
                       Northfield, Minnesota 55057
```
```

ily in Chicago. I am seeking employment in the Chicago area.

Enclosed is my résumé for your consideration again. Thank you for your attention. I will look forward to hearing from you in the near future.

Sincerely,

Dear Mr. ———:

I am seeking a challenging position in marketing and consumer relations with a company in the Chicago area. I am particularly drawn to your firm because it is a utility, and utilities must maintain a proper balance between serving the public and protecting their own corporate interests. The challenge of maintaining this balance strongly appeals to me.

I have studied both marketing and consumer relations. At Monmouth College, from which I will shortly receive a B.A. in business administration, I took courses in such subjects as Consumer Attitudes, Marketing Strategies, and Principles of Retail Management.

Along with my education, I have had job experience which has given me frequent contact with the public. Working in a small business for two summers, I learned firsthand how to deal with consumers, and in the second summer I was promoted from sales-clerk to acting assistant manager.

I hope you will review the attached résumé. Although a position in my field of interest may not be open at this time, I would appreciate your consideration for future management or marketing opportunities.

Yours truly,

These two letters make quite different impressions. The first writer opens by misspelling *scheduled* and by recalling that he once canceled an interview with the man to whom he is now writing for a job; the second writer opens with a clear-cut statement of his ambition. The first writer tells almost nothing about his interest in the company; the second tells exactly what makes the company appealing. The first writer asks to be hired because he wants to see more of his family; the second asks to be hired because his studies in marketing and consumer relations and his experience in selling will enable him to help the company. Which of these two applicants do you think the hiring officer will want to see?

If you can answer that question, you know the difference between a weak covering letter and a strong one. A weak letter speaks of what the company can do for the writer; a strong letter speaks of what the writer can do for the company. (On thinking about your reader, see section 3.5, pp. 37–40.) If your own covering letter can at least begin to indicate how your experience and qualifications will help the company, the hiring officer will probably read your résumé with more than usual interest.

*Format of a business letter*

Return address
{
14 Sunset Drive
Interlaken, N.J. 08074
October 1, 1979
}

**← Date**

Inside address
{
Mr. Roy A. Blodgett
Director, Research Division
Baker Games, Inc.
502 Broad Street
Buffalo, N.Y. 14216
}

Salutation ➤ Dear Mr. Blodgett:

Body
{
I am writing at the suggestion of Ms. Grace Smith, owner of the Nifty Novelty Shop in Interlaken, N.J. She has carried your games for more than fifteen years.

Ms. Smith thinks you would be interested in a game I have invented. It resembles backgammon but requires the two players to use mini-computers rather than dice when making a move. This step reduces the element of chance and rewards the players' skill. Friends tell me the game is more exciting than backgammon or chess.

If you would like to see the game, I would be glad to give a demonstration when you come to New York City for a meeting with your buyers in the area. I can be reached at the following number: 1-609-555-2468.
}

Complimentary close ⟶ Sincerely yours,

Signature ⟶ *George A. Andrews*

Typed name ⟶ George A. Andrews

*Format of a business envelope*

George A. Andrews
14 Sunset Drive
Interlaken, N.J. 08074

Mr. Roy A. Blodgett
Director, Research Division
Baker Games, Inc.
502 Broad Street
Buffalo, N.Y. 14216

**510 Beyond Freshman English**

(For the format of a covering letter, which is a kind of business letter, see the next section.)

## 28.4 Writing a Business Letter—The Proper Format

The covering letter that accompanies a résumé is just one example of a business letter—a letter designed to initiate or transact business. Such a letter should be concise and forthright. In relatively short paragraphs it should accurately state all the information that the writer needs to convey.

The format of a business letter is shown opposite. For a business letter you normally use medium-weight typing paper of standard size (8½ by 11 inches). Center the letter as well as you can, leaving side margins of at least 1½ inches. Unless the body of the letter is extremely short, use single-spacing and block form; type the paragraphs without indentation, and separate one from the next by a double space. Also leave a double space between the inside address and the salutation, between the salutation and the body, and between the body and the complimentary close. Leave at least four spaces for your signature between the complimentary close and the typed name.

Fold the completed letter in two places—a third of the way down from the top and up from the bottom—and insert it in a business envelope (4⅛ by 9½ inches) addressed as shown on p. 510.

## 28.5 Writing for Your Rights—The Letter of Protest

We live in a world of huge and increasingly impersonal corporations. Most of the bills and probably most of the letters you get come not from human beings but from machines. Bills are processed automatically; letters are clacked out by computers that know your address and your social-security number and have been taught to use your name in every other sentence, but nonetheless have not the faintest idea who you are or what your problems might be. How do you shout back at all this machinery? When you have a problem that can't be solved by a computerized explanation, how do you make yourself heard?

In a word, write. Do not accept the computerized explanation. Do not accept the words of a machine. If you think you have been overcharged or incorrectly billed or stuck with defective goods or shoddy service, don't keep silent. Fight back. Write a letter to the company or the institution, and demand to have your letter answered by a live human being. If the facts are on your side and you state them plainly, you may win your case without ever going to court or spending one cent for legal advice.

A friend of ours was recently billed $46.00 for an emergency service which he thought his medical insurance should cover. When the insurance company denied the claim, he phoned the company, got the name of the president, and wrote this letter directly to him:

> Dear Sir:
>
> In connection with the enclosed bill for emergency-room service provided to my son Andrew on October 15, 1980, I write to ask an explanation for your company's refusal to pay for this service.
>
> Your company's statement for October 1980 indicates that the charge for emergency-room service is not covered because "use of emergency room is covered when in connection with accident or minor surgery." Does this mean that use of the emergency room is covered *only* when in connection with accident or minor surgery? Andrew had neither of these, but his condition was a genuine emergency, and I don't see why you refuse to cover treatment for it.
>
> Andrew has asthma. He has long been treated for it by Dr. ———, who is an allergy specialist, but from time to time he has severe respiratory attacks that require emergency treatment— or rather, that require adrenalin, which is available *only* at the emergency room of ——— Hospital. If Andrew could have received adrenalin anywhere else, I could understand your denial of our claim, but so long as the hospital dispenses adrenalin *only* to emergency-room patients, we have to take him there. If we hadn't taken him there on October 15, he might have stopped breathing.
>
> I can fully understand why you stop short of indiscriminately reimbursing all visits to the emergency room, since that would be an open invitation for your subscribers to use the emergency room for any and all ailments. But I believe you must distinguish between genuine emergencies and routine problems. I therefore expect your company to pay this particular bill in full.
>
> Yours truly,

This letter got fast results. The president of the company referred it to the vice-president in charge of claims, and within a week the vice-president wrote to say that an asthma attack was indeed a genuine emergency, so the company would pay the bill in full. Thus the letter writer saved himself $46.00—not bad pay for the half hour he took to write the letter.

To see the effect that a letter of protest can have is to discover the power of the written word. Whether you realize it or not right now, the way you write can make a real difference in the life you lead after you have completed freshman English. In a composition course, you are writing only for a grade. But when you write a statement for an admissions officer, you are writing for a place in a school, and getting that place may determine the rest of your career. When you write a letter of application to a hiring officer, you are writing for a job. And when you write a letter of protest, you are writing for your rights.

What writing ability finally gives you, then, is the power to express yourself on paper for any purpose you choose. The more you write, the better you will write; and the more kinds of writing you do, the more you will discover what writing can do for you. If you care about your writing, you will continue to refine and develop it long after the composition course is over. Very few things that college can give you will be more important to you afterward than the ability to put your thoughts and feelings into words.

28.5

# GLOSSARIES

# GLOSSARY OF USAGE

**accept, except**

*Accept* means "receive" or "agree to."

Medical schools accept less than half the students who apply.

As a preposition, *except* means "other than."

I can resist anything except temptation.        Oscar Wilde

As a verb, *except* means "exclude," "omit," "leave out."

If you except Eisenhower, no U.S. president since Roosevelt has served a full two terms in office.

**A.D., B.C.**

A.D. stands for *anno Domini,* "in the year of our Lord." It designates the period since the birth of Christ, and precedes the year number.

The emperor Claudius began the Roman conquest of England in A.D. 43.

B.C. designates the period before the birth of Christ, and follows the year number. For this period, the lower the number, the more recent the year.

Alexander the Great ruled Macedonia from 336 B.C. to his death in 323.

**advice, advise**

*Advice* is a noun meaning "guidance."

When a man is too old to give bad examples, he gives good advice.                —La Rochefoucauld

*Advise* is a verb meaning "counsel," "give advice to," "recommend," or "notify."

Shortly before the stock market crash of 1929, Bernard Baruch advised investors to buy bonds.

**affect, effect**

*Affect* means "change," "disturb," or "influence."

The rising cost of gas has drastically affected the automobile industry.

517

It can also mean "feign" or "pretend to feel."

> She knew exactly what was in the package, but she affected surprise when she opened it.

As a verb, *effect* means "bring about," "accomplish," or "perform."

> With dazzling skill, the gymnast effected a triple somersault.

As a noun, *effect* means "result" or "impact."

> His appeal for mercy had no effect on the judge.

**afraid** *See* frightened.

**aggravate, irritate**

*Aggravate* means "make worse."

> The recent bombing of a school bus has aggravated racial hostilities.

*Irritate* means "annoy" or "bring discomfort to."

> His tuneless whistling began to irritate me.

**all** *See* almost.

**all ready, already**

Use *all ready* when *all* refers to things or people.

> At noon the runners were all ready to start. [The meaning is that *all* of the runners were *ready*.]

Use *already* to mean "by this time" or "by that time."

> I reached the halfway mark, but the front-runners had already crossed the finish line.

**all right, *alright**

*All right* means "completely correct," "safe and sound," or "satisfactory."

> My answers on the quiz were all right. [The meaning is that *all* of the answers were *right*.]

> The car was demolished, but aside from a muscle bruise in my shoulder and a few minor cuts, I was all right.

In formal writing, do not use *all right* to mean "satisfactorily" or "well."

> *In spite of a bruised shoulder, Ashe played all right.

> REVISED: In spite of a bruised shoulder, Ashe played well.

In formal writing, do not use *all right* before a noun to mean "very good" or "excellent."

> *The Casio calculator is an all right electronic device.

> REVISED: The Casio calculator is an excellent electronic device.

Do not use *alright* anywhere; it is a misspelling of *all right*.

**all together, altogether**

Use *all together* when *all* refers to things or people.

> The demonstrators stood all together at the gate of the nuclear power plant.

Use *altogether* to mean "entirely" or "wholly."

> Never put off till tomorrow what you can avoid altogether. (Preston's Axiom)

**allude, refer**

*Allude* means "call attention indirectly."

> When the speaker mentioned the "Watergate scandal," he

alluded to a chain of events which led to the resignation of President Richard Nixon.

*Refer* means "call attention directly."

In the Declaration of Independence, Jefferson refers many times to England's mistreatment of the American colonies.

**allusion, delusion, illusion**

An *allusion* is an indirect reference.

Prufrock's vision of his own head "brought in upon a platter" is an allusion to John the Baptist, whose head was presented that way to Salome, Herod's daughter.

A *delusion* is a false opinion or belief, especially one that springs from self-deception or madness.

A megalomaniac suffers from the delusion that he or she is fabulously rich and powerful.

An *illusion* is a false impression, especially one that springs from false perception (an optical illusion, for example) or from wishful thinking.

The sight of palm trees on the horizon proved to be an illusion.

The so-called "free gifts" offered in advertisements feed the illusion that you can get something for nothing.

**almost, most, mostly, all, *most all**

*Almost* means "nearly."

By the time we reached the gas station, the tank was almost empty.

Almost all the Republicans support the proposed amendment.

As an adjective or noun, *most* means "the greater part (of)" or "the majority (of)."

Most birds migrate in the fall and spring.

Most of the land has become a dust bowl.

As an adverb, *most* designates the superlative form of long adjectives and adverbs.

Truman thought MacArthur the most egotistical man he ever knew.

*Mostly* means "chiefly," "primarily."

Milk is mostly water.

*All* means "the whole amount," "the total number of," or "entirely."

All art is useless.                                                —Oscar Wilde

The manufacturer has recalled all (of) the new models.

The new buildings are all finished.

In formal writing, do not use *most all*. Use *almost all* or *most*.

*Most all of the plants looked healthy, but two of the roses were dying.

REVISED: Almost all of the plants looked healthy, but two of the roses were dying.

*Most all of the refugees suffered from malnutrition.

REVISED: Most of the refugees suffered from malnutrition.

**a lot, \*alot**   *See* lots of.

**already**   *See* all ready.

**\*alright**   *See* all right.

**altogether**   *See* all together.

**alumnus, alumni; alumna, alumnae**

Use *alumnus* for one male graduate of a school, college, or university, and *alumni* for two or more male graduates or for a predominantly male group of graduates.

Dartmouth alumni are extraordinarily loyal to their college.

Use *alumna* for one female graduate, and *alumnae* for two or more female graduates or for a predominantly female group of graduates.

Vassar's alumnae include Mary McCarthy and Meryl Streep.

If you can't cope with all those Latin endings, use *graduate* for an individual of either sex, and just remember that *alumni* designates a male group, *alumnae* a female group. Do not refer to any one person of either sex as an *alumni*.

\*He is an alumni of Florida State.

REVISED: He is an alumnus [or "a graduate"] of Florida State.

**among, between**

Use *among* with three or more persons, things, or groups.

There is no honor among thieves.

In general, use *between* with two persons, two things, or two groups.

Political freedom in America means the right to choose between a Democrat and a Republican.

**amoral, immoral**

*Amoral* means "without morals or a code of behavior," "beyond or outside the moral sphere."

Rich, riotous, and totally amoral, he lived for nothing but excitement and pleasure.

*Immoral* means "wicked."

The Roman emperor Nero was so immoral that he once kicked a pregnant woman to death.

**amount, number**

Use *amount* when discussing uncountable things.

No one knows the amount of damage that a nuclear war would do.

Use *number* when discussing countable things or persons.

The store offered a prize to anyone who could guess the number of marbles in a large glass jug.

**anyone, any one**

*Anyone* is an indefinite pronoun (like *everyone, everybody*).

Anyone who hates dogs and children can't be all bad.

—W. C. Fields

*Any one* means "any one of many."

I felt wretched; I could not answer any one of the questions on the test.

**apt**   *See* likely.

**as, as if, like**

Use *as* or *as if* to introduce a clause.

> As I walked up the driveway, a huge dog suddenly leaped out at me.

> Susan looked as if she had just seen a ghost.

Use *like* to mean "similar to."

> At first glance the organism looks like an amoeba.

**assure, ensure, insure**

> *Assure* means "state with confidence to."

> > The builders of the *Titanic* assured everyone that it could not sink.

> *Ensure* means "make sure" or "guarantee."

> > There is no way to ensure that every provision of the treaty will be honored.

> *Insure* means "make a contract for payment in the event of specified loss, damage, injury, or death."

> > I insured the package for fifty dollars.

**awfully** *See* very.

**bad, badly**

> *Bad* is an adjective meaning "not good," "sick," or "sorry."

> > We paid a lot for the meal, but it was bad.

> > In spite of the medicine, I still felt bad.

> > She felt bad about losing the ring.

> *Badly* is an adverb meaning "not well."

> > Anything that begins well ends badly. (Pudder's Law)

> Used with *want* or *need, badly* means "very much."

> > The fans badly wanted a victory.

> Do not use *bad* as an adverb.

> > *We played bad during the first half of the game.

> > REVISED: We played badly during the first half of the game.

**B.C.** *See* A.D.

**because, since, *being that**

> Use *since* and *because* to introduce clauses. Do not use **being that*.

> > Since fossil fuels are becoming scarce, scientists are working to develop synthetic forms of energy.

> > The soldiers could not advance because they had run out of ammunition.

**because of** *See* due to.

*****being that** *See* because.

**beside, besides**

> *Beside* means "next to."

> > A little restaurant stood beside the wharf.

> As a preposition, *besides* means "in addition to."

> > Besides working with the sun and the wind, engineers are seeking to harness the power of tides.

> As a conjunctive adverb, *besides* means "moreover" or "also."

> > Randy's notion of bliss was a night at the disco, but discos made me dizzy; besides, Randy stepped on my toes whenever we danced.

**between** *See* among.

**can hardly, *can't hardly**

*Can hardly* means virtually the same thing as *cannot* or *can't*. Do not use **can't hardly*.

> **We can't hardly bomb Moscow without getting bombed in return.

> REVISED: We can hardly bomb Moscow without getting bombed in return.

**capital, capitol**

*Capital* means the seat of government of a country or state, the type of letter used at the beginning of a sentence, or a stock of accumulated wealth.

> Paris is the capital of France.

> This sentence begins with a capital *T*.

> What does capital consist of? It consists of money and commodities. —Karl Marx

*Capitol* means the building that houses the state or federal legislature. Remember that the *o* in *capitol* is like the *o* in the dome of a capitol.

> The new governor delivered his first official speech from the steps of the capitol.

**censor, censure**

As a verb, *censor* means "exercise censorship."

> Television networks usually censor X-rated movies before broadcasting them.

As a noun, *censor* means "one who censors."

> Censors cut the best part of the film.

As a verb, *censure* means "find fault with" or "reprimand."

> In the 1950s, Senator Joseph McCarthy was censured for publicly questioning the integrity of President Eisenhower.

As a noun, *censure* means "disapproval" or "blame."

> Ridicule often hurts more than censure.

**childish, childlike**

*Childish* means "disagreeably like a child."

> The childish whining of a chronic complainer soon becomes an unbearable bore.

*Childlike* means "agreeably like a child."

> Picasso's brilliant canvases express his childlike love of color.

**cite**   *See* sight.

**compare, comparison, contrast**

*Compare* means "bring together in order to note similarities and differences."

> In *A Stillness at Appomattox*, Bruce Catton compares Lee and Grant not only to show the difference between a Virginia aristocrat and a rough-hewn frontiersman but also to show what these two men had in common.

Use *compare to* to stress similarities.

> Lewis Thomas compares human societies to ant colonies, noting that individuals in each of these groups sometimes work together as if they were part of a single organism.

Use *compare with* to stress differences.

> Compared with Texas, Rhode Island is a postage stamp.

*Comparison* means "act of comparing."

> Catton's comparison of Lee and Grant shows the difference between the South and the frontier.
>
> In comparison with Texas, Rhode Island is a postage stamp.

As a transitive verb, *contrast* means "bring together to show differences."

> In *Huckleberry Finn,* Clemens contrasts the peaceful, easy flow of life on the river with the tense and violent atmosphere of life on shore.

As an intransitive verb, *contrast* means "show one or more differences."

> In *Huckleberry Finn,* the peaceful flow of life on the river contrasts vividly with the violent atmosphere of life on shore.

As a noun, *contrast* means "striking difference."

> To drive across America is to feel the contrast between the level plains of the Midwest and the towering peaks of the Rockies.

**complement, compliment**

As a verb, *complement* means "bring to perfect completion."

> A red silk scarf complemented her white dress.

As a noun, *complement* means "something that makes a whole when combined with something else" or "the total number of persons needed in a group or team."

> Experience is the complement of learning.
>
> Without a full complement of volunteers, a small-town fire department cannot do its job.

As a verb, *compliment* means "praise."

> The teacher complimented me on my handwriting but complained about everything else.

As a noun, *compliment* means "expression of praise."

> Everyone loves a compliment, but scarcely anyone will accept one without objecting to it.

**conscience, conscious**

*Conscience* is a noun meaning "inner guide or voice in matters of right and wrong."

> A pacifist will not fight in any war because his or her conscience says that all killing is wrong.

*Conscious* is an adjective meaning "aware" or "able to perceive."

> Conscious of something on my leg, I looked down to see a cockroach crawling over my knee.
>
> I was conscious during the whole operation.

**consul** *See* council.

**continual, continuous**

*Continual* means "going on with occasional slight interruptions."

> I grew up next to an airport. What I remember most from my childhood is the continual roaring of jet planes.

*Continuous* means "going on with no interruption."

In some factories the assembly line never stops; production is continuous.

**contrast**    *See* compare.

**council, counsel, consul**

*Council* means "group of persons who discuss and decide certain matters."

The city council often disagrees with the mayor.

As a verb, *counsel* means "advise."

President John F. Kennedy was badly counseled when he approved the American attack on Cuba at the Bay of Pigs.

As a noun, *counsel* means "advice" or "lawyer."

Camp counselors tend to give orders more often than counsel.

When the prosecution showed a picture of the victim's mangled corpse, the defense counsel vigorously objected.

A *consul* is a government official working in a foreign country to protect the interests of his or her country's citizens there.

If you lose your passport in a foreign country, you will need to see the American consul there.

**credible, credulous**

*Credible* means "believable."

A skillful liar can often sound highly credible.

*Credulous* means "overly ready to believe."

Some people are credulous enough to believe anything they read in a newspaper.

*See also* incredible, incredulous.

**criterion, criteria**

A *criterion* is a standard by which someone or something is judged.

In works of art, the only criterion of lasting value is lasting fame.

*Criteria* is the plural of *criterion*.

What criteria influence voters in judging a presidential candidate?

**data**

*Data* is the plural of the Latin *datum* (literally, "given"), meaning "something given"—that is, a piece of information. *Data* should be treated as plural.

The data transmitted by space satellites tell us much more about distant planets than we have ever known before.

**delusion**    *See* allusion.

**different from, *different than**

In formal writing do not use *than* after *different*. Use *from*.

An adult's idea of a good time is often very different from a child's.

**differ from, differ with**

*Differ from* means "be unlike."

Black English differs from Standard English not only in its sounds but also in its structure.       —Dorothy Z. Seymour

*Differ with* means "disagree with."

Jung differed with Freud on the importance of the sex drive.

**disinterested, uninterested**

> *Disinterested* means "impartial," "unbiased," "objective."
>> Lawyers respect Judge Brown for his disinterested handling of controversial cases.
>
> *Uninterested* means "indifferent," "not interested."
>> Some people are so uninterested in politics that they do not even bother to vote.

**due to, because of**

> *Due to* means "resulting from" or "the result of."
>> Home-insurance policies sometimes fail to cover losses due to "acts of God," such as hurricanes and tornadoes.
>> The senator's failure to win reelection was largely due to his lackluster campaigning.
>
> *Because of* means "as a result of."
>> Fighting persists in Northern Ireland because of animosities nearly three hundred years old.
>
> Do not use *due to* to mean *because of.*
>> *Due to a sprained ankle I had to drop out of the race.
>> REVISED: Because of a sprained ankle I had to drop out of the race.

**effect**   *See* affect.

**emigrate**   *See* immigrate.

**eminent, imminent, immanent**

> *Eminent* means "distinguished," "prominent."
>> An eminent biologist has recently questioned the theory of evolution.
>
> *Imminent* means "about to happen."
>> The leaden air and the black, heavy clouds told us that a thunderstorm was imminent.
>
> *Immanent* means "inherent," "existing within."
>> Pantheists believe that God is immanent in all things.

**ensure**   *See* assure.

**envelop, envelope**

> *EnVELop* (second syllable accented) is a verb meaning "cover" or "enclose."
>> Fog seemed to envelop the whole city.
>
> *ENvelope* (first syllable accented) is a noun meaning "container used for mailing."
>> The small white envelope contained a big check.

**\*etc., et al.**

> The abbreviation *\*etc.* stands for *et cetera,* "and other things." You should avoid it in formal writing. Instead, use *and so on,* or tell what the other things are.
>> *Before setting out that morning, I put on my hat, mittens, etc.
>> REVISED: Before setting out that morning, I put on my hat, mittens, scarf, and boots.
>
> The abbreviation *et al.* stands for *et alii,* "and others." Use it only in a footnote or bibliography, when citing a book written by three or more authors.

Maynard Mack et al., eds., *World Masterpieces*, 3rd ed. (New York: Norton, 1973), pp. 73–74.

**everyday, every day**

*Everyday* means "ordinary" or "regular."

The governor has a common touch; even in public speeches he likes to use everyday words.

*Every day* means "daily."

While in training, Mary Thomas commonly runs at least ten miles every day.

**except**  *See* accept.

**factor**

*Factor* means "contributing element" or "partial cause." It can be used effectively, but far too often it simply clutters and obscures the sentence in which it appears. In general, you should avoid it.

One factor in the decay of the cities is the movement of middle-class families to the suburbs.

REVISED: One reason for the decay of the cities is the movement of middle-class families to the suburbs.

**farther, further**

*Farther* means "a greater distance."

The trail went farther into the bush than the hunter had expected.

As an adjective, *further* means "more."

After high school, how many students really need further education?

As a conjunctive adverb, *further* means "besides."

Lincoln disliked slavery; further, he abhorred secession.

As a transitive verb, *further* means "promote" or "advance."

How much has the federal government done to further the development of solar energy?

**fatal, fateful**

*Fatal* means "sure to cause death" or "resulting in death."

Even a small dose of cyanide is fatal.

In a fruitless and fatal attempt to save the manuscript which he had spent ten years to produce, the novelist rushed back into the burning house.

*Fateful* means "momentous in effect," and can be used whether the outcome is good or bad.

In the end, Eisenhower made the fateful decision to land the Allies at Normandy.

**few, little, less**

Use *few* or *fewer* with countable nouns.

Few pianists even try to play the eerie music of George Crumb.

Use *little* (in the sense of "not much") or *less* with uncountable nouns.

A little honey on your hands can be a big sticky nuisance.

In spite of his grandiloquent title, the vice-president of the United States often has less power than a congressman.

**former, formerly, formally**

As an adjective, *former* means "previous."

When we moved in, the apartment was a mess. The former tenants had never even bothered to throw out the garbage.

As a noun, *former* refers to the first of two persons or things mentioned previously.

Muhammad Ali first fought Leon Spinks in February 1978. At the time, the former was an international celebrity, while the latter was a twenty-four-year-old unknown.

*Formerly* means "at an earlier time."

Most of the men in the tribe were formerly hunters, not farmers.

*Formally* means "in a formal or ceremonious manner."

The president is elected in November, but he does not formally take office until the following January.

**frightened, afraid**

*Frightened* is followed by *at* or *by*.

Many people are frightened at the thought of dying.

As I walked down the deserted road I was frightened by a snarling wolfhound.

*Afraid* is followed by *of*.

Afraid of heights, Sylvia would not go near the edge of the cliff.

**further**   *See* farther.

**good, well**

Use *good* as an adjective, but not as an adverb.

The proposal to rebuild the chapel sounded good to many in the congregation.

*She ran good for the first twenty miles, but then she collapsed.

REVISED: She ran well for the first twenty miles, but then she collapsed.

Use *well* as an adverb when you mean "in an effective manner," "ably."

Fenneman did so well in practice that the coach decided to put him in the starting lineup for the opening game.

Use *well* as an adjective when you mean "in good health."

My grandfather hasn't looked well since his operation.

**\*got to**   *See* has to.

**hanged, hung**

*Hanged* means "executed by hanging."

The prisoner was hanged at dawn.

*Hung* means "suspended" or "held oneself up."

I hung my coat on the back of the door and sat down.

I hung on the side of the cliff, frantically seeking a foothold.

Do not use *hung* to mean "executed by hanging."

*They hung the prisoner at dawn.

REVISED: They hanged the prisoner at dawn.

**has to, have to, *got to**

In formal writing, do not use *got to* to denote an obligation. Use *have to, has to,* or *must.*

*Anyone who wants to win the nomination has got to run in the primaries.

REVISED: Anyone who wants to win the nomination has to run in the primaries.

**hopefully**

Use *hopefully* to modify a verb.

As the ice-cream truck approached, the children looked hopefully at their parents. [*Hopefully* modifies *looked,* telling how the children looked.]

Do not use *hopefully* when you mean "I hope that," "we hope that," or the like.

*Hopefully, the company will make a profit in the final quarter.

REVISED: The stockholders hope that the company will make a profit in the final quarter.

**human, humane**

*Human* means "pertaining to human beings."

To err is human.

*Humane* means "merciful," "kindhearted," or "considerate."

To forgive is both divine and humane.

**illusion**   *See* allusion.

**immanent, imminent**   *See* eminent.

**immigrate, emigrate**

*Immigrate* means "enter a country in order to live there permanently."

Professor Korowitz immigrated to the United States in 1955.

*Emigrate* means "leave one country in order to live in another."

My great-great-grandfather emigrated from Ireland in 1848.

**immoral**   *See* amoral.

**imply, infer**

*Imply* means "suggest" or "hint at something."

The manager implied that I could not be trusted with the job.

*Infer* means "reach a conclusion on the basis of evidence"; it is often used with *from.*

From the manager's letter I inferred that my chances were nil.

**in, into, in to**

Use *in* when referring to a direction, location, or position.

Easterners used to think that everyone in the West was a cowboy.

Use *into* to mean movement toward the inside.

Before he started drilling, the dentist shot Novocain into my gum.

Use *in to* when the two words have separate functions.

The museum was open, so I walked in to look at the paintings.

**incredible, incredulous**

*Incredible* means "not believable."

Since unmanned exploration of Mars has revealed no signs of life there, the idea that "Martians" could invade the earth is now incredible.

In formal writing, do not use *incredible* to mean "amazingly bad," "compelling," "brilliant," or "extraordinary." In speech, you can indicate the meaning of *incredible* by the way you say it, but in writing, this word may be ambiguous and confusing.

*Marian gave an incredible performance. [The reader has no way of knowing whether the performance was not believable, amazingly good, or amazingly bad.]

REVISED: Marian gave a brilliant performance.

*Incredulous* means "unbelieving" or "skeptical."

When Columbus argued that his ship would not fall off the edge of the earth, many of his hearers were incredulous, for they believed the earth was flat.

**infer** *See* imply.

**inferior to, *inferior than**

Always use *to* after *inferior*. Do not use *than*.

*America once led the world in its technology, but now many of its products—including the automobile—are inferior than those made elsewhere.

REVISED: America once led the world in its technology, but now many of its products—including the automobile—are inferior to those made elsewhere.

**insure** *See* assure.

***irregardless** *See* regardless.

**irritate** *See* aggravate.

**its, it's**

*Its* is the possessive form of *it*.

We liked the house because of its appearance, its location, and its price.

*It's* means "it is."

It's a pity that we seldom see ourselves as others see us.

**kind of, sort of**

In formal writing, do not use *kind of* or *sort of* to mean "somewhat" or "rather."

*When I got off the roller coaster, I felt sort of sick.

REVISED: When I got off the roller coaster, I felt rather sick.

**later, latter**

Use *later* when referring to time.

Russia developed the atomic bomb later than the United States did.

During our century, aerospace technology has progressed with astounding speed. In 1903 the Wright brothers invented the first successful airplane; sixty-six years later, America put a man on the moon.

Use *latter* when referring to the second of two persons or things mentioned previously.

Muhammad Ali first fought Leon Spinks in February 1978. At the time, the former was an international celebrity, while the latter was a twenty-four-year-old unknown.

**lay**   *See* lie.

**lead, led**

> *Lead* (rhymes with *seed*) is the present-tense and infinitive form of the verb meaning "cause," "guide," or "direct."
>> Deficit spending leads to inflation.
>> An effective president must be able to lead Congress without bullying it.
>
> *Led* is the past-tense form and past participle of *lead.*
>> During the Civil War, General Robert E. Lee led the Confederate forces.
>> Some buyers are led astray by simple-minded slogans.

**learn, teach**

> *Learn* means "gain knowledge, information, or skill."
> *Teach* means "give lessons or instructions."
>> If you want to know how well you have learned something, teach it to someone else.

**leave, let**

> *Leave* means "go away from" or "put in a place."
>> I had to leave the house at 6:00 A.M. in order to catch the bus.
>> Just as I got to the bus station, I suddenly realized that I had left my suitcase at home.
>
> *Let* means "permit," "allow."
>> Some colleges let students take courses by mail.

**led**   *See* lead.

**less**   *See* few.

**let**   *See* leave.

**let's, *let's us**

> Use *let's* before a verb. Do not follow *let's* with *us;* that would mean "let us us."
>> *Let's us finish the job.
>> REVISED: Let's finish the job.

**liable**   *See* likely.

**lie, lay**

> *Lie* (*lie, lying, lied, lied*) means "tell a falsehood."
>> He sometimes lies about his age.
>> He should stop lying about his age.
>> He lied about his age when he talked to the recruiter.
>
> *Lie* (*lie, lying, lay, lain*) means "rest," "recline," or "stay."
>> I love to lie on the sand in the hot sun.
>> Lying on the sand, I watched the clouds and listened to the pounding of the surf.
>> After she lay in the sun for three hours, she looked like a boiled lobster.
>> On April 26, 1952, workers digging peat near Grueballe, Denmark, found a well-preserved body that had lain in the bog for fifteen hundred years.

*Lay* (*lay, laying, laid, laid*) means "put in a certain position."

> A good education lays the foundation for a good life.
>
> The workers were laying bricks when an earthquake struck.
>
> He laid the book on the counter and walked out of the library.
>
> The earthquake struck after the foundation had been laid.

**like**   *See* as.

**likely, apt, liable**

*Likely* indicates future probability.

> As gas becomes scarcer and more expensive, battery-powered cars are likely to become popular.

*Apt* indicates a usual or habitual tendency.

> Most cars are apt to rust after two or three years.

*Liable* indicates a risk or adverse possibility.

> Cars left unlocked are liable to be stolen.

**little**   *See* few.

**loose, lose**

*Loose* (rhymes with *moose*) means "free" or "not securely tied or fastened."

> The center grabbed the loose ball and ran for a touchdown.
>
> From the rattling of the door, I could tell that the catch was loose.

*Lose* (sounds like *Lou's*) means "fail to keep" or "fail to win."

> In some cultures, to lose face is to lose everything.
>
> The hard truth about sports is that whenever somebody wins, somebody else loses.

**lots of, a lot of, \*alot of**

*A lot of* and *lots of* are colloquial and wordy. In formal writing, use *much* for "a great amount" and *many* for "a great number." Do not use \*alot anywhere; it is a misspelling of *a lot.*

> Lots of students come to college with no clear notion of what they want to do.
>
> BETTER: Many students come to college with no clear notion of what they want to do.

**many, much, \*muchly**

Use *many* with countable nouns.

> Many hands make light work.

Use *much* with uncountable nouns.

> Much of the work has been done.

Use *much* or *very much*, not \**muchly*, as an adverb.

> \*The long sleep left me muchly refreshed.
>
> REVISED: The long sleep left me much [or "very much"] refreshed.

**maybe, may be**

*Maybe* means "perhaps."

> Maybe all cars will be electric by the year 2000.

*May be* is a verb phrase.

> Before the year 2000, the president of the United States may be a woman.

**might have, \*might of.**

Use *might have,* not *\*might of.*

\*Oklahoma might of won the game if it had lasted just two minutes longer.

REVISED: Oklahoma might have won the game if it had lasted just two minutes longer.

**moral, morale**

*MORal* (first syllable accented) is an adjective meaning "ethical" or "virtuous."

To heed a cry for help is not a legal duty but a moral one.

Piety and morality are two different things: a pious man can be immoral, and an impious man can be moral.

*MoRALE* (second syllable accented) is a noun meaning "spirit," "attitude."

Eisenhower's habit of mixing with his troops before a battle kept up their morale.

**most, mostly, \*most all**   *See* almost.

**much, \*muchly**   *See* many.

**not very, none too, \*not too**

In formal writing, use *not very* or *none too* instead of *\*not too.*

\*Not too pleased with the dull and droning lecture, the students filled the air with catcalls, spitballs, and paper planes.

REVISED: None too pleased with the dull and droning lecture, the students filled the air with catcalls, spitballs, and paper planes.

**nowhere, \*nowheres**

Use *nowhere,* not *\*nowheres.*

\*The child was nowheres to be seen.

REVISED: The child was nowhere to be seen.

**number**   *See* amount.

**OK, O.K., okay**

Avoid all three in formal writing. In business letters or informal writing, you can use *OK* as a noun meaning "endorsement" or "approval," or *okay* as a verb meaning "endorse," "approve."

The stockholders have given their OK.

Union negotiators have okayed the company's latest offer.

**only**

Place *only* carefully. It belongs immediately before the word, phrase, or clause it modifies.

\*At most colleges, students only get their diplomas if they have paid all their bills.

REVISED: At most colleges, students get their diplomas only if they have paid all their bills.

\*Some busy executives only relax on Sundays.

REVISED: Some busy executives relax only on Sundays.

**ourselves, ourself**

Use *ourselves,* not *ourself,* when the antecedent is plural.

Nearly an hour after the front-runners had come in, Sally and I dragged ourselves across the finish line.

**passed, past**

*Passed* means "went by" or "threw."

The idiot passed me on the inside lane.

Conversation ground to a painful halt, and minutes passed like hours.

Seymour passed to Winowski, but the ball was intercepted.

As a noun, *past* means "a certain previous time" or "all previous time."

Prehistoric monuments like Stonehenge speak to us of a past that we can only speculate about.

As an adjective, *past* means "connected with a certain previous time" or "connected with all previous time."

Past experience never tells us everything we want to know about the future.

As a preposition, *past* means "beyond."

The space probe *Pioneer 10* will eventually travel past the limits of the solar system.

**persecute, prosecute**

*Persecute* means "pester" or "harass."

As Nero persecuted the Christians, Hitler persecuted the Jews.

*Prosecute* means "bring charges against someone in a formal, legal way."

Al Capone ran his criminal empire so shrewdly that authorities took years to prosecute him.

**personal, personnel**

*PERsonal* (first syllable accented) is an adjective meaning "private" or "individual."

In writing or speaking, you can sometimes use a personal experience to illustrate a general point.

*PersonNEL* (last syllable accented) is a noun meaning "persons in a firm or a military group."

If you want a job with a big company, you normally have to see the director of personnel.

**phenomenon, phenomena**

*Phenomenon* means "something perceived by the senses" or "something extraordinary."

A rainbow is a phenomenon caused by the separation of sunlight into various colors as it passes through raindrops.

Old Barney is a phenomenon. At eighty years of age he still swims five miles every day.

*Phenomena* is the plural of *phenomenon.*

The Northern Lights are among the most impressive phenomena in nature.

**precede, proceed, proceeds, proceedings, procedure**

To *precede* is to come before or go before in place or time.

A dead calm often precedes a hurricane.

To *proceed* is to move forward or go on.

With the bridge washed out, the bus could not proceed, so we had to get out and take a ferry across the river.

The bishop proceeded toward the cathedral.

After the judge silenced the uproar, he told the prosecutor to proceed with her questioning.

*Proceeds* are funds generated by a business deal or a money-raising event.

The proceeds of the auction went to buy new furniture for the Student Center.

*Proceedings* are formal actions, especially in an official meeting.

During a trial, a court stenographer takes down every word of the proceedings for the record.

A *procedure* is a standardized way of doing something.

Anyone who wants to run a meeting effectively should know the rules of parliamentary procedure.

**principal, principle**

As a noun, *principal* means "administrator" or "sum of money."

The school principal wanted all of us to think of him as a pal, but none of us did.

The interest on the principal came to $550 a year.

As an adjective, *principal* means "most important."

In most American households, television is the principal source of entertainment.

*Principle* means "rule of behavior," "basic truth," or "general law of nature."

Whenever we officially recognize a government that abuses its own citizens, we are tacitly accepting the principle that might makes right.

**proceed,** *See* precede.

**proceeds, proceedings, procedure** *See* precede.

**prosecute** *See* persecute.

**quote, quotation**

*Quote* means "repeat the exact words of."

In his "Letter from Birmingham Jail," Martin Luther King, Jr., quotes Lincoln: "This nation cannot survive half slave and half free."

Do not use *quote* to mean "refer to" or "paraphrase the views of." Use *cite*.

In defense of his stand against segregation, King cites more than a dozen authorities, and he quotes Lincoln: "This nation cannot survive half slave and half free."

Do not use *quote* as a noun to mean "something quoted." Use *quotation*.

\*A sermon usually begins with a quote from Scripture.

REVISED: A sermon usually begins with a quotation from Scripture.

*Quotation* means "something quoted," as in the preceding example. But you should not normally use it to mean something *you* are quoting.

\*In a quotation on the very first page of the book, Holden expresses his opinion of Hollywood. "If there's one thing I hate," he says, "it's the movies." [Holden is not quoting any-body. He is speaking for himself.]

REVISED: In a statement on the very first page of the book, Holden expresses his opinion of Hollywood. "If there's one thing I hate," he says, "it's the movies."

You can improve this passage even further by compressing the first sentence.

Holden states his opinion of Hollywood on the very first page of the book.

### raise, rise

*Raise* (*raise, raising, raised, raised*) is a transitive verb—one followed by an object.

Moments before his hanging, Dandy Tom raised his hat to the ladies.

My grandmother has raised ten children.

*Rise* (*rise, rising, rose, risen*) is an intransitive verb—one that has no object.

Puffs of smoke rose skyward.

The farmhands rose at 5:00 A.M. Monday through Saturday.

Have you ever risen early enough to see the sun rise?

### rational, rationale, rationalize

*Rational* means "able to reason," "sensible," or "logical."

Can a rational person ever commit suicide?

Is there such a thing as a rational argument for nuclear war-fare?

*Rationale* means "justification," "explanation," or "underlying rea-son."

The rationale for the new bypass is that it will reduce the flow of traffic through the center of town.

*Rationalize* means "justify with one or more fake reasons."

He rationalized his extravagance by saying that he was only doing his part to keep money in circulation.

### real, really

*Real* means "actual."

The unicorn is an imaginary beast, but it is made up of fea-tures taken from real ones.

*Really* means "actually."

Petrified wood looks like ordinary wood, but it is really stone.

In formal writing, do not use *real* to modify an adjective.

*In parts of the country synthetic fuels have met real strong resistance.

REVISED: In parts of the country synthetic fuels have met really strong resistance.

FURTHER REVISED: In parts of the country synthetic fuels have met strong resistance. [This version eliminates *really*, which—like *very*—often weakens rather than strengthens the word it modifies.]

### reason . . . is that, *reason . . . is because

Use *reason* with *that*, not with *because*, or use *because* by itself.

*The reason many college freshmen have trouble with writing is because they did little or no writing in high school.

REVISED: The reason many college freshmen have trouble with writing is that they did little or no writing in high school. [or] Many college freshmen have trouble with writing because they did little or no writing in high school.

**refer**   *See* allude.

**regardless, *irregardless**

Use *regardless,* not *irregardlesss.*

*Irregardless of what happens to school systems and public services, some cities and towns have voted to cut property taxes substantially.

REVISED: Regardless of what happens to school systems and public services, some cities and towns have voted to cut property taxes substantially.

**respectively, respectfully, respectably**

*Respectively* means "in turn" or "in the order presented."

The college presented honorary degrees to Harriet Brown and Emanuel Lee, who are, respectively, an Olympic medalist and a concert pianist.

*Respectfully* means "with respect."

Parents who speak respectfully to their children are most likely to end up with children who speak respectfully to them.

*Respectably* means "presentably" or "in a manner deserving respect."

She ran respectably but not quite successfully for the Senate.

**rise**   *See* raise.

**set, sit**

*Set (set, setting, set, set)* means "put" or "place."

I filled the kettle and set it on the range.

When daylight saving changes to standard time, I can never remember whether to set my watch forward or back.

*Sit (sit, sitting, sat, sat)* means "place oneself in a sitting position."

On clear summer nights I love to sit outside, listen to crickets, and look at the stars.

Grandfather sat in an easy chair and smoked his pipe.

**sight, cite, site**

As a verb, *sight* means "observe" or "perceive with the eyes."

After twenty days on the open sea the sailors sighted land.

As a noun, *sight* means "spectacle," "device for aiming," or "vision."

Some travelers care only for the sights of a foreign country; they have no interest in its people.

The deadliest weapon of all is a rifle with a telescopic sight.

Most of us take the gift of sight for granted; only the blind know how much it is worth.

*Cite* means "refer to," "mention as an example or piece of evidence."

Anyone opposed to nuclear power cites the case of Three Mile Island. But just how serious was the accident that occurred there?

As a verb, *site* means "locate" or "place at a certain point."

> The architect sited the house on the side of a hill.

As a noun, *site* means "location" or "place," often the place where something has been or will be built.

> The site of the long-gone Globe Theatre, where Shakespeare himself once trod the boards, is now occupied by a brewery.

**since** *See* because.

**sit** *See* set.

**site** *See* sight.

**so** *See* very.

**sometimes, sometime**

*Sometimes* means "occasionally."

> Sometimes I lie awake at night and wonder what I will do with my life.

As an adjective, *sometime* means "former."

> In the presidential campaigns of 1952 and 1956, Eisenhower twice defeated Adlai Stevenson, sometime governor of Illinois and later U.S. ambassador to the United Nations.

As an adverb, *sometime* means "at some point."

> A slot machine addict invariably thinks that he or she will sometime hit the jackpot.

**somewhere, *somewheres**

Use *somewhere,* not **somewheres.*

> *Somewheres in that pile of junk was a diamond necklace.
> REVISED: Somewhere in that pile of junk was a diamond necklace.

**sort of** *See* kind of.

**stationary, stationery**

*Stationary* means "not moving."

> Before you can expect to hit a moving target, you need to practice with a stationary one.

*Stationery* means "writing paper," "writing materials."

> Since my parents sent me off to college with a big box of personalized stationery, I guess I'd better write to them occasionally.

**statue, statute**

*Statue* means "sculpted figure."

> The Statue of Liberty in New York harbor was given to America by France.

*Statute* means "law passed by a governing body."

> Some people are upset by the new statute governing the registration of motorcycles.
> Though the Supreme Court has ruled that abortion is legally permissible, some state legislatures have enacted statutes restricting the conditions under which it may be performed.

**such a**

Do not use *such a* as an intensifier unless you add a result clause beginning with *that.*

WEAK: The commencement speech was such a bore.

BETTER: The commencement speech was such a bore that I fell asleep after the first five minutes.

**supposed to, \*suppose to**

Use *supposed to* when you mean "expected to" or "required to." Do not use *\*suppose to.*

\*Truman was suppose to lose when he ran against Dewey, but he surprised almost everyone by winning.

REVISED: Truman was supposed to lose when he ran against Dewey, but he surprised almost everyone by winning.

\*I was suppose to get up at 5:30 A.M., but I overslept.

REVISED: I was supposed to get up at 5:30 A.M., but I overslept.

**teach** *See* learn.

**than, then**

Use *than* when writing comparisons.

Many people spend money faster than they earn it.

Use *then* when referring to time.

Lightning flashed, thunder cracked, and then the rain began.

**that, which, who**

Use *which* or *that* as the pronoun when the antecedent is a thing.

There was nothing to drink but root beer, which I loathe.

Any restaurant that doesn't serve grits ought to be closed.

Use *who* as the pronoun when the antecedent is a person or persons.

Anyone who hates dogs and children can't be all bad.

—W. C. Fields

**themselves, \*theirselves, \*theirself**

Use *themselves,* not *\*theirselves* or *\*theirself.*

\*Fortunately, the children did not hurt theirselves when they fell out of the tree.

REVISED: Fortunately, the children did not hurt themselves when they fell out of the tree.

**then** *See* than.

**there, their, they're**

Use *there* to mean "in that place" or "to that place," and in the expressions *there is* and *there are.*

I have always wanted to see Las Vegas, but I have never been there.

There is nothing we can do to change the past, but there are many things we can do to improve the future.

*There is* and *there are* should be used sparingly, since most sentences are tighter and better without them.

We can do nothing to change the past, but many things to improve the future.

Use *their* as the possessive form of *they.*

The immigrants had to leave most of their possessions behind.

Use *they're* when you mean "they are."

I like cats because they're sleek, quiet, and sly.

**thus, therefore, \*thusly**

Use *thus* to mean "in that manner." In formal writing, do not use *\*thusly.*

> Carmichael bought a thousand shares of IBM when it was a brand-new company. Thus he became a millionaire.

Do not use *thus* to mean "therefore," "so," or "for this reason."

> A heavy storm hit the mountain. \*Thus the climbers had to take shelter.
>
> REVISED: A heavy storm hit the mountain, so the climbers had to take shelter.

**to, too, two**

Use *to* when writing about place, direction, or position, and with infinitives.

> We drove from Cleveland to Pittsburgh without stopping.
>
> Like many before him, Fenwick was determined to write the great American novel.

Use *too* when you mean "also" or "excessively."

> In spite of the cast on my foot, I too got up and danced.
>
> Some poems are too confusing to be enjoyable.

Use *two* when you mean "one plus one."

> In some mathematical systems, two and two do not make four.

**try to, \*try and**

Use *try to,* not *\*try and.*

> \*Whenever I feel depressed, I try and lose myself in science fiction.
>
> REVISED: Whenever I feel depressed, I try to lose myself in science fiction.

**two**  *See* to.

**-type**

Do not attach *-type* to the end of an adjective.

> \*He had a psychosomatic-type illness.
>
> REVISED: He had a psychosomatic illness.

**uninterested**  *See* disinterested.

**unique**

*Unique* means "one of a kind."

> Among pop singers of the fifties, Elvis Presley was unique.

Do not use *unique* to mean "remarkable," "unusual," or "striking."

> \*She wore a unique dress to the party.
>
> REVISED: She wore a striking dress to the party.

**used to, \*use to**

Write *used to,* not *\*use to,* when you mean "did regularly" or "was accustomed to."

> \*She use to run three miles every morning.
>
> REVISED: She used to run three miles every morning.

**very, awfully, so**

Use *very* sparingly, if at all. It can weaken the effect of potent modifiers.

> The very icy wind cut through me as I walked across the bridge.

BETTER: The icy wind cut through me as I walked across the bridge.

Do not use *awfully* to mean "very."

*We were awfully tired.

REVISED: We were very tired.

FURTHER REVISED: We were exhausted.

Do not use *so* as an intensifier unless you add a result clause beginning with *that*.

*They were so happy.

REVISED: They were so happy that they tossed their hats in the air.

**wait for, wait on**

To *wait for* is to stay until something is provided or something happens.

The restaurant was so crowded that we had to wait half an hour for a table.

To *wait on* is to serve.

Monica waited on more than fifty people that night. When the restaurant closed, she could barely stand up.

**way, ways**

Use *way*, not *ways*, when writing about distance.

*A short ways up the trail we found a dead rabbit.

REVISED: A short way up the trail we found a dead rabbit.

**well**   *See* good.

**were, we're**

Use *were* as a verb or part of a verb phrase.

The soldiers were a sorry sight.

They were trudging across a wheat field.

Use *we're* when you mean "we are."

We're trying to build a telescope for the observatory.

Most Americans have lost the urge to roam. With television scanning the world for us, we're a nation of sitters.

**which, who**   *See* that.

**would have, *would of**

Use *would have*, not *would of*.

*Churchill said that he would of made a pact with the devil himself to defeat Hitler.

REVISED: Churchill said that he would have made a pact with the devil himself to defeat Hitler.

*Have*, not *of*, is also customary after *may, might, must,* and *should.*

# GLOSSARY OF TERMS

**absolute phrase**

>A modifier usually made from a noun or noun phrase and a participle. It modifies the whole of the base sentence to which it is attached.
>
>>*Teeth chattering,* we waited for hours in the bitter cold.
>>
>>Who is best for the job, *all things considered?*

**active voice** *See* voice.

**adjective**

>A word that modifies a noun, specifying such things as how many, what kind, and which one.
>
>>For a *small* crime, he was made to spend *seven* years in a *tiny* cell of the *old* prison.

**adjective phrase**

>A phrase that modifies a noun.
>
>>On the table was a bouquet *of red roses.*
>>
>>The man *in the center of the picture* has never been identified.

**adjective (relative) clause**

>A subordinate clause that is used as an adjective within a sentence. It normally begins with a relative pronoun, a word that relates the clause to a preceding word or phrase and thus makes it modify that word or phrase.
>
>>Pablo Picasso, *who learned to paint by the age of twelve,* worked at his art for nearly eighty years.

**adverb**

>A word that modifies a verb, an adjective, another adverb, or a clause. It tells such things as how, when, where, why, and for what purpose. It often ends in *-ly.*
>
>>The cyclist breathed *heavily.*
>>
>>She spoke *forcefully.*
>>
>>Trains are *frequently* late.

**adverb clause**

A subordinate clause that is used as an adverb within a sentence. It commonly modifies another entire clause, but can also modify a word or phrase. It begins with a subordinator, a term like *before, because, when, since,* or *although.*

Because he faltered in the seventh inning, the pitcher was taken off the mound.

Smiling *when the guests arrived,* she was miserable *by the time they left.*

To cut all the grass *before the rains came,* I had to work fast.

**adverb phrase**

A phrase that modifies a verb, an adjective, another adverb, or a clause.

The fox jumped *over the hedge.*

Wary *at first,* he soon threw caution *to the winds.*

The Amazon runs *through some of the most densely vegetated land in the world.*

*On the eve of the battle,* the valley seemed peaceful.

**agreement of pronoun and antecedent**

Correspondence in gender and number between a pronoun and its antecedent.

Nellie Bly, the American journalist, was noted for *her* daring. [*Her* is feminine and singular.]

Ms. Stearns handed Mr. Nichols *his* briefcase. [*His* is masculine and singular.]

You can't tell a book by *its* cover. [*Its* is neuter and singular.]

The Andrews Sisters sang some of *their* best-known songs during World War II. [*Their* is plural and used for all genders.]

**agreement of subject and verb**

Correspondence in number between the form of a verb and its subject. In most cases, the subject affects the form of the verb only in the present tense; when the subject is a singular noun or a third-person singular pronoun, the present tense is made by the addition of *-s* or *-es* to the bare form.

Naomi *paints* houses.

He *fishes* every summer.

When the subject is not a singular noun or a third-person singular pronoun, the present tense is normally the same as the bare form.

I *paint* houses.

The men *fish* every summer.

The verb *be* has special forms in the present and the past, as shown on p. 322.

**analogy**

A noting of the similarities between two or more things of different classes. It is commonly used to clarify an abstract or specialized subject by linking it with something concrete, ordinary, and familiar.

Electrical energy is like the force that travels through a row of falling dominoes.

**antecedent**

The word or word group that a pronoun refers to.

> *Oliver* said that he could eat a whole pizza. [*Oliver* is the antecedent of *he*.]
>
> *The police*, who have surrounded the building, expect to free the hostages tonight. [*The police* is the antecedent of *who*.]
>
> *A snake* sheds its skin several times a year. [*A snake* is the antecedent of *its*.]

**appositive**

A noun or noun phrase that is used to identify another noun or noun phrase, or a pronoun.

> The blackjack player, *an expert at counting cards in play*, was barred from the casino.
>
> He was denied his favorite foods—*ice cream, pizza, and peanut butter*.
>
> He and she—*brother and sister*—decided to run away from home together.

**article**

A short word commonly used before a noun or noun equivalent. The articles are *a, an,* and *the*.

> *The* bombing of *the* village provoked *a* storm of protest.

**auxiliary (helping verb)**

A verb used with a base verb to make a verb phrase.

> I *have* seen the Kennedy Library.
>
> It *was* designed by I. M. Pei.

**bare form**

The verb form used in the present tense with every subject except a singular noun and a third-person singular pronoun.

> When the children *laugh*, we *laugh* too.

**base predicate** *See* predicate.

**base sentence**

A sentence without modifiers.

> Borg lost.
>
> McEnroe beat him.

**base verb**

The principal verb in a verb phrase made with an auxiliary.

> She has *earned* a promotion.
>
> He might *sell* the house.

**case**

The form that a noun or pronoun takes as determined by its role in a sentence. The **subject case** is used for a pronoun that is the subject of a verb.

> The dog was far from home, but *he* still wore a leather collar.

The **object case** is used for a pronoun that is the object of a verb or preposition, or that immediately precedes an infinitive.

> I found *him* trailing a broken leash behind *him*.
>
> I wanted *him* to come with *me*.

The **possessive case** of a noun or pronoun is used to indicate ownership of something or close connection with it. The possessive case is the only one for which the noun has a special form.

The *dog's* hind feet were bleeding, and *his* coat was muddy.

The **reflexive/emphatic case** of a pronoun is used to indicate a reflexive action—an action affecting the one who performs it. This case is also used for emphasis.

The dog had injured *himself;* I *myself* had seen him do so.

**clause**

A word group consisting of a subject and a predicate.

> S          P
> We  /  bought an old house. [one clause]

> S          P          S        P
> After we  /  bought the house,  we  /  found a crack in the foundation. [two clauses]

> S          P       S        P
> Furthermore, the roof  /  leaked,  the floors  /  sagged,
> S          P
> and the furnace  /  was out of order. [three clauses]

**comma splice (comma fault)**

The error of joining two independent clauses with nothing but a comma.

> *Sir Richard Burton failed to trace the source of the Nile, John Hanning Speke discovered it in 1862.
>
> REVISED: Sir Richard Burton failed to trace the source of the Nile; John Hanning Speke discovered it in 1862.

**common and progressive forms**

Tense forms of the verb. The **common form** indicates a momentary, habitual, or completed action.

> She *cooks* on weekends.
>
> He *cooked* dinner last night.
>
> I *will cook* next month.

The **progressive form** indicates a continuing action.

> Divers *are searching* for the sunken ship.
>
> *Was* I *doing* it right?
>
> We *will be seeing* you.

The progressive consists of some form of the auxiliary *be* followed by a present participle—a verb with *-ing* on the end.

**comparative and superlative**

Forms of the adjective and adverb. The **comparative** is used to compare one person, thing, or group with another person, thing, or group.

> Los Angeles is *bigger* than Sacramento.
>
> Cal was *more ambitious* than his classmates.
>
> Sheila argued *more persuasively* than Tim did.
>
> In general, women live *longer* than men.

The **superlative** is used to compare one person, thing, or group with all others in its class.

Joan's quilt was the *most colorful* thing on display.
Whales are the *largest* of all mammals.
George was the *most eagerly* awaited bachelor at the party.

**comparison**

A noting of the similarities and differences—or just the similarities—between two or more things of the same class.

Like a tramp, a hobo is a homeless vagrant with little or no money; but unlike a tramp, a hobo will sometimes do odd jobs.

**complete subject**  *See* subject.

**complex sentence**

A sentence consisting of one independent clause and at least one subordinate clause. The independent clause in a complex sentence is usually called the main clause.

Although Frank pleaded with Ida [subordinate clause], she would not give him the money [main clause].

**compound-complex sentence**

A sentence consisting of two or more independent clauses and one or more subordinate clauses.

When I moved to Chicago [subordinate clause], I first applied for a job [main clause], and then I looked for an apartment [main clause].

**compound phrase**

Words or phrases joined by a conjunction, a comma, or both.

The plan was *simple but shrewdly conceived.*

We saw an *old, rough-skinned, enormous* elephant.

The kitten was *lively, friendly, and curious.*

You must *either pay your dues on time or turn in your membership card.*

**compound sentence**

A sentence consisting of two or more independent clauses.

I won the contest, and I sailed for Europe.

He practiced many hours each day, but he never learned to play the piano well.

**conditional sentence**

A sentence normally consisting of an *if* clause, which states a condition, and a result clause, which states the result of that condition.

If it rains on the Fourth of July, the fireworks will be canceled.

If Social Security were abolished, million of retirees would be destitute.

**conjunction (coordinating conjunction)**

A word used to show a relation between words, phrases, or clauses. The conjunctions are *and, yet, or, but, nor,* and—for joining clauses only—*for* and *so.*

The tablecloth was red, white, *and* blue.

Small *but* sturdy, the cabin had withstood many winters.

Al *and* Joan walked to the meeting, *for* they liked exercise.

**conjunctive adverb**

A word or phrase used to show a relation between clauses. Conjunctive adverbs include *nevertheless, as a result, therefore, however,* and *likewise.*

> The ship was supposed to be unsinkable; *nevertheless,* it did not survive its collision with an iceberg.
>
> The lawyer spoke for an hour; the jury, *however,* was unimpressed.

**connotation and denotation**

> **Connotation** is the feeling, attitude, or set of associations that a word conveys. **Denotation** is the specific person, object, sensation, idea, action, or condition that a word signifies or names. *Home* connotes the warmth of familial affections; it denotes a place in which one or more persons or creatures live.

**contrast**

> A noting of the differences between two or more things of the same class.
>
> Unlike a motorcycle, which can usually carry two riders, a moped can carry just one.

**coordinating conjunction** *See* conjunction.

**coordination**

> An arrangement that makes two or more parts of a sentence equal in grammatical rank.
>
> Martha *took the script* home and *read it* to her husband.
> *The fight ended,* and *the crowd dispersed.*

**correlatives**

> Words or phrases used in pairs to join words, phrases, or clauses. Correlatives include *both . . . and, not only . . . but also, either . . . or, neither . . . nor,* and *whether . . . or.*
>
> He was *both* rich *and* handsome.
> She *not only* got the part *but also* played it brilliantly.
> *Either* they would visit us, *or* we would visit them.

**dangling modifier**

> A modifier without a headword—a word or phrase that it can modify.
>
> *\*Running angrily out the back way,* a couple of milk bottles were overturned.
> REVISED: Running angrily out the back way, he overturned a couple of milk bottles.

**deductive argument**

> A type of argument in which a conclusion is drawn from one or more assumptions and one or more statements of fact.

**definite pronoun** *See* pronoun.

**denotation** *See* connotation and denotation.

**dependent clause** *See* subordinate clause.

**direct object** *See* object.

**fallacy**

> An unsound or illogical way of arguing.

**faulty parallelism**

> An error in which two or more parts of a sentence are parallel in meaning but not parallel in form.
>
> *\* I want to learn how to write *with simplicity, clarity, and logically.*

REVISED: I want to learn how to write with simplicity, clarity, and logic.

**faulty predication**

The use of a linking verb between two expressions that are not equivalent.

*What surprised me was when she canceled the party.

REVISED: What surprised me was her cancellation of the party.

**faulty tense shift**

An unjustified shift from one tense to another, or an inconsistency between the tense of a subordinate verb and the tense of the main verb.

*I lit a candle, but the darkness *is* so thick I saw nothing.

REVISED: I lit a candle, but the darkness was so thick I saw nothing.

*Though he *blows* as hard as he could, the drummer drowned him out.

REVISED: Though he blew as hard as he could, the drummer drowned him out.

**fragment**   *See* sentence fragment.

**fused sentence**

Two or more independent clauses run together with no punctuation or conjunction between them.

*Mosquitoes arrived at dusk they whined about our ears as we huddled in our sleeping bags.

REVISED: Mosquitoes arrived at dusk, and they whined about our ears as we huddled in our sleeping bags.

**future perfect tense**   *See* tense.

**future tense**   *See* tense.

**gender**

The form of a pronoun as determined by the sex of its antecedent, which may be masculine, feminine, or neuter.

Bill [antecedent] brought *his* fishing rod, and Sally [antecedent] brought *her* paints.

The sun [antecedent] shed *its* rays over the lake.

**gerund**   *See* verbal noun.

**headword**

A word or phrase modified by another word or phrase, or by a clause.

Running for the elevator, *Pritchett* nearly knocked over Mr. Givens. [*Pritchett* is the headword of *Running for the elevator.*]

I found *the dog* digging for bones in the town dump. [*The dog* is the headword of *digging for bones in the town dump.*]

*The bullet* that killed him came from a high-powered rifle. [*The bullet* is the headword of *that killed him.*]

**helping verb**   *See* auxiliary.

**imperative mood**   *See* mood.

**indefinite pronoun**   *See* pronoun.

**independent clause**
> A clause that begins without a subordinator, a relative pronoun, or any other subordinating word, such as *whatever* or *whoever*. Such a clause can stand by itself as a simple sentence.
>> The roof leaks.
>
> It can be combined with one or more other independent clauses in a compound sentence.
>> The roof leaks, and the floor sags.
>
> And it can serve as the main clause in a complex sentence.
>> Whenever it rains, the roof leaks.

**indicative mood**  *See* mood.

**indirect object**  *See* object.

**inductive argument**
> A type of argument in which a conclusion is drawn from a set of examples.

**infinitive**
> A form usually made by the placing of *to* before the bare form of a verb.
>> Some say that politicians are born *to run*.
>>
>> The prisoners of war refused *to continue* their forced march.
>
> After some verbs the *to* in the infinitive is omitted. Compare:
>> Jack wanted the little boy *to feed* the ducks.
>>
>> Jack watched the little boy *feed* the ducks.

**infinitive phrase**
> A phrase formed by an infinitive and its object, its modifiers, or both.
>> She hates *to see horror movies*.
>>
>> It was beginning *to rain furiously*.
>>
>> I hope *to find a job soon*.

**intransitive verb**  *See* transitive and intransitive verbs.

**irregular verb**  *See* regular and irregular verbs.

**linking verb**
> A verb followed by a word or word group that identifies or describes the subject.
>> This machine *is* a drill press.
>>
>> I *feel* good today.
>>
>> That perfume *smells* sweet.

**main clause**
> The independent clause in a complex sentence.
>> Since there was no food in the house, *we went to a restaurant*.

**main verb**
> The verb of the independent clause in a complex sentence.
>> I *cut* the grass before the storm came.
>>
>> Since the store was closed, we *drove* away.

**metaphor and simile**
> A **metaphor** is a figure of speech in which two things of different classes are implicitly compared.
>> She was *burning with new ideas*. [Her new ideas are implicitly compared to fire.]

He was *drowning in self-pity*. [His self-pity is implicitly compared to water.]

Only *the skeleton of the building* remained. [The framework of the building is implicitly compared to a skeleton.]

A **simile** is a figure of speech in which two things of different classes are explicitly compared.

The office ran *like clockwork*.

**misplaced modifier**

A modifier that does not clearly point to its headword—the word or phrase it modifies.

*\*Crawling slowly up the tree*, the elderly Mrs. Cartwright spotted a bright green worm.

REVISED: The elderly Mrs. Cartwright spotted a bright green worm crawling slowly up the tree.

**modal auxiliary**

A helping verb that indicates the subjunctive mood.

The children *should* be here on Father's Day this year.

I'm not so sure that the average citizen *can* fight City Hall.

Besides *should* and *can*, the modal auxiliaries include *would*, *could*, *may*, *might*, *must*, and *ought*.

**modifier**

A word or phrase that describes, limits, or qualifies another word or phrase in a sentence

Pat smiled *winningly*.

I *rarely* travel *anymore*.

*The big gray* cat seized *the little* mouse.

*Polished to a high gloss, the mahogany* table *immediately* drew *our* attention.

**mood**

The form of a verb that indicates the writer's attitude toward a particular statement as it is made. The **indicative** is the mood used in statements of actuality or strong probability.

He *lingered* over his second cup of coffee.

We *will sleep* well tonight.

The **imperative** is the mood of commands and requests made directly.

*Be* quiet!

Please *go* away.

*Let us pray.*

*Down,* Fido!

The **subjunctive** is the mood used in statements of hypothetical conditions or of wishes, recommendations, requirements, or suggestions. Normally the subjunctive requires either a modal auxiliary or a subjunctive verb form.

I wish I *could* say yes, but I'm busy on Saturday night. [wish]

I wish I *were* a rock star. [wish]

Each member *must* pay her dues by December 1. [requirement]

The rules require that each member *pay* her dues by December 1. [requirement]

**nonrestrictive modifier**  *See* restrictive and nonrestrictive modifiers.

**noun**

A word that names a person, creature, place, thing, activity, condition, or idea.

**noun clause**

A subordinate clause that is used as a noun within a sentence. It serves as subject, object, predicate noun, or object of a preposition.

> *Whoever contributed to the office party* deserves many thanks.
> I said *that I was hungry.*
> You are *what you eat.*
> She was amazed by *what I said.*

**noun equivalent**

A verbal noun or a noun clause.

**noun phrase**

A phrase formed by a noun and its modifiers.

> She floated happily on *a big, fat, black inner tube.*
> *The eighteenth-century building* was declared a landmark last week.

**number**

The form of a word as determined by the number of persons or things it refers to. Most nouns and many pronouns may be singular or plural.

> A *carpenter* [singular] works hard.
> *Carpenters* [plural] work hard.
> Jeff said that *he* [singular] would give the party.
> All *his* [singular] friends said that *they* [plural] would come.

**object**

A word or word group naming a person or thing affected by the action that a verb, an infinitive, or a participle specifies.

> I hit *the ball.*
> Sighting *the bear,* he started to aim *his rifle.*
> Splitting *wood* is hard work.

A **direct object** names the person or thing directly affected by the action specified.

> The accountant prepared *my tax return.*

An **indirect object** names the person or thing indirectly affected by the action specified.

> I gave *Joe* a bit of advice.
> She bought *her father* a shirt.

Objects also include any word or word group that immediately follows a preposition.

> For *her,* the meeting was crucial.
> I found the sponge under *the kitchen sink.*

**object case**  *See* case.

**object complement**

A word or word group that immediately follows a direct object and identifies or describes it.

> I find card games *boring.*
> They named their son *Franklin.*
> The president appointed Smathers *ambassador to India.*

**parallel construction**

The arrangement of two or more elements of a sentence in grammatically equivalent patterns: noun lined up with noun, verb with verb, phrase with phrase, and clause with clause.

*Sink or swim, live or die, survive or perish,* I give *my hand* and *my heart* to this vote. —Daniel Webster

We must *take the risk* or *lose our chance.*

**participle**

A term usually made by the addition of *-ing, -d,* or *-ed* to the bare form of a verb.

| **Present Participle:** | calling | living | burning | lifting |
| **Past Participle:** | called | lived | burned | lifted |

A **perfect participle** is made by the combination of *having* or *having been* with the past participle.

having called    having been lifted

**participle phrase**

A phrase formed by a participle and its object, its modifiers, or both.

*Screaming the lyrics of its hit song,* the rock group could hardly be heard above the cheers of the crowd.

*Wearied after their long climb,* the hikers were glad to stop and make camp.

Harriet picked at the knot, *loosening it gradually.*

**passive voice**   *See* voice.

**past participle**   *See* participle.

**past perfect tense**   *See* tense.

**past tense**   *See* tense.

**perfect participle**   *See* participle.

**phrase**

A word group that forms a unit but lacks a subject, a predicate, or both.

*On his way to the elevator,* Hawkins sneezed.

*Encouraged by her friends,* Helen bought the house.

*A bright red kimono* caught my eye.

**possessive case**   *See* case.

**predicate**

A word or word group that tells what the subject of a sentence does, has, or is, or what is done to it.

The strong man *can lift 450 pounds.*

The pastry chef *makes doughnuts, napoleons, and éclairs.*

Venice *is a golden city interlaced with canals.*

A **base predicate** is a predicate without its modifiers.

Simon and Garfunkel *sang* for a crowd of almost half a million.

The little boys *threw snowballs* at all of the passing cars.

They *were* therefore *punished.*

**predicate adjective**

A word that follows a linking verb and describes the subject.

Henry seems *upset.*

Velvet feels *soft.*

**predicate noun**

A word that follows a linking verb and identifies the subject.

Bill Gorham is *treasurer*.
"Ma Bell" is a *nickname*.
Time was our only *enemy*.
Children eventually become *adults*.

**preposition**

A word used to show the relationship of a noun, pronoun, or noun equivalent to another word or word group in a sentence.

The table was set *under* a tree.

Hounded *by* his creditors, he finally declared himself bankrupt.

Besides *under* and *by*, prepositions include *with, at, of, in,* and *on*.

**prepositional phrase**

A phrase that starts with a preposition. Phrases of this type are regularly used as adjectives or adverbs.

Helen is the woman *with the quizzical expression on her face*.

Have you ridden *on the Ferris wheel?*

**present participle**   *See* participle.

**present perfect tense**   *See* tense.

**present tense**   *See* tense.

**principal parts**

The present, present participle, past, and past participle of a verb.

| PRESENT (BARE FORM) | PRESENT PARTICIPLE | PAST | PAST PARTICIPLE |
|---|---|---|---|
| see | seeing | saw | seen |
| work | working | worked | worked |

**progressive form**   *See* common and progressive forms.

**pronoun**

A word that commonly takes the place of a noun or noun phrase. Pronouns may be definite or indefinite. A **definite pronoun** refers to an antecedent, a noun or noun phrase appearing before or shortly after the pronoun.

As soon as Grant [antecedent] saw the enemy, *he* ordered the men to fire.

Janis Joplin [antecedent] was only twenty-seven when *she* died.

Though *he* won the battle, Nelson [antecedent] did not live to savor the victory.

An **indefinite pronoun** refers to unspecified persons or things. It has no antecedent.

*Everyone* likes Marvin.

*Anything* you can do, I can do better.

*Nobody* around here ever tells me anything.

**pronoun-antecedent agreement**   *See* agreement of pronoun and antecedent.

**reflexive/emphatic case**   *See* case.

**regular and irregular verbs**

A **regular verb** is one for which the past and past participle are formed by the addition of *-d* or *-ed* to the present.

| PRESENT (BARE FORM) | PAST | PAST PARTICIPLE |
| --- | --- | --- |
| work | worked | worked |
| tickle | tickled | tickled |
| walk | walked | walked |

An **irregular verb** is one for which the past, the past participle, or both are formed in other ways.

| sew | sewed | sewn |
| --- | --- | --- |
| have | had | had |
| eat | ate | eaten |

**relative clause**  *See* adjective clause.

**relative pronoun**

A pronoun that introduces an adjective clause.

> Women *who* like engineering are hard to find.
> Some companies now make furnaces *that* burn wood as well as oil.

The relative pronouns are *which, that, who, whom,* and *whose.*

**restrictive and nonrestrictive modifiers**

A **restrictive modifier** identifies or restricts the meaning of its headword.

> All taxpayers *who fail to file their returns by April 15* will be fined.

A restrictive modifier is essential to the meaning of a sentence; without the modifier, the meaning of the preceding sentence would be fundamentally different.

> All taxpayers will be fined.

A **nonrestrictive modifier** does not identify or restrict the meaning of its headword.

> Daphne, *who loves football,* cheered louder than anyone else.

A nonrestrictive modifier is not essential to the meaning of a sentence; without the modifier, the meaning of the preceding sentence remains basically the same.

> Daphne cheered louder than anyone else.

**run-on sentence**

A fused sentence or a sentence with a comma splice.

**sentence**

A word group containing at least one independent clause.

> The telephone was ringing.
> By the time I got out of the shower, the caller had hung up.

**sentence fragment**

A part of a sentence punctuated as if it were a whole one.

> The plant drooped. *And died.*
> I could not get into the house. *Because I had forgotten my key.*

**sequence of tenses**

The relation between the tenses of the verbs in a sentence that contains more than one verb, or in a passage of several sentences.

By the time I *arrived,* everyone else *had left.*

When the parade *goes* through town, all the townspeople *come* to see it.

**simile**   *See* metaphor and simile.

**simple sentence**

A sentence consisting of one independent clause.

The rat ate the cheese.

Her desk was piled high with papers.

**simple subject**   *See* subject.

**split infinitive**

An infinitive in which one or more adverbs are wedged between *to* and the verb.

The purchasing department is going *to carefully check* each new order.

BETTER: The purchasing department is going to check each new order carefully.

**subject**

A word or word group that tells who or what performs or undergoes the action named by a verb, or experiences the condition named by the verb.

*Gossip* amuses me.

*Morgan* hit one of Johnson's best pitches.

*Piccadilly Circus* is the Times Square of London.

Does *your allergy* cause a rash?

*Jan and I* were pelted by the rain.

A **simple subject** is a subject without its modifiers.

The old dusty *volumes* fell to the floor.

A **complete subject** is a subject with its modifiers.

*The old dusty volumes* fell to the floor.

**subject case**   *See* case.

**subject-verb agreement**   *See* agreement of subject and verb.

**subjunctive mood**   *See* mood.

**subordinate (dependent) clause**

A clause that normally begins with a subordinator, a relative pronoun, or some other subordinating word, such as *whoever* or *whatever.* Such a clause cannot stand alone as a sentence. It must be connected to or included in a main clause.

*Because Mrs. Braithwaite was writing her memoirs,* she reviewed all her old diaries and correspondence.

The essay *that won the prize* was written by a freshman.

I didn't know *where she had left the key.*

**subordinate verb**

The verb of a subordinate clause in a complex sentence.

I cut the grass before the storm *came.*

Since the door *was* open, I walked in.

**subordinating conjunction**   *See* subordinator.

**subordination**

An arrangement that makes one or more parts of a sentence grammatically subordinate to another part.

WITHOUT SUBORDINATION: The dog ate his dinner, and then he took a nap.

WITH SUBORDINATION: After the dog ate his dinner, he took a nap.

**subordinator (subordinating conjunction)**

A word or phrase used to introduce an adverb clause.

*Before* we left, I locked all the doors.

Besides *before,* subordinators include *because, after, since, while,* and *even though.*

**superlative**   *See* comparative and superlative.

**tense**

The form of a verb that helps to indicate the time of an action or condition.

**Present:** I jump.
**Past:** I jumped.
**Future:** I will jump.

**Present Perfect:** I have jumped.
**Past Perfect:** I had jumped.
**Future Perfect:** I will have jumped.

**transitive and intransitive verbs**

A **transitive verb** names an action that directly affects a person or thing specified in the predicate.

He *struck* the gong.
Water *erodes* even granite.
Did you *mail* the letters?
We *elected* Sloan.

An **intransitive verb** names an action that has no direct impact on anyone or anything specified in the predicate.

Wilson *smiled* at the comedian's best efforts, but he did not *laugh.*

**verb**

A word or phrase naming an action done by or to a subject, or a condition experienced by a subject.

Cavanaugh *runs* every day.
Salmon *swim* upstream each year.
My aunt *has lived* in Chicago.
Reagan *was elected* by a landslide.

**verbal noun**

A word or phrase formed from a verb and used as a noun.

*Hunting* was once the sport of kings.
I want *to travel.*
*Fixing bicycles* keeps me busy.
*To sacrifice his rook* would have been Gilman's best move.

A verbal noun made with a present participle—such as *hunting* or *fixing*—is sometimes called a **gerund.**

**verb phrase**

A phrase formed by two or more verbs—a base verb and at least one auxiliary.

Richard *may complete* his experiment by July.

Alison *would have come* earlier if you *had called* her.

**voice**

The aspect of a verb that indicates whether the subject acts or is acted upon. A verb is in the **active voice** when the subject performs the action named by the verb.

She *raised* her hand.

He *painted* the ceiling.

They *built* a house.

A verb is in the **passive voice** when the subject undergoes the action named by the verb.

I *was told* to do it that way.

The operation *was performed* by a famous surgeon.

*Is* this form *preferred*?

# INDEX

subordination for, 267–70
word placement for, 109
encyclopedias
forms for citations of, in bibliographies, 479
forms for citations of, in notes, 470–71
specialized, 425
standard, 425
endnotes, 460–62
advantages of, 461
*See also* notes.
*ensure, assure, insure,* 521
*envelop, envelope,* 525
*Environment Index,* 435
*Essay and General Literature Index,* 435
essays
conclusion of, 49–51
examination, 499–503
first draft of, 39–40, 145
format for, 166–69
goals for, 21–22
introduction of, 40–46
length of, 39–40
outlines of. *See* outlines for essays.
paragraph organization in, 48–49, 97–99. *See also* paragraphs.
proofreading of, 167–69
research papers vs., 421
revision of, 39–40, 145–48, 155–66
summaries of, 187
essays, examination, 499–503
*et al.,* in citations, 466
*etc., et al.,* 525–26
etymology
definition by, 64
in dictionaries, 135
euphemisms, 132
*everyday, every day,* 526
evidence, use of, 78–80, 86–87
examination essays, 499–503
examples
definition by, 64
in exposition, 58–59
in inductive argument, 81–84, 86–88

*except, accept,* 517
exclamation points, 34, 387
experience, personal
exposition illustrated by, 56–58
topics connected to, 16–17, 21
explanations
reporting, 70–71
teaching, 70–71
*See also* exposition.
explanatory notes, 462–63
exposition, 56–74
analogies in, 59–62
analysis in, 65–69
argument vs., 76–78, 89–90
of cause and effect, 71–72
comparison in, 59–62
contrast in, 59–62
definitions in, 63–65
examples in, 58–59
narration and description in, 56–58
of processes, 69–71
as strategy of development, 52
*factor,* 526
facts, opinions vs., 187–89
*Facts on File,* 434
fallacies, logical, 88–91, 546
*ad hominem* argument, 90
arguing by association, 88
improper analogies, 89–90
*post hoc, ergo propter hoc* argument, 90–91
undefended assumptions, 88–89
undistributed middle, 88
*farther, further,* 526
*fatal, fateful,* 526
faulty comparisons, 286–87
faulty parallelism, 263–64, 546–47
faulty predication, 208–9, 547
faulty tense shifts
defined, 360, 547
in paragraphs, 362
in sentences, 360–61
*few, little, less,* 526
figurative comparisons, 142–44
figures. *See* numbers.
first drafts
of essays, 39–40, 145

paragraphs (*continued*)
  change of speakers indicated by,
    381–82
  coherence in, 101, 110–15, 164
  conclusions in, 121–22
  emphasis in, 101, 108–10
  in essay organization, 48–49
  in examination essays, 501
  faulty tense shifts in, 362
  length of, 164
  main point in, 102, 108, 121–22,
    164
  outline as basis for, 48
  purpose of, 97–101
  sequence of tenses in, 358–60,
    362
  structure of, 101–7
  topic sentence in, 102
  transitions between, 97, 122–25
  unity in, 101–7
parallel construction, 260–66
  correlatives in, 262
  defined, 260, 551
  faulty, 263–64, 546–47
  functions of, 260–61
  types of, 261–62
paraphrasing
  citations to avoid plagiarism in,
    457–59
  in note-taking, 441
  in research papers, 455
parentheses
  for interruptions, 400, 401, 402
  for numerals, 401
  other punctuation with, 401
  in source citations, 465. *See also*
    parenthetical references.
parenthetical references
  in paper with bibliography,
    460–61, 463–65, 466. *See also*
    notes.
  in paper with reference list,
    480–82
participle phrases, 241
  defined, 551
  as modifiers, 219–21
  as verbal nouns, 241
participles
  commas with, 221
  defined, 218, 551

as modifiers, 218–21
past, 218, 219–20, 336, 349–53,
  551
perfect, 218, 220–21, 551
present, 218–19, 240, 336,
  349–53, 551
tenses of, 348
as verbal nouns, 240
parts of speech, dictionary designa-
  tions for, 134
*passed, past,* 533
passive voice, 157–58, 203–4,
  365–71
  changing from active voice to,
    366–67
  defined, 203, 556
  misuse of, 371
  use of, 369–71
past participles, 219–20
  defined, 551
  formation of, 218, 336
  of irregular verbs, 349–53
past perfect tense, 337, 343–44, 555
  subjunctive, 376
past tense, 337, 342–43, 555
  of irregular verbs, 349–53
  subjunctive, 376
perfect participles, 218, 220–21,
  551
periodicals
  forms for citations of, in bibliog-
    raphies, 479–80
  forms for citations of, in notes,
    471–73
  general vs. specialized, 425–26
  indexes to, 426–27, 435–36
  location of, in library, 437
  source cards for, 438–39
periods, 385–86
  in abbreviations, 385–86
  in acronyms, 385–86
  at end of sentences, 385
  in source citations, 465, 477
*persecute, prosecute,* 533
*personal, personnel,* 533
personal statements, for applications, 503–7
  avoiding errors in, 506
  detail in, 505
  diction in, 506

experience presented in, 505–6

organization of, 505–6

*personnel, personal,* 533

persuasion, 75–96

emotional, 76–78, 95–96

as strategy of development, 52

*See also* argument; deductive argument; inductive argument.

*phenomenon, phenomena,* 533

phrases

absolute, 227–28, 541

adjective, 212–13, 541

adverb, 214–15, 542

compound, 207, 247–49, 545

defined, 551

exclamatory, 387

infinitive, 224–25, 241, 548

noun, 205, 550

participle, 219–21, 241, 551

prepositional, 147–48, 212–13, 552

verb, 202–3, 555–56. *See also* auxiliary verbs.

plagiarism, 457–59

acknowledgment of sources and, 457–59

as copying key word or phrase, 459

as copying many words and phrases, 459

as paraphrasing without citation, 459

as using author's ideas without citation, 459

as word-for-word copying, 458–59

plays

forms for citations of, in bibliographies, 478

forms for citations of, in notes, 464–65

plot summaries

comprehensive, 186–87

sequential, 186–87

plurals

of letters, 411

of nouns, 151, 325–26, 328–29

of numbers, 411

poetry

quoting from, 405–6, 408, 457

form for citations of, in bibliographies, 479

forms for citations of, in notes, 464–65, 470

possessive case, 316, 318, 410, 543–44

postgraduate programs, personal statements for applications to 503–7

*post hoc, ergo propter hoc* argument, 90–91

*precede, proceed, proceeds, proceedings, procedure,* 533–34

predicate adjectives, 203, 212, 551

predicate nouns

defined, 203, 551–52

noun clauses as, 272–73

predicates, 201–4

base, 551

defined, 201, 551

predication, faulty, 208–9, 547

prefixes, 409

prepositional phrases, 212–13

defined, 212, 552

replacement of, 147–48

prepositions, 212, 552

present participles, 218–19

defined, 551

formation of, 218, 336

of irregular verbs, 349–53

as verbal nouns, 240

present perfect tense, 337, 341–42, 555

present tense, 336, 339–40, 555

of irregular verbs, 349–53

subjunctive, 376

pretentious words, 131–32

prewriting

for essays, 19–24

for research papers, 421

primary sources, 428–29. *See also* sources for research papers.

*principal, principle,* 534

principal parts of verbs, 336, 349–53, 552

*proceed, precede, proceeds, proceedings, procedure,* 533–34

processes, explanations of, 69–71

plagiarism and, 457–59
of poetry, 405–6, 408, 457
punctuation of, 403–8, 444–46,
 456–57
review of, in revision, 166
summaries as alternatives to, 453
tags for, 381, 404
*quote, quotation,* 534–35

*raise, rise,* 535
*rational, rationale, rationalize,* 535
raw material
 for essays, 25–26
 for research papers, 421
readers, thinking of, 37–40
 considering background of,
  37–38, 130–31, 451–52
 considering expectations of,
  38–39
 overcoming resistance of, 38. *See
  also* persuasion.
*Readers' Guide to Periodical Literature,*
  426–27, 435
reading, 171–98
 as aid to writing essays, 17–18,
  171–98
 analytical response in, 176–93
 detecting bias in, 191
 detecting tone in, 176–80
 distinguishing facts and opinions
  in, 187–89
 identifying main point in, 180–85
 imitative response in, 194–98
 judging supporting points in,
  187–91
 judging whole argument in,
  191–94
 subjective response in, 172–75
reading for research papers,
  424–27, 439–40. *See also* note-
  taking.
*real, really,* 535
*reason . . . is that, reason . . . is
  because,* 535–36
*refer, allude,* 518–9
reference books, 424–25, 434–35
 bibliographical information in,
  434–35
 biographical, 425
 direct information in, 434

encyclopedias, 425
government publications, 436
indexes to periodicals, 435–36
textbooks as, 425
reference lists, 482–83. *See also* bibliographies.
reference of pronouns
 clear, 307–8
 unclear, 308–9
reflexive/emphatic case, 316, 319,
 544
*regardless, irregardless,* 536
regular verbs
 defined, 336, 552–53
 principal parts of, 336, 552
relative clauses. *See* adjective
 clauses.
relative pronouns, 274–77
 adjective clauses introduced by,
  274–75
 antecedents of, 275–77
 defined, 553
 sentence fragments beginning
  with, 300
repetition, 108–9, 146
reporting explanations, 70–71
reporting of discourse, 380–84
 direct, 380–82, 383
 indirect, 272, 380, 382–84
reprints
 form for citations of, in bibliographies, 478
 forms for citations of, in notes,
  469
research papers, 421–98
 as analysis, 422, 453–55
 bibliography for, 476–80
 combining quotations and commentary in, 452–53, 456–57
 conclusion of, 454–55
 essays vs., 421
 excessive use of quotations in,
  441, 452–53
 filling gaps in research for,
  447–48
 first draft of, 451–57
 goal, choice of, 447
 introduction of, 451–52
 notes for, 460–74
 note-taking for, 440–46